LEITH'S
SEASONAL
BIBLE

LEITH'S SEASONAL BIBLE

BY

C.J. JACKSON &
BELINDA KASSAPIAN

FOREWORD BY CAROLINE WALDEGRAVE
PHOTOGRAPHS BY GRAHAM KIRK

BLOOMSBURY

First published in Great Britain in 1998
Bloomsbury Publishing Plc, 38 Soho Square, London W1V 5DF

Text copyright © 1998 by Leith's School of Food and Wine

The moral right of the authors has been asserted

A CIP catalogue record for this book is available from the British Library

ISBN 0 7475 3178 1

10 9 8 7 6 5 4 3 2 1

Photographs by: Graham Kirk
Stylist: Helen Payne
Home Economists: Puff Fairclough, C.J. Jackson and Belinda Kassapian
Assisted by: Leith's Diploma Students 1996–97

Typeset by Hewer Text Limited, Edinburgh
Printed in Great Britain by The Bath Press, Bath

CONTENTS

CONTENTS

THE SEASONS

SPRING

SUMMER

CONTENTS

AUTUMN

WINTER

Basic Recipes

ACKNOWLEDGEMENTS

We have enjoyed the challenges of writing this book, but couldn't have done it without a great number of people who listened, encouraged and ate their way through the contents.

In particular we would like to thank: Caroline Waldegrave, Principal of Leith's School of Food and Wine, for giving us the opportunity to be creative. David Reynolds and Monica Macdonald from the publishers, Bloomsbury for their help, and Helen Dore, the editor, who painstakingly worked her way through the manuscript giving suggestions and advice and also Meg Calvert for the hours that she spent proofreading. The skills and creativity of our photographer Graham Kirk and stylist Helen Payne, and for Puff Fairclough who styled the food with the help of many ex-students and home economists including Terry Farris.

A team of dedicated recipe testers carefully worked their way trying and retesting each recipe: we would like to thank Jacqui Thomas, Viv Pigeon, Netty Nicholson, Sarah Kidd and Kate Jay as well as all the staff and students of the Leith's Diploma group of 1995–1997.

Seana Lyneham Wood for her help with the wine selection and for Philippa Carr MW for stepping in at the last moment to complete the suggestions.

Annie Simmonds and Julia Kerslake for their computing skills.

Laura Ponsonby and John Jackson for their help with some of the fruit and vegetable sections. Alison Cavaliero for her potato chart.

AIJ for her help with recipe testing, the herb section and loan of a huge amount of gardening books! Helen Clare for garden produce and use of kitchen library.

Last, but not at all least, Mark, Toby and Rory for eating too much over the past two years.

FOREWORD

by Caroline Waldegrave

As soon as C.J. said that she was keen to write a book based on the seasons of the year, I wondered why we had not thought of it before.

We have almost lost our sense of the seasons in food, as strawberries or raspberries have become available throughout the year, flown in from around the world. The imported fruits taste as good in December as in June, but are never as good as fresh home-grown ones in their proper month of June. So we thought we would try to reintroduce the idea of eating our own produce when it is in season. For example, wild garlic and asparagus in May, and artichokes in August. Wait for vegetables to come into season and plan your menus. How dull to have mangetout all year round!

Whilst researching for this book we began to find out that our instinctive prejudices were thoroughly justified. When you compare the taste of perfect soft fruits served in summer, you wonder why restaurants bother to have raspberry coulis on the menu in December. And where are the old seasonal foods? Gooseberries and elderflowers in summer, chanterelles in August, and game and root vegetables in autumn. If you think like this menus begin to write themselves.

Leith's School began in 1975, and when we started we taught that it was important to cook food that was in season. During the late eighties we began to say, cook things that are suitable for the time of the year, but given that virtually all ingredients are always available all the year round we placed more emphasis on cooking food suitable for the occasion and type of guests. We are now teaching that all the factors are essential when planning a menu – and that seasonality should not be forgotten. I do hope that you enjoy cooking and eating from this book.

INTRODUCTION

INTRODUCTION

Over the last few years supermarket shelves have expanded enormously to accommodate a wonderful array of fruits, vegetables and other fresh produce. These are imported from all over the world to provide a continuous supply all year round of foods that were once only found when in season in this country. Only ten years ago, for example, you would not have been able to find raspberries in February for anything less than a king's ransom, paying up to ten times more for them than in the summer months. Now prices are much more realistic.

We have found recently that some of our younger students have no concept of what fruits and vegetables are in season, as the notion of seasonal change is unfamiliar to them. We have written this book to remember the seasons and to celebrate the produce that each one brings to our tables. In the recipes that follow you will find some old favourites such as casseroles and crumbles, and many new ideas that incorporate fruits, vegetables, meats, fish and game in season that all deserve never to be forgotten. Some of our fruit and vegetable recipes have been inspired from produce grown in our own gardens, and we have both thoroughly enjoyed watching the seasons change over the last couple of years. We have looked with new eyes at cold, frosty winter moving into budding spring, followed by a glorious summer through to a golden autumn, and all that the different seasons have to offer.

'Season watching' requires a certain amount of forethought on the part of the cook – weather plays a large part in the arrival of the produce that we grow. A late frost may see some crops fail or a warm spring may hasten the harvest. If you are aware of each season's produce you will want to seize the opportunity to make the most of it as and when it appears,

whether it be Seville oranges in January or blackberries and quinces in September, in the certain knowledge that these truly seasonal fruits will not reappear until the following year.

Certain fruits and vegetables may not appear in the supermarkets as they are not considered 'commercial' enough – mulberries, damsons and quinces to name but a few. You may need either to become or adopt an avid gardener who will enjoy growing different things in the vegetable garden, or find a greengrocer who will search out some of the virtually forgotten fruits and vegetables.

The Henry Doubleday Foundation advertised an Adopt a Vegetable campaign a couple of years ago to encourage gardeners to grow different types of traditional or old-fashioned vegetables, such as Elephant garlic and cardoons which have long since gone out of fashion. The idea was to prevent these from becoming extinct. The addition of vegetables such as these add an extra dimension to the excitement of gardening and provide something unusual for the cook.

Summer produces huge quantities of fruits and vegetables and we found that recipe development for this time of the year was easy and a joy. Autumn and winter provided the ingredients for rich game dishes and the warming foods such as casseroles and substantial vegetables we all crave when the days become shorter and chilly. Spring was the hardest season by far for recipe development as there is little in the garden at that time, and waiting to see the first vegetables coming through proved rather frustrating. So in the spring season we made the most of the superb tropical fruits and vegetables available in the supermarkets.

We hope that you enjoy using this book as much as we enjoyed writing it.

SEASONAL FOODS

FRUIT AND VEGETABLES

With farming techniques highly advanced, a tremendous variety of fruit and vegetables, both home-grown and imported, is available for the table most of the year round. The growing of fruit and vegetables is not an exact science; however, the non-commercial gardener is at the mercy of the weather. Fruit and vegetables need rain, frost, warmth and sun in varying degrees. All these elements come in differing quantities and rarely at the same time. It is therefore impossible to give exact seasons for any fruit or vegetable. One year a warm wet winter may produce crops early, and after a cold winter and hard frost everything appears much later.

We have attempted to give approximate seasons for fruit and vegetables, subdividing each seasonal chart into easily recognized botanical groups. Tonnes of fruit and vegetables are imported and exported to and from northern and southern hemisphere countries throughout the year, making most produce available year-round. Produce grown and sold locally is often much more flavoursome than that which is gathered and transported thousands of miles to our tables. The distance that the produce has to travel makes it essential to pick it when still under-ripe, therefore the flavour will never be quite the same as if grown, ripened and picked locally. Some imported fruits and vegetables are grown under glass and tend to lack the flavour that is enhanced by the elements. Hot-house imported strawberries that are available during the winter will lack the aroma and flavour of strawberries grown outdoors during our own summer, and there is nothing quite like the first home-grown asparagus of late spring that appears in our shops in May.

We have a plentiful supply of many home-grown fruit and vegetables during both summer and winter. It is important to make the most of these, especially when in glut, and spend time preserving, whether it be making jams, jellies, chutneys and pickles or freezing or drying the surplus.

Be mindful of the seasons, keep looking for prized fruits and vegetables and store whatever you can.

We have listed most of the fruit and vegetables available in supermarkets, most of which now offer a great choice. Fruit and vegetables indicated in italics are readily available, but not grown commercially in this country, and so are not strictly seasonal. Under each heading we have indicated when each fruit or vegetable is in season in the UK and where imports will have come from at other times of year, either northern or southern hemisphere. At the beginning of each seasonal section the fruit and vegetables in season at that time of year are listed again under a botanical category, e.g. broccoli under brassicas.

CATEGORIES OF FRUIT AND VEGETABLES

FRUIT

Fruit is subdivided into three main groups:

Top fruit or tree fruit: This term is used to describe fruit that grows on trees and includes apples, pears, plums, figs, mulberries and nuts. Some of these top fruits have a hard central stone containing a kernel and we have referred to these in some of our recipes as **stone fruit**. They include apricots, peaches, plums and greengages.

Soft fruit: This term is used to describe fruit that grows perennially on small shrubs and includes gooseberries and currants, strawberries, raspberries and hybrids such as loganberries.

Rhubarb has been included in the vegetable section as a 'vegetable fruit' because although we have used it as a spring fruit, many gardeners regard it as a vegetable.

Exotic or tropical fruit: This term encompasses a huge variety of well- and lesser-known fruits grown in tropical and sub-tropical climates. Because they are not grown in this country, they are not strictly seasonal. We have made the most of these fruits during the winter and spring months, when there is a dearth of home-grown seasonal produce.

VEGETABLES
These have been subdivided into several different recognized categories:

Alliums are members of the onion family. Onions, shallots and garlic are harvested in the summer months, and depending on the variety store well into the following year. Leeks, on the other hand, weather well through frost and are a popular winter and spring vegetable. Spring onions are available all year round.

Brassicas or 'flowering shoots' are staple green vegetables, very popular in the kitchen. Fortunately members of the brassica family are available most of the year round. They include brussels sprouts, cabbages, broccoli and cauliflowers. Like many vegetables, most brassicas are not native to the UK. Some do not like frost while others, such as certain varieties of cabbage and brussels sprouts, cope well with a cold winter. Different varieties of cabbage grow throughout the year.

Pods, beans and seeds: This group includes both fresh peas and beans and some of the more popular dried variety. We have also included sweetcorn in this category.

Lettuce, spinach, salad plants and leaves: This group includes lettuces and salads and is ever-increasing as we see more and more varieties of oriental salad leaves such as Japanese mizuna, and the popular bitter winter chicorys coming into the shops.

Tubers: The principal member of this group is one of the most versatile of vegetables, the potato. The other vegetable included here is the Jerusalem artichoke.

Root crops: This group includes all the vegetables that mainly grow underground and which we regard as winter warmers. They include swedes, celeriac, carrots, beetroot, parsnips and radishes. As with most of the other groups, a steady supply of different members of these are available all year round, and they do of course store well. We have made use of them in spring, summer, autumn and winter.

Stalks and shoots: This group includes a mixture of shoots such as the aristocratic asparagus and stalks including Florence fennel and celery.

Vegetable fruits: This last group encompasses the sweet vegetables such as the tomato, and rhubarb which can be used for desserts.

Fungus: This category includes both wild and cultivated mushrooms sold commercially in the UK.

Herbs: This section includes all the herbs that we have used in our recipes and some others that are also well worth utilizing. For full information on herbs, see the chart on pages 112–114.

WHERE TO BUY FRUIT AND VEGETABLES
For most people the supermarket is often the best and most convenient choice for shopping. However, it is worth remembering that fruits in season, particularly through the summer and early autumn months, can be purchased at lower cost from Pick Your Own farms. It is a satisfying and enjoyable task to search out,

choose and pick your own fruit and vegetables, with the added bonus that your own labour in turn reduces the cost.

In some of our recipes we have used increasingly popular exotic fruits and vegetables such as yams, plantains and galangal, that are not always available from supermarkets. Specialist ethnic grocers can often supply these. Keep a look-out for them and make the most of supplies.

COOKING VEGETABLES

For further information on cooking methods, see under individual categories.

Always wash fruit and vegetables thoroughly before using. To avoid loss of vitamins, do not prepare too far in advance.

Baking vegetables: This is a particularly good method for stuffed vegetables such as aubergines, peppers, tomatoes and Spanish onions.

Cooking root vegetables and tubers: On the whole, these vegetables take some time to cook through; adding a little salt to the water not only adds seasoning but increases the water temperature slightly, thus reducing the cooking time. Put the prepared vegetables into cold water, bring to the boil and cover the pan with a lid. Cook over a low heat until tender.

Cooking green vegetables: Steaming vegetables has become popular because it prevents loss of vitamins and the leaching of minerals. The only drawback is that they are less likely to keep a good colour than if they are quickly cooked in plenty of boiling water, again lightly salted. This method prevents minimal loss of minerals and vitamins. Do not cover the pan; the acid from condensation collects in the lid and can give the vegetables an unappetizing khaki colour. Under no circumstances add bicarbonate of soda to the cooking water; this old-fashioned method keeps the colour of the vegetables but destroys most of the vitamin content. Refreshing lightly boiled green vegetables by passing them quickly under cold running water helps them retain their fresh green colour.

Cooking vegetables in the microwave: Cooking green vegetables for a few seconds in the microwave steams them and prevents the loss of vitamins. Add a little water to the prepared vegetables in a microwave dish, cover with microwave-proof cling wrap, prick and cook for anything from 30 seconds to 2 minutes. Some supermarkets sell ready-prepared vegetables that can be cooked in the bag they are sold in.

Stir-frying vegetables: Stir-frying vegetables in a little oil in a wok or frying pan is a healthy and delicious way of cooking many vegetables, such as leeks, spring onions, cabbage, broccoli, mushrooms and baby sweetcorn. Even thinly sliced carrots can be cooked in this way. The vegetables retain their colour and goodness, and have an appetizing 'bite'. All vegetables for stir-frying must be cut to a uniform size.

Deep-frying vegetables: This traditional method of cooking potatoes, either as crisps or chips, can be used for a multitude of root vegetables. Deep-fried vegetable crisps are very popular today and can be made from beetroot, parsnips, sweet potatoes and celeriac as well as potatoes. Slice the vegetables finely and pat dry on kitchen paper. (Potatoes require soaking in cold water for 15–20 minutes to remove the excess starch and should be dried thoroughly before frying.) Heat the oil until a cube of bread browns within 30 seconds and add the prepared vegetables. Once golden-brown, lift from the oil, drain on kitchen paper and sprinkle lightly with salt. If the oil is too hot the vegetables will brown too quickly and taste bitter; if not hot enough, they absorb too much oil and taste greasy.

Roasting vegetables: True roasting was traditionally done on a spit over a roaring fire. We use the same term today for cooking meat in a hot oven with fat to baste. Roasting is also traditionally associated with potatoes which are served as an accompaniment to the meat. We have included a few roast vegetable recipes as roasting is a useful and particularly flavoursome method, especially for root vegetables, tubers, pumpkins and squash, onions and aubergines. Prepare the vegetable and if necessary parboil for a few minutes to soften the outside, then dry on kitchen paper. The fat for the roasting can vary, but be sure to choose one that can be used for cooking at high temperatures: lard and dripping are typical choices, but a healthier option would be sunflower oil, which is high in polyunsaturates. Heat the fat in the oven, add the vegetables, baste and season with salt and pepper. The oven temperature varies according to the type of vegetable – roast until the vegetable is tender and crisp on the outside.

Grilling vegetables: We grill some soft-fleshed vegetables such as courgettes and aubergines, either for a salad or in the case of peppers to char and blister the skin so that it peels away easily. The vegetable should be sliced, brushed with oil and seasoned. Cook under a preheated grill until tender and lightly browned. Do not allow to burn.

COOKING FRUIT

For further information on cooking methods, see under individual categories.

Stewing and poaching are the most popular methods for cooking fruit; hard top fruit benefits from long slow cooking, the softer stone and berry fruits cook in a short space of time and break up easily. As with vegetables, do not prepare top fruit too far in advance as many fruits, particularly apples and pears, will discolour as well as lose valuable vitamin and mineral content.

Poaching top fruit: The method of poaching is most often done on the stove. Prepare the fruit as necessary, submerge in a sugar syrup (see page 661) and cover closely with a piece of damp greaseproof paper. Cook, covered, over a very low heat so that the liquid around the fruit barely simmers. The length of cooking time

greatly depends on the type of fruit. Apples and pears can take up to an hour to cook through completely, whereas ripe stone fruit such as plums and peaches will be cooked within 20 minutes.

It is useful to note that whenever ripe fruit are required for a recipe, under-ripe fruit may be used if poached briefly first to soften the flesh.

Stewing top fruit: For apples and denser fruits such as pears, medlars and quinces, submerge the prepared fruit in a syrup, cover and cook in a low oven until tender. Soft stone fruit can produce a lot of its own juice, therefore a splash of water is all that is required to cook it.

Baking fruit: Large dense fruits such as apples, pears and quinces can be successfully baked. The fruit needs to be washed, but not peeled. Leave the fruit whole, but remove the core. Make a slit through the skin to prevent the fruit from bursting in the oven. Put the fruit into a roasting tin with a little liquid to help create some steam, cover and bake until tender. Cooked at 180°C/350°F/gas mark 4, most fruit will be tender within 1 hour.

Cooking soft berry fruits: Berry fruits are most often served just as they are, ripe and fresh. At times of glut, not only can these fruits be preserved or frozen for use later in the year, but they can be gently poached in syrup, to make a thick compote, or alternatively may be stewed in the oven.

All soft berry fruit will give off a lot of juice during cooking, therefore it is only necessary to add a little liquid, if any, while cooking. To poach, barely cover with a light syrup and cook over a very low heat for a few minutes. The fruit cooks quickly and will break up if overcooked or allowed to boil. Avoid overcooking as soft fruits lose their fresh fruity flavour easily and take on a jam-like flavour instead.

FRUIT

TOP OR TREE FRUIT
APPLES

UK SEASON: Various, mainly late summer through to early winter; some types of apple store well.

IMPORTS:

Northern hemisphere: August–May
Southern hemisphere: April–November
FREEZING: Not normally frozen raw as they store well; cooked apples will freeze for up to 6 months.

Entire books have been written exclusively about the apple, and we could easily write many pages, not just a short paragraph, about this most well-used and popular fruit. In brief, there are thousands of apple varieties from around the world; some, like Bramley, Cox's Orange Pippin, Granny Smith and Golden Delicious have become household names.

There is always such a good selection of cookers and dessert apples in the supermarkets that we can tend to become a little complacent about this fruit, which in turn may become less favoured than the more exciting exotic fruits. We are inundated with apples from abroad, but do have an extensive supply of our own varieties from all counties across the UK. Recently there has been a revival of some of the old varieties like Russets, Beauty of Bath, James Grieve and Jonagold.

Apple harvesting starts with some early varieties in July and finishes with late developers in December. Varieties such as Discovery are at their best early in the season, from late summer onwards. Cox's Orange Pippins store well and are a perfect variety for Christmas, although home-grown Coxes are not good after January. Choosing varieties of apple at their best in supermarkets tends to be a matter of trial and error. We obtained our information about apples from Common Ground (see Bibliography), who promote varieties grown in the UK. Their list shows that we can enjoy a good selection of home-grown apples virtually all year.

Crab apples: Like a lot of other fruit, including pears, varieties of apple grow wild in the UK. Crab apples are one of these. They are the size of a large cherry, varying in colour from yellow to red. They are very tart and therefore not suitable for dessert eating. They are mainly used for jelly, where the fruit is cooked to a pulp and sets perfectly because of the high pectin and acid content, giving a lovely red clear jelly. Crab apples also make a great accompaniment to pork or a rich game dish.

PREPARATION AND COOKING
The flesh of apples oxidizes and turns brown quickly, therefore it is advisable to peel just before eating or cooking. Try to avoid peeling apples and leaving to soak in acidulated water; this does help prevent discoloration, but a lot of the flavour will leach into the water and there is also a certain amount of mineral and vitamin loss. When removing the core, take care to remove the tough seed beds.

Dessert apples tend to have a firm texture and hold together well in cooking. Cookers' high acid and water content means they break up more easily, making them ideal for purées and preserving purposes.

Puréeing, poaching, frying and baking are all perfect ways of cooking apples. Coarsely grated apple will give a stuffing lots of added moisture. Drying is a good way of utilizing this fruit. Classic pork and duck recipes often suggest the use of glazed apples to garnish the dish. Dessert apples are most commonly used as they hold together well. Cored and cut into thick slices, the apple can be fried in a little butter and sugar for 2–3 minutes until caramelized and sticky.

APRICOTS

UK SEASON: Not grown commercially. Apricots ripen from mid-summer to early autumn in the warmer parts of this country.
IMPORTS:
Northern hemisphere: May–September
Southern hemisphere: November–February
FREEZING: Halve and stone the fruit, open freeze or poach in a syrup and freeze cooked.

PREPARATION AND COOKING

Choose undamaged apricots. Wash and make an incision around the natural indentation of the fruit, twist in half and remove the stone. Industrious cooks then split open the stone to reveal the apricot kernel which has a surprising almond flavour. The kernels can be added to the fruit when making jam, their flavour giving it an extra dimension.

Apricots are delicious served raw, but cooking them can enhance the flavour. Poaching, baking and stewing are all perfect methods. Dried and canned apricots can be substituted for fresh in many recipes.

CHERRIES

UK SEASON: June–August
IMPORTS:
Northern hemisphere: May–September
Southern hemisphere: October–January
FREEZING: For jam-making cherries can be frozen raw or cooked in a light sugar syrup. Native to Europe and some parts of Asia, cherries are divided into two main groups:

Acid or sour cherries: The best-known varieties are the Morello and Montmorency. These bitter-sweet cherries are used for cooking purposes, requiring the addition of sugar. They are often sold commercially already cooked in jars. Dried cherries are also available.

Dessert or sweet cherries: There are many different varieties of this wonderfully 'moreish' fruit, ranging from pink through yellow to a deep blood red.

PREPARATION AND COOKING

A truly seasonal fruit, cherries do not store well and need to be eaten soon after picking as they bruise easily. Choose those that are obviously undamaged and on a tender, pliable stalk, which becomes brittle after a few days' storage. The only preparation needed is washing and de-stalking. Stoning can be tedious without the aid of a cherry stoner, a kitchen implement which is also useful in the pitting of olives.

Acid or sour cherries make excellent sauces,

especially for duck. As cherries are one of the most delightful fruits to eat raw, it seems a pity to cook them unless you have a glut; should this be the case, cherries are delicious in pies, tarts and clafoutis, the French batter pudding, and as an addition to classic summer pudding.

CITRUS FRUITS

UK SEASON: *Not grown commercially.*
IMPORTS:
Northern hemisphere: November–May
Southern hemisphere: May–December
FREEZING: *The fruit can be frozen whole for marmalade, or cooked to a pulp.*

The genus citrus covers a multitude of types of lemon, orange, lime and grapefruit and the many hybrids of each. They grow in warm, temperate climates where there are periods of heavy rain, drought and short cold periods. Some varieties, lemons in particular, can cope with cooler environments and are grown in glasshouses in the UK. They need much light, but do not like excessive heat. Too much water can kill the plant.

We are fortunate in having a steady year-long supply of these fruits. The true season of many varieties is winter and early spring.

TYPES OF CITRUS

Citron: Similar in appearance to a lemon, this is usually only used in the making of candied peel.

Grapefruit and pomelo: As with other citrus fruits there are many varieties, some with a very acidic flavour, others with a very sweet juice. Grapefruit is widely used for its juice, or raw, segmented for a refreshing breakfast fruit or in salsas. It is used in the making of marmalades and candied peel. The flavour of grapefuit is not enhanced by cooking.

Kumquat: These tiny oranges, oval in shape, are not normally peeled or eaten whole, but thinly sliced to make an attractive if sharp addition to a fruit salad and for use in bottling and preserving. Cooked in a little sugar syrup, they make an interesting accompaniment to rich game and fish dishes.

Lemon: The lemon is one of the cook's most valued and widely used assets as there are countless uses for both zest and juice.

Lemons are grown extensively in the Mediterranean, in particular Sicily, and in California, from where they are imported. Lemons cope well with a drop in temperature, with the fruit turning from green to the distinctive yellow colour during cooler spells. Cooler weather is said to heighten the acidity of the fruit. Lemon plants need lots of light but not excessive heat, and hate being overwatered. The tree flowers and produces fruit simultaneously. Most fruit appears in winter, and as it stores well is usually picked when still green and allowed to turn yellow in cold storage, which makes lemons easily available all year.

Lime: A relative of the lemon, which flourishes in warmer tropical climates and is far less resistant to the cold. The lime has become very popular over the last few years, but its higher acidity, smaller size and greater cost still make it second in line to the lemon. Unlike lemons, limes are usually sold green; some varieties turn yellow in cool conditions.

The **Kaffir lime** has a knobbly skin and aromatic flavour. The leaves from the tree as well as the fruit are used extensively in Thai cookery.

Hybrids of the lime include the **limequat**, a cross between a lime and kumquat.

Mandarins: This term also encompasses a whole group of citrus fruits including the clementine, tangerine and satsuma as well as the mandarin itself, all distinctive by their loose, baggy skin that peels away very easily. The main commercial season for these fruits is the winter and they are always available around Christmas.

Orange: The many varieties of orange include sweet oranges and the bitter Seville. **Sweet oranges** include the navel orange, so called because of the thick pith at one end resembling a tummy button; they are usually large and practically seedless. Common sweet oranges include the Valencia, Maroc and Jaffa. **Blood oranges**, sometimes known as **Malta oranges**, have streaks of red pigment throughout and are very sweet. The addition of blood orange juice turns a classic hollandaise sauce into sauce maltaise.

Seville orange: This orange, essential for marmalade, is truly seasonal and worth keeping an eagle eye out for as the season seems to come and go before you have blinked! This bitter orange appears in the shops for a very short period during January and February, when marmalade cooks are planning their year's supply. If you see them, but do not have the time to make marmalade immediately, it is worth buying the fruit and freezing them for a later date, rather than missing the season altogether.

Bergamot orange: Similar to the Seville, the oil from the zest is used in aromatherapy.

PREPARATION AND COOKING
Many citrus fruits are waxed and therefore need careful washing before preparation. To remove the zest successfully, rub the fruit over the finest gauge of a grater. Take care to remove the zest (coloured part of the skin) only and not the pith, which is exceedingly bitter. Use a pastry brush to remove the zest stuck in the teeth of the grater. Squeeze the fruit, strain and use as required.

Some cooks suggest heating citrus fruit in a microwave for 20–30 seconds to increase the quantity of juice. If you are lucky enough to have access to a citrus tree, the leaves can be used to flavour olive oil-roasted potatoes.

To obtain more information about growing this rewarding group of fruits, contact the Citrus Centre, Marehill Nursery, West Mare Lane, Marehill, Pulborough, West Sussex RH20 2EA, which has a wonderful selection of citrus plants and all the information that you need to grow them very successfully. The owners are passionate about their fruit – they will vet your green-finger ability and then suggest what variety to buy. Some citrus plants are much easier to grow than others.

FIGS

UK SEASON: Not grown commercially, but like apricots and peaches can grow and produce fruit in the late summer and autumn in warmer parts of the UK.
IMPORTS:
Northern hemisphere: May–November
Southern hemisphere: December–March
FREEZING: Will store if cooked in a sugar syrup.

The fig is often regarded as a Mediterranean fruit – most imported figs come from Greece and Turkey – but it does grow quite happily in protected pockets of the garden in the UK. Where it grows will determine the quantity of fruit produced – in the tropics it can yield three crops of fruit a year, in the cooler climate of the UK only one.

PREPARATION AND COOKING
Choose your fruit carefully. Figs with a good dark-coloured skin are preferable; if very green the fruit will have a fluffy texture and not a lot of flavour. Stored in a cool room, figs will keep for 10–14 days. They freeze quite well for use as preserves, but as a general rule avoid refrigeration if serving raw. Figs are best eaten very ripe and raw, or baked in a liqueur.

MULBERRIES

UK SEASON: Late summer to autumn, not grown or imported commercially.
FREEZING: Freeze individually or in a sugar syrup.

The mulberries are in danger of becoming one of the forgotten fruits. They rarely appear in the supermarket, but can be found occasionally in more adventurous greengrocers. Befriend someone who has a tree in their garden. Take care when picking, as mulberry juice stains anything it touches to a vivid red.

PEACHES AND NECTARINES

UK SEASON: Not grown commercially, but grown in warmer parts of the UK. Will produce fruit from mid- to late summer through to early autumn.
IMPORTS:
Northern hemisphere: April–October
Southern hemisphere: October–May
FREEZING: Best if skinned, halved, stoned and poached in a syrup.

Peaches and nectarines were introduced to Europe from China. They thrive in a warm, temperate climate and grow profusely in the Mediterranean.

Choose unbruised, firm-fleshed fruit and allow to ripen in a mixed fruit bowl at room temperature. When buying from a supermarket, one can usually guarantee that they will have been squeezed and pressed by many fingers to assess their ripeness and will therefore be bruised.

PREPARATION AND COOKING
Both the velvet skin of the peach and the smooth skin of the nectarine are perfectly edible, but the fruit should always be washed first. If a recipe requires the fruit to be cooked, it is advisable to remove the skin as it may become tough during cooking. Submerge the fruit in boiling water, reduce the heat and simmer slowly for about 30 seconds – if the fruit is under-ripe it may need a little longer. Rinse under cold running water and peel away the loosened skin. Avoid soaking in hot water for too long as the fruit may become soft.

Sun-ripened peaches and nectarines are at their best eaten raw or macerated in a little crème de cassis. The flavour of some can be a little bland, in which case poaching or baking in a syrup or with other fruit, such as blackcurrants, is a lovely way to serve them.

PEARS

UK SEASON: Various, mainly late summer to early winter.

IMPORTS:

Northern hemisphere: July–February

Southern hemisphere: February–June

FREEZING: Halved, cored and poached in a syrup.

Like apples, pears are native to Northern Europe and can be found wild in some parts of Britain. Although pears are considered an autumnal fruit, this depends on the variety and locality in which they are grown. Some of the early varieties are ripe and ready to eat by August, some winter varieties are not available until December. Like apples, too, pears are subdivided into dessert and cooking varieties, although the majority available in the supermarkets are the old dessert favourites, such as the elongated russet-looking Conference, always reliable to eat, shiny-skinned Williams Bon Chrétien or Bartlett pear, and the rotund Comice. The Catillac, a traditional cooking pear, is well worth buying to use for poaching in the traditional recipe with red wine or port.

When choosing loose pears, it is often sensible to buy them when they are slightly under-ripe and allow them to ripen in a cool larder or refrigerator. However, a crisp under-ripe pear can be delicious eaten with a mature cheese.

Pre-packaged pears, sometimes sold as 'Ripe and Ready to Eat', will be relatively unbruised as they are protected from the fingers of other supermarket customers.

For the most part, pears do not store as well as apples; they are harvested when only just ripe and left to mellow in a cool dark room or shed. If stored for too long in warm conditions or if harvested too early they become 'sleepy', that is, the flesh turns brown and has a soft mealy texture.

PREPARATION AND COOKING

Careful peeling with a stainless-steel peeler is essential to prevent the fruit from discolouring. Remove the calix, but leave the stalk intact if cooking whole. If slicing, carefully remove the core which can taste bitter.

Unlike some top fruit, gentle cooking greatly enhances the texture of pears, with no loss of flavour.

Baking or poaching in red wine has long been a favourite method of cooking pears. Thick slices of pear lightly sautéed in a little butter and sprinkling of sugar turns the fruit into an excellent accompaniment for game or other rich meat dishes.

Pears can be preserved, most appealingly by bottling them peeled but whole in a liqueur such as Kirsch. Dried pears make a great addition to warm dried fruit salads.

PLUMS, *DAMSONS, GREENGAGES, SLOES AND BULLACES*

UK SEASON FOR PLUMS AND GREENGAGES: Various, late summer to early autumn.

UK SEASON FOR DAMSONS, SLOES AND BULLACES: Not grown commercially, but found throughout the UK in season from late summer to late autumn.

IMPORTS:

Northern hemisphere: June–October

Southern hemisphere: November–April

FREEZING: The smaller fruits can be frozen whole for use in jams and jellies. Plums and greengages are best halved, stoned and cooked in a syrup or dry frozen with sugar.

Obscurity surrounds its family origins, but the plum is thought to be a hybrid of the wild sloe and cherry plum, combining the tartness of the sloe with the sweetness of the cherry plum. The members of this group are autumn fruits, but like many others have an extended season depending on variety.

Sweet dessert plums like Early Laxton and Victoria, and the 'green' plum, the greengage, ripen any time from mid-July onwards. Later varieties including Monach and Marjories Seedling are more likely to appear in September.

PREPARATION AND COOKING

Plums are prepared in the same way as peaches and nectarines, although the skin does not become so tough during cooking. In fact the skin, the most colourful part of the fruit, gives the syrup of poached plums a great warmth. Plums make first-class pies, crumbles and jams and combine well with rich meats such as pork and duck.

Cooking plums, damsons, sloes and bullaces are all found during the autumn months. All these are acidic and therefore used for cooking purposes. Damsons and its close relative the bullace can be found wild and cultivated in this country. The large stones in damsons and bullaces make them tedious to prepare but the results are well worth the effort for the wonderful rich flavour and colour. Cook the washed fruit in a little water until soft, sieve to remove the stones and then sweeten to taste with caster sugar. The purée can then be used as a base for soufflés, mousses and ice creams.

The wild sloe can be utilized in much the same way as the damson; the flavour is similar but extremely tart. This flavour comes into its own when the sloe is added to alcohol and left to mature. Sloe gin is the best-known combination, although sloe brandy or sloe whisky can also help fend off the winter blues very well; lightly warmed through, they make a perfect toddy for a bad cold.

Sloes appear in early October, but if you can avoid the temptation of picking them before the first frost, you will find the flavour infinitely superior and less tart. The only drawback is that the birds may get to the fruit first. Sloes also make a wonderful jelly to serve with pork or game.

QUINCES AND MEDLARS

UK SEASON: Not grown commercially, but found throughout the UK during the autumn months.
FREEZING: Like apples, these do not freeze well uncooked. They are best cooked to a purée or in the case of a fruit jelly, cook the fruit, drip through a bag and freeze the liquid.

These autumnal fruits should be utilized more often, but sadly do not appear in supermarkets as often as they should.

The quince is related to the pear, not to the oriental quince or japonica as it is better known. Quinces grown in the UK tend to be very tart and are therefore not eaten raw. The fruit grown in warmer climates has sweetened in the sun and can therefore be eaten raw. Quinces vary in shape and size – for our recipes we chose the pear-shaped golden-coloured quince. The colour of this variety is such that once cooked it turns a delicate shade of pink. The apple-shaped quince has less flavour and the white flesh hardly colours at all.

Quinces are picked when just ripening, but before a frost can get to them. They have a strong, characteristic flavour and an unforgettable perfumed aroma.

The medlar is related to the quince, but is less popular and not usually available commercially. Its flavour is not dissimilar to that of the quince. The fruit is russet-coloured and has a sharp, tart flavour which makes cooking essential. Medlars are ready to cook when they have 'bletted', a term used to describe half-rotten fruit. The bletting softens the fruit and makes it suitable for cooking, mainly jellies, which turn a beautiful clear red.

PREPARATION AND COOKING

For jelly-making it is preferable to leave the skin, core and seeds intact as they contain acid and pectin which help the jelly to set. Peeling and coring quinces can be quite tedious and is best done using a small sharp knife. Like apples, they will discolour quickly, so do not prepare until required. Long slow poaching, stewing and baking are the most effective methods of cooking.

POMEGRANATES

No UK season.
IMPORTS: From warm climates. Northern and Southern hemispheres: August–April
FREEZING: Remove the pips, juice and freeze.

The seeds of the pomegranate are colourful, slightly tart but distinctive in flavour. The pomegranate is a typical Mediterranean fruit that ripens at the end of a long hot summer and appears in the shops shortly before Christmas.

PREPARATION AND COOKING

Cut the pomegranate open and scoop out the seeds, taking care to remove the very bitter pith in which they are embedded. Do this over a bowl to catch any escaping juice.

The Italians use pomegranates as a macerated accompaniment to Panna Cotta (see page 583), the sharp flavour making the perfect contrast to a rich pudding. Duck in a pomegranate sauce is a classic Iranian dish.

The seeds can also be added to a fruit salad to add colour and an interesting flavour. Pomegranate juice mixes beautifully with vodka.

SOFT FRUITS

BERRIES

FREEZING: All the berry fruits freeze brilliantly either individually or packed in sugar. Once defrosted they can be used for jams, jellies, fruit compotes or any recipe where the fruit requires cooking.

LOGANBERRIES AND TAYBERRIES

UK SEASON: Grown commercially in the UK they appear from mid-June to August.
IMPORTS: Northern hemisphere only: June–August

These hybrid berries are the result of crossing blackberries and raspberries and should be used in the same way.

BLACKBERRIES

UK SEASON: July–September
IMPORTS:
Northern hemisphere: March–September
Southern hemisphere: October–June

Although blackberries are cultivated for supply to supermarkets, in the country wild blackberries are very much food for free. They lose their flavour after frost. Cooked and puréed, especially with apples and pears, they make excellent pies and crumbles and coulis to serve with ice creams or other poached fruit. Bramble jelly is one of the very best preserves.

BLUEBERRIES

UK SEASON: Found in UK markets from July to October.
IMPORTS:
Northern hemisphere: May–October
Southern hemisphere: November–April

Blueberries are a favourite addition to American muffins and mix well with other fruits for fruit salad or coulis.

CRANBERRIES

UK SEASON: Not grown commercially.
IMPORTS:
Northern hemisphere: September–January
Southern hemisphere: April–May

Cranberries appear in supermarkets towards the end of November in time to serve with turkey for Thanksgiving and Christmas. They have a tart flavour and benefit from slow cooking in sugar syrup.

CURRANTS (Black, white and red)

UK SEASON: June–August
IMPORTS:
Northern hemisphere: May–November
Southern hemisphere: December–January

Currants are essential in summer pudding and make excellent preserves.

PREPARATION AND COOKING

Wash well and pull the currants away from the stalks using the prongs of a fork. Cook with sugar with only a small amount of water as they produce a lot of juice. They need minimal cooking to become soft. The washed fruit still on the stalk can be dipped into egg white and then dredged with caster sugar to give a frosted look. Clusters of frosted currants make a lovely decoration for summer fruit puddings and cheesecakes.

ELDERFLOWERS AND ELDERBERRIES
Elderflowers
UK SEASON: Late spring to early summer.

Elderberries
UK SEASON: Early autumn.

These are the blossom and fruit of the common elder, a tree native to Europe, North Africa and Asia. It grows wild in the UK.

Elderflowers have a strong aromatic muscat flavour, often associated with the bouquet of a Sauvignon blanc wine. The frothy, creamy-white heads are called umbels.

Elderberries are shiny-black when ripe and grow in clusters.

PREPARATION AND COOKING
Elderflowers should be picked when newly in flower, shaken to release debris and tiny insects and rinsed under cold running water. They are classically associated and cooked with gooseberries, both coming into season at the same time. They should be tied in muslin and added to the gooseberries during cooking to enhance the flavour. The umbels also contain natural yeast, which when left to ferment with sugar and lemon juice give off CO_2 which gives a refreshing sparkle to elderflower cordial or sparkling wine.

Elderberries need to be prepared in much the same way as currants, washed and stripped carefully from the branch with the prongs of a fork. They need to be cooked with sugar to bring out their strong, distinctive flavour. They are used in the making of wine and in preserves. They can be mixed with other autumnal fruits to make a lovely hedgerow jelly.

CAPE GOOSEBERRIES
UK SEASON: September–December (hot-house)
IMPORTS: All year round from Colombia. Imports also from South Africa, Zimbabwe, Egypt and Kenya.

Cape gooseberries, also known as physalis and Chinese Lantern, are thought of as a luxury fruit. They are sold still encased in a brittle lantern-like jacket which needs to be removed, revealing a small orange berry. Once the berry has been washed, they can be used in exotic fruit salads and dipped in chocolate or fondant icing and served as a petit four. They are high in pectin and therefore make good jam.

RASPBERRIES AND STRAWBERRIES
UK SEASON:
Raspberries: May–October
Strawberries: April–October
IMPORTS:
Northern hemisphere: April–November
Southern hemisphere: November–March
FREEZING: As with other berry fruits these will freeze very well either individually or packed in sugar.

The most popular of all the summer fruits, raspberries and strawberries grow in abundance in this country during summer months and in the case of raspberries in autumn as well. We have become so used to seeing imported strawberries at other times of year that they have lost their seasonality. Strawberries imported from abroad during the winter and spring months seem to lack the wonderful sweet aroma that English varieties have. Wild or Alpine strawberries grow happily in the UK and appear from early June onwards.

Cultivated raspberries have two seasons. Summer varieties produce fruit from early July onwards. In the autumn, just as we think that all that summer has to offer has gone, the second season begins and we can enjoy raspberries for a few short weeks in September. Like strawberries, raspberries also grow wild in some parts of the UK and other Northern European countries.

PREPARATION AND COOKING
Both raspberries and strawberries should be rinsed before eating. Strawberries usually need to be hulled before eating; raspberries, if carefully picked, can be eaten straight away.

Both raspberries and strawberries are delicious on their own with cream, or mixed with other berries such as blueberries. They make superb mousses, ice creams, tarts, cheesecakes and sauces.

In years of a glut of either fruit, jam-making is the best option to preserve them. Both can be frozen, although raspberries seem to fare better in the freezer. Raspberries also make wonderful vinegar. Sweet raspberry vinegar can be made by steeping the fruit over a few days; the resulting sticky vinegar can be used in dressings or as a sauce for ice cream.

GOOSEBERRIES
UK SEASON: Late spring to mid-summer.
IMPORTS:
Northern hemisphere: May–August
Southern hemisphere: November–February
FREEZING: Like other berry fruits, gooseberries will freeze well either individually or packed in sugar. As with other frozen fruits they are only suitable for recipes that require cooked fruit such as jam, chutneys or compotes.

The gooseberry is native to Northern Europe and is grown commercially in the UK. The fruit of a thorny shrub, the small bristly fruits that appear in late May are sweet straight from the bush. If left too long before picking, they will either be eaten by birds or have a tendency to become bitter.

PREPARATION AND COOKING
Wash, top and tail and stew slowly with a little water until soft, sweetening to taste with sugar. Elderflower umbels (see above) can be added to the cooking fruit to enhance the flavour. Gooseberry purée can be sieved (it freezes well) and used for fools, soufflés and ice creams. The fruit is high in pectin and can be added to low-pectin fruits, such as strawberries, in the making of jam.

GRAPES
UK SEASON: Dessert grapes are not grown commercially but found from late summer to mid-winter in warmer parts of the UK or grown in glasshouses.
IMPORTS:
Northern hemisphere: June–November
Southern hemisphere: December–May

FREEZING: Seedless varieties of grape will freeze whole, otherwise, halve, remove the pips and pack in sugar.

EXOTIC FRUITS
The variety of exotic fruits available in supermarkets and ethnic grocers increases each year; with every passing month something new adorns the shelves. We take for granted that pineapple and kiwi fruit are exotic as they are practically part of our daily lives, but we are still hesitant to try the very newest arrivals. We only cover the most popular fruits that we use in our recipes, but do look out for and try new ideas when you see them.

BANANAS
UK SEASON: Not applicable.
IMPORTS: From tropical parts of Northern and Southern hemisphere.

The banana, the most favoured and familiar addition to our fresh fruit bowls, has been a popular import for many years. Tonnes of bananas are imported yearly from as far afield as St Lucia, Jamaica, Costa Rica and Belize. Best peeled and eaten raw, the flesh may be heated, but it is not good cooked or frozen as the flesh turns brown. The larger and less sweet relative, the plantain, is mainly imported from Africa and Asia where they are used in many savoury dishes.

DATES
UK SEASON: Not applicable.
IMPORTS: July–February mainly from hot climates in the Northern hemisphere.

Fresh dates are a real treat, but we more often find the semi-dried vacuum-packed variety in the supermarket. The very best are the fat sweet medjool dates that are imported from California and the Middle East; they have a high carbohydrate content and are perfect served with mature cheddar or as a petit four. Once the stone is removed they can be either stuffed or served plain.

KIWI FRUIT

UK SEASON: Not applicable (though they can be grown in a glasshouse).
IMPORTS:
Northern hemisphere: October–May
Southern hemisphere: April–September

Kiwi fruit, or Chinese gooseberries as they are often known, have become part of our everyday diet. They pip the orange at the post by having the highest vitamin C content of any fruit. They are normally peeled of their mohair-textured skin, but it is edible and the fruit is served 'skin on' in some countries of origin. Kiwi is at its best served raw, either on its own or in a salad; the texture is not pleasant cooked.

LYCHEES

UK SEASON: Not applicable.
IMPORTS:
Northern hemisphere: May–September
Southern hemisphere: October–February

Lychees are most often seen on the menu of an oriental restaurant. They appear fresh in the supermarket at Christmas when they are imported from South Africa, Madagascar and Australia. Like many exotic fruits, they are fiddly to prepare; not only does the thick, bitter skin need to be peeled away, but the large stone needs to be removed from the centre. They need to be eaten raw and make a wonderful addition to an exotic fruit salad. Peeled and stoned canned lychees are a good alternative to fresh.

MANGOES AND PAPAYA

UK SEASON: Not applicable.
IMPORTS:
Northern hemisphere: May–September
Southern hemisphere: October–July

There are practically as many different varieties of mango imported into this country as there are apples, but to the untrained eye they can all look identical. The papaya is less popular and mainly comes from South America, whereas the majority of mangoes are imported from Asia.

They say the only way to eat a mango is in the bath; it is a notoriously messy business and can be wasteful. The best way is to slice off the flesh on either side of the large flat stone, peel and slice. The remaining flesh around the stone can be cut away, peeled and sliced. Like melons and pineapple, a ripe mango will smell strongly through the skin; the colour of the skin is not always a good indication of ripeness. Likewise if the fruit is very soft when pressed, it may be an indication that it is bruised.

Papaya should be cut in half and the seeds removed. The flesh should be peeled and sliced.

PASSION FRUIT

UK SEASON: Not applicable.
IMPORTS:
Northern hemisphere: March–July
Southern hemisphere: September–May

The passion fruit is the one fruit that is at its best when it looks at its worst. The pips are completely under-ripe when the skin is smooth. Once the skin has shrunk and is wrinkled the seeds will be sweet and not too hard. An under-ripe fruit tastes tart and the seeds are very hard. To serve passion fruit, cut the top off, just like a boiled egg, and scoop out the seeds with a teaspoon. The seeds freeze well and can be frozen in ice cube trays to make an unusual addition to a soft drink during hot summer months.

PINEAPPLE

UK SEASON: Not applicable.
IMPORTS: North and South America, Asia and Africa.

This popular exotic fruit is so commonplace now that we probably take it for granted. It is tedious to prepare but the effort of peeling a fresh pineapple is well worthwhile.

To choose a fresh pineapple: Don't be tempted to press the fruit, but smell the skin instead. A ripe pineapple will smell strongly sweet and aromatic; the cut stalk on the underside should not be too dry or rotten and a leaf will pull easily from the top. Fresh pineapple is notoriously difficult to cook with. The enzyme, bromlin, in the flesh prevents gelatine setting efficiently. For cooking purposes it is better to use canned fruit; the fruit does not freeze well, but can be candied. It has a low pectin content and therefore is not ideal for jam.

MELONS

The sweet melon is a tropical fruit, native to central Africa. Melons vary enormously in shape, size and flavour and we are fortunate enough to have supplies of various types all through the year. The most popular include Cantaloupe, Charentais, Galia, honeydew and Ogen.

TAMARILLO

UK SEASON: *Not applicable.*
IMPORTS: *Mainly from the Southern hemisphere, Zimbabwe and New Zealand in particular.*

This colourful and tart fruit makes the perfect refreshing accompaniment to a rich creamy pudding.

Tamarillo should be peeled in the same way as a tomato, halved and cooked in a light syrup until tender. Raw, they are dark cranberry-red in colour; once cooked the seeds and juice turn a sensational dark purple.

VEGETABLES

ALLIUMS (the onion family)

There are over 400 varieties of allium, most of which are ornamental. The few that can be eaten give us variety all year round. We produce a large majority of our own alliums. Imports from the Northern hemisphere, as a general rule, occur most of the year round. Few alliums are imported from the Southern hemisphere

with the exception of garlic, some onions and shallots.

The allium family are most often preserved in pickles rather than frozen. If frozen, they must be prepared as for cooking and then ideally cooked and carefully wrapped to prevent cross-flavouring other foods.

GARLIC

UK SEASON: *From mid-summer onwards. Some varieties store well and are therefore in season, from store, all year round.*

Garlic has the strongest flavour of all the edible alliums and should therefore be used in moderation in most dishes, with one or two exceptions.

Like the onion, garlic has been traditionally used for its medicinal value as well as for cooking, and it is well known that it was used to ward off evil spirits.

When the garlic bulbs are harvested, some are sold as green, wet or fresh. The flavour of the garlic at this stage is pungent and well pronounced. Other bulbs are dried briefly, then strung on to ropes for storage through the winter. Some varieties store well, some need eating within a few months. Strings of garlic, which look so decorative in a kitchen, will dry and shrivel much quicker than bulbs kept covered in the refrigerator. A variety that has been growing in this country for many years, but is in danger of dying out, is the Elephant garlic, which has huge cloves: a single clove can weigh up to 85g/3oz. This sounds like a garlic fanatic's dream, but in fact the flavour is very subtle and mild.

PREPARATION AND COOKING

The finer garlic is crushed, the stronger the flavour, therefore for stews, casseroles, aïoli, or wherever pungency is needed, crush finely. For a more subtle flavour chop or leave whole, then remove after cooking. For those who find that raw garlic in aïoli is too overpowering, blanching for 1 minute in boiling water will lessen the strong taste.

The use of a garlic-crusher is fine – until you

need to clean it! Trying to remove pieces of garlic embedded in the holes is tedious. It is far easier to squash the garlic flat with the blade of a knife, then remove the skin and pulverize the garlic, with a good pinch of salt, to a paste. This takes the same amount of time and there is no mess to clean up. As with onions, wash your hands carefully afterwards in cold water, then hot soapy water, or the flavour of the garlic will be with you for a few days.

Care needs to be taken when sweating or roasting garlic. If it is allowed to brown it becomes very bitter, so always add it towards the end of cooking to get the full flavour.

LEEKS

UK SEASON: Depending on variety, mid-autumn to late spring.

The leek is one of the most desirable winter vegetables. At a time when little else is growing in the garden, they add colour to any menu, and are an inexpensive vegetable to buy. Most varieties are resistant to frost; the only disadvantage is trying to dig them up when the ground is rock-solid with the cold.

The delicate part of the leek is the white or 'blanched' base. This part has been underground and therefore has not had the opportunity to turn green in the winter sun. Many recipes call for the white part of the leek as the flavour is less defined and adds subtlety to a recipe.

PREPARATION AND COOKING

Choose even-sized leeks with plenty of blanched area. Trim away the root and shave off the thick, tough outside green leaves. Leeks are grown in sand, and if the weather has been wet they can be very gritty. Either split the leek in half lengthways or slice crossways, then wash in several changes of water. Cook, uncovered, in boiling salted water for 2–3 minutes or until tender. Steaming leeks will prevent them from breaking up too much.

Leeks can be successfully roasted, baked or even finely shredded, rolled in seasoned flour and deep-fried. Whatever the recipe, it is always a good idea to blanch them for a minute or so first.

Leeks are good in soups and quiches, or served in a vinaigrette as part of a mixed hors d'oeuvre.

ONIONS, SHALLOTS AND PICKLING ONIONS

UK SEASON: Late summer to early autumn. For the most part onions store well, so strictly speaking they remain in season all year long.

The most used and oldest vegetable known in the kitchen, onions contribute many different assets to a legion of dishes, and cooking wouldn't be the same without them. They were brought to Britain by the Romans who revered the onion not only for its culinary uses, but for its medicinal properties as well. To this day, baked or boiled onions are still considered to be one of the best cures for a cold.

One of the mainstays of the vegetable garden, some varieties of onion are planted in the autumn, others when the weather warms in spring. They are harvested during the summer, dried a little then strung into bunches to last through the long cold winter.

The mild-flavoured shallot, used in many recipes that require a more subtle version of onion, has been much used by the French through the centuries. Its lilac hue makes it an attractive alternative to onion, and it is better suited to serving raw. It must however, be very finely sliced or chopped.

Button or pickling onions are another mild-flavoured variety that are grown particularly for preserving, but are also excellent cooked whole in stews and casseroles. Varieties of button onion include cocktail and silverskin, which are very often used for commercial pickling.

PREPARATION AND COOKING

Slicing and chopping an onion has become something of an art form but is often a tearful experience. There are many different opinions on how to prevent crying during preparation, which probably depends on the type of onion and its acidity. Very fresh onions are much worse to peel than onions that have been stored for a few weeks.

Cut the onion in half through the root. Peel away the skin, taking care to peel enough of the outside layers away as any brown membrane left on will be tough.

To slice the onion, work from the top of the onion, leaving the root to keep the onion together. To chop an onion, cut horizontal slices then vertical slices, leaving the root intact.

To rid onions of their acidity, which is strong enough to curdle milk, they can be sweated very slowly in butter until completely soft and transparent. Onions contain a lot of natural sugar and therefore burn very easily. A helpful but not foolproof tip when cooking onions is to cover them closely in damp greaseproof paper and put a lid on top. Cook over a very low heat, stirring from time to time to prevent sticking. The sweating process can take up to 30 minutes, or for recipes that require colour as well, up to an hour. For recipes that require the use of whole button or pickling onions, it is advisable to blanch them before peeling by placing in boiling water for 2–3 minutes, then drain and peel while still warm. This will start the cooking and makes the thin skin much easier to pull away.

As well as lending essential flavour to many recipes, onions feature as a principal ingredient in a variety of dishes, from soups and tarts to sauces, marmalades and relishes.

SPRING AND WELSH ONIONS
UK SEASON: Various, but in the garden from mid-spring onwards.

Spring or salad onions, sometimes known as scallions, lend themselves well to stir-fries, salads and any dishes that require a subtle flavour.

Welsh onions make a good substitute for spring onions during winter and early spring. Like spring onions, they have a subtle onion flavour that can be used in many dishes.

PREPARATION
Trim the root away and cut off the coarse green leaves about 2.5cm/1in above the split. Slice as required. Spring onions sliced on the diagonal with a sharp knife are a pleasing garnish for many dishes.

CHIVES: *See herbs.*

BRASSICAS
The brassica group includes a large selection of the green vegetables that feature in our day-to-day diet, including cabbages and cauliflowers, broccoli, kale, kohlrabi and brussels sprouts. Turnips and swedes are also true brassicas but in this chapter we have included them in our roots section.

The different varieties of all these vegetables makes it possible to have a supply of one or other all through the year for use in the kitchen.

As with other vegetables, we produce large quantities of our own brassicas although we do import from Northern hemisphere countries such as the Netherlands, Canada and Europe. As a general rule little is imported from the Southern hemisphere.

Some members of the brassica family may be frozen. Wash well, prepare and pack carefully before freezing.

CABBAGE AND KALE
UK SEASON: Various all year round.

Immensely popular with the Romans and accredited with medicinal powers to cure many ills, nowadays the cabbage is not always so favourably looked upon by the cook and can be seen as dull and uninteresting. 'School dinners' in this country may account for this. Cabbage was often served drastically overcooked and left covered in warming ovens for a long period of time, so that the resulting mass looked, smelt and tasted unpleasant. If cabbage is cooked briefly it can be delicious, however.

Dutch, Savoy and the various red cabbages are probably the best-known autumn and winter varieties. Spring and summer yield the less hearted, loose-leaf varieties. Whatever the cabbage, it is an economical way of providing a good source of greenery and roughage in the diet.

Curly kale is a loose-leafed variety of cabbage that has no heart. It is at its best during January and February when there is a lack of other green vegetables. It can be cooked in the same way as cabbage.

PREPARATION AND COOKING

Pull away the outer leaves, cut in quarters and cut out the core. Shred finely. The cabbage may then be stir-fried in butter or oil or cooked briefly in boiling salted water. Some find the smell of cabbage (and cauliflower) quite overpowering: a bay leaf added to the water reduces the smell considerably.

Cabbage can be braised slowly in stock or vinegar: red cabbage cooked in this way makes a wonderful splash of colour in many autumn and winter menus, whether it is served with bangers and mash or with roast goose. Served raw, cabbage is popular in coleslaw. The leaves may also be stuffed and steamed, like dolmades.

CHINESE CABBAGE
UK SEASON: Mainly summer and autumn.

This is one of the brassicas that can be used raw in the making of salads. It is a hearted variety of cabbage, resembling the cos lettuce, which has a delicate flavour and is also good shredded and stir-fried.

Pak choi, or Bok choi as it is sometimes known, is a non-hearted variety of Chinese cabbage that has always been a popular vegetable in oriental cuisine and is now available in supermarkets. Steamed, blanched or stir-fried with other oriental ingredients it can be quite delicious.

CAULIFLOWER
UK SEASON: Various, depending on varieties.

In the last century cauliflowers were a miniature version of the large flowering head that we know so well, no bigger than a tennis ball. These small cauliflowers are now making a reappearance and are available pre-packed in supermarkets. At its best the head of cauliflower should be creamy white, with no blemishes, and is quite a challenge for even the experienced gardener to grow. If cooked well it is a wonderful vegetable with much potential; if cooked badly it can be soggy and flavourless.

PREPARATION AND COOKING

Pull away the tough outer green leaves and break the head into even-sized florets, wash well to remove any debris and cook for 2–3 minutes, depending on the size of the florets, in boiling salted water. As with cabbage, a bay leaf can be added to the water to reduce the smell.

Once cooked, drain and refresh briefly. Press the cauliflower gently to remove any excess water and then use as required.

Cauliflower coated in cheese sauce made with good mature cheddar must be the ultimate in comfort food. It is also good served raw and we often use it at Leith's in a display of crudités served with a dip.

BROCCOLI AND CALABRESE
UK SEASON: Various, depending on varieties.

Strictly speaking, broccoli is the sprouting variety, grown for its sprout, rather than a headed variety. Calabrese, on the other hand, is a type of headed broccoli, sometimes called summer cauliflower and ready for harvesting from July onwards.

The spring and winter varieties are the purple and white sprouting broccoli that appears from January onwards. This is one of the most popular of all the brassicas, which needs only light cooking. Blanching, steaming, stir-frying or deep-frying as for tempura are all great ways to cook broccoli.

BRUSSELS SPROUTS
UK SEASON: Winter to spring.

These miniature cabbages are an essential part

of Christmas dinner, cooked until just tender, tossed in butter and served mixed with chestnuts. There are a number of varieties: recently a little red brussels sprout has been developed which has a nutty flavour and is really worth trying if you see it.

PREPARATION AND COOKING
Choose the smallest sprouts you can find. Trim away the stalk and peel away enough of the outside leaf to reveal a shiny clean baby cabbage underneath. Avoid cutting a cross in the bottom of sprouts as this only makes them waterlogged. Cook, uncovered, in simmering salted water for 6–10 minutes or until tender – like cabbage, brussels sprouts can be bitter and unpleasant if overcooked. Once cooked, refresh well and avoid keeping them warm for any period of time as they lose their colour and become acidic.

KOHLRABI
UK SEASON: Winter.

This member of the brassica family is sometimes looked upon as a root crop. Its crisp, firm-textured flesh tastes very much like cabbage. It has an odd shape with shoots all around the outside, and varieties include a red-skinned as well as a green. Kohlrabi can be peeled and shredded to make a great addition to a winter salad, stir-fried to add texture to a dish, or plainly roasted with other root crops.

BEANS, PODS AND SEEDS
There is a vast array of different types and varieties of beans and peas, cultivated all around the world. Beans were popular with the Romans, who in turn introduced them to the countries of Northern Europe.

In this country we grow a huge amount of our own beans and pods. Many varieties are imported from Northern hemisphere countries. Peas are imported during the winter months from Spain, Portugal and Egypt. Mangetout and sweetcorn are the main varieties imported from Southern hemisphere countries during the winter months in the UK.

Surplus from the garden can be frozen. There is also always a particularly large selection of frozen beans and peas in supermarkets. Prepare as for cooking and seal in a polythene bag.

BROAD BEANS
UK SEASON: June to September.

Broad beans were once a staple of the peasant farmer's diet as they are very easy to grow. The beans can also be dried, which adds to their versatility. When cooking fresh, choose small pods as they contain sweeter beans.

PREPARATION AND COOKING
Open the pod and remove the beans. Blanch for a minute in boiling water (some say that adding salt to beans and peas toughens the outer skin). Drain and refresh. Peel away the tough outer skin, a tedious job but really worth the effort. Toss in hot seasoned butter or add cold to salads.

If freezing broad beans, this is best done after the first blanching.

FRENCH BEANS (HARICOTS VERTS/ STRING BEANS)
UK SEASON: July to September.

The French bean is said to have come from Central and South America to Europe, where the French Huguenots cultivated it.

As a green vegetable, young French beans are best, but when allowed to grow, the pod yields the haricot bean, which is dried and becomes a staple during the winter months (see dried beans below). There are many varieties and colours of haricot bean and when eaten very young they are wonderful.

PREPARATION AND COOKING
Many recipes suggest topping and tailing the bean, but if young and tender it is only necessary to trim off the tops and the tails can be left on. Wash and cook in boiling salted water until tender – this can take anything from 30 seconds to 10 minutes depending on size. French beans can become disappointing later on in the season. Drain and refresh before serving.

RUNNER BEANS

UK SEASON: July to October, depending on frost.

The runner bean, like the French bean, comes from the New World. They make a decorative centrepiece in any vegetable garden, running or climbing up a standing frame, as they give lovely orange flowers and a multitude of produce later on.

PREPARATION AND COOKING

Choose small beans if possible; older ones are stringy and the beans inside can be tough.

Wash, top and tail, pulling away the tough string down the outside of the bean. Pull through a 'stringer' which shreds them finely, or practise your knife skills by cutting them very finely on the diagonal. Runner beans need little cooking if cut carefully: simmer in boiling salted water until *al dente*.

DRIED BEANS

During the winter months make the most of dried haricot, black-eyed and kidney beans as well as the other dried legumes that pack the supermarket shelves. They are a wonderful source of fibre and introduce many differing textures and flavours.

PEAS

UK SEASON: Various, depending on variety, from late spring to late summer.

Like so many of the vegetables we enjoy today, peas were cultivated by the Greeks and brought to us by the Romans. They soon became favoured and were dried like other legumes to become a staple of the winter diet.

Like potatoes, peas are classified according to the time when they are ready for harvesting. Early varieties are ready for harvesting in late spring and main crop varieties from mid-July through to September.

Mangetout, also known as sugar snaps or snow peas, is a variety grown and picked before the peas have had time to develop in the pod. They are popular though quite expensive. The asparagus pea, with its frilly, caterpillar-shaped pod, is another delicious 'eat-all' variety with a distinct asparagus flavour, well worth trying if you come across it.

PREPARATION AND COOKING

Peas: Choose smallish peas with heavy pods. Open the pod and remove the peas, which can be blanched and frozen for use later on in the season or cooked straight from the pod. Add a pinch of sugar and a sprig of mint to the cooking water to add sweetness; do not add salt, this can toughen the skin. Serve as a classic accompaniment to poached salmon, lamb, duck and other roasts. Peas are good in risottos, especially the Italian risi e bisi.

Mangetout: Top and tail and boil or steam for 30 seconds, drain and refresh. Use as a vegetable accompaniment or in stir-fries.

OKRA

UK SEASON: Not applicable.
IMPORTS: From Northern and Southern hemispheres all year round.

Okra, bhindi and ladies' fingers are all names for this versatile and popular vegetable. It is a main ingredient in many ethnic cuisines, particularly in Indian and Sri Lankan dishes. It is also well known as the main ingredient in the Cajun dish, gumbo, where it is used to thicken this spicy stew. Gumbo was the name given to it by African slaves taken to the USA 200 years ago.

SWEETCORN

UK SEASON: August to September.

The appearance of inexpensive corn on the cob in the supermarket heralds the end of summer and beginning of autumn. A type of maize, sweetcorn is grown extensively in this country. It originated in Mexico thousands of years ago. The Americans took to it in a big way: the corn from the cob was dried and 'pop corn' was invented.

PREPARATION AND COOKING

For barbecuing, the husk can be left on and the

cob wrapped in foil and cooked on the barbecue for 20–30 minutes until tender.

The husk can also be removed and the cob simmered in unsalted water for 15–20 minutes, depending on size, until just *al dente*. It is then most popular served with hot butter and plenty of black pepper.

If sweetcorn 'nibs' are required, for salads or to make corn fritters to serve with Southern-style fried chicken, remove the corn from the cooked cob with the prongs of a fork.

Baby sweetcorn, available pre-packed from supermarkets, are ideal for stir-fries and can be found as part of a stir-fry vegetable selection.

LETTUCE, SALAD LEAVES AND SPINACH

UK SEASON: Differing varieties throughout the year: we are never without!

Every visit to the supermarket reveals a new leaf on the chilling shelves. A few years ago all the bitter leaves such as frisée and radicchio became hugely popular, then Chinese and other oriental cabbage, followed by rocket, and now we have Japanese green mustard leaves such as mizuna and shiso, Japanese basil, to try along with mitzuba – Japanese cress.

LETTUCES

There is a huge selection of lettuces to choose from. Some varieties are imported. Cos lettuce types are imported from Israel and Morocco during our winter months. Hearted cabbage-type lettuces such as Iceberg are imported from the USA all year round as are the non-hearting butterhead lettuces from the Irish Republic.

As most lettuce and salad leaves are eaten raw, freezing is not a suitable method of storing with the exception of spinach.

Cos lettuce: Characterized by the elongated, crisp leaf, there are many varieties, some of which are resistant to cold and can withstand winter, the best-known being Winter Density. Little Gem is another Cos variety and a popular salad choice.

Soft cabbage lettuces: One of the best-known varieties is Tom Thumb. On the whole these lettuces are early maturing types. Sown throughout spring and summer, they ensure a steady supply.

Hearted cabbage lettuces: These include Webb's Wonder and Iceberg.

Non-hearting lettuces ('cut-and-come-again' or 'salad bowl'): The oak leaf and the lollo rosso are probably the best known. They are prolific all year round, grown mainly under cloche in winter.

Oriental lettuces: These include the Celtuce and are grown for their edible stems.

CHICORYS

These bitter-leafed salad plants are hugely popular in Italy whence the name radicchio, Italian for chicory, derives. Some wonderful varieties include variegated and red types, and we are seeing more of these in the supermarkets now. Some varieties grow and heart in late summer, others are cut back, the root replanted and kept in the dark until a forced chicon develops. Chicory winters well in protected areas. Red chicory provides a welcome splash of colour in winter *salades tièdes*.

Endives: Rather confusingly, chicory is also known as Belgian endive, endives being members of the chicory family. Again, the leaves are bitter. Many varieties winter well, including the ever-popular frisée.

PREPARATION AND COOKING

Avoid cutting salad leaves with a knife as this bruises them and they will soon look tired in a salad. All salad leaves are best washed well and torn into bite-sized pieces.

Some lettuces can be cooked and served with a creamy sauce. The best variety for cooking is probably the Cos, as it is firm and will not lose its shape. Lettuce can also be used to make a refreshing chilled summer soup.

SPINACH

UK SEASON: Spring, summer and autumn.

Different varieties of this delicate leaf, home-grown and from abroad, are available all year round. Spinach needs little introduction. Its very distinctive flavour has made it the most tasty of leaves: young leaves are excellent in salads or large leaves cooked until just lightly wilted.

FREEZING: Choose young leaves, blanch for 30 seconds, then refresh under cold running water. Press very well to remove excess water, then freeze.

PREPARATION AND COOKING
Spinach needs careful washing in several changes of water. The leaves wilt very quickly so the most effective way of cooking spinach is to toss it in hot seasoned butter or olive oil for a few seconds until it wilts. Or cook lightly with just the water adhering to the leaves after washing, but with no added water. Overcooked spinach is bitter and unpleasant.

As an accompaniment, spinach goes especially well with fish and chicken, and also makes beautiful soup or quiche filling.

ROOTS AND TUBERS

We import many varieties of roots and tubers from both Northern and Southern hemisphere countries. Storage and the numerous varieties of home-grown carrots and potatoes that we have on offer make them in season all year round. Jerusalem artichokes on the other hand appear mainly during late autumn and the winter, they are not imported on a large scale. Parsnips, swedes, turnips and beetroot are available in large quantities from store, although a few are imported from as far away as Australia and Tasmania during May, June and July.

POTATOES: In Britain potatoes are often classified according to when they are harvested:
First earlies (new): end May to July
Second earlies (new): end August to March
Main crop: September to May.

The growing season for early potatoes is short. They are harvested when the tubers are immature; the skin is not 'set' and can be rubbed off easily, and they should be eaten soon after purchase as they do not keep well.

Main crop varieties are lifted when fully mature and will keep through to next year's harvest if correctly stored.

The three most popular varieties of main crop potatoes grown in Britain are, in descending order: Maris Piper, Record and Cara.

Look for potatoes that are well-shaped, firm and free from blemishes. Avoid those with green patches as these indicate exposure to light and the production of toxins (non-deadly poisons) under the skin. Buy new potatoes in small quantities as they do not keep well.

Always remove potatoes from the plastic bag in which they have been sold.

Main crop potatoes will keep well if they are stored, unwashed, in a dark, cool, frost-free, airy place away from smells. Light turns potatoes green, and warmth and dampness can cause them to sprout, shrivel and rot.

SELECTION OF POTATO VARIETIES

NAME	CROP	USES	COMMENTS
ARRAN PILOT	First early.	Salads, chipped, baked.	White skin and flesh; waxy texture when cooked.
ASPERGE LA RATTE/ CORNICHON	Second early.	Salads, steamed.	Yellow skin; creamy flesh; waxy texture when cooked.
CARA	Main.	All rounder.	Large; round; white skin; pink eyes; creamy flesh; creamy texture when cooked.

NAME	CROP	USES	COMMENTS
CHARLOTTE	Second early	Salads, steamed, boiled.	Pale yellow skin and flesh; good flavour; waxy texture when cooked.
DESIRÉE	Main.	All rounder.	Red skin; pale yellow flesh; waxy texture when cooked.
ESTIMA	Second early.	Baked, chipped, boiled.	Pale yellow skin and flesh; waxy texture when cooked.
GOLDEN WONDER	Main.	Salads, baked, mashed.	Brown skin; pale yellow flesh; floury texture when cooked.
KING EDWARD	Main.	All rounder.	Large; pale skin with pink patches; creamy flesh; floury texture when cooked.
MARIS BARD	First early.	Salads, boiled, baked when mature.	White skin and flesh; waxy texture when cooked.
MARIS PIPER	Main.	All rounder.	Thin white skin; cream-coloured flesh; floury texture when cooked.
PENTLAND DELL	Main.	All rounder.	Long oval shape; white flesh and skin; firm texture when cooked.
PENTLAND JAVELIN	First early.	Salads, boiled, steamed.	Smooth white skin; white flesh; waxy texture when cooked.
PENTLAND SQUIRE	Main.	Baked, roasted, chipped, mashed.	White skin (russeted); white flesh; floury texture when cooked.
PINK FIR APPLE	Main.	Salads, boiled.	Pink skin; pinky-yellow flesh; new potato characteristics; waxy texture when cooked.
ROMANO	Main.	Baked, boiled, roasted, chipped.	Red skin; creamy flesh; waxy texture when cooked.
RECORD	Main.	Grown mainly for processing, such as crisps, waffles, etc.	Short oval; yellow skin; pigments on exposure to light; yellow flesh; firm; slightly waxy texture.

NAME	CROP	USES	COMMENTS
ULSTER SCEPTRE	First early.	Salads, boiled.	Elongated oval shape; white skin and flesh; very waxy; firm texture when cooked.
WILJA	Second early.	Boiled, baked, chipped.	Rough yellow skin; pale yellow firm flesh; slightly dry but firm texture when cooked.

MOST SUITABLE COOKING METHODS

BOILING	MASHING	BAKING	CHIPPING
Cara	Golden Wonder	Arran Pilot	Arran Pilot
Charlotte	King Edward	Cara	King Edward
Desirée	Maris Piper	Estima	Maris Piper
Estima	Pentland Dell	Golden Wonder	Maris Bard
King Edward	Pentland Squire	King Edward	Pentland Dell
Maris Piper	Romano	Maris Piper	Romano
Maris Bard	Wilja	Pentland Dell	Desirée
Pentland Javelin	Desirée	Romano	
Pentland Squire		Wilja	
Pink Fir Apple		Desirée	
Romano			
Ulster Sceptre			
Wilja			

ROASTING	SALADS	STEAMING	PROCESSING
King Edward	Asperge	Asperge	Record
Maris Piper	Desirée	Pentland Javelin	
Pentland Dell	Golden Wonder	Ulster Sceptre	
Romano	Maris Bard	Wilja	
Wilja	Pentland Javelin		
Desirée	Pentland Squire		
	Wilja		
	Charlotte		
	Pink Fir Apple		
	Ulster Sceptre		

ARTICHOKES (JERUSALEM)

UK SEASON: Late autumn through winter.

Jerusalem artichokes are indigenous to North America and have no connection with the holy city of Jerusalem at all. How they became so called is something of a mystery, but a common theory is that the name is linked to the Italian name for the sunflower, which is a close relative.

This winter vegetable does not store at all well. As with some types of potato, Jerusalem artichokes begin to soften once removed from the ground. They are well known to provoke flatulence so it may be worth cooking them with a strip of kombu seaweed, which is used by the Japanese when cooking beans to help prevent wind.

PREPARATION AND COOKING

The knobbly shape makes Jerusalem artichokes very difficult to peel; a small paring knife is the best utensil to use. Once peeled they should be kept covered in lightly acidulated water, which helps prevent discoloration.

They can be cooked in much the same way as potatoes, either boiled or roasted, and the unusual nutty flavour makes a great addition to a selection of winter roast vegetables.

A close relative of the Jerusalem artichoke is the Chinese variety, which has a more subtle taste.

CARROTS

UK SEASON: Late spring onwards. Carrots store fairly well and are therefore available all year round.

Established and cultivated in this country since Elizabethan times, the carrot has become a great favourite and staple of the kitchen. Many varieties are grown in this country and we are so used to them that perhaps we have become a little complacent about their versatility and uses.

For serving as a vegetable accompaniment, choose small young carrots, ideally in bunches with the stems and leaves still attached, that have not had a chance to develop a woody core: those can be relegated to the stock pot or used in casseroles and soups or grated for salads.

PARSNIPS

UK SEASON: October onwards through the winter months.

This is one of the few vegetables that is thought to be native to Britain. It is hardy and can withstand winter conditions.

PREPARATION AND COOKING

Choose parsnips that are not too big, lest they be woody. Peel and cut into quarters for cooking. Parsnips are usually parboiled in boiling water before roasting. Its texture and distinctive flavour makes the parsnip a perfect addition to roast vegetables or for a purée.

SWEDE

UK SEASON: October through to early winter.

Swede is also known as Swedish turnip and in Scotland is still referred to as a turnip.

With its colourful look and texture it needs much the same treatment as parsnips and turnips in cooking. Bashed Neeps, from north of the border, is a classic swede recipe, traditionally served with haggis.

TURNIPS

UK SEASON: Summer and autumn.

The turnip was the staple root vegetable in Europe before the appearance of the potato. Turnips ended up as animal fodder from the eighteenth century onwards. They are often thought of as a rather old-fashioned vegetable and consequently ignored, which is a pity, because baby turnips make a wonderful addition to stir-fries, while the large ones are a good addition to roasts.

SWEET POTATOES AND YAMS

Not native to the UK but are very popular. We import them from warmer Northern hemisphere countries such as Israel and Egypt and from as far away as South Africa and Madagascar in the Southern hemisphere. Again, they can be used in the same way as parsnips and potatoes.

SALSIFY AND SCORZONERA (BLACK SALSIFY)

UK SEASON: October onwards through the winter.

These vegetables are sensational. The long white salsify and the black scorzonera roots do not look particularly appealing, but once cooked and peeled they reveal wonderful texture and flavour, slightly reminiscent of asparagus.

PREPARATION AND COOKING

Wash well, but do not peel. Cook in boiling

salted water for 30–40 minutes or until the skin peels away easily. Rinse in hot water, drain and serve either with hot butter or, more traditionally, Hollandaise sauce.

BEETROOT
UK SEASON: Early summer to mid-autumn (will store through winter).

This wonderful Northern European vegetable is not seen much on menus these days, which is a great shame. Perhaps this is because it stains everything it comes in contact with and takes an age to cook. It is widely used in Eastern Europe and Russia, however, where it is especially well known in borscht, the classic beetroot soup.

PREPARATION AND COOKING
Choose even-sized beetroot that are not too big. Wash well, do not peel or trim off stalks as the colour will leach into the water. Cook slowly in boiling salted water for 1–1½ hours or until the skin will peel away easily. Avoid the temptation of stabbing the vegetable or it will lose colour. Serve hot with a béchamel sauce or sliced in salads.

RADISHES
UK SEASON: Spring through to summer.

These fiery little turnip lookalikes are at their best washed, trimmed and tossed in a salad or as part of a crudités selection served with a dip.

At Leith's we used to blanch them in boiling water for a stir-fried vegetable dish. We discovered that this was a complete waste of time, as the radishes would lose their pink tinge and come out completely white, looking just like turnips.

CELERIAC
UK SEASON: October onwards through the winter months.

Celeriac is the root version of celery and has a similar taste to salad celery. It is gaining popularity in Britain as a versatile winter vegetable for roasting and mashing. It is a traditional accompaniment to roast game.

HORSERADISH
UK SEASON: Most of the year.

Horseradish is one of those plants that gardeners spend time trying to rid themselves of as it is likely to take over if not checked. The root can bury itself to extraordinary depths, so careful digging is required to lift it in its entirety.

The leaves of this plant can be poisonous; it is the root that is edible. Peeled and grated, it is used not only for horseradish cream to serve with roast beef or smoked fish, but also in mustards.

STALKS AND SHOOTS
ARTICHOKES (GLOBE)
UK SEASON: Mid-summer to early Autumn.

Some globe artichokes are imported from warmer Northern hemisphere countries during the winter months. (Baby artichokes appear earlier in the season.) The globe artichoke is basically an edible thistle. History relates that it was thought to have had aphrodisiac qualities. It has been popular with 'foodies' since the Middle Ages, particularly with the Italians, who still eat vast quantities of artichokes. They grow to a considerable size, but are considered by gardeners to be fairly easy to cultivate. They are not suitable for freezing.

PREPARATION AND COOKING
Artichokes are served in a variety of ways. The baby artichoke has not had time to develop a thistle choke and can be cooked whole, the more mature plant head needs careful preparation. The stalk of a young globe artichoke is also edible and is referred to as a 'chard'. The whole globe is served with just the 'choke' removed as a first course.

Wash the artichoke thoroughly in salty water to rinse off any bugs that may be hiding in the leaves. Cut off the fibrous stalk so that the artichoke will sit comfortably on a plate. Trim the sharp thistle tips to the leaves either before or after cooking.

Cook for 35–40 minutes in boiling salted water. Artichokes discolour easily which can be avoided by adding a slice of lemon or a splash of vinegar to the cooking water. Try to keep the artichokes completely submerged by weighting down with a sieve or plate; as with any green vegetable, avoid covering with a lid. The artichokes are cooked when a central leaf will pull away easily. Refresh the artichokes under cold running water and allow to drain for a few minutes.

The 'choke' needs to be removed just before serving. Carefully pull back the outside leaves to reveal the soft downy centre leaves, which can be pulled away. Using a teaspoon, scoop out the thistle-like fibres underneath, but take care not to remove too much of the artichoke bottom. Fill the centre with melted butter, hollandaise sauce or a well-flavoured French dressing.

One word of caution – artichokes are notoriously difficult to match to a wine as they have a strong flavour.

Also, as they can be messy to eat, it is essential to provide a hand bowl of hot water for your guests.

Globe artichokes can be purchased canned and ready prepared as artichoke hearts where the centre leaves are still intact, or as artichoke bottoms where the centre leaves and choke have been removed. For most recipes calling for prepared bottoms there is no shame in purchasing them in cans.

CARDOON

The cardoon, also a member of the thistle family, is a vegetable long gone out of fashion though it was grown extensively during the Victorian era. This tall stalk resembles celery in shape but has a flavour not dissimilar to that of globe artichokes. The tender young inner stalks and heart are edible. They need to be cooked by boiling gently or braising. Once cooked cardoons are best served drizzled with melted butter.

ASPARAGUS

UK SEASON: Late April through to late June.

A large quantity of asparagus is imported from Spain. It is grown in Thailand year-round, making it readily available through the winter months. This coveted vegetable is found in the market towards the end of spring. In Europe it is blanched by growers to a creamy white colour; picked straight from the garden it is a greenish-purple colour. It is usually expensive because the plant takes from 3 to 5 years from cultivation to mature ready for picking.

The flavour of asparagus is sensational and as popular now as it was with the Romans. Purists would say the only way to serve it is either steamed or boiled and then drizzled with melted butter. However, there are various other ways to make the most of this popular vegetable.

Freezing is suitable if the asparagus is to be used in cooking recipes such as flans and tarts. The stalks should be trimmed and packed in airtight containers.

PREPARATION AND COOKING

Buy asparagus that has tightly closed tips and is not too closely packed in polythene (the smell of decaying asparagus is particularly unpleasant). To remove the fibrous part of the stalk, avoid cutting with a knife, but bend it until it snaps (the tough part of the stalk will not snap easily). The shoots on the stalk itself should be trimmed away with a peeler, but avoid peeling too deep into the stalk itself as this is wasteful.

Cooking asparagus can be hazardous as the tips cook a lot quicker than the stalks. Either invest in an asparagus steamer, which is a tall saucepan that will hold the asparagus upright, or alternatively lay it in a roasting tin, add a little boiling water and cook it on the hob, with only the stalks over direct heat. An ingenious friend suggested cooking it standing upright in an old baked bean tin with the top and bottom removed, so that the stalks can be submerged in boiling liquid and the tips can steam gently. Depending on size, asparagus takes 3–8 minutes to cook through.

Canned asparagus is readily available, but is a poor reflection of the real flavour of the fresh vegetable.

Asparagus is a perfect first course with melted butter, vinaigrette, hollandaise sauce or sauce maltaise and is also good in tartlets, risottos and salads. It makes luxurious soup and combines very well with fish and chicken.

CELERY

UK SEASON: Late autumn through winter.

Celery has been eaten both raw and cooked for centuries, not only because it is a delicious salad vegetable, but for its medicinal properties. It is notoriously difficult to grow, taking a long time and then requiring a period of earthing up and blanching to give the characteristic crisp white stalk.

PREPARATION AND COOKING
Washed and trimmed, tough celery stalks benefit from being de-stringed. Snap the base and pull upwards and any tough fibres will pull away easily. It is delicious served raw, in salads or a crudités selection, or cooked in soups. As a vegetable accompaniment it is good stir-fried or braised. Celery has a special affinity with cheese.

FLORENCE FENNEL
UK SEASON: Late spring through to autumn.

The plant grows from seed and as it matures develops a swollen bulb, which is cut when about the size of a tennis ball. The leaves are used as herb fennel and the seeds gathered when it flowers.

PREPARATION AND COOKING
Remove the tough outer skin, cut out the core and slice thinly. The aniseed flavour of Florence fennel gives summer salads and purées an unusual flavour. It is a pity to blanch it for use in salads as the flavour and texture are lost. Fennel bulbs are good baked in a cheese sauce.

RHUBARB
UK SEASON: Forced November–April
Outdoor April–September

Rhubarb is a great asset in the vegetable garden. It is easy to grow and useful during months when many fruits and vegetables are sparse. Imported rhubarb comes from the Netherlands and France. Rhubarb freezes very well: trimmed, washed and cut into short lengths, it can be frozen individually or packed in sugar.

Rhubarb is often considered a fruit, but a vegetable by gardeners. Everyone has different ideas. In our recipes we have used it as a fruit in most cases.

At the end of each year the crown is trimmed to the base and then covered over with a terracotta forcer or something similar. Pale pink, delicately flavoured forced rhubarb has appeared by early April. Later on in the season the dark red stalks can become quite tough and acidic.

PREPARATION AND COOKING
Wash, peel and stew with a little water, orange zest or rosewater. Rhubarb makes wonderful pies and crumbles. Puréed rhubarb can be used in mousses, soufflés, ice creams and fools. In savoury dishes the acidity of rhubarb matches rich meats and oily fish well.

SILVER BEET, CHARDS AND SEA KALE
UK SEASON: Some varieties summer and autumn, others throughout the year.

Silver beet is related to beetroot. The leaf has a similar texture to that of spinach but a less refined flavour.

Swiss and rhubarb chards are fairly hardy leafy vegetables. When the leaves are young the whole stalk and leaf can be used; later on in the year, only the leaves can be eaten, as the stalks will have become too tough.

Sea kale has grown wild around the coasts of the UK and Europe for many years. During winter months it is forced (and therefore blanched) under terracotta pots, making it a good late spring vegetable.

PREPARATION AND COOKING
Wash carefully, then simmer in boiling salted water for 2–3 minutes or until cooked, or stir-fry.

VEGETABLE FRUITS
AUBERGINES
UK SEASON: Late summer through to mid-autumn.
IMPORTS: From Northern and Southern hemisphere countries year-round.

Aubergines can be disappointing in flavour and when they are out of season during winter and spring it is best to look for those grown in warmer climates, where they would have had the benefit of autumn sun. Those grown under glass or in the hot-house can be very bland. Aubergines can be frozen for cooked dishes. Prepare as for cooking and store in an airtight container.

This handsome vegetable is often considered to be Mediterranean but actually originates from Asia. The word aubergine derives from Sanskrit. In Asia it was considered to prevent flatulence. It can, however, be quite indigestible and with that in mind many recipes suggest that salting or degorging the aubergine before cooking will lessen these effects. The various species vary from creamy egg-shaped white, deep purple and striped through to the little green pea aubergine which is used extensively in Thai food, particularly green curries.

In some parts of the world the name eggplant is used for aubergine, as is brinjal, familiar from Indian menus.

PREPARATION AND COOKING

As aubergine has a high water content, the most suitable methods of cooking are either baking, frying or grilling. If cooked whole it is worth piercing the aubergine to prevent an explosion in the oven. Once sliced or diced, lightly salting the flesh will draw out the excess moisture. Wipe the salt and moisture away before cooking. Grilling is the healthiest method of cooking, but once degorged aubergines can burn easily. If fried they have a tendency to absorb a lot of oil during cooking, so proceed with caution.

AVOCADOS

UK SEASON: Not grown commercially.
IMPORTS:
Northern hemisphere: July–March
Southern hemisphere: May–October

The avocado is a relative of the laurel. Grown in the tropics, it has gained immense popularity over the last few years. Avocados are well known for their high calorific value and should be recognized for their nutritional qualities. They have the highest protein level of any vegetable and are low in sugar and high in vitamins A, B, C and iron. They contain mainly unsaturated fatty acids.

Grown in tropical climates, avocados are gathered from mid-summer onwards. As with many other fruit and vegetables they are gathered while still unripe so that they will store and travel well. Once exported they are allowed to ripen in the country to which they are exported. Gone are the days when it was necessary to buy an avocado 10 days before it was required in order to let it ripen. In most cases these days, they are often sold 'ripe and ready to eat'. To hasten the ripening of an avocado, put it into a bowl with other ripe fruit and leave it for 48 hours. The fruit is ripe when the stalk end gives when lightly pressed.

Favourite varieties include the Israeli, dark, warty-skinned Hass. The bright green smooth-skinned Fuerte is imported from South America. The flesh is creamy to yellow when ripe.

Avocados are traditionally served raw in salads and used in the savoury dip guacamole. They are not suitable for either cooking or freezing as the high tannin content can make them bitter.

CAPSICUMS AND CHILLIES

UK SEASON: Mid-summer to mid-autumn.
IMPORTS: Both capsicums, or peppers, and chillies are native to Central and South America. When not in season in the UK, look for those from warmer climates. They need a fair amount of warmth and are therefore mainly grown in the greenhouse in this country. They both grow quite happily on a sunny kitchen window-sill too, so are a good pot plant for flat dwellers who like the idea of growing vegetables. They do not freeze well raw, but once grilled and skinned will freeze successfully for a few months.

There are numerous capsicums or peppers and the range of colours can be quite confusing. Peppers change colour during the ripening stage. The majority start out green ripening to red, but other varieties ripen to orange or yellow and some to a dark chocolate colour. As red peppers are a ripe green variety, they inevitably taste a lot sweeter.

Pimiento peppers are a variety used for canning purposes.

The many different varieties of chilli are fast becoming more and more popular and most supermarkets stock a good selection. They vary from the mild paprika chilli to the breathtakingly hot scotch bonnet or Habanero chilli. It is advisable to read the label before cooking with them, so be warned.

PREPARATION AND COOKING
Peppers can be halved, the seeds and pith removed and used as required.

Chillies require more careful preparation. Halve the chilli, remove the seeds, which are very hot, and chop the flesh finely. It is advisable either to wear rubber gloves or to deal with the chilli with a knife and fork. The burning sensation of the seeds on sensitive skin is something not easily forgotten!

Home-grown peppers available during the summer months in the UK are wonderfully sweet. Eaten raw or char-grilled and skinned they add flavour and texture to salads and other vegetables.

Chillies give characteristic hotness to curries and other spicy dishes.

CUCUMBERS
UK SEASON: July to October.

Two types of cucumber are available: the ridge and the greenhouse cucumber, which has fewer seeds and thinner, smoother skin.

There was a time when it was necessary to degorge cucumber, to draw out excess moisture, but with commercial growing as it is that is no longer necessary. The high water content of cucumbers makes them unsuitable for freezing; pickling in brine is the most successful method of preserving.

Cucumber has become favoured as a good salad vegetable, for its colour and texture, but in centuries gone by when it was habitually cooked the results were sadly disappointing. We teach the students at Leith's the classic fish recipe, sole Doria, which has a garnish of blanched cucumber, a delicious combination.

PREPARATION
Peel the cucumber if desired (the skin does add good colour to a pale salad), halve and de-seed as required. Slice and use as required.

COURGETTES, MARROWS
UK SEASON: Late summer through to late autumn.

Courgettes remain a great favourite in the UK as a green vegetable, but the adult courgette, the marrow, is not so popular, which is a pity as marrows store better than courgettes and can be eaten right into the winter. They grow happily on rich manured soil and one plant provides many vegetables. Courgette flowers are well liked in Italy, where they stuff or fry them early on in the season.

PREPARATION AND COOKING
Courgettes: Washed and sliced, they suit many methods of cooking, in particular stir-frying or steaming.
Marrows: Peeling is usually essential (though not for stuffed marrow), and the seeds and central pith should be removed before boiling or baking.

SQUASHES AND PUMPKINS
UK SEASON: Late summer through to late autumn.
IMPORTS: Many varieties are imported from both Northern and Southern hemisphere countries.

Relatives of the courgette and marrow, pumpkins and squashes, are native to the USA where they are most widely used in pies, purées and roasts. Numerous varieties such as spaghetti squash, butternut, patty pan and acorn are available in supermarkets. Around the time of Hallowe'en the large pumpkin varieties used for lanterns make their appearance.

There are many different varieties which once germinated will grow in cooler climates, but they must be picked before heavy frosts appear. The high water content makes them unsuitable for freezing raw, but the cooked pulp will freeze well.

PREPARATION AND COOKING
Tough-skinned squash and pumpkins usually need peeling first. Then remove the seeds, cut the flesh into pieces, steam, boil or roast – the texture suits many methods of cooking.

Do not discard the seeds; they can be cleaned and roasted to make a good nibble served with drinks.

TOMATOES
UK SEASON: Late summer to mid-autumn.

Tomatoes were brought to Europe in the sixteenth century, originally used as a decorative plant. The first people to use them for cooking were the Italians.

The different varieties of tomato seem to multiply yearly and the types available in the supermarket do likewise. There are cherry tomatoes, beef tomatoes, plum tomatoes and just – tomatoes. All are used for differing purposes.

PREPARATION AND COOKING
On the whole slicing is all that is necessary, but some recipes do call for skinning the tomatoes. To do this successfully, dip the tomatoes into boiling water for the count of 10, remove and dip into a bowl of cold water. Cut away the tough stalk and peel away the skin. Some of our recipes call for de-seeding the tomatoes; this is done for appearance, but also to remove acidity.

Cherry and beef tomatoes are perfect for salads, and beef also for stuffing and baking. Plum are disappointing served raw but make a wonderful tomato sauce. Recently baby plum tomatoes have made an appearance in some supermarkets; baked slowly so as to oven-dry them, they make the usual sun-dried tomato taste passé. Vine-ripened tomatoes, usually sold still on the stalk, also make lovely salad tomatoes and although relatively expensive taste much better than the pale apologies found on supermarket shelves in the late winter and early spring. Tomatoes are best frozen as a pulp.

NUTS
A huge amount of nut varieties are imported yearly, some fresh, but many packaged ready for eating. They include:

ALMONDS: *Found in the UK but not grown commercially. Imports come from several countries, but the bulk are from the USA. Northern hemisphere season September–May; Southern hemisphere season, mainly in Chile, March–August.*

BRAZIL NUTS: *Not grown in the UK. The majority are imported from Brazil and Bolivia. In season in November and December and therefore popular in the UK at Christmas.*

CASHEW NUTS: *This other great favourite is not grown in the UK but imported from Brazil and India. In season year round.*

CHESTNUTS: *Although we have hundreds of chestnut trees in the UK, they are not a commercial commodity here. The large chestnuts that are available come from Spain and Portugal; they are grown mainly in the Northern hemisphere and are in season September–January.*

HAZELNUTS/FILBERT NUTS: *Both these nuts are fruits of the hazelnut or 'cobnut' bushes. The filbert is the more popular with a strong robust flavour which is pronounced when toasted.*

Both are grown commercially in many countries including Turkey, Italy and the USA. They ripen, ready for picking, in mid-August and are in season until November.

They are traditionally used in pâtisserie and desserts. The tight-fitting skin comes away easily after toasting in the oven until the skin darkens. The nuts should be rolled in a cloth to rub off the skins and allowed to cool. Once cooled they may be ground and give a wonderful intense flavour to pastries and meringues.

MACADAMIAS: *Tremendously popular in Australia, these nuts are grown in warmer climates, mainly in the Southern hemisphere. They are in season March–December.*

PECANS: *These favourite US imports are in season November–March. They are utilized in the famous pecan pie.*

PISTACHIOS: *Grown commercially in Iran, Iraq, Sicily and the USA, they are in season all year.*

WALNUTS: *Walnuts are grown commercially in the UK where they are in season during the autumn months of September and October. At other times of the year they are imported from Chile where they are available all the year* round. They are often pickled while young and allowed to mature during the winter months. Sweet pickled walnuts make a wonderful addition to rich meat stews or accompaniments to cheese.

FOOD IN THE WILD

Keep your eyes peeled for goodies that grow wild in our countryside and are therefore for free (but be sure you do not trespass).

Look out for the first crop of elderflower; as they only last for a few short weeks, gather them when you have the opportunity. In the summer, from early July onwards, samphire, or sea asparagus as it is sometimes called, can be collected on salt marshes from Norfolk. Later in autumn, the eldertrees will be heavy with fruit and you will need to pick them before the birds get to them. Blackberries, sloes and some nuts – especially cob nuts – are all there for the gathering.

Hips and haws and rowan berries are worth looking out for too. Rosehips are the seed pods of the rose; they are not suitable for eating raw but with their high acidity and wild rose flavour make excellent syrup and jelly. High in vitamin C, they are a traditional remedy for colds and flu. Haws, the fruit of the hawthorn, are small cherry-red berries which make particularly good jelly to serve with game, either used by themselves or a combination with rowan berries (the fruit of the Mountain ash) for a hedgerow jelly.

When picking wild mushrooms, only contemplate gathering them if you know exactly what you are looking for. Extreme caution must be exercised, as an extremely poisonous toadstool can be mistaken for a perfectly edible mushroom. Information on wild mushrooms can be found below.

Having gathered your fare, make the most of them with preserves, jams, jellies, chutneys and sloe gin or whisky – all make wonderful Christmas presents.

Happy gathering!

WILD MUSHROOMS AND TRUFFLES

Mushrooms are the fruit body of a type of fungus, which develops to form and distribute the spores to enable it to reproduce. Conditions of nutrition, humidity, temperature and light are essential for the mushrooms to grow and the autumn season provides all these criteria perfectly.

Hunting for wild mushrooms needs to be done with care. There are approximately 3,000 varieties in the UK, 18 of which are the best and most commonly eaten species. There are 8 poisonous species of mushroom and therefore if you are at all unsure of the type of mushrooms you are picking, get them identified by an expert before eating. Symptoms can be delayed for several hours or even days and can make diagnosis difficult, and incorrect treatment can mean death. Identifying mushrooms is often very difficult as a novice because the same species can look totally different at different stages of growth.

COOKING MUSHROOMS

Mushrooms have a high water content and when cooked over a gentle heat with a little fat the liquid is released. If these juices are discarded much of the mushroom flavour is lost so it is important to evaporate the water to condense the flavour. With cultivated mushrooms it is possible to cook them over a high heat so that the water evaporates as they are cooking, but wild mushrooms tend to burn at high temperatures and must be cooked gently – this is particularly important when cooking expensive varieties such as cèpes.

Field Mushroom (*Agaricus campestris*)

Culinary uses:	Baked and stuffed, grilled or fried.
Season:	Late summer to autumn.
Habitat:	Pastureland.

The cap is 3–10cm/1¼–4in in diameter, domed in earlier stages, white or creamy yellow, scaly or smooth. The stem is 3–10cm/1¼–4in in length and the flesh is white with deep pink, even gills, darkening to brown.

Cèpe or Penny Bun (*Boletus edulis*)

Culinary uses: Use in stuffings and sauces, good with foie gras.
Season: Summer to late autumn.
Habitat: Coniferous, broad-leaved or mixed woodland.

The cap is 8–20cm/3½–8in in diameter, brown in colour with a white line at the edge. The skin is smooth and dry, becoming greasy in later stages. The stem is 3–23cm/1¼–9in long and the flesh is white, but a pale brown straw colour inside the cap.

Chanterelle (*Cantharellus cibarius*)

Culinary uses: Rich reduction sauces, good with poultry and game.
Season: Summer to late autumn.
Habitat: All types of woodland, but usually associated with frondnose trees in Britain.

The cap is 3–10cm/1¼–4in in diameter, at first flat and curvy on the outside, then becoming depressed at the centre with wavy, lobed edges and pale to deep egg-yellow fading with age. The stem is 3–8cm/1¼–3½in long with yellow flesh and narrow, vein-like gills, irregularly forked at the edges.

Shaggy Ink Cap or Lawyer's Wig (*Coprinus comatus*)

Culinary uses: Fried in butter and garlic – simple supper dishes.
Season: Late summer to autumn.
Habitat: Grass by roadsides, on rubbish heaps or lawns, particularly on recently disturbed soil.

The cap is 5–15cm/2–6in in diameter and is high and cylindrical, white in colour with a buff centre. The rim of the cap eventually breaks up into large white shaggy, brownish-tipped scales. The stem is 10–37cm/4–15in in length with white/pink gills that eventually turn black.

Horn of Plenty (*Craterellus cornucopioides*)

Culinary uses: Accompaniment to poultry and game birds in sauces and stuffings.
Season: Late summer to late autumn.
Habitat: Clustered amongst leaf litter of deciduous woods.

The cap is 2.5–8cm/1–3½in in across and is deeply tubular with a flared mouth, wavy at the edges and thin and leathery in texture. It is dark brown to black in colour and scaly when moist, drying to a paler greyish-brown. The stem is 10cm/4in long and ash-grey in colour, initially smooth but undulating with age.

Hedgehog Fungus (*Hydnum repandum*)

Culinary uses: Fried in butter or made into soup – commonly sold in European markets.
Season: Late summer to late autumn.
Habitat: Deciduous or coniferous trees.

The cap is 3–17cm/1¼–7in in diameter, flat with a slight depression in the centre. It is cream, yellowish or pale flesh colour and velvety in texture. The stem is 3.5–7.5cm/1½–3in long and finely downed. Spines on the underside of the cap are whitish to salmon-pink.

Chicken of the Woods or Sulphur Polypore (*Laetiporus sulphureus*)

Culinary uses: Stir-fries, omelettes, stuffing for chicken.
Season: Late spring to autumn.
Habitat: Deciduous trees, usually oak but common also on yew, cherry, sweet chestnut and willow.

The fungus forms a 'bracket' on the tree trunks, 10–40cm/4–16in in diameter. It is fan shaped, thick and fleshy and usually in large tiered groups. The top surface is uneven and wrinkled, with a suede-like texture. It is lemon-yellow or orange drying to a pale straw colour. The flesh is succulent, producing a yellowish juice, but becomes white and crumbly with age.

Giant Puff-ball (*Langermannia gigantia*)

Culinary uses: Sliced and fried with bacon (see recipe, page 394).
Season: Summer to autumn.
Habitat: Gardens, pasture and woods.

The puff-ball is a large white, irregularly shaped ball 7–80cm/3–30in in diameter. The flesh is firm, with a slightly leathery outer skin.

Parasol Mushroom (*Lepiota procera*)

Culinary uses: Fried in butter, sauces and casseroles.
Season: Summer and autumn.
Habitat: Open woods and pastures.

The cap is 10–25cm/4–10in in diameter. It is round, spherical or egg-shaped at first, expanding to a flat disc which is pale grey-brown in colour, covered in darker shaggy scales. The stem is 15–30cm/6–12in long with a grey-brown felty covering which splits into snake-like markings as it develops. The flesh is thin, soft and white with white gills.

Shaggy Parasol (*Lepiota rhacodes*)

Culinary uses: as above.
Season: Summer to late autumn.
Habitat: Woods and shrubberies of all kinds, often with conifers.

The cap is 5–15cm/2–6in across, egg-shaped before expanding to an almost flat disc with slightly curling scales on a fibrous background which gives a shaggy, torn appearance. The stem is 10–15cm/4–6in in length. The flesh starts off white, turning to orange and red when cut with white and red-tinged gills.

Field Blewitt or Blue Leg (*Lepista saeva*)

Culinary uses: Simple sauces and creamy poultry dishes.
Season: Autumn to early winter.
Habitat: Often in rings, in pastureland.

The cap is 6–10cm/2½–4in in diameter, convex to start with then flattening with an indented centre. The edges are generally wavy and muddy brown in colour. The stem is 3–6cm/

1¼–2½in in length and the flesh is whitish to flesh coloured with crowded gills of the same colour.

Wood Blewitt (*Lepista nuda*)

Culinary uses: as above.
Season: Autumn to early winter.
Habitat: Woodland, hedgerows and gardens.

The cap is 6–12cm/2½–5in in diameter, flattened with a convex top, which becomes depressed and wavy later. It is bluish-lilac in colour, turning browner with age. The stem is 5–9cm/2–3¾in in length and the flesh is thick and bluish-lilac with crowded gills of the same colour.

Common Morel (*Morchella vulagaris*)

Culinary uses: An accompaniment to game bird dishes with cream and sherry, or fried with butter and garlic.
Season: Late spring.
Habitat: Gardens and wasteland.

The body is 5–12cm/2–5in high and looks as though it is inside out, with large ridges and irregular holes on the outside. It is dark grey-brown in colour becoming a little creamier with age.

Oyster Mushroom (*Pleurotus ostreatus*)

Culinary uses: Chinese stir-fries and sauces.
Season: All year.
Habitat: Large clusters on stumps and fallen or standing trunks of usually deciduous trees, especially beech.

The cap is 6–14cm/2½–5½in in diameter and shell-shaped, convex at first, then flattening and often wavy or lobed and sometimes splitting at the edges. The colour can vary from flesh-brown or deep blue-grey turning to a more grey-brown. The flesh is white with gills starting white then becoming tinged with yellow.

Cauliflower or Brain Fungus (*Sparassis crispa*)

Culinary uses: Dipped in seasoned flour and deep-fried, served with lemon wedges.

Season: Autumn.

Habitat: At the base of conifer trees or nearby.

The body is 20–50cm/8–20in across and appears cauliflower-like, buff in colour and darkening with age.

St George's Mushroom (*Tricholoma gambosum*)

Culinary uses: Simple supper dishes, fried in butter.

Season: Traditionally found on 23 April, St George's Day, although it generally matures a week later.

Habitat: Grass on roadsides, at the edge of woods or in pastureland.

The cap is 5–15cm/2–6in in diameter, rounded then expanding into an irregularly wavy circle which sometimes cracks at the edge. It is white with a pale brown tinge in colour. The stem is 2–4cm/¾–1½in in length. The flesh is white with narrow, crowded spores of the same colour.

TRUFFLES

Truffles are the ultimate prize in many fungi hunters' eyes, though the two most esteemed varieties – the black Périgord truffle from France and the white truffle of Alba in Italy – cannot be found in England. We do, however, have a black truffle called the summer truffle which has quite a good flavour, if not as powerful.

Hunting for truffles

The only way of finding truffles, which bury themselves just under the ground and therefore cannot be seen by the naked eye, is to sniff them out. Traditionally pigs were used for this purpose, but it is sometimes difficult to retrieve a truffle from a pig who has worked hard to find such a prize. Nowadays, dogs are used to rout them out, and the truffles can be gathered, still intact, from the undergrowth.

Culinary uses

Truffles are generally used as a flavouring ingredient, in olive oil for example – their taste and smell goes a long way. Black truffles are good finely diced and used in terrines and pâtés or in rich wine sauces with the finest fillet of beef or venison. They are often served with foie gras or simply in an omelette. Putting a good fresh truffle into a box of eggs and leaving it for a few days will be enough to flavour them for the most wonderful scrambled eggs. The white truffle is delicious when grated and served raw with risottos or in salads.

Summer Truffle

Season: Late summer to autumn.

Habitat: Buried near beech trees on calcareous soil.

An uneven round ball which is 3–7cm/1¼–2¾in in diameter, blackish-brown in colour and covered with a rough, warty skin. The flesh is whitish, becoming marbled grey-brown.

Périgord Truffle

Season: Autumn.

Habitat: At the base of oak trees in the chalky, unfertile soil of the Dordogne.

This is similar in appearance to the summer truffle, but the flesh is blackish-brown and marbled with white veins.

White Truffle of Alba

Season: October–January.

Habitat: At the roots of trees on the lower slopes of Italy's Langhe hills and in the valleys around Alba in the Piedmont where the soil is a mixture of clay and limestone.

It is an irregular shape, approximately 2.5–5cm/1–2in in diameter, and is a creamy pale brown with a greyish tinge. Once unearthed it must be eaten within days or the flavour is lost.

CULTIVATED MUSHROOMS

Growing cultivated mushrooms

Cultivated mushrooms originated in France, grown in the dark humid caves of the Saumur region. Nowadays mushrooms are grown in specially prepared compost in a temperature- and humidity-controlled environment, with each crop taking approximately 6 weeks to mature.

Oyster mushrooms are cultivated on straw which is enclosed in plastic bags with holes in the sides. This encourages the mushrooms to grow in clusters outside the bags, emulating their natural habitat on the trunks of trees.

Shiitake mushrooms were first grown in China and Japan where they were cultivated on dead or decaying deciduous tree logs. Today they are grown on blocks of sawdust contained in a polythene mesh.

White Cap (*Agaricus bisporus*)

Culinary uses: Frying, stuffings, sauces, casseroles.

These mushrooms are subdivided into 4 categories according to their size:

Button:
(1cm/½in–3.5cm/1¼in)
Pale in colour and firm to touch.
Closed cup:
(3.5cm/1¼in–6cm/2½in)
Round with a closed veil.
Open cup:
(4cm/1½in–6cm/2½in)
Partly broken veil and pinkish gills visible under the cap, still retaining their cap shape.
Large open or flat:
(4cm/1½in–6cm/2½in)
Completely broken veils, darker brown gills and flatter caps – 'T' shaped.

Chestnut or Brown Cap (*Agaricus bisporus*)

Culinary uses: Salads and casseroles.

These mushrooms are also graded into 'closed cup' and 'flat' according to size. They are grown like the White Cap but the strain is slightly different, producing a mushroom with a brown outer skin and a firmer texture and nutty flavour.

Shiitake (*Lentinus edodes*)

Culinary uses: Chinese cooking – stir-fries, soups, salads and vegetarian dishes.

They have dark brown umbrella-shaped caps with pure white gills underneath and relatively thick stems. They range in size from 3cm/1¼in–7.5cm/3in. They have a unique steak-like texture and subtle meaty flavour with a faint peppery bite when eaten raw.

Enoki Dake
This thin spindly fungus closely resembles a pin. It has a mild flavour and is very popular in Japanese cookery.

BUYING AND STORING MUSHROOMS

When buying mushrooms handle them as little as possible. Keep them loosely packed in a paper bag in the salad drawer of a refrigerator. Do not wash the mushrooms before storage as they will deteriorate rapidly. To clean mushrooms before use wipe them with a piece of damp kitchen paper – or rinse them quickly under cold running water just before use. Avoid soaking them in water because they will discolour.

GAME

'Game' is the term used to describe wild animals or birds shot for sport and then eaten for pleasure. Following the recent development of the Game Marketing Board, a very positive move is taking place to make game much more widely available to the general public, and as a result it can now be purchased from many of our larger supermarkets.

Although much game, such as quail and venison, is now farmed, if you are able to buy 'wild' game you will undoubtedly benefit from the flavour and texture. Wild game is naturally lean, and because its muscles have developed through working for its food, it will generally take longer to cook than a farmed animal.

However, the flesh of wild game will be richer and will have picked up the wonderful natural flavours of the countryside such as heather or blackberries – you can usually tell what it has been eating by the colour of its fat.

Hanging

All game should be hung to develop the flavour and to allow the enzymes in the flesh of the muscles to start to break down the muscle fibres, which will help tenderize the meat. Hanging should take place as soon as possible after shooting in a cool (3–5°C/36–40°F), dry, well-ventilated place. Only one bird or animal should be hung from each hook. Birds are generally hung by the neck and animals by the hoof. Air should be allowed to flow easily, and different game should not be hung from the same hook. The length of hanging time depends on the conditions, but in general, the longer game is hung the more its flavour will develop.

Methods of Cooking

This is the most important decision to make when cooking game, and often the most difficult. To tell the age of a bird or animal you need to look at its head and mouth/beak, then at its feet. In most cases, and in supermarkets in particular, the meat is presented beautifully skinned, plucked and trussed and therefore you have to rely on the cooking method on the back of the packaging – or trust your butcher. As a general rule young game should be cooked quickly in dry heat, as in roasting or grilling, and can be served 'pink', whereas older game should be cooked very slowly in moist conditions in order to have time to tenderize. There is always an exception to the rule and this would apply with farmed game which can often be cooked successfully in a dry heat, although to be sure of success, I would opt for a moist method if at all unsure. Alternatively, check the seasonal chart that follows and if the season is in its early stages then a quick cooking method would probably work well.

Game will often benefit from a marinade, using a good-quality oil which can be used to baste the meat during cooking, and a wine or vinegar which will help to tenderize the meat as well as give magnificent flavour. It is essential to provide some extra fat during either cooking process to ensure the meat doesn't dry out. For roasting, cover the bird with a piece of fat, streaky bacon or caul (this is known as barding, see page 127). For braising or stewing the meat can be larded – fine strips of pork fat threaded through larger pieces of lean meat at regular intervals which will melt during cooking and disappear, but keep the joint really moist. For smaller joints or birds, adding streaky bacon to the recipe or marinating with olive oil will achieve the same result. For slow cooking, make sure the casserole dish has a heavy, well-fitting lid and check the meat regularly to make sure it doesn't dry out.

Traditionally game birds were served with their heads intact and, in the case of snipe and woodcock, their long beaks were used to truss them together and hold them in shape for cooking. Woodcock were left undrawn and their entrails are traditionally served on a croûte (a piece of fried bread) – these birds defecate when they take flight and therefore their entrails will be clean when shot.

Traditional Accompaniments

Roast game is classically served on a croûte with game chips (potato crisps are a quick substitute), fried crumbs, bread sauce and gravy, often made with red wine or port. The sweetness of damson cheese or hedgerow jellies goes extremely well with all game and is often used in gravy or sauces if not served as an extra accompaniment. A few blackberries and apples are often put in the cavity of a bird before cooking for flavour as well as moisture.

Casseroles and stews often have the addition of double cream or butter to finish off the sauce for extra flavour and richness. Fortified wines such as port, sherry or Madeira go extremely well with game cookery, and the autumn fruits added as described above.

Grouse

Season: 12 August–10 December
Hanging times: 2/3 days–2 weeks
Best eating: August–October
Classic accompaniments:

                  Bread sauce, orange, whisky, soft fruit, purée of root vegetables and smoked bacon.

The race is on for the 'Glorious 12th' when the first young grouse are rushed to the finest hotels and restaurants at the start of the season. The flavour, rich and powerful, is quite distinctive. For this reason, grouse is generally considered to be the finest of all game and is expensive. The red grouse is only found in Britain on moorland, though its cousin – the willow grouse – is common in North America, Northern Europe and Russia.

Guinea fowl

Season:	All year
Hanging times:	3–5 days
Best eating:	All year
Classic accompaniments:	
	As for pheasant or chicken, very adaptable.

Guinea fowl are widely farmed, and being similar in many ways to pheasant, can be adapted to most pheasant recipes. They are particularly popular in France.

Partridge

Season:	1 September–1 February
Hanging times:	2/3 days–2 weeks
Best eating:	October–November
Classic accompaniments:	
	Apples, Calvados, sauerkraut, Savoy cabbage, root vegetables.

The French red-legged partridge is considered the best for eating, although the grey-legged partridge, slightly smaller, has a good flavour too. Nowadays their numbers are considerably reduced due to modern farming techniques and the loss of hedgerows. Many partridge are farmed and released for the start of the season.

Pigeon

Season:	All year
Hanging times:	–
Best eating:	April–October
Classic accompaniments:	
	Red wine, mushrooms, smoked bacon, sauerkraut.

Pigeons are plentiful and cheap. They have a dark, rich flesh which is full of flavour. As there is little meat on the legs and wings, the breasts are generally taken off and cooked separately. The carcass can be roasted separately and used for a rich game stock. Pigeon will be at their most tender from May to September, and can be barbecued or pan-fried. In the winter, they can lend contrast and flavour to terrines.

Pheasant

Season:	1 October–1 February
Hanging times:	5 days–3 weeks
Best eating:	October–December
Classic accompaniments:	
	Chestnuts, Calvados, sauerkraut, Madeira, peppercorns, vegetable purées, fruit berries and herbs.

Pheasant is bred all over the countryside and is therefore widely available. Its appeal probably has something to do with its size – a large bird can feed up to 3 people. The flavour can often be disappointing if the bird has not been hung for long enough. When roasted the breast meat dries out very quickly, so it is important to bard it and baste it frequently. The breasts can be taken off and cooked separately for a dinner party, saving the legs to casserole or braise slowly on a separate occasion.

Quail

Season:	All year
Hanging times:	3–5 days
Best eating:	All year
Classic accompaniment:	Grapes.

The Japanese quail is farmed extensively in England and is available all year round. The flesh is tender and sweet and cooks very well on the barbecue. It is a small bird and you really need to cook 2 per person, unless boning and filling the central cavity with meat stuffing. Quail's eggs are also a delicacy in plentiful supply as the birds lay one egg a day from approximately 6 weeks old to one year.

Wild duck

Season: August–March
Hanging times:
   Mallard: 4/5 days–10 days
   Teal: 3/4 days–1 week
Best eating:
   Mallard: November–December
   Teal: October–November
Classic accompaniments:
          Black cherries, cider, apples,
          peppers, olives, garlic, mint,
          Jerusalem artichokes and
          parsnip purée.

Mallard and teal are the most widely available, the mallard being the larger and plumper of the two. Young duck are good roasted, though the breast is best served pink. Often the breast is carved first and the rest of the body is returned to a slightly cooler oven to continue cooking a little longer and is then served for 'seconds'. Old birds need to be cooked really slowly and suited to the Chinese style of steaming and roasting. Sometimes the 'fishy' taste of a wild duck can be a little off-putting.

Snipe

Season: 12 August–31 January
Hanging times: 2–5 days
Best eating: August–October
Classic accompaniment:
          Flamed with brandy.

The snipe is a tiny, long-legged, long-beaked marsh bird found only in parts of Ireland and Scotland.

Woodcock

Season: October–January
Hanging times: 2/3 days–10 days
Best eating: October–November
Classic accompaniment: As for snipe.

The woodcock is recognized by its short legs and long beak. As mentioned earlier, the head is classically left on the bird, using the beak to truss it neatly together. This is also because the brain is considered a delicacy, and the head is often split after cooking for this reason. It has a very good flavour.

Hare

Season: September–March
Hanging times: 2/3 days–1–3 weeks
Best eating: October–January
Classic accompaniments:
          Cranberry, beetroot, wild
          mushrooms, red cabbage.

Hare has a very dark rich flesh and can sometimes feed up to 8 people. The most classic hare dish is jugged hare where the blood is collected and used to thicken and enrich the sauce just before the end of cooking.

Rabbit

Season: All year
Hanging times: 3–5 days
Best eating: September–November
Classic accompaniments:
          Cabbage, mustard, prunes,
          root vegetables and white
          wine.

Widely available all year round, rabbit has a very lean and mild flavour similar to that of chicken. It can be quickly pan-fried or simmered slowly in a sauce, though farmed rabbit rarely takes longer than 1 hour to cook.

Venison

Season: See chart
Hanging times:
   Roe: 5 days–2 weeks
   Fallow/Red/Sika: 1–3 weeks
Best eating:
   Roe: Bucks: October, Does:
          December–February
   Red: Stags: July–August, Hinds:
          December–February
Classic accompaniments:
          Peppercorns, oranges, sour
          cherries, red wine, redcurrant
          jelly and red cabbage.

The season for venison is complicated, differing between breed and sex. It is simpler to note that with the farmed venison available nowadays it can be bought at any time of year (see chart for seasons).

There are 4 main varieties to look out for: the native red deer found mainly in Scotland, the Sika which is a large Japanese deer excellent for eating, the fallow deer and roe deer which have the finest flavour of all. It is important that the deer are well fed for the flavour of the meat to be at its best – fat around the kidneys is a good sign of this. The meat is dark and close-textured with little fat. The fat is generally very strong and is often discarded before cooking and another milder fat or oil used to baste in its place. The cuts dictate the method of cooking: the haunch, loin and best end are best served rare, while the neck, shoulder and shin need long slow cooking. Venison liver can be fried or made into pâtés and the kidneys can also be used.

Wild boar

Season: All year
Hanging times: 4–12 days
Best eating: –
Classic accompaniments:
            Red wine, apples, sultanas.

Wild boar are best eaten up to the age of 2 years, though they are at their very best before 6 months. Wild boar is much more widely available nowadays, though it can often lack any distinct flavour and can be disappointing. Diet plays an important role in the flavour of the meat as with all game – when they are farmed like pigs they tend to taste the same. A conversation with a pig farmer who bred wild boar for a short while revealed that pork could be just as good if the pigs were allowed to roam the forests eating wild food. The meat is dark and is best marinated to bring out the gamey flavour.

STATUTORY CLOSE SEASONS FOR DEER

Species	Sex	England and Wales	Scotland
Red	Stags	1 May – 31 July	21 October – 30 June
	Hinds	1 March – 31 October	16 February – 20 October
Fallow	Bucks	1 May – 31 July	1 May – 31 July
	Does	1 March – 31 October	16 February – 20 October
Roe	Bucks	1 November – 31 March	21 October – 31 March
	Does	1 March – 31 October	1 April – 20 October
Sika	Stags	1 May – 31 July	21 October – 30 June
	Hinds	1 March – 31 October	16 February – 20 October
Red/Sika	Stags		21 October – 30 June
Hybrids	Hinds		16 February – 20 October

In addition The British Deer Society recommends the following close seasons for which there is no statutory provision at present

Muntjac	Bucks	1 March – 31 October	
	Does	1 March – 31 October	
Chinese Water	Bucks	1 March – 31 October	
Deer	Does	1 March – 31 October	

CONVERSION TABLES

The tables below are approximate, and do not conform in all respects to the conventional conversions, but we have found them convenient for cooking. Use either metric or imperial measurements: do not mix the two.

Weight

Imperial	Metric	Imperial	Metric
¼oz	7–8g	½oz	15g
¾oz	20g	1oz	30g
2oz	55g	3oz	85g
4oz (¼lb)	110g	5oz	140g
6oz	170g	7oz	200g
8oz (½lb)	225g	9oz	255g
10oz	285g	11oz	310g
12oz (¾lb)	340g	13oz	370g
14oz	400g	15oz	425g
16oz (1lb)	450g	1¼lb	560g
1½lb	675g	2lb	900g
3lb	1.35kg	4lb	1.8kg
5lb	2.3kg	6lb	2.7kg
7lb	3.2kg	8lb	3.6kg
9lb	4.0kg	10lb	4.5kg

Australian cup measures

	Metric	Imperial
1 cup flour	140g	5oz
1 cup sugar (crystal or caster)	225g	8oz
1 cup brown sugar, firmly packed	170g	6oz
1 cup icing sugar, sifted	170g	6oz
1 cup butter	225g	8oz
1 cup honey, golden syrup, treacle	370g	12oz
1 cup fresh breadcrumbs	55g	2oz
1 cup packaged dry breadcrumbs	140g	5oz
1 cup crushed biscuit crumbs	110g	4oz
1 cup rice, uncooked	200g	7oz
1 cup mixed fruit or individual fruit, such as sultanas	170g	6oz
1 cup nuts, chopped	110g	4oz
1 cup coconut, desiccated	85g	3oz

Approximate American/European conversions

Commodity	USA	Metric	Imperial
Flour	1 cup	140g	5oz
Caster and granulated sugar	1 cup	225g	8oz
Caster and granulated sugar	2 level tablespoons	30g	1oz
Brown sugar	1 cup	170g	6oz
Butter/margarine/lard	1 cup	225g	8oz
Sultanas/raisins	1 cup	200g	7oz
Currants	1 cup	140g	5oz
Ground almonds	1 cup	110g	4oz
Golden syrup	1 cup	340g	12oz
Uncooked rice	1 cup	200g	7oz
Grated cheese	1 cup	110g	4oz
Butter	1 stick	110g	4oz

Liquid measures

Imperial	ml	fl oz
1 teaspoon	5	
2 scant tablespoons	28	1
4 scant tablespoons	56	2
¼ pint (1 gill)	150	5
⅓ pint	190	6.6
½ pint	290	10
¾ pint	425	15
1 pint	570	20
1¾ pints	1000 (1 litre)	35

Australian

250ml	1 cup
20ml	1 tablespoon
5ml	1 teaspoon

Approximate American/European conversions

American	European
1 teaspoon	1 teaspoon/5ml
½fl oz	1 tablespoon/½fl oz/15ml
¼ cup	4 tablespoons/2fl oz/56ml
½ cup plus 2 tablespoons	¼ pint/5fl oz/150ml
1¼ cups	½ pint/10fl oz/290ml
1 pint/16fl oz	1 pint/20fl oz/570ml
2½ pints (5 cups)	1.1 litres/2 pints
10 pints	4.5 litres/8 pints

Useful measurements

Measurement	Metric	Imperial
1 American cup	225ml	8fl oz
1 egg, medium	56ml	2fl oz
1 egg white	28ml	1fl oz
1 rounded tablespoon flour	30g	1oz
1 rounded tablespoon cornflour	30g	1oz
1 rounded tablespoon caster sugar	30g	1oz
2 rounded tablespoons fresh breadcrumbs	30g	1oz
2 level teaspoons gelatine	8g	¼oz

30g/1oz granular (packet) aspic sets
570ml/1 pint liquid.

15g/½ oz powdered gelatine, or 4 leaves, will set 570ml/1 pint liquid. (However, in hot weather, or if the liquid is very acid, like lemon juice, or if the jelly contains solid pieces of food and is to be turned out of the dish or mould, 20g/¾oz should be used.)

Wine quantities

Imperial	ml	fl oz
Average wine bottle	750	25
1 glass wine	100	3½
1 glass port or sherry	70	2
1 glass liqueur	45	1

Lengths

Imperial	Metric
½in	1cm
1in	2.5cm
2in	5cm
6in	15cm
12in	30cm

Oven temperatures

°C	°F	Gas mark	AMERICAN	AUSTRALIAN
70	150	¼	COOL	VERY SLOW
80	175	¼	COOL	VERY SLOW
100	200	½	COOL	VERY SLOW
110	225	½	COOL	VERY SLOW
130	250	1	VERY SLOW	
140	275	1	VERY SLOW	
150	300	2	SLOW	SLOW
170	325	3	MODERATE	MODERATELY SLOW
180	350	4	MODERATE	MODERATELY SLOW
190	375	5	MODERATELY HOT	MODERATE
200	400	6	FAIRLY HOT	MODERATE
220	425	7	HOT	MODERATELY HOT
230	450	8	VERY HOT	MODERATELY HOT
240	475	8	VERY HOT	HOT
250	500	9	EXTREMELY HOT	HOT
270	525	9	EXTREMELY HOT	VERY HOT
290	550	9	EXTREMELY HOT	VERY HOT

CATERING QUANTITIES

Few people accurately weigh or measure quantities as a control-conscious chef must do, but when catering for large numbers it is useful to know how much food to allow per person. As a general rule, the more people you are catering for the less food per head you need to provide: thus 225g/8oz stewing beef per head is essential for 4 people, but 170g/6oz per head would feed 60 people.

SOUP

Allow 290ml/½ pint soup per head, depending on the size of the bowl and the thickness of the soup. If a thick chowder is being served for a first course, 200ml/7fl oz will be sufficient, but be more generous if it is for a light lunch.

POULTRY

Chicken and Turkey: Allow 450g/1lb per person, weighed when plucked and drawn. An average chicken serves 4 people on the bone and 6 people off the bone.
Duck: A 2.7kg/6lb bird will feed 3–4 people; a 1.8kg/4lb bird will feed 2 people; 1 duck makes enough pâté for 6 people.
Goose: Allow 3.6kg/8lb for 4 people; 6.8kg/15lb for 7 people.

GAME

Partridge: Allow 1 bird per person.
Pigeon: Allow 1 bird per person.
Pheasant: Allow 1 bird for 2 people (roast); 1 bird for 3 people (casseroled).
Grouse: Allow 1 young grouse per person (roast); 2 birds for 3 people (casseroled).
Quail: Allow 2 small birds per person or 1 large boned stuffed bird served on a croûton.
Venison: Allow 170g/6oz lean meat per person; 1.8kg/4lb cut of haunch weighed on the bone for 8–9 people. With steaks, allow 170g/6oz per person.

MEAT

BEEF
Stewed: Allow 225g/8oz boneless trimmed meat per person.
Roast (off the bone): If serving men only, allow 225g/8oz per person; if serving men and women, 200g/7oz per person.
Roast (on the bone): Allow 340g/12oz per person.
Roast whole fillet: Allow 1.8kg/4lb piece for 10 people.
Grilled steaks: Allow 200–225g/7–8oz per person.

MINCE
Allow 170g/6oz per person for **shepherd's pie, hamburgers,** etc.
Allow 110g/4oz per person for **steak tartare.**
Allow 85g/3oz per person for **lasagne, cannelloni,** etc.
Allow 110g/4oz per person for **moussaka.**
Allow 55g/2oz per person for **spaghetti sauce.**

LAMB OR MUTTON
Casseroled: Allow 285g/10oz per person (boneless, with fat trimmed away).
Roast leg: Allow 1.35kg/3lb for 3–4 people; 1.8kg/4lb for 4–5 people; 2.7kg/6lb for 7–8 people.
Roast shoulder: Allow 1.8kg/4lb shoulder for 5–6 people; 2.7kg/6lb shoulder for 7–9 people.
Grilled best end cutlets: Allow 3–4 per person.
Grilled loin chops: Allow 2 per person.

PORK

Casseroled: Allow 170g/6oz per person.
Roast leg or loin (on the bone): Allow 340g/12oz per person.
Roast leg or loin (off the bone): Allow 200g/7oz per person.
2 average fillets will feed 3–4 people.
Grilled: Allow 1 × 170g/6oz chop or cutlet per person.

VEAL

Stews or pies: Allow 225g/8oz per person.
Fried: Allow 1 × 170g/6oz escalope per person.

FISH

Whole large fish (e.g. sea bass, salmon, haddock), weighed uncleaned, with head on: Allow 340–450g/12oz–1lb per person.
Cutlets and steaks: Allow 170g/6oz per person.
Whole small fish (e.g. trout, slip soles, small plaice, small mackerel, herring): Allow 225–340g/8–12oz weighed with head for main course; 170g/6oz for first course.
Fish off the bone (in fish pie, with sauce, etc.): Allow 170g/6oz per person.
Fillets (single): Allow about 170g/6oz per person.
Lemon sole and other small flat fish fillets: Allow 2 per person for a first course; 3 per person for a main course.
Sea bass, trout and whiting fillets: Allow 1 per person for a first course; 2 per person for a main course.
Haddock, cod and larger fish fillets: Allow ½ per person for a first course; 1 per person for a main course.
Fish off the bone: Where it is going to be served as an integral part of a dish (mixed with a sauce), allow 140–170g/5–6oz per person.
Sea urchins (oursins): Allow 3 per person.
Caviar: Allow 30g/1oz per person.

PRESERVED AND SALTED FISH

Smoked and salted fish are much denser than fresh as the moisture has evaporated away in the preserving process. As a general rule, less fish is needed.

Cold smoked fish to eat raw (e.g. smoked salmon and halibut): Allow 85–110g/3–4oz per person.
Cold smoked fish to cook (e.g. smoked haddock and smoked cod): Allow 110–170g/4–5oz per person for a main course; 1 smoked trout per person; ½ smoked mackerel (1 fillet) per person.
Hot smoked fish: Allow 110g/4oz per person for a main course.
Smoked roes: Allow 55g/2oz per person.
Salted fish (e.g. salt cod): Allow 85–110g/3–4oz per person for a main course.

SHELLFISH

Quantities are given here in 450g/1lb, although many smaller shellfish are traditionally measured by the pint.
Mixed shellfish: Allow 55–85g/2–3oz per person as a first course; 140g/5oz per person as a main course.

CRUSTACEANS

Lobster: For a first course a 675g/1½lb lobster, in the shell, will feed 2 people. For a main course, be more generous and serve a 450g/1lb lobster each.

As lobster is expensive, one way of stretching it further is to remove it from the shell, slice it and combine with another firm-fleshed fish, such as monkfish, or with other shellfish.
Crab: For dressed crab, a 675g/1½lb crab will feed 2 people. For crab claws as a first course, 4–5 claws per person is sufficient. 170g/6oz crabmeat (white and brown) is sufficient for a main course.

Prawns: These vary in size enormously, but as a general rule:
Fresh-water tiger prawns (raw/green, unpeeled): Allow 6–8 per person for a first course; 12–14 per person for a main course.
There are approximately 30 to 450g/1lb.
King prawns (raw/green, unpeeled): Allow 3–4 per person for a first course; 5–6 per person for a main course.
Atlantic prawns (cooked, shell-on): Allow 8–10 per person for a first course; 14–15 per person for a main course.

There are approximately 25 to 570ml/1 pint and 30 to 450g/1lb.

Madagascar king prawns (cooked, shell-on): Allow 2–3 for a first course; 4–5 for a main course.

There are approximately 6–8 to 450g/1lb.

Brown shrimps: These are so small that they are usually sold as a portion. Allow 110–170g/ 4–6oz per person.

Fresh-water crayfish: Allow 8–10 per person.

MOLLUSCS

Mussels: Served in the shell, allow 12–15 per person.

There are about 15 to 450g/1lb. Allow 450g/ 1lb or 570ml/1 pint per person, taking into account wastage of cracked and dead mussels.

Green-lipped mussels: Allow 4–5 per person.

Scallops

King or bay scallops: Allow 2 fresh or frozen for a first course; 4 fresh or frozen for a main course.

Queen scallops: Allow 3–4 fresh or frozen for a first course; 5–6 fresh or frozen for a main course.

Princess scallops: Allow 8–10 for a first course; 10–12 for a main course.

Oysters: Usually sold by the ½ dozen. Allow ½ dozen per person if served as a first course with a heavy main course to follow; 1 dozen per person as a main course for lunch.

Whelks: Allow 290ml/½ pint per person for a first course.

There are approximately 15–20 per 570ml/1 pint.

CEPHALOPODS

Squid: Allow 170g/6oz unprepared, 110g/4oz prepared, per person for a first course; 285g/ 10oz unprepared, 170g/6oz prepared, per person for a main course.

Octopus and cuttlefish: Allow 170g/6oz unprepared, 110g/4oz prepared, per person for a first course; 285–340g/10–12oz unprepared, 170–225g/6–8oz prepared, per person for a main course.

VEGETABLES

Weighed before preparation and cooking, and assuming 3 vegetables, including potatoes, served with a main course: allow 110g/4oz per person, except (per person):

French beans: 85g/3oz
Peas: 85g/3oz
Spinach: 340g/12oz
Potatoes: 3 small (roast); 170g/6oz (mashed); 10–15 (Parisienne); 4 (château); 1 large or 2 small (baked); 110g/4oz (new).

SALADS

Obviously, the more salads served, the less guests will eat of any one salad. Allow 1 large portion of salad in total per head, i.e. if only one salad is served, make sure there is enough for 1 helping each. Conversely, if 100 guests are to choose from 5 different salads, allow a total of 150 portions, i.e. 30 portions of each salad.

Tomato salad: 450g/1lb tomatoes (average 6 tomatoes), sliced, serves 4 people.

Coleslaw: 1 small cabbage, finely shredded, serves 10–12 people.

Grated carrot salad: 450g/1lb carrots, grated, serves 6 people.

Potato salad: 450g/1lb potatoes (weighed before cooking) serves 5 people.

Green salad: Allow a loose handful of leaves for each person (a large Cos lettuce will serve 8, a large Webb's will serve 10, a Dutch hothouse 'butterhead' will serve 4).

RICE

Plain, boiled or fried: Allow 55g/2oz per person (weighed before cooking) or 1 breakfast cup (measured after cooking).

In risotto or pilaf: Allow 30g/1oz per person (weighed before cooking) for first course; 55/ 2oz per person for main course.

PASTA

Allow 55g/2oz per person for a first course; 110g/4oz per person for a main course.

As part of composite dishes such as lasagne, allow 55g/2oz per person.

PUDDINGS

Cooking apples: Allow 225g/8oz per head for puddings.

Fruit salad: Allow 8 oranges, 2 apples, 2 bananas and 450g/1lb grapes for 8 people.

Mousses: Allow 290ml/½ pint double cream inside and 290ml/½ pint to decorate a mousse for 8 people.

Strawberries: Allow 110g/4oz per head.

COCKTAIL PARTIES

Allow 10 cocktail canapés per head.

Allow 14 cocktail canapés per head if served at lunchtime when guests are unlikely to go on to a meal.

Allow 4–5 canapés with pre-lunch or pre-dinner drinks.

Allow 8 cocktail canapés, plus 4 miniature sweet cakes or pastries per head, for a wedding reception.

MISCELLANEOUS

Sliced bread: A large loaf, thinly sliced, generally makes 18–20 slices.

Brown bread and butter: Allow 1½ slices (3 triangular pieces) per person.

French bread: Allow 1 large loaf for 10 people; 1 small loaf for 6 people.

Butter: Allow 30g/1oz per person if bread is served with the meal; 45g/1½oz per person if cheese is served as well. 30g/1oz soft butter will cover 8 large bread slices.

Cheese: After a meal, if serving one blue-veined, one hard and one soft cheese, allow 85g/3oz per person for up to 8 people; 55g/2oz per person for up to 20 people; 30g/1oz per person for over 20 people.

At a wine and cheese party: allow 110g/4oz per person for up to 8 people; 85g/3oz per person for up to 20 people; 55g/2oz per person for over 20 people. Inevitably, if catering for small numbers, there will be cheese left over but this is unavoidable if the host is not to look mean.

Cheese biscuits: Allow 3 each for up to 10 people; 2 each for up to 30 people; 1 each for over 30 people.

Cream: Allow 1 tablespoon per person for coffee; 3 tablespoons per person for pudding or dessert.

Milk: Allow 570ml/1 pint for 18–20 cups of tea.

Bacon: A good-sized rasher weighs about 30g/1oz.

Sausages: 450g/1lb is the equivalent of 32 cocktail sausages; 16 chipolata sausages; 8 pork sausages.

Bouchées: 675g/1½lb packet of puff pastry makes 60 bouchées.

Chicken livers: 450g/1lb chicken livers will be enough for 60 bacon and chicken liver rolls.

Dates: 50 fresh dates weigh about 450g/1lb.

Prunes: A prune (with stone) weighs about 10g/⅓oz.

Mushrooms: A button mushroom weighs about 7g/¼oz.

Button onions: A button onion weighs about 15g/½oz.

Choux pastry: 6-egg quantity choux paste makes 150 baby éclairs. They will need 570ml/1 pint cream for filling and 225g/8oz chocolate for coating.

Short pastry: 900g/2lb pastry will line 150 tartlet tins; 110g/4oz pastry will line a 15cm/6in flan ring; 170g/6oz pastry will line a 20cm/8in flan ring.

MENU PLANNING

Knowing how to plan and balance a menu successfully is essential for any good cook. Once a menu is planned cooking becomes much easier. It is making the decisions that can be so daunting – a non-cook always overfeeds guests. Here are a few hints that may help.

One of the most important things is to make the menu relevant to the people you are cooking for: food that you serve for a barbecue would be totally unsuitable for a black-tie dinner. The menu should stay in style throughout. Although today chefs combine many flavours from around the world, choosing a menu that leaps from traditional English fare in one course to Thai in another would give your guests an uncomfortable culture shock. If you are cooking for old-fashioned friends we would not recommend giving them the warm Pinto Beans with Red Chilli and Lemon dressing, for example. One of the many skills of cooking is to think of the people for whom you are cooking and choosing a menu you know they would like.

Here is a set of guidelines.

PLANNING A MENU

1. Season of year: hot or cold?
2. Availability of ingredients (and seasonal constraints).
3. Cost/budget: how much do you want to spend?
4. Type of people: young or old?

5. Special diets: this is important. Not only may you have vegetarians to cater for, but allergies and certain illnesses may require careful consideration.
6. Style of occasion: formal or informal.
7. Capabilities of staff in kitchen and serving area: never over-estimate your own abilities: if you feel under-confident, keep it simple.
8. Size and equipment of kitchen.
9. Size and equipment of dining area.

BALANCING A MENU

1. Avoid repetition of:
Ingredients
Colour
Method of cooking
Names of dishes
Texture
Sauces – use only one mother sauce
Garnishes.

2. Overall balance:
Seasonings – weak and strong
Good balance of simple and exotic tastes
Style: avoid Chinese, French and English dishes together.

3. Food value and nutrition:
Particularly important if you are cooking for a group of people over a period of time.

DICTIONARY OF COOKING TERMS AND KITCHEN FRENCH

Abats French for offal (hearts, livers, brains, tripe, etc.). Americans call them 'variety meats'.

Bake blind To bake a flan case while empty. In order to prevent the sides falling in or the base bubbling up, the pastry is usually lined with paper and filled with 'blind beans'. See below.

Bain-marie A roasting tin half filled with hot water in which terrines, custards, etc. stand while cooking. The food is protected from direct fierce heat and cooks in a gentle, steamy atmosphere. Also a large container that will hold a number of pans standing in hot water, used to keep soups, sauces, etc. hot without further cooking.

Bard To tie bacon or pork fat over a joint of meat, game bird or poultry, to be roasted. This helps to prevent the flesh from drying out.

Baste To spoon over liquid (sometimes stock, sometimes fat) during cooking to prevent drying out and to promote flavour.

Bavarois Creamy dish made with eggs and cream and set with gelatine, traditionally a pudding.

Beignets Fritters.

Beurre manié Butter and flour in equal quantities worked together to a soft paste, and used as a liaison or thickening for liquids. Small pieces are whisked into boiling liquid. As the butter melts it disperses the flour evenly through the liquid, thereby thickening it without causing lumps.

Beurre noisette Browned butter; *see* Noisette.

Bisque Shellfish soup, smooth and thickened.

Blanch Originally, to whiten by boiling, e.g. to boil sweetbreads or brains briefly to remove traces of blood, or to boil almonds to make the brown skin easy to remove, leaving the nuts white. Now commonly used to mean parboiling, as in blanching vegetables when they are parboiled prior to freezing, or precooked so that they have only to be reheated before serving.

Blanquette A stew made without prior frying of the meat. Usually used for lamb, chicken or veal. The sauce is often thickened with an egg and cream liaison.

Blind beans Dried beans, peas, rice and pasta used to fill pastry cases temporarily during baking.

Bouchées Small puff pastry cases like miniature vol-au-vents.

Bouillon Broth or uncleared stock.

Bouquet garni Parsley stalks, small bay leaf, fresh thyme, celery stalk, sometimes with a blade of mace, tied together with string and used to flavour stews, etc. Removed before serving.

Braise To bake or stew slowly on a bed of vegetables in a covered pan.

Brunoise Vegetables cut into very small dice.

Canapé A small bread or biscuit base, sometimes fried, spread or covered with savoury paste, egg, etc., used for cocktail titbits or as an accompaniment to meat dishes. Sometimes used to denote the base only, as in champignons sur canapé.

Caramel Sugar cooked to a toffee.

Châteaubriand Roast fillet steak from the thick end for 2 people or more.

Chine To remove the backbone from a rack of ribs. Carving is almost impossible if the butcher has not 'chined' the meat.

Clarified butter Butter that has been separated from milk particles and other impurities which cause it to look cloudy when melted, and to burn easily when heated.

Collops Small slices of meat, taken from a tender cut such as neck of lamb.

Concasser To skin, de-seed and dice.

Consommé Clear soup.

Coulis Essentially a thick sauce, such as coulis de tomates, thick tomato sauce; raspberry coulis, raspberry sauce.

Court bouillon Liquid used for cooking fish.

Cream To beat ingredients together, such as butter and sugar when making a sponge cake.

Crêpes Thin French pancakes.

Croquettes Pâté (stiff purée) of mashed potato and possibly poultry, fish or meat, formed into small balls or patties, coated in egg and breadcrumbs and deep-fried.

Croustade Bread case dipped in butter and baked until crisp. Used to contain hot savoury mixtures for a canapé, savoury or as a garnish.

Croûte Literally crust. Sometimes a pastry case, as in fillet of beef en croûte, sometimes toasted or fried bread, as in Scotch woodcock or scrambled eggs on toast.

Croûtons Small evenly sized cubes of fried bread used as a soup garnish and occasionally in other dishes.

Dariole Small castle-shaped mould used for moulding rice salads and sometimes for cooking cake mixtures.

Déglacer To loosen and liquefy fat, sediment and browned juices stuck at the bottom of a frying pan or saucepan by adding liquid (usually stock, water or wine) and stirring while boiling.

Deglaze See Déglacer.

Dégorger To extract the juices from meat, fish or vegetables, generally by salting then soaking or washing. Usually done to remove indigestible or strong-tasting juices.

Dépouiller To skim off the scum from a sauce or stock: a splash of cold stock is added to the boiling liquid. This helps to bring scum and fat to the surface, which can then be skimmed more easily.

Dropping consistency The consistency where a mixture will drop reluctantly from a spoon, neither pouring off nor obstinately adhering.

Duxelles Finely chopped raw mushrooms, sometimes with chopped shallots or chopped ham, often used as a stuffing.

Egg wash Beaten raw egg, sometimes with salt, used for glazing pastry to give it a shine when baked.

Emulsion A stable suspension of fat and other liquid, e.g. mayonnaise, hollandaise.

Entrée Traditionally a dish served before the main course, but usually served as a main course today.

Escalope A thin slice of meat, sometimes beaten out flat to make it thinner and larger.

Farce Stuffing.

Fecule Farinaceous thickening, usually arrowroot or cornflour.

Flamber To set alcohol alight. Usually to burn off the alcohol, but frequently simply for dramatic effect. (Past tense flambé or flambée; English: to flame).

Flame See Flamber.

Fleurons Crescents of puff pastry, generally used to garnish fish or poultry.

Fold To mix with a gentle lifting motion, rather than to stir vigorously. The aim is to avoid beating out air while mixing.

Frappé Iced, or set in a bed of crushed ice.

Fricassé White stew made with cooked or raw poultry, meat or rabbit and a velouté sauce, sometimes thickened with cream and egg yolks.

Fumet Strong-flavoured liquor used for flavouring sauces. Usually the liquid in which fish has been poached, or the liquid that has run from fish during baking. Sometimes used of meat or truffle-flavoured liquors.

Glace de viande Reduced brown stock, very strong in flavour, used for adding body and colour to sauces.

Glaze To cover with a thin layer of shiny jellied meat juices (for roast turkey), melted jam (for fruit flans) or syrup (for rum baba).

Gratiner To brown under a grill after the surface of the dish has been sprinkled with breadcrumbs and butter and, sometimes, cheese. Dishes finished like this are sometimes called gratinée or au gratin.

Hors d'oeuvre Usually simply means the first course. Sometimes used to denote a variety or selection of many savoury titbits served with drinks, or a mixed first course (hors d'oeuvres variés).

Infuse To steep or heat gently to extract flavour, as when infusing milk with onion slices.

Julienne Vegetables or citrus rind cut in thin matchstick shapes or very fine shreds.

Jus or jus de viande God's gravy, i.e. juices that occur naturally in cooking, not a made-up sauce. Also juice.

Jus lié Thickened gravy.

Knock down or knock back To punch or knead out the air in risen dough so that it resumes its pre-risen bulk.

Knock up To separate slightly the layers of raw puff pastry with the blade of a knife to facilitate rising during cooking.

Lard To thread strips of bacon fat (or sometimes anchovy) through meat to give it flavour, and, in the case of fat, to make up any deficiency in very lean meat.

Lardons Small strips or cubes of pork fat or bacon generally used as a garnish.

Liaison Ingredients for binding together and thickening sauce, soup or other liquid, e.g. roux, beurre manié, egg yolk and cream, blood.

Macerate To soak food in a syrup or liquid to allow flavours to mix.

Mandolin Frame of metal or wood with adjustable blades set in it for thinly slicing cucumbers, potatoes, etc.

Marinade The liquid described below. Usually contains oil, onion, bay leaf and vinegar or wine.

Marinate To soak meat, fish or vegetables before cooking in acidulated liquid containing flavourings and herbs. This gives flavour and tenderizes the meat.

Marmite French word for a covered earthenware soup container in which the soup is both cooked and served.

Medallions Small rounds of meat, evenly cut. Also small round biscuits. Occasionally used of vegetables if cut in flat round discs.

Mirepoix The bed of braising vegetables described under Braise.

Moule-à-manqué French cake tin with sloping sides. The resulting cake has a wider base than top, and is about 2.5cm/1in high.

Napper To coat, mask or cover, e.g. éclairs nappés with hot chocolate sauce.

Needleshreds Fine, evenly cut shreds of citrus zest (French julienne) generally used as a garnish.

Noisette Literally 'nut'. Usually means nut-brown, as in beurre noisette, i.e. butter browned over heat to a nut colour. Also

hazelnut. Also boneless rack of lamb rolled and tied, cut into neat rounds.

Nouvelle cuisine Style of cooking that promotes light and delicate dishes often using unusual combinations of very fresh ingredients, attractively arranged.

Oyster Small piece of meat found on either side of the backbone of a chicken. Said to be the best-flavoured flesh. Also a bivalve mollusc!

Panade or panada Very thick mixture used as a base for soufflés or fish cakes, etc., usually made from milk, butter and flour.

Paner To egg and crumb ingredients before frying.

Papillote A wrapping of paper in which fish or meat is cooked to contain the aroma and flavour. The dish is brought to the table still wrapped up. Foil is sometimes used, but as it does not puff up dramatically, it is less satisfactory.

Parboil To half-boil or partially soften by boiling.

Parisienne Potato (sometimes with other ingredients) scooped into small balls with a melon baller and usually fried.

Pass To strain or push through a sieve.

Pâte The basic mixture or paste, often used of uncooked pastry, dough, uncooked meringue, etc.

Pâté A savoury paste of liver, pork, game, etc.

Pâtisserie Sweet cakes and pastries. Also a cake shop.

Paupiette Beef (or pork or veal) olive, i.e. a thin layer of meat, spread with a soft farce, rolled up, tied with string and cooked slowly.

Piquer To insert in meats or poultry a large julienne of fat, bacon, ham, truffle, etc.

Poussin Baby chicken.

Praline Almonds cooked in sugar until the mixture caramelizes, cooled and crushed to a powder. Used for flavouring desserts and ice cream.

Prove To put dough or yeasted mixture to rise before baking.

Purée Liquidized, sieved or finely mashed fruit or vegetables.

Quenelles A fine minced fish or meat mixture formed into small portions and poached. Served in a sauce, or as a garnish to other dishes.

Ragoût A stew.

Réchauffée A reheated dish made with previously cooked food.

Reduce To reduce the amount of liquid by rapid boiling, causing evaporation and a consequent strengthening of flavour in the remaining liquid.

Refresh To hold boiled green vegetables under cold running water, or to immerse them immediately in cold water to prevent them cooking further in their own steam, and set the colour.

Relax or rest Of pastry: to set aside in a cool place to allow the gluten (which will have expanded during rolling) to contract. This lessens the danger of shrinking in the oven. Of batters: to set aside to allow the starch cells to swell, giving a lighter result when cooked.

Render To melt solid fat (e.g. beef, pork) slowly in the oven.

Revenir To fry meat or vegetables quickly in hot fat in order to warm them through.

Roux A basic liaison or thickening for a sauce or soup. Melted butter to which flour has been added.

Rouille Garlic and oil emulsion used as flavouring.

Salamander A hot oven or grill used for browning or glazing the tops of cooked dishes, or a hot iron or poker for branding the top with lines or a criss-cross pattern.

Salmis A game stew sometimes made with cooked game, or partially roasted game.

Sauter Method of frying in a deep-frying pan or sautoir. The food is continually tossed or shaken so that it browns quickly and evenly.

Sautoir Deep-frying pan with a lid used for recipes that require fast frying and then slower cooking (with the lid on).

Scald Of milk: to heat until on the point of boiling, when some movement can be seen at the edges of the pan but there is no overall bubbling. Of muslin, cloths, etc.: to immerse in clean boiling water, generally to sterilize.

Sear or seize To brown meat rapidly usually in fat, for flavour and colour.

Season Of food: to flavour, generally with salt and pepper. Of iron frying pans, griddles, etc.: to prepare new equipment for use by placing over high heat, generally coated with oil and sprinkled with salt. This prevents subsequent rusting and sticking.

Slake To mix flour, arrowroot, cornflour or custard powder to a thin paste with a small quantity of cold water.

Soft ball The term used to describe sugar syrup reduced by boiling to sufficient thickness to form soft balls when dropped into cold water and rubbed between finger and thumb.

Suprême Choice piece of poultry (usually from the breast).

Sweat To cook gently, usually in butter or oil, but sometimes in the food's own juices, without frying or browning.

Tammy A fine muslin cloth through which sauces are sometimes forced. After this treatment they look beautifully smooth and shiny. Tammy cloths have generally been replaced by blenders or liquidizers, which give much the same effect.

Tammy strainer A fine mesh strainer, conical in shape, used to produce the effect described under Tammy.

Terrine Pâté or minced mixture baked or steamed in a loaf tin or earthenware container.

To the thread Of sugar boiling. Term used to denote degree of thickness achieved when reducing syrup, i.e. the syrup will form threads if tested between a wet finger and thumb. Short thread: about 1cm/½in; long thread: 5cm/2in or more.

Timbale A dish that has been cooked in a castle-shaped mould, or a dish served piled high.

Tomalley Greenish lobster liver. Creamy and delicious.

Tournedos Fillet steak. Usually refers to a one-portion piece of grilled fillet.

To turn vegetables To shape carrots or turnips to a small barrel shape. To cut mushrooms into a decorative spiral pattern.

Velouté See under Sauces, p. 630.

Vol-au-vent A large pastry case made from puff pastry with high raised sides and a deep hollow centre into which chicken, fish, etc. is put.

Well A hollow or dip made in a pile or bowlful of flour, exposing the tabletop or the bottom of the bowl, into which other ingredients are placed prior to mixing.

Zest The skin of an orange or lemon, used to give flavour. It is very thinly pared without any of the bitter white pith.

CLASSIC GARNISHES

Anglaise Braised vegetables such as carrots, turnips and quartered celery hearts (used to garnish boiled salted beef).

Bolognaise A rich sauce made from chicken livers and/or minced beef flavoured with mushrooms and tomatoes. Usually served with pasta.

Bonne femme To cook in a simple way. Usually, of chicken: sautéed and served with white wine gravy, bacon cubes, button onions and garnished with croquette potatoes. Of soup: a simple purée of vegetables with stock. Of fish: white wine sauce, usually with mushrooms and served with buttered mashed potatoes.

Boulangère Potatoes and onions sliced and cooked in the oven in stock. Often served with mutton.

Bouquetière Groups of very small carrots, turnips, French beans, cauliflower florets, button onions, asparagus tips, etc. Sometimes served with a thin demi-glace or gravy. Usually accompanies beef or lamb entrées.

Bourgeoise Fried diced bacon, glazed carrots and button onions. Sometimes red wine is used in the sauce. Used for beef and liver dishes.

Bourguignonne Button mushrooms and small onions in a sauce made with red wine (Burgundy). Used for beef and egg dishes.

Bretonne Haricot beans whole or in a purée. Sometimes a purée of root vegetables. Usually served with a gigot (leg) of lamb.

Chasseur Sautéed mushrooms added to a sauté of chicken or veal.

Chiffonnade Chopped lettuce or sorrel cooked in butter to garnish soup.

Doria A garnish of cucumber, usually fried in butter.

Flamande Red cabbage and glazed small onions used with pork and beef.

Florentine Spinach purée, or leaf spinach. Also a sixteenth-century name for a pie.

Lyonnaise Denotes the use of onions as garnish – the onions are frequently sliced and fried.

Meunière Of fish, lightly dusted with flour, then fried and served with beurre noisette and lemon juice; also frequently (but not classically) chopped fresh parsley.

Milanese With a tomato sauce, sometimes including shredded ham, tongue and mushrooms. Frequently served with pasta.

Minute Food quickly cooked, either fried or grilled. Usually applied to a thin entrecôte steak.

Mornay With a cheese sauce.

Nantua With a lobster sauce.

Napolitana Tomato sauce and Parmesan cheese (for pasta). May also mean a three-coloured ice cream.

Niçoise Name given to many dishes consisting of ingredients common in the South of France, such as tomatoes, olives, garlic, fish, olive oil.

Normande Garnish of mussels, shrimps, oysters and mushrooms. Or creamy sauce containing cider or Calvados, and sometimes apples.

Parmentier Denotes the use of potato as a base or garnish.

Paysanne Literally, peasant. Usually denotes the use of carrots and turnips sliced across in rounds.

Portugaise Denotes the use of tomatoes or tomato purée.

Princesse Denotes the use of asparagus (usually on breast of chicken).

Printanière Early spring vegetables cooked and used as a garnish, usually in separate groups.

Provençal Denotes the use of garlic, and sometimes tomatoes and/or olives.

Rossini With collops of foie gras and truffles tossed in butter, served with a rich meat glaze.

St Germain Denotes the use of peas, sometimes with pommes Parisienne.

Soubise Onion purée, frequently mixed with a béchamel sauce.

Vichy Garnish of small glazed carrots.

METHODS OF COOKING

WAYS OF COOKING MEAT

The tougher the meat, or the larger its volume, the more slowly it must be cooked. The quick methods of cooking – frying, deep-fat frying and grilling – are suitable for small pieces of tender meat, whereas the slower methods – braising, stewing, etc. – are best for the tougher cuts.

Three factors determine the toughness of a particular cut of meat: the age of the animal (the older it is the tougher it will be); the activity of the particular joint (the neck, shoulders, chest and legs are used far more than the back of a quadruped and are therefore tougher); and finally the texture of the fibres.

Muscle tissue is made up of long thin cells or muscle fibres bound together by sheets of connective tissue. Individual fibres can be as long as the whole muscle. Bundles of fibres are organized in groups to form an individual muscle. The lengthways structure of muscles is known as the grain of the meat. It is easier to carve and also to chew in the direction of the grain, which is why meat is cut across the grain. The connective tissue is the harness of the muscle and is visible as gristle, tendons, etc. Connective tissue is made up of three main proteins: collagen, which can be converted by long, slow cooking into gelatine; elastin, which is elastic and not changed by heat; and reticulen, which is fibrous and not changed by heat.

Tender cuts of meat such as sirloin steak have relatively few connective tissues and as they cook the meat fibres shrink and lose moisture. If overcooked, the juices finally dry up and a once tender piece of meat becomes tough and dry. However, a tough cut of meat such as oxtail, which has a lot of connective tissue, can become very moist during cooking. The collagen is converted into gelatine and the meat becomes almost sticky in its succulence.

As meat should be tender and juicy rather than dry and tough, it is important to cook it in such a way as to minimize fluid loss and to maximize the conversion of the tough collagen in the connective tissue into water-soluble gelatine.

It is possible to tenderize meat before cooking it. This can be done by cutting, pounding and grinding to break down the structure of the muscle bundles. It can also be done by marinating. The acid in citrus fruit or wine produces protein-digesting enzymes that can break down muscle and connective tissue.

POT-ROASTING

Pot-roasting is not really roasting but rather baking food enclosed in a pot, either in the oven or over a low heat. It is an ancient, economical method of cooking that was much used in the days before domestic ovens. Roasting proper is a much faster, 'dry' method used for cooking choicer, more tender cuts of meat and poultry by exposing them to direct heat. (Full instructions for roasting meat are given on page 116.) Pot-roasting involves cooking meat in its own juices and might better be called a simpler, quicker version of braising. It is ideal for cooking joints with plenty of connective tissue. On the other hand, a tender joint will toughen when pot-roasted or braised.

Traditionally there is very little liquid in a pot-roast, other than the fat needed for browning, as moisture from the meat provides most of the liquid during cooking.

A casserole with a tightly fitting lid creates a small oven. Steam is formed inside the pot from the moisture given off by the added liquid or by the food itself, and this tenderizes and cooks the meat. If the lid does not fit tightly, the steam can escape. Similarly, if the casserole or pan is too big, the liquid spreads over too large an area and is more likely to boil away. To make sure a lid fits tightly, cover the top of the casserole or pan with a piece of greaseproof paper and place the lid on top, jamming it down firmly.

If you have a flameproof casserole, you can brown meat on the hob and pot-roast in the oven in one vessel. Otherwise, brown the meat in a frying pan and transfer it with all the pan juices to a casserole for pot-roasting.

A traditional tip when pot-roasting is to cook the browned meat on a piece of pork rind. This adds flavour, and prevents the meat from scorching. Coarsely cut root vegetables are sometimes placed under the meat for the same reason. They can be either raw or browned in the same fat as the meat, though the meat should be removed from the pan while browning the vegetables. Once cooked, they can be served with the meat.

One way to ensure tender meat, is to marinate it before cooking. A mixture of oil, wine and other flavourings penetrates the outer layer of the meat when it is left to marinate overnight in the refrigerator. The acid in the marinade also helps to break down tough fibres, and the oil prevents moisture evaporation and adds richness. Save some of the marinade to use as the cooking liquid.

Another way to make sure that a large piece of pot-roasted meat is succulent is to lard it. This is especially important with some lean joints such as the beef 'leg of mutton' cut. Cut thin strips of pork back fat longer than the joint and thread them all the way through the meat about 1cm/½in apart. This is easily done with a larding needle which, when removed, leaves the strips of fat in place. As the meat cooks, the fat partially melts, making the meat juicy and adding flavour and richness to the sauce. As long as the meat cooks slowly, the liquid in the pan is not likely to boil, or, more importantly, to evaporate. This liquid becomes a richly flavoured sauce for the meat after cooking. Any vegetables cooked with the meat will help to thicken it.

Transfer the pot-roasted joint to a warmed serving dish or board to carve and remove any strings or skewers. If there is too much liquid left in the pan, simply reduce it by boiling or thicken it with beurre manié (see page 108). Serve separately.

GRILLING

Intense heat is the secret of successful grilling. Although this method requires active attention from the cook, its advantages are that the food cooks quickly and the charred surface gives great flavour.

To produce succulent, perfectly grilled meat with a crisp brown outside and pink juicy inside, it is absolutely essential to preheat the grill to its highest setting. This may take 10 or even 20 minutes for the grill on a good domestic cooker. Under a cooler grill, the meat's surface will not brown quickly, leaving the meat tasteless and unattractive by the time it is cooked through. If the grill cannot be adequately preheated to brown meat and fish quickly, fry the steaks instead.

When grilling over an open charcoal fire, it may take 2 hours before the embers are flameless yet burn with the necessary intensity. But their fierce heat will cook a small lamb cutlet perfectly in 2 minutes and the charcoal will give it a wonderfully smoky flavour. Charcoal, when ready, glows bright red in the dark and has an ashy grey look in daylight.

Unlike braising, grilling will not tenderize meat, so only tender, choice cuts should be grilled. They should not be much thicker than 5cm/2in because of the high temperatures involved. Any thicker and the meat will remain cold and raw when the outside is black. Even so, unless the cut of meat is fairly thin, once it browns it must be moved further away from the heat source so that the interior can cook before the surface burns. Basting with the delicious pan juices or with olive oil or butter adds flavour and shine. Turning is necessary for even cooking, and should be done halfway through the estimated cooking time, when the first surface is attractively brown.

When grilling over, rather than under, heat, use a fine grill rack or wire mesh grill to support delicate cuts of fish and grease the grill rack or mesh well. Fish cuts can be wrapped in greased foil and cooked over heat, but they then cook in their own steam rather than grill in the true sense.

The following points should be remembered when grilling:

1. Take food out of the refrigerator or freezer in plenty of time to bring it to room temperature before grilling. An almost frozen steak will still be cold inside when the outside is brown and sizzling. This is particularly important if the steak is to be served very rare (blue, see below).
2. Do not salt food much in advance. The salt draws moisture from the food. Salt after, during or immediately before grilling.
3. Brush the food with butter, oil or a mixture of the two to keep it moist and to speed the browning process. This is also essential to prevent delicate foods such as fish from sticking.
4. The more well done meat or fish is, the tougher it will be to the touch and the palate.
5. To avoid piercing the meat and allowing the juices to escape, turn the grilling food with tongs or spoons, not a sharp instrument.
6. Serve immediately. Grilled food, even if well seared, inevitably loses moisture, dries up and toughens if kept hot for any length of time.

GRILLING STEAKS

All grilled meats should be well browned on the surface, but the varying degrees of 'doneness' are defined as follows:

BLUE The inside is almost raw (but hot).
RARE Red inside with plenty of red juices running freely.
MEDIUM RARE As rare, but with fewer free-flowing juices and a paler centre.
MEDIUM Pink in the centre with juices set.
WELL DONE The centre is beige but the flesh is still juicy.

The best way to tell if meat is done is by its texture. Feel the meat by pressing firmly with a finger. Rare steak feels soft, almost raw; medium steak is firmer with some resilience to

it; well-done steak feels very firm. With practice there will soon be no need to cut-and-peep.

COOKING TIME FOR STEAKS varies with the heat of the grill, the distance of the food from the heat, the thickness of the cut and its fat content. The density of the meat also affects the cooking time. Open-textured steak such as sirloin will cook faster than the same thickness and weight of closer-textured rump.

GRILLING FISH

Lay fish steaks and fillets on greased foil on the grill rack, and set close under the preheated grill. This prevents the delicate flesh from sticking to the rack and breaking up when turned.

FRYING AND SAUTÉING

Frying, sometimes referred to as 'shallow frying', and sautéing are both quick cooking methods which are suitable for small, not-too-thick, tender pieces of meat and other foods. The difference between the two methods is the amount of fat used in cooking. For sautéing, an almost dry pan with no more than 1 tablespoon of fat is used; for frying, food is cooked in 5mm/¼in of fat.

The processes are similar to grilling but when grilling small pieces of meat some fat is lost in the pan juices which may or may not be eaten with the meat. When fried, the meat cooks in fat, at least some of which is eaten with the meat. For this reason the fat used for frying is an important consideration as its distinctive flavour – or the lack of it – will affect the taste of the dish. Olive oil, butter, bacon dripping, lard and beef dripping will each give distinctive flavour to fried foods, while corn, safflower, peanut and most other vegetable oils have little or no flavour. Potatoes fried in goose fat may taste delicious, but not when they are served with fish.

When choosing a fat, remember that some can be heated to much higher temperatures than others before they break down and start to burn. For example, clarified butter – butter with all its milk solids removed (see page 637) – can be heated to a higher temperature than untreated butter; pure bacon dripping, lard, beef dripping and solid frying fat can generally withstand more heat than margarine, butter or vegetable oil. Fats tend to lose their molecular structure ('break down') if heated for too long, and this causes them to smoke (and smell) unpleasantly at a lower temperature than when fresh. Eventually they will give an unappetizing flavour to any food fried in them. However, even solid fresh fats (if they contain an emulsifier) will smoke and burn at cooler temperatures than pure fats without additives.

FRYING

Techniques vary depending on the texture and size of the food and the effect the cook wishes to achieve. For instance, when frying steaks or chops remember to:

1. Fry in an uncovered wide pan. A lid traps the steam and the food stews or steams rather than frying crisply.
2. Preheat the fat. If the fat is cool when the food is put into it, the food will not brown. It will then lack flavour, look unattractive and may even absorb some of the cool fat and become too greasy.
3. Fry a little at a time. Adding too much food at one time to hot fat lowers the temperature and, again, hinders the browning.
4. Fry fast until the meat is completely browned on all sides. Then turn down to medium heat to cook the inside through.

Fried food should be served as soon as possible after cooking. Juices gradually seep out and meat toughens on standing; potatoes lose their crispness, become leathery and tough-skinned; fritters deflate, and everything loses its newly fried shine.

Fish is cooked à la meunière by dusting it with flour and shallow-frying in butter until it is brown on both sides. The slight coating of flour helps to prevent sticking and adds crispness to the skin. The fish is then put on a warmed platter. Chopped fresh parsley, lemon juice, salt and pepper are added to the butter in the pan and, once sizzling, this is poured over the fish.

STIFFENING Some recipes require gentle frying without a coating of flour. When this method is used, the fat, though hot, is not fearsomely so, and the food can be gently fried to a very pale brown, or cooked without browning. This is particularly useful with kidneys and liver, which tend to burst and become grainy if fried too fast; with shellfish, which toughens if subjected to fierce heat; and with thin slices of fish (such as salmon to be served in a sorrel sauce), where the taste of butter-frying is required without a browned surface.

ENGLISH BREAKFAST FRYING Eggs should be fried in clean fat. Frying them in a pan in which bacon or sausages have been cooking leads to sticking and possible breaking of the yolks. If eggs are to be fried in the same pan as other items, fry the bacon, ham, sausages, potatoes, mushrooms and bread first as this will all keep in a warm oven for a few minutes. Tip the fat into a cup. Rinse the pan, removing any stuck sediment, dry it, then pour the fat back into the pan. Using enough sizzling fat to spoon over eggs speeds up the process and prevents the edges of the whites from overcooking before the thicker parts are set.

Sausages generally have skins which, as the stuffing expands in the hot pan, can burst or split open. Avoid this by pricking them carefully all over with a thin needle (large holes like those made by the prongs of a fork provide weak points where the skin will split), and/or by cooking slowly. Shake the pan with rapid but careful side-to-side or forward-and-backward movements; this will dislodge any pieces that are stuck with less damage than a prodding utensil. Fry the sausages slowly until evenly browned all over and firm to the touch.

Bacon rashers can be fried in an almost dry pan as they readily produce their own fat. However, they cook faster and more evenly in shallow fat.

GLAZING VEGETABLES Vegetables are sometimes given a final shiny, slightly sweet glaze by frying them in a mixture of butter and sugar. The sugar melts and caramelizes to a pale toffee and the vegetables brown in the butter and caramel mixture. Constant shaking of the pan is necessary to prevent burning and sticking. This method is particularly successful with shallots, baby onions, mushrooms and root vegetables.

SAUTÉING is used on its own to cook foods such as chicken pieces, mushrooms or apple rings, but is most frequently used in conjunction with other forms of cooking. For example, whole small onions may be sautéed to brown them before they are added to liquid in a stew or a sauce. Sautéing is also employed after boiling to give cooked or partially cooked foods, such as potatoes, a lightly browned and buttered exterior.

Browning gives a sautéed dish its essential character. After browning, some meats, such as liver or veal escalopes, are often removed and then served with a relatively small amount of well-flavoured sauce which has been made in the same pan. Meats such as pork chops or chicken pieces may be given an initial browning and then cooked with added ingredients that will eventually form the sauce. The range of such sauces is almost endless – as various as the liquids and other flavourings that can be used in making them. Stages in sautéing are as follows:

1. Fry the main ingredients together with any others, browning them in minimal fat. Remove them from the pan and keep them hot.
2. Deglaze (see page 56) the pan with a liquid such as stock, cream or wine.
3. Add the flavourings for the sauce.
4. If the initial browning has cooked the main ingredients sufficiently, reduce the sauce by rapid boiling and pour it over the dish. Garnish and serve immediately.
5. If the main ingredients need further cooking, simmer them in the sauce until they are tender, then proceed as above.

DEEP-FRYING

Deep-frying is one of the fastest possible methods of cooking small, tender cuts of meat and fish. It is also suitable for many vegetables, and for dough mixtures such as fritters and doughnuts.

Because of the very high temperatures the fat reaches, most foods are given a protective coating before frying. This seals in their juices and prevents overcooking as well as too much spluttering of the hot fat, caused by moisture rapidly vaporizing on the surface of uncoated wet food.

Some foods, such as potato crisps, are in and out of the hot fat so quickly that they do not need any coating. Chips are given a first frying at a low temperature to cook them through, then a second frying at a higher temperature to brown them.

Most other foods need a coating, either of flour or crumbs or a flour-and-liquid batter. While the coating fries to a crisp brown, the food stays moist and tender. One of the pleasures of deep-fried food is the contrast between interior and exterior. For the driest and crispest coating, drain off all excess fat on kitchen paper after cooking and serve as soon as possible.

If the coating covers the food completely, as it should, the flavour of the fried food will not contaminate the fat, which may then be used again. Filter the fat clean of any food particles after frying. As soon as it shows signs of breaking down, by becoming dark, odorous or cloudy, it should be replaced. Such fat smokes and burns at a lower temperature than fresh fat, smells stale and gives an unpleasant flavour to anything cooked in it.

BATTER Batter is a farinaceous mixture of a thick liquid consistency. It is used to give a crisp protective coating to food that might otherwise burn or splatter when deep- or shallow-fried.

USING A DEEP-FRYER
1. If the deep-fryer is not thermostatically controlled, use a thermometer to test the temperature of the fat by dropping a crumb or cube of bread into it. If the bread browns in 60 seconds, the fat is about 182°C/360°F and suitable for gentle frying; if it browns in 40 seconds, the oil is moderately hot, about 190°C/375°F; if it browns in 20 seconds, the fat is very hot, about 195°C/385°F. If the bread browns in 10 seconds, the fat is dangerously hot and should be cooled down. Turn off the heat and fry several slices of bread in it to speed up the cooling.

2. Cook food in small amounts. Adding too many pieces at one time lowers the temperature of the fat so that the coating will not form a crisp crust. The food then absorbs fat and loses its juices in the cooking fat. This is particularly important if you are frying food that is still frozen, such as fish fingers, commercially prepared chips or Chinese spring rolls, which will of course cool the fat greatly. However, do not attempt to remedy this problem by frying in very hot fat. Comparatively cool fat is needed (about 180°C/350°F) to allow the inside to thaw and cook before the coating browns.

3. Drain the cooked food well on kitchen paper.

4. If the food is not served right away, spread it out in a single layer on a hot baking sheet or tray and keep it uncovered in a warm oven with the door ajar to allow the free circulation of air. Covering or enclosing the food will make the crust soggy. Try not to fry far ahead of serving.

5. Add salt, or a sprinkling of caster sugar if the food is sweet, after frying. This accentuates the flavour and the dry, crisp texture.

6. After use, cool the fat and strain it through muslin or a coffee filter paper. This removes food particles which, if left in the fat, will become black and burned with repeated fryings. As soon as the fat becomes at all dark, it should be changed, as it is beginning to break down, will smoke readily and give a rancid flavour to fried food.

STIR-FRYING

Choose a carbon iron wok with a round base and one long wooden handle. The best size is about 35cm/14in. The advantage of stir-frying is that there is a large surface area all at the same temperature, so the food cooks fast and retains all its flavour, colour and texture. The trick is to stir with a Chinese ladle, strainer or spoon with one hand while shaking and jerking the wok with the other. When stir-frying vegetables add the firmest vegetables first, and the more tender ones a few minutes later.

BRAISING

Braising, in the true sense of the word, is a method of slowly cooking meat on a mirepoix, a thick bed of finely diced mixed vegetables with the addition of strong stock. In practice, the term braising is often confused with pot-roasting, as in both methods food is cooked slowly in a pan with a tightly fitting lid to give deliciously tender results. The main difference is that pot-roasted food is cooked with little, if any, liquid other than the fat used for browning the ingredients, and braising involves some liquid and at least some cut-up vegetables to add moisture to the pan, even if a true mirepoix is not used. A pot-roast should taste 'roasted' and be decidedly fattier than a braise, which is closer to a stew and depends more on juices and stocks than on fat for flavour.

Braising can also mean 'sweating'. This is a method of gently cooking vegetables, frequently onions and shallots, in butter or oil in a covered pan, which is shaken frequently to prevent burning and sticking. Once cooked through, softened and exuding their juices but not coloured, the vegetables are usually added to stews, sauces or soups, to which they give a subtle flavouring but no colouring. For example, to braise red cabbage, a finely chopped onion is sweated in butter until tender, then shredded cabbage, a little vinegar, sugar, apple and seasoning are added. These are left over a low heat, covered tightly, to sweat for 2–3 hours. The result is braised red cabbage, even though neither meat nor mirepoix has been included.

Occasionally the term braising is used to mean baking in a covered pan with only a little liquid. Braised celery hearts, for example, consists of quarters of celery head cooked in a little stock in a covered pan in the oven. Braised fennel is cooked with lemon juice, butter and stock.

Beef fillet and sirloin or lamb best end should be roasted or grilled, but otherwise whole joints or smaller pieces of meat can be braised with advantage. The meat should be fairly lean and any fat that melts into the stock should be skimmed off before serving. Poultry may be braised unless it is old and tough, when stewing or poaching are more suitable cooking methods as all the flesh, which will tend to be stringy and dry, is submerged in liquid.

The vegetables for the mirepoix should be browned quickly in hot fat and stirred constantly to ensure even colouring, then transferred to a heavy casserole or pan. The meat can be browned in the same fat before it is placed on top of the vegetables and stock is added. As the vegetables cook they will disintegrate, helping to thicken the stock.

Making a strong, reduced, well-flavoured stock is time-consuming, but it is one of the key factors in good braising. The best stock is one made from chopped-up chicken and veal bones that have been browned all over and then simmered and skimmed frequently for hours (see page 625).

As with pot-roasting, meat may be marinated overnight in the refrigerator and large pieces of exceptionally lean meat may be larded to ensure that they remain moist. Dry the meat well before browning it.

The exact and by no means easy steps for braising red meat to ideal tenderness and almost sticky juiciness are as follows:

1. Fry the mirepoix of vegetables and a few tablespoons of diced salt pork or bacon slowly in oil and butter, shaking the pan and stirring until they are evenly browned all over.

2. Brown the meat on all sides and place it on top of the vegetable bed in a heavy casserole.

3. Add stock, made from gelatinous meats such as knuckle of veal, to cover the meat. If the stock is not rich and solidly set when cold, the braise will not have the correct 'melting' stickiness. Then stew, without basting, until half-cooked.

4. Lift out the meat, strain the stock, and discard the mirepoix, which will by now have imparted all its flavour.

5. Return the meat to the casserole and reduce the stock by rapid boiling until it is thick and syrupy, then pour it over the meat.

6. There will no longer be enough stock to cover the meat and there is a danger, even in a covered pan, of the exposed top drying out, so turn the meat every 15 minutes and baste it with the stock.

By the end of the cooking time, when the meat is tender, the stock should be so reduced as to provide a shiny coating that will not run off the meat. It will penetrate the flesh, moistening it and giving it the slightly glutinous texture of perfectly braised meat.

STEWING

The term stew is so widely used that it can mean almost anything. A stew is essentially food that has been slowly and gently cooked in plenty of liquid. Most cooks envisage meat cut into smallish pieces before cooking, but the term is sometimes used for sliced, sautéed meat or poultry served in a sauce, or for a whole joint or bird poached in liquid. Many stews require preliminary frying of the meat, and sometimes of onions, shallots, carrots or mushrooms too. This gives a richer flavour to the ingredients and adds colour and flavour to the sauce, which will be made using the browned sediment and dried-on juices sticking to the pan after frying. These are called brown stews. White stews are made without preliminary browning and are less rich, less fatty, altogether gentler and more easily digestible than brown ones.

Both brown and white stews are served in their cooking liquid, which is usually thickened to a syrupy sauce.

The principles of shallow-frying (see page 64) apply to the preliminary frying for a brown stew. If the sauce is not to taste insipid, or be pale in colour, you must start with a good even colour on both sides of each slice or all sides of each cube of meat. Good stews are made or lost in the early stages – so take care to fry only a few pieces at a time, to keep the temperature hot enough to sizzle and to take the time to get an even colour. Deglaze the pan as often as necessary. Deglazing serves three essential purposes: it prevents the stuck sediment in the pan from burning; it allows the flavour of that sediment to be captured and incorporated into the sauce; and it cleans the pan ready for the next batch of meat.

Beef stew with suet crust is a traditional stew, classically made. But the same principles can be used to make a lamb navarin, for example. Follow the same procedure, using lean cubes of lamb instead of the beef and omitting the suet crust. Young spring vegetables such as broad beans, French beans, tiny whole carrots, peas or sprigs of cauliflower, can be added to the stew for the last 10 minutes of stewing time to give a navarin d'agneau printanier.

BOILING AND POACHING

BOILING is a blanket term for cooking food submerged in liquid by one of several techniques: from fast, agitated bubbling – a rolling boil – to a gentle simmer, when bubbles will appear in one part of the pan only, or to the barest tremble of the liquid, which is poaching. The techniques suit different foods and achieve different effects.

Cooking green vegetables quickly in rapidly boiling water in an open pan tenderizes them, yet ensures they retain their crispness and bright colour. The water should be well salted (1 tablespoon for every 1.75 litres/3 pints), as it then boils at a higher temperature, cooking the vegetables even more quickly.

Rapid boiling in an open pan protects the vivid colours of some vegetables, such as runner beans, while enhancing the colours of others, such as artichokes. When covered, discoloration can be caused by enzymes from the vegetables, which collect in the condensation on the lid and fall back into the water. The best method is to bring the water to the boil without the vegetables, add the vegetables and cover with a lid to bring them back to the boil as fast as possible, then remove the lid to allow the escape of steam.

Vegetables that would be damaged by vigorous boiling are cooked by the more gentle simmering methods. Vegetables unlikely to discolour, like potatoes, carrots, parsnips, beetroot and other root vegetables, are traditionally cooked in a covered pan to preserve heat and control fuel costs. Hence the adage: 'If it grows in the light, cook it in the open; if it grows in the dark, keep it covered.'

REFRESHING Once cooked, refresh the vegetables by rinsing them briefly under cold running water, then put them into a warmed serving dish. Refreshing prevents further cooking by the heat retained in the vegetables, and thus sets the colour. Vegetables that hold their colour well, such as carrots, or small quantities of vegetables, such as French beans for 4 people, do not need refreshing, but for large quantities it is vital, especially if there is to be any delay before serving. They can be reheated briefly before serving by any of the following methods: by being dipped in boiling water; by rapid steaming; by being given 30–60 seconds in a microwave oven; by being tossed quickly in butter over high heat. Slow reheating in the oven will discolour most green vegetables, frozen peas being the exception, although even these will eventually lose their brilliant hue.

BLANCHING Some foods, especially vegetables and fruit, are immersed in boiling water without being fully cooked. This is called blanching and has various uses:

1. To remove strong flavours, e.g. from liver or kidneys before frying.
2. To facilitate the removal of skin, e.g. from tomatoes or peaches.
3. To lessen the salt content, e.g. from ham before cooking.
4. To destroy enzymes in vegetables destined for the freezer and to prevent discoloration.
5. To shorten the roasting time of vegetables such as potatoes, onions and parsnips by parboiling first.
6. Simply to semi-cook or soften food, e.g. fennel in salad.

FAST BOILING Rice and pasta cook well at a good rolling boil. The boiling water expands the starch granules and makes them tender, while the rapid agitation prevents the pieces of pasta or rice grains from sticking together or to the pan. Adding 1 tablespoon oil to the water also helps to prevent sticking. Long-grain rice boiled in a large pan of heavily salted water takes 10–11 minutes to cook. The grains should then mash to a paste when pressed between the thumb and index finger, though a little 'bite' is preferable to an all-over soft texture.

Similarly, pasta should always be cooked *al dente*, i.e. firm to the bite. Remember that fresh or home-made pasta, which already contains moisture, cooks 4 times faster than the dried commercial equivalents. The cooking time also depends on the thickness. Dried vermicelli cooks in 2–3 minutes, while dried lasagne takes 15–16.

Sometimes rapid boiling is used to drive off

moisture and reduce liquids to a thicker consistency. With sugar mixtures, the essential high temperatures are most rapidly achieved by a galloping boil.

EGGS are often boiled, yet there is considerable confusion about the correct method of doing this. The easiest and most foolproof is as follows:

1. Prick the rounded end of the egg with an egg-pricker or a needle to allow air to escape.
2. Bring a pan of water to the boil. Have the eggs at room temperature. (If chilled, add 30 seconds to cooking time.)
3. Carefully lower the eggs into the water on a slotted spoon.
4. Time the cooking from the moment of immersion, keeping the water simmering or gently boiling, and not boiling too vigorously, which tends to crack the shells and toughen the whites.

Three minutes will cook a medium-sized egg until the white is barely set; indeed, the white closest to the yolk will still be slightly jelly-like. Four minutes give a runny yolk and a just-set white. Six minutes give a well-set white and moist but runny yolk (set on the rim and thick but wet inside). Eight minutes give a nicely hardboiled egg. Ten minutes will give a yolk sufficiently cooked to be dry and crumbly when mashed. Fifteen minutes will give a yellow-green rim to the dry yolk and make the white tough and unpalatable.

SIMMERING Dried pulses are also cooked by boiling. As there is no colour loss to worry about, and the process is a long one, they may be simmered rather than fast-boiled. Rapidly boiling water evaporates very fast, risking boiling dry and burning. They may even, with advantage, be slowly stewed – cooked in a covered pan in liquid that only partially covers them – either on top of the stove or in the oven. If the proportion of liquid to pulses is right, they absorb all the liquid during cooking. There is nothing to throw away and little loss of flavour and nutrients. The amount of water needed obviously depends on the age, and therefore dryness, of the pulses and the speed of boiling, but twice the volume of water to pulses is a good guide.

It is often recommended that pulses be soaked in water before cooking, but this is not always necessary, especially if the pulses are last season's crop. Dried beans that are known to be 2–3 years old can be cooked without any prior soaking, but they will absorb more water, take longer to become tender, and will not taste as good as fresher pulses. As a general rule, soaking is a good idea, especially for the larger beans.

Pressure-cooking works well for pulses and eliminates the need for soaking. Pressure cookers vary and it is obviously sensible to consult the manufacturer's instructions. As a general rule, 450g/1lb dried peas or beans, unsoaked, will need 1 litre/1¾ pints water and will cook in 30 minutes at 7kg/15lb pressure.

Like pulses, some vegetables can be slowly stewed until all the liquid is either absorbed or has evaporated. For example, even-sized pieces of carrot can be put into very lightly salted water with a lump of butter. The carrots are cooked slowly so that when all the water has evaporated they are just tender, and coated in the butter. They are then called Vichy carrots.

POACHING is another long, slow, gentle cooking method, but the food is generally completely submerged in liquid that is barely trembling, either on the hob or in the oven. It is an excellent method for delicate items, such as eggs, fish or soft fruit, which would break up if subjected to vigorous agitation.

Tough meat becomes more tender and succulent the more slowly it is cooked. A cut such as oxtail takes at least 3 hours of simmering on the hob until it is acceptably tender. Poached in the oven at 150°C/300°F/gas mark 2 for 5 hours, it would be even more tender, falling from the bone and gelatinous.

A ham or large piece of bacon is cooked when the meat has shrunk back from the bone or, if boneless, when it has visibly shrunk in size by about one-fifth. The rind or skin will then peel off easily and a skewer will penetrate the meat unimpeded. But until you are experienced and confident, it is wise to stick to the cooking times given in recipes.

STEAMING

Steaming is the cooking of food in hot vapours over boiling liquid (usually water) rather than in liquid. It occurs to some extent in braising and pot-roasting, because of the closed pans and the relatively small amounts of liquid used. In true steaming, however, the food never touches the liquid, so the loss of many vitamins is significantly reduced. Furthermore, steamed food is not browned first, so it can be cooked without fat. This makes the food more easily digestible and particularly suitable for invalids and those on low-fat diets. The method has regained great favour with the new-wave nouvelle cuisine chefs because of its simplicity and purity. But excellent ingredients are essential for steaming – there is no browning, so the food must taste good without such assistance.

A variety of equipment for steaming food is available. Most common are oval or round steamers, which are like double saucepans, except that the top has holes in its base. Steam from boiling water in the lower pan rises through the holes to cook the food, while the lid on the upper pan keeps in the steam.

Another popular steaming device is a stainless steel or aluminium basket that opens and folds shut and is used with an ordinary lidded saucepan. The basket stands on its own short legs to keep it clear of the boiling water. It fits inside most saucepans and is particularly suitable for foods that do not need long cooking time as otherwise the water underneath the short legs would have to be replaced too frequently. The saucepan must have a tightly fitting lid.

VEGETABLES are the food most commonly steamed as they cook quickly and retain more of their colour and texture this way. Careful timing is essential as steamed food can be tasteless if even slightly overcooked. Today steaming times for vegetables are short, giving bright-coloured, *al dente*, palpably fresh results. Some vegetables can be steamed in their own juices. Spinach, for example, may be trimmed and put wet from washing into a covered saucepan over medium heat, and shaken occasionally until limp and cooked, but still very green. This takes about 5 minutes.

Floury potatoes that tend to break up when boiled before they are cooked are best steamed; choose potatoes that are about the same size, so that they cook at the same time. If they are very large or different sizes, cut them into bite-size pieces before steaming. For most other root vegetables, such as turnips, parsnips and swedes, cut them into 1cm/½in dice and steam them until tender before seasoning and adding butter to serve.

FISH AND POULTRY Steaming fish is simple and quick and always produces a delicate result if the fish is not allowed to overcook. Put the fish on to a piece of muslin or cheesecloth to prevent it from sticking to the steamer bottom. Oval steamers and folding baskets are suitable for small quantities of fish, but for larger fish or cooking a number of small fish, shellfish, fish steaks or fillets, a fish kettle (usually used for poaching whole fish) may be used. Made of metal, these come in sizes to take whole fish on a perforated rack inside the kettle. Ramekins can be placed under the rack to keep it well above the boiling liquid. Whole fish can be stuffed and cooked over liquid in a covered kettle on top of the stove. Allow about 8 minutes per 450g/1lb of fish.

Delicate poultry such as chicken breasts or whole small quail may be steamed similarly.

Plate steaming is an excellent method of cooking small quantities of fish in their own juices. Put the fish fillets or steaks on a lightly buttered plate, season well and cover with another upturned buttered plate or buttered kitchen foil. Set the covered plate on top of a pan of gently boiling water or on a trivet inside a large frying pan of bubbling water and cook for 8–10 minutes, depending on the thickness of the fish.

STEAMED PUDDINGS Traditional English sweet and savoury puddings (particularly suet crust puddings) are also cooked by steaming, but here the food is cooked in a container heated by steam. This gives the suet mixture its distinctive soft, open texture. The easiest way to cook the pudding is to put its container in a saucepan with hot water that comes halfway up the sides of the container. The pan is covered and the pudding cooked over low heat to steam gently for a long time, and water is added to the pan as necessary. Take care to cover the pudding with a double thickness of kitchen foil, pleated to allow for expansion of the crust, and put a band of folded foil under the basin with ends projecting up the sides to act as handles.

CHINESE COOKING traditionally involves a good deal of steaming. Fish, shellfish and tender cuts of meat, often wrapped in pastry or vegetable leaves, are quickly steamed. Food in one or more stacked rattan or metal baskets with a lid is placed over steaming liquid in a pan or wok for quick cooking.

MICROWAVING In conventional oven cooking the air is heated and the heat is passed slowly into the centre of the food by conduction. In microwaving the microwaves cause the moisture molecules in the food to vibrate, causing friction which results in heat. The heat that is generated in the food begins to cook it from the inside. Microwaves only penetrate about 5cm/2in into the food. The centre of large pieces of food is cooked by the conduction of the heat produced near the food's surface. The microwaves are reflected off the metal cavity of the oven and form criss-cross patterns. The food absorbs waves from all directions. The waves pass through china, glass, paper, etc., all of which make suitable microwave containers. Metal must not be used for microwaving as the waves are reflected and bounce off.

Microwave ovens can cook all foods but with varying results. They are very useful for cooking vegetables that would normally be boiled, such as peas and asparagus, saving on washing up and preserving vitamins and minerals, but not so good for those that would naturally be baked – a microwave-'baked' jacket potato tastes boiled.

A microwave is excellent for reheating, melting butter and defrosting food in small quantities. However, it is less suitable for defrosting large joints of meat or poultry; as the food begins to thaw, the microwaves are attracted to the defrosted water molecules and keep causing vibration/friction in the same place, while other parts remain frozen. The joint or bird should be removed from the oven and left to stand every so often so that the heat can be conducted to the centre. The speed at which a microwave cooks means that food benefiting from long cooking, such as roast beef, simply does not have the depth of flavour that a conventionally cooked piece has. On the other hand, it is good for cooking fish, which it will steam or poach beautifully.

There is no need to preheat a microwave oven but the colder the food is the longer it will take to cook. There is only a set amount of energy coming into the oven so when more than one item of food is put in, the energy is divided between them. Thus five potatoes will take considerably longer to cook than one. The shape of the food should also be taken into account – the more even the shape the more evenly it will cook. Thinner areas of food can be covered with smooth-edged tin foil to prevent further cooking. Very dense foods, such as shepherd's pie, are more difficult to reheat than those with a light, open texture, such as a sponge pudding.

Do not cover food to be microwaved with tin foil, which reflects the waves; instead use clingfilm, which should be pierced to prevent it from bursting. As a general rule moist food should be pricked.

At Leith's we have decided that a microwave is most useful for:

- Melting butter
- Softening butter for cake making (be careful not to oversoften and melt)
- Cooking vegetables in a minimum of water
- Cooking small pieces of fish
- Cooking chestnuts (pierce the tops and place on kitchen paper, cook on High for 2 minutes and peel while warm)
- Reheating plated meals and cups of coffee
- Making caramel (make it in a dish.)

Do not use the following utensils in the microwave:

- Metal containers, which reflect the waves
- Dishes with gold or silver decoration, which cause arcing (blue flashes)

- Packets with a gold line, which will get so hot that the paper will burst into flames
- Anything containing glue
- Pottery, which often has a metallic glaze
- Melamine or similar, which will absorb the waves
- Crystal glass, which contains lead
- Thin-stemmed glasses, which may break
- Jagged pieces of tin foil, which may cause arcing. If foil is used to prevent cooking, make sure it has smooth edges.

BARBECUING This popular method is perfect for informal summer entertaining or for cooking out of doors whenever the weather permits. There are various types of barbecue, from home-made to the sophisticated kettle barbecue. Whatever type is used, the principle is always the same. The barbecue must be made up well in advance so that any fire and smoke has died down and the embers are red-hot and smouldering.

Choose meat or fish cut into thick steaks for best results. The best cuts would include fillet or sirloin steaks, chicken breasts or legs, chump chops, taken from leg of lamb, and pork chops. If using fish it is advisable to marinate it first, particularly if using white fish, which is low in fat and can tend to become dry in the intense heat of the barbecue. Cook on each side until done to your liking.

Some vegetables, such as aubergines, peppers and potatoes, and some fruits, such as bananas, can be successfully barbecued. Wrapping them in kitchen foil will protect them from the intense heat.

HOME-SMOKING Smoking food can be a fairly messy business, therefore attempting it at home requires a certain degree of determination.

A selection of domestic smokers is available, varying in price and sophistication. All home-smokers are for hot-smoking, where the food cooks and smokes at the same time.

The home-smoker is a simple affair, easily assembled. We use a tall metal cylinder with a trivet which sits on the bottom and an assortment of baskets that fit inside the cylinder or hang from the lid. The wood shavings are sprinkled on the bottom; the trivet, containing a little water or other liquid, sits on top, and then the food is arranged over the trivet and the smoking takes place.

The smoke is created by the use of wood shavings. Oak, beech or fruit wood shavings are best as they give a subtle flavour and burn easily. Resinous woods such as pine should never be used. Other flavourings can be mixed with the shavings to give an extra dimension. Whole spices such as dried chilli peppers, cumin, caraway, coriander, cinnamon sticks and star anise are excellent. Tea leaves also give an interesting flavour.

The shavings and flavourings are sprinkled, dry, on to the base of the smoker. The food can be either very lightly smoked, giving a very subtle flavour, or heavily smoked for a pronounced flavour, according to the amount of wood shavings used. The small amount of liquid in the trivet is essential during the smoking, as the steam created helps to keep the food moist. Water can be infused with herbs and spices, or wine or a marinade can be used.

The food is then arranged in the baskets. It is important that they do not touch; the smoker must not be overcrowded with food. The smoker is set over a low heat and the food is cooked for 30–45 minutes, depending on size. Avoid lifting the smoker lid too much during cooking or smoke will escape. The end-result is delicious and well worth the effort.

It is perfectly possible to smoke food at home without the use of a special smoker. Instead, a large roasting tin can be effectively used, with a cake tin or small metal dish acting as the trivet, and a wire cake rack placed over the tin can hold the food. When the shavings, liquid and food are in place, the whole thing can be covered in kitchen foil and the smoking process begun.

Smoking can also be done on a barbecue by sprinkling mesquite wood chips on to the burning embers just before arranging the food on top.

FOOD PRESENTATION

If food looks delicious, people are predisposed to find that it tastes delicious. If you have spent a long time cooking, it is a shame just to dump the food on a plate. At Leith's School we have gradually developed a set of rules which can be used as guidelines when presenting food. Fashion may dictate the method – be it stylish nouvelle cuisine or chunky real food – but the guidelines are the same.

1. Keep it simple
Over-decorated food often looks messed about – no longer appetizing, but like an uncertain work of art. The more cluttered the plate, the less attractive it inevitably becomes.

2. Keep it fresh
Nothing looks more off-putting than tired food. Sprigs of herbs used for garnish should always be absolutely fresh. Pot herbs now widely available in supermarkets make this easy to ensure. Salad wilts when dressed in advance, sautéed potatoes become dull and dry when kept warm for hours, and whipped cream goes buttery in a warm room, so don't risk it.

3. Keep it relevant
A sprig of fresh watercress complements lamb cutlets nicely. The texture, taste and colour all do something for the lamb. But scratchy sprigs of parsley, though they might provide the colour, are unpleasant to eat. Gherkins cut into fans do nothing for salads, tomato slices do not improve the look of a platter of sandwiches – they rather serve to confuse and distract the eye. It is better by far to dish up a plate of chicken mayonnaise with a couple of suitable salads to provide the colour and contrast needed, than to decorate it with undressed tomato waterlilies or inedible baskets made out of lemon skins and filled with frozen sweetcorn.

4. Centre height

Dishes served on platters, such as chicken sauté, meringues, profiteroles or even a bean salad, are best given 'centre height' – arranged so the mound of food is higher in the middle with sides sloping down. Coat carefully and evenly with the sauce, if any. Do not overload serving platters with food, which makes dishing up difficult. Once breached, an over-large pile of food looks unattractive.

5. Contrasting rows
Biscuits, petits fours, little cakes and cocktail canapés all look good if arranged in rows, each row consisting of one variety, rather than dotted about. Pay attention to contrasting colour, taking care, say, not to put 2 rows of chocolate biscuits side by side, or 2 rows of white sandwiches.

6. Diagonal lines
Diamond shapes and diagonal lines are easier to achieve than straight ones. The eye is more conscious of unevenness in verticals, horizontals and rectangles.

7. Not too many colours
As with any design, it is easier to get a pleasing effect if the colours are controlled – say, just green and white, or just pink and green, or chocolate and coffee colours or even 2 shades of one colour. Coffee icing and hazelnuts give a cake an elegant look. Adding multi-coloured icings to a cake, or every available garnish to a salad, tends to look garish. There are exceptions of course: a colourful salad Niçoise can be as pleasing to the eye as a dish of candy-coated chocolate drops.

8. Contrasting the simple and the elaborate
If the dish or bowl is elaborately decorated, contrasting simple food tends to show it off better. A Victorian fruit epergne with ornate stem and silver carving will look stunning filled with fresh strawberries. Conversely, a plain

white plate sets off pretty food design to perfection.

9. Uneven numbers

As a rule, uneven numbers of, say, rosettes of cream on a cake, baked apples in a long dish, or portions of meat on a platter look better than even numbers. This is especially true of small numbers. Five and three invariably look better than four, but there is little difference in effect between eleven and twelve.

10. A generous look

Tiny piped cream stars, or sparsely dotted nuts, or mean-looking chocolate curls on a cake look amateurish and stingy.

11. Avoid clumsiness

On the other hand, the temptation to cram the last spoonful of rice into the bowl, or squeeze the last slice of pâté on to the dish leads to a clumsy look, and can be daunting to the diner.

12. Overlapping

Chops, steaks, sliced meats, even rashers of bacon, look best evenly overlapping. This way, more of them can be fitted comfortably on the serving dish than if placed side by side.

13. Best side uppermost

Usually the side of a steak or a cutlet that is grilled or fried first looks the best, and should be placed uppermost. Bones are generally unsightly and, if they cannot be clipped off or removed, they should be tucked out of the way.

14. Individual plating

Until the advent of nouvelle cuisine in the 1970s it was considered a caterer's short-cut trick to plate dishes individually. Suddenly it became the only way to present food. When plating individually the same rules apply to presentation. Keep it simple and keep it relevant. We add two extra caveats. First, think of the rim of the plate as a picture frame: do not put any food on the 'frame'. Second, stick to your original idea. If a dish has been plated up and then changed, it will inevitably look messy.

SERVING STYLE

How much formal convention is followed at an informal family table or at a simple supper with friends, depends of course on the character and personal style of the host or hosts. But it is useful to know how things ought to be done, so that, at an elegant dinner party or if cooking for someone else, the cook at least won't make any blunders.

LAYING THE TABLE

As a rule, cutlery is laid so that the diner works from the outside in – his first-course knife will be furthest from the plate, and on the right, because he is to pick it up with his right hand. His first-course fork will be on his left, and furthest from his plate. Similarly, if the first course is soup, the soup spoon will be on the right (because most people are right-handed), at the extreme outside of the cutlery collection.

If a knife-and-fork first course is followed by soup, the soup spoon will be in second place, and so on, working inwards to dessert spoon and fork, or cheese knife. Dessert or pudding cutlery is sometimes put across the top of the diner's place, the spoon above or beyond the fork and the handles pointing towards the hand that will pick them up – i.e. spoon handle towards the right hand, fork handle towards left hand.

Logic prevails in the same way with glasses, which are set out just beyond the knife tip, in a diagonal row, first one (say for a white wine to go with the first course) a little further away, and the dessert wine glass at the end of the row. The bread plate is placed on the diner's left, to the left of the cutlery. Napkins either go on this plate, or in the middle of the diner's place if the first course is not yet on the table. Individual ashtrays, fingerbowls, salt cellars are placed within comfortable reach.

The commonest mistakes made in laying tables are: to fail to leave enough space between the banks of cutlery for the dinner plate to fit comfortably (leaving the guest foraging under his plate for a knife or fork), to line up the tips of the cutlery instead of the bases, which gives an untidy unprofessional look, and to arrange flowers or candles in such a way that diners cannot see each other across the table. Low flowers are best, and candles should be checked to make sure they do not confuse sight lines. Nothing is so irritating as having to peer round an obstruction to carry on a conversation.

THE ETIQUETTE OF SERVING

At a formal dinner, convention holds that women are served before men, starting with the most important female guest and ending with the hostess. Usually the top female guest will be seated on the right of the host. The men are then served, the most important male guest (who will be seated at the right of the hostess) being served first, then the others and, lastly, the host. Once everyone is served the hostess starts to eat which is a signal for everyone else to begin.

HOW MUCH TO SERVE

A daunting plateful tends to take away the appetite, so do not over-help guests to food. Take trouble to arrange things neatly and attractively on the plate. Place the first spoonful (say the meat) to one side, not in the middle, then work round with vegetables and garnishes, keeping them separate. Slops and drips look bad, so take time when spooning a sauce to let any excess run off the spoon before moving away from the main dish, and make sure the serving dish and diner's plate are as close together as possible.

If waiting formally, by the diner's side, hold the platter with one hand almost over his plate and use a spoon and fork in the other hand to serve him. This is called 'silver service'. If the diner is helping himself, hold the platter very low close to the table and close to his plate, to the side of it, so he can manage the awkward business of turning and wielding spoon and fork. This is called 'butler service'. With silver service the server serves food to the diners' left. With butler service diners are offered food to their right. Plates are always cleared from the diners' right. But in awkward or crowded corners it is better to forget convention and do whatever is least likely to disturb conversation.

SERVING WINE

The wine should be served at the same time as the food, or even before, but not too long afterwards – waiting is a strain and drinking is permitted straight away even if eating is not. The host tastes the wine – if he has not already done so – then everyone is served, ladies then men.

Good waiters, or hosts, do not constantly top up glasses, but do so positively when they are down to about a third. Glasses should not be filled more than two thirds full – the idea is to leave room for the drinker to be able to get his nose into the glass to smell it without getting the tip wet! It also means he can swill the wine about, which encourages the release of its bouquet.

CLEARING THE TABLE

This should happen as unobtrusively as possible. Nothing should be touched until everyone has finished his food and indicated the fact by putting knife and fork firmly together. Then the plates are removed, but not stacked one on top of the other or scraped within sight of the diners. Such unattractive operations should be performed out of sight. When the plates are cleared, everything connected with the just-removed course is cleared too – salt and pepper, mustard, sauces, salad dishes and, if the savoury courses are now over, bread plates and bread and butter. Nothing connected with the pudding should go on the table before everything pertaining to the previous course is off it. The same goes for coffee – it should not appear, nor should the bitter mints or petits fours, until the pudding has vanished, with its sauce jugs, cream, etc.

HEALTHY EATING

by Caroline Waldegrave

Healthy recipes form an integral part of this book, in that you will find some that are low in saturated fat, sugar and salt. It is not a health book as it is designed to cover all aspects of cooking that most of us need to know about. However, I am very keen on bringing up my children as healthily as possible and many of our ex-students are asked to cook carefully for overweight, over-stressed businessmen.

Nutritionists seem to have changed their advice dramatically over the past few years and this can be very confusing. But in fact they are responding to the considerable advance in knowledge made recently as well as to changing social conditioning. Earlier this century, the national diet was high in inexpensive carbohydrate foods like bread and potatoes and often dangerously low in the more costly protein foods like meat. The more affluent post-war years have seen a great change in the way the nation eats, however, and now the danger is seen to be not so much in an excess of protein as in too much saturated fat in the diet. Saturated fat comes from high-protein foods like meat and cheese as well as from more obvious sources like butter and cream. Moreover, we no longer eat enough carbohydrate to provide adequate dietary fibre.

We are told now to reduce our intake of saturated fat, but we are also sometimes told that a small increase in polyunsaturated fat may be a good thing. What is the difference between these two types of fat? It is a matter of the chemical structure of the fatty acids that make them up. Fatty acids are long chains of carbon atoms joined by a chemical bond, which may be either double or single. A fatty acid with no double bonds is called saturated; where there is only one double bond, it is known as monounsaturated, and where there are two or more, polyunsaturated. Most fats are made up of a mixture of many fatty acids. For example, the fat in butter is 63 per cent saturated, 3 per cent polyunsaturated and 34 per cent monounsaturated fatty acids. So when you hear that butter is a saturated fat, this really means that it is higher in saturated fat than in any other kind. Unsaturated bonds can be converted back into single (saturated) bonds by a process called hydrogenation; a food that undergoes this process, therefore, will become higher in saturated fats. Hydrogenation is used in some food-refining processes to make liquid fats solidify.

Why are saturated fats now considered to be bad for us? Medical research suggests that a high level of saturated fat in the blood blocks and damages the arteries and impedes blood circulation. This increases the risk of cardiovascular disease, which is one of the major killers in this country. Polyunsaturated fat makes the blood less 'sticky' and so prevents it from attaching itself to arterial walls and causing blockages. Thus it has a beneficial effect on health, unless you eat so much of it that your weight starts to become a health problem. Monounsaturated fat has no effect on the blood.

Saturated fat is also thought to be a factor in the level of cholesterol in the blood. Cholesterol is a common source of confusion. It is a substance associated with fat and can originate in two ways.

Blood (serum) cholesterol is manufactured by the human liver and is an essential part of all healthy cells. The liver makes enough cholesterol for our needs, and in some people a high level of saturated fat in the diet makes the liver produce more cholesterol than is needed by the body.

Dietary cholesterol is cholesterol found in foods. Animal foods that are high in saturated fat are also high in cholesterol; some low-fat foods contain high levels as well. You should be concerned about eating too much fat overall, but not about eating prawns, brains, liver and kidney which, although high in cholesterol, are low in other fats. The important point is still to reduce the proportion of saturated fats in your diet.

All fat is fattening, that is, high in calories: 1 gram of fat releases about 9 calories, while 1 gram of carbohydrate releases only about 4. Calories are a unit of heat energy, but if the food you eat releases more calories than you need, your body will store the extra energy as body fat. If you are trying to lose weight, cutting fats out of your diet is therefore the best way. You would find it hard, and it would be foolish, to cut them out entirely, however, as some intake of fat is essential to several metabolic processes.

It is now recommended that no more than 30–35 per cent of daily calories should come from fats of any sort, even if you are not trying to lose weight. Fat in the diet comes from many sources, from the obvious fatty foods such as butter, cream and cheese to hidden sources such as many ready-prepared and processed foods. Meat products, such as sausages, pork pies and so on, are generally high in fat, and especially high in saturates. Some cuts of meat are very fatty and, again, the fat is mostly saturated. The leanest meats are chicken – especially when skinned – turkey, rabbit, game, liver and kidney. Many fish, such as tuna, salmon, herrings and mackerel, are oily, but the fat is mainly monounsaturated and polyunsaturated. If you buy fish canned in oil, however, drain away the oil as it may be high in saturated fat unless, for example, soya oil is used. White fish and shellfish are low in fat.

Nutritionists also advise us to reduce the amount of sugar we eat. Too much sugar has no direct link with heart disease, but sugar is quite fattening and obesity is a major cause of heart disease. Sugar is also bad for your teeth. The calories released by sugar are 'empty', that is, they provide no nutritional advantages.

I am always amazed when I go into health food shops. They are often stuffed full of jars of honey (another form of sugar), 'healthy' bars (often full of more sugar) and mueslis (often far from free of sugar). Also in health food shops you sometimes see cheesy pies (full of saturated fat) and carob cakes (full of another form of sugar). Sometimes they also have spring rolls and samosas (often deep-fried and actually tasting greasy).

The basic message is to cut down on fat – saturated fat in particular – sugar, salt and processed foods. And to increase your intake of fresh fruit, vegetables and cereals. Obviously one must not go 'over the top' by sprinkling bran on everything. Apart from making food fairly unpalatable, this can cause diarrhoea and bowel obstructions. Eating no salt at all would be harmful and everything would taste deadly dull.

At home, I avoid saturated fats in my cooking. This means I do not use butter, lard, cream, dripping, coconut oil, blended cooking fat, mixed blended vegetable oil, solid vegetable fat, or margarines unless they are labelled 'high in polyunsaturated fat'. For general cooking purposes I use sunflower or grapeseed oil as they are both high in polyunsaturated fat. Corn oil is also a good choice but it has a strong flavour, and safflower is high in polyunsaturated fat but very expensive. For special occasions, I buy walnut oil, as it is fairly high in polyunsaturated fat and tastes delicious, as does hazelnut oil, which is high in monounsaturated fatty acids. I also like to use extra virgin olive oil, which is high in monounsaturated fatty acids. Use a polyunsaturated margarine instead of butter, but most low-fat spreads are not suitable for cooking, because they tend to separate on contact with heat.

When cooking conventionally, cream is often an important part of a recipe. Cream is high in saturated fat, so I use low-fat natural yoghurt, buttermilk, low-fat soft cheese (quark), tofu, fromage frais and cottage cheese in place of cream.

Greek yoghurt is higher in fat than ordinary natural yoghurt but makes a very good cream substitute for special occasions when you would normally serve cream as an accompaniment.

Unfortunately none of these substitutes is capable of remaining stable if boiled, so they must be added at the last minute. Cottage cheese must be whizzed or sieved before use and the others should be slaked. Greek yoghurt can be momentarily boiled.

Skimmed or semi-skimmed milk can easily be substituted for full-fat milk and after a couple of weeks you will not notice the difference. Nuts are a high-fat food although their fat is mainly monounsaturated and polyunsaturated. There are two exceptions: coconut contains saturated fat and chestnuts are very low in fat.

Of all the foods high in saturated fats, cheese is the one I find hardest to give up. On the whole I try to eat low-fat cheese such as quark or cottage cheese, but for a treat I have Brie and, for a real treat, farmhouse Cheddar. Looking at labels on cheese can be confusing, as in other parts of Europe the fat content is measured at a different stage in the manufacturing process. They measure the amount of fat in the 'dry matter', that is, the fat content of the cheese minus water. Many French cheeses, like Brie, have a high water content. Here in Britain the amount of fat given per 100g is the amount of fat you actually eat. When you see a Brie labelled in the French way as containing 45 per cent fat, it is only about 23 per cent fat by British standards: that is, the same as the rather bland Edam that dieters have always been told to eat.

A change to healthy eating can involve imitating conventional recipes in a healthier way, making shepherd's pie with more vegetables and less mince, for example. But there are some dishes that you cannot imitate. What is the point of a yoghurt-based crème brûlée? Or a carob, polyunsaturated oil, wholemeal flour and raw sugar chocolate cake? Either you allow yourself the occasional treat, or you try to find equally sophisticated puddings that are low in fat. You want, after all, to keep to your new way of eating. Although after 10 years of healthy eating my tastebuds have learned to appreciate slightly different tastes, it has taken time and patience: much better to go slowly and stick to it than be too dramatic and too restrictive and then give it up. Begin by allowing yourself occasional treats – after 6 months you will not want them any more! The gentle and almost subversive route to health is a smooth path.

FAT CONTENTS OF VARIOUS FOODS

Bacon	Fat (g/100g)
Collar joint, boiled, lean and fat	27.0
Collar joint, boiled, lean only	9.7
Gammon, boiled or grilled, lean and fat	18.9
Gammon, boiled or grilled, lean only	5.5
Rashers, grilled, lean only	18.9
Rashers, back, lean and fat	33.8
Rashers, streaky, lean and fat	36.0
Rashers, middle, lean and fat	35.1

Beef	
Brisket, boiled, lean and fat	23.9
Forerib, roast, lean and fat	28.8
Forerib, roast, lean only	12.6
Rump steak, grilled, lean and fat	12.1
Rump steak, grilled, lean only	6.0
Stewing steak, lean and fat	11.0
Topside, roast, lean and fat	12.0
Topside, roast, lean only	4.4

Lamb	
Breast, roast, lean and fat	37.1
Breast, roast, lean only	16.6
Chops, grilled, lean and fat } without	29.0
Chops, grilled, lean only } bone	12.3
Leg, roast, lean and fat	17.9
Leg, roast, lean only	8.1
Scrag and neck, stewed, lean and fat	21.1
Scrag and neck, stewed, lean only	15.7

Pork	
Chops, grilled, lean and fat } without	24.2
Chops, grilled, lean only } bone	10.7
Leg, roast, lean and fat	19.8
Leg, roast, lean only	6.9

Veal	Fat (g/100g)
Cutlets, grilled	5.0
Fillet, roast	11.5

Chicken	
Roast, meat and skin	14.0
Roast, meat only	5.5

Grouse	
Roast	3–5

Partridge	
Roast	4–7

Pheasant	
Roast	5–10

Pigeon	
Roast	5–13

Turkey	
Roast, meat and skin	6.5
Roast, meat only	2.7

Rabbit	
Stewed	3–7

Hare	
Stewed	3–7

Offal	
Hearts, stewed	3–6
Kidneys	5–7
Liver, grilled, etc.	5

Cooking Fat	Total fat content (g/100g)
Butter	82.0
Margarine	82.0
Gold	40.7
Outline	40.7
Cream, single	21.2
Cream, soured	21.2
Cream, whipping	35.0
Cream, double	48.2

Cheese	
Camembert, Brie, etc.	23.2
Cheddar, Cheshire, Gruyère, Emmental, etc.	33.5
Danish Blue, Roquefort, etc.	29.2
Edam, Gouda, St. Paulin, etc.	22.9
Parmesan	29.7
Stilton	40.0
Cream cheese	47.4
Low-fat cottage cheese (see carton)	0–4
Medium-fat curd cheese	25
Medium-fat Mozzarella, etc.	25

Fish	
Eel, stewed	13.2
Herring, grilled	13.0
Bloater, grilled	12.9
Kipper, baked	6.2
Mackerel, grilled	6.2
Salmon, steamed	13.0
Sardines, canned (drained)	13.0
Sprats, grilled (estimated value)	13.0
Trout, steamed	3.0
Tuna, canned (includes oil)	22.0
Tuna, canned (drained, estimated value)	13.0

FOOD SAFETY

Food safety and hygiene are essential in the kitchen as many foods may contain harmful organisms. The cook must be aware of these bacteria and of how to prevent them multiplying to dangerous levels in food which would cause food poisoning.

Salmonella is one of the commonest causes of food poisoning and is most often brought into the kitchen on poultry and meat. Campylobacter (the symptoms of which may not appear for 10 days) usually enters on raw poultry. Clostridium perfringens is often present on raw meats, or unwashed vegetables. The origin of Staphylococcus aureus is usually a food handler with an inadequately covered skin infection. The latter two organisms can produce illness within a few hours of eating. Listeria is commonly found in many foods but listeriosis is very rare as most people's immune systems cope well. Special dietary advice regarding listeriosis applies only to vulnerable groups who are particularly at risk. These are pregnant women and those with an underlying illness which results in impaired resistance to infection. These special groups are advised to avoid pâtés and soft ripened cheeses of the Brie, Camembert and blue-vein types, and to reheat cooked chilled meals and ready-to-eat poultry until piping hot rather than eat them cold.

PREVENTING THE GROWTH OF BACTERIA

Bacteria will grow to toxic levels if given the chance. What they need to do their evil work is warmth, time and moisture – ideal conditions, from the bugs' point of view, would be lukewarm food left out in a hot kitchen for several hours. A tiny (and therefore harmless) colony of bacteria could multiply rapidly to such an extent that anyone eating that food could become very ill and require hospitalization. If the victim was a baby (with an immune system not fully developed) or an elderly person or invalid (whose immunity might be impaired), death could result.

Fortunately, some simple precautions can be taken to prevent food poisoning. You can wash off bacteria (such as listeria from salad vegetables, etc.); you can kill the organisms with heat; you can arrest their growth by refrigeration; and you can prevent cross-contamination by practising good hygiene in the kitchen.

THE GOLDEN RULES ARE:

BUYING Buy only very fresh food from suppliers you can trust.

WASHING Wash all food if it is to be eaten raw. It is good practice to wash all fruits and vegetables, even if they are to be peeled, as they could contaminate other foods. Wash free-range eggs just before cooking – salmonella is more likely to be present on the egg shell than in the egg.

REFRIGERATION Refrigerate all meat, fish and chicken, all dairy products and eggs. Until the discovery of salmonella in eggs, refrigeration of eggs was not thought to be necessary. The danger is still small, but why take any unnecessary risks? Besides, eggs lose their freshness and become stale much more quickly when they are not stored in a refrigerator.

Keep food refrigerated as much as you can. Never leave it on the side in the kitchen waiting to be used, and never leave cold, cooked food at room temperature for more than an hour or so.

Although the original cooking will have destroyed any bacteria, food can be re-infected and, if left in a warm atmosphere, can become harmful.

Do not put hot food in the refrigerator. It will warm up the atmosphere inside and encourage the growth of any bacteria present in other foods in the cabinet.

As far as possible, always keep raw and cooked food separated until serving. Bacteria can enter the kitchen on raw food, and can then be transferred to cooked food where they might easily be left to multiply in peace if the food is not to be re-cooked.

COOKING Cook food sufficiently to kill any bacteria that may be present. In particular chicken, chopped meats, rolled joints, burgers and re-formed steaks must be cooked thoroughly as food-poisoning bacteria may be present in the centres of these. If cooking for the very young, the very old or the infirm, egg yolks should be cooked hard. (Soft-cooked eggs may not have reached a sufficiently high temperature to kill salmonella.)

RAW MEAT AND FISH Consumption of raw meat and fish carries a risk of food poisoning. Meat and fish that are traditionally served raw, such as sushi and steak tartare, must be of the freshest, best quality, and should be prepared and eaten on the day they are purchased. Some traditional dishes, such as gravad lax, smoked salmon, or Parma ham, although they are raw, can be kept safely under refrigeration because they have been cured either with salt or smoke, or both.

REHEATING If reheating food, make sure that you serve it really hot, i.e. near boiling point, even right in the middle.

Do not pour hot sauces on to cold food unless you are going to reheat it right through at once. Don't add warm food to cold food. Don't mix yesterday's soup with today's without reboiling. Always reheat any mixture immediately if adding two things of different temperatures together. Remember that the cool one might contain a few bacteria, and the hot one will provide enough heat to start them

multiplying, but not enough to kill them.

Reboil stocks, soups and sauces frequently in hot weather. Even in winter, reboil them every three days. In theory, you can keep the same stockpot on the go for ever if you reboil it every time you add anything to it. And remember that the stronger the stock, the firmer the jelly it will set to, and the better it will keep in the refrigerator. If reheating aspic, bring to the boil, then let it cool enough to use.

KEEPING FOOD WARM If food must be kept warm, first make sure that it is heated through sufficiently to kill all bacteria; then keep it really hot, not lukewarm. Do not pour a warm sauce over, say, cold poached eggs and keep them warm in a hot cupboard or warming drawer.

FREEZING Do not refreeze completely thawed food without cooking it first. Although the freezing and thawing do not harm, it is easy to forget just how many periods at room temperature the food has had, and it is therefore impossible to guess how large the concentration of bacteria may be. Never refreeze chicken that has been frozen and thawed.

COOKING FROM FROZEN Do not cook large items (such as whole chickens) when frozen. When the bird looks cooked, the inside (where salmonella is most likely to be present on the surface of the cavity) may still be lukewarm and raw. For the same reason, it is unwise to stuff large birds. The stuffing may prevent the heat from penetrating the cavity and killing any bacteria present.

THAWING Thaw food slowly in the refrigerator or in a leakproof plastic bag under cold water. Do not try to thaw things fast by putting them in a warming drawer or under hot water. The outer layer will stay at incubating temperature too long. However, microwaving to thaw is safe because it is so fast that the bacteria do not have time to breed. But cook the food as soon as it is thawed, just in case your microwave has warmed it up too much.

COOLING Cool large quantities of food fast. If a stew is left to cool in a heavy pan, the centre of it will provide perfect bacteria breeding conditions: warmth, moisture and time. And a stir with a non-sterile wooden spoon could easily provide the parent bacteria to start the colony. Commercial caterers cool food in a blast chiller, but small kitchens do not have this luxury. So either tip the stew into shallow flat containers to cool, or cool the pot fast by standing it in a bowl in the sink, and continuously running the cold tap into the bowl, to keep the waterjacket round the pan cool. Give it an occasional stir to speed things up.

Nor should you leave hot food covered with a heavy lid. Open food cools quicker. If you want to avoid the food drying out or forming a skin, place some wet greaseproof paper (which is thin enough not to hinder cooling) flat on the surface of the food.

WRAPPING Take care when wrapping hot food in clingfilm – if there are any air spaces between the food and the film, greenhouse-like incubating conditions will be produced. Instead, wrap the food loosely in kitchen foil, and refrigerate as soon as it is cold.

UTENSILS Don't use the same knife or board for raw and cooked food without washing it between jobs. If you have just jointed a raw chicken and then slice cooked beef with the same knife, you could transfer bacteria from the chicken to the beef. The micro-organisms in the chicken will get cooked to death, but they could grow with impunity in the beef. Caterers have separate refrigerators and boards for storing and preparing hot and cold food, and large-production kitchens very often have separate kitchen areas and separate cooks. The home cook, however, who is dealing with small quantities of food that are cooked, eaten or refrigerated fast need not go to such lengths but should practise good food hygiene and take sensible precautions, always washing utensils thoroughly after use.

Keep the kitchen area clean. This means frequently washing tools in near-boiling water, scrubbing boards and surfaces with detergent, washing out the refrigerator weekly with weak bleach, and making sure that tea-towels and cloths are changed as soon as they are dirty or damp. A damp cloth left over a warm cooker, or a crack in the wooden handle of a much-used knife, provides the perfect incubating conditions for germs.

'OFF' FOODS Don't ever serve food that smells or looks at all peculiar. Although salmonella is completely tasteless and has no discernible odour, unpleasant odours or appearance are an indication of age and poor condition, and food-poisoning organisms are likely to be present along with the ones causing the obvious deterioration. Always err on the safe side and throw out any food that looks or smells dubious – don't take risks.

SALMONELLA IN EGGS Consumption of raw eggs or uncooked dishes made from them, such as home-made mayonnaise, mousse and ice cream, carries the risk of food poisoning. However, if you do use raw eggs to make these dishes, make sure you use only the freshest, that the dishes are eaten as soon as possible after making and that they are never left for more than 1 hour at room temperature.

For healthy people there is little risk from eating cooked eggs, however they have been prepared – boiled, fried, scrambled or poached. Vulnerable people such as the elderly, the sick, babies, toddlers and pregnant women should only eat eggs that have been thoroughly cooked until the white and yolk are solid. These vulnerable people should avoid egg recipes which require light cooking, such as meringues and hollandaise sauce.

Lightly cooked egg dishes should be eaten as soon as possible after cooking and if the dishes are not for immediate use they should be stored in the refrigerator after cooling. Pasteurized egg, which is free from harmful bacteria, is often used by caterers in these dishes and is available as a useful alternative in the home.

POISONOUS FOODS Some foods are naturally poisonous and must be treated with care. For example, red kidney beans must be boiled for 15 minutes to destroy an enzyme which is potentially fatal. Cooking the beans until soft at a very low temperature is not sufficient to do this, so, if using a 'slow cooker', give the beans a good boil before putting them into the pot.

Green potato skins, rhubarb leaves and many wild mushrooms are mildly poisonous and can cause gastric upsets in some people. Indeed, a few wild mushrooms are lethal. Do not cook mushrooms unless purchased from a reputable supplier and you are certain they are safe. Do not gather and cook wild mushrooms unless you have the knowledge to distinguish between the safe and poisonous varieties.

CHOOSING AND STORING PRODUCE

This chapter has been written to offer a few guidelines on how to recognize good-quality food and how best to store it. For freezability please see the chapter on freezing (see page 95). When shopping we would always suggest buying organic ingredients as their taste is naturally better. Organic foods are more highly priced than non-organic ingredients so the purse inevitably dictates your final decision.

MEAT

When choosing meat, the general principle is to look for signs that it has come from a young animal. It should not be too fatty, the joints should be reasonably small, it should be of a firm texture and not have too much gristle; although obviously there are different expectations about the quantity of acceptable fat and gristle depending on the particular cut of meat. Meat should never be slimy; it should be moist but not gelatinous and it should not smell. Any exposed bones should be pinkish-blue in colour and the paler the fat the better.

STORAGE

Always allow meat to breathe, so if it comes tightly wrapped up, pierce the clingfilm and refrigerate for not more than 2–3 days. Raw meat should always be stored at the bottom of the refrigerator so that no raw blood can drop on to cooked food – this can be a cause of food poisoning.

BEEF

Generally you should look for a deep, dull red piece of meat rather than a bright, orange-red joint. This is difficult in a supermarket because managers assume that their customers want 'bright' meat so there is much use of clever lighting as well as the widespread use of adding anti-oxidants. The fat on beef should be a pale creamy yellow colour. When choosing beef, ask for meat from a traditional beef herd.

VEAL

The flesh should be pale pink, soft but not flabby, and finely grained. There should be very little creamy white fat. Do not worry if there is a lot of gelatinous tissue around the meat as this is a natural characteristic of a very immature animal.

LAMB

The colour of the meat varies with the breed of lamb. The fat should be creamy white (if it is yellow it indicates old age) and it should not be oily. All joints should be plump and compact rather than long and thin. The skin should be pliable – not hard and wrinkled. Welsh or English lamb is considered to be superior to New Zealand lamb.

PORK

The meat should be pale pink, close-grained and firm to the touch. It should not have enlarged glands or abscesses (pigs kept too close together, reasonably enough, bite each other). The fat should be firm and white, not oily, and without a greyish tinge. There should be an even covering of fat. Try to find free-range pork; it has an excellent flavour.

OFFAL

Offal has often been called 'awful offal' in the past, but at last it is gaining the recognition it deserves as a delicacy. It tends to be low in fat and high in iron and is very healthy. All offal must be eaten very fresh.

LIVER

It should not have a strong smell; it should be shiny and a little bloody.

CALVES' LIVER It should be a pale milky brown colour with a fine even texture. Dutch liver is considered better than English.

LAMBS' LIVER This is darker in colour than calves'.

PIGS' LIVER This is dark and close-textured. It is used in pâtés and terrines.

OX LIVER This is dark bluish-brown with a very strong flavour. Used occasionally in stews and pies but it is very inferior to other sorts of liver and is best avoided.

KIDNEY

Kidneys are sold loose or still in their suet. To store kidneys, remove them from the suet and refrigerate for a maximum of 24 hours. Make sure that they are not tightly wrapped in clingfilm – they must be allowed to breathe.

VEAL KIDNEYS These are delicious. They should be a pale milky brown with a creamy white suet. They look rather like a bunch of grapes.

LAMBS' KIDNEYS These are medium brown, faintly bluish, firm-textured and egg-shaped.

PIGS' KIDNEYS These are pale brown with a rather strong flavour, similar in shape to lambs' kidneys.

OX KIDNEYS These look like huge veal kidneys but are much darker in colour. They are only suitable for pies and puddings.

SWEETBREADS As with all offal, the calves' sweetbreads are the best, then the lambs' and then the ox breads. Pigs' sweetbreads are not sold.

HEADS AND BRAINS

CALVES' HEADS These are sometimes available if ordered specially. They are used mainly for boiling and serving hot. Salted, they are used for brawn.

CALVES' BRAINS The most delicate and expensive, they are soaked and blanched to remove all traces of blood before cooking, and skinned of membrane and sinew after blanching. They are excellent fried plain or in a crumb coating and have an almost creamy texture when cooked.

PIGS' HEADS These are made into brawn, fresh or salted, and can be used for sausages. The cheeks of certain long-faced breeds of pig are lightly salted and sold as Bath Chaps. They are rather fatty, but have a good flavour, and are usually eaten crumbed and fried, or cold like ham. A pig's head is sometimes used on banqueting tables as a stand-in for the now unavailable boar's head. Pigs' brains are sold in the heads.

SHEEP'S HEADS These can be boiled or stewed for use in broths and pie fillings, but are seldom available, and involve a lot of labour for very little meat.

SHEEP'S BRAINS These are less fine and delicate than calves', but more readily available. They are treated in exactly the same way.

OX CHEEK This is sold for brawns and stews.

HEART

Heart is highly nutritious, but needs slow cooking to tenderize it. It is also very lean, and requires a sauce or plenty of basting to keep it moist. Hearts must be cleaned of all sinew and the tubes removed before cooking.

OX HEART This is large, very tough, strongly flavoured, coarse and muscular and bluish-red. It is generally used chopped or minced with other ingredients – perhaps for a pie.

LAMBS' HEARTS The smallest and most tender of the hearts, but stuffing to add flavour, slow cooking and careful basting are still necessary to moisten and tenderize the naturally lean and tough flesh.

PLUCK

The pluck is the name given to the lights (lungs), liver, pancreas and spleen. Today, lights are sold generally for pet food. The liver is sold separately. Sheep's pluck is sometimes minced for haggis.

FEET AND TROTTERS

CALVES' FEET These are seldom sold to the public. They are good for stock and calf's foot jelly due to the high concentration of gelatine present in the feet. Pigs' trotters are high in gelatine, and good for setting stocks, and for brawn. They can be boned, stuffed, braised, served hot with mustard sauce, or hot or cold with vinaigrette. Sheep's trotters and ox feet are not sold. Cow heel is treated before sale, and looks and tastes similar to tripe. It consists of the whole foot and heel of the animal.

TRIPE

Tripe can come from all cud-chewing animals, being the first and second stomachs, but in practice only ox tripe is sold. The first stomach (blanket tripe) is smooth, the second honeycombed.

Tripe is sold parboiled, but needs further long boiling to tenderize it. It is wise to ask the butcher how much more boiling it will need. Grey, slimy, flabby, strong-smelling tripe should be avoided. It should be thick, firm and very white. Tripe can be stewed, boiled or deep-fried. A specialist taste, it's either loved or loathed!

OXTAIL

Oxtail is sold skinned and usually jointed. Choose large fat tails, with plenty of meat on them. Cow tails, which are skinny and rather tasteless, are sometimes passed off as oxtail. The meat should be dark and lean, and the fat creamy white and firm. Oxtail is high in gelatine content, so it cooks to a tender, almost sticky, stew. It is good for soups and very rich in flavour.

MARROW BONES

Marrow bones are from the thigh and shoulder bones of beef. They are sawn across in short cylinders by the butcher. They are boiled whole and served in a napkin, the diner extracting the soft rich marrow and eating it on toast. Marrow is also used as a flavouring in other dishes, such as entrecôte à la Bordelaise, where it moistens and flavours the steak.

TONGUE

To get a pig's tongue you must buy the whole head, while calves' tongues are very rarely available. Ox and lambs' tongues can be bought, however.

OX TONGUE It should feel soft to the touch, though it may have a rough, pigmented skin.

LAMBS' TONGUES They are very small and are generally sold by the kilo. They should be pale pink; the roughish skin may be light or dark grey.

BLOOD

Pigs' blood is used in the making of black pudding. It is mixed with fat, and stuffed into intestines like a sausage.

NOTE: Brains, oxtail and marrow-bones are currently not eaten because of the BSE controversy. Doubtless they will come back into fashion.

GAME

If you want to roast your game, try to buy young tender birds or animals. You can recognize a young bird by its smooth legs and pliable feet and beaks. If it has already been plucked, feel it for pliability in the backbone.

STORAGE

If it has not been hung already, you should hang game, undrawn (except for rabbits, which are paunched, or gutted, as soon as they are killed), in a cool, dry place. Birds are hung by the neck and animals by the feet. The hanging time varies according to the animal and the weather, but a rough guide is given below with a brief description of each bird or animal. The less well hung it is, the easier it is to pluck and draw. If the game is already prepared, store it loosely wrapped in the bottom of the refrigerator.

GROUSE
Hanging time: anything from 2–10 days.
After 2 days it does not have a strong flavour but after 10 it will be very gamey. Red or Scottish grouse is best. Allow one grouse per head.

PARTRIDGE
Hanging time: 3–4 days.
We think that a partridge, particularly the grey British as opposed to the French red leg, is the nicest of all game birds. Plucked birds should have a pale skin and plump breast. Allow one partridge per head (some people can eat 2).

RABBIT
Hanging time: 24 hours.
Wild or farmed rabbit is available all the year round. Rabbits are paunched (gutted) as soon as they are killed. Wild rabbit is gamier and less tender than farmed, whose pale flesh is rather like chicken. If the rabbit has not been skinned, look for smooth, sharp claws and delicate soft ears.

HARE
Hanging time: 5–6 days, unpaunched.
If the hare has not been skinned, look for smooth sharp claws and delicate soft ears. A leveret (young hare) has a hardly noticeable hare lip – this becomes deeper and more pronounced in an older animal. If the hare has been skinned, look for deep claret flesh. Only young tender joints of hare are suitable for roasting, and even they need much basting. Older hares and the tougher joints are traditionally jugged.

POULTRY
STORAGE OF ALL POULTRY
If the bird has been sold with giblets remove them as soon as you get home, and unwrap the bird so that it can breathe. Store at the bottom of the refrigerator for not more than 2–3 days.

CHICKENS
The more you spend on a chicken, the better it will probably taste. A frozen supermarket bird, battery-raised and fed on fishmeal until the moment of slaughter, has little chance of tasting good, however well cooked. Try to buy free-range birds. They may look scrawnier than the plump-breasted oven-ready bird but the flavour is far superior.

POUSSINS These are 4–6 weeks old. They serve one person and look appetizing but have very little flavour.

DOUBLE POUSSINS These are 6–10 weeks old. They serve 2 people and have quite a good flavour.

SPRING CHICKENS These are 10–12 weeks old. They serve 3 people and have a similar flavour to that of double poussins.

ROASTERS These are usually over 3 months old and can have an excellent flavour as long as they have been reasonably raised. They normally serve 4 people.

CORN-FED CHICKENS These are normally free-range chickens fed on corn. They are yellow in colour and have a very good flavour. The French corn-fed chickens generally seem to have a better flavour than the English ones.

POULET NOIR This is a French black-legged chicken. It is more like a guinea fowl than a chicken in both shape and texture. The poulet noir is more expensive than a conventional chicken but is really worth the occasional burst of extravagance.

CAPONS These were castrated cockerels who, having lost their interest in sex, ate voraciously and became very plump and tender. They have been banned by the EC.

BOILING FOWLS These are very rare today. They require long, slow cooking and have an excellent flavour.

DUCK

Most ducks sold today are ducklings of 7–9 weeks. A 1.8kg/4lb duck feeds only 2–3 people. Young duck is delicious, but do not buy frozen duck as you will not be able to judge the pliability of the backbone, which is the tell-tale sign of age. The skin of a fresh duck should be dry, soft and smooth. It should not be slimy and should not smell strongly. The Aylesbury duck is a very superior bird.

GOOSE

This is at its best when it weighs 4.5kg/10lb, i.e. when it is 6–9 months old. A goose can be utterly delicious but make sure that you choose a young bird as old geese can be very tough. Fresh goose has a clean white skin, which is soft and dry to the touch.

TURKEY

Try to buy fresh rather than frozen turkeys as they tend to have a better flavour. The flesh should be snow-white and firm, and the skin dry and soft. A turkey can often smell a little high. Remove all the giblets as soon as possible because they deteriorate quickly, and wipe the bird inside and out before storing.

GUINEA FOWL

This is normally a little smaller than the average-sized chicken and looks rather scrawny. The taste is that of a very delicious, slightly gamey chicken. Be warned: it needs careful cooking as it should have very little fat.

DAIRY PRODUCTS

EGGS

CHICKEN EGGS There is no nutritional difference between a battery and a free-range egg, but somehow the idea of a battery egg is depressing. If the box says 'farm eggs' it simply means battery-farmed eggs. You cannot judge the freshness of an egg from its outward appearance so buy eggs from somewhere with a rapid turnover. You can test for freshness by breaking an egg into a saucer: the yolk should be well domed and there should be 2 distinct layers of egg white, the inner circle being rather gelatinous and the outer circle a little thinner. When an egg is stale, the yolk is flatter and the 2 layers of white intermingle. Store eggs pointed end downwards so that the air pocket in the rounded end is uppermost. They should keep for a minimum of 2 weeks in the refrigerator. If the eggs have been separated, the whites can be frozen and the yolks kept refrigerated for 2–3 days. Cover them with a little cold water to prevent a hard crust from forming, then cover with clingfilm.

Eggs can be tainted easily so keep them well separated from other foods. The easiest thing is to keep them in the egg box in which they have been bought.

GOOSE, DUCK, PLOVER, GULLS', TURKEY AND QUAIL EGGS All eggs should be stored in the same way as chicken eggs. The following eggs are now available fresh from farms, from specialist shops and from the occasional supermarket.

TURKEY, GOOSE AND DUCK EGGS These have too strong a flavour to be eaten in the normal way as eggs but are useful for cooking. Goose eggs make particularly good sponge cakes.

QUAIL, GUINEA FOWL AND GULLS' EGGS These make very good first courses served with celery salt, paprika, brown bread and butter. Quail eggs take 3 minutes to boil, guinea fowl eggs take 5, and gull eggs are always sold ready cooked and are only in season in May and June.

MILK, CREAM AND YOGHURT

Always refrigerate milk as quickly as possible and keep it covered as it can easily be tainted by other foods in the refrigerator. An open bottle or carton of milk will go off more quickly than an unopened one. Milk keeps for about 3 days. Milk is standardized by its fat content. Most milk has been pasteurized to kill off harmful bacteria.

SKIMMED MILK A thin, slightly grey-coloured milk from which virtually all the fat has been removed. It goes off a little more quickly than 'fattier' milks.

SEMI-SKIMMED MILK As skimmed milk but with a little more fat.

'REGULAR' MILK This is the standard milk with about 3.8 per cent fat.

'RAW' MILK This unpasteurized milk is very rarely available.

HOMOGENIZED MILK This has been pasteurized and then homogenized to distribute the cream evenly throughout the milk. It has a particularly unpleasant flavour.

LONG-LIFE MILK This is milk that has been sterilized or heat-treated to give it a long shelf life unrefrigerated. It is a useful emergency stopgap but has a rather nasty flavour. Once opened, treat as fresh.

BUTTER
This is either salted or unsalted, and either pasteurized or ripened. Most English and New Zealand butter is pasteurized. Whether you buy salted or unsalted depends on your personal taste, but unsalted butter is better (although more expensive) for cooking as it contains less sediment and is consequently less likely to burn. It should be used for all butter sauces.

Unsalted butter will keep for only 2 weeks whereas salted butter can be kept for up to 4 weeks. It must always be refrigerated and should be kept tightly wrapped to prevent it drying out or becoming tainted by other foods in the refrigerator.

CHEESE
CHOOSING CHEESE Many shops sell unpasteurized cheese. If the milk is not pasteurized it is probably not filtered either as the filter is an integral part of the pasteurizing machine. It might have been filtered into the milk lorry but there will be lots of twigs, hairs and worse still left in the milk. Pasteurization does not change the consistency or the taste of the milk; it only heats it up to 74°C/160°F (boiling is 100°C/212°F) and it simply kills any bugs. No responsible parent would give their children unpasteurized milk, nor should they give them unpasteurized cheese.

It is difficult to choose cheese in a supermarket if it has been tightly wrapped in clingfilm and is deceptively coloured by supermarket lighting.

HARD CHEESE (E.G. CHEDDAR, DOUBLE GLOUCESTER) Try to find a mature cheese that has a rind. It should have a good strong smell but should not smell of whey (i.e. sour milk) and nor should it smell of ammonia. If there is no odour at all, it is probably too bland. It should feel hard rather than soft and should not be sweaty, or have any mould or be cracked.

SOFT FRESH CHEESES (E.G. COTTAGE CHEESE, CURD CHEESE) They should look and smell fresh and the packaging should be un-damaged.

SOFT MATURED CHEESES (E.G. BRIE, CAMEMBERT) There are a huge number of soft matured cheeses available but many of them are rather dull. We think that the best are Brie and Camembert, but fear that the imitation Somerset Brie bears little resemblance to the real thing. Buy a soft runny cheese that does not have a chalky white rind. If it has a strong smell of ammonia do not buy it as it will have an unpleasant flavour.

FIRM MATURED CHEESES (E.G. PONT L'ÉVÊQUE, REBLOCHON) These cheeses can vary from the rather tasteless (Port Salut) to the utterly delicious and very strong Pont l'Évêque. Firm matured cheeses should be pale, creamy and fairly firm in texture.

BLUE CHEESES (E.G. STILTON, ROQUEFORT) These cheeses can be soft or firm, and should have strong blue veins with no brown blotches.

STORING CHEESE
Ideally cheese should be kept in a larder, but as few houses have one, the next best thing is to wrap it tightly in clingfilm and keep it in the refrigerator. Remove at least 1 hour before serving. If left in the warmth of a centrally heated house it will sweat.

YOGHURT
CHOOSING YOGHURT There are many different types of yoghurt now widely available. Take no notice of the labels that proudly say 'live' – all yoghurt is live unless specified as having been pasteurized, in which case it cannot be used as a

starter for making your own yoghurt. Most yoghurt is labelled 'low fat' as it is made from skimmed milk. Greek yoghurt, which is now widely available in supermarkets as well as delicatessens, is a little higher in fat than most yoghurts but the taste is utterly delicious.

STORAGE

Store in the refrigerator for 3–4 days. Note that Greek yoghurt tends to go off more quickly than other yoghurts.

FISH

For fish classifications and methods of preparation see the chapter on fish (page 131).

Fish must be purchased and eaten when it is still very fresh. Some fish is frozen on board trawlers, so do not be put off buying a frozen fish as it may well be significantly fresher than a 'fresh' fish. It is easy to tell if fish is fresh, firstly by its smell – if it has a strong fishy smell it is probably quite stale. Scaly fish should have plenty of scales and all fish should have bright eyes, red gills and firm flesh. If you press your finger into a fish and the flesh does not spring back into place immediately, it is probably not fresh.

Shellfish are often sold live in order to guarantee freshness – if buying raw shellfish, I would opt for frozen rather than for dead raw shellfish. Chinese supermarkets are often the best place to buy good-quality raw frozen shellfish. If you want to buy cooked shellfish it must be very fresh. Some fishmongers will buy and cook lobsters and crayfish to order. Cooked 'shell-on' prawns are delicious but they must be bought from a reputable source and eaten on the day of purchase. If you just need a few cooked prawns for a recipe, I would recommend that you buy frozen ones and defrost them slowly sprinkled with a little lemon juice and freshly ground black pepper.

STORING FISH

Store fish, gutted, for as short a time as possible. Refrigerate it, lightly covered with clingfilm, and eat on the day of purchase. Smoked fish will keep for a couple of days and vacuum-packed smoked fish will stay fresh for much longer (check the sell-by date), but as with all 'long-life' products it must be treated as fresh once opened. To store live shellfish, such as crabs, lobsters, mussels and oysters, put them curved side down to prevent them losing their juices on a tray in the bottom of the refrigerator and cover with a damp cloth. They can be kept overnight.

VEGETABLES AND HERBS

See the vegetable chapter (page 111) for detailed descriptions and uses for vegetables and herbs.

CHOOSING

The most important thing about choosing vegetables is that they should be young and fresh. Old-fashioned gardeners and many producers take pride in their enormous turnips and giant parsnips but, in fact, nothing can be nicer than a tiny roasted parsnip or a minute braised turnip. The only vegetables that I like reasonably old (but not stale) are carrots. Young carrots can be rather flavourless compared to large, deep orange ones. Very old carrots, however, are horrid as they have woody cores.

TO CHOOSE GOOD-QUALITY VEGETABLES It is obvious from a carrot's wrinkled skin that it is old, or from a lettuce's limp leaves that it has wilted. As a general rule of thumb, the vegetables you choose should be small (of their type), brightly coloured, unwrinkled, unblemished and should look 'alert' – for example, pea pods should snap open. Fruit vegetables, such as tomatoes, avocado pears and aubergines, can be large but they should still look and feel ripe. They should also feel heavy for their size.

STORING

Unwrap any vegetables that have been sold tightly wrapped in clingfilm. Store them in the warmest part of the refrigerator (i.e. the salad compartment) or in a larder. The air in a refrigerator is very dry and, to prevent dehydration, you should store root vegetables (which like to be in the dark) in brown paper bags, and above-ground vegetables in polythene bags. Make sure that the vegetables are not squeezed into too small a space. If there is no room in the refrigerator and the vegetables have to be kept in a warm room, do not put them in polythene bags as they will sweat and rot. Small packets of fresh herbs will keep in their cartons for a day or two. Large bunches can be kept in polythene bags or, like flowers, in jugs of water. Watercress is best kept leaves downwards in a jug of water.

CHOOSING FRUIT

It is fairly easy to choose good-quality fresh fruit – it should look bright-skinned and, usually, should be heavy for its size. It should also have a fairly strong scent without being overpowering. Some fruits, such as pears, are very rarely perfect in the shops as they are only perfectly ripe for one day and should therefore be purchased in advance and ripened at home.

STORING FRUIT

SOFT FRUIT Do not store for more than 2 days in the refrigerator. Do not prepare until ready for use – an unhulled strawberry will keep longer than a hulled one. If the fruit cannot be used in time, freeze and use for dishes such as ice creams, purées and pies.

CITRUS FRUITS AND HARD FRUITS Ideally these should be kept refrigerated in polythene bags. If there is no room in the refrigerator, do not leave them in polythene bags as they will rot. To store these fruits for more than a week, wrap each piece of fruit individually in newspaper and place in a box in a cool place. Some fruits (especially if under-ripe), such as quinces, apples and pears, will keep well like this for 2–3 months. Citrus fruits can be kept for 2–3 weeks. Seville oranges will only keep for 1 week but may be frozen. (Freezing will not spoil the marmalade.)

BANANAS AND AVOCADO PEARS Do not refrigerate but leave in a cool place. To ripen firm avocado pears, place in a paper bag and keep in a warm place.

STONE FRUITS (E.G. APRICOTS, PLUMS, GRAPES, ETC.) Store in a cool place, preferably the refrigerator.

NOTE: Strong-smelling fruit, such as cut pineapple or melon, must be well wrapped if kept in the refrigerator as their fragrance will taint cheese, butter and milk.

BOTTLING FRUIT

The preservation of food by bottling works on the principle of destruction by heat of all micro-organisms present in the fruit or syrup. Because a partial vacuum is created in the jar, by expelling air during processing, a tight seal is formed between the lid and jar, keeping the sterilized contents uncontaminated.

The procedure described here applies to the bottling of fruit only. Because vegetables and meat contain little or no acid, and are therefore likely to harbour bacteria they need considerably longer processing at higher temperatures to become safe. This lengthy heating tends to spoil the texture and flavour of the food. In general, bottling meat and vegetables is not worth the effort, time and risks involved. But fruit and tomatoes, because they are fairly acid, do not contain bacteria; and the relatively harmless yeasts and moulds are more easily destroyed.

Fruit may be bottled in plain water or in salted water.

JARS

Kilner jars come with a glass lid and a rubber ring. The lid is kept in place by a metal screwband. The rubber ring must not be re-used as it will not give a good seal twice, and is perishable. Kilner jars are closed loosely before processing, and only tightened fully when they come out of the sterilizer or saucepan, while still hot. As the hot air cools it will contract, pulling the lid on tightly as it does so.

Parfait jars are similar to Kilner jars but the lid is held in place by a metal gimp or clip. It is clipped shut before processing. There is sufficient spring in the gimp to allow the escape of steam during heating. The lid tightens automatically as the jar cools after processing.

PREPARING THE FRUIT

Fruit can be bottled raw or cooked. If the fruit is cooked the processing time need only be long enough for sterilization, not for tenderizing the fruit. If raw, the fruit is cooked and sterilized at the same time, and may need longer processing. Fruits that cook to a pulp easily, such as berries and cooking apples, are generally processed from raw as the minimum time at great heat is the objective. Other fruits, such as pears and peaches, which require an uncertain time to soften, are frequently precooked as it is then possible to tell if they are tender. Precooking has a further advantage. Once the fruit is cooked and softened, more of it can be packed into the jars. Also, it will not rise up in the jar when sterilized. Fruit bottled from raw frequently rises.

POINTS TO REMEMBER

1. Make sure the bottling jars are not cracked and that the tops are in good condition. Jars must have new rubber rings fitted each year. Screw bands or metal clips should work properly and jars should be clean.
2. Make the sugar syrup before peeling the fruit.
3. Choose perfect, not over-ripe fruit.
4. If fruit needs cutting or peeling, use a stainless steel knife.
5. If it is likely to discolour (apples or pears), drop the pieces into cold water containing a teaspoonful of ascorbic acid (vitamin C powder or a fizzy Redoxon table will do) until you are ready to process them.
6. Pack the fruit (cooked or raw) up to the necks of the jars.

PROCESSING THE FRUIT

The fruit can be processed (or sterilized) in the following ways:

1. In a sterilizer (sometimes called a pressure canner). This is a purpose-made machine like a large pressure cooker. It is reliable and easy to use, but by no means essential. Follow the manufacturer's instructions.
2. In a pressure cooker, which works like a sterilizer but holds fewer jars and will not hold tall ones. About 2.5cm/1in of water in the

bottom is sufficient, as no evaporation will take place. The process is very quick, and the jars and fruit sterilize in the steam. Wedge the jars with cloths to stop them rattling. Allow the pressure to fall before opening the cooker. Consult the manufacturer's manual.
3. In a deep saucepan or bath of boiling water. Stand the jars in the container and wedge them with cloths to stop them rattling or cracking. Fill with hot water right over the tops of the jars, or at least up to their necks. Cover as best you can with a lid or foil and tea-towels to keep in the steam.

NOTES: Processing in the oven is not recommended. The temperatures cannot be reliably checked and the jars sometimes crack or explode, or boil over.

If the fruit has been cooked in an open pan with its syrup, it is possible to get a good seal by closing the jar as soon as the hot fruit and boiling syrup are in it, without further sterilization, but the method is not reliable and processing according to the instructions above is recommended.

TESTING FOR SEALING

After processing, the jars should be lifted on to a board. Kilner jars should be screwed up tight. Jars should be left undisturbed for 24 hours. They must then be tested for sealing. Remove the bands on the Kilner jars, or loosen the clips on the Parfait jars. It should be possible to lift the jars by the lids, without breaking the seal. If the lid of a jar comes off, the jar must be reprocessed with a new rubber ring or the contents must be eaten within a day or two.

STORING

Wipe the jars with a damp clean cloth, label them with the date of bottling, and store in a dark place. They will keep for at least 18 months, probably for many years.

GELATINE

Gelatine, available powdered and in leaves, is obtained from the bone and connective tissue of certain animals. Connective tissue is the physical harness of muscles, it is made up of three basic proteins – collagen, elastin and reticulen. Collagen is converted by long slow cooking into gelatine.

Acids weaken the setting power of gelatine so when following a recipe such as lemon soufflé an increased amount of gelatine is called for.

How to use powdered gelatine
1. Pour a small amount of liquid into a saucepan.
2. Slowly sprinkle on the required amount of gelatine.
3. Leave the gelatine to 'sponge' i.e. swell, for 3–5 minutes.
4. Melt the gelatine over a very low heat. Do not allow to boil. Do not stir. It should become clear and warm.
5. Pour into the mousse/soufflé base. Stir briskly – if the base is too cold the gelatine can set quickly in streaks. Gelatine is generally poured from a height to help cool it down.
6. When the mousse has reached setting point other light ingredients such as cream or whisked egg whites can be added. If the cream or egg whites are added too early the base mix will not support their weight and the soufflé will separate into layers. If the cream or whites are added too late the mixture has to be beaten hard to incorporate the additions and the result is heavy.

Setting point is when the base mixture will support its own weight and when a spoon is drawn through the mixture the bottom of the mixing bowl will remain visible for 2–3 seconds.

How to use leaf gelatine
1. Soak the leaves in a small amount of cold water for 5 minutes.
2. Dissolve over a gentle heat until liquid.
3. Use as powdered gelatine.

Gelatine Conversion Table

1 level teaspoon	5–7g	¼oz	1½ leaves
3 level teaspoons	15g	½oz	3 leaves
6 level teaspoons	30g	1oz	6 leaves

AGAR AGAR

Agar agar, a seaweed, is cooked, pressed, freeze-dried and then flaked or powdered for use as a setting agent in vegetarian cooking. 1 teaspoon powder has the setting power of 1 tablespoon flakes. Agar agar's setting qualities are affected by the nature of the food to which it is added, and so required quantities will vary, but as a general rule 1 teaspoon powder or 1 tablespoon flakes will set 570ml/1 pint, and twice the quantity should be used to set a firm jelly.

How to use agar agar
1. Soak the agar agar in the full liquid measurement specified in the recipe, in a saucepan; leave powder for 5 minutes, flakes for 10–15 minutes.
2. Dissolve the agar agar in the pan over a medium heat, stirring continuously. Turn up the heat and boil for 2–3 minutes, continuing to stir to prevent sticking. Use as required. (Agar agar may be reboiled without impairing its setting ability.)
3. If properly prepared, agar agar sets quickly on contact with anything much cooler than itself. Therefore, the ingredients to which it is added must be no colder than room temperature. To test whether it is ready for use, spoon a small quantity on to a cold plate – a skin should form very quickly, and wrinkle if a finger is pulled over the surface.

FREEZING

Freezing is a method of preserving food – not indefinitely, but for some weeks or months. Bacterial action, which causes spoilage, is prevented by keeping the food at extremely low temperatures. Note that some deterioration in the taste, texture and colour of food will take place if it is kept frozen for longer than the recommended times. Providing that the following simple instructions for freezing are followed religiously, many foods can be stored successfully without any loss of nutritional value or quality.

RAPID FREEZING

The quicker the freezing process, the smaller will be the ice crystals formed in the food. Large ice crystals, resulting from slow freezing, damage the cell walls of the food itself, and consequently, when it is thawed, liquid will be lost, including some soluble nutrients. Meat, in particular, will lose moisture on thawing if frozen too slowly, and will be dry when cooked.

PACKING THE FREEZER

In order to facilitate rapid freezing, only small amounts of unfrozen food should be put into the freezer at one time. Large quantities of food at room temperature would raise the temperature in the freezer and, inevitably, the freezing process would be slower. For the same reason, food should not be packed in large parcels, and the items should be separated in the freezing compartment, allowing the air to circulate around them. Once they are frozen, however, they can be – and indeed should be for economy's sake – packed tightly together with as little space between them as possible. A full freezer costs less to run than a half-empty one. Many freezers contain a fast-freeze compartment for the actual freezing process, and larger compartments for storage.

WRAPPING THE FOOD

Because the cold atmosphere of a freezer is very drying, and direct contact with the icy air causes 'freezer burn' (dry discoloured patches) on some foods, most foods need careful wrapping before freezing. Heavyweight polythene bags are the cheapest and best wrappers, because it is possible to see through them, and they take various shapes of food without creating too many air spaces. However, an airtight container will suffice. Foil is sometimes used, as are rigid plastic containers, old yoghurt cartons, bowls with lids, etc.

Whatever container you use, it must be robust enough to withstand some rough handling in the freezer, and it must be possible to label it clearly. Freezer labels, or polythene bags with white labels on which it is possible to write with a freezer pen, are best. Once the food is packed into the container, as closely wrapped as possible, it should be labelled with the contents and the date, and frozen immediately. Liquids can be poured into a polythene bag set in square containers and frozen. Once solid, the bag is lifted out of the outer container and thus stored. This means fewer kitchen containers are out of use in the freezer, and liquids can be stored in space-saving rectangular shapes. Liquids in plastic tubs or containers should be frozen with a 2.5cm/1in gap between bowl and lid to allow for expansion. Food should be used up in the right order – for example, peas frozen the previous week should not be eaten before the batch that was frozen 2 months ago. To facilitate this, a record or inventory of what is in the freezer can be kept on it, in it or near it, with additions and subtractions made each time food is put in or taken out.

OPEN FREEZING

If frozen in a mass, fruit and vegetables will emerge from the freezer in a solid block. This can be inconvenient for thawing in a hurry, or if only a small quantity of the food is needed, and the fruit and vegetables may also lose their individual shape and texture. For this reason, many foods are frozen on open trays so that each raspberry, pea, broad bean or sprig of cauliflower is individually frozen before packing into bags. The frozen produce will then be free-flowing and separate. Use this method for sausages, beefburgers, breadcrumbs, bread rolls, etc. as well as for fruit and vegetables. Decorated cakes and puddings can be open frozen, then packed when the decoration is hard enough to withstand the tight wrapping around it.

MASS FREEZING

If the food to be frozen is not suitable for open freezing, make sure that the block is not too thick. This will make cooking and thawing easier and quicker. For example, meatballs in tomato sauce should be laid one deep in a plastic box, not piled one on top of each other; spinach should be in a flattish pack so that it can be cooked from frozen (a thick block would mean overcooked outside leaves while the middle was still frozen). Air should be excluded as far as possible. This is especially important with casseroles, where the chicken or meat should be coated or covered completely by the sauce. Otherwise, the meat may become dry and fall apart on reheating.

THAWING

Thawing should be as slow as possible. Rapid thawing leads to loss of moisture and subsequent dryness or tastelessness of the food. However, it is sometimes imperative to thaw food in a hurry. To do this, put it into an airtight polythene bag and immerse it in cold, not hot, water. Hot water tends to cook the outside of the food and encourages bacterial activity which would cause the food to go bad if not completely cooked immediately. Meat should be thawed completely, and should be at room temperature before it is cooked.

RE-FREEZING FROZEN FOOD

Freezing does not kill bacteria present in food; it simply inhibits growth. So when food is removed from the freezer the bacteria in it will multiply normally. When put back, the now considerably increased population of bacteria will cease breeding, to start afresh when the food is brought back into the warmth. For this reason, frozen food manufacturers caution purchasers not to refreeze the product once it has been thawed. They are justly nervous that if the food is taken in and out of the freezer, it could contain germs in dangerous concentrations. However, the cook may still regard the product as being perfectly fresh because it has just emerged from the freezer. The foods most likely to cause illness are commercial ice cream and seafood, as both deteriorate rapidly. But this is not to say that no food should ever be refrozen. It is merely a matter of common sense.

FOODS THAT CANNOT BE FROZEN SUCCESSFULLY

Although most food will be prevented from going bad if kept at freezing point, some foods cannot be frozen successfully as their texture is ruined by freezing. This is particularly true of foods with a high water content. However, some of these may be frozen if wanted for soups or purées, in which case they should normally be frozen in purée form. Examples are bananas, cucumbers, lettuce and watercress.

Emulsions such as mayonnaise or hollandaise sauce do not freeze successfully as they separate when thawed.

Yoghurt, milk and cream can be frozen but will not be totally smooth when thawed. Double cream freezes better if whipped first. Storage time: 4 months.

Eggs cannot be frozen in the shell, but both whites and yolks freeze well, either lightly beaten together or separated. Storage time: 9 months.

Jelly, both savoury and sweet, loses its texture if frozen, and would have to be reboiled and allowed to set again after thawing if required jellied.

Mousses and soufflés set with gelatine tend to go rubbery.

Strawberries keep their colour and flavour well, but become soft on thawing.

Melon is too watery to remain crisp when thawed. It is best frozen in balls in syrup, but even this is not totally satisfactory.

Tomatoes emerge mushy when thawed, but are good for soups and sauces. One bonus of freezing tomatoes whole is that they can be easily peeled if placed, still frozen, under running hot water. They can, of course, be frozen as purée or juice.

Fats, or foods with a high fat content, freeze less successfully as a rule than less fatty foods. They have a tendency to develop a slightly rancid flavour if stored for more than 3 months.

FOODS THAT FREEZE SUCCESSFULLY

Most foods freeze well if some care is taken with wrapping, etc. But some foods freeze so well that no one would ever know that they had been frozen. Baked or raw pastries, breads, bread or biscuit doughs, cakes and sandwiches containing not-too-wet fillings, are good examples. As a general rule, raw food keeps better and longer than cooked. But cooked food, especially if well covered in a sauce, or under a potato or pastry crust, keeps well.

Vegetables freeze well if they are to be eaten cooked. They cannot be frozen if intended to be eaten raw. In order to prevent enzyme activity, green vegetables are boiled briefly, then cooled rapidly, before freezing. They may be frozen without this 'blanching' but their storage time would be reduced, and it is foolish to lose food through lazy freezing. Only the best vegetables, very fresh, should be used. They should be washed, or picked over, or otherwise prepared as if for immediate cooking. A large saucepan of water is brought to a rapid boil, and the vegetables (not more than 450g/1lb or so at a time) lowered into it. Accurate timing of the blanching process is important: the minutes are counted from the time the water reboils. As soon as the time is up, the vegetables are lifted out, and immediately cooled in a sink full of cold water, if possible. Once stone-cold, the vegetables are lifted out, drained well, patted dry if necessary, and frozen. The same blanching water can be used for several batches of vegetables. Some vegetables (onions, mushrooms, potatoes) may be cooked completely in butter or blanched in oil instead of water. They are allowed to cool normally before freezing.

Fruits (storage time: 9 months) Only freeze fruit that is in prime condition. Unripe, over-ripe or blemished fruit gives poor results. Three methods, as follows, are generally used to freeze raw fruit. (Cooked fruit may also be frozen whole or puréed.)

OPEN FREEZING

Suitable for most soft fruit such as raspberries and currants. Spread the fruit out on a baking sheet or tray and place in the freezer uncovered. When hard, pack into polythene bags or a rigid container, with or without adding sugar.

DRY SUGAR PACK

Suitable for most fruit to be used in cooked puddings. Prepare the fruit, toss it in sugar and freeze, with any juices that may have run from it during preparation. Care should be taken to exclude air, which may cause discoloration of the fruit.

PURÉE

Suitable for any fruits. Stew the fruit and mash, liquidize or sieve. Allow the purée to cool. Pack into containers, leaving head space, cover, label and freeze. Raw purées freeze well, too.

HERBS

(Storage time: 3 months) Herbs should be frozen dry in small polythene bags or packets, or chopped finely, put into ice trays and just covered with water. The frozen cubes can be transferred to labelled bags.

MEAT AND FISH
(Storage time: raw meat, 9 months; cooked meat, 4 months; raw fish, 5 months; cooked fish, 3 months) Special care should be taken in wrapping to prevent freezer burn.

CAKES AND BREAD
(Storage time: 12 months) Both raw and cooked doughs and pastries freeze well.

STOCKS
Reduce stocks by boiling rapidly until very concentrated. Freeze in ice trays and when thawed use as stock cubes.

VEGETABLES

Where a choice of times is given, the shorter time is for smaller vegetables, the longer for larger ones.

Vegetable	Preparation	Blanching time in minutes	Storage time in months
Asparagus	Do not tie in bunches.	3–4	12
Artichoke (globe)	Remove stalks and outer tough leaves.	7	6
Artichoke (Jerusalem)	Freeze once cooked into a purée.	–	6
Beans, broad	Sort by size.	3	12
Beans, French	Trim ends.	2–3	12
Beans, runner	Slice thickly.	1½–2	6
Beetroot	Freeze completely cooked and skinned. Slice if large.	–	6
Broccoli	Trim stalks.	2½–4	12
Brussels sprouts	Choose small, firm sprouts. Remove outer leaves.	4–6	12
Carrots	Choose small young ones with good colour. Scrape. Freeze whole.	5–6	12
Cauliflower	Break heads into florets.	3–4	6
Celery	Will be soft when thawed, but good for soups and stews.	3	12
Corn on the cob	Remove husks and silks.	6–10	9
Courgettes	Use only very small ones. Do not peel.	1	12
Kale	Remove stalks.	1	6
Leeks	Slice thinly, chop in chunks or leave whole.	1–3	12
Mushrooms	Do not peel. Freeze unblanched for up to 1 month. For longer storage, cook in butter.	–	4
Onions	Store unblanched onions sliced or chopped, for up to 3 months. Sliced or chopped onions can be blanched in water or oil. Button onions can be blanched whole.	1–3	5

VEGETABLES—*contd*

Vegetable	Preparation	Blanching time in minutes	Storage time in months
Peas	Choose young, very fresh peas.	1–2	12
Potatoes	Chips: blanch in oil. Boiled or mashed: freeze cooked and cold.	4	6
Root vegetables	Cut into chunks, blanch, or cook completely.	3	12
Spinach	Move about in water to separate leaves.	1	12
Tomatoes	Do not blanch. Freeze whole, in slices or as juice or purée, cooked or raw.		

FRUITS

FRUIT	PREPARATION
Apples/Pears/Quinces, etc.	Best frozen as a purée, peel, core and cook to a pulp, cool and freeze.
Citrus Fruit	The fruit can be cooked and then frozen for a later date for marmalade, alternatively, wrap the fruit individually and freeze, particularly useful method for the Seville orange season.
Figs	Can be frozen raw, but store better if cooked in a sugar syrup first.
Peaches, Nectarines and other stone fruit	Smaller stone fruits can be frozen whole for use in jams. Large fruits such as peaches, plums and greengages are best halved, stoned and poached in syrup.
Soft berry fruits Currants/Cranberries/Blackberries, etc.	Open freezing, dry sugar packing or cooked are all suitable. Remove stalks wherever possible.
Pomegranates	Scoop out seeds and freeze.

PRESERVING

The term 'preserves' covers all food that has been treated to keep for longer than it would if fresh. Frozen food, dried food, salted food and smoked food are all preserves. But in household language, the word means jams, jellies, marmalades, pickles and sometimes bottled food; in short, the sort of preserves found on a good countrywoman's larder shelf.

Jellies are clear preserves, made from strained fruit juice. They should be neither runny nor too solid. Jams are made from crushed fruit. They should almost hold their shape, but be more liquid than jelly. Conserves are jams containing a mixture of fruits, generally including citrus fruit, and sometimes raisins or nuts. Marmalade is jam made exclusively from citrus fruit. Fruit butters are made from smooth fruit purées, cooked with sugar to the consistency of thick cream. Fruit cheese are made in the same way but cooked until very thick. Butters and cheeses, because they are not set solidly and generally contain less sugar than jams, should be potted in sterilized jars. Curds generally contain butter and eggs, are best kept refrigerated, and will not keep for more than a couple of months.

JAMS, JELLIES AND MARMALADES

These preserves depend on four main factors to make them long-lasting:

1. The presence of pectin This is a substance, converted from the gum-like pectose found to some degree in all fruit, which reacts with the acids of the fruit and with the sugar to form a jelly-like set. Slightly under-ripe fruit is higher in pectin than over-ripe fruit, and some types of fruit are higher in pectin than others, notably apples, quinces, damsons, sour plums, lemons and redcurrants. Jam made from these will set easily. Jam from low-pectin fruit such as strawberries, rhubarb, mulberries and pears may need added commercial pectin or lemon juice (or a little high-pectin fruit) to obtain a good set.

TO TEST FOR PECTIN: before you add the sugar, take 1 teaspoon of the simmered fruit juice and put it into a glass. When it is cold add 1 tablespoon methylated spirit. After a minute a jelly will have formed. If it is in 1 or 2 firm clots there is adequate pectin in the fruit. If the jelly clots are numerous and soft the jam will not set without the addition of more pectin.

2. A high concentration of sugar Sugar is itself a preservative, and without sufficient sugar the pectin will not act to form the set.

3. The presence of acid which, like sugar, acts with the pectin to form a gel or set. Acid also prevents the growth of bacteria, and it helps to prevent the crystallization of the sugar in the jam during storage. If the fruit is low in acid, then tartaric acid, ascorbic acid or lemon juice may be added.

4. The elimination and exclusion of micro-organisms The jam itself is sterilized by rapid boiling. Jam jars need not normally be sterilized since the heat of the jam should be sufficient to sterilize them. However, harmless moulds do sometimes form round the rim and on the surface of jams potted in this way, and sterilizing the jars does help to prevent this. Jam jars may be soaked in solutions bought at chemists for sterilizing babies' bottles, etc. Ordinary household bleach will also be effective, but the bottles should be rinsed in boiling water afterwards. The jam funnel should be sterilized with the jars. It is not necessary to sterilize ladles or spoons except by leaving them in the bubbling jam for a minute or two. Jelly cloths or bags need not be sterilized as the juice is dripped through them before being boiled.

Once put into the clean, dry jars, the jam is sealed to prevent the infiltration of mildew spores, etc. Melted paraffin wax (melted white candles will do) poured over the surface of the jam makes a good old-fashioned and most effective seal, but most cooks rely on ordinary paper jam covers and a bit of luck.

Ideally, the jam should be sealed while boiling hot, i.e. before any fresh mildew spores can enter. However, if liquid wax is used on hot jam, it may disturb the flat surface, so the slightly cooled but still clear wax is poured on once the jam is set. Two applications of wax are necessary if the first covering shrinks away from the sides of the jar, leaving a gap.

Perhaps the best method of sealing is to use metal screwtops. They should be sterilized and checked for a tight fit. The jam should be poured up to the shoulder of the jars, leaving a good 1cm/½in. The caps are screwed on tightly as soon as the jars are filled. The cooling jar will form a partial vacuum in the neck, tightly sealing the jar. Plastic lids do not give a reliable seal.

If, in spite of all precautions, mould appears on the top of the jams, it can be scraped off and the jam beneath is perfectly good to eat; but it should be eaten quite quickly as mould spores in the air could re-infect it. Scraping off visible mould will not prevent the invisible spores from multiplying. Jam that is fizzy or fermented should be thrown away.

YIELD

The amount of finished jam obtained from a given quantity of fruit varies according to type, jellies giving comparatively little, marmalades and whole fruit jams much more. As a general rule, the mixture will yield between 1½ times and double the weight of sugar used. It is wise to over-estimate the amount of jars needed, rather than to have to prepare more at the last minute.

EQUIPMENT

Making jam is easy enough, but it requires a little organization. First the equipment should be assembled. You will need:

Accurate scales
Preserving pan or a large, heavy saucepan with a solid base
Sharp knives
Grater
Mincer
Long-handled wooden spoons
Slotted spoon
Metal jug with a large lip or a jam funnel
Jam jars
Jam covers, labels and rubber bands (available from chemists and stationers) or metal screwtop lids
Sugar thermometer (not essential but useful)
Perforated skimmer (not essential but useful)

POINTS TO REMEMBER

1. Make sure all equipment is absolutely clean.
2. Use dry, unblemished, just-ripe fruit.
3. Use preserving, lump, granulated or caster sugar. Modern white sugars are highly refined and therefore suitable. They need little skimming and give a clear preserve. Using preserving sugar has a slight advantage because the crystals are larger and the boiling liquid circulates freely round them, dissolving them rapidly. Caster sugar is inclined to set in a solid mass at the bottom of the pan and takes longer to dissolve. Brown sugar gives an unattractive colour to preserves.
4. Covering lukewarm jam could lead to mildew. If the jam is covered immediately, any bacteria or mildew spores present in the atmosphere are trapped between jam and seal and will be killed by the heat. If the atmosphere is lukewarm and steamy, perfect incubating conditions are created.

BASIC PROCEDURE

1. Wash and dry the jam jars and warm them in the oven.
2. Pick over the fruit, wash or wipe and cut up if necessary.
3. Put the fruit and water into the pan and set to simmer.
4. Warm the sugar in a cool oven for 20

minutes. When it is added to the fruit it will not lower the temperature too much, necessitating prolonged cooking which could impair the colour of the jam.

5. Bring the fruit to a good boil. Tip in the sugar and stir, without reboiling, until the sugar has dissolved.

6. Once the sugar has dissolved, boil rapidly, stirring gently but frequently.

7. When the mixture begins to look like jam – usually after about 10 minutes – test for setting. It is important not to overboil since this can make the colour too dark and the texture too solid. It will also ruin the flavour. Overboiling can sometimes even prevent a set by destroying the pectin. If you are using a thermometer, you can check the setting point: 105°C/220°F for jam and 106°C/222°F for marmalade. To test for setting, put a teaspoon of the jam on to an ice-cold saucer and return it to the ice compartment or freezer to cool rapidly. When cold, push it gently with a finger. The jam should have a slight skin, which will wrinkle if setting point is reached. If a finger is drawn through the jam, it should remain separated, not run together. Also, clear jam or jelly should fall from a spatula not in a single stream, but forming a wavy curtain and dripping reluctantly from more than one point.

8. As soon as a setting test proves positive, remove the jam from the heat. Skim carefully and then, if the jam contains whole fruit or large pieces of fruit, allow to cool for 15 minutes. This will prevent the fruit rising to the top of the jam jars.

9. Put the hot jars close together on a wooden board or tray. Fill them with hot jam with the aid of a jug or jam funnel.

10. Seal at once with screwtops or put waxed paper discs, waxed side down, on the surface of the jam, and cover the tops of the jars with cellophane covers, securing them with a rubber band. Brush the cellophane tops with water to stretch them slightly. Carefully pull them tight. As they dry they will shrink tightly around the jars.

11. Wipe the sides of the jars with a hot, clean, damp cloth to remove any drips of jam.

12. Label each jar with the type of jam and the date.

13. Leave undisturbed overnight.

14. Store in a cool, airy, dark place.

MILDEW on the surface of the jam is probably caused by one of the following:

1. Using wet jars.
2. Covering the jam when lukewarm.
3. Imperfect sealing.
4. Damp or warm storage place.
5. Equipment that is less than spotless.
The mildew should be removed, and the jam consumed fairly quickly.

CRYSTALLIZATION of the sugar in jam is caused by:

1. Insufficient acid in the fruit.
2. Boiling the jam before the sugar has dissolved.
3. Adding too much sugar.
4. Leaving jam uncovered.
5. Storing in too cold an atmosphere, such as a refrigerator.

FERMENTATION of jam is caused by:

1. Insufficient boiling leading to non-setting.
2. Insufficient acid leading to non-setting.
3. Insufficient pectin leading to non-setting.
4. Insufficient sugar leading to non-setting.
5. A storage place that is too warm.
6. Jars that are less than spotless.

PICKLES

Pickles are foods, usually vegetables or fruit, preserved in vinegar. Fruit for pickles is generally cooked in sugared vinegar, and stored in this sweetened vinegar syrup. Vegetables are usually, but not always, pickled raw, and are generally salted in dry salt, or steeped in brine, before being immersed in the vinegar. Salting draws moisture out of the food. If salting is omitted, the juices from the vegetables leak into the vinegar during storage, diluting it and impairing its keeping quality. Salt also has preservative powers, and its penetration into the food helps to prevent it going bad, but the main preservative in pickles is vinegar, which prevents the growth of bacteria.

The best salt is pure rock salt or crushed block salt. Pure sea salt is good too, but very expensive. Table salt has additives to make it conveniently free-flowing, but these may cause the pickle to go cloudy.

NOTE: Brass, old-fashioned iron or copper preserving pans or saucepans should not be used in the preparation of foods containing vinegar. The acid reacts with the metal, spoiling both colour and flavour.

BRINING

Brine is a solution of salt in water, and is suitable for the steeping of vegetables for pickling. Firm vegetables such as shallots should be pierced with a needle to allow the brine to penetrate.

225g/8oz pure salt (not table salt) 2.3 litres/4 pints water

1. Heat the salt and water slowly together until the salt has dissolved.
2. Allow to cool.
3. Prepare (peel, cut up, prick, etc.) the vegetables to be pickled, put them into a bowl and pour over the cold brine. Put a plate on top to keep the food submerged.
4. After 24 hours (usually, but check individual recipes) drain well, pat dry and pack into clean jars ready for pickling.

DRY-SALTING

This is particularly suitable for 'wet' vegetables such as marrow and cucumber.

110g/4oz dry pure salt (not table salt) per 1kg/2¼lb prepared vegetables

1. Prepare (peel, cut up, etc.) the vegetables. If they are tough (like onions or shallots) pierce them deeply with a needle.
2. Put them in a bowl, sprinkling each layer liberally with salt. Cover and keep cool for 24 hours.
3. Drain off all the liquid, rinse the vegetables in cold water and pat dry in a clean cloth.
4. Pack into clean jars ready for pickling.

THE VINEGAR

Pickling vinegar should be strong, containing at least 5 per cent acetic acid. Most brand vinegars contain sufficient acid, but home-made vinegars or draught vinegars are not suitable. Brown malt vinegar is the best for flavour, especially if the pickle is to be highly spiced or is made with strong-tasting foods. White vinegar has less flavour, but obviously gives a clearer pickle. Wine vinegar is suitable for delicate mild-tasting foods. Commercial cider vinegar is good too. The vinegar may be spiced and flavoured according to taste by the addition of cayenne pepper, ginger or chillies, or aromatic spices such as cardamom seeds, cloves or nutmeg. Whole spices are best as they can be removed easily, and will not leave the vinegar murky. Ready-spiced pickling vinegar may also be purchased.

CHUTNEYS

Chutneys are the easiest preserves to make. They are mixtures, always sweet and sour, somewhere between a pickle and a jam. They are generally made of fruit, or sometimes soft vegetables such as tomato or marrow, with vinegar, onion and spices.

Both sugar and salt, themselves preservatives, are present in chutneys, but they are there for flavour more than for their keeping powers. As with jams, boiling the ingredients destroys micro-organisms, but with chutneys obtaining a set is not necessary – like pickles, they depend on vinegar for their keeping qualities.

Fruit and vegetables for chutneys should be sliced or cut small enough to be lifted with a teaspoon, but not so small as to be unidentifiable in the chutney. As the ingredients are seldom used whole, you can use damaged or bruised fruit, with the imperfect bits removed.

Chutneys improve with keeping. They can generally be eaten after 2 months (before this their taste is harsh) but are at their best between 6 months and 2 years. If the chutney is to be kept for more than 6 months a more secure seal than a jam cover is advisable. See the notes for jars and lids on pages 102, 105.

BASIC PROCEDURE FOR CHUTNEY

1. Prepare the ingredients: wash fruit and vegetables, peel where necessary, cut up, etc. Wash dried fruit if bought loose. Chop or mince onions. Use a stainless steel fruit knife for fruit or vegetables liable to discolour.

2. Put all the ingredients, except the sugar and vinegar, into a saucepan (not an unlined copper, brass or old-fashioned iron one: see note on page 104). The spices should be tied in a muslin bag if they are to be removed later.

3. Add enough of the vinegar to easily cover the other ingredients.

4. Cook slowly, covered or not, until the fruit or vegetables are soft, and most of the liquid has evaporated.

5. Add the sugar and the rest of the vinegar and stir until the sugar has dissolved.

6. Boil to the consistency of thick and syrupy jam.

7. Put into clean, hot jars. Cover as for jam if to be eaten within 6 months. Use non-metal lids or stoppers if the chutney is to be kept longer.

NOTE: In recipes for chutneys that do not require prolonged cooking to soften the ingredients the sugar and vinegar may be added with the other ingredients, the whole lot being boiled together.

BOTTLING FRUIT

The preservation of food by bottling works on the principle of destruction by heat of all micro-organisms present in the fruit or syrup. Because a partial vacuum is created in the jar, by expelling air during processing, a tight seal is formed between the lid and jar, keeping the sterilized contents uncontaminated.

The procedure described here applies to the bottling of fruit only. Because vegetables and meat contain little or no acid, and are therefore likely to harbour bacteria, they need considerably longer processing at higher temperatures to become safe. This lengthy heating tends to spoil the texture and flavour of the food. In general, bottling meat and vegetables is not worth the effort, time and risks involved. But fruit and tomatoes, because they are fairly acidic, do not contain bacteria; and the relatively harmless yeasts and moulds are more easily destroyed.

Fruit may be bottled in plain water or in salted water.

JARS

Kilner jars come with a glass lid and a rubber ring. The lid is kept in place by a metal screw band. The rubber ring must not be re-used as it will not give a good seal twice, and is perishable. Kilner jars are closed loosely before processing, and only tightened fully when they come out of the sterilizer or saucepan, while still hot. As the hot air inside cools it will contract, pulling the lid on tightly as it does so.

Parfait jars are similar to Kilner jars but the lid is held in place by a metal gimp or clip. It is clipped shut before processing. There is sufficient spring in the gimp to allow the escape of steam during heating. The lid tightens automatically as the jar cools after processing.

PREPARING THE FRUIT

Fruit can be bottled raw or cooked. If the fruit is cooked the processing time need only be long enough for sterilization, not for tenderizing the fruit. If raw, the fruit is cooked and sterilized at the same time, and may need longer processing. Fruits that cook to a pulp easily, such as berries and cooking apples, are generally processed from raw as the minimum time at great heat is the objective. Other fruits, such as pears and peaches, which require an uncertain time to soften, are frequently precooked as it is then possible to tell if they are tender. Precooking has a further advantage. Once the fruit is cooked and softened, more of it can be packed into the jars. Also, it will not rise up in the jar when sterilized. Fruit bottled from raw frequently rises.

POINTS TO REMEMBER

1. Make sure the bottling jars are not cracked and that the tops are in good condition. Jars must have new rubber rings fitted each year. Screw bands or metal clips should work properly and jars should be clean.

2. Make the sugar syrup before peeling the fruit.

3. Choose perfect, not over-ripe fruit.

4. If fruit needs cutting or peeling, use a stainless steel knife.

5. If it is likely to discolour (apples or pears), drop the pieces into cold water containing a teaspoonful of ascorbic acid (vitamin C powder or a fizzy Redoxon tablet will do) until you are ready to process them.

6. Pack the fruit (cooked or raw) up to the necks of the jars.

PROCESSING THE FRUIT

The fruit can be processed (or sterilized) in the following ways:

1. In a sterilizer (sometimes called a pressure canner). This is a purpose-made machine like a large pressure cooker. It is reliable and easy to use, but by no means essential. Follow the manufacturer's instructions.

2. In a pressure cooker, which works like a sterilizer but holds fewer jars and will not hold tall ones. About 2.5cm/1in of water in the bottom is sufficient, as no evaporation will take place. The process is very quick, and the jars and fruit sterilize in the steam. Wedge the jars with cloths to stop them rattling. Allow the pressure to fall before opening the cooker. Consult the manufacturer's manual.

3. In a deep saucepan or bath of boiling water. Stand the jars in the container and wedge them with cloths to stop them rattling or cracking. Fill with hot water right over the tops of the jars, or at least up to their necks. Cover as best you can with a lid or foil and tea-towels to keep in the steam.

NOTES: Processing in the oven is not recommended. The temperatures cannot be reliably checked and the jars sometimes crack or explode, or boil over.

If the fruit has been cooked in an open pan with its syrup, it is possible to get a good seal by closing the jar as soon as the hot fruit and boiling syrup are in it, without further sterilization, but the method is not reliable and processing according to the instructions on page 277 is recommended.

TESTING FOR SEALING

After processing, the jars should be lifted on to a board. Kilner jars should be screwed up tight. Jars should be left undisturbed for 24 hours. They must then be tested for sealing. Remove the bands on the Kilner jars, or loosen the clips on the Parfait jars. It should be possible to lift the jars by the lids, without breaking the seal. If the lid of a jar comes off, the jar must be reprocessed with a new rubber ring or the contents must be eaten within a day or two.

STORING

Wipe the jars with a damp clean cloth, label them with the date of bottling, and store in a dark place. They will keep for at least 18 months, probably for many years.

STOCKS AND SAVOURY SAUCES

Behind every great soup and behind many a sauce stands a good strong stock. Stock is flavoured liquid, and the basic flavour can be fish, poultry, meat or vegetable. Stock cubes and bouillon mixes are usually over-salty and lack the intense flavour of properly made stock, making food taste the same. As an emergency measure, or to strengthen a rather weak stock, they are useful. But a good cook should be able to make a perfect stock. For individual stock recipes, see Basic Recipes (pages 625–8).

MAKING A STOCK

The secret of stocks is slow, gentle simmering. If the liquid is the slightest bit greasy, vigorous boiling will produce a murky, fatty stock. Skimming, especially for meat stocks, is vital; as fat and scum rise to the surface they should be lifted off with a slotted spoon, perhaps every 10–15 minutes.

Rich, brown stocks are made by first frying or baking the bones, vegetables and scraps of meat until a good, dark, even brown. Only then does the cook proceed with the gentle simmering. Care must be taken not to burn the bones or vegetables; one burned carrot can ruin a gallon of stock. Brown stocks are usually made from red meats or veal, and sometimes only from vegetables for vegetarian dishes. Brown fish stock can be very useful.

White stocks are more delicate and are made by simmering only. They are usually based on white poultry or vegetables.

The longer meat stocks are simmered the better flavoured they will be. A stockpot will simmer all day in a restaurant, being skimmed or topped up with water as the chef passes it, and only strained before closing time. However, it is important not to just keep adding bits and pieces to the stockpot and to keep it going on the back burner for days, because the pot will become cluttered with cooked-out bones and vegetables that have long since given up any flavour. At least 3, and up to 8 hours over the gentlest flame, or in the bottom oven of an Aga, is ample cooking time.

In the Aga, skimming is unnecessary – as the liquid hardly moves there is no danger of fat being bubbled into the stock, and it can be lifted off the top when cold.

Fish stocks should never be simmered for more than 30 minutes. After this the bones begin to impart a bitter flavour to the liquid. For a stronger flavour the stock can be strained, skimmed of any scum or fat, and then boiled down to reduce and concentrate it.

Similarly, vegetable stocks do not need long cooking. As they contain very little fat, even if the vegetables have been browned in butter before simmering, they are easily skimmed, and can then be boiled rapidly to concentrate the flavour. An hour's simmering or 30 minutes' rapid boiling is generally enough.

THE BONES Most households rarely have anything other than the cooked bones from a roast available for stocks. These will make good stock, but it will be weaker than that made with raw bones. Raw bones are very often free from the butcher, or can be had very cheaply. Get them chopped into manageable small pieces in the shop. A little raw meat, the bloodier the better, gives a rich, very clear liquid.

WATER The water must be cold, as if it is hot the fat in the bones will melt immediately and when the stock begins to boil much of the fat will be bubbled into the stock. The stock will then be murky, have an unattractive smell and a nasty flavour. Cold water encourages the fat to rise to the surface; it can then be skimmed.

JELLIED STOCK Veal bones produce a particularly good stock that will set to a jelly. A pig's trotter added to any stock will have the same jellifying effect. Jellied stock will keep longer than liquid stock, but in any event stocks should be reboiled every 2 or 3 days if kept refrigerated, or every day if kept in a larder, to prevent them going bad.

SALT Do not add salt to stock. It may be used later for something that is already salty, or boiled down to a concentrated glaze (glace de viande), in which case the glaze would be over-salted if the stock contained salt. (Salt does not boil off with the water, but remains in the pan.)

STORAGE A good way of storing a large batch of stock is to boil it down to double strength, and to add water only when using. Or stock can be boiled down to a thick, syrupy glaze, which can be used like stock cubes. Many cooks freeze the glaze in ice cube trays, then turn the frozen cubes into a plastic box in the freezer. They will keep for at least a year if fat-free.

SAUCES

Larousse defines a sauce as a 'liquid seasoning for food', and this covers anything from juices in a frying pan to complicated and sophisticated emulsions.

FLOUR-THICKENED SAUCES The commonest English sauces are those thickened with flour, and these are undoubtedly the most practical for the home cook. The secret is not to make them too thick (by not adding too much flour), to beat them well and to give them a good boil after they have thickened to make them shine. They will also look professionally shiny if they are finished by whizzing in a blender, or if they are 'mounted' with a little extra butter, gradually incorporated in dice, at the end.

The butter and flour base of a sauce is called a roux. In a white roux, the butter and flour are mixed over a gentle heat without browning; in a blond roux, they are allowed to cook to a biscuit colour; and in a brown roux, they are cooked until distinctly brown.

Another way of thickening a sauce with flour is to make a beurre manié. Equal quantities of butter and flour are kneaded to a smooth paste and whisked into a boiling liquid. As the butter melts the flour is evenly distributed throughout the sauce, thickening the liquid without allowing lumps to form. Cornflour and arrowroot are also useful thickeners. They are 'slaked' (mixed to a paste with cold water, stock or milk), added to a hot liquid and allowed to boil to thicken it for a couple of minutes.

EMULSIONS AND LIAISONS Emulsions are liquids that contain tiny droplets of oil or fat evenly distributed in suspension. Like liaisons, they may be unstable.

STABLE EMULSIONS Mayonnaise is the best known of the cold and stable emulsion sauces, in which oil is beaten into egg yolks and held in suspension. If the oil is added too fast the sauce will curdle.

WARM EMULSIONS The most stable warm emulsions, like cold emulsions, are based on egg yolks and butter. The best known is hollandaise. Great care has to be taken not to allow the sauce to curdle.

EGGLESS EMULSIONS These have become the more fashionable butter sauces. The classic is beurre blanc. Eggless emulsions curdle very easily, so great care should be taken to follow the recipe precisely.

UNSTABLE EMULSIONS French dressing will emulsify if whizzed or whisked together, but will separate back to its component parts after about 15 minutes.

SABAYONS Egg yolks are whisked over heat and the flavouring ingredient is gradually whisked in. The suspension is temporary and most sabayons collapse after 30–40 minutes.

LIAISONS Egg yolk can be mixed with cream to form a liaison. It is then used to thicken and enrich sauces. The yolks must not boil or the sauce will curdle.

SAUCE TABLE

Flour-thickened		Emulsions		Combinations and other
Mother	Daughter	Mother	Daughter	
White sauce	Anchovy	Mayonnaise	Aïoli	Apple sauce
	Béchamel		Rémoulade	Tomato sauce
	Cardinale		Tartare	Mint sauce
	Crème		Andalouse	
	Egg		Elizabeth	**Savoury butters**
	Cheese			Almond, Anchovy,
	Onion	Hollandaise	Béarnaise	Garlic, Green,
	Parsley		Choron	Maître d'hotel,
	Green		Moutarde	Mint and Mustard
			Mousseline	
Blond (velouté)	Aurore		Maltaise	Cumberland sauce
	Poulette	Beurre blanc	Chicken	Yoghurt sauce, Cranberry
	Suprême		Fish	sauce
	Mushroom		Orange	Bread sauce, Horseradish
			Saffron	cream
				Soured cream, Onion sauce,
				Mint sauce
				Tomato and cream sauce
Brown	Chasseur			Red pepper sauce, Black
	Robert			bean sauce
	Madeira	French dressing		Ginger and tomato sauce
	Bordelaise			Uncooked pasta sauce
	Poivrade			Exotic sauce
	Diane			Tomato and whisky sauce
	Réforme			Salsa Pizzaiola, Salsa
	Périgueux			Romesco
				Sabayons
				Leek and watercress
				Liaisons
				As in Blanquette de Veau
				Reduction and Pan sauces
				Wild mushroom sauce

VEGETABLES

Vegetables in Britain are usually served as an accompaniment to a main meat course. It is worth considering them, however, as first courses on their own, or as main courses if served in sufficient variety or with a sauce. For a salad or first course they may be served raw or cooked, warm or cold, and with a dressing.

TO PREPARE VEGETABLES

Always wash vegetables before preparing them. Vegetables are an excellent source of vitamins and minerals but these can easily be leached if the vegetables are cut up too far in advance of cooking, if they are left to soak in cold water (vitamin C particularly is lost in this way), if they are cut up with a blunt knife, which damages the cells, or if they are cooked with bicarbonate of soda in an attempt to preserve colour.

FRESH GREEN VEGETABLES

BLANCHING AND REFRESHING This method of cooking vegetables is commonly used in restaurants where some advance preparation is vital. It is worth doing when coping with a large selection of vegetables.

BOILING Boil the vegetables separately; bring the water to a good boil and drop in the vegetables. Use enough water to barely cover them and add 1 teaspoon salt for each 570ml/1 pint water. Boil as rapidly as you dare (delicate vegetables like broccoli can break up if too rapidly boiled.) As soon as they are tender, drain them and serve or rinse under cold running water to prevent further cooking and to set the colour. This is called refreshing. Just

before serving, toss the vegetables separately in melted butter over a good heat.

NOTE: As the cooking liquid contains most of the vitamins and minerals it should, if possible, be preserved and used for soups or sauces.

SWEATING Put the prepared vegetables into a heavy saucepan with 1 tablespoon butter or oil. Cover tightly with a lid. Cook over a very low heat. Shake the pan frequently until the vegetables are tender. Season with salt and dish up.

STEAMING Steaming in a proper steamer is an excellent method of cooking root vegetables, but is less successful with green ones as their bright colour is sometimes lost. It is nutritionally superior to boiling – although vegetables take longer to cook, there is no leaching of vitamins or minerals into the water.

STIR-FRYING This cooking method, much beloved of Chinese cooks, is excellent for green vegetables. It preserves vitamins and minerals, and the vegetables remain bright in colour. The disadvantage is that you must stand over the vegetables while they cook, but cooking time is short.

Slice the vegetables as thinly as you can, then put into a large deep-sided frying pan (a Chinese wok is perfect) with a splash of oil. Toss the vegetables in the hot oil over a fierce heat. Shake the pan, and stir and turn the vegetables continually until they are just tender. Sprinkle with salt and serve.

FRESH NON-GREEN VEGETABLES

BOILING Put the vegetables into cold salted water and bring slowly to the boil. Cook, covered, until completely tender. With the exception of carrots (which are good with a bit of bite to them), root vegetables should be cooked until tender. Drain and brush with melted butter if required. New potatoes are usually put into boiling salted water.

REFRESHING It is sometimes advisable to rinse carrots briefly in cold water after cooking, as this sets the bright colour, but it is not necessary.

SWEATING OR HALF-STEAMING Slice the vegetables fairly thickly. Cook them slowly in butter or oil in a covered saucepan. They will absorb more fat than green vegetables. This is a very good method for mushrooms.
STEAMING This is excellent for all root vegetables, particularly for large potatoes, which might otherwise break up while boiling.

DRIED PULSES

Dried peas and beans (lentils, split peas, chick-peas, green peas, black-eyed beans, haricot beans, lima beans, butter beans, brown beans, red kidney beans, etc.) are generally cheaper than their fresh or canned equivalents, are easy to cook and are very nutritious. They should be bought from grocers with a good turnover, and as a rule small butter beans are better than large ones.

Most pulses need soaking until softened and swollen before cooking. Soaking can take as much as 12 hours (butter beans) or as little as 20 minutes (lentils). Do not soak for more than 12 hours in case the beans start germinating or fermenting. If there is no time for preliminary soaking, unsoaked pulses may be cooked either in a pressure cooker or very slowly in a saucepan; but remember that enough water must be used to allow the beans first to swell and then to cook. Preliminary soaking is less hazardous.

To cook the pulses, cover them with fresh cold water, bring to the boil and then simmer for 5 minutes. Change the water and cook until tender. Boiling times vary according to the age and size of the pulses; new season's pulses will cook faster. Small lentils may take as little as 15 minutes and large haricot beans or chickpeas can take as long as 2 hours.

NOTE: Red kidney beans must be boiled fast for at least 15 minutes to destroy dangerous toxins.

HERBS AND SEEDS

HERB/SEED	SEASON	CULINARY USE
Alfalfa	Grown indoors all year round.	Young shoots used in salads or stir-fries are rich in vitamins and minerals.
Angelica	3-year biennial after which it sets seed and dies. In flower April–November.	Young stems candied and used for decoration of desserts. Sometimes used to cook with acidic fruit to remove acidity.
Aniseed	Annual, grows in a sunny position. Spring and summer herb.	Old medicinal use to help digestion. Now used to flavour bread, cakes and Pernod.
Basil (many types)	Annual or short-lived perennial. In season April–November.	First introduced to the UK in the early sixteenth century. Perfect with tomatoes and pasta.
Sweet Bay	Continuous.	Classic part of bouquet garni. Excellent in small quantities.

HERBS AND SEEDS—*contd*

HERB/SEED	SEASON	CULINARY USE
Bergamot	Summer.	Young leaves used in salads.
Borage	June–August.	Lovely blue flowers for salads. A must for Pimms.
Caraway	Summer.	Seed used in cakes and breads. Leaves used in salads.
Chervil	Summer.	Delicate garnish, good with fish.
Chives	Late spring through to late autumn.	Onion flavour, good in salads and for garnish.
Coriander	Late spring to autumn.	Classic in Middle Eastern and Asian food. Seed helps wind!
Cumin	Summer.	Common in Indian cookery. Aids digestion.
Curry plant	Continuous.	A pinch can give stews interesting flavour.
Dill	June–October.	Used in pickles and classic with fish, particularly gravad lax.
Fennel	May–October.	Classic herb for fish.
Wild garlic	May–June.	Used to flavour soups, good in salads and wonderful with seafood.
Garlic mustard	May–July.	Raw leaves in salad. Root edible.
Good King Henry	May–June.	Used in place of spinach in salads.
Lemon balm	April–November.	Good with fish, poultry and in stuffings.
Lavender	Flowers: July–August. Leaves: June–September.	Classic in herbes de Provence.
Lemon grass	Only indoors in UK.	Sorbets, tea and Thai food.
Lovage	Spring–December.	Distinctive celery flavour. Makes a pretty garnish.
Marjoram	Continuous.	Classic in Italian food.
Mint (various types)	Spring–autumn.	Many uses.
Nasturtium	Late spring–autumn.	High in vitamin C. Peppery leaves and flowers good in salad.
Nigella	May–August.	Flavouring for stews.

HERBS AND SEEDS—*contd*

HERB/SEED	SEASON	CULINARY USE
Purple Orach	May–October.	Similar to spinach.
Parsley	Spring–autumn. Winter under cover.	Classic in bouquet garni. Use chopped for a garnish.
Rocket	Spring–October. Can winter under cover.	Wonderful salad ingredient. Peppery leaves easy to grow.
Rosemary	Continuous.	Classic with lamb and chicken. Lovely with oily fish dishes.
Rose Geranium	Summer.	Leaves used in jam-making.
Savory	Summer.	Used to flavour dried bean dishes.
Sage (various types)	Continuous.	Strong flavour good for rich meat, classic with duck and pork.
Sorrel	March–November. In warmer winters can last right through.	Sorrel sauce classic with fish particularly salmon.
Sesame	June–September.	Dried seeds used in breads and tahini paste. Roast seeds in sesame oil.
Skirret	Spring–November.	Roots used like horseradish. Good in stews.
Star Anise	Tropical, dried use as a spice.	One of the spices in Chinese five spice.
Stinging nettle	Spring.	Use gloves to pick young leaves. Wilts like spinach.
Sweet Cicely	April–first frosts.	Good with rhubarb, counteracts acidity.
Tansy	Spring–late autumn.	Tansy used to flavour traditional custard puddings.
Tarragon	March–September.	Classic with chicken. Pungent flavour can be overpowering.
Thyme (various types)	Continuous.	Classic in bouquet garni used to flavour casseroles and stocks.

MEAT AND OFFAL

The younger the animal, and the less exercise it has taken, the more tender its meat will be, but its flavour will be less pronounced. For example, a week-old calf will be tender as margarine, and about as flavourless. An ox that has pulled a cart all its long life will be quite the reverse – good on flavour, but tough as old boots. A relatively young, and therefore tender, animal will have white or pale fat, rather than yellow; the meat will be less dark, and the bones more pliable than in an older, tougher animal. So rump steak with a bright red hue and white fat may well be more tender than the dark flesh and yellow fat of older meat, but it will probably lose in flavour what it gains in texture.

Because tenderness is rated highly today, the most expensive cuts of meat are those from the parts of the animal's body that have had little or no exercise. For example, the leg, neck and shoulder cuts of beef are tougher (and therefore cheaper) than those taken from the rump or loin.

But apart from the age of the animal, there are other factors that affect tenderness. Meat must not be cooked while the muscle fibres are taut due to rigor mortis, which can last, depending on the temperature at which the carcass is stored, for a day or two. The state of the animal prior to slaughter can also affect the tenderness of the meat; for example, if it is relaxed and peaceful the meat is likely to be more tender. Injections of certain enzymes (proteins that produce changes in the meat without themselves being changed) given to the animal before slaughter will produce the same result artificially.

But the most crucial factor affecting tenderness is the length of time that meat is stored before cooking. If hung in temperatures of 2°C/35°F it

will, due to enzyme activity, become increasingly tender. Temperatures should not be higher than this, because although the enzyme activity would be greater, the risk of spoilage due to bacterial action would become high. For beef, 7 days is the minimum hanging time, while 3 weeks or a month are more desirable. However, with the commercial demands for quick turnover, the weight-loss during storage and the expense of storing, good hanging is rare these days. Some enzyme activity continues if the meat is frozen, and the formation, and subsequent melting, of ice-crystals (which, in expanding, bruise the fibres of the meat) mean that freezing meat can be said to tenderize it. However, the inevitable loss of juices from the meat (and subsequent risk of dryness after cooking) is a disadvantage that outweighs the minimal tenderizing effect.

Hanging is most important in beef, as the animals are comparatively old, perhaps 2 or 3 years, when killed. It is less important for carcasses of young animals, such as calves and lambs, as their meat is relatively tender anyway.

Because, inevitably, some bacterial action (as well as enzyme action) must take place during hanging, the flavour of well-hung meat is stronger, or gamier, than that of under-hung meat. The colour will also deepen and become duller with hanging. But the prime reason for hanging meat is to tenderize it, rather than to increase or change its flavour. This is not so with game, including venison, which is hung as much to produce a game flavour as to tenderize the meat.

The last, and probably most important, factor that affects the ultimate tenderness of meat is the method of cooking. Half-cooked or rare meat will be tender simply because its fibres have not been changed by heat, and will still retain the softness of raw meat. But as the heat penetrates the whole piece of meat the fibres set rigidly and the juices cease to run. Once the whole piece of meat is heated thoroughly, all the softness of raw meat is lost and it is at its toughest. This explains the natural reluctance of chefs to serve well-done steaks – it is almost impossible to produce a tender well-done grilled steak.

But, paradoxically, further cooking (though not fast grilling or frying) will tenderize that tough steak. This is seen in stewing, when long, slow cooking gradually softens the flesh. A joint from an older animal, which has done much muscular work during its lifetime and is coarse-grained and fibrous, can be made particularly tender by prolonged gentle cooking. This is because much of the connective tissue present in such a joint, if subjected to a steady temperature of, say, 100°C/200°F, will convert to gelatine, producing a soft, almost sticky tenderness.

Joints with finer graining and little connective tissue, such as rump or sirloin, will never become gelatinous, and are consequently seldom cooked other than by roasting or grilling, when their inherent tenderness (from a life of inaction) is relied on. But they will never be as tender as the slow-cooked shin or oxtail, which can be cut with a spoon.

It does not matter that few people have any idea which part of the animal their meat comes from. But it is useful to know, if not how to do the butcher's job, at least which cuts are likely to be tender, expensive, good for stewing, or not worth having, and what to look for in a piece of meat.

ROASTING MEAT

1. Weigh the joint and establish the length of cooking time (see below).
2. Preheat the oven (electric ovens take longer to heat up than gas ovens).
3. Prepare the joint for roasting; see the relevant recipe.
4. Heat some dripping in a roasting pan and if the meat is lean, brown the joint over direct heat so that it is well coloured. Pork and lamb rarely need this but many cuts of beef do.
5. Place the joint in the pan, on a grid if you have one available, as this aids the circulation of hot air; roast for the time calculated.

ROASTING TIMES
Obviously a long thin piece of meat weighing 2.3kg/5lb will take less time to cook than a fat round piece of the same weight, so the times below are meant only as a guide. The essential point is meat must reach an internal temperature of 60°C/140°F to be rare, 70°C/150°F to be medium pink, and 80°C/170°F to be well done. A meat thermometer stuck into the thickest part of the meat, and left there during cooking, eliminates guesswork.

BEEF: Beef is generally roasted in the hottest of ovens for 20 minutes to brown the meat (or it may be fried all over in fat before being transferred to the oven). Whatever the method, calculate the cooking time after the browning has been done, and allow 10–15 minutes per 450g/1lb for rare meat, 20 minutes for medium and 25 for well done, roasting the meat in an oven preheated to 190°C/375°F/gas mark 5.

LAMB: Put the lamb into the hottest of ovens for 20 minutes, then allow 20 minutes per 450g/1lb at 190°C/375°F/gas mark 5. This will produce very slightly pink lamb. If lamb without a trace of pinkness is wanted, allow an extra 20 minutes after the calculated time is up.

PORK: Pork must be well cooked. Allow 40 minutes per 450g/1lb at 170°C/325°F/gas mark 3. If crackling is required, roast at 200°C/400°F/gas mark 6 for 25 minutes per 450g/1lb, plus 25 minutes over.

VEAL: Brown in hot fat over direct heat. Or roast for 20 minutes at maximum temperature. Then allow 20 minutes per 450g/1lb at 180°C/350°F/gas mark 4.

CUTS OF MEAT
BEEF
For roasting: sirloin, fore rib, fillet.
For pot-roasting: topside, silverside, brisket, thick flank.

For stewing, braising and boiling, and for salting and boiling: chuck, shin, brisket, flank, neck, topside, silverside.

For grilling and frying: fillet, rump and sirloin. But the names for steaks can be confusing:

Rump steaks (rumsteck in French): These are thick (about 2cm/¾in) slices cut across the grain of the rump, and then, if for individual servings, cut into smaller neat pieces.

Fillet steak: This comes in various guises. Cut across into neat thick (2.5cm/1in) slices, it becomes tournedos. A neat piece for 2–3 people, weighing perhaps 225g/8oz cut from the thick end (but with all the coarser meat trimmed from it), can be grilled, spitted or roasted as a châteaubriand. Medallions are thin neat slices cut across the fillet.

Beef cuts

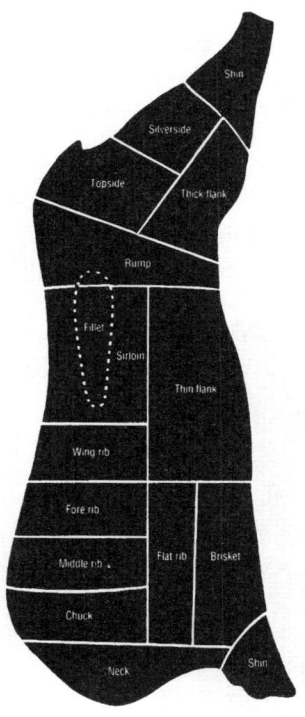

Sirloin steaks: The name sirloin covers steak from the upper side of the true sirloin, wing rib and fore rib. The French entrecôte means only the true tender sirloin, which is cut in individual steaks or as T-bone steaks (on the rib, with the sirloin on one side of the T and the fillet or undercut on the other). French côte de boeuf or our rib of beef are thick steaks on the rib bone, from the slightly less tender wing rib or fore rib.

Porterhouse is a double-sized T bone, or double-sized wing rib.

For pies: chuck, brisket, thick flank, shin (foreleg), shin or leg (hind leg).

VEAL

The cuts of veal, and their names, more closely resemble those of a lamb or sheep than those of grown-up beef.

Veal cuts

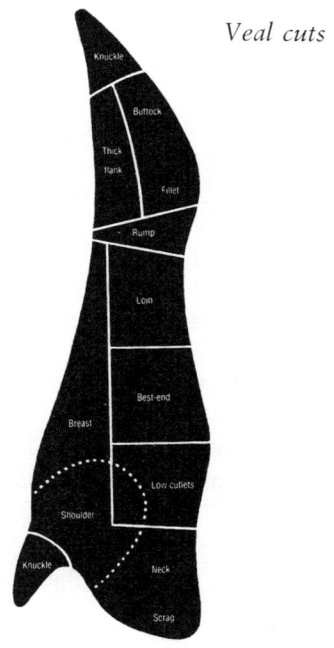

As veal is more tender than beef, most of the animal is suitable for quick cooking (roasting, frying). But as there is little fat on a calf, care must be taken to moisten the meat frequently during cooking to prevent dryness. Because of the absence of fat, veal is seldom grilled.

Much Dutch veal is milk-fed and expensive. It has a pale pink colour and the best cuts are exceptionally tender. But the taste is mild to the point of insipidity, and it needs good seasoning, usually plenty of lemon, pepper or a good sauce. English veal is cheaper, has more flavour, and generally has a slightly more reddish hue. This is because the animals are killed older than their Dutch fellows, and are generally, though not always, grass-fed. But veal should never look bloody or really red.

For roasting: leg, loin, best end, breast.

For braising and stewing: leg, shoulder, middle neck, scrag, breast.

For frying (and possibly grilling if frequently basted): cushion (fillet), loin chops, best end cutlets, rump, round (buttock).

For stock: knuckle, foot or scrag end of neck.

NOTE: The more tender cuts from the forequarter, from a top-quality milk-fed calf, may also be boned out and sliced for escalopes.

VENISON

Venison is the meat of deer. Good deer meat should be dark red with a fine grain and firm white fat.

When preparing venison remove as much of the membrane as possible. Venison is very low in fat so it is often recommended that the meat be marinated before cooking. If roasting, the meat can be barded with bacon to help retain moisture.

For roasting: haunch, saddle, either whole or in fillets.

For grilling and frying: steaks from the fillet or chops made from the saddle.

For stewing: shoulder, neck, flank.

For braising in one piece: shoulder.

For mincing: flank, neck.

PORK

Pork used to be eaten mainly in winter, or as bacon, because of the difficulty of keeping it fresh. But with modern methods of refrigeration, pork is eaten all the year round.

The flesh should be pale pink, not red or bloody. Pork killed for the fresh meat market is generally very young and tender, carrying little fat. Suckling pigs, killed while still being milk-fed, may be roasted or barbecued whole, and are traditionally served with the head on, and with an apple or an orange between the jaws.

Crackling is the roasted skin of pork. The skin must be scored deeply with a sharp knife before roasting. Salt is rubbed on the skin, making it crisp and bubbly when cooked.

For roasting: any part of the pig (bar the head, trotters and knuckle) are suitable.

For grilling and frying: spare rib chops, loin chops, chump chops from the saddle, best end cutlets, belly bones or American spare ribs (usually with a marinade), fillet, tenderloin, trotters.

For boiling: leg, belly, hand and spring, trotters.

For pies: any meat is suitable.

For sausages: any fatty piece, especially belly.

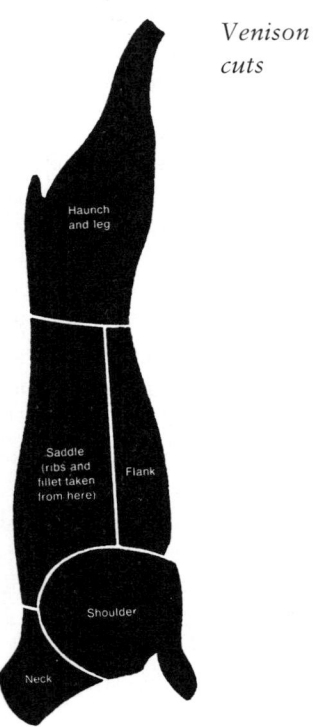

Venison cuts

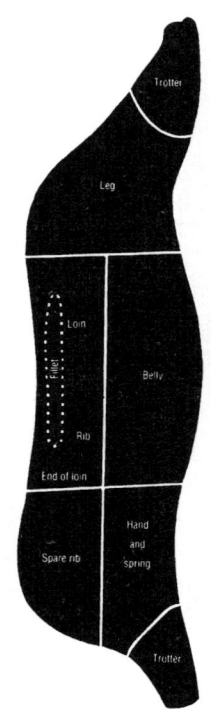

Pork cuts

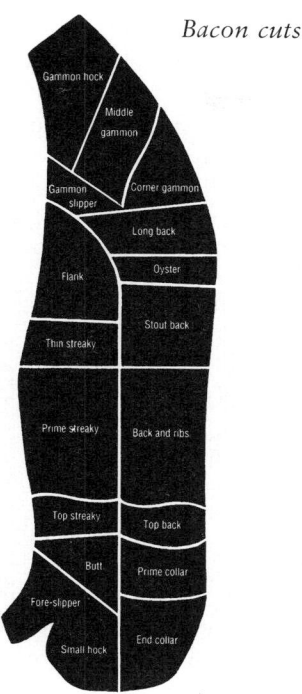

Bacon cuts

(Diagram labels: Gammon hock, Middle gammon, Gammon slipper, Corner gammon, Long back, Flank, Oyster, Stout back, Thin streaky, Prime streaky, Back and ribs, Top streaky, Top back, Butt, Prime collar, Fore-slipper, End collar, Small hock)

BACON

Bacon pigs are killed when heavier than pigs destined for the fresh pork market, so the comparable cuts of bacon should contain more fat than those of fresh pork.

Almost the whole of the pig is salted in brine for up to a week then matured. Green bacon (unsmoked) is sold at this stage. Smoked bacon is hung in cool smoke for up to a month. Gammon is bacon from a hind leg, and ham is bacon from a hind leg that has been brined or cured in dry salt separately from the rest of the pig. Gammon is cured while still attached to the body. Hams are salted and possibly smoked according to varying local traditions. Parma ham and Bayonne ham, for example, are salted and smoked but not cooked further before eating. English hams are generally cooked before eating hot or cold. The most famous are the well-hung Braddenham ham and the sweet milk York ham. American Virginia hams are said to owe their sweet flavour to the fact that the hogs are fed on peanuts and peaches, and the hams are cured in salt and sugar and smoked over apple and hickory wood for a month. Westphalian ham from Germany is eaten raw in thin slices like Parma ham. Paris ham is similar to English York ham.

Since good refrigeration is now widely available, pork need no longer be salted as a preservative measure. Today pork is turned into bacon mainly for the flavour. Smoked bacon keeps slightly longer than green but, again, modern smoking is done more for the flavour than for preservation.

Commercially produced bacon is generally mild. Bacon cured at home, without chemical preservatives, vacuum packs, etc., is likely to have more flavour and saltiness, but needs soaking before cooking.

Smoked and green bacon flesh look similarly reddish-pink. It should not be dry, hard, dark or patchy in colour. Smoked rind is yellowish-brown; green bacon rind is white.

English bacons vary according to manufacturer and price, some being saltier than others, so care should be taken if boiling without prior soaking. It is wise to soak large pieces to be cooked whole, such as gammons or forehocks. Smaller cuts, steaks and rashers, rarely need soaking.

Danish pigs are all cured in the same manner, giving a good quality, mild-tasting, not very salty bacon.

For boiling and stewing: all cuts are suitable, but the lean pieces (forehock, gammon, collar) are sometimes casseroled or stewed whole, tied with string.
Streaky and flank are used diced for soups, or to add flavour to stews.
For frying or grilling: all cuts are suitable but rashers are usually cut from the back, streaky or collar. Steaks are cut from the gammon or prime back.
For baking (usually boiled first): large lean pieces are generally used (whole gammon or ham, whole gammon hock, large piece of back, whole boned and rolled forehock or either of the collars).

LAMB AND MUTTON

Animals weighing more than 36kg/80lb are graded as mutton. Real mutton is seldom available in butchers' shops since all the animals are killed young enough to be called lamb. But there is a difference between the small sweet joints of the new season's spring lamb, and the larger lambs killed later in the year.

Really baby lambs, killed while still milk-fed, are extremely expensive, with very pale, tender flesh. A leg from such a lamb would feed only 2 or perhaps 3 people at most.

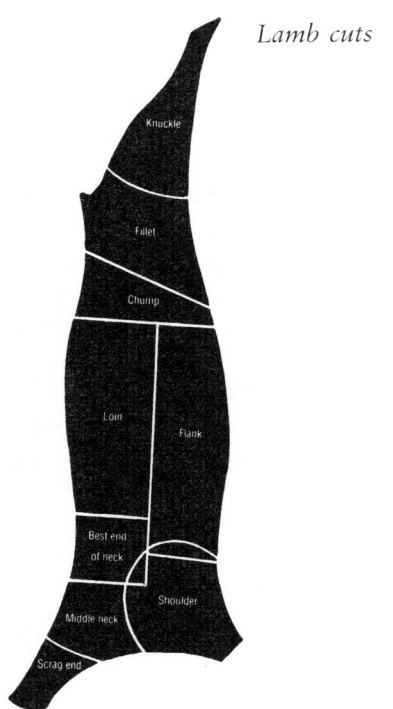

Lamb cuts

British lamb is very fine in flavour, but good imported New Zealand lamb is usually cheaper. As a general rule, New Zealand lamb joints come from smaller animals than the full-grown English lambs, but it should be remembered that 3 grades of New Zealand lamb are imported into Britain, ranging from excellent to very tough. All New Zealand lamb comes into the country frozen, so it stands to reason that some lambs have been more recently killed than others. The best time to buy New Zealand lamb is from Christmas through to the summer months.

Lamb should be brownish-pink rather than grey in colour, but not bloody. Because the animal is killed young, almost all the cuts are tender enough for grilling, frying or roasting, but the fattier, cheaper cuts are used for casseroles and stews too.

For roasting: saddle or loin, best end of neck (rack of lamb), shoulder, leg, breast.
For braising: chump chops, loin, leg.

For grilling and frying: best end cutlets, loin chops, chump chops, steaks from fillet end of leg.
For boiling and stewing: knuckle, scrag and middle neck, breast, leg.

BUTCHERY AND MEAT PREPARATION

Most cuts of meat are available ready prepared from the shop or market. But it is useful to know how to bone and tie certain French and English cuts that a busy butcher may be unwilling to tackle.

BONING

Boning is easier than most people imagine. A short sharp knife is essential. Tunnel-boning – where the bone, say from a leg, is extracted from the hole from which it protrudes, without opening out the meat – is more difficult than open-boning where the flesh is split along the bone, the bone worked out and the meat rolled up and tied or sewn. But, whether tunnel-boning or open-boning it is essential to work slowly and carefully, keeping the knife as close to the bones as possible, and scraping the meat off the bone rather than cutting it. Any meat extracted inadvertently with the bone can be scraped off and put back into the joint.

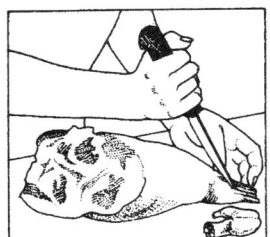 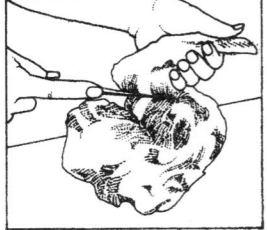

To make a butterfly joint, work from the knuckle end

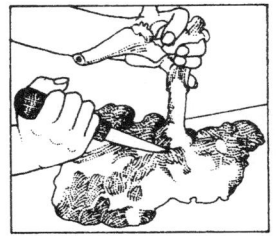 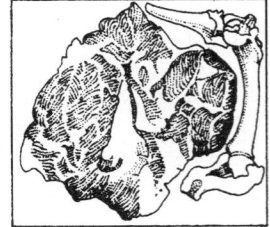

Gradually ease out the three bones

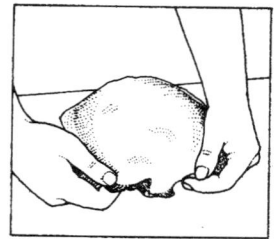

After stuffing, fold the butterfly flaps under the joint

With most bones it is possible, when tunnel-boning, to work from both ends – for example, a leg of lamb can be worked on where the knuckle bone sticks out of the thin end, and the leg bone out of the fillet end. But in most cases it is simpler to cut neatly through the flesh, along the length of the bone, from the side nearest to the bone, and work the bone out all along its length. After all, some sewing or tying is necessary at the ends of the joints even if tunnel-boned, and it is simpler to sew up the length of the joint.

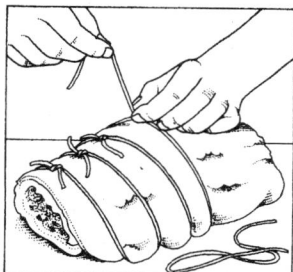

Tie with short pieces of string or cotton

Trainee butchers are taught to use the knife in such a way that should it slip it will not hurt them. This means never pulling the knife directly towards the body. In addition, the knife is held firmly like a dagger when working, with the point of the knife down. But the safest precaution that cooks can take is to see that their knives are sharp. Blunt knives need more

pressure to wield, and are therefore more inclined to slip.

BUTTERFLY JOINTS
To make a butterfly joint, open-bone a leg of lamb. Hold a sharp, sturdy butcher's knife like a dagger and cut, from the knuckle end, down the non-fleshy side of the leg and gradually work out the three bones.

LAMB 'EN BALLON'
This is stuffed boned shoulder of lamb that is tied up to look like a balloon. To reassemble the shoulder, spread the stuffing on one half of the boned lamb and fold the other half close up over to cover it. If the shoulder has been tunnel-boned, push the stuffing into it. Turn the shoulder over, skinned side up. Tie the end of a 3m/9ft piece of string firmly round the shoulder, making a knot in the middle at the top. Take the string around again, but this time at right angles to the first line, again tying at the first knot. Continue this process until the 'balloon' is trussed about 8 times. Tuck in any loose flaps of meat or skin.

ROLLING AND TYING
Once a joint, such as loin, is boned, remove most of the fat and lay it, meat side up, on the board. Season it or spread sparingly with stuffing. Roll it up from the thick end and use short pieces of thin cotton (not nylon) string to tie round the meat at 2.5cm/1in intervals. These can easily be cut off when serving, or the carver can slice between them when cutting the meat into thick slices.

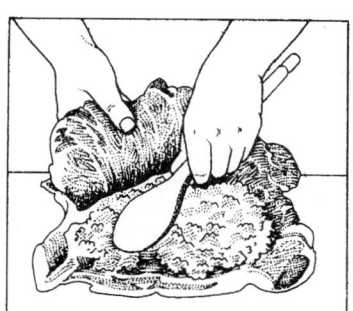
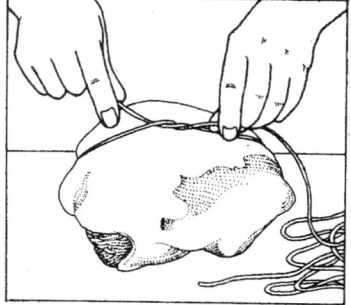
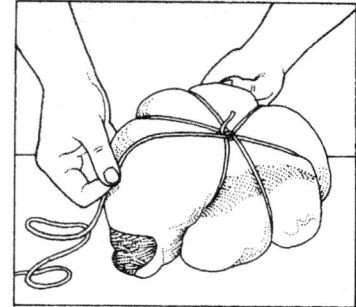

To assemble lamb 'en ballon', stuff a boned shoulder and tie

SEWING UP WHOLE JOINTS AFTER STUFFING

Use a larding needle or large darning or upholstery needle. Some of these are curved slightly which makes the job easier. Use thin old-fashioned white string, not nylon which will melt under heat. If the string is not very thin it can be 'untwined' quite easily and used as required. Leave a good length of string at the beginning and end, but do not tie elaborate knots, which are difficult to undo when dishing the meat. Simple, large, fairly loose stitches are best – the whole length of string can be pulled out in one movement when dishing.

LARDING

Some very lean or potentially tough meat is larded before roasting. This promotes tenderness and adds flavour. The technique is most commonly used for slow-roasted dishes like boeuf à la mode or roast veal. A special larding needle is used.

To lard a joint, cut the larding fat (usually rindless back pork fat) into thin strips and put one of them into the tunnel of the needle, clamping down the hinge to hold it in place. The fat should extend a little way out of the needle. Thread through the meat, twisting the needle gently to prevent the fat pulling off. Then release the clamp, and trim the 2 ends of fat close to the meat. Repeat this all over the lean meat at 2.5cm/1in intervals.

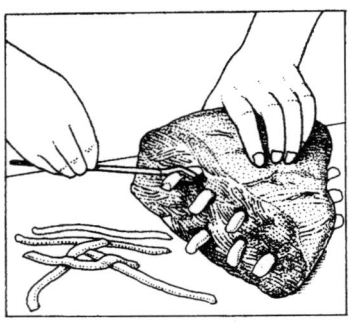

To lard: thread with strips of pork fat

PREPARING BEEF

STEAKS FOR GRILLING OR FRYING

Cut across the grain of the meat, if possible into thickish slices. Trim neatly, and cut rump slices into 2–3 individual steaks.

MINUTE STEAKS

Cut large thin steaks. Put them between 2 sheets of paper or clingfilm and bat gently with a cook's mallet or rolling pin to flatten the meat.

TOURNEDOS STEAKS

Cut 2.5cm/1in slices across the trimmed fillet.

FOR STEWING

Remove the gristle, but not all the fat (it will add moisture and flavour). Cut into 2.5cm/1in cubes, or larger. Too-small pieces shred up, becoming dry and tough during cooking.

FOR STROGANOFF

Cut into small strips about the thickness of a pencil across the grain of the meat.

FOR ROASTING

If the meat has no fat on it, tie a piece of pork fat, or fatty bacon, round it. Tie up as described on page 121.

PREPARING LAMB

SADDLE

This consists of both loins of lamb, left attached at the backbone, in the same way as a baron of beef.

First remove the skin: with a small knife lift a corner of the skin, hold this firmly with a tea-towel to get a good grip and tug sharply to peel off. Trim off any very large pieces of fat from the edges of the saddle, but leave the back fat. Tuck the flaps under the saddle. Cut out the kidneys but keep them (they can be brushed with butter and attached to the end of the saddle with wooden skewers 30 minutes before the end of the roasting time). Using a sharp knife, score the back fat all over in a fine criss-cross pattern.

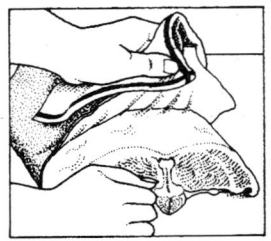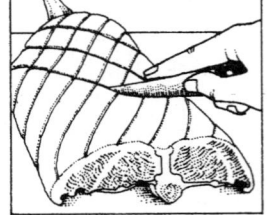

Preparing a saddle of lamb

The pelvic or aitch bone, protruding slightly from one end of the saddle, can be removed, or left in place and covered with a ham frill when the saddle is served.

FRENCH-TRIMMED BEST END CUTLETS

Skin the best end: lift a corner of the skin from the neck end with a small knife, hold it firmly, using a cloth to get a good grip, and peel it off. Chine if the butcher has not already done so. This means sawing carefully through the chine bone (or spine) just where it meets the rib bones. Take care not to saw right through into the eye of the meat. Now remove the chine bone completely. Chop off the cutlet bones so that the length of the remaining bones is not more than twice the length of the eye of the meat. Remove the half-moon shaped piece of flexible cartilage found buried between the layers of fat and meat at the thinner end of the best end. This is the tip of the shoulder blade. It is simple to work out with a knife and your fingers. Remove the line of gristle to be found under the meat at the thick end.

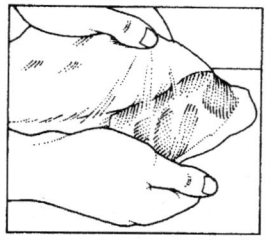 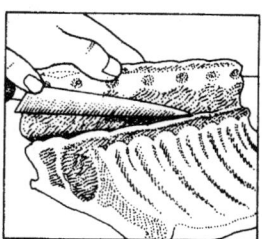

For cutlets: skin and chine

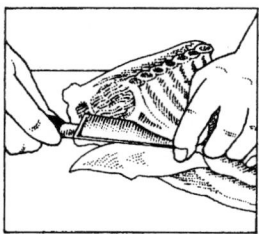 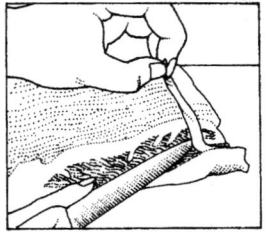

Remove the shoulder blade and gristle

If thin small cutlets are required, cut between each bone as evenly as possible, splitting the rack into 6–7 small cutlets. If fatter cutlets are required, carefully ease out every other rib bone. Then cut between the remaining bones

into thick cutlets. Now trim the fat from the thick end of each cutlet, and scrape the rib bones free of any flesh or skin.

NOISETTES

These are boneless cutlets, tied into a neat round shape with string. They are made from the loin or best end. Skin the meat: lift a corner of the skin with a small knife, holding it firmly with a cloth to get a good grip, and pull it off.

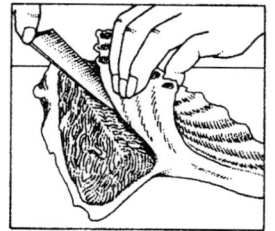 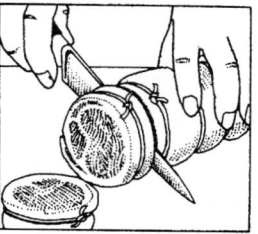

For noisettes: ease out the bones, then roll, tie and cut

Chine the meat (see above). Now remove first the chine bone and then all the rib bones, easing them out with a short sharp knife. Remove the half-moon-shaped piece of flexible cartilage found buried between the layers of fat and meat at the thinner end of the best end. This is the top of the shoulder blade. Remove the line of gristle to be found under the meat at the thick end.

Trim off any excess fat from the meat and roll it up tightly, starting at the meaty thick side and working towards the thin flap. Tie the roll neatly with separate pieces of string placed at 3cm/1½in intervals. Trim the ragged ends of the roll to neaten them. Now slice the roll into pieces, cutting accurately between each string. The average English best end will give 4 good noisettes. The string from the noisette is removed after cooking.

COLLOPS

These are small slices of meat taken from the best end neck of lamb. They are a very extravagant lamb steak. Lay the best end neck down and prepare the meat partly as for noisettes (see above), i.e. remove the chine bone, gristle and shoulder blade. With a sharp knife (and making small cuts close to the rib bones), ease the bones, in one piece, away from the meat. Gradually separate the whole 'eye' of the meat (the fat-free cylinder) from the bones. Using a sharp flexible knife, remove all fat and membranes from the meat. Finally, slice into meat rounds or 'collops'.

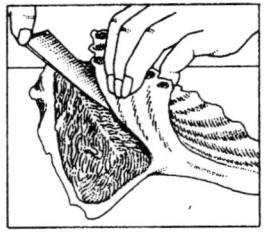
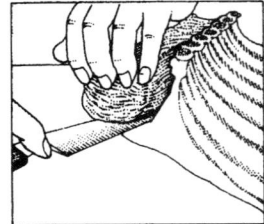

For collops: ease out the bones and separate the eye

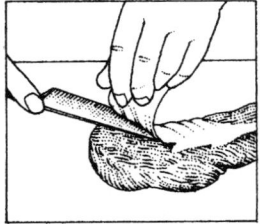
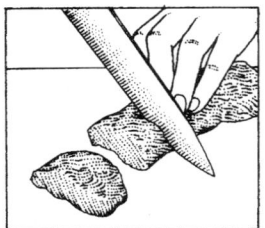

Remove fat and membrane, and slice

CROWN ROAST

Two racks (best ends) are needed. The rack is prepared similarly to one destined for cutlets (see page 123) but the rib bones are left slightly longer, and the rack is not split into cutlets.

However, it is skinned and chined, the shoulder cartilage and the line of gristle are removed. The excess fat is cut off (stages 1 and 2 below) and the top inch of the bones are scraped clean (stage 3). Remove an even layer of fat from the prepared rack (stage 4). Bend each best end into a semi-circle, with the fatty side of the ribs inside. To facilitate this it may be necessary to cut through the sinew between each cutlet, from the thick end for about 2.5cm/1in. But take care not to cut into the fleshy eye of the meat. Sew the ends of the racks together to make a circle, with the meaty part forming the base of the crown. Tie a piece of string round the 'waist' of the crown (stage 5). A crown roast is traditionally stuffed, but this can result in undercooked inside fat.

GUARD OF HONOUR (RACK OF LAMB)

Prepare 2 best end racks exactly as for the crown roast, above. Score the fat in a criss-cross pattern.

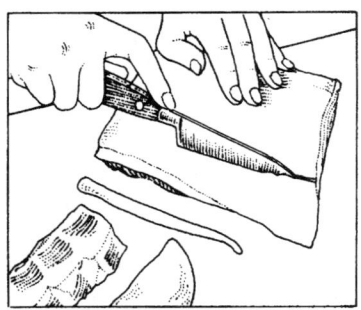

Stage 1

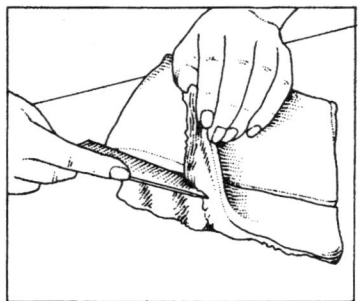

Stage 2

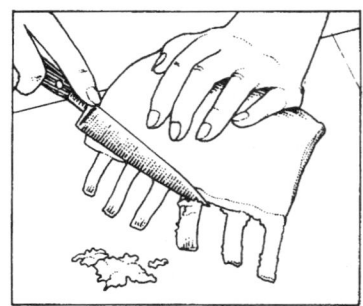

Stage 3

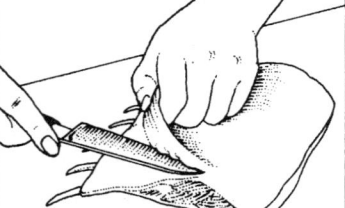

Stage 4

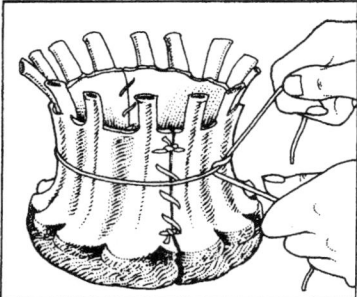

Stage 5

To make a crown roast: see the numbered stages in the text above

POULTRY AND GAME

TO PREPARE AND DRAW A GAME BIRD FOR THE OVEN

Some birds are easier to pluck than others, ducks being notoriously tedious. All birds are easier to pluck if still warm when tackled. Work away from draughts, as the feathers fly about, and pluck straight into a dustbin. Tug the feathers, working from the tail to the head, pulling against the way the feathers grow. If the bird is very young or if there is a lot of fat, pull downwards towards the tail to avoid tearing the flesh.

Once plucked, the bird should be singed. This can be done with a burning taper, or directly over a gas flame, but care should be taken to singe only the down and small feathers, and not to blacken the flesh. The bird should then be rubbed with a clean tea-towel to remove any remaining stubble. It is now ready for drawing.

Surprisingly, birds keep better, when hanging, with their insides intact. Once eviscerated they must be cooked within a day or two. So when you are ready to cook the bird, take it down, and proceed as follows.

1. Pluck it.

2. Cut round the feet, at the drumstick joint, but do not cut right through the tendons. Pull the legs off the bird, drawing the tendons out with them. If the bird is small this is easy enough – just bend the foot back until it snaps, and pull, perhaps over the edge of a table. Turkeys are more difficult: snap the feet at the drumstick joint by bending them over the end of the table, then hang the bird up by the feet from a stout hook, and pull on the bird. The feet plus tendons will be left on the hook, the turkey in your arms. All too often birds are sold with the tendons in the legs, making the drumsticks tough when cooked.

3. Now for the head and neck. Lay the bird breast side down on a board. Make a slit through the neck skin from the body to the head. Cut off the head and throw it away. Pull back the split neck skin, leaving it attached to the body of the bird (it will come in useful to close the gap if you are stuffing the bird). Cut the neck off as close to the body as you can.

4. Put a finger into the neck hole, to the side of the stump of neck left on the bird, and move the finger right round, loosening the innards from the neck. If you do not do this you will find them difficult to pull out from the other end.

5. With a sharp knife slit the bird open from the vent to the parson's (or pope's) nose, making a hole large enough to just get your hand in. Put your hand in, working it so the back of your hand is up against the arch of the breastbone, and carefully loosen the entrails from the sides of the body cavity, all the way round. Pull them out, taking care not to break the gall bladder, the contents of which would embitter any flesh they touched. Covering the gutting hand with a cloth helps extract the intestines intact. The first time you do this it is unlikely that you will get everything out in one motion, so check that the lungs and kidneys come too. Have another go if necessary. Once the bird is empty, wipe any traces of blood off with a clean damp cloth.

The neck and feet go into the stockpot with the heart and the cleaned gizzard. To clean the gizzard, carefully cut the outside wall along the natural seam so that you can peel it away from the inner bag of grit. Throw the grit bag away, with the intestines and the gall bladder. Do not put the liver in the stockpot: it may make the stock bitter. It may be fried and served with the dish, or fried, chopped and added to the sauce, or kept frozen until enough poultry liver has been collected to make pâté. But if the liver is to be used, carefully cut away the discoloured portion of it where it lay against the gall bladder (it will be bitter) and trim off any membranes.

The bird is trussed to keep it in a compact, neat shape, usually after stuffing. Trussing large birds is unnecessary as the bird is to be carved up anyway, and trussing serves to prevent the inside thigh being cooked by the time the breast is ready. Small birds, especially game birds where underdone thighs are desirable, are trussed, but their feet are left on. Their feet may simply be tied together for neatness sake, and the pinions skewered under the bird. Or they may be trussed in any number of ways, one of which is described below.

1. Arrange the bird so that the neck flap is folded over the neck hole, and the pinions turned under and tucked in tight. They will, if folded correctly, hold the neck flap in place, but if the bird is well stuffed the neck flap may have to be skewered or sewn in place.

2. Press the legs down and into the bird to force the breast into a plumped-up position. Thread a long trussing needle with thin string and push it through the wing joint, right through the body and out of the other wing joint.

3. Then push it through the body again, this time through the thighs. You should now be back on the side you started.

4. Tie the two ends together in a bow to make later removal quick.

5. Then thread a shorter piece of string through the thin end of the two drumsticks and tie them together, winding the string round the parson's nose at the same time to close the vent. Sometimes a small slit is cut in the skin just below the end of the breastbone, and the parson's nose is pushed through it.

Small birds such as quail are invariably cooked whole, perhaps stuffed, and perhaps boned (see pages 127–8). But medium-sized ones, like chickens and guinea fowl, are often cut into 2, 4, 6 or 8 pieces. Use a knife to cut through the flesh and poultry shears or scissors to cut the bones.

TO SPLIT A BIRD IN HALF

Simply use a sharp knife to cut right through flesh and bone, just on one side of the breastbone, open out the bird and cut through the other side, immediately next to the backbone. Then cut the backbone away from the half to which it remains attached. The knobbly end of the drumsticks and the fleshless tips to the pinions can be cut off before or after cooking. In birds brought whole to the table they are left on.

TO JOINT A BIRD INTO 4

First pull out any trussing strings, then pull the leg away from the body. With a sharp knife cut through the skin joining the leg to the body, pull the leg away further and cut through more skin to free the leg. Bend the leg outwards and back, forcing the bone to come out of its socket close to the body. Turn the bird over, feel along the backbone to find the oyster (a soft pocket of flesh at the side of the backbone, near the middle). With the tip of the knife, cut this away from the carcass at the side nearest the backbone and farthest from the leg. Then turn the bird over again, and cut through the flesh, the knife going between the end of the thigh bone and the carcass, to take off the leg, bringing the oyster with it. Using poultry shears or a heavy knife, split the carcass along the breastbone. Cut through the ribs on each side to take off the fleshy portion of the breast, and with it the wing. Trim the joints neatly to remove scraps of untidy skin.

For six joints, proceed as above but split the legs into thigh portions and drumsticks. The exact join of the bones can easily be seen if the leg is laid on the board, skin side down. Cut through the fat line. With a cleaver, or the heel end of a knife, chop the feet off the drumsticks.

TO JOINT INTO 8

1. Turn the chicken over so the backbone is uppermost. Cut through to the bone along the line of the spine.

2. Where the thigh joins the backbone there is a fleshy 'oyster' on each side. Cut round them to loosen them from the carcass so that they come away when the legs are severed.

3. Turn the bird over and pull a leg away from the body. Cut through the skin only, as far round the leg as possible, close to the body.

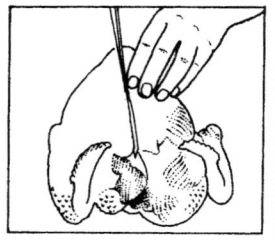 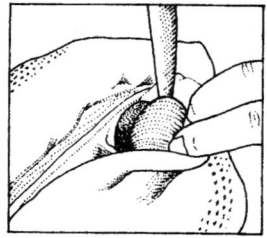 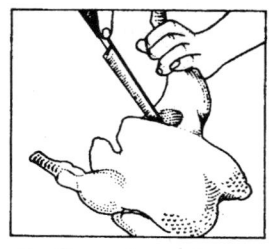 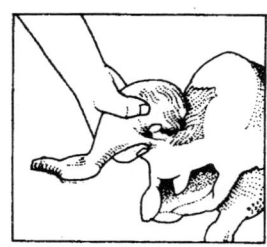

Jointing a chicken: Stages 1 and 2 (numbers refer to text)   Stages 3 and 4

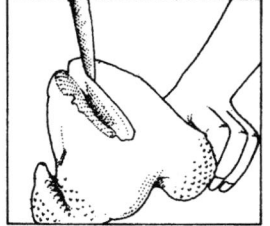 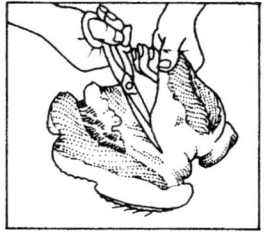 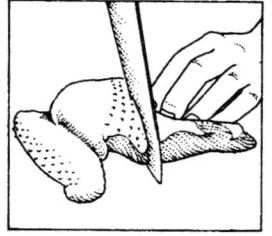 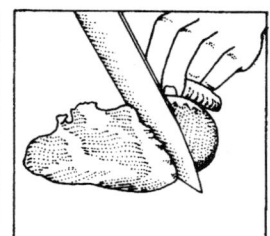

Stages 6, 7 and 8   *Stages 9 and 11*

4. Pull the leg away from the body and twist it down so that the thigh bone pops out of its socket on the carcass and is exposed.
5. Cut the leg off, taking care to go between thigh bone and carcass and to bring the 'oyster' away with the leg. (Turn over briefly to check.) Repeat the process for the other leg.
6. Carefully cut down each side of the breastbone to free the flesh a little.
7. Use scissors to cut through the small bone close to the breast. Cut away the breastbone.
8. Open up the bird. Cut each wing and breast off the carcass with scissors. Start at the tail end and cut to and through the wing bone near the neck.
9. Cut the wing joint in two, leaving about one third of the breast attached to the wing.
10. Cut off the pinions from each wing. They can go into the stockpot with the carcass.
11. Separate the drumsticks and thighs, lay the legs skin side down on the board, and cut through where the thigh and lower leg bones meet, on the obvious fat line.
12. With a cleaver, or the heel end of a heavy knife, chop the feet off the drumsticks.

BARDING

Poultry liable to dry out during cooking is often barded: lay fatty bacon or rindless pork back fat strips over the body of the bird, and secure or tie in place. The barding is removed during cooking to allow the breast to brown.

BONING

1. Put the bird breast side down on a board. Cut through to the backbone.
2. Feel for the fleshy 'oyster' at the top of each thigh and cut round it. Cut and scrape the flesh from the carcass with a sharp knife held as close as possible to the bone.
3. Continue along both sides of the backbone until the ribcage is exposed. At the joint of the thigh and pelvis, cut between the bones at the socket so that the legs stay attached to the flesh and skin, and not to the body carcass.
4. Keep working right round the bird, then use scissors to cut away most of the ribcage, leaving only the cartilaginous breastbone in the centre.
5. Using a heavy knife, cut through the foot joints to remove the knuckle end of the drumsticks.
6. Working from the inside thigh end scrape one leg bone clean, pushing the flesh down towards the drumstick until you can free the thigh bone. Repeat on the other leg.
7. Working from the drumstick ends, scrape the lower leg bones clean in the same way and remove them. Remove as many tendons as possible from the legs as you work.

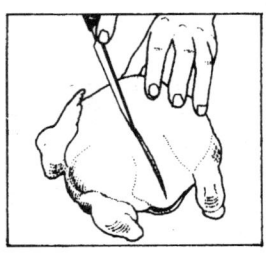
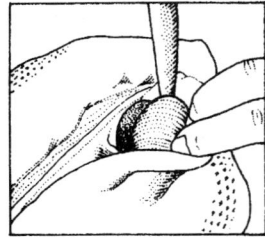

Boning a chicken: Stages 1 and 2 (numbers refer to text)

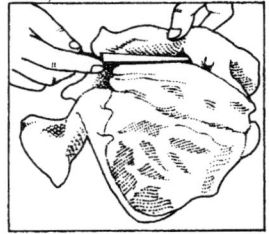
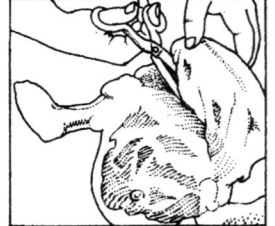

Stages 3 and 4

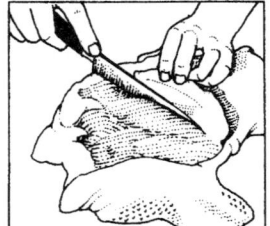
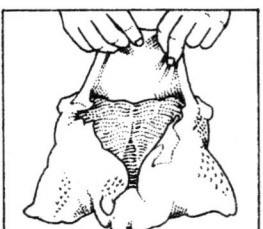

Stages 10 and 12

8. Now for the wings. Cut off the pinions with a heavy knife.

9. Scrape the wing bones clean as you did the leg bones.

10. Carefully free the breastbone with the knife, working from the middle of the bird towards the tail.

11. Take great care not to puncture the skin, which has no flesh under it at this point so is easily torn.

12. You should now have a beautifully boned bird. Keep the neck flap of skin intact to fold over once the chicken is stuffed.

ROASTING TABLES

If using a fan (convection) oven, reduce the cooking times by 15 per cent or lower the oven temperature by 20°C/40°F.

Meat		Temperature			Cooking time	
		°C	°F	Gas	per kg	per lb
Beef	Brown	220	425	7	20 mins +	
	Rare roast	170	325	3	35 mins	15 mins
	Medium roast				45 mins	20 mins
Pork	Roast	200	400	6	65 mins	25 mins
Veal	Brown	220	425	7	20 mins +	
	Roast	180	350	4	55 mins	25 mins
Lamb	Brown	220	425	7	20 mins +	
	Roast	190	375	5	55 mins	20 mins
Chicken		200	400	6	35–45 mins	15–20 mins
NOTE: Few chickens, however small, will be cooked in much under an hour.						
Turkey	Small (under 6kg/13lb)	200	400	6	25 mins	12 mins
	Large	180	350	4	35 mins	15 mins
(Few turkeys, however small, will be cooked in under 2 hours.)						
Duck, goose	Small (under 2.3kg/5lb)	190	375	5	45 mins	20 mins
	Large	180	350	4	55 mins	25 mins
Pigeon		200	400	6	25–35 minutes	
Grouse		190	375	5	25–35 minutes	
Guinea fowl		190	375	5	70 minutes	
Partridge		190	375	5	20–25 minutes	
Pheasant		190	375	5	45–60 minutes	
Wild duck		200	400	6	40 minutes	
Woodcock		190	375	5	20–30 minutes	
Quail		180	350	4	20 minutes	
Snipe		190	375	5	15–20 minutes	

FISH AND SHELLFISH

Freshwater fish are divided into coarse fish, fished mainly for sport and generally thrown back live into the rivers, and game fish, which are caught both for sport and commercially. Much freshwater fish in fact comes from fish farms. Many freshwater fish, such as bass, sturgeon, sea trout and salmon spend most of their adult lives in the sea, swimming back up the rivers to spawn, but they are still classified as freshwater fish despite the fact that most of them are caught by trawler in the sea. Coarse river fish, such as roach, gudgeon and tench, are not sold commercially and are seldom eaten except by anglers' families.

Most of our fish comes from the sea. It is increasingly difficult today to get locally caught fish. Fish is frozen or deep-chilled on trawlers and immediately exported. For the cook this is sad. Fish is a valuable source of protein, vitamin D (in oily fish), calcium and phosphorus (found especially in the edible bones of whitebait, sardines, etc.), iodine, fluorine and some of the B vitamins. Fish contains very little fat, and even oily fish seldom has more than 20 per cent fat content. The fat in fish is polyunsaturated and contains essential fatty acids that cannot be obtained elsewhere.

Like meat, fish is composed of muscle fibres that vary in length and thickness according to type. For example, lobster has long and coarse fibres and herring very fine fibres.

The fibres are generally shorter than in meat and are packed in flakes with very little connective tissue between them. The fat is dispersed among the fibres. The connective tissue is very thin and is quickly converted to gelatine when cooked. Because of its structure, fish is naturally more tender than meat, and over-vigorous or overlong cooking will cause dryness and disintegration as the connective tissue dissolves and the flakes fall apart. The protein in the fibres coagulates, the fish begins to shrink and the juices are extracted – in dry heat there is a more rapid loss of juices. In moist heat soluble nutrients and flavouring minerals are lost into the liquid, making an overcooked fish dry, tough and tasteless.

Fish should be cooked quickly by grilling or frying, or slowly by poaching. If frying or grilling, the fish should be protected from the fierce heat by a coating of seasoned flour, beaten egg, breadcrumbs or a batter. If poaching, use a well-seasoned court bouillon and then use this liquid to make the sauce so that none of the flavour is lost. Do drain fish well after it has been poached, and do not keep it warm as it will dry out and become tough and tasteless. Fish does not keep well and should be eaten as fresh as possible. A plausible theory explaining this is that as fish live in cold water, they are cold-blooded and their enzymes work at very low temperatures. Thus they continue, unlike meat, to deteriorate in the refrigerator.

PREPARATION FOR COOKING

REMOVING THE SCALES Large fish have dry scales which should be removed before cooking. To do this, scrape a large knife the wrong way along the fish (from tail to head). This can be a messy business as the scales tend to fly about; it can be cleanly done in a plastic carrier bag to prevent this. However, unless you are buying fish from a wholesale market, the fishmonger will do it for you.

GUTTING AND CLEANING The fishmonger will probably clean the fish, but if you are to do it yourself you will need a very sharp knife. Fish skin blunts knives faster than anything else. If

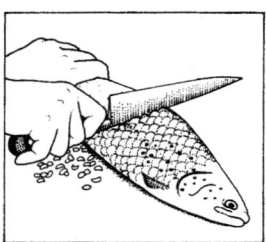

Remove the scales with the back of a knife

the fish is to be stuffed or filleted it does not matter how big a slit you make to remove the entrails. If it is to be left whole, the shorter the slit the better. Start just below the head and slit through the soft belly skin. After pulling out the innards, wash the fish under cold water. If it is large, and of the round type, make sure all the dark blood along the spinal column is removed. Now carefully cut away the gills. Take care not to cut off the head if you want to serve the fish whole. If you do not, cut off head and tail now. To remove the fins, cut the skin round them, take a good grip (if you salt your fingers well it will stop them slipping) and yank sharply towards the head. This will pull the fin bones out with the fin.

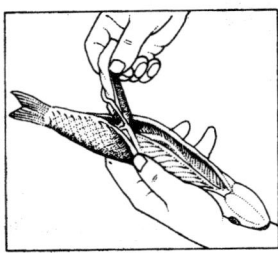

Remove the innards and wash thoroughly

STUFFING FISH Round fish are more suitable for stuffing whole than flat fish, as there is more space in the body cavity after gutting. Stuffings usually contain breadcrumbs, which swell during cooking, so care should be taken not to overfill the fish. Fish fillets can be sandwiched with stuffing, or rolled up round the mixture. Well-flavoured expensive fish is less often stuffed than the more tasteless varieties, which need the additional flavour of an aromatic filling.

FILLETING AND SKINNING ROUND FISH
Round fish are filleted before skinning. If they are to be cooked whole, the skin is left on and peeled away when the fish is about to be served, as in the case of a whole poached salmon. The skin gives flavour to the fish and prevents the flesh from drying out.

To fillet a round fish, lay it on a board. Hold the fish taut against the board with your left hand, and cut through the flesh down to the backbone from the head to the tail. Insert a sharp, pliable knife between the flesh and the bones, and slice the fillet away from the bones, working with short strokes from the backbone and from the head end. Remember to keep the knife as flat as possible, and to keep it against the bones. When the fillet has almost been removed from the fish, you will need to cut through the belly skin to detach it completely.

Some round fish, such as John Dory, with its deep rather than wide body, should be filleted into double or cross-cut fillets. Very large round fish can be filleted into four, following the flat fish method, or the whole side can be lifted as described here, and then split in two once off the fish by cutting down the centre.

SKINNING AND FILLETING FLAT FISH Fish skin is easier to remove after cooking. But sometimes the fish must be skinned beforehand. Most whole fish are not skinned or filleted before grilling, but sole (and lemon sole, witch and plaice) are skinned on at least the dark side, and sometimes on both sides. To do this, make a crossways slit through the skin at the tail, and push a finger in. You will now be able to run the finger round the edge of the fish loosening the skin. When you have done this on both edges, salt your fingers to prevent slipping, take a firm grip of the skin at the tail end with one hand, and with the other hold the fish down. Give a quick strong yank, peeling the skin back towards the head. If necessary, do the same to the other side.

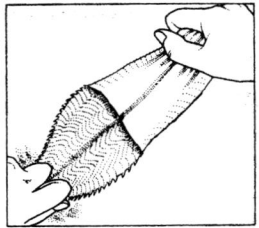
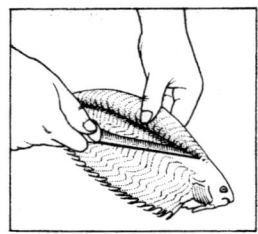

Remove the skin from a flat fish in one piece

To fillet a flat fish, stroke the flesh away from the bones

Flat fish are generally filleted into four half or single fillets. To do this, lay the fish on a board with the tail towards you. Cut through the flesh to the backbone along the length of the fish. Then, using a sharp, pliable knife, lift the left-hand fillet away with a long sweeping action, keeping the blade almost flat and close to the bone. Then swivel the fish round so the head is towards you, and cut away the second fillet in the same way. Turn the fish over and repeat the process on the other side. (If you are left-handed, tackle the right-hand fillet first.)

It is possible to fillet the fish into two double or cross-cut fillets, as fishmongers do, but most people find it easier to take off a single fillet at a time.

SKINNING A FISH FILLET

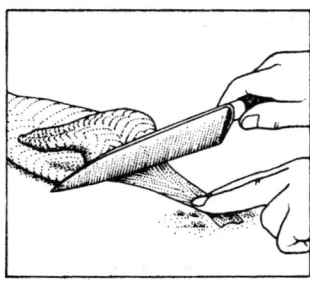

To skin a fillet, grip the tail with one hand and with a gentle sawing action push the flesh off the fillet with a filleting knife

Lay the fillet skin side down on a board. Hold the tail end down, using a pinch of salt to help get a firm grip. With a sharp knife, using a gentle sawing action, cut through the flesh, starting at the tail end. Keep a very tight grip on the skin, taking care not to cut right through it. Keep the knife at a flat or you will leave too much of the flesh behind. Avoid putting too much pressure on the knife – if it is really sharp it will remove all the flesh easily.

BONING A FISH FOR STUFFING

Skin both sides of the fish as described. Lay it on a board and cut through the flesh down the backbone. Using a long, stroking action, lift the fillet from the bone, stopping at the fins. Leave the fillet attached to the head and tail. Swivel the fish around and lift the fillet on the other side in the same way. Turn the fish over and lift the underside fillets from the

bone, still leaving them attached to the fins, in the same way as before. All four fillets should now be loose and free from bone. Using a pair of kitchen scissors, cut the backbone at the head and tail to loosen it, and carefully snip the outside of the bone, keeping as close to the fillets as possible, but not cutting through.

Lay the fish on a baking sheet and reassemble the four fillets so that the fish is re-formed into its original shape. For stuffing, roll the two upper fillets back to form a lip. The small, frilly fins can be pulled away after cooking.

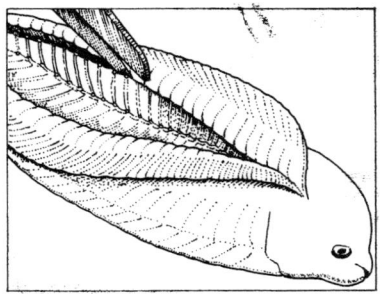

Using a pair of kitchen scissors, cut the backbone at the head and tail to loosen it, carefully snip the outside of the bone

PINBONING FISH

This is done to remove all the small irritating bones that run along the flanks of the fish, and which are the reason why some people do not enjoy eating fish.

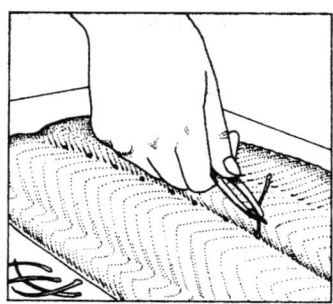

Remove the bones with tweezers or pliers

Any cut of fish should be pinboned before cooking. Run the tips of the fingers of one hand over the surface of the flesh to locate the ends of the small bones. Pull the bones out with tweezers or pliers. The fish is now ready for cooking.

PREPARING A FISH NOISETTE

Carefully remove the bones from the fish cutlet. Using a sharp knife, slice the skin away from the flesh halfway round the cutlet. Fold the skinned piece of fish into the centre and wrap the rest of the cutlet round the outside. Tie with string.

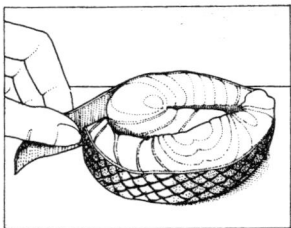

Fold the skinned piece of fish into the centre and wrap the rest of the skin round the outside

SKINNING EEL

Some fishmongers will supply a live eel, which needs to be killed first, then skinned immediately. Cut through the skin round the neck and slit the skin down the length of the body. Hang the eel up by its head – a stout hook through the eyes is best. Using a cloth to get a good grip, pull hard to peel off the skin from neck to tail.

PREPARATION OF RAW FISH FOR SASHIMI AND CEVICHE

It is recommended that fish that is to be eaten in raw dishes should be left in the freezer at −18°C for at least 24 hours before using. As with eating raw meat or eggs, the consumption of raw fish carries some risk.

PREPARING SHELLFISH

COOKED SHELLFISH

Boiling shellfish is covered here as an extension of preparation, rather than in the Methods of Cooking section, which deals with general cooking techniques.

LOBSTER AND CRAB

There are two main methods of cooking a live lobster, depending on the dish. If using a live lobster for a hot dish, freeze, then split it in half (see below) and cook it. For salads, the lobster should be boiled in salted water, ideally sea water, first, then allowed to cool. As sea water is not always available, use a concentration of 3 tablespoons salt to 1 litre/1¾ pints water for boiling any shellfish. For Boiled Lobster, see page 158.

Dealing with a live lobster can be disconcerting for the cook. Plunging a lobster into boiling water or stabbing it requires a strong stomach and a keen appetite! The RSPCA have set down guidelines for the killing of crustaceans, which they consider to be humane.

The traditional method of cooking crustaceans is by boiling. Small crustaceans, such as prawns or crayfish, will die very quickly if placed in boiling water. The RSPCA set guidelines as to the most humane method of dealing with live crayfish: they should be submerged in boiling court bouillon, covered with a lid and boiled for 3–4 minutes.

Lobsters and crabs can react violently to immersion by shooting their claws. It is therefore more humane to kill them prior to boiling. A lobster will become sleepy and then hibernate if cold. Therefore, the RSPCA suggest putting it into a freezer at −18°C for at least 2 hours: it will hibernate, then die. This method is only humane if done rapidly in a large freezer; the ice box of a small refrigerator is *not* acceptable.

Before boiling a crab, it should be rendered unconscious by piercing the main nerve centres behind the eyes and on the underside of the 'apron' (the small flap on the underside of the carapace). This is done using an awl or other sharp instrument. Like lobster, crab can then be boiled. A well-flavoured court bouillon is the best cooking liquid to use. A crab has a thicker shell than a lobster and should be boiled for about 15 minutes per 450g/1lb. A lobster will take about 10 minutes per 450g/1lb.

It is always quite difficult to tell when either lobster or crab is cooked. The lobster turns a cardinal red colour, but that is not a perfect indication, as the claws usually need a little longer to cook, even after the change of colour.

To tell if smaller crustacea, such as langoustines and prawns, are cooked, check the underside of the body. It should have lost its translucency and will look white.

SPLITTING A LOBSTER

Put the lobster into a large freezer at − 18°C for

a minimum of 2 hours, not to kill it but to make it very sleepy. Place the lobster on a board, cover the tail end with a tea-towel and hold down firmly. Take a sharp knife and quickly push it through the nerve centre in the head (this is marked by a well-defined cross on the back of the carapace), turn the lobster around and cut the tail shell and the rest of the body in half. Lay it open on the board. Remove and discard the little stomach sac and the thread-like intestine. Both the coral and tomalley are edible, so do not discard.

KILLING/SPLITTING AND PREPARING A LIVE LOBSTER

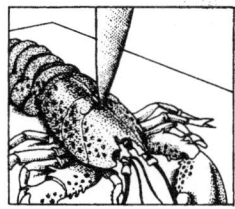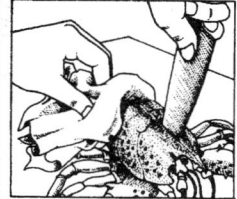

Push a sharp knife through the lobster's nerve centre

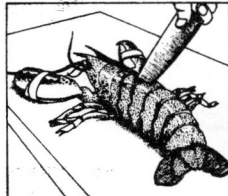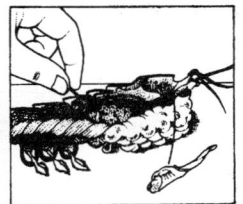

Split the lobster in half and remove the stomach sac

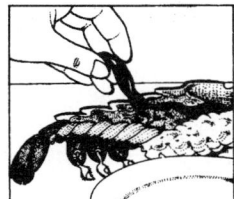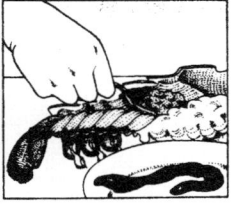

Remove the thread-like intestine and the greeny black roe.

PREPARING AN UNCLEANED SQUID

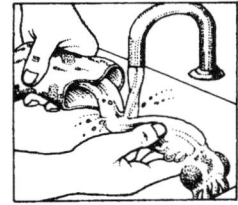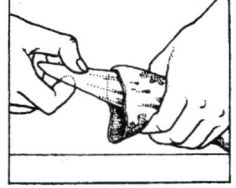

Remove the entrails and cartilage

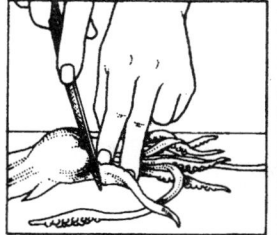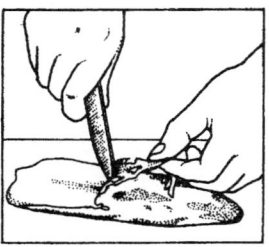

Cut off the head and scrape away the membrane

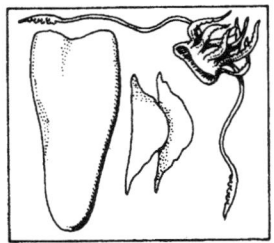

Body, fins and tentacles

PREPARING OCTOPUS

Octopus usually comes ready-cleaned. If not, split the top of the octopus in two and remove the ink sac and entrails. Rinse well under cold running water. To skin, blanch the octopus in boiling water for 5 minutes, drain and refresh. Scrape the skin away with a sharp knife. Before cutting up the octopus, tenderize it by beating with a rolling pin or meat mallet.

DEBEARDING AND CLEANING MUSSELS

It is not a good idea to soak shellfish in cold water, particularly filter feeders or bivalve molluscs such as mussels and clams, if you want them to stay alive. When mussels are harvested they go through several screening stages, which filters out any unwanted matter and cleans them thoroughly, leaving them sterilized. They do, however, need a little preparation before cooking. First scrub the mussels to remove any barnacles. Pull away the 'beard' or byssus thread, the stringy thread on the outside of the shell which helps the mussel attach itself to rocks and other surfaces. If the mussel is open and will not close on sharp tapping, it is dead and should be discarded before cooking. Also throw away any that feel heavy or have a shattered or cracked shell. Use as required.

PREPARING A MUSSEL

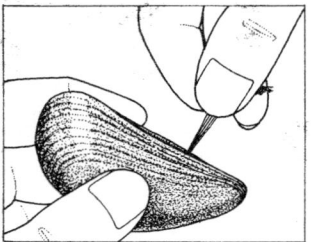

Pull away the 'beard' or byssus thread

PREPARING A SCALLOP

Opening the scallop: prise open the shell with a strong knife and detach the scallop from the lower shell. Scoop out the scallop with a spoon, catching all the juice in a strainer lined with a clean cloth placed over a bowl.

Cleaning the scallop: pull away and discard the membrane or frill and the black stomach parts. Wash the scallop thoroughly under cold running water and pat dry on absorbent paper. Remove the thick white muscle around the outside of the scallop. Separate the coral (roe) from the white meat as required.

PREPARING A SCALLOP

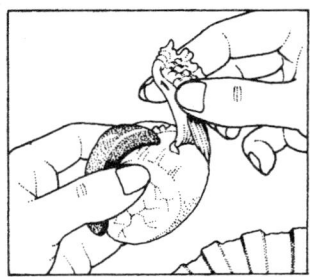

Remove the muscular white frill found opposite the coral (roe)

SHUCKING AN OYSTER

Holding the oyster in a cloth, insert a shucking knife at the hinge of the shell. Twist the knife and prise open the shell. Work above a bowl, to catch as much of the juice as possible. Take great care with this tricky operation as if the knife slips it can cause a nasty injury.

PEELING A RAW PRAWN

Remove the prawn's head by pulling gently from the body. Carefully peel away the body shell.

DE-VEINING A PRAWN

Using a sharp knife, make a small incision the length of the back of the prawn. Carefully pull away the dark intestinal vein, which can be gritty and bitter.

SHUCKING (OPENING) AN OYSTER

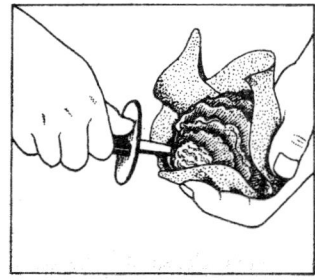

Slip an oyster shucking knife or short kitchen knife under the shell hinge and push and twist it into the oyster

DE-VEINING A PRAWN

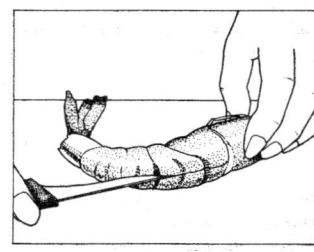

Using a sharp knife, make a small incision the length of the back of the prawn

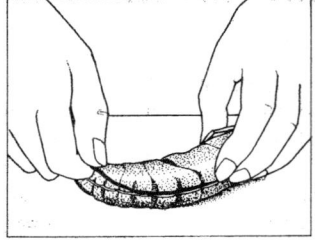

Carefully pull away the dark intestinal vein

After preparing shellfish and other fish, to avoid retaining its odour on your hands, rinse first under cold running water, then wash thoroughly with detergent in hot water.

SPECIAL INGREDIENTS

As we use a large variety of ingredients in our recipes, it may be helpful to give a few guidelines as to what these are.

Anchovy essence Pounded anchovies in liquid form.

Arachide oil Groundnut or peanut oil.

Arborio rice The classic Italian rice traditionally used in the making of risotto. There are several types of risotto rice, but this is definitely the best. It is high in starch and able to absorb a tremendous amount of water without disintegrating.

Balsamic vinegar Dark, sweet vinegar aged in oak over a period of some years, which gives a rich, sweet flavour. It can vary in price, but generally the older and longer it has been aged the sweeter it is and the more it costs. The best comes from Modena, in Italy. Many supermarkets sell own brands.

Basmati rice Aromatic rice from the foothills of the Himalayas, gives a wonderful flavour and scent to many rice dishes. It is a long-grain rice, suitable for pilafs and boiled and steamed rice dishes. It is readily available. Wash it very thoroughly before use.

Bouquet garni The classic ingredients of this bundle of herbs for flavouring stews, stocks, etc. are a bay leaf, a sprig of thyme and a parsley stalk. Tie the herbs together with a stick of celery and remove after cooking.

Buckwheat flour Classic flour used in the making of Russian blinis, it was originally used as an inexpensive alternative to white wheat flour. It is available from healthfood shops and larger supermarkets.

Bulghar wheat Also known as cracked wheat, this is the essential ingredient in kibbeh and tabouleh, two traditional recipes from Lebanon.

Capers The flower-buds of a shrub, readily available, preserved in vinegar, in most supermarkets. They are also available packed in salt which some consider to be superior. Whichever type you use, capers need to be rinsed and dried before use.

Chinese five spice A combination of star anise, cloves, fennel seeds, anise pepper and cassia. Now readily available in most supermarkets.

Couscous Sometimes confused with bulghar wheat, but actually grains of semolina. For cooking, look for the quick or pre-cooked variety.

Crème fraîche This cream has a slight sourness to it. It also has a high fat content, which means that it can be boiled without separating. In the absence of crème fraîche, whipping or double cream can be used with a little lemon juice. Fromage frais (see below) is not a particularly good substitute, as it is more likely to separate on boiling.

Curry leaf This leaf when fresh looks similar to a bay leaf. It has a pronounced spicy, curry flavour and is much used in Thai and Indonesian cooking. Available both fresh and dried from many supermarkets and specialist grocers.

Daikon White radish or Mouli. This is often shredded and used as a garnish.

Dashi Fish stock, sold dry in a packet, or in a tea-bag for infusion. Made with fish, dried bonito flakes and seaweed, kombu, it is used as the base for many soups, sauces and Japanese dishes. The recipe for fish stock on page 627 can be used for all recipes calling for dashi.

Fromage frais Fresh curd cheese made from skimmed cow's milk. Fat content varies from virtually nil to about 8 per cent, depending on whether it has been enriched with cream.

Galangal The fresh root does not look

dissimilar to ginger, and has a slightly peppery flavour. It is used in food from South East Asia, particularly Thailand. Some supermarkets and specialist grocers sell it. Dried powdered galangal is available from many supermarkets, but is inferior to fresh.

Garam masala Like Chinese five spice, garam masala is a mixed spice. The quantities and proportions of the spices depend on the food it is to be served with: they generally include black pepper, ground cloves, whole cardamom, cumin, fenugreek and chilli.

Gari Pink ginger served with sushi. The ginger is thinly sliced and marinated in sugar, vinegar and a little red food colouring before use (see Pickled Ginger, page 638).

Ghee Ghee is clarified butter that has had all of its milk solids removed, so that the fat can be used for frying, but without burning.

Ginger Available in powdered, crystallized and preserved forms as well as the fresh root. The root needs to be peeled and is usually grated or chopped before use.

Gobi Fresh ginger.

Gumbo African name for okra, which is the main ingredient in the Creole stew, gumbo.

Horseradish Mainly bought as creamed horseradish, this root, if you are able to buy it fresh, should be peeled and grated. Leftover horseradish can be stored in vinegar in the refrigerator for future use. Horseradish features widely in Scandinavian fish cooking and is a good accompaniment to smoked fish.

Japanese rice The Japanese regard rice with great reverence. It is a pure food and is usually plainly steamed and served with as little adulteration as possible. White or brown Japanese rice is a short-grained rice with a very high starch content, which becomes sticky when cooked. Japan is completely self-sufficient in this staple food.

Kaffir lime This leaf, also called Makrut, comes from a tree of the lime family and is a typical ingredient in many Thai and Indonesian dishes. It has a distinctive flavour and can be found in many supermarkets and specialist grocers.

Krachai Chinese chives.

Lentils The most superior variety is the little green French Puy lentil. They are not always easy to find in the supermarkets and they are the most expensive. Alternatives are the much bigger brown or green lentils. They hold together well during cooking and are ideal for some of the lentil dishes in this book. Yellow and orange lentils purée easily and are therefore ideal for dahls and soups.

Mascarpone A soft cream cheese from Italy with a rich, creamy texture. Traditional cream cheese is an alternative.

Mirin A sweet version of sake. If unavailable, use sugar.

Miso Fermented soya bean sauce. The soup of the same name is made using miso, dashi and kombu.

Nam pla Fermented fish paste, used extensively in Thai food and available from specialist grocers.

Pancetta Italian streaky bacon, which, like British bacon, is available green (unsmoked) or smoked.

Parmesan cheese A hard Italian cheese available ready grated or fresh in a block. At Leith's we always try to use the fresh block, which we grate ourselves; there is a big difference in flavour.

Pastas See page 651.

Pinenuts A traditional ingredient in pesto. An expensive ingredient, as the harvesting is a time-consuming business and occasionally the crop fails. Most supermarkets sell them. They tend to go stale after a few months so avoid buying them in large quantities.

Peppercorns Availability of this seasoning spice includes dried black and white peppercorns, and green and pink varieties, which although available dried, are also sold in brine. Pink peppercorns in particular are thought to bring on palpitations, so should be used with caution. Many supermarkets now sell mixtures of different-coloured peppercorns.

Polenta A fine, rich yellow cornmeal. Most supermarkets stock it, but if you are unable to buy it, semolina can be substituted.

Pulses We use a selection of pulses in our recipes, such as haricot, kidney and aduki beans and chickpeas. Most supermarkets sell all these either dried or in tins. The canned variety are much more convenient, but need to be rinsed thoroughly before use. If you have to use dried, first soak for 6–8 hours, then blanch in plenty of boiling water for 5 minutes, to get rid of the enzymes that can cause flatulence. Drain the beans, then cover with fresh water, bring to the boil and continue to cook until soft, which may take anything from 45 minutes to 2 hours in the case of chickpeas. Make sure that you boil the beans fast for the first 10 minutes of cooking as this kills any enzymes that can cause food poisoning.

Rice vinegar Until recently rice vinegar was available only from specialist foodstores, but it is now catching on and is much more readily available. This is the main vinegar used in Japanese cooking. It is sweet and makes a dressing with a different flavour.

Saffron The most expensive spice on earth, this stamen of the saffron crocus is harvested by hand. Not only does it colour, it has a subtle but distinctive taste which is suited to other subtle flavours. It can be bought in powdered form, which is less expensive, or as strands. The strands need to be soaked in boiling water for 1–2 minutes before use to get the full benefit of the colour and flavour.

Sake Dry Japanese rice wine. If sake is unavailable, use sugar.

Salt In some recipes we specify coarse sea salt, which has a superior taste to table salt.

Shiso A leaf that looks similar to a horse chestnut leaf, used for garnish. Available in Japanese supermarkets. Sometimes known as Japanese basil. The Red Shiso leaf is used as a food colorant.

Shrimp paste Dried shrimps pulverized to a paste, used in Thai and Malaysian food and available from specialist grocers (see Suppliers, page 141).

Sichuan pepper Otherwise known as anise pepper, this is an ingredient of Chinese five spice. It has a pungent aroma not dissimilar to pepper, but is not of the pepper family, but from a type of ash. It is available from specialist food stores. Some recipes suggest roasting first, which should be done in a dry frying pan over a medium heat, until the pepper begins to darken in colour. Do not allow to burn.

Soy sauce As Japanese soy sauce is noticeably more subtle than other oriental soys, it is worth looking out for the Japanese version.

Tahini A sesame seed paste used extensively in Middle Eastern cooking.

Tamarind Sometimes known as the Indian date, this is a dark brown, sticky paste that has a slightly sharp, distinctive but refreshing taste. It is available from specialist food stores, Asian grocers and some supermarkets in the form of a dried paste, which needs to be soaked first. Other acids, such as lemon and vinegar, are sometimes suggested as alternatives, but are not ideal.

Tofu Soy bean curd, of which there are several types, has now become recognized in countries other than the Orient as a high-protein, low-fat food. In Japan it is traditionally cubed and served as a garnish for soups.

Vanilla This is the dried seed pod of an orchid. It has a distinct, strong flavour and is usually associated with sweet dishes. The pods are quite expensive, but a whole one can be cut into smaller pieces.

Wasabi Japanese green horseradish.

SPECIALIST SUPPLIERS AND INFORMATION

For further information about exotic fruits and vegetables
The Education Department
The Royal Botanic Gardens
Kew
Richmond
Surrey TW9 3AB

For purchase of citrus fruits
The Citrus Centre
Marehill Nursery
West Mare Lane
Marehill
Pulborough
West Sussex RH20 2EA

Seed catalogues for keen gardeners
Thompson and Morgan (UK Ltd)
Poplar Lane
Ipswich
Suffolk IP8 3BU
Tel: 01473 688821 (catalogues free)

'The largest illustrated seed catalogue in the world':
Unwin Seeds Ltd
Mail Order Department
Histon
Cambridge
Cambs CB4 4LE

Simpson Seeds
27 Meadow Brook
Old Oxted
Surrey RH8 9LT
Tel: 01883 715 242

HERBS
Many of our recipes call for fresh herbs, including the more exotic ones such as shiso leaves or Japanese basil. If you are unable to find these, it is worth attempting to grow your own.

Mail order companies include:
Cheshire Herbs
Fourfields
Forest Road
Nr Tarporley CW6 9EF
Tel: 01829 760578

Jekka's Herb Farm
Rose Cottage
Shellards Lane
Alveston
Bristol BS12 2SY
Tel: 01454 418878

Suffolk Herbs
Monks Farm
Coggeshall Road
Kelvedon, Essex CO5 9PG
Tel: 01376 572456

For purchase of unusual wild food
Taste of the Wild
For mail order:
Tel: 0171 498 5654
Fax: 0171 498 5419

Specialist ingredients
Leathams plc
114 Camberwell Road
London SE5 0EE
Tel: 0171 703 7031
Specialist French and Italian provisions including dried seaweed.

Heritage Fine Foods Ltd
Lakeside
Bridgewater Road
Barrow Gurney
Nr Bristol BS19 1BA
Tel: 01275 474707
Fax: 01275 474708
This mail order company specializes in wild
salmon and supplies just about anything from
samphire to hand-picked scallops.

Weald Smokery
Mount Farm
Flimwell
East Sussex TN5 7QL
Tel: 01580 879601
Fax: 01580 879564
Mail order company specializing in smoked fish
and shellfish.

WINE INTRODUCTION

by Philippa Carr MW

The sun shining on a June wedding, poached salmon, fresh garden peas and a glass of chilled Chablis – what could be more fitting? Some combinations of food and wine seem so natural that we hardly consider what makes them so. Seasonality certainly would not spring to mind since many classic wines are made to mature over a period of years. How they progress will depend to a great degree on the weather conditions when the grapes were picked, and vintage charts predict when those wines will be ready for drinking and when at their peak. However, other wines also have times when they are at their best and most appealing: in a sense, their season. Most of the wines available nowadays in supermarkets and off-licences are made to be drunk within a year or two of the vintage, with lower tannin for the reds and more upfront fruit in both reds and whites, so those are freshest when first appearing on the shelves.

In the northern hemisphere, and particularly in Northern Europe, grapes are picked in September or October and the first wines, the Nouveaus, are ready for drinking as early as mid-November. Then in January some German wines are released, followed by other light whites at Eastertime. Light red wines leave the cellars in May and heavier reds mature until at least the following year.

In the southern hemisphere the seasons are reversed and grape picking starts in late February – in some countries this can be long and protracted. In Australia the vintage continues until around May times because the wide range of grape varieties ripen at different times in diverse regions. In Chile, however, the period of picking is more concentrated.

Medium-priced Australian whites are bottled in June or July and arrive in the UK in late August and the reds are bottled in the August of the following year to arrive on our shelves in the October.

So in spring and early summer we can choose from inexpensive light reds and whites from Europe, and from late summer the southern hemisphere whites arrive, followed by the reds of the previous year. In the autumn we can enjoy Australian white wines when light European styles are losing their freshness, the Nouveaus arrive in November, whilst a selection of serious, classic wines from both hemispheres are available year round.

Knowing what wines are likely to be most appealing according to season, how do you select a wine to accompany a meal? Whilst there are no longer any firm rules, some guidelines will help to improve the enjoyment of both food and wine.

First, match the body of the dish to that of the wine – a meat dish with a rich sauce will be better served by a very full-bodied, oaky Chardonnay than a light, fruity red.

Second, an acidic wine can make an acidic dish taste less so, and vice versa: lime in a recipe cries out for New Zealand Sauvignon Blanc.

Third, a pudding wine should always be sweeter than the dessert itself, otherwise the combinations will taste metallic and unpleasant.

Beyond these basic suggestions, do not be afraid to experiment: pair food and wine from the same country or region, partner Australian and New Zealand wines with recipes influenced by the cuisine of the Pacific region, watch the supermarket shelves and wine press for new releases, make friends with your local wine merchant or off-licence manager and . . . enjoy.

SPRING
March – April – May

INTRODUCTION

There is palpable excitement in the air as spring fever hits us all. The countryside wakes up and suddenly we notice the longer, warmer days as the clocks go forward. Lambs leaping, tiny green shoots appearing on the trees and thoughts of Easter give hope on days when the weather can still be chilly and damp.

It can be an awkward time of year in the kitchen with little English produce available until the weather becomes warmer, but when winter stretches on it is time to make use of all the pickles and preserves now mature from the previous summer. At these times you can make use of some of the Mediterranean produce which comes into season a little earlier and is widely available in supermarkets, to liven up your menus. Frequently, though, we get a warm spell before Easter which brings forward all the early summer produce and we can enjoy asparagus and cherries long before summer.

Also to be enjoyed at this time are globe artichokes, spring greens and Swiss chard. Jersey Royal new potatoes will arrive in the shops, perfect with the fresh mint growing rapidly now. Tender baby vegetables are delicious to eat and quick to prepare as they only need a quick wash or scrub instead of peeling, cooking much faster than their older winter relatives. Young lamb will be at its most tender and can be roasted with fresh rosemary, always easy to grow in abundance in the garden, garlic and more fresh mint.

In spring we want food to look and taste exciting and with the weather not entirely reliable it needs to be warm, fresh and vibrant. Make use of oriental spices to liven up winter recipes when the weather is cold, but when the sun comes out keep the style simple and enjoy the true natural flavours of the tender meat and vegetables. Fresh ingredients simply prepared will give you the energy needed for the year ahead.

With all seasons starting and finishing at approximate times, you may find yourself jumping ahead to the summer section, or delaying the spring chapter for a while, but when you feel that the time is right and the ingredients have arrived, try some of these recipes – Spiced Wild Garlic Soup (see photo to make sure you know what the leaf looks like), Asparagus with Lemon Sesame Butter, Leek and Olive Beer Bread Tart, and Penne with Chicken Livers and Swiss Chard. For puddings try the Rhubarb Strudel or Elderflower Sorbet and when the occasion requires something more elegant, Spring Mint Parfait.

Celebrate the spring at Easter, a time of new birth and life – not forgetting new and old love on Valentine's Day. Roast lamb is traditional for Easter Sunday, but many enjoy cooking something different, perhaps roast goose. When guests are staying, keep things simple. Leftovers from a large joint can be enjoyed when served with warm home-made bread – fresh mint, onion and garlic naan, for example – and green tomato chutney.

FRUIT AND VEGETABLES IN SEASON

TOP FRUIT	March	April	May
Apricots (Mediterranean)			XXXXXXXXX
Alliums			
Leeks	XXXXXXXXX	XXXXXXXXX	
Spring Onions		XXXXXXXXX	XXXXXXXXX
Welsh Onions	XXXXXXXXX	XXXXXXXXX	XXXXXXXXX
In store: Garlic	XXXXXXXXX	XXXXXXXXX	XXXXXXXXX
Onions	XXXXXXXXX	XXXXXXXXX	XXXXXXXXX
Shallots	XXXXXXXXX	XXXXXXXXX	XXXXXXXXX
BRASSICAS			
Cabbage/Savoys	XXXXXXXXX	XXXXXXXXX	
Kale	XXXXXXXXX	XXXXXXXXX	XXXXXXXXX
Cauliflower	XXXXXXXXX	XXXXXXXXX	XXXXXXXXX
Broccoli	XXXXXXXXX	XXXXXXXXX	
Brussels sprouts	XXXXXXXXX		
Spring greens	XXXXXXXXX	XXXXXXXXX	XXXXXXXXX
Kohlrabi	XXXXXXXXX		
BEANS AND PODS			
Use dried			
LETTUCE/SPINACH			
Spinach	XXXXXXXXX	XXXXXXXXX	
Sea kale	XXXXXXXXX	XXXXXXXXX	XXXXXXXXX
Chicorys if not too cold	XXXXXXXXX		
Autumn sowing lettuces	XXXXXXXXX	XXXXXXXXX	XXXXXXXXX
Lamb's lettuce	XXXXXXXXX	XXXXXXXXX	
Rocket (under cloche)	XXXXXXXXX		
ROOTS AND TUBERS			
Potatoes in store	XXXXXXXXX	XXXXXXXXX	XXXXXXXXX
Parsnips	XXXXXXXXX		
Swede	XXXXXXXXX		
Celeriac	XXXXXXXXX		
Radishes		XXXXXXXXX	XXXXXXXXX
Carrots in store	XXXXXXXXX		
STALKS/SHOOTS			
Asparagus			XXXXXXXXX
Rhubarb	XXXXXXXXX	XXXXXXXXX	XXXXXXXXX
VEGETABLE FRUITS			

148

FRUIT AND VEGETABLES IN SEASON—*contd*

HERBS	March	April	May
Mint		XXXXXXXX	XXXXXXXX
Chives		XXXXXXXX	XXXXXXXX
Sage	XXXXXXXX	XXXXXXXX	XXXXXXXX
Rosemary	XXXXXXXX	XXXXXXXX	XXXXXXXX
Thyme	XXXXXXXX	XXXXXXXX	XXXXXXXX

WILD			
Wild Garlic		XXXXXXXX	XXXXXXXX
Elderflowers			XXXXXXXX

FISH IN SEASON

SALMON FAMILY
Farmed Atlantic and Pacific Salmon
Farmed Trout and Char
Wild Atlantic Salmon
Wild Brown Trout
Wild Rainbow Trout

SHELLFISH
Brown Crab
Spider Crab
Lobster
Dublin Bay Prawn
Crayfish
Prawns (various)
Shrimp
Whelk
Winkle
Cockle
Clam
Mussel
Native Oyster
Pacific Oyster
Scallop (all species)
Sea Urchin
Octopus
Squid

BEST FROM HOME
Monkfish
John Dory
Red Mullet
Sea Bass
Wrasse
Rockfish/Catfish

FLAT FISH
Plaice
Halibut
Lemon Sole
Dab
Flounder
Turbot
Megrim
Witch
Skate

MACKEREL FAMILY
Mackerel
Tuna
Bonito/Wahoo

HERRING FAMILY
Herring
Pilchard/Sardine
Whitebait
Sprat
Shad

COD FAMILY
Haddock
Pollock
Ling
Hake

FIRST COURSES
AND SOUPS

FIRST COURSES

ASPARAGUS WITH LEMON SESAME BUTTER

SERVES 4

675g/1½lb asparagus
salt
20g/¾oz sesame seeds
85g/3oz unsalted butter, softened
lemon juice or balsamic vinegar
freshly ground white pepper
1 small, thick French stick

1. Preheat the oven to 180°C/350°F/gas mark 4.
2. Cut the woody stalks off the ends of the asparagus on the diagonal. Bring a large pan of salted water to the boil.
3. Roast the sesame seeds in the preheated oven for 10–15 minutes, or until golden-brown. Tip them on to a plate to cool.
4. Make the lemon sesame butter: whizz the butter with the cold sesame seeds in a food processor with 1 tablespoon lemon juice, and season to taste with salt and pepper, adding more lemon juice if needed.
5. Put the bread in the oven for 5 minutes. Warm 4 large individual plates.
6. Put the asparagus into the boiling water and simmer gently for 5 minutes, or until just tender. Strain carefully in a large colander.
7. To serve: cut 4 thick slices from the French stick on the diagonal and arrange them on their sides on the plates.
8. Arrange the asparagus spears with their tips leaning on top of the bread. Spoon a dollop of the lemon sesame butter over the tips so that it drips on to the bread as it melts. Serve immediately.

 *SANCERRE*

BAKED FIELD MUSHROOMS WITH TAPENADE

SERVES 4

4 large field mushrooms
4 teaspoons tapenade (see page 633)
1 clove of garlic, crushed
55g/2oz soft goat's cheese
freshly ground black pepper
55g/2oz Parmesan cheese, grated

To garnish
1 teaspoon chopped fresh parsley

1. Preheat the oven to 200°C/400°F/gas mark 6.
2. Wipe the mushrooms with a damp cloth and trim off the stalks.
3. Mix the tapenade with the garlic and goat's cheese and season to taste with pepper.
4. Place the mushrooms gill side up on a baking sheet and spread each one with a quarter of the tapenade.
5. Sprinkle over the Parmesan cheese and bake at the top of the preheated oven for 10–15 minutes, or until tender and golden-brown on top. Sprinkle with the parsley and serve immediately.

 *DOLCETTO D'ALBA*

HUMMUS

SERVES 8

1 × 400g/14oz can of chickpeas, drained
110g/4oz low-fat cottage cheese
1 clove of garlic, crushed
juice of 1 large lemon
4 tablespoons low-fat fromage frais
4 tablespoons extra virgin olive oil
salt and freshly ground black pepper

To serve
2 tablespoons extra virgin olive oil
a few sprigs of fresh flat-leaf parsley
pitta bread, toasted

1. Rinse the chickpeas in cold water and drain thoroughly.
2. Put the chickpeas into a food processor with the cottage cheese, garlic and lemon juice and whizz until the mixture forms a thick purée. Add the fromage frais, oil and plenty of pepper and whizz for a few more seconds. Season with salt and more pepper.
3. Tip the hummus into a bowl, cover and chill for 1 hour.
4. To serve: drizzle over the olive oil, garnish with the parsley and serve with warm, toasted pitta bread.

 WHITE RIOJA

ROCKET RAVIOLI WITH GARLIC AND GOAT'S CHEESE

SERVES 4

1 × 225g/8oz flour quantity rocket pasta II (see page 652)

For the filling
225g/8oz hard mature goat's cheese, grated
1 egg

55g/2oz fresh white breadcrumbs
1 clove of garlic, crushed
2 carrots, peeled, grated, blanched, refreshed and dried on kitchen paper
salt and freshly ground black pepper

To garnish
3 tablespoons extra virgin olive oil
30g/1oz hard goat's cheese, grated
a few fresh rocket leaves

1. Roll out the pasta as thinly as you can, or if using a pasta machine, pass it through on the finest setting. Using a 10cm/4in biscuit cutter, cut out circles of pasta using enough flour to prevent the pasta from sticking. Cover with clingfilm to prevent drying out while making the filling.
2. Mix all the filling ingredients together and season to taste with a little salt and plenty of pepper.
3. Place a large teaspoon of the filling in the centre of each pasta circle, brush the edges with a little water and fold over to create a half-moon shape. Leave the ravioli to dry out on a large tray sprinkled lightly with flour. Turn them over every 10 minutes to prevent them from sticking to the tray.
4. To serve: bring a large saucepan of salted water to the boil, tip in the ravioli and simmer very gently for about 5 minutes, or until the pasta is *al dente*. Drain, toss with the olive oil and season with plenty of pepper.
5. Transfer to a warmed serving dish and garnish with the grated goat's cheese and rocket. Serve immediately.

 ITALIAN RED OR WHITE

SMOKED HADDOCK, WATERCRESS AND GRAPEFRUIT SALAD

SERVES 4

*450g/1lb smoked haddock fillet (preferably
    dyed for the colour)*
½ small onion, sliced
1 bay leaf
a few parsley stalks, crushed
6 black peppercorns
110g/4oz basmati rice
2 pink grapefruit
*1 small bunch of watercress, washed and stalks
    removed*

For the dressing
2 tablespoons white wine vinegar
6 tablespoons olive oil
1 teaspoon English mustard
salt and freshly ground black pepper
lemon juice

1. Preheat the oven to 180°C/350°F/gas mark 4.
2. Place the haddock in a roasting tin, skin side
up, with the onion, bay leaf, parsley stalks and
peppercorns. Pour over cold water to cover the
fillets. Cover the roasting tin with kitchen foil
and bake in the preheated oven for 20 minutes,
or until the skin of the haddock peels off easily.
3. Strain the cooking liquor into a large
saucepan and bring to the boil. Add the rice and
cook for 8–10 minutes, or until just tender.
Drain immediately and allow to steam-dry in
the pan. Set aside to cool.
4. Cut the tops and bottoms off the grapefruit
so that the flesh is exposed. Carve the pith away
from the sides in 2.5cm/1in strips, removing all
the pith. Cut out the segments, leaving the
membrane behind. Squeeze any juice out of the
remaining membrane and reserve it for the
dressing. Remove any pips from the segments if
necessary.
5. Pat the watercress dry on kitchen paper.
6. Make the dressing: place the vinegar, oil and
mustard in a large bowl and whisk together

vigorously. Season to taste with salt, pepper
and lemon juice.
7. Stir the rice into the dressing and check the
seasoning. Skin the haddock fillet and flake it
into large pieces, removing any bones at the
same time. Gently fold the haddock into the rice
with the grapefruit segments and watercress.
8. Divide the salad between 4 individual plates
to serve.

 *SAUVIGNON DE TOURAINE*

WARM SALMON MOUSSELINE WITH SCALLOPS

SERVES 4

*340g/12oz fresh salmon fillet, skinned and
    boned (see page 133)*
1 egg white
salt and freshly ground white pepper
*4 large fresh scallops with coral, cleaned (see
    page 136)*
15g/½oz butter, melted
ice
290ml/½ pint double cream, chilled
ground mace

To serve
1 quantity shellfish butter sauce (see page 239)
a few large sprigs of fresh chervil

1. Preheat the oven to 150°C/300°F/gas mark 2.
2. Whizz the salmon with the egg white, salt
and pepper in a food processor for 30 seconds,
then pass through a fine-meshed drum sieve.
Chill for 30 minutes.
3. Remove the outer membrane and white
muscle from the scallops and separate the coral
from the white flesh, then cut the white flesh in
half horizontally. Chill for 15 minutes.
4. Brush out 4 timbale moulds or ramekins with
the melted butter, place upside down on a tray
and chill for 5 minutes, then brush out with a
second layer of butter.

5. Fill a roasting tin with ice and water. Put the salmon purée into a large metal bowl and set on top of the ice. Gradually beat in the cream with a wooden spoon, slowly at first, then fold in gently with a spatula. Season with salt, pepper and mace.

6. Place a scallop coral in the bottom of each mould and season with salt and pepper. Spoon half the salmon mousseline on top of the corals, then arrange 2 scallop slices on top of each mould. Season with salt and pepper. Spoon the remaining salmon mousseline on top.

7. Fill a roasting tin two-thirds full with boiling water and place the timbales in it. Cover each timbale with a disc of oiled greaseproof paper and bake in the preheated oven for 15 minutes, or until just firm.

8. Remove from the oven and leave to stand for 5 minutes.

9. To serve: carefully turn each mousseline out of its mould on to a fish slice and drain any juices on to some kitchen paper before arranging on the centre of 4 warmed individual plates. Spoon a little shellfish butter sauce around the mousselines and garnish with a few sprigs of chervil.

 *CHABLIS*

WARM SMOKED COD'S ROE BLINIS

SERVES 8

110g/4oz smoked cod's roe
85g/3oz unsalted butter
juice of 1 lemon
freshly ground black pepper
8 quick chive blinis (see page 649)
24 tiger prawns, cooked and peeled

To serve
2 tablespoons chopped fresh chives
8 lemon wedges

1. Scrape the cod's roe out of the skin and put it into a bowl. Add the butter and lemon juice and season with pepper. Beat well together, then

transfer the cod's roe butter on to a piece of clingfilm and roll it up to form a sausage. Chill for 30 minutes.

2. Preheat the oven to 180°C/350°F/gas mark 4.

3. Arrange the blinis in a single layer on 2 baking sheets. Arrange 3 prawns on each blini. Cut 24 thin discs of the smoked cod's roe butter and arrange 3 slices over each blini.

4. Bake the blinis at the top of the preheated oven for 5 minutes, until the butter starts to melt.

5. To serve: sprinkle the blinis with the chives, place 2 on each individual plate and arrange the lemon wedges to one side. Serve immediately.

 TOP-QUALITY AUSTRALIAN OR NEW ZEALAND SPARKLING WINE, PREFERABLY ROSÉ

CRAB, AVOCADO AND BEANSPROUT SALAD

SERVES 4

450g/1lb fresh white crabmeat (see page 134)
2 ripe avocados
340g/12oz beansprouts
juice of 2–3 lemons
few drops of Tabasco sauce
4 tablespoons basic vinaigrette (see page 634)
salt and freshly ground black pepper

To garnish
2 spring onions, sliced on the diagonal

1. Pick over the crabmeat to remove any bits of remaining shell.

2. Cut the avocados in half and remove the stones. Peel off the skin and cut the flesh into 1cm/½in chunks.

3. Put the crabmeat, avocado, beansprouts, lemon juice and Tabasco to taste into a large bowl. Pour over the French dressing, season well with salt and pepper and gently toss the salad together.

4. Pile the salad on to 4 individual plates and garnish with the spring onions. Serve immediately.

 BARSAC OR MONBAZILLAC

KING PRAWNS IN FILO WITH DIPPING SAUCE

SERVES 4

24 raw shell-on king prawns
salt and freshly ground black pepper
juice of 1 lemon
6 sheets of filo pastry
55g/2oz butter, melted
1 egg
oil for deep-frying

For the dipping sauce
170g/6oz granulated sugar
150ml/¼ pint water
75ml/2½ fl oz white wine vinegar
2.5cm/1in piece of fresh root ginger, peeled and
   finely chopped
1 clove of garlic, finely chopped
6 star anise
6 cloves
½ red chilli, finely chopped
2 strips of lemon zest, cut into julienne strips

To garnish
julienne of spring onion

1. Take the heads off the prawns and peel the shell from the body, leaving the tail intact. Make a shallow cut along the back of each prawn and remove the black intestine. Put the prawns into a bowl and season with salt, pepper and lemon juice.
2. Take one sheet of filo and brush all over with melted butter. Cut into 6 strips and wrap each prawn in a filo strip, leaving the tail shell exposed. Repeat with the remaining sheets of filo and prawns.
3. Beat the egg with a pinch of salt and brush the filo parcels lightly on all sides with the glaze. Lay out separately on a large tray ready to deep-fry.
4. Make the dipping sauce: dissolve the sugar in a small pan with the water and vinegar. Simmer for 5 minutes. Add all the remaining ingredients and leave to stand for 30 minutes before serving.

5. Pour the oil into a large pan. It should not be more than one-third full. Heat the oil until a cube of bread will sizzle and brown in 30 seconds.
6. Deep-fry the prawns a few at a time until golden-brown (be careful they do not brown too quickly or the prawns may not be cooked through). Drain on kitchen paper and sprinkle with salt. Garnish with the spring onions and serve immediately with the dipping sauce.

 *GEWÜRZTRAMINER*

SPRING VEGETABLES AND RICE NOODLES WITH SESAME SEED PURÉE

SERVES 4

225g/8oz asparagus spears
225g/8oz baby carrots
225g/8oz sugarsnap peas
12 radishes
340g/12oz rice noodles

For the sesame seed sauce
6 tablespoons sesame seeds
4 tablespoons light soy sauce
4 tablespoons dry sherry
2 tablespoons sesame oil
5cm/2in piece of fresh root ginger, peeled and
   grated
1½ teaspoons chilli powder
3 teaspoons caster sugar
3 tablespoons plum jam
salt and freshly ground black pepper

1. Blanch the vegetables separately in boiling water for 2–3 minutes, or until tender. Drain and refresh under cold running water, set aside.
2. Cook the noodles in boiling water for 1–2 minutes or until tender, drain thoroughly and set aside.
3. Put the sesame seeds into a dry frying pan and shake the pan over a medium heat until the seeds are lightly browned.

4. Transfer the seeds to a blender with all the remaining sauce ingredients and whizz to form a paste.

5. Transfer the paste to a frying pan and bring to the boil.

6. Divide the noodles between 4 plates and spoon the sauce over the top. Arrange the vegetables around the noodles. Serve immediately.

 *CHILEAN PINOT NOIR*

BOILED LOBSTER

SERVES 4

2 × 900g/2lb live lobsters

For the court bouillon
1 litre/1¾ pints water
225g/8oz carrots, sliced
1 medium onion, sliced
1 bay leaf
1 sprig of fresh thyme
30g/1oz salt
150ml/¼ pint white wine vinegar
1 bunch of fresh parsley
10 black peppercorns

To serve hot
hollandaise sauce (see page 633), or melted butter

To serve cold
mayonnaise (see page 632)

1. Combine all the court bouillon ingredients in a saucepan and simmer for 30 minutes.
2. Weigh the lobsters, then put them into the court bouillon.
3. Bring to the boil, cover and simmer for 8 minutes per 450g/1lb. Lift the lobsters out. Allow to cool before splitting if to be served cold.
4. Split the lobsters in half, remove the stomach sac near the head and the intestine, a thin grey or black line running the length of the body.
5. Serve with Hollandaise sauce or melted butter if to be eaten hot, with mayonnaise if cold.

NOTE: A fresh live lobster turns bright red when cooked and the tail tightens considerably.

 *CHABLIS*

DRESSED CRAB

SERVES 3

1 × 900g/2lb live crab

To season
lemon juice
salt and freshly ground black pepper
mustard
fresh white breadcrumbs

To garnish
hardboiled egg yolks, sieved
chopped fresh parsley

To serve
mayonnaise (see page 632)
tartare sauce (see page 632)
brown bread and butter

1. Place the crab in a pan of well-salted water (about 170g/6oz salt to 2.3 litres/4 pints water), cover and bring to the boil. Simmer, allowing 15 minutes per 450g/1lb crab. Remove from the pan and allow to cool.
2. Lay the crab on its back. Twist off the legs and claws. Cracking round the natural line (visible near the edge), remove the pale belly shell and discard it. Remove and throw away the small sac at the top of the crab body and the spongy lungs which line the edge (they look rather like grey fish gills).
3. Have 2 bowls ready, one for white meat, one for brown. Lift out the body of the crab, cut into 2–4 pieces and carefully pick out all the meat that you can. This is fiddly and could take up to 15 minutes. If you have a lobster pick it can be very useful. Wash and dry the shell.
4. Crack the large claws, remove the meat and put it into the white-meat bowl.

5. With a lobster pick or toothpick poke out the remaining meat from the legs, and add it to the white meat in the bowl.

6. Dress the crab: cream the brown meat, season with lemon juice, salt, pepper and mustard. Add enough breadcrumbs to bind the mixture. Arrange this down the centre of the shell and pile the white meat up at each side.

Garnish with neat lines of egg yolk and parsley.

7. Place on a serving plate with the claws. Serve with mayonnaise or tartare sauce and brown bread and butter.

 *LOIRE WHITE*

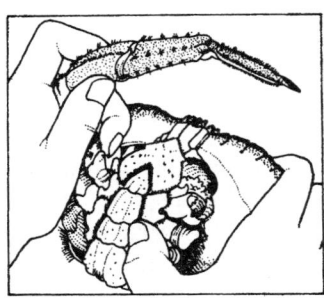 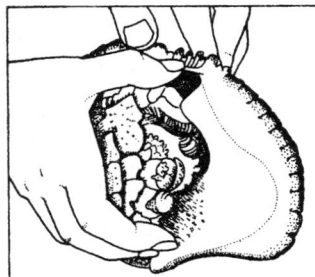 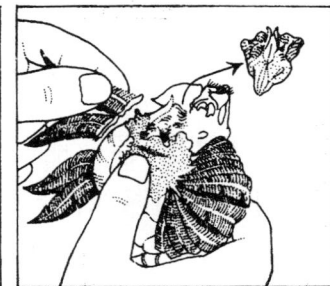

Twist off the legs and claws; remove and throw away the pale belly shell; discard the spongy lungs and small stomach sac

STEAMED DIM SUM

The dim sum in this selection are easy to make. Wonton wrappers and barbecued pork are widely available at Chinese supermarkets.

MAKES 36

36 wonton skins

For the prawn filling
225g/8oz raw tiger prawns, peeled
30g/1oz pork fat, minced (optional)
1 tablespoon dry sherry
1 tablespoon sesame oil
1 tablespoon cornflour
1 teaspoon clear honey or sugar
110g/4oz water chestnuts, finely chopped
1–2 tablespoons finely chopped fresh coriander
salt and freshly ground black pepper

For the pork filling
340g/12oz Chinese barbecued pork
1 tablespoon sesame oil
3 tablespoons soft light brown sugar
5 tablespoons white stock, made with chicken bones (see page 625)
1 tablespoon dark soy sauce
1 tablespoon oyster sauce
1 tablespoon hoisin sauce

2 tablespoons cornflour
½ teaspoon Sichuan peppercorns, roasted and crushed
salt and freshly ground black pepper

For the vegetable filling
1 tablespoon groundnut oil
1 tablespoon sesame oil
1 tablespoon dark soy sauce
1 small carrot, cut into small julienne strips
1 stick of celery, cut into small julienne strips
55g/2oz bamboo shoots, cut into lengths
55g/2oz shiitake mushrooms, thinly sliced
55g/2oz water chestnuts, thinly sliced
2.5cm/1in piece of fresh root ginger, peeled and grated
2 cloves of garlic, crushed
4 spring onions, very thinly sliced
salt and freshly ground black pepper

1. Prepare the fillings. For the prawn filling: peel and de-vein the prawns and chop finely. Mix with all the remaining ingredients, season with salt and pepper and set aside.

2. For the pork filling: chop the barbecued pork finely, mix with all the remaining ingredients, season with salt and pepper and set aside.

3. For the vegetable filling: heat the oils in a large wok, add the soy sauce and vegetables and stir-fry over a high heat until just cooked. Turn on to a plate and allow to cool. Season with salt and pepper.

4. Assemble the dim sum: put a tablespoon of filling on each wonton wrapper, lightly dampen the edges and draw the wrappers together to form a parcel.

5. Lightly grease a steamer (a tier of bamboo steamers is perfect for this), arrange the dim sum in a single layer and steam over a medium heat for 12–15 minutes, or until the dim sum are firm and translucent. Serve warm.

 SOUTH AFRICAN CHARDONNAY

BABY SPRING VEGETABLES WITH ROQUEFORT BUTTER

SERVES 4

225g/8oz baby carrots, scraped
225g/8oz baby turnips, scrubbed
225g/8oz young peas, shelled
8 small spring onions, trimmed
2 tablespoons extra virgin olive oil
225g/8oz baby leaf spinach

For the Roquefort butter
85g/3oz Roquefort cheese, diced
30g/1oz unsalted butter, softened
1 tablespoon chopped fresh mint
freshly ground black pepper

1. Blanch the carrots, turnips, peas and spring onions in boiling water for 2–3 minutes, or until just tender. Drain and refresh under cold running water and set aside.

2. Put the Roquefort cheese and butter into a food processor, add the mint and whizz until the mixture is well combined. Season with pepper.

3. Heat half the oil in a large frying pan until very hot. Add the spinach and cook for 30 seconds, then place on 4 individual plates. Heat the remaining oil, add the blanched vegetables and toss over a high heat for a further few seconds or until very hot. Arrange attractively on top of the spinach. Spoon a large spoonful of the Roquefort butter on top and serve immediately.

 *VALPOLICELLA*

SWEET SUSHI RICE SALAD

SERVES 6

1 quantity sweet vinegar rice (see page 659)
110g/4oz smoked salmon, thinly sliced
½ cucumber, peeled, de-seeded and diced
2 spring onions, thinly sliced
110g/4oz fine asparagus spears, blanched
1 tablespoon capers, rinsed
juice of 1 lemon
salt and freshly ground black pepper

1. Put the rice into a large bowl, add the smoked salmon, cucumber, spring onions, asparagus and capers. Toss together.

2. Add the lemon juice, salt and pepper. Toss together and pile into a serving dish. Chill for 15 minutes, then serve.

SWEET VINEGAR-FLAVOURED BASMATI RICE

Japanese sushi rice can be difficult to find, and Thai and basmati rice are much more readily available. This recipe was given to us by Roz Denny, one of our popular guest demonstrators at Leith's, who is an authority on rice. This method of cooking sushi rice gives a good result, but is a lot less sticky than the authentic Japanese recipe on page 162.

MAKES ENOUGH FOR ABOUT 6–8 ROLLS OF 5 PORTIONS EACH

200g/7oz Thai jasmine or basmati rice
425ml/¾ pint water
2 strips of kombu seaweed

For the dressing
2 tablespoons rice wine vinegar
1½ tablespoons caster sugar
1 teaspoon salt

1. Put the rice, water and kombu into a large saucepan and bring to the boil, then reduce the heat, cover and cook over a slow heat for 12–15 minutes or until the rice has absorbed the moisture and is cooked through.

2. Remove from the heat and allow to stand, covered, for 15 minutes.

3. Tip the rice into a large bowl and remove the kombu. Combine the dressing ingredients, fork into the rice and allow to cool as quickly as possible. Do not chill.

4. Use as required.

NOTE: Kombu is a type of sea kelp. Thick and tough, it is usually used to flavour rice and miso soup, but is removed before serving. It can also help tenderize pulses during cooking.

TRADITIONAL NORI SUSHI ROLLS

Smoked or raw fish can be included in this simple roll as desired.

SERVES 4

2 eggs
1 tablespoon light soy sauce
freshly ground black pepper
1 tablespoon oil
½ cucumber, peeled
4 sheets of nori seaweed
Full quantity sweet vinegar rice (see page 162)

For dipping
3 tablespoons dark soy sauce
1 red chilli, de-seeded and chopped
wasabi paste or powder (see below)

1. Beat the eggs and soy sauce together and season with pepper. Heat the oil in a frying pan, add the egg mixture and cook over a low heat until the egg is cooked and resembles an omelette. Remove from the pan and allow to cool.

2. Cut the cucumber into long pencil lengths. Cut the omelette into strips.

3. Lay a sushi mat or thick napkin on a work surface. Using kitchen scissors, trim the nori to

fit the mat. Pass the nori sheets through a gas flame to toast them. Lay them on the mat and spoon a layer of rice over two-thirds of each sheet up to the edges.

4. Arrange a couple of cucumber and omelette strips on the rice, then roll up firmly as for a Swiss roll, using the sushi mat or napkin to help you. Press the roll well to compress it and allow it to stand for 15 minutes while you make up the rest.

5. Cut each roll crosswise into 5–6 even slices and arrange on a black or dark unpatterned plate.

6. Mix the soy and chilli together and hand separately in a little dish. Hand the wasabi separately too.

NOTES: Nori is a type of sea kelp, typically dried in sheets, toasted and used as a wrap for sushi.

Wasabi – Japanese horseradish – is extremely hot and should be used with caution.

FILLINGS FOR TRADITIONAL SUSHI ROLLS

Prawn and avocado
1 avocado and 8 cooked tiger prawns

Smoked salmon or gravad lax
110g/4oz smoked salmon or gravad lax

Grilled squid
8 cooked squid bodies, sliced

Seared scallops
8 scallops, sliced

SUSHI SELECTION

SWEET VINEGAR RICE

This is the recipe for the rice used in sushi. As with any cooked rice dish, keep refrigerated and eat within 24 hours of cooking.

MAKES ENOUGH FOR 15–20 PIECES OF SUSHI

225g/8oz Japanese sushi short-grain rice
425ml/¾ pint water
1 piece of kombu seaweed
75ml/2½fl oz rice wine vinegar
1 tablespoon caster sugar
2 teaspoons salt

1. Put the rice into a sieve and rinse under cold running water for 1 minute, to remove excess starch.
2. Put into a saucepan, cover with the water, add the kombu and allow to soak for 45 minutes.
3. After the soaking time, cover the saucepan with a well-fitting lid and bring to the boil. Reduce the heat and continue to cook the rice for 10–12 minutes or until cooked through.
4. Meanwhile, put the vinegar into a small saucepan, add the sugar and salt, and heat slowly until dissolved. Remove from the heat and allow to cool.
5. When the rice is cooked, turn it on to a flat plate and remove and discard the kombu.
6. Pour the sweetened vinegar over the rice, toss with a fork and allow to cool. Use as required.

CORNUCOPIAS OF SUSHI

SERVES 2

8 nori seaweed sheets
½ teaspoon wasabi paste (see page 161)
1 quantity sweet vinegar rice (see above)
55g/2oz smoked salmon, finely shredded

To garnish
shiso or fresh coriander

For dipping
3 tablespoons dark soy sauce
1 red chilli, de-seeded and chopped
wasabi paste or powder

1. Cut enough nori sheets to make 8 × 10cm/4in squares. Cut each square in half to make 2 triangles. Pass the nori triangles through a gas flame to toast them.
2. Lay the nori triangles on a chopping board. Spread a tiny amount of wasabi on each piece of nori and spread a thin layer of the sushi rice on top of each piece.
3. Arrange a small piece of smoked salmon on the rice, dampen the edges of the nori with water, then fold each triangle into a cornucopia or cone. Each cone should have rice and fish showing through the top.
4. Arrange the smoked salmon sushi with the other sushi of your choice on an unpatterned serving dish. Garnish with shiso or coriander leaves. Serve with the dipping ingredients as for nori rolls.

NOTE: Shiso – Japanese basil – has leaves similar in shape to nettles. It is used to garnish sashimi and sushi. It has a delicate flavour and there are two main varieties, red and green.

IDEAS FOR FILLINGS FOR CORNUCOPIAS OF SUSHI

Raw or Seared Salmon
110g/4oz salmon steak

Seared Rare Tuna
110g/4oz tuna steak

Tiger prawns
8 cooked prawns

Oysters
8 Pacific oysters

Tofu
110g/4oz tofu

SOUPS

SMOKED HADDOCK AND PEA SOUP

SERVES 4

450g/1lb undyed smoked haddock fillet
570–860ml/1–1½ pints milk
1 onion, thinly sliced
1 bay leaf
6 black peppercorns
a few parsley stalks, crushed
450g/1lb peas, fresh or frozen
juice of 1 lemon
salt and freshly ground black pepper

To serve
4 tablespoons plain yoghurt
1 tablespoon chopped fresh chives

1. Preheat the oven to 180°C/350°F/gas mark 4.
2. Place the haddock in a roasting tin, skin side
up. Pour over the milk and add the onion, bay
leaf, peppercorns and parsley stalks.
3. Cover the roasting tin with kitchen foil and
bake in the centre of the preheated oven for 20
minutes, or until the skin peels off the top of the
fish fillet easily.
4. Strain off the milk, reserving it for later, and
leave the haddock until it is cool enough to
handle. Flake the fish into small pieces,
discarding the skin and bones. Taste the milk
and, if it is very salty, pour half of it away.
5. Pour the fish milk into a heavy-based
saucepan (adding the extra 290ml/½ pint if
necessary) and bring to the boil. Add the peas
and simmer until tender. Liquidize the peas
with the milk until smooth. Stir in the lemon
juice.

6. Return the pea purée to the pan and add the
flaked haddock. Season to taste with a little salt
if needed and pepper. Add extra milk as
required to make the soup the desired
consistency. Check the seasoning and pour into
4 warmed soup bowls. Swirl a tablespoon of
yoghurt and a few chives on each and serve
immediately.

 CHARDONNAY VIN DE PAYS D'OC

SPICED WILD GARLIC SOUP

SERVES 4

225g/8oz wild garlic leaves
225g/8oz spinach, washed and de-stalked
2 tablespoons extra virgin olive oil
1 Spanish onion, finely chopped
55g/2oz long-grain rice
1 teaspoon garam masala
570ml/1 pint white stock, made with chicken
    bones, or vegetable stock (see pages 625 and
    627)
salt and freshly ground black pepper

To serve
4 tablespoons Greek yoghurt
2 teaspoons lemon juice

1. Wash the wild garlic leaves and set aside with
the spinach.
2. Heat the oil in a saucepan, add the onion and
cook over a low heat until soft and transparent.
3. Add the rice and garam masala to the
softened onion and cook for a further 1–2
minutes. Add the garlic and spinach leaves to
the pan with the stock, bring to the boil and

season lightly with salt and pepper. Cover the pan with a lid and cook over a very low heat for 8–10 minutes, or until the rice is cooked and the leaves are wilted and soft.

4. Put the contents of the pan into a blender and whizz to form a purée. Return to the rinsed-out pan and season to taste with salt and pepper. If the soup is a little thick, dilute it with a little water.

5. To serve: ladle into 4 warmed soup bowls. Swirl a spoonful of the Greek yoghurt on each bowl and sprinkle with a little lemon juice. Serve immediately.

 *CHILEAN PINOT NOIR*

SHELLFISH AND SOBA NOODLE BROTH

SERVES 4

225g/8oz raw shell-on tiger prawns
225g/8oz live mussels
225g/8oz fresh or frozen squid
1 tablespoon sunflower oil
1 clove of garlic, bruised
2.5cm/1in piece of fresh ginger root, unpeeled and chopped
1 red chilli, halved and de-seeded
1 litre/1¾ pints shellfish stock (see page 627)
5 tablespoons mirin
1 tablespoon rice wine vinegar
110g/4oz soba noodles
4 spring onions, thinly sliced
1–2 tablespoons light soy sauce

1. Peel and de-vein the prawns. Reserve the shells. Scrub the mussels and discard any that are cracked and do not shut when sharply tapped. Clean the squid (see page 135).

2. Heat the oil in a large saucepan, add the prawn shells, garlic, ginger and chilli and cook over a low heat for 3–4 minutes. Add the shellfish stock, mirin and rice wine vinegar. Bring to the boil, then simmer for 30 minutes. Strain.

3. Meanwhile, cook the noodles in plenty of

boiling water for 12 minutes. Drain and cut into 7.5cm/3in lengths. Set aside.

4. Return the strained stock to a clean saucepan, add the prawns and mussels, bring to the boil and cook over a low heat until the prawns are pink and the mussels begin to open. Add the squid and spring onions and cook for a further 30 seconds.

5. Add the noodles and soy sauce to the broth and serve in a warmed tureen. Discard any mussels that remain shut.

NOTES: Mirin is a sweet version of sake, Japanese rice wine. If unavailable, use sugar instead.

Soba noodles are long thin noodles made from buckwheat flour.

 NEW ZEALAND SAUVIGNON BLANC

SPRING LOVAGE AND JERUSALEM ARTICHOKE SOUP

SERVES 4

450g/1lb Jerusalem artichokes, peeled
720ml/1¼ pints white stock, made with chicken bones (see page 625)
4 cloves of garlic, peeled and sliced
1 tablespoon rice wine vinegar
salt and freshly ground black pepper
2 tablespoons chopped young fresh lovage leaves
150ml/¼ pint double cream

1. Slice the artichokes thinly. Bring the chicken stock to the boil in a large saucepan, add the artichokes, garlic and vinegar and cook for 30–40 minutes, or until the artichokes are completely tender.

2. Liquidize the cooked artichokes until smooth, then return to the rinsed-out pan. Season the purée to taste with salt and pepper and add the lovage and double cream. Bring slowly to the boil, check the seasoning and serve immediately in 4 warmed soup bowls.

 VERY YOUNG MIDI ROSÉ

CLEAR CRAYFISH BOUILLON WITH SPRING LOVAGE

SERVES 4

450g/1lb live crayfish
1 tablespoon olive oil
1 small bulb of Florence fennel, sliced
6 spring onions, sliced
2 cloves of garlic, chopped
2 small carrots, peeled and sliced
1.7 litres/3 pints shellfish stock (see page 627)
1 teaspoon tomato purée
5 tablespoons dry white wine
5 tablespoons red wine
3 tablespoons port
1 sprig of fresh rosemary
1 bouquet garni
10 black peppercorns

To clarify the bouillon
2 egg whites
2 egg shells, washed and crushed

To serve
sprigs of fresh spring lovage

1. Put the live crayfish into the freezer for 1–1½ hours. Do not allow to freeze solid.

2. Place the chilled crayfish in a saucepan of well-salted, boiling water, bring back to the boil and simmer for 2–3 minutes. Drain and cool.

3. Shell the crayfish by removing the claws and pulling off the body shell. Reserve the shells for the bouillon. De-vein the body meat and set aside.

4. Heat the oil in a large saucepan, add the fennel, spring onions, garlic and carrots and fry over a medium heat until lightly browned. Add the crayfish shells and fry for a further 1–2 minutes. Add the shellfish stock, tomato purée, wines, port, herbs and peppercorns. Bring to the boil, then lower the heat and poach for 30 minutes, skimming from time to time.

5. Strain the bouillon and allow to cool. Season to taste with salt and pepper.

6. To clarify the bouillon: put the bouillon into a large saucepan and set over a low heat. Put the crushed egg shells into a bowl, add the egg whites and whisk until frothy. Pour into the warming stock and keep whisking steadily (preferably with a balloon whisk) until a crust begins to form. Allow the mixture to come just to the boil. Stop whisking immediately and remove the pan from the heat. Allow the mixture to subside. Take care not to break the crust formed by the egg white. Cool for 2 minutes.

7. Bring the bouillon up to the boil again, then allow to subside again. Cool for 5 minutes.

8. Strain the bouillon through a double layer of fine scalded muslin over a clean saucepan; do not hurry the process by squeezing the cloth. When strained, discard the egg white 'filter'.

9. Heat the bouillon, add the crayfish meat and small sprigs of spring lovage. Season with salt if necessary and serve.

NOTE: Live crayfish are not always easy to find. The alternative is to use langoustines (Dublin Bay prawns) which are usually readily available shell-on, raw and frozen.

 AMONTILLADO SHERRY

MAIN COURSES

Fish and Shellfish
Poultry and Game
Beef
Lamb
Pork
Veal
Offal
Vegetarian

FISH AND SHELLFISH

HOT POACHED MONKFISH WITH SAGE BUTTERED NOODLES

SERVES 4

4 × 170g/6oz pieces of monkfish fillet, skinned
1 litre/1¾ pints court bouillon (see page 626)
225g/8oz pappardelle (wide ribbon noodles)
salt
85g/3oz butter
freshly ground black pepper
2–3 tablespoons chopped fresh sage
1 clove of garlic, crushed
juice of 1 lemon

To serve
4 sprigs of fresh sage
4 lemon wedges

1. Preheat the oven to 140°C/275°F/gas mark 1.
2. Trim the monkfish fillets of any remaining white cartilage or grey membrane.
3. Place the monkfish in a large sauté pan and pour over the cold court bouillon. Gently poach the fillets for 10 minutes, or until opaque. Turn off the heat.
4. Boil the pasta in salted water until just tender, drain and stir in 30g/1oz of the butter. Season with plenty of pepper. Pile the pasta on to a large serving dish and cover with wet greaseproof paper. Keep warm in the oven while finishing the monkfish.
5. Remove the fillets from the court bouillon with a slotted spoon and drain on kitchen paper. Place the fillets on the pasta.
6. Melt the remaining butter in a frying pan. When foaming, quickly add the sage and garlic

and season with salt and pepper. Turn off the heat and pour in the lemon juice. Swirl the juice around the pan and pour immediately over the monkfish fillets. Garnish with the sprigs of sage and lemon wedges before serving immediately.

NOTE: This recipe is good made using fresh lobster. Poach the lobster for 8 minutes per 450g/1lb and follow the recipe as for monkfish.

 CHABLIS PREMIER CRU

INDIAN SPICED MONKFISH DOLMADES WITH A WARM CAPER AND RED ONION VINAIGRETTE

SERVES 4

For the dolmades
675g/1½lb monkfish fillet, skinned
200g/7oz long-grain rice, cooked
salt
6 cardamom pods, cracked
3 tablespoons olive oil
1 onion, finely chopped
1 clove of garlic
1 teaspoon peeled and grated fresh root ginger
1 tablespoon chopped fresh coriander
1 teaspoon soft dark brown sugar
1 teaspoon ground turmeric
½ teaspoon cumin seeds
100ml/3½fl oz plain yoghurt
juice of 1 lemon

freshly ground black pepper
1 packet of 12 vine leaves in brine
290ml/½ pint dry white wine

For the vinaigrette
3 tablespoons red wine vinegar
9 tablespoons extra virgin olive oil
½ red onion, finely chopped
2 tablespoons capers, rinsed
1 tablespoon lemon juice

1. Preheat the oven to 180°C/350°F/gas mark 4.
2. Cut the monkfish into 1cm/½in cubes.
3. Boil the rice in plenty of salted water with the cardamom pods until *al dente*. Drain well and leave to steam-dry. Remove the cardamom pods.
4. Heat 1 tablespoon of the olive oil in a frying pan, add the onion and cook over a low heat for 20 minutes, or until soft. Add the garlic, ginger, coriander, sugar, turmeric and cumin seeds and stir over the heat for 1 further minute. Remove from the heat and allow to cool. Stir in the monkfish.
5. Mix the monkfish with the rice, yoghurt and lemon juice and season to taste with salt and pepper.
6. Simmer the vine leaves in a large pan of boiling water for 15 minutes. Drain and refresh under cold running water, drain again and pat dry on kitchen paper.
7. Place a spoonful of the monkfish mixture in the centre of each vine leaf and wrap up to form a sausage shape. Repeat with all the vine leaves.
8. Arrange the dolmades in a casserole dish, and pour over the wine and the remaining olive oil. Cover and bake in the preheated oven for 30 minutes.
Make the vinaigrette:
9. Mix all the ingredients together in a small pan and bring to the boil. Simmer for 2 minutes and keep warm.
10. Arrange 3 dolmades on each of 4 individual plates and spoon over the vinaigrette.

 *VIOGNIER VIN DE PAYS D'OC OR BEER*

CRISP PLAICE FILLETS STUFFED WITH BROCCOLI AND CHEESE

SERVES 4

16 × 85g/3oz single plaice fillets, skinned (see page 133)
salt and freshly ground black pepper

For the stuffing
225g/8oz broccoli florets, blanched and refreshed
45g/1½oz butter
45g/1½oz plain flour
a pinch of cayenne pepper
a pinch of dry English mustard
290ml/½ pint milk
110g/4oz strong Cheddar cheese, grated

For the coating
seasoned plain flour (see page 637)
2–3 eggs, beaten with a pinch of salt
225g/8oz dry white breadcrumbs
oil for frying

To garnish
4 lemon wedges
4 sprigs of fresh flat-leaf parsley

1. Season the plaice fillets with salt and pepper and chill.
2. Make the stuffing: dry the broccoli well on kitchen paper and chop it up into small pieces.
3. Melt the butter in a small heavy-based saucepan and add the flour, cayenne and mustard. Stir over a low heat for 1 minute.
4. Add the milk and stir continuously until the sauce thickens and comes to the boil. Turn off the heat and stir in the cheese. Season well with salt and pepper. Pour the sauce into a deep plate to cool.
5. Gently stir the broccoli into the thick cheese sauce and check the seasoning.
6. Take half the plaice fillets and lay them bone side down on a flat surface. Divide the broccoli and cheese stuffing between them and spread it evenly over the fillets. Cover with the remaining fillets. Chill for 30 minutes.

7. Preheat the oven to 140°C/275°F/gas mark 1.

8. Put the seasoned flour, beaten eggs and breadcrumbs into separate shallow trays.

9. Dip the fillets into the flour and shake off the excess. Then dip them in the egg and finally into the crumbs, making sure they are all evenly coated. Chill for 30 minutes.

10. Heat 2.5cm/1in oil in a large sauté pan until a breadcrumb browns instantly. Carefully lower one or two sandwiched fillets (depending on the size of the pan) at a time into the oil. When they are brown on the underside, carefully turn them over, using a palette knife and fish slice. Brown them on the second side, then lift them out carefully, drain them on kitchen paper and sprinkle with salt to absorb excess oil.

11. Place the cooked fillets on a baking sheet in the warm oven while the remaining fillets are being cooked.

12. Serve the fillets on warmed individual plates and garnish with lemon wedges and parsley.

 CÔTE D'OR WHITE BURGUNDY OR ALSACE PINOT BLANC

GLAZED RARE SALMON WITH ASPARAGUS

Wild salmon and young asparagus are both ingredients that are in season in late spring, and there are several classic recipes that combine the two. Wild salmon can be very expensive – good-quality farmed fish is perfectly acceptable instead.

SERVES 4

4 × 170g/6oz salmon fillets

For the cure
2 tablespoons soft light brown sugar
2 tablespoons coarse sea salt
1 tablespoon white peppercorns, crushed

8 young asparagus spears, blanched
2-egg quantity hollandaise sauce (see page 633)
2 teaspoons chopped fresh chives

To serve
4 handfuls of young salad leaves, washed

1. Pinbone the salmon fillets but do not skin them (see page 133). Mix together the sugar, salt and peppercorns. Put half this mixture in the bottom of a large dish. Place the salmon fillets on top of the cure and cover with the remainder. Cover tightly and refrigerate for 4–6 hours.

2. Remove the salmon from the cure, clean off any excess and pat the fish dry with kitchen paper.

3. Preheat the grill and place a sheet of well-buttered kitchen foil on top of the grilling tray. Place the salmon fillets, skin side uppermost, on the foil and grill for 1 minute.

4. Remove the salmon skin and turn the fillets over. Grill on the second side for 1 further minute.

5. Arrange 2 asparagus spears on each salmon fillet and spoon a little hollandaise over each. Sprinkle with the chives. Grill for a further 20–30 seconds, or until lightly browned.

6. Divide the salad leaves between 4 individual plates and arrange a salmon fillet on each. Serve immediately.

 *SOUTH AFRICAN CHARDONNAY*

SALMON, FENNEL AND WILD RICE GALETTE

This is suitable for a summer buffet.

SERVES 4

340g/12oz quantity pâte à pâté (see page 645)
340g/12oz salmon fillet, pinboned (see page 133)
5 tablespoons white wine
1 bay leaf
3–4 sprigs of fresh fennel
1 medium bulb of Florence fennel
15g/½oz butter
85g/3oz wild rice, cooked
85g/3oz basmati rice, cooked
55g/2oz pinenuts, toasted
2 tablespoons sultanas
1 egg, beaten
salt and freshly ground black pepper

171

1. Roll the pastry out into 2 circles, one about 25cm/10in in diameter, the second slightly larger. Chill for 20 minutes.

2. Preheat the oven to 190°C/375°F/gas mark 5.

3. Put the smaller of the two circles on to a baking sheet, prick all over with a fork. Bake in the preheated oven for 15 minutes, or until lightly brown and crisp. Leave to cool on a wire rack.

4. Put the salmon into an ovenproof dish, pour over the wine, add the bay leaf, sprigs of fresh fennel and cover with lightly buttered greaseproof paper. Bake in the preheated oven for 12–15 minutes, or until just cooked. Lift the salmon from the cooking liquor, remove the skin and any bones and break into large flakes. Allow to cool.

5. Slice the fennel very thinly and blanch in boiling water for 1 minute, then drain and refresh under cold running water. Melt the butter in a saucepan, add the fennel and cook over a low heat for 5–7 minutes, or until beginning to brown. Tip into a bowl and allow to cool.

6. Add the rice, pinenuts and sultanas to the fennel, add a little beaten egg to bind, and season to taste with salt and pepper. Scatter half this mixture over the baked pastry, leaving a good 1cm/½in clear all round the edge.

7. Arrange the salmon flakes over the rice and pile the remaining rice on top. Season with salt and pepper. Wet the edge of the bottom piece of pastry with beaten egg and put the top circle of pastry in place, pressing the edges to seal it well.

8. Use any pastry trimmings to decorate the pie and brush all over with beaten egg.

9. Bake in the preheated oven for 25–30 minutes, or until the pastry is crisp and pale brown. Serve hot or cold.

 *WHITE BURGUNDY*

LEMON SOLE WITH CHICORY AND BABY BEETROOT

SERVES 4

12 baby beetroots, washed and trimmed
salt
2 heads of chicory
3 × 675g/1½lb lemon sole, filleted and skinned (see page 132)
seasoned plain flour (see page 637)
85g/3oz unsalted butter
grated zest of 1 orange
freshly ground black pepper
juice of 2 lemons

To garnish
4 lemon wedges

1. Preheat the oven to 140°C/275°F/gas mark 1.

2. Boil the beetroots in salted water for 15 minutes, or until tender. Drain and refresh under cold running water. Scrape off the outer skin and trim off the roots. Cut the stalks off to ½cm/¼in.

3. Separate the chicory into individual leaves. Wash them well and cut them into 5cm/2in pieces, leaving the small inner leaves whole.

4. Dip the lemon sole fillets in seasoned flour. Lay them on a plate but do not allow them to touch each other or they will become soggy.

5. Heat 15g/½oz of the butter in a heavy-based saucepan. Add the orange zest and beetroot and cook for a few minutes to reheat them. Season well with salt and pepper.

6. Heat a little more butter in a frying pan. When foaming, put in a batch of sole fillets. Fry them for about 1 minute until golden-brown, then turn them and transfer to an ovenproof dish. Keep these fillets warm in the oven. Fry the remaining fillets in the same way.

7. When all the fillets are cooked, add a little more butter to the pan. When foaming, add the chicory and fry over a high heat for 1 minute, just until they start to colour. Season with salt and pepper. Turn off the heat and pour in the lemon juice.

8. Immediately divide the chicory between 4 warmed individual plates. Arrange the sole fillets on top and garnish with the beetroot and lemon wedges.

 CALIFORNIAN FUMÉ BLANC

ROAST TUNA LOIN MARINATED WITH CHILLI AND LIME

SERVES 6

1.2–1.35kg/2.5–3lb fresh tuna loin, skinned (see page 133)
1 tablespoon olive oil

For the marinade
1 teaspoon chilli flakes
grated zest and juice of 2 limes
3 tablespoons demerara sugar
8 tablespoons medium sherry
2 tablespoons soy sauce
8 tablespoons olive oil
salt and freshly ground black pepper

To garnish
2 limes cut into wedges

To serve
1 quantity beet greens and sesame rice timbales (see page 204)

1. Put the tuna into a large bowl. Combine all the marinade ingredients and add to the bowl. Turn the tuna over to make sure it is well coated and chill for 1 hour, turning the tuna over in the marinade after 30 minutes.
2. Preheat the oven to 200°C/400°F/gas mark 6.
3. Drain the tuna, reserving the marinade.
4. Heat the oil in a small roasting tin. Put the tuna in the pan on one side and cook over a high heat until golden-brown. Turn the tuna over on to another side and continue until all the sides are seared, adding a little more oil if necessary. (This should only take a few minutes.)

5. Pour the marinade over the tuna and place in the top of the preheated oven. Cook for 10 minutes per 450g/1lb (about 20–30 minutes), basting frequently.
6. To test if the tuna is done, insert a metal skewer into the centre of the loin and leave it for 10 seconds. Pull the skewer out and if it feels warm the tuna is cooked.
7. Transfer the tuna to another plate, cover with kitchen foil and allow to rest for 10 minutes before carving. Taste the juices in the tin and if necessary boil rapidly to a sticky, syrupy consistency.
8. Carve the tuna into slices and arrange on 6 warmed individual plates. Spoon over the marinade and garnish with the lime wedges. Serve with beet greens and sesame rice timbales.

 TOP-QUALITY NEW ZEALAND SAUVIGNON BLANC

SUGAR-MARINATED TUNA WITH SPRING GREENS

SERVES 4

4 × 170g/6oz tuna steaks, skinned (see page 133)
2 tablespoons olive oil

For the marinade
2 tablespoons soft light brown sugar
2 tablespoons dark soy sauce
1 tablespoon treacle
1 tablespoon sherry
1 teaspoon Sichuan peppercorns, roasted and ground

For the spring greens
675g/1½lb spring greens, washed and tough stalks removed
3 tablespoons sesame oil
1 tablespoon light soy sauce
freshly ground black pepper

1. Place the tuna steaks in a shallow dish. Mix

together the marinade ingredients. Pour over the tuna steaks and turn them in the marinade so that they are well coated. Cover and refrigerate for 1 hour.

2. Tear the spring greens into large bite-sized pieces. Wash again and dry thoroughly.

3. Heat the sesame oil in a large wok, add the spring greens and stir-fry over a very high heat until wilted. Add the soy sauce and season with pepper. Set aside and keep warm.

4. Brush a frying pan with the olive oil and heat until smoking hot.

5. Add the tuna steaks, 2 at a time, and fry on both sides for 1–2 minutes, or until very well browned.

6. Divide the spring greens between 4 warmed individual plates. Arrange a tuna steak on the top of each. Serve very hot.

 *CHILEAN PINOT NOIR*

LEMON AND PRAWN RISOTTO

SERVES 4

900g/2lb cooked shell-on prawns
1.75 litres/3 pints water
100ml/3½fl oz dry white wine
freshly ground black pepper
1 bouquet garni
110g/4oz unsalted butter
1 large onion, finely chopped
grated zest of 2 lemons
2 cloves of garlic, crushed
400g/14oz risotto (arborio) rice
salt and freshly ground black pepper
juice of 1 lemon
55g/2oz Parmesan cheese, freshly grated
2 tablespoons chopped fresh chives

1. Peel all the prawns and reserve. Put the shells into a saucepan with the water, wine, pepper and bouquet garni. Bring to the boil, then lower the heat and simmer for 15 minutes. Strain and reserve the liquor. Put the stock back into the saucepan and keep hot. Allow to simmer gently.

2. Meanwhile, melt the butter in a large saucepan, add the onion and cook over a low heat until soft and lightly coloured. Add the lemon zest and garlic and continue to cook for a further 1–2 minutes.

3. Add the rice to the pan with one ladleful of the stock, cook until the stock is absorbed (about 3 minutes), then lower the heat and continue to cook, stirring gently and continuously.

4. Continue to add the hot stock to the rice a little at a time, stirring gently. Allow the stock to become absorbed after each addition. Keep stirring constantly. Season with salt and pepper, and keep adding the stock until the rice is cooked but still *al dente* (about 30 minutes).

5. Remove the pan from the heat, add the prawns, lemon juice, Parmesan cheese and chives and mix well with a wooden spoon until the prawns are very hot and the cheese is absorbed. Serve immediately, with additional grated Parmesan cheese handed separately if desired.

 *SANCERRE*

ORIENTAL FILO PARCELS WITH SPRING GREENS AND CRISP CARROTS

SERVES 4

8 tiger prawns, cooked, peeled and de-veined
340g/12oz salmon fillet, skinned and cut into
*   1.5cm/¾in cubes (see page 133)*
3 tablespoons medium sherry
2 tablespoons light soy sauce
1cm/½in piece of fresh root ginger, peeled and
*   grated*
1 clove of garlic, crushed
2 spring onions, thinly sliced
freshly ground black pepper
8 × 20cm/8in squares of filo pastry
6 tablespoons sesame oil
30g/1oz butter, melted

For the spring greens and crisp carrots
450g/1lb spring greens, washed and tough
  stalks removed
oil for deep-frying
2 tablespoons olive oil
salt and freshly ground black pepper
1 tablespoon sesame seeds, toasted
1 large carrot, peeled and cut into julienne strips
seasoned plain flour (see page 637)

1. Mix the prawns and salmon in a bowl with the sherry, soy sauce, ginger, garlic and spring onions. Season with pepper and leave, covered, to marinate for 20 minutes.
2. Preheat the oven to 200°C/400°F/gas mark 6.
3. Lay a square of filo pastry on a flat surface. Brush completely with sesame oil and place a second square on top. Brush again with sesame oil.
4. Pile one-quarter of the fish mixture on to the centre of the pastry and gather up the edges to form a pouch. Make 3 further parcels with the remaining ingredients.
5. Place the parcels on a baking sheet and brush all over with melted butter. Bake in the centre of the preheated oven for 15 minutes, or until golden-brown all over.
6. Finely shred the spring greens by layering the leaves together and rolling them into a cigar shape.
7. Preheat the deep-frying oil to a high setting.
8. Heat the olive oil in a wok and stir-fry the greens until they are just starting to wilt. Season well with salt and pepper and sprinkle in the sesame seeds.
9. Toss the carrot in the seasoned flour, tip into a sieve and shake off the excess. Deep-fry the carrots until just starting to turn golden. Drain and allow to dry on kitchen paper sprinkled with salt.
10. To serve: place a pile of spring greens on each of 4 warmed individual plates and place a filo parcel on top, sprinkling the crisp carrots attractively around.

*DRY ALSACE OR AUSTRALIAN
RIESLING*

LANGOUSTINE AND MUSSEL RISOTTO

SERVES 4

16 fresh langoustines
30g/1oz butter, melted
salt and freshly ground black pepper
900g/2lb fresh mussels, scrubbed
150ml/¼ pint dry white wine
1 onion, finely chopped
55g/2oz butter
3 shallots, finely chopped
400g/14oz risotto (arborio) rice
1.5 litres/2½ pints shellfish stock (see page 627)
  using langoustine shells
juice of 1 lemon
85g/3oz Parmesan cheese, freshly grated
30g/1oz unsalted butter
2 tablespoons chopped fresh parsley

To garnish
2 tablespoons freshly grated Parmesan cheese
4 sprigs of fresh flat-leaf parsley

1. Preheat the oven to 230°C/450°F/gas mark 8.
2. Place the langoustines in a large roasting tin, brush with melted butter and season with salt and pepper. Roast at the top of the preheated oven for 10 minutes, or until the shells have turned a brighter pink. Allow to cool.
3. Take the langoustines out of their shells and chill.
4. Check over the mussels and throw away any that are open.
5. Put the wine and onion into a large saucepan, bring to the boil and simmer for 2 minutes. Add the mussels, cover and steam for 5 minutes, stirring them from time to time, until the shells are open.
6. Place a large colander over a bowl and tip in the mussels, reserving the juices in the bowl. When the mussels are cool, remove, discard the shells, and chill until needed.
7. Melt the butter in a large saucepan and gently cook the shallots until soft but not coloured. Add the rice and cook for 1 minute.
8. Meanwhile, heat the shellfish stock with the mussel liquor in a second pan.

9. Start adding the hot stock to the rice a little at a time, stirring gently. Allow the stock to become absorbed after each addition. Keep stirring constantly. Season with salt and pepper and continue to add the stock until the rice is cooked but still *al dente* (about 30 minutes).
10. Add the langoustines and mussels to the risotto and season again, adding the lemon juice.
11. Stir in the Parmesan cheese, unsalted butter and parsley.
12. To serve: pile into 4 warmed shallow soup plates, sprinkle with the extra Parmesan cheese and add a parsley sprig to each serving.

 CHABLIS PREMIER CRU

LOBSTER, LEEK AND CHIVE TART

SERVES 4

170g/6oz rich shortcrust pastry (see page 642)
30g/1oz butter
450g/1lb young tender leeks, washed, trimmed and very thinly sliced
4 egg yolks
290ml/½ pint double cream
225g/8oz cooked lobster meat, chopped
2 tablespoons chopped fresh chives
Tabasco sauce
salt and freshly ground black pepper
1 tablespoon freshly grated Parmesan cheese

1. Preheat the oven to 200°C/400°F/gas mark 6.
2. Roll out the pastry and use to line a 20cm/8in loose-based flan ring. Chill for 20 minutes to relax – this prevents shrinkage during baking.
3. Melt the butter in a large pan, add the leeks, cover and cook over a very low heat until soft but not coloured. Transfer to a large bowl to cool.
4. Bake the pastry blind (see page 640), then reduce the oven temperature to 170°C/325°F/gas mark 3.
5. Add the egg yolks, cream, lobster and chives to the leeks and season to taste with a little

Tabasco, salt and pepper. Pour into the prepared flan case and spread the lobster and leek about evenly. Sprinkle with the Parmesan cheese.
6. Place the flan near the bottom of the oven and cook for 20–30 minutes, or until just set.

 *CHABLIS OR SINGLE VINEYARD MOSEL SPÄTLESE*

POULTRY AND GAME

ROAST CHICKEN WITH LEEKS AND YOGHURT

SERVES 4

1 × 1.35kg/3lb chicken, jointed into 4 (see page
   126)
2 teaspoons medium curry paste
150ml/¼ pint plain yoghurt
1 clove of garlic, crushed
freshly ground black pepper
4 large leeks, washed and thinly sliced
30g/1oz butter
salt

To serve
30g/1oz flaked almonds, lightly toasted
a few sprigs of fresh coriander
1 quantity fresh cucumber and mango chutney
   (see page 235)
150ml/¼ pint plain yoghurt

1. Put the chicken into a bowl. Smear the curry
paste over the 4 pieces and stir in the yoghurt
and garlic. Season with pepper, cover and
refrigerate for 2 hours, turning the chicken from
time to time.
2. Preheat the oven to 200°C/400°F/gas mark 6.
3. Cook the leeks in the butter in a heavy-based
saucepan over a low heat until they are soft, but
not brown. Season with salt and pepper and tip
them into the bottom of a shallow casserole
dish.
4. Arrange the chicken pieces over the top of the
leeks in a single layer, skin side up.
5. Roast the chicken near the top of the
preheated oven for 45–50 minutes, or until the
chicken is golden-brown and tender.

6. Sprinkle over the toasted almonds and
coriander and serve with the fresh cucumber
and mango chutney and plain yoghurt.

 SOUTH AFRICAN CHENIN BLANC

ROAST CHICKEN WITH WILD GARLIC

SERVES 4

1 × 1.35kg/3lb roasting chicken
1 small bunch of wild garlic leaves
thinly pared zest of 1 lemon
30g/1oz butter
salt and freshly ground black pepper
5 tablespoons white stock, made with chicken
   bones (see page 625)
5 tablespoons dry white wine

For the gravy
150ml/¼ pint white stock, made with chicken
   bones (see page 625)
1 teaspoon arrowroot
2 teaspoons water

1. Preheat the oven to 200°C/400°F/gas mark 6.
2. Singe the chicken with a flame and remove
any small feathers.
3. Wash the garlic leaves and put into the cavity
of the chicken with the lemon zest, a little of the
butter and some salt and pepper. Rub the
remaining butter over the breast of the chicken
and season with more salt and pepper.
4. Put the stock and wine into a roasting tin and
sit the chicken in the liquid, breast side up.
Roast in the preheated oven for 1–1¼ hours,

basting frequently, or until the chicken is cooked (the juices should run clear when the thigh is pierced).

5. Lift the chicken from the roasting tin and keep it warm for 10 minutes.

6. Skim off any fat from the cooking juices left in the roasting tin. Add the remaining stock, bring to the boil and simmer for 5 minutes. Slake the arrowroot with the water, add to the boiling liquid and bring back to the boil. Season to taste with salt and pepper and strain into a gravy boat.

7. Carve or joint the chicken and serve with the gravy.

 *CHILEAN PINOT NOIR*

BAKED CHICKEN WITH RED ONIONS AND BLACK OLIVES

SERVES 4

1 × 1.6kg/3½lb chicken
2 red onions, cut into thick wedges
2 cloves of garlic, crushed
55g/2oz Kalamata olives
375ml/½ bottle red wine
1 bouquet garni
4 tablespoons extra virgin olive oil
110g/4oz field mushrooms, quartered
30g/1oz plain flour
1 tablespoon soft dark brown sugar
salt and freshly ground black pepper

To garnish
a few sprigs of fresh flat-leaf parsley

1. Joint the chicken into 8 pieces (see page 126).

2. Put the chicken pieces into a non-metallic bowl and add the onions, garlic, olives, red wine and bouquet garni. Cover and leave to marinate in the refrigerator overnight, turning the chicken from time to time. Strain the marinade out of the bowl and reserve. Remove the chicken.

3. Preheat the oven to 220°C/425°F/gas mark 7.

4. Heat 2 tablespoons of the oil in a frying pan,

add the marinated onions, olives and bouquet garni and fry until golden-brown. Tip into a large, shallow roasting tin.

5. Heat the remaining oil in the frying pan, add the mushrooms and fry until golden-brown. Lower the heat and stir in the flour. Pour in the marinade, increase the heat and stir constantly while bringing up to the boil. Simmer for 5 minutes. Pour into the roasting tin.

6. Arrange the chicken pieces on top of the mushrooms and onions, skin side uppermost, and sprinkle the sugar on to the skin. Season well with pepper.

7. Cook the chicken near the top of the preheated oven for 20 minutes. Reduce the oven temperature to 180°C/350°F/gas mark 4 and cook for a further 20 minutes, or until the chicken is tender.

8. Arrange the chicken on a warmed serving dish. If the sauce is rather thin, reduce it by boiling rapidly in a frying pan. Season to taste with salt and pepper. Pour over the sauce and garnish with the parsley.

 *MINERVOIS*

CAUL-WRAPPED CHICKEN BREASTS WITH GARLIC HERB STUFFING

This delicious chicken dish is adapted from a recipe by Alistair Little.

SERVES 4

4 × 225g/8oz boneless chicken breasts, skinned
1 tablespoon chopped fresh parsley
1 tablespoon finely chopped fresh tarragon
1 clove of garlic, crushed
grated zest of 1 lime
1 tablespoon lime juice
30g/1oz unsalted butter, softened
salt and freshly ground black pepper
pig's caul, soaked in cold water
2 tablespoons olive oil

To serve
chicken and rosemary jus (see following recipe)
sprigs of fresh rosemary

1. Lightly bat the chicken breasts between 2 pieces of clingfilm. Refrigerate until required.
2. Mix the herbs, garlic, lime zest and juice and butter together and season with salt and pepper. Wrap in a piece of greaseproof paper and chill.
3. Cut the flavoured butter into 4 pieces. Make a slit on the underside of each chicken breast and put a piece of butter into each.
4. Drain the caul and cut out 4 large pieces. Wrap each chicken breast in a piece of caul, securing if necessary with a cocktail stick.
5. Preheat the oven to 200°C/400°F/gas mark 6.
6. Heat the oil in a large frying pan. Season the chicken with salt and pepper and brown all over in the hot oil. Transfer the chicken to a roasting tin and cook in the preheated oven for 12–18 minutes, or until the chicken is cooked (it should feel firm to the touch).
7. Arrange the chicken on 4 warmed individual plates and pour the sauce around the outside. Garnish with the rosemary and serve immediately.

 *NEW ZEALAND SAUVIGNON BLANC*

CHICKEN AND ROSEMARY JUS

SERVES 4

450g/1lb chicken wings
2 tablespoons sunflower oil
1 leek, sliced
1 small carrot, sliced
1 stick of celery, sliced
2 shallots, sliced
2 tomatoes, halved and de-seeded
2 cloves of garlic, bruised
4 sprigs of fresh rosemary
1 bay leaf
1 sprig of fresh parsley
6 black peppercorns

290ml/½ pint dry white wine
425ml/¾ pint dry red wine
3 litres/5¼ pints well-flavoured white stock, made with chicken bones (see page 625)

1. Brown the chicken wings thoroughly in the oil in a large saucepan. Lift out and set aside.
2. Add the leek, carrot, celery and shallots to the pan and fry over a low heat until golden-brown. Add the tomatoes and garlic and cook for a further 2–3 minutes. Add the herbs and peppercorns.
3. Return the browned chicken wings to the pan. Pour over the white wine, bring to the boil and allow to simmer slowly until the wine is reduced to 1–2 tablespoons.
4. Add the red wine to the pan and bring to the boil, then lower the heat and allow to simmer slowly until reduced to 2–3 tablespoons.
5. Pour over the stock and bring to the boil, then lower the heat and cook very slowly for 2–3 hours, skimming frequently. On no account allow the liquid to boil.
6. Strain into a clean saucepan, discarding the bones and vegetables. Bring to the boil, then lower the heat and allow to simmer until the liquid is reduced to 425ml/¾ pint. Strain through a chinois and season to taste with salt and pepper.

GREEN CHICKEN CURRY

SERVES 4

1 tablespoon oil
2 cloves of garlic, sliced
2 tablespoons green curry paste (see following recipe)
290ml/½ pint thick coconut milk
2 tablespoons nam pla
1 teaspoon sugar
4 boneless chicken breasts, skinned and cut into strips
3 small green aubergines
150ml/¼ pint white stock, made with chicken bones (see page 625)
3 kaffir lime leaves, shredded
20 basil leaves

1. Heat the oil in a flameproof casserole, add the garlic and fry until golden-brown. Add the green curry paste, then gradually blend in the coconut milk, nam pla and sugar.
2. Add the chicken and aubergines and stir for 2–4 minutes. Add the stock and simmer for 20 minutes, or until tender.
3. Stir in the lime leaves and basil and serve immediately.

NOTE: Nam pla – fermented fish sauce – is used extensively in Thai cooking and is available from oriental supermarkets.

 *CHILEAN GEWÜRZTRAMINER*

GREEN CURRY PASTE

10 green chillies, de-seeded and roughly
    chopped
2 sticks of lemon grass, chopped
4 shallots
1 piece of galangal
1 piece of krachai (optional)
2–3 tablespoons chopped fresh coriander leaves
    and stalks
2 teaspoons ground cumin
3 kaffir lime leaves, chopped
1 teaspoon nam pla
6 black peppercorns

1. Pound or blend all the ingredients to a paste.

NOTES: Galangal – a rhizome similar to root ginger – has a peppery, perfumed taste. It is used extensively in the cooking of South East Asia, particularly Thai cookery.

Krachai – Chinese chives – is a member of the allium family, with a mild flavour.

CHICKEN AND SAGE TART WITH WHOLEMEAL GRUYÈRE PASTRY

SERVES 6

For the pastry
110g/4oz wholemeal flour
55g/2oz plain flour
a pinch of salt
a pinch of cayenne pepper
a pinch of dry English mustard
55g/2oz butter, diced
45g/1½oz Gruyère cheese, finely grated
1 egg, lightly beaten

For the filling
2 Spanish onions, thinly sliced
55g/2oz butter
3 tablespoons chopped fresh sage
110g/4oz Gruyère cheese, grated
2 egg yolks
4 tablespoons double cream
450g/1lb poached chicken, cut into bite-sized
    pieces
salt and freshly ground black pepper

To garnish
a few sprigs of fresh sage

1. Preheat the oven to 200°C/400°F/gas mark 6.
2. Sift the flours with the salt, cayenne and mustard into a large bowl and add the bran from the sieve. Rub in the butter until the mixture resembles coarse breadcrumbs.
3. Add the Gruyère cheese and stir in enough egg to bind the pastry to a firm dough. Roll out the pastry and use to line a 20cm/8in loose-based fluted flan ring. Chill for 30 minutes.
4. Bake the pastry blind (see page 640). Reduce the oven temperature to 180°C/350°F/gas mark 4.
5. Make the filling: cook the onions in the butter in a heavy-based saucepan over a low heat until they are soft and pale golden-brown

Spiced Wild Garlic Soup

Rocket Ravioli with Garlic and Goat's Cheese

King Prawns in Filo with Dipping Sauce

Salmon, Fennel and Wild Rice Galette

Venison Burgers with Sour Cherry Relish

Potato Gnocchi with Creamy Nettles, Ham and Gruyère

Leek and Olive Beer Bread Tart

Hot Asparagus and Jersey Royal New Potatoes with Mint Butter

Spring Mint Parfait

Rhubarb Strudel

Chocolate Meringue Torte with Kumquat and Date Compote

White Praline Meringues with Pink Grapefruit Curd Cream

(this will take up to 30 minutes). Stir in the sage and cook for a further 2 minutes. Tip the onions into a large bowl and allow to cool.
6. Stir in the Gruyère cheese, egg yolks, cream and chicken and season to taste with salt and pepper.
7. Spread the filling in the prepared flan case and bake in the centre of the preheated oven for 20–30 minutes, or until the filling is golden on top. Allow to cool slightly before serving garnished with fresh sage leaves.

 DRY WHITE WINE/NEW WORLD CHARDONNAY

BRAISED GUINEA FOWL WITH SALTED LEMONS AND OLIVES

SERVES 4

2 guinea fowl
2 teaspoons olive oil
4 cloves of garlic, unpeeled
5 tablespoons Madeira or sherry
1 tablespoon sherry vinegar
salt and freshly ground black pepper
225g/8oz couscous
1 red onion, finely chopped
1 tablespoon extra virgin olive oil
8 slices of salted lemons (see page 236)
110g/4oz Kalamata olives
1–2 tablespoons chopped fresh coriander

To garnish
sprigs of fresh coriander

1. Preheat the oven to 180°C/350°F/gas mark 4.
2. Remove any feathers from the guinea fowl and wipe them clean inside with a damp cloth.
3. Heat the oil in a flameproof casserole. Add the guinea fowl and brown them all over.
4. Lower the heat, add the garlic, Madeira or sherry and vinegar to the casserole and season with salt and pepper.
5. Cover the casserole and cook in the

preheated oven for 1 hour.
6. Meanwhile, prepare the couscous: put the couscous into a large saucepan, cover with water and bring to the boil. Remove from the heat and allow to stand for 15 minutes. Drain very thoroughly.
7. In a separate saucepan, fry the onion in the oil until softened and lightly coloured. Add the drained couscous and stir until very hot, then season with salt and pepper. Pile into a large, deep ovenproof dish and keep warm.
8. Remove the guinea fowl from the casserole and joint them as you would a pheasant (see page 126). Arrange on top of the couscous and keep warm.
9. Skim as much fat as possible from the cooking liquor and strain it into a clean saucepan, pressing the garlic to extract the soft flesh from the skins (discard the skins). Bring to the boil and skim again, boil rapidly for 2–3 minutes. Add the salted lemons, olives and coriander, season to taste with salt and pepper and pour over the guinea fowl. Garnish with the sprigs of coriander and serve very hot.

 ASTI SPUMANTE

PAN-FRIED PIGEON BREASTS WITH MULBERRY GIN

SERVES 4

570ml/1 pint white stock, made with chicken
* bones (see page 625)*
225g/8oz mulberries, fresh or frozen
8 pigeon breasts, skinned
55g/2oz seasoned plain flour (see page 637)
1 tablespoon sunflower oil
100ml/3½fl oz mulberry gin (see page 495)
55g/2oz unsalted butter, diced
salt and freshly ground black pepper

To serve
1 quantity polenta potato cakes (see page 571)
110g/4oz fresh mulberries

1. Preheat the oven to 130°C/250°F/gas mark 1.
2. Boil the stock with the mulberries in a wide, heavy-based saucepan until the stock has reduced to 150ml/¼ pint.
3. Coat the pigeon breasts with the seasoned flour and pat off the excess.
4. Heat the oil in a frying pan, add the pigeon breasts in batches and fry for 2 minutes. Turn and cook for a further 2 minutes until browned but still pink inside. Transfer to a baking sheet and place in the oven while finishing the sauce.
5. Add the mulberry gin to the pan and stir well to remove any sediment stuck to the bottom of the pan. Boil rapidly until reduced to 4 tablespoons. Strain the reduced stock into the frying pan with the gin.
6. Whisk in the butter, over a medium heat, piece by piece. If the sauce becomes a little thick or oily, add a tablespoon of water before adding the remaining butter. Add any juices that have run from the pigeon breasts to the sauce at this point. Season to taste with salt and pepper.
7. To serve: place a polenta potato cake on to each plate, arrange 2 pigeon breasts on top and pour the sauce around. Garnish with the fresh mulberries and serve immediately.

 *BARDOLINO*

BAKED RABBIT WITH RED ONIONS, TOMATO AND TURMERIC

SERVES 4

2 tablespoons olive oil
1 large rabbit, skinned and jointed
seasoned plain flour (see page 637)
2 large red onions, sliced
2 large cloves of garlic, crushed
1 tablespoon ground turmeric
290ml/½ pint dry white wine
450g/1lb ripe tomatoes, skinned and chopped
1 tablespoon tomato purée
1 bay leaf

a pinch of sugar
290ml/½ pint white stock, made with chicken bones (see page 625)
salt and freshly ground black pepper

To garnish
2 tablespoons roughly chopped fresh flat-leaf parsley

To serve
1 quantity spring greens and Gorgonzola polenta (see page 196)

1. Preheat the oven to 170°C/325°F/gas mark 3.
2. Heat the oil in a large, heavy-based casserole. Dip the rabbit joints into the seasoned flour and pat off the excess. Gently brown the rabbit joints on all sides. Transfer them to a plate.
3. Add the onions to the pan and cook until golden-brown, adding more oil if necessary. Add the garlic and turmeric and cook for 1 minute.
4. Pour in the wine and boil rapidly, stirring any sediment off the bottom of the pan, until almost completely reduced.
5. Add the tomatoes, tomato purée, bay leaf, sugar and stock and season with salt and pepper.
6. Bring to the boil, cover with a close-fitting lid and cook in the preheated oven for 45 minutes–1 hour, or until the rabbit is tender. Lift the rabbit out of the sauce and transfer to a warmed serving dish.
7. Bring the sauce back to the boil and reduce to a syrupy consistency. Season to taste before pouring over the rabbit.
8. To serve: sprinkle over the parsley and serve with the spring greens and Gorgonzola polenta.

 *AUSTRALIAN SHIRAZ-CABERNET*

VENISON BURGERS WITH SOUR CHERRY RELISH

SERVES 4

450g/1lb venison fillet
110g/4oz pork fat, minced
salt and freshly ground black pepper
1 tablespoon finely chopped fresh sage
1 tablespoon Worcestershire sauce
1 tablespoon whisky
1 small onion, grated
1 clove of garlic, crushed
2 tablespoons olive oil

For the relish
110g/4oz dried sour Montmorency cherries
5 tablespoons water
1 red chilli, finely chopped
2 tablespoons rice wine vinegar
grated zest and juice of 1 orange
3 tablespoons soft dark brown sugar
salt and freshly ground black pepper

To serve
wholemeal bread rolls
small sprigs of fresh sage

1. Trim the venison of any membrane. Put into a food processor and whizz until finely chopped. Transfer to a bowl and mix with all the remaining ingredients except the oil.
2. Preheat the grill to its highest setting.
3. Meanwhile, make the relish: put all the ingredients into a saucepan and bring to the boil, then lower the heat and simmer for 15–20 minutes, or until the liquid has evaporated and the cherries are sticky. Do not allow to burn.
4. Shape the minced venison into 4 burgers, brush with oil and season with salt and pepper. Grill on the second grill shelf for 2–3 minutes on each side, or until just cooked.
5. Cut the bread rolls in half and toast under the grill. Divide the burgers and relish between the rolls. Garnish with the sage and serve very hot.

 *CHÂTEAUNEUF DU PAPE*

BEEF

BRAISED FILLET OF BEEF IN MADEIRA

SERVES 4

900g/2lb fillet of beef, trimmed
salt and freshly ground black pepper
2 tablespoons olive oil or dripping
1 onion, chopped
1 carrot, chopped
1 stick of celery, chopped
55g/2oz mushrooms, sliced
2 tablespoons brandy
150ml/¼ pint Madeira
150ml/¼ pint brown stock (see page 625)
1 bouquet garni
55g/2oz unsalted butter, diced

1. Preheat the oven to 170°C/325°F/gas mark 3.
2. Tie 4 pieces of string along the length of the fillet of beef to keep its shape. Season with salt and pepper.
3. Heat the oil or dripping in a flameproof casserole and fry the fillet on all sides until well browned, then remove from the casserole and set aside.
4. Add the vegetables to the casserole with a little more oil or dripping if needed and fry for 5 minutes or until a good russet-brown. Return the fillet to the casserole and flame it with the brandy, shaking the pan until the flames subside. Add the Madeira, stock and bouquet garni, and season with salt and pepper. Bring to the boil, cover with a lid and cook in the preheated oven for 15–20 minutes, or until a metal skewer inserted into the centre of the meat is just hot.
5. Remove the casserole from the oven, transfer the fillet to a carving board and cover with kitchen foil. Leave to rest for 15 minutes before carving. Strain the juices in the casserole into a small saucepan, pressing the vegetables to extract as much flavour as possible.
6. Reduce the sauce by boiling rapidly until syrupy, then whisk in the butter, piece by piece, until you have a smooth shiny sauce. Check the seasoning.
7. Remove the string from the fillet of beef and carve into thin slices. Serve immediately on warmed individual plates with the sauce.

 *AUSTRALIAN SHIRAZ OR NORTHERN RHÔNE*

STIR-FRIED BEEF FILLET WITH CHILLI SAUCE AND PAK CHOI

SERVES 4

For the chilli sauce
3 tablespoons groundnut oil
1 large onion, finely chopped
4 red chillis, de-seeded and finely chopped
4 cloves of garlic, crushed
5 tablespoons water
1 teaspoon sugar
salt and freshly ground black pepper
2 teaspoons chopped fresh basil

225g/8oz rice noodles
450g/1lb fillet of beef
110g/4oz mangetout, topped, tailed and
*   blanched*
225g/8oz pak choi, sliced and blanched

1. Make the chilli sauce: heat 2 tablespoons of

the oil in a wok or frying pan, add the onion and cook until completely soft. Add the chillies and garlic and cook for a further 8–10 minutes, or until the chillies are soft. Add the water, sugar and salt to taste and simmer for 5 minutes. Whizz in a food processor until smooth, then stir in the basil and allow to cool.

2. Cook the noodles in boiling water for 2–3 minutes, or until tender. Drain, mix with the chilli sauce and set aside.

3. Cut the fillet of beef into thick strips. Heat the remaining oil in the wok and stir-fry the beef briskly for 1 minute, or until lightly browned. Add the mangetout and pak choi and heat through for 30 seconds. Stir the mixture into the chilli rice noodles and season with salt and pepper. Serve hot or cold.

 YOUNG RED VIN DE PAYS D'OC

LAMB

ROSEMARY LAMB BURGERS WITH RED ONION AND GOAT'S CHEESE

SERVES 4

675g/1½lb lean minced lamb
1 clove of garlic, crushed
1 tablespoon Worcestershire sauce
salt and freshly ground black pepper

For the filling
1 tablespoon olive oil
1 large red onion, thinly sliced
1 tablespoon chopped fresh rosemary
110g/4oz soft mild goat's cheese

1. Preheat the grill to its highest setting.
2. Mix the lamb with the garlic and Worcestershire sauce and season well with salt and pepper.
3. Make the filling: heat the oil in a frying pan, add the onion and cook for 5 minutes over a low heat, or until nearly soft, then increase the heat and lightly caramelize the onion. Add the rosemary and cook for 1 further minute, then set aside to cool.
4. Mix the onion with the goat's cheese and season well with salt and pepper.
5. With wet hands divide the seasoned minced lamb into 4 equal portions. Mould each portion around a quarter of the cheese and onion mixture to form burger shapes.
6. Place the burgers on a wire rack over a roasting tin and grill for 8 minutes on each side, or until golden-brown and hot in the middle. Serve immediately.

 AUSTRALIAN CABERNET SAUVIGNON

SLOW-COOKED LAMB WITH SPINACH AND COCONUT MILK

SERVES 4

4 × 225g/8oz pieces of lamb neck fillet, trimmed and cut into 2.5cm/1in lengths
salt and freshly ground black pepper
1 teaspoon ground coriander
2 tablespoons sunflower oil
1 onion, chopped
1 clove of garlic, crushed
1 stick of lemon grass, very thinly sliced
450g/1lb potatoes, scrubbed and cut into 2.5cm/1in cubes
1 teaspoon ground cumin
290ml/½ pint brown stock (see page 625)
290ml/½ pint coconut milk
1 bay leaf
450g/1lb fresh spinach leaves, washed and roughly chopped

To serve
warm lemon grass and carrot basmati rice (see page 204)

1. Preheat the oven to 170°C/325°F/gas mark 3.
2. Season the lamb well with the salt, pepper and coriander.
3. Heat 1 tablespoon of the oil in a heavy-based

186

frying pan and brown the lamb all over, a few pieces at a time. Put the lamb into a flameproof casserole. Deglaze the frying pan with a little water to remove all the sediment stuck to the bottom. Reserve the deglazing liquid if it does not taste burnt.

4. Fry the onion in the remaining oil in the frying pan until golden-brown. Add the garlic and lemon grass and cook for 1 further minute. Stir in the potatoes and cumin and cook for a further 2 minutes.

5. Add the stock and bring to the boil, stirring constantly to avoid lumps. Tip the mixture into the casserole with the lamb and add the coconut milk and bay leaf.

6. Bring the casserole to a simmer over direct heat. Cover with a close-fitting lid and cook near the bottom of the preheated oven for 1½–2 hours, or until the lamb is tender.

7. Blanch the spinach in salted water for a few seconds until it wilts. Drain and refresh in cold water. Squeeze out the excess liquid and chop roughly.

8. Remove the bay leaf from the casserole and stir in the spinach. Check the seasoning before serving with the lemon grass and carrot basmati rice.

 *SPANISH RIOJA OR OTHER SPICY FULL-BODIED RED*

ROAST SPRING LAMB AND RED WINE PAELLA

SERVES 4

4 × 225g/8oz lamb leg steaks, cut 2.5cm/1in thick
salt and freshly ground black pepper
2 red peppers, quartered and de-seeded
12 shallots, peeled
2 tablespoons olive oil
4 shiitake mushrooms, wiped and quartered
55g/2oz sultanas
1 tablespoon chopped fresh rosemary
2 cloves of garlic, crushed
290ml/½ pint red wine

55g/2oz black olives
570ml/1 pint brown stock (see page 625)
225g/8oz Spanish short-grain rice

To garnish
chopped fresh parsley

1. Preheat the grill to its highest setting and the oven to 180°C/350°F/gas mark 4.

2. Season the lamb steaks with salt and pepper on both sides and place on a grill rack with the red pepper, skin side uppermost. Place as close as possible to the heat under the grill and cook for 2 minutes, or until the lamb is well browned. Turn the lamb over and continue to grill it with the peppers until the second side is brown and the skin of the peppers is blackened.

3. Put the peppers into a bowl, cover with clingfilm and leave to steam for 5 minutes. Peel off the skins and cut the pepper quarters in half on the diagonal.

4. Fry the shallots in the oil in a large sauté or paella pan, tossing them frequently until they are well browned all over.

5. Add the mushrooms to the pan and cook for a further 2 minutes.

6. Add the sultanas, rosemary and garlic and cook together for 1 minute. When you can really smell the garlic, add the wine. Bring to the boil, then lower the heat and simmer for 5 minutes.

7. Place the lamb in the dish with the peppers and olives. Pour over half the stock and cover the whole dish with kitchen foil. Bring to a simmer, then cook the paella in the preheated oven for 20 minutes.

8. Check the paella and add a little more stock and the rice. Be careful not to add too much liquid or the rice will end up soggy. Season well with salt and pepper. Return to the oven for a further 20–30 minutes, or until the rice is cooked and the lamb is tender. Sprinkle with parsley before serving.

 *SPANISH RED*

CHILLI ROAST LAMB WITH APRICOT SALSA

SERVES 2

1 rack (best end) of lamb, chined, trimmed and
*   skinned*
1 clove of garlic, thinly sliced
1 red chilli, de-seeded and sliced
salt and freshly ground black pepper

For the salsa
255g/9oz ripe apricots, halved and stoned
2 spring onions, thinly sliced
2 tablespoons chopped fresh coriander
1 teaspoon ground coriander
1 clove of garlic, chopped
1 red chilli, de-seeded and chopped
2.5cm/1in piece of fresh root ginger, peeled and
*   cut into julienne strips*
julienned zest and juice of 1 lime
1–2 tablespoons rice wine vinegar
salt and freshly ground black pepper

To garnish
sprigs of fresh coriander

1. Preheat the oven to 220°C/425°F/gas mark 7.
2. Trim some of the fat from the rack of lamb.
Make slits in the remaining fat and insert slices
of garlic and chilli into the slits. Season with
salt and pepper.
3. Place the lamb, fat side up, in a roasting tin
and roast in the preheated oven for 25 minutes
for a 7-cutlet best end, less for a smaller one.
This will give pink, slightly underdone lamb.
4. Meanwhile, make the salsa: dice the apricots
and mix with the remaining ingredients. Chill
until required.
5. To serve: slice the lamb into cutlets and
arrange overlapping on a large warmed serving
plate. Spoon the salsa around one side and
garnish with sprigs of coriander.

 *YOUNG RED CORBIÈRES*

LAMB, ROSEMARY AND WILD GARLIC SALAD

This quick and easy *salade tiède* or warm salad
makes a delicious light lunch or supper. New
season's lamb is perfect for this dish, but choose
a cut that can be stir-fried, such as the fillet
from the best end of neck or the chump end of
the leg.

SERVES 4

450g/1lb lamb, suitable for stir-frying
salt and freshly ground black pepper
110g/4oz baby asparagus spears
170g/6oz Jersey Royal new potatoes, scrubbed
1 handful of wild garlic leaves
salad leaves, such as lamb's lettuce, Little Gem,
*   frisée*
4 tablespoons olive oil
1 tablespoon chopped fresh rosemary
1 tablespoon rice wine vinegar

To serve
pitta bread
hummus (see page 154)

1. Remove any fat from the lamb and cut the
meat into strips the size of your little finger.
Season with salt and pepper and set aside.
2. Cook the asparagus in a small amount of
boiling salted water until tender. Drain and
refresh under cold running water and set aside.
Cook the potatoes in boiling salted water, drain
and cut in half. Set aside.
3. Wash the garlic leaves and salad, dry well
and put into a large salad bowl.
4. Heat the oil in a large frying pan, add the
rosemary and fry for 1–2 minutes. Fry the lamb
strips a few at a time for 2–3 minutes, or until
lightly browned on the outside but still pink in
the middle. Lift on to a plate and fry the
remaining lamb in the same way.
5. When all the lamb is cooked, transfer to the
salad bowl with the asparagus and potatoes.
Toss together, sprinkle over the vinegar and
season with salt and pepper. Serve immediately
with the warm pitta bread and hummus handed
separately.

 *BEAUJOLAIS*

PORK

PORK FILLET WITH SAGE AND MADEIRA

SERVES 4

2 × 340g/12oz pork fillets
freshly ground black pepper
225g/8oz rindless streaky bacon rashers
1 handful of fresh sage leaves
1 teaspoon plain flour
570ml/1 pint white chicken stock, made with
   chicken bones (see page 625)
150ml/¼ pint Madeira

1. Trim the pork fillets of any outer membrane or fat and season with pepper. Stretch each bacon rasher and cut in half.
2. Lay 8 rashers of bacon side by side on a piece of clingfilm, season with pepper and cover with sage leaves. Lay a pork fillet along one edge of the strips of bacon, folding in the narrow end of the fillet, and roll up tightly in the bacon and clingfilm. Repeat with the second fillet. Leave in the refrigerator for 2 hours or overnight.
3. Preheat the oven to 230°C/450°F/gas mark 8 and the grill to its highest setting.
4. Remove the clingfilm from the fillets and place them in a shallow roasting tin (seam side down). Roast at the top of the preheated oven for 15 minutes. (If the bacon has not browned you may need to put the fillets under the grill for a minute.) Transfer the fillets to a tray while you make the gravy.
5. Put the flour in the roasting tin and stir over a low heat until the fat is absorbed. Add the stock and Madeira and bring to the boil. Skim off any excess fat, then reduce by boiling rapidly to a syrupy consistency. Season to taste with salt and pepper and pass through a fine sieve.

6. Cut the pork into slices on the diagonal and arrange on 4 individual plates. Pour the Madeira sauce around and serve immediately.

 CALIFORNIAN CHARDONNAY OR PINOT NOIR

PORK AND MIXED BEAN CASSOULET

SERVES 10

450g/1lb dried haricot beans
450g/1lb red kidney beans
225g/8oz black-eyed beans
110g/4oz piece of salt pork or unsmoked bacon
1 onion, halved
5 cloves
1 bouquet garni
2 cloves of garlic, peeled
225g/8oz pork belly
450g/1lb good-quality pork sausages, such as
   Cumberland or Lincoln
4 small chorizo sausages
450g/1lb piece of gammon, soaked
1 tablespoon tomato purée
2 tablespoons chopped fresh sage
salt and freshly ground black pepper
4 tablespoons fresh white breadcrumbs

1. Wash the beans well in cold water and leave to soak overnight. Drain and blanch in fresh boiling water for 5 minutes, then drain again.
2. Rinse the beans well and place in a saucepan of fresh cold water, making sure they are covered. Add the rind of the salt pork or bacon, the onion and cloves, bouquet garni and garlic.
3. Bring to the boil, then skim and simmer for

1¾ hours, or until the beans are tender.

4. Meanwhile, preheat the oven to 190°C/ 375°F/gas mark 5. Place the pork belly and sausages in a roasting tin and roast in the preheated oven for 30 minutes, or until the meat is cooked and the sausages browned.

5. Meanwhile, put the gammon into a saucepan of cold water, bring to the boil and simmer for 30–35 minutes, or until the rind will pull away easily. Strain the cooking liquor and reserve. Skin the gammon and cut into 2.5cm/1in chunks.

6. Remove the pork belly and sausages from the oven and tip off and reserve the fat. Slice the sausages into 2.5cm/1in pieces and cut the pork belly into same-sized chunks.

7. When the beans are cooked, strain them, reserving 290ml/½ pint of the cooking liquor. Discard the pork or bacon rind, onion and bouquet garni. Add the tomato purée.

8. Reduce the oven temperature to 170°C/ 325°F/gas mark 3.

9. Place a layer of beans in a deep ovenproof dish. Cover with a layer of meats and sprinkle with sage. Continue to layer up, finishing with a layer of beans. Season generously with salt and pepper. Pour over the cooking liquor and 290ml/½ pint of the reserved gammon liquor. Sprinkle the breadcrumbs on the top.

10. Cook uncovered in the preheated oven for 1½ hours. If the breadcrumbs become dry and crusty, stir them into the cassoulet, add more liquid if necessary and sprinkle more breadcrumbs on top. At the end of the cooking time, the meat and beans should be very tender and creamy and the top crisp and brown.

 *PINOT NOIR*

POTATO GNOCCHI WITH CREAMY NETTLES, HAM AND GRUYÈRE

This dish is best made using young spring nettles. However, if it is the wrong time of the year you will simply need to blanch the nettles for a little longer than the recipe suggests.

SERVES 4

450g/1lb young nettle leaves, washed
  thoroughly
salt
450g/1lb potato gnocchi (see page 571)
1 tablespoon olive oil
225g/8oz cooked ham, cut into strips
freshly ground black pepper
freshly grated nutmeg
570ml/1 pint double cream
dry English mustard
170g/6oz Gruyère cheese, grated

1. Preheat the oven to 200°C/400°F/gas mark 6.

2. Prepare the nettles: bring a large saucepan of salted water to the boil and blanch the nettle leaves for a few seconds, or until they wilt. Remove with a slotted spoon and refresh quickly in a bowl of cold water. Drain the leaves and dry them on kitchen paper. Chop roughly.

3. Boil the gnocchi in the nettle water with the oil for 2 minutes, then drain in a colander and refresh in cold water to prevent them sticking together. Drain again.

4. Toss the nettles, gnocchi and ham together and season well with salt, pepper and nutmeg. Tip into a 5cm/2in deep ovenproof dish.

5. Season the cream well with salt, pepper and mustard. Pour over the gnocchi and sprinkle the Gruyère cheese on top.

6. Place the dish on a baking sheet and cook at the top of the preheated oven for 20 minutes, or until golden-brown and bubbling.

NOTE: Potato gnocchi are readily available, pre-prepared, at large supermarkets where they can usually be found near the fresh pasta.

 *FRASCATI OR NORTHERN ITALIAN CHARDONNAY*

VEAL

VEAL STEAKS WITH ROSEMARY, RED ONION AND SHERRY

SERVES 4

4 × 170g/6oz veal steaks
1 tablespoon olive oil
1 large red onion, thinly sliced
1 tablespoon chopped fresh rosemary
30g/1oz unsalted butter
4 tablespoons medium sherry
150ml/¼ pint white stock, made with chicken
   bones (see page 625)
150ml/¼ pint double cream
salt and freshly ground black pepper

To garnish
4 small sprigs of rosemary

1. Preheat the oven to 110°C/225°F/gas mark ½.
2. Trim the veal steaks of excess fat and season with salt and pepper.
3. Heat the oil in a frying pan and add the onion. Cook over a low heat for 10 minutes until soft and golden in colour, add the rosemary, season with salt and pepper and cook for 1 further minute. Tip on to a plate and set aside.
4. Heat half the butter in the frying pan and when the foam subsides add 2 of the veal steaks and cook for 3 minutes on each side. Remove from the pan and keep in the warm oven. Heat the remaining butter and fry the remaining veal steaks in the same way.
5. Return the onions to the empty pan, add the sherry and cook over a high heat until it has almost completely reduced. Add the stock and

cream and bring to the boil, stirring every so often to prevent the cream from catching, until the sauce is of a syrupy consistency. Season with salt and pepper.
6. Take the veal steaks out of the oven, pour any juices back into the pan and arrange the steaks on a warmed serving dish. Pour over the sauce and garnish with the rosemary. Serve immediately.

 *SPANISH RED*

OFFAL

PENNE WITH CHICKEN LIVERS AND SWISS CHARD

SERVES 4

450g/1lb chicken livers
450g/1lb Swiss chard, washed thoroughly
salt
225g/8oz penne
3 tablespoons olive oil
30g/1oz butter
freshly ground black pepper
100ml/3½fl oz medium sherry

To garnish
55g/2oz Parmesan cheese, shaved

1. Remove any membranes from the chicken livers and cut off any green bits. Dry the livers on kitchen paper.
2. Pull the leaves off the stalks of the chard. If the stalks are quite thick and tough-looking, use a peeler to remove the stringy ridge on the curved side. Chop the stalks up into 2.5cm/1in pieces on the diagonal. Tear the leaves into smaller pieces, keeping the leaves separate from the stalks.
3. Bring 2 large saucepans of salted water to the boil.
4. Boil the penne in one of the pans, with 1 tablespoon of the oil, until just tender (the timing will depend on whether you are using fresh or dried penne).
5. Boil the chard stalks for 3–5 minutes, or until just tender. Add the leaves to the pan and allow them to wilt, then pour the leaves and stalks into a colander. Press out the excess water with the back of a wooden spoon.
6. Heat half the remaining oil and half the butter in a large frying pan until the butter is melted and foaming. Season the chicken livers with salt and pepper.
7. Fry half the livers in the oil and butter over a high heat for 1 minute, so that the livers brown on the outside but remain pink in the middle. Tip the browned livers on to a plate and keep warm while you fry the remaining livers in the remaining oil and butter.
8. In a very large saucepan or wok, toss the livers with the penne and the chard. Pour the sherry into the frying pan in which the livers were cooked, and stir over a high heat for a minute to remove the sediment from the bottom of the pan.
9. Add the sherry and juices to the pasta. Season to taste with salt and pepper, adding a little extra olive oil if the mixture seems a little dry, then tip into a large warmed serving bowl. Sprinkle over the shavings of Parmesan cheese before serving.

 *DRY WHITE/ITALIAN CHARDONNAY OR LIGHT RED*

CHICKEN LIVER MASALA

SERVES 2

225g/8oz chicken livers, rinsed
55g/2oz clarified butter
1 large onion, finely chopped
2 cloves of garlic, crushed
1 tablespoon garam masala (see page 637)
150ml/¼ pint white stock, made with chicken
    bones (see page 625)
150ml/¼ pint soured cream
salt and freshly ground black pepper

To serve
hot spice mash (see page 206)

1. Pick over the chicken livers and remove and discard any discoloured pieces as they may taste bitter.

2. Melt half the butter in a frying pan, add the onion and cook over a very low heat until meltingly soft and golden-brown. Add the garlic and continue to cook for 2 minutes. Tip into a bowl and set aside.

3. Melt the remaining butter in the pan, add the garam masala and fry over a low heat for 2–3 minutes. Add the chicken livers a few at a time, increase the heat a little and fry until the livers are brown on the outside but still slightly pink in the middle. Lift on to a plate as they are cooked. When all the livers are cooked, add the stock to the pan and bring to the boil, then lower the heat and simmer for 2–3 minutes. Add the soured cream and reheat. Return the livers and onion to the pan and season to taste with salt and pepper. Serve very hot, with the hot spice mash handed separately.

 AUSTRALIAN CHARDONNAY

BLACK PUDDING WITH HOT BEETROOT AND SOURED CREAM

SERVES 4

675g/1½lb best-quality black pudding, skin
*   removed*
salt and freshly ground black pepper
45g/1½oz butter
15g/½oz caster sugar
2 red dessert apples, cored and each cut into 12
*   even segments*
4 medium beetroots, peeled and coarsely grated
juice of 1 lemon

To garnish
100ml/3½fl oz soured cream
½ tablespoon chopped fresh parsley

1. Preheat the oven to 150°C/300°F/gas mark 2.
2. Slice the black pudding into 1cm/½in oval slices. Season with salt and pepper. Fry the

pudding in 15g/½oz of the butter until crisp on the outside and hot in the middle. Keep warm.
3. Melt another 15g/½oz butter in a frying pan. Add the sugar and cook until the sugar starts to caramelize. Fry the apples until they are caramelized on both sides. Keep warm.
4. Heat the remaining butter in the frying pan, add the beetroot and season well with salt and pepper. Toss over a high heat for a minute or until just hot, then stir in the lemon juice. Pile the beetroot on to a warmed serving dish. Sprinkle the caramelized apples on top and arrange the black pudding slices on top.
5. Drizzle over the soured cream, sprinkle with the parsley and serve immediately.

 BEAUJOLAIS–VILLAGES

LAMB SWEETBREADS WITH SPRING VEGETABLES AND HOLLANDAISE

SERVES 4

450g/1lb lamb's sweetbreads
seasoned flour (see page 637)
30g/1oz butter

For the vegetables
225g/8oz baby carrots, scrubbed and blanched
225g/8oz young peas, blanched
225g/8oz baby turnips, blanched
1 teaspoon finely chopped fresh rosemary
salt and freshly ground black pepper

To serve
110g/4oz butter quantity hollandaise sauce (see
*   page 633)*
lemon wedges

1. Soak the sweetbreads in cold water for 4 hours. Change the water every time it becomes pink (probably 4 times). There should be no blood at all when the sweetbreads are ready for cooking.

2. Place them in a saucepan of cold water and bring to the boil. Lower the heat and poach for 2 minutes.

3. Drain the sweetbreads and rinse under cold running water. Dry well. Pick them over, removing all the skin and membrane.

4. Toss the sweetbreads in the seasoned flour.

5. Fry the sweetbreads in half the butter for 2–3 minutes, or until well browned. Remove to a serving dish and keep warm.

6. Wipe out the frying pan, melt the remaining butter, add the vegetables and toss over the heat until very hot, then add the rosemary. Season to taste with salt and pepper. Arrange the vegetables around the sweetbreads.

7. Hand the hollandaise sauce separately and garnish the dish with the lemon wedges. Serve very hot.

 *CÔTES DU RHÔNE*

VEGETARIAN

SWISS CHARD AND GRUYÈRE PUFF PASTRY TART

SERVES 10–12

450g/1lb flour quantity puff pastry (see page 643)

For the filling
30g/1oz butter
1 bay leaf
½ teaspoon dry English mustard
a pinch of cayenne pepper
30g/1oz plain flour
290ml/½ pint milk
340g/12oz Gruyère cheese, grated
salt and freshly ground black pepper
1kg/2¼lb Swiss chard, washed
170g/6oz pancetta or smoked ham, thinly sliced (optional)

1. Preheat the oven to 220°C/425°F/gas mark 7.
2. Cut the pastry in half. Roll out one half into a 35cm/14in square. Place a 25cm/10in fluted, loose-based flan ring on a baking sheet and lay over the pastry, easing it down into the corners of the ring rather than stretching it. Do not trim off any excess pastry. Roll the second half of the pastry into a 27.5cm/11in square, and lay on a baking sheet. Chill both pastry squares for 30 minutes.
3. Bake the pastry case blind (see page 640).
4. Carefully trim off the overlapping edges with a sharp knife.
5. Melt the butter in a saucepan, add the bay leaf, mustard, cayenne and flour. Stir over a low heat for 1 minute, then remove the pan from the heat and add the milk. Return to the heat and bring to the boil, stirring continuously. Simmer for 2 minutes, then remove from the heat and stir in the Gruyère cheese. Season to taste with salt and pepper. Leave to cool.
6. Separate the stalks from the leaves of the Swiss chard. Simmer the stalks in salted water until they are tender, then add the leaves to the water until they wilt. Drain quickly in a colander. Immediately refresh the Swiss chard in a large bowl of cold water. When it is cold drain well, squeeze out any excess water and pat dry with kitchen paper. (It is important to do this quickly in order to keep the bright green colour of the leaves.)
7. Spread half the cold cheese sauce on to the base of the pastry case, arrange the Swiss chard over the top and season well with salt and pepper. Spread over the remaining sauce and top with a layer of pancetta or ham, if using.
8. Brush the edges of the pastry lid with a little egg glaze and lay over the tart. Press the edges together and, using the blade of a sharp knife horizontally, cut into the edge of the pastry to neaten it. Brush the top with the egg glaze, then bake at the top of the preheated oven for 20–30 minutes until the pastry is well risen and golden.
9. Allow the tart to cool a little before removing from the flan ring to serve.

 *ALSACE PINOT BLANC*

SHIITAKE AND GORGONZOLA RISOTTO WITH PURPLE SPROUTING BROCCOLI

SERVES 4

85g/3oz unsalted butter
1 large onion, very finely chopped
110g/4oz shiitake mushrooms, thickly sliced
400g/14oz risotto (arborio) rice
150ml/¼ pint dry white wine
1.7 litres/3 pints white stock, made with
  chicken bones (see page 625)
450g/1lb purple sprouting broccoli
salt
freshly ground black pepper
225g/8oz Gorgonzola cheese

To serve
30g/1oz Parmesan cheese, freshly grated

1. Melt the butter in a large saucepan, add the onion and cook over a low heat until soft and lightly coloured. Add the mushrooms and cook for 2 minutes.
2. Add the rice and wine and bring to the boil, then lower the heat and simmer until the wine is absorbed (about 3 minutes). Lower the heat again and stir gently and continuously.
3. Meanwhile, reheat the stock in a second pan and allow to simmer gently.
4. Start adding the stock to the rice a little at a time, stirring gently. Allow the stock to become absorbed after each addition, stirring continuously until the rice is cooked but still *al dente* (about 30 minutes in total).
5. Trim the broccoli and discard any tough outer leaves. Boil the broccoli in salted water for 5 minutes or until just tender. Drain well and season with pepper.
6. Remove the risotto pan from the heat and stir in the Gorgonzola cheese. Check the seasoning.
7. Spoon the risotto on to a warmed serving dish and pile the purple sprouting broccoli on top. Sprinkle over the Parmesan cheese and serve immediately.

 RED BORDEAUX CRU CLASSÉ

SPRING GREENS AND GORGONZOLA POLENTA

Polenta is a good accompaniment to game bird dishes or chicken, served as an alternative to potatoes.

SERVES 4

225g/8oz spring greens, washed
720ml/1¼ pints strong white stock, made with
  chicken bones (see page 625)
salt
140g/5oz quick-cook polenta
110g/4oz Gorgonzola cheese, cubed
30g/1oz Parmesan cheese, freshly grated
freshly ground black pepper

1. Remove the thick stalks from the spring greens. Layer the leaves together, roll into a cigar shape and slice very thinly.
2. Put the stock and a teaspoon of salt into a large saucepan and bring to the boil.
3. Add the spring greens and simmer for 2 minutes. Remove from the heat and sprinkle on the polenta, stirring quickly to prevent lumps from forming. Reduce the heat.
4. Continue cooking until the polenta is thick, stirring often to prevent sticking and burning. If the polenta becomes very thick add a little extra stock or water.
5. Stir in the Gorgonzola and Parmesan cheeses and season to taste with pepper. Serve immediately.

NOTE: If you are not using quick-cook polenta, it will take 35–40 minutes to cook at stage 4, therefore add the spring greens 5 minutes before the end of the cooking time instead of before the polenta is added.

 *AUSTRALIAN CHARDONNAY*

POACHED EGG AND RHUBARB CHARD FLORENTINE

SERVES 4

900g/2lb rhubarb chard
salt and freshly ground black pepper
freshly grated nutmeg
4 large fresh eggs
570ml/1 pint béchamel sauce (see page 629)
paprika

1. Preheat the oven to 150°C/300°F/gas mark 2.
2. Tear the leaves away from the stalks of the chard. Trim the stalks and cut them into 5cm/2in lengths. Wash the leaves and stalks thoroughly.
3. Boil the stalks in a very large saucepan of salted water for 5 minutes, or until just tender. Add the chard leaves and boil for a minute or two, or until they go limp (this will depend on the age of the chard). Drain the chard in a large colander and press out the excess water with a wooden spoon. Season the chard with salt, pepper and freshly grated nutmeg. Pile into a gratin dish. Cover with wet greaseproof paper and place in the preheated oven to keep warm.
4. Poach the eggs: fill a large saucepan with water and bring to simmering point. Crack an egg into a cup and tip into the pan, holding the cup as near to the water as possible. Raise the temperature so that the water bubbles gently.
5. Using a slotted spoon, draw the egg white close to the yolk. Poach the egg for 2–3 minutes, then transfer to another pan of hot water to keep warm while the remaining eggs are poached. (If the pan is large enough you should be able to poach 2 eggs at a time.)
6. Lift the eggs out with a slotted spoon, drain on kitchen paper and place them on top of the chard. Coat the poached eggs and chard with the béchamel sauce and garnish with a little paprika. Serve immediately.

ALSACE PINOT BLANC

LEEK AND OLIVE BEER BREAD TART

SERVES 4

4 large leeks, sliced
55g/2oz butter
1 clove of garlic, crushed
150ml/¼ pint double cream
1 egg yolk
1 whole egg
110g/4oz green olives, pitted and halved
55g/2oz Kalamata olives, pitted and halved
1 teaspoon chopped fresh sage
salt and freshly ground black pepper
225g/8oz quantity beer bread dough (see following recipe)
55g/2oz feta cheese, crumbled

1. Preheat the oven to 200°C/400°F/gas mark 6.
2. Wash the leeks thoroughly and dry on kitchen paper. Heat the butter in a large saucepan, add the leeks and cook over a very low heat for about 20 minutes, or until soft but not brown. Add the garlic and continue to cook for a further 5 minutes.
3. Add the cream, bring to the boil and simmer for 5 minutes. Remove from the heat and allow to cool. Add the egg yolk and whole egg, olives and sage and season to taste with salt and pepper. Set aside.
4. Meanwhile, knock back the risen beer bread dough and roll out into a circle about 27.5cm/11in in diameter. Place on a lightly floured baking sheet.
5. Spread the leek mixture over the surface, leaving a 2.5cm/1in border all the way around the edge. Sprinkle over the feta cheese.
6. Bake the tart in the centre of the preheated oven for 30–40 minutes, or until golden-brown and the leek mixture has set. Reduce the oven temperature if the tart shows signs of burning. Serve warm.

 *RIOJA*

BEER BREAD

MAKES 1 450G/1LB LOAF

55g/2oz butter
2 teaspoons soft light brown sugar
290ml/½ pint brown ale
30g/1oz fresh yeast
2 teaspoons salt
1 egg
225g/8oz wholemeal flour
225g/8oz strong plain white flour

1. Grease a 1kg/2¼lb loaf tin.
2. Bring the sugar, beer and the remaining butter to boiling point, then allow to cool until lukewarm.
3. Use 1–2 spoonfuls of this liquid to cream the yeast. Add the creamed yeast, salt and lightly beaten egg to the beer mixture.
4. Sift the flours into a warmed large mixing bowl. Make a well in the centre and pour in the liquid. Mix, first with a knife, and then with your fingers, to a soft but not sloppy dough. Knead for 10 minutes or until smooth, a little shiny and very elastic.
5. Put the dough back into the bowl and cover with a piece of oiled clingfilm. Leave in a warm place until it has doubled in bulk.
6. Take the dough out of the bowl, knock it down and knead until smooth again. Shape the dough into a loaf shape and put into the tin. Cover again with oiled clingfilm and return to the warm place to prove (rise again) until doubled in size and the shape of the finished loaf.
7. Meanwhile, preheat the oven to 200°C/400°F/gas mark 6. Bake the loaf in the middle of the oven for 35 minutes, or until it is brown on top and sounds hollow when tapped on the underside. Cool on a wire rack.

THAI VEGETABLE CURRY

SERVES 4

1 aubergine
110g/4oz shiitake mushrooms
1 red pepper
110g/4oz asparagus
110g/4oz baby sweetcorn
110g/4oz mangetout

For the curry
2 tablespoons sunflower oil
1 large onion, sliced
2 cloves of garlic, crushed
2.5cm/1in piece of galangal, peeled and grated
1 stick of lemon grass, finely chopped
1 tablespoon ground coriander
2 kaffir lime leaves
2 curry leaves
1 green pepper, blanched
2 green chillies, de-seeded and chopped
2 red chillies, de-seeded and chopped
290ml/½ pint coconut milk
salt and 1 teaspoon freshly ground black pepper

To serve
a few sprigs of fresh coriander

1. Cut the aubergine into a 2.5cm/1in dice, sprinkle lightly with salt and leave to degorge for 5 minutes. Wipe the mushrooms and cut into thick slices.
2. Cut the pepper in half and remove any pith and seeds, then cut into thick slices. Blanch the asparagus, sweetcorn and mangetout in boiling water until nearly tender, refresh under cold running water and set aside.
3. Make the curry paste: heat half the oil in a frying pan, add the onion and cook until soft, then add the garlic and cook for a further 2 minutes. Add the galangal, lemon grass and ground coriander and cook for a further minute. Add the lime and curry leaves and the green pepper and chillies and cook for a further 2–3 minutes, then remove from the heat.
4. Put the curry ingredients into a liquidizer and whizz to form a smooth paste.

5. Heat the remaining oil in a second frying pan. Wipe the aubergine dry, add to the hot oil and sauté over a medium heat for 2–3 minutes, or until soft. Add the mushrooms and cook for a further 2 minutes. Add the red pepper, mangetout, asparagus and sweetcorn and stir-fry over a medium heat for a further minute, or until the vegetables are very hot.

6. Add the curry paste and the coconut milk to the pan and stir over a low heat until very hot. Stir in the coriander leaves and season to taste with salt and pepper. Pile into a warmed serving dish and serve very hot.

 *ALSATIAN TOKAY/PINOT GRIS*

VEGETABLES AND SALADS

VEGETABLES

HOT ASPARAGUS AND JERSEY ROYAL NEW POTATOES WITH MINT BUTTER SAUCE

SERVES 4

225g/8oz asparagus, trimmed
450g/1lb baby Jersey Royal potatoes, scrubbed
salt
225g/8oz baby carrots with stalks, scrubbed
   and trimmed, leaving 1cm/½in stalk

For the mint butter sauce
1 shallot, chopped
3 tablespoons white wine vinegar
3 tablespoons water
55g/2oz unsalted butter, diced
1 tablespoon chopped fresh mint
2 tablespoons double cream
a pinch of caster sugar
freshly ground black pepper

1. If the asparagus stalks are long, cut in half on the diagonal. Gently boil in salted water for about 5 minutes, or until tender. Remove with a slotted spoon and refresh under cold running water.
2. Add the new potatoes to the asparagus water and boil until tender. Drain, again reserving the liquid, and refresh under cold running water.
3. Boil the carrots in the vegetable water for about 2 minutes, or until just tender, and refresh under cold running water.
4. Top up the vegetable water with tap water, making sure there is enough to cover all the vegetables to reheat them just before you are ready to serve.

5. Make the sauce: put the shallot, vinegar and water into a small pan, heat gently and cook for 5 minutes. Boil until reduced to about 2 tablespoons.
6. Lower the heat under the pan. Using a wire whisk, gradually add the butter piece by piece, whisking vigorously all the time, until the sauce is thickened, creamy and pale, rather like a thin hollandaise. If it starts to look a little oily at the edges, add a tablespoon of water. Strain the sauce into a small saucepan.
7. Whisk in the mint, cream and sugar and season to taste with salt and pepper.
8. Bring the vegetable water back to the boil and put in the potatoes for 1 minute, then add the carrots and asparagus for 30 seconds. Drain all the vegetables well and pile into a warmed serving dish. Pour over the mint butter sauce and serve immediately.

BABY CARROTS WITH CASHEWS

SERVES 4

85g/3oz whole cashew nuts, shelled
675g/1½lb baby carrots, stalks attached
salt
30g/1oz unsalted butter
freshly ground black pepper
1 teaspoon caster sugar
juice of ½ lemon
4 spring onions, thinly sliced on the diagonal

1. Preheat the oven to 180°C/350°F/gas mark 4.
2. Place the cashew nuts on a baking sheet and roast in the preheated oven for 15 minutes, or until pale golden-brown. Tip on to a cool plate

to stop them browning further and burning.

3. Trim the carrot stalks down to 1cm/½in and scrape the carrots with a small knife. Cut off the roots.

4. Bring a saucepan of salted water to the boil and blanch the carrots for 3 minutes in the water, then drain.

5. Melt the butter in a large frying pan or wok and when foaming add the carrots, pepper and sugar. Toss over a high heat until the sugar just starts to caramelize. Toss in the cashews, lemon juice and spring onions. Serve immediately.

SPRING CABBAGE WITH CREAM AND NUTMEG

SERVES 4–6

675g/1½lb spring cabbage
salt and freshly ground black pepper
a pinch of freshly grated nutmeg
15g/½oz butter
2 tablespoons soured cream

1. Shred the cabbage finely and rinse it under cold running water. Place in boiling salted water and return to the boil. Boil rapidly for 3–5 minutes until slightly soft but crunchy.

2. Drain the cabbage well, then return it to the heat to evaporate excess moisture, shaking the pan and tossing the cabbage so that it dries but does not burn.

3. Sprinkle with pepper and nutmeg. Toss in the butter. Remove from the heat and stir in the soured cream.

BEET GREENS AND SESAME RICE TIMBALES

These timbales are served as an accompaniment to roast tuna loin marinated with chilli and lime (see page 173).

SERVES 6

oil for greasing
225g/8oz young beetroot leaves, stalks removed
    and washed thoroughly

1 tablespoon sesame oil
1 tablespoon olive oil
salt and freshly ground black pepper
2 tablespoons sesame seeds, toasted
340g/12oz sweet vinegar rice (see page 659)

1. Lightly oil 6 ramekins or timbale moulds.

2. Lay the beetroot leaves together and roll them into a cigar shape. Cut the leaves into shreds.

3. Heat the oils in a large frying pan or wok. Stir-fry the beetroot leaves in the oil until they have just wilted. Season with salt and pepper.

4. Carefully fold the sesame seeds and beet greens into the hot sweet vinegar rice. Divide the rice between the ramekins and press it in firmly.

5. To serve: turn the rice out of the moulds on to warmed individual plates and serve immediately.

WARM LEMON GRASS BASMATI RICE WITH CARROT RIBBONS

SERVES 4

225g/8oz basmati rice, rinsed in plenty of cold
    water
1 teaspoon salt
1 tablespoon mustard seeds
3 cardamom pods, cracked
2 sticks of lemon grass, outer leaves removed
    and very thinly sliced
1 tablespoon olive oil
2 large carrots, peeled and cut into ribbons with
    a peeler
salt and freshly ground black pepper

1. Put the rice into a large heavy-based saucepan and pour in enough water just to cover. Add the salt and leave to soak for 30 minutes.

2. Heat a heavy-based frying pan and dry-fry the mustard seeds until the toasted aroma comes through.

3. Add the mustard seeds, cardamom, lemon

grass, oil and carrots to the rice and season with pepper.

4. Bring the pan of rice to the boil and stir everything well together. Cover the pan with a close-fitting lid and turn the heat right down to a gentle simmer. Cook for 5 minutes, then turn off the heat. Leave for a further 5 minutes, covered.

5. Remove the lid, check the seasoning and gently toss the rice with a fork before serving.

NEW POTATO AND BACON GRATIN

SERVES 4

85g/3oz streaky bacon, grilled and chopped
1 bunch of spring onions, thinly sliced
1 clove of garlic, crushed
450g/1lb baby new potatoes, parboiled
290ml/½ pint double cream
salt and freshly ground black pepper
30g/1oz Gruyère or strong Cheddar cheese, grated
1 tablespoon dry white breadcrumbs

1. Preheat the oven to 200°C/400°F/gas mark 6.
2. Combine the bacon, spring onions, garlic, potatoes and cream in a bowl. Season to taste with salt and pepper.
3. Pour into a shallow ovenproof dish. Mix the cheese with the crumbs and sprinkle over the top.
4. Bake near the top of the preheated oven for 20 minutes, or until golden and bubbling at the edges.

BRAISED BABY JERSEY ROYAL POTATOES WITH GARLIC BUTTER

SERVES 4

450g/1lb baby Jersey Royal potatoes
570ml/1 pint white stock, made with chicken bones, or vegetable stock (see pages 625 and 627)

salt and freshly ground black pepper
4 cloves of garlic
2 sprigs of fresh mint
55g/2oz butter
1 tablespoon chopped fresh mint
1 tablespoon chopped fresh chives

1. Scrape the potatoes to remove as much skin as possible.
2. Put into a flameproof casserole with the stock, season with salt and pepper and add the garlic and mint. Cover the casserole and bring to the boil, then lower the heat and simmer very gently for 15–20 minutes, or until the potatoes are tender.
3. Remove the lid from the casserole, increase the heat and continue to simmer until the liquid has evaporated and the potatoes are covered in a sticky glaze. Remove from the heat. Remove the garlic and mint. Crush the garlic and discard the mint.
4. Melt the butter in a large saucepan, add the garlic and cook for 1–2 minutes. Add the potatoes, season with salt and pepper and add the herbs. Serve hot or warm.

JERSEY ROYAL POTATOES AND SAGE EN PAPILLOTE

SERVES 2

225g/8oz Jersey Royal potatoes
1–2 teaspoons coarse sea salt
6 sprigs of fresh sage, chopped
4 tablespoons extra virgin olive oil
freshly ground black pepper

1. Preheat the oven to 200°C/400°F/gas mark 6.
2. Scrape the potatoes, wash well and dry.
3. Put the potatoes on a large piece of greaseproof paper. Sprinkle with the salt, sage and olive oil and season with pepper.
4. Wrap the potatoes up in the greaseproof paper, sealing the parcel tightly so that the steam does not escape.
5. Bake in the preheated oven for about 40–50

minutes, or until the potatoes are tender. To test, push a skewer through the paper into the potatoes.

6. Serve the potatoes wrapped in the paper.

HOT SPICE MASH

SERVES 4

450g/1lb potatoes, peeled
450g/1lb parsnips, peeled
55g/2oz butter
1 bunch of spring onions, sliced
1 clove of garlic, crushed
½ teaspoon ground ginger
½ teaspoon ground cumin
salt and freshly ground black pepper
150ml/¼ pint Greek yoghurt

1. Boil the potatoes and parsnips in boiling salted water until tender. Drain and push through a sieve. Keep warm.
2. Melt the butter in the rinsed-out pan, add the spring onions and fry briskly for 1–2 minutes. Add the garlic, ginger and cumin and fry for a further 1–2 minutes. Add the sieved vegetables.
3. Season with salt and pepper, add the yoghurt and stir together until very hot. Pile into a warmed serving dish and serve immediately.

GARLIC AND MINT MASH

SERVES 4

675g/1½lb potatoes, peeled
45g/1½oz butter
2 cloves of garlic, crushed
5 tablespoons crème fraîche
salt and freshly ground black pepper
a pinch of freshly grated nutmeg
1 tablespoon chopped fresh mint

1. Boil the potatoes in salted water until tender. Drain thoroughly.
2. Push the potatoes through a sieve or mouli.

Return them to the dry pan. Heat carefully, stirring to allow the potato to steam-dry.
3. Meanwhile, melt the butter in a saucepan, add the garlic and cook over a low heat for 4–5 minutes to soften the garlic.
4. Push the potato to one side of the pan. Set the exposed part of the pan over direct heat and add the crème fraîche and garlic butter. Season with salt, pepper and nutmeg.
5. When the crème fraîche is just coming to the boil, beat it into the potatoes. Check the seasoning and stir in the mint.

BRAISED SPRING ONIONS

SERVES 4

2 tablespoons extra virgin olive oil
3 large bunches of spring onions, trimmed and
    thickly sliced
salt and freshly ground black pepper
5 tablespoons red wine
150ml/¼ pint vegetable stock (see page 627)
2 tablespoons red wine vinegar
30g/1oz butter, diced

To garnish
1 tablespoon chopped fresh chives

1. Heat the oil in a large casserole, add the spring onions and fry over a high heat for 1–2 minutes, or until they begin to colour. Season with salt and pepper.
2. Pour the wine, stock and vinegar over the spring onions, cover and cook slowly for 8–10 minutes, or until the onions are tender.
3. Lift the onions from the cooking liquid and keep warm. Reduce the cooking liquid to 5 tablespoons by boiling rapidly. Whisk in the butter piece by piece, adjust the seasoning and pour over the onions. Sprinkle with the chives.

SALADS

BABY ASPARAGUS AND LEMON SALAD

SERVES 4

340g/12oz baby asparagus spears
3 sprigs of fresh mint
grated zest and juice of 1 lemon
4 tablespoons extra virgin olive oil
salt and freshly ground black pepper
4 handfuls of salad leaves, such as rocket,
    radicchio, chicory and frisée

To garnish
2–3 tablespoons roughly chopped herbs, such as
    chives, mint and thyme

1. Cook the asparagus in boiling salted water
with the mint for 2–3 minutes, or until just
tender. Drain and refresh lightly under cold
running water. Drain well again.
2. Mix together the lemon zest, juice and olive
oil and pour over the warm asparagus. Season
with salt and pepper.
3. Arrange the salad leaves on 4 individual
plates. Divide the asparagus between the leaves
and pour over the dressing. Sprinkle with the
herbs and serve warm.

BABY BEETROOT AND CHICKPEA SALAD WITH SESAME DRESSING

SERVES 4

675g/1½lb baby beetroots, trimmed leaving
    1cm/½in stalk
225g/8oz cooked chickpeas

For the dressing
4 tablespoons extra virgin olive oil
juice of 1 lemon
1 teaspoon light tahini
1 teaspoon Dijon mustard
salt and freshly ground black pepper

1. Wash the beetroot, then boil in salted water
until tender. Drain in a colander and when they
are cool enough to handle, peel off the skins.
2. Place the warm beetroot and chickpeas in a
large bowl.
3. Mix all the dressing ingredients together,
seasoning to taste with salt and pepper. Stir the
dressing into the beetroot and chickpeas and
allow to stand for 30 minutes before serving.

NOTE: If the beetroot are really tiny, there will be
no need to remove the skins after cooking them.

PINK FIR APPLE POTATO AND HAZELNUT SALAD

The nutty texture of these little potatoes makes
them perfect for a salad. In the absence of these
use Jersey Royals in early summer or Charlotte
potatoes later on in the year.

SERVES 4

675g/1½lb pink fir apple potatoes, scrubbed
1 teaspoon salt
1 sprig of fresh mint
2 cloves of garlic
110g/4oz hazelnuts, skinned, toasted and
    roughly chopped

For the dressing
2 tablespoons hazelnut oil
2 tablespoons olive oil

207

grated zest of 1 lemon
1 teaspoon Dijon mustard
1 tablespoon white wine or champagne vinegar
salt and freshly ground black pepper

To garnish
1 tablespoon chopped fresh chives

1. Put the potatoes into a large saucepan and add the salt, mint and garlic. Bring to the boil, then lower the heat and simmer for 12–15 minutes, or until the potatoes are tender. Drain and discard the mint.
2. Remove the garlic and crush. Set aside.
3. Put the hazelnuts into a bowl with the potatoes.
4. Put the dressing ingredients into a bowl, add the crushed garlic and whisk together to form an emulsion, then season to taste with salt and pepper.
5. Pour the dressing over the potatoes while they are still warm and leave to marinate for a few minutes. Sprinkle with the chives and serve warm or cold.

WILD GARLIC AND MIXED LEAF SALAD

Wild garlic is one of the delights of late spring. It grows abundantly in most woodland, where the strong pungent smell is quite overpowering.

SERVES 4

10 large leaves of wild garlic
225g/8oz baby spinach
30g/1oz rocket
1 Little Gem lettuce

For the dressing
grated zest and juice of 1 lemon
4 tablespoons extra virgin olive oil
½ teaspoon Dijon mustard
½ teaspoon soft light brown sugar
salt and freshly ground black pepper

To serve
55g/2oz Parmesan cheese, shaved

1. Wash and spin the wild garlic. Shred finely.
2. Tear the spinach, rocket and Little Gem into bite-sized pieces. Wash and spin-dry.
3. Put all the dressing ingredients into a bowl and whisk together until well emulsified.
4. To serve: put the salad leaves and wild garlic into a bowl and toss with the dressing. Pile on to a serving dish and scatter the Parmesan cheese shavings over the top. Serve immediately.

PUDDINGS

Fruit Puddings
Mousses, Soufflés and Creams
Ice Creams and Sorbets
Meringues
Pastries, Pies and Tarts
Cakes and Pâtisserie

FRUIT PUDDINGS

ROAST PINEAPPLE WITH RUM BUTTER

SERVES 4

4 baby pineapples or 2 medium pineapples, washed
170g/6oz butter
170g/6oz soft light brown sugar
4 tablespoons golden or dark rum

To serve
rich vanilla ice cream (see page 665)

1. Preheat the oven to 230°C/450°F/gas mark 8.
2. Cut the pineapples in half lengthways. Carefully cut the flesh out of the shells, reserving the 4 best halves for presentation.
3. Remove the core from the flesh and neatly slice the flesh lengthways. Pile the flesh back into the 4 reserved shells and place them on a large baking sheet.
4. Cream the butter with the sugar. Add the rum a little at a time according to taste. Spread one-quarter of the butter over the top of each pineapple and bake near the top of the preheated oven for 5–10 minutes. Serve immediately.

 MUSCAT DE BEAUMES DE VENISE

KUMQUAT AND DATE COMPOTE

SERVES 4

225g/8oz kumquats
225g/8oz dates

170g/6oz caster sugar
150ml/¼ pint water
1 cinnamon stick
3 tablespoons Armagnac

1. Wash the kumquats and slice them thinly, removing any pips. Cut the dates in half and remove the stones.
2. Dissolve the sugar in the water, bring to the boil and add the cinnamon stick. Lower the heat and simmer for 5–7 minutes, or until syrupy.
3. Add the kumquats and simmer for 2 minutes. Add the dates and cook for a further 2 minutes.
4. Remove the cinnamon and add the Armagnac. Serve warm or chilled.

RHUBARB AND ORANGE-FLOWER WATER COMPOTE

SERVES 4

290ml/½ pint orange-flower water
110g/4oz granulated sugar
4 star anise
450g/1lb rhubarb

To serve
vanilla Greek yoghurt cream (see page 618)

1. Make the poaching syrup: put the orange-flower water, sugar and star anise into a saucepan. Heat slowly until the sugar has completely dissolved, then bring to the boil and simmer for 5 minutes. Remove from the heat and allow to cool for 10 minutes, then remove the star anise with a slotted spoon.

2. Cut the rhubarb into 2.5cm/1in pieces. Put into the syrup and return to the heat. Cook very slowly for 10–12 minutes, or until the rhubarb is tender but not breaking up. Remove from the heat and allow to cool. Serve warm or cool, with the yoghurt cream handed separately.

 *SWEET WHITE*

SPICED BAKED BANANAS

SERVES 4

4 large ripe bananas
30g/1oz butter
grated zest and juice of 1 lime
1 teaspoon ground cardamom
1 teaspoon ground coriander
a large pinch of ground cinnamon
2 tablespoons clear honey
4 tablespoons plain yoghurt
4 teaspoons soft light brown sugar

1. Preheat the oven to 190°C/375°F/gas mark 5.
2. Peel and thickly slice the bananas and arrange in 4 ramekins.
3. Melt the butter in a small saucepan and stir in the lime zest and juice, spices and honey. Bring to the boil, then pour over the bananas.
4. Bake in the preheated oven for 10 minutes, or until very hot. Remove the ramekins from the oven and spoon a tablespoon of yoghurt over each. Sprinkle with the sugar. Serve immediately.

 *MUSCAT DE BEAUMES DE VENISE*

WILD RICE, JASMINE AND COCONUT PUDDING

SERVES 4

30g/1oz wild rice
110g/4oz jasmine Thai rice
570ml/1 pint coconut milk
2 star anise
110g/4oz creamed coconut
110g/4oz caster sugar

To serve
mango dipping sauce (see page 376)

1. Put the wild and jasmine rice into a large bowl, cover with cold water and stir well. Strain and allow to drip-dry in the strainer for 10 minutes.
2. Meanwhile, put the coconut milk, star anise, creamed coconut and sugar into a saucepan. Heat gently until the liquid just comes to the boil, stir occasionally to prevent the mixture from burning. Remove from the heat and allow to stand for 10 minutes.
3. Preheat the oven to 150°C/300°F/gas mark 2.
4. Put the rice into a large ovenproof casserole, pour over the coconut liquid, cover and bake in the preheated oven for 1½ hours, or until the rice is cooked and the liquid has been absorbed. Remove from the oven every 20 minutes and stir.
5. Transfer to warmed ramekins and serve hot. Just before serving spoon the cold dipping sauce on top.

 *SWEET WHITE*

MOUSSES, SOUFFLÉS AND CREAMS

WHITE CHOCOLATE MOUSSE

SERVES 8

100g/3½oz granulated sugar
water
5 egg yolks
285g/10oz white chocolate, chopped
3 tablespoons Cointreau
570ml/1 pint double cream, lightly whipped

1. Put the sugar into a small heavy saucepan and pour in just enough water to cover the sugar. Heat gently until the sugar has completely dissolved, then bring to the boil.
2. Boil to the short thread stage (when a little syrup is placed between a wet finger and thumb and the fingers are opened, it should form a thread about 2.5cm/1in long).
3. Pour the sugar syrup over the egg yolks, whisking all the time. Carry on whisking until the mixture is thick and mousse-like.
4. Bring a saucepan of water to the boil and turn off the heat. Set a heatproof bowl over the pan, place the chocolate and Cointreau in the bowl and melt carefully. Fold the melted chocolate into the egg mixture.
5. Immediately and carefully fold in the cream. Pour into a serving bowl or individual ramekins. Chill for 2 hours before serving.

 *LOUPIAC OR SAINTE-CROIX-DU-MONT*

WARM STEM GINGER MOUSSE WITH CARDAMOM SABAYON

SERVES 6

290ml/½ pint milk
150ml/¼ pint double cream
55g/2oz roasted coffee beans, lightly crushed
2 eggs
1 teaspoon ground ginger
4 tablespoons syrup from the stem ginger jar
2 teaspoons arrowroot
4 pieces of stem ginger, chopped

For the sabayon
2 egg yolks
1 teaspoon ground cardamom
2 tablespoons caster sugar
5 tablespoons Marsala
2 tablespoons white wine

To serve
coffee dragees
chocolate brandy snaps (see page 229)

1. Preheat the oven to 150°C/300°F/gas mark 2.
2. Put the milk, cream and coffee beans into a large saucepan and bring to scalding point (just below boiling), then remove from the heat and allow to infuse for 30 minutes. Strain.
3. Mix the eggs, ground ginger, stem ginger syrup and arrowroot together in a bowl until well mixed. Stir in the infused cream and strain into a clean bowl, taking care to sieve as much

of the egg through as possible. Stir in the stem ginger. Taste and add more stem ginger if desired.

4. Divide the mixture between 6 ramekins. Do not fill them more than two-thirds full. Put into a large roasting tin half filled with boiling water and bake in the preheated oven for 40–50 minutes, or until set. Remove from the oven and place each ramekin on an individual plate. The mousses can be served warm or cold.

5. Ten minutes before the mousses are to be served, make the sabayon: put the egg yolks, cardamom, sugar, Marsala and wine into a bowl set over, not in, a saucepan of simmering water. Whisk for 6–8 minutes, or until frothy. Spoon a little of the sabayon over each mousse and decorate with the coffee dragees. Hand the chocolate brandy snaps separately.

NOTE: Coffee dragees are chocolate-coated coffee beans.

 *MARSALA*

MILK CHOCOLATE BAVAROIS WITH BLUEBERRY SAUCE

SERVES 4

oil for greasing
3 tablespoons water
7g/¼oz powdered gelatine
150ml/¼ pint milk
3 egg yolks
15g/½oz caster sugar
140g/5oz milk chocolate, chopped
290ml/½ pint double cream, lightly whipped

For the blueberry sauce
225g/8oz blueberries
85g/3oz caster sugar
4 tablespoons water
1 tablespoon lemon juice

To decorate
milk chocolate caraque (see page 664)

1. Lightly oil 4 ramekins and line the bottom of each with a disc of oiled greaseproof paper.

2. Place the water in a small pan and sprinkle over the gelatine. Leave for 5 minutes to become spongy.

3. Bring the milk to the boil in a saucepan. Beat the egg yolks and sugar together with a wooden spoon and gradually stir in the milk. Return the mixture to the pan and heat gently, stirring constantly with a wooden spoon until the custard will coat the back of the spoon.

4. Put the chocolate into a bowl and pour on the custard. Stir well to melt the chocolate (you may need to strain the chocolate custard if there are pieces of chocolate floating around).

5. Dissolve the gelatine over a low heat without boiling until liquid and clear, then add to the custard. Stir gently and when the mixture is on the point of setting, fold in the cream. Divide the mixture evenly between the 4 ramekins. Chill until set.

6. Make the sauce: put the blueberries into a large saucepan with the sugar, water and lemon juice. Stir over a low heat to melt the sugar. Increase the heat and stir until the blueberries just begin to collapse. Remove from the heat and allow the compote to cool.

7. To serve: turn each bavarois out carefully on to an individual plate, using a knife to loosen the edges, or dip the ramekins very quickly in boiling water. Remove the greaseproof paper from the tops.

8. Spoon a little compote on to the side of each plate and decorate with the chocolate caraque.

 *CALIFORNIAN ORANGE MUSCAT*

GOOSEBERRY AND ELDERFLOWER FOOL

SERVES 4

450g/1lb gooseberries, washed
290ml/½ pint elderflower muscat syrup (see page 362)
5 tablespoons mascarpone
150ml/¼ pint Greek yoghurt
150ml/¼ pint whipping cream

To decorate
fresh mint leaves
icing sugar

1. Put the gooseberries and syrup into a saucepan, bring to the boil, then cover, lower the heat and simmer for 7–10 minutes, or until the gooseberries are completely soft.
2. Push the gooseberries with the cooking liquor through a sieve into a clean bowl and allow to cool completely.
3. Mix together the mascarpone and yoghurt and stir into the gooseberry mixture.
4. Whisk the cream until it leaves a trail and fold into the gooseberry mixture. Turn into a glass bowl, cover and allow to chill for at least 2 hours. Decorate with mint leaves and dust the top with icing sugar.

NOTE: If elderflowers are not in season, apple and elderflower juice drink can be used in their place.

 *SAUTERNES*

IRISH COFFEE JELLIES

SERVES 6

100ml/3½fl oz Irish whiskey
45g/1½oz powdered gelatine
110g/4oz caster sugar
1 litre/1¾ pints strong fresh coffee
290ml/½ pint double cream
2 tablespoons Kahlua or other coffee liqueur

To decorate
a few chocolate coffee beans
6 amaretti biscuits, crushed

1. Put the whiskey into a small saucepan and sprinkle over the gelatine.
2. Dissolve the sugar in the hot coffee.
3. Melt the gelatine over a low heat without boiling and pour into the coffee, stirring continuously.
4. Taste the coffee and add extra sugar if necessary. Pour into 6 stemmed glasses and

leave until cool. Chill for 2–3 hours, or until set.
5. Whisk the cream with the coffee liqueur until it just holds its shape. Pile it on to the jellies and sprinkle over a few chocolate coffee beans and amaretti. Serve immediately.

 *SAINTE-CROIX-DU-MONT*

ICE CREAMS AND SORBETS

INDIVIDUAL WHITE CHOCOLATE AND COFFEE BOMBES

SERVES 8

For the ice cream
6 egg yolks
a pinch of salt
110g/4oz caster sugar
570ml/1 pint single cream
2 tablespoons instant coffee powder
55g/2oz chocolate coffee beans, roughly chopped
1 quantity white chocolate ganache (see page 241)

To serve
1 quantity chocolate brandy snap cups (see page 229)
bitter chocolate sauce (see page 241)
cocoa powder for dusting

1. Whisk the egg yolks, salt and sugar together in a bowl.
2. Place the cream and coffee powder in a saucepan and heat slowly until the coffee dissolves.
3. Add the coffee cream to the egg yolk mixture, stirring all the time.
4. Pour the mixture into a clean, heavy-based saucepan and stir continuously over a low heat until thick and creamy. Do not allow to boil.
5. Strain into a bowl and allow to cool, whisking occasionally. Chill, then pour into a freezerproof container and freeze.
6. When the ice cream is almost frozen, remove from the freezer and whizz in a food processor, using the pulse mode to break up the ice

crystals. Stir in the coffee beans before returning to the freezer for a further 2–3 hours, or until firm.
7. Using an ice-cream scoop or soup spoon dipped into hot water, scoop 8 balls of ice cream on to a baking sheet lined with silicone paper and return to the freezer for 30 minutes.
8. Melt the ganache in a heatproof bowl set over, not in, a saucepan of simmering water. Allow to cool.
9. Pick up one ice cream ball at a time with a fork. Using a large spoon, coat the ice cream with the ganache. Allow the ganache to set in a smooth layer before returning the bombe to the freezer. Repeat with the remaining ice cream and ganache.
10. To serve: place each bombe in the centre of a chocolate brandy snap. Place on a large individual flat plate, pour a little bitter chocolate sauce around and dust with cocoa powder.

 AUSTRALIAN LIQUEUR MUSCAT

SPRING MINT PARFAIT

SERVES 6

oil for greasing
170g/6oz granulated sugar
2 sprigs of fresh mint
thinly pared zest of 1 lemon
water
3 egg whites
380ml/⅔ pint double cream
190ml/⅓ pint Greek yoghurt
20g/¾oz (a large handful) fresh mint leaves, finely shredded

To decorate
6 small sprigs of fresh mint
1 egg white
caster sugar

1. Prepare a 12.5cm/5in soufflé dish: wrap a double-thickness piece of greaseproof paper around the dish and secure with string or an elastic band, so that the paper comes 5cm/2in over the top of the dish. Lightly oil the inside edge of the paper.

2. Put the sugar, sprigs of mint and lemon zest into a heavy-based saucepan with enough water to cover. Bring slowly to the boil without stirring, then, when the sugar has dissolved, simmer for 5 minutes. Remove the mint and lemon zest and continue to boil the syrup to the firm ball stage (see page 662).

3. Meanwhile, whisk the egg whites in a clean bowl until they form stiff peaks (preferably using an electric hand whisk), and when the sugar syrup is just ready pour it on to the whites, whisking continuously and being careful not to let the hot sugar touch the beaters. Work as quickly as possible.

4. When all the syrup has been added, whisk hard until the mixture is stiff, shiny and absolutely stable. When the whisk is lifted the meringue should not flow at all.

5. Lightly whip the cream and fold it into the meringue mixture with the yoghurt and shredded mint. Pour into the prepared soufflé dish and freeze for 2 hours before serving.

6. Prepare the decoration: brush a very little egg white all over each sprig of mint and dip into the caster sugar. Arrange in a single layer on a baking sheet lined with silicone paper and leave to dry in a warm, dry place for 1 hour.

7. To serve: remove the greaseproof paper from the sides of the parfait and arrange the mint sprigs on top.

 *MOSCATO D'ASTI*

ELDERFLOWER SORBET

SERVES 4

290ml/½ pint elderflower cordial (see page 361)
juice of 1 lemon
150ml/¼ pint water
½ egg white
1 tablespoon chopped fresh mint

1. Mix the elderflower cordial with the lemon juice and water. Pour the liquid into a freezerproof container and freeze for 3–4 hours, or until firm.

2. Transfer the sorbet to the refrigerator for 15 minutes to soften the ice crystals a little.

3. Cut the sorbet into cubes, transfer to a food processor with the egg white and mint and whizz, using the pulse button, until the ice crystals have broken up and you have a smooth purée.

4. Refreeze the sorbet for 1 hour before serving.

 ASTI SPUMANTE OR MOSCATO D'ASTI

GRAPEFRUIT, PINK PEPPERCORN AND VODKA SORBET

SERVES 4

225g/8oz granulated sugar
570ml/1 pint freshly squeezed grapefruit juice
150ml/¼ pint vodka
2 tablespoons pink peppercorns, crushed
½ egg white

1. Melt the sugar in the grapefruit juice in a saucepan over a low heat. Stir in the vodka and peppercorns and set aside to cool.

2. Pour the mixture into a freezerproof container and freeze overnight.

3. Transfer the sorbet to the refrigerator for 20 minutes. Cut the sorbet into rough cubes, place in a food processor with the egg white and whizz, using the pulse button, until the crystals have broken up and you have a smooth, thick, frozen purée. Immediately return the sorbet to the freezer and freeze for 2 hours before serving.

NOTE: If you have an ice-cream machine, tip the mixture into it at stage 2 and churn until frozen with the egg white.

 *MOSCATO D'ASTI*

BLUEBERRY AND MUSCAT SORBET

SERVES 4

450g/1lb blueberries
170g/6oz granulated sugar
juice of 1 lemon
150ml/¼ pint water
150ml/¼ pint muscat or other sweet dessert
  wine
1 egg white

1. Place the blueberries, sugar, lemon juice and water in a heavy-based saucepan. Stir gently over a low heat until the sugar has dissolved.
2. Whizz the blueberries in a food processor and pass through a sieve. Allow to cool.
3. Stir in the wine and taste. The mixture should have a good strong flavour and be a little too sweet. Add a little extra lemon juice to bring out the flavour of the blueberries if necessary.
4. Pour into a freezerproof container and freeze overnight.
5. Transfer the sorbet to the refrigerator for 15 minutes. Cut the sorbet into cubes, and place with the egg white in a food processor and whizz, using the pulse button, until the ice crystals have broken up and you have a smooth, thick purée. Be careful not to whizz for too long or the ice crystals will melt. Return to the freezer until firm before serving. (If the sorbet is still granular you may need to repeat step 5 for a really smooth consistency.)

NOTE; If you do not have a food processor, whisk the egg white until it forms stiff peaks and fold into the sorbet when it is half frozen, then freeze until firm.

 *MOSCATO D'ASTI*

RHUBARB CURD YOGHURT ICE CREAM

SERVES 4

450g/1lb rhubarb
4 tablespoons water
2 teaspoons stem ginger, chopped
4 egg yolks
170g/6oz caster sugar
110g/4oz unsalted butter
290ml/½ pint Greek yoghurt

To serve
ginger and brown sugar meringues (see page 592)

1. Slice the rhubarb and cook with the water over a low heat until completely tender. Put into a food processor and whizz until smooth, then sieve.
2. Put the rhubarb purée, stem ginger, egg yolks, sugar and butter into a saucepan. Set over a low heat and stir with a wooden spoon until the butter has melted and the curd is thick enough to coat the back of the spoon.
3. Remove from the heat and allow the curd to cool, then stir in the yoghurt. Cover closely and freeze.
4. Transfer the ice cream to the refrigerator about 1 hour before serving. Serve in scoops accompanied by the meringues.

NOTE: This ice cream is also delicious made with good-quality shop-bought lemon curd.

 *SAUTERNES*

CITRUS GRANITA

SERVES 4

thinly pared zest of 1 orange
thinly pared zest of 1 lime
thinly pared zest of 1 grapefruit
170g/6oz granulated sugar
150ml/¼ pint water
juice of 6 oranges
juice of 1 lime
juice of 1 grapefruit

1. Put the citrus zest, sugar and water into a saucepan and dissolve over a low heat, then bring to the boil, lower the heat and simmer for 4–5 minutes.
2. Remove from the heat and allow to cool completely. When the syrup is cold, add the citrus juice and strain.
3. Freeze in a shallow tray for 1 hour, or until nearly frozen. Break up the ice crystals with a fork and freeze again until firm.
4. To serve: transfer the granita to the refrigerator for 10 minutes, then pile into individual chilled serving glasses.

 *MUSCAT DE BEAUMES DE VENISE*

MERINGUES

CHOCOLATE AND STRAWBERRY PAVLOVA

SERVES 8

4 egg whites
a pinch of salt
225g/8oz caster sugar
1 teaspoon vanilla essence
1½ teaspoons white wine vinegar or lemon
    juice
30g/1oz cocoa powder, sifted
425ml/¾ pint double cream, lightly whipped
450g/1lb strawberries, hulled

To finish
icing sugar

1. Preheat the oven to 140°C/275°F/gas mark 1.
2. Line a large baking sheet with silicone paper.
3. Whisk the egg whites with the salt in a large, clean bowl until they form stiff peaks, then quickly add a tablespoon of the sugar and whisk again until very stiff and shiny.
4. Gradually add the remaining sugar, 1 tablespoon at a time, beating until very stiff between each addition.
5. Add the vanilla and vinegar or lemon juice.
6. Sift the cocoa powder on to the egg whites mixture and gently fold in. Pile the mixture on to the lined baking sheet, shaping it into a circle 4cm/1½in thick. Make an indentation in the centre to make room for the filling.
7. Bake at the bottom of the preheated oven for 1–1½ hours, or until firm and dry to touch. Leave to cool, then carefully peel off the silicone paper.
8. When quite cold, spoon the cream into the centre of the pavlova and pile the strawberries on top. Sift icing sugar over the top to decorate.

 TOP ESTATE NEW ZEALAND PINOT NOIR

CHOCOLATE MERINGUE TORTE

SERVES 8–10

oil for greasing
225g/8oz almonds, toasted
225g/8oz good-quality dark chocolate
225g/8oz pitted dates
6 egg whites
30g/1oz caster sugar
225g/8oz soft light brown sugar, sifted
225g/8oz mascarpone

To serve
icing sugar
kumquat and date compote (see page 211)

1. Preheat the oven to 180°C/350°F/gas mark 4.
2. Line 2 × 20cm/8in moule-à-manqué tins with lightly oiled kitchen foil.
3. Put the almonds, chocolate and dates into a food processor and pulse on and off until they are roughly chopped. Set aside.
4. Whisk the egg whites until they form stiff peaks, then add the caster sugar and continue to whisk until shiny.
5. Add the brown sugar and chopped almond, chocolate and date mixture, folding the ingredients into the egg whites with a large metal spoon until they are just combined.

Divide the mixture between the prepared tins and spread to flatten.

6. Bake the tortes towards the bottom of the preheated oven for 45 minutes. Remove from the oven and allow to cool in the tins.

7. When the meringues are cold, peel away the foil.

8. Place one meringue bottom side up on a board and spread with the mascarpone, then place the second meringue on top.

9. Dust the torte with icing sugar and serve with the compote handed separately.

 *SAUTERNES*

WHITE PRALINE MERINGUES WITH PINK GRAPEFRUIT CURD CREAM

MAKES ABOUT 24

4 egg whites
a pinch of salt
2 tablespoons caster sugar
1 × 225g/8oz sugar quantity white praline (see page 605)
2–3 drops of almond essence

For the pink grapefruit curd cream
290ml/½ pint whipping or double cream
5 tablespoons pink grapefruit curd (see following recipe)

To serve
a little icing sugar

1. Preheat the oven to 110°C/225°F/gas mark ½.
2. Line 2 baking sheets with silicone paper.
3. Whisk the egg whites with a pinch of salt until very stiff but not dry. Add the sugar and whisk again until very stiff and shiny. Carefully fold in the praline and the almond essence.
4. Put the meringue mixture into a piping bag fitted with a 1cm/½in plain nozzle. Squeeze

gently to get rid of any pockets of air. Pipe the meringue into 5cm/2in shells set fairly far apart on the prepared baking sheets.

5. Bake the meringues near the bottom of the preheated oven for 1–1½ hours, or until they will lift cleanly from the paper. Using your thumb, make an indentation in the base of each meringue. Bake for a further 15 minutes.

6. Carefully lift the meringues from the paper, transfer to a wire rack and leave to cool completely.

7. Whip the cream to soft peaks and fold in the pink grapefruit curd. Use to sandwich the meringues together and pile on to a serving dish. Dust with icing sugar and serve within 1 hour.

 AUSTRALIAN ORANGE MUSCAT AND FLORA

PINK GRAPEFRUIT CURD

MAKES 450G/1LB

1 large pink grapefruit, washed
85g/3oz unsalted butter
225g/8oz granulated sugar
3 eggs, lightly beaten

1. Grate the zest of the grapefruit on the finest gauge on the grater, taking care to grate the zest only, not the pith.
2. Squeeze and strain the juice from the grapefruit.
3. Put the grapefruit zest and juice, butter, sugar and eggs into a heavy-based saucepan or double boiler and heat gently, stirring all the time, until the mixture is thick.
4. Pour into warm, dry, sterilized jars (see page 277), cover and label.

NOTE: This curd will keep in the refrigerator for about 3 weeks.

PASTRIES, PIES AND TARTS

APRICOT AND HAZELNUT STRUDEL

SERVES 4

*285g/10oz flour quantity strudel pastry (see
    page 647), stretched to a rectangle at least
    40 × 60cm/16 × 24in*
900g/2lb fresh apricots
55g/2oz soft light brown sugar
85g/3oz toasted hazelnuts, ground
grated zest and juice of 1 lemon
2 tablespoons ground rice
1 teaspoon ground cinnamon
85g/3oz butter, melted

To decorate
icing sugar

1. Preheat the oven to 200°C/400°F/gas mark 6.
Grease a baking sheet.
2. Prepare the fillings: halve the apricots and
remove the stones. Mix with the sugar,
hazelnuts, lemon zest and juice, ground rice and
cinnamon.
3. Flour a large tea-towel. Lay the pastry on
this.
4. Brush the pastry with melted butter. Place the
filling on one end of the pastry. Using the tea-
towel to help, roll up as for a Swiss roll, trying
to maintain a fairly tight roll. Lift the tea-towel
and gently tip the strudel on to the prepared
baking sheet. Brush with melted butter. Trim
the edges neatly.
5. Bake in the preheated oven for about 40
minutes, or until golden-brown. Dust with icing
sugar while still warm.

AUSTRALIAN LIQUEUR MUSCAT

CARAMELIZED PINEAPPLE AND MASCARPONE TART

SERVES 6–8

1 × 170g/6oz pâte sucrée (see page 645)
1 large pineapple
55g/2oz butter
55g/2oz soft light brown sugar
255g/9oz mascarpone
30g/1oz icing sugar

To decorate
a few sprigs of fresh mint

1. Preheat the oven to 190°C/375°F/gas mark 5.
2. Roll out the pastry and use to line a 20cm/8in
loose-based flan ring. Chill for 30 minutes.
3. Bake the flan ring blind for 15 minutes (see
page 640) until pale brown in colour and dry to
the touch. Remove the lining paper and beans
and leave the pastry case in the flan ring on a
wire rack to cool. When cold, take the pastry
case out of the flan ring and place on a flat
serving plate.
4. Cut the leaves and skin off the pineapple and
remove the core. Cut the pineapple in half
lengthways and cut each half into 1cm/½in
slices.
5. Melt half the butter with half the sugar in a
frying pan, and when sizzling add a few
pineapple slices. Cover over a low heat, turning
once, until the pineapple starts to caramelize.
Tip the slices on to a plate to cool slightly and
repeat with the remaining butter, sugar and
pineapple.

6. Mix the mascarpone with the icing sugar and spread over the base of the pastry case. When the pineapple is just warm, arrange the slices, overlapping, on top.

7. Arrange the sprigs of fresh mint on the top before serving.

NOTE: The pineapple is best served slightly warm so that the butter does not solidify. If you need to prepare the tart in advance keep the pineapple separate and warm it in a preheated oven (150°C/300°F/gas mark 2) for 10–15 minutes, then arrange it on top of the mascarpone.

 *MONBAZILLAC*

RHUBARB STRUDEL

SERVES 4

900g/2lb rhubarb
grated zest of 1 orange
3 tablespoons redcurrant jelly
4 pieces of stem ginger, finely chopped
30g/1oz caster sugar
4 sheets of filo pastry
55g/2oz butter, melted
55g/2oz ground rice

To decorate
icing sugar

To serve
1 quantity orange crème anglaise (see page 505)

1. Preheat the oven to 200°C/400°F/gas mark 6.
2. Cut the rhubarb into 1cm/½in chunks. Put into a saucepan with the orange zest, redcurrant jelly, stem ginger and caster sugar and cook over a low heat for 7–10 minutes, or until the rhubarb is soft. Taste for sweetness and add more sugar if necessary. Remove from the heat and allow to cool.
3. Lay the pieces of filo on a clean work surface,

brush generously with butter (see diagram) and sprinkle with ground rice.

4. Pile the rhubarb mixture on one end of the filo and roll up like a Swiss roll (see diagram on page 647). Brush the outside with melted butter. Bake in the preheated oven for 20–25 minutes, or until golden-brown. Remove from the oven and dust generously with icing sugar. Serve warm, with the orange crème anglaise handed separately.

 *SAUTERNES*

INDIVIDUAL RHUBARB MILLE-FEUILLES

SERVES 4

225g/8oz flour quantity cinnamon puff pastry
  (see page 646)
340g/12oz rhubarb, sliced
grated zest of ½ orange
4 tablespoons cranberry or redcurrant jelly
290ml/½ pint mascarpone

To decorate
icing sugar

1. Preheat the oven to 220°C/425°F/gas mark 7.
2. On a floured board, roll the pastry into a thin rectangle about 30 × 20cm/12 × 8in. Place on a baking sheet. Prick all over with a fork.
3. Leave the pastry to relax, covered, for 20 minutes. Bake in the preheated oven for 7–10 minutes, or until browned. Remove from the oven and allow to cool.
4. Meanwhile, put the rhubarb into a saucepan with the orange zest and cranberry or redcurrant jelly and cook over a low heat for 7–8 minutes, or until the rhubarb is soft but not broken up. Allow to cool.
5. Cut the pastry into 12 strips, each 7.5 × 4cm/ 3 × 1½in. Divide half the mascarpone between 4 strips of pastry and spread flat. Spoon a little of the rhubarb on top. Cover each with a second

strip of pastry. Spread each with the remaining mascarpone and rhubarb. Put a strip of pastry on top of each and dust very generously with icing sugar.

6. To serve: dust a plate with a little icing sugar and arrange a mille-feuille on top. Serve within 1 hour.

 *SAUTERNES*

CAKES AND PÂTISSERIE

BANANA CAKE

MAKES A 22.5CM/9IN CAKE

225g/8oz butter, softened
225g/8oz soft light brown muscovado sugar
3 eggs, lightly beaten
3 medium-ripe bananas, mashed with a fork
1 teaspoon vanilla essence
285g/10oz self-raising flour
1 teaspoon ground mixed spice
½ teaspoon salt
½ teaspoon baking powder
a little milk

To serve
1 quantity cream cheese icing (see page 664)

1. Preheat the oven to 180°C/350°F/gas mark 4. Grease and line the base of a 22.5cm/9in deep loose-based cake tin with lightly oiled greaseproof paper.
2. Cream the butter and when soft add the sugar and beat until light and fluffy. Beat in the eggs a little at a time to prevent curdling. (If the mixture starts to curdle, add 1 tablespoon of the flour.)
3. Stir in the bananas and vanilla essence.
4. Sift the flour, mixed spice, salt and baking powder into a bowl. Fold into the banana mixture, adding a little milk to give a dropping consistency.
5. Tip the mixture into the prepared cake tin and bake in the centre of the oven for 1–1¼ hours, or until the cake is golden-brown, firm to the touch and is coming away from the edges of the tin. (You may need to cover the cake with kitchen foil after about 30 minutes if it is browning a little too fast.)

6. Allow to cool completely before turning out of the tin.
7. To serve: spread the cream cheese icing over the top of the cake.

HAZELNUT AND ORANGE GRIESTORTE WITH RHUBARB CREAM

Griestorte is a classic semolina and almond cake. This is a variation.

SERVES 4

15g/½oz butter, melted
3 eggs, separated
110g/4oz caster sugar
grated zest and juice of 1 orange
55g/2oz fine semolina
2 tablespoons ground hazelnuts

To serve
150ml/¼ pint double cream
1 quantity rhubarb and orange-flower water
    compote (see page 211)
icing sugar

1. Preheat the oven to 180°C/350°F/gas mark 4.
2. Brush a moule-à-manqué or 20cm/8in cake tin with the melted butter. Line the base with a circle of greaseproof paper and brush with melted butter.
3. Cream the egg yolks, sugar, orange zest and juice together in a bowl until light, fluffy and thick.
4. Mix the semolina and hazelnuts together and fold into the cake mixture.

5. Whisk the egg whites until stiff and fold into the cake.

6. Pile the mixture into the prepared tin and smooth the top with a spatula. Bake in the preheated oven for 35–40 minutes, or until the cake is firm to the touch and just shrinking away from the sides of the tin. Cool on a wire rack. Peel off the lining paper.

7. Whip the cream and fold into the rhubarb and orange-flower water compote. Split the cake in half and fill with the mixture. Dust the top with icing sugar.

 *AUSTRALIAN ORANGE MUSCAT AND FLORA*

LEMON SYRUP CAKE

SERVES 4

butter for greasing
110g/4oz butter, softened
170g/6oz caster sugar
170g/6oz self-raising flour, sifted
4 tablespoons milk
grated zest of 1 lemon
2 large eggs, beaten
a pinch of salt

For the lemon syrup
4 tablespoons lemon juice
85g/3oz icing sugar, sifted

To serve
icing sugar

1. Grease a 900g/2lb loaf tin with a little butter. Line the tin with buttered greaseproof paper. Preheat the oven to 180°C/350°F/gas mark 4.

2. Place all the cake ingredients in a large bowl and beat with an electric mixer for 3 minutes or until well blended. Pour the mixture into the loaf tin and smooth the top. Bake in the centre of the preheated oven for 45 minutes, or until golden, firm to the touch and coming away from the edges of the tin.

3. Leave the cake to cool on a wire rack.

4. Make the lemon syrup: gently warm the lemon juice and icing sugar in a saucepan until the sugar dissolves. Prick the top of the cake all over with a fork and pour the warmed syrup over the top.

5. Leave the cake until cold before turning out. Serve sprinkled with icing sugar.

RICH LEMON ROULADE

SERVES 6

200g/7oz cream cheese
grated zest and juice of 2 large lemons
5 eggs, separated
140g/5oz caster sugar
icing sugar

For the filling
4 tablespoons lemon curd
190ml/⅓ pint double cream, whipped

1. Preheat the oven to 200°C/400°F/gas mark 6.

2. Line a large roasting tin with a sheet of silicone paper.

3. Put the cream cheese into a large bowl and gradually stir in the lemon zest and juice, making sure there are no lumps.

4. Whisk the egg yolks and sugar together until pale and creamy. Put the egg whites into a clean glass or metal bowl and whisk until they form medium peaks.

5. Gently stir the egg yolk mixture into the lemon and cream cheese, then fold in the egg whites. Tip into the roasting tin and bake for 10 minutes, or until the mixture is just set.

6. When the roulade is cool, turn it on to a piece of greaseproof paper sprinkled with icing sugar and peel off the backing paper.

7. Spread with the lemon curd and then the whipped cream and roll up, leaving the final seam tucked underneath. Transfer to a serving dish and sift a little more icing sugar over just before serving.

 *MONBAZILLAC*

WARM LIME AND PISTACHIO SYRUP LOAF

SERVES 6

140g/5oz plain flour
1 teaspoon baking powder
a pinch of salt
55g/2oz butter
110g/4oz caster sugar
grated zest of 3 limes
1 large egg
5 tablespoons buttermilk or soured cream

For the syrup
juice of 3 limes
55g/2oz pistachio nuts, roughly chopped
110g/4oz caster sugar

1. Preheat the oven to 180°C/350°F/gas mark 4.
2. Prepare a 20 × 7.5cm/8 × 3in loaf tin and line with greaseproof paper.
3. Sift the flour with the baking powder and salt and set aside.
4. Cream the butter, sugar and lime zest together until light and fluffy.
5. Beat the egg in a separate bowl and beat into the creamed mixture a little at a time, adding 1 tablespoon of the flour if the mixture begins to curdle.
6. Alternately fold in the flour and buttermilk until thoroughly mixed.
7. Spoon the mixture into the prepared tin. Bake in the centre of the preheated oven for 30–35 minutes, or until the loaf is well risen and a skewer inserted into the centre comes out clean.
8. Make the syrup: combine the lime juice, pistachios and sugar in a saucepan and dissolve over a low heat, stirring occasionally.
9. Prick the cake all over with a skewer and pour over the hot syrup. Allow to cool for 15 minutes in the tin, then lift out and slice. Serve warm.

APRICOT, NECTARINE AND MASCARPONE BRIOCHE PIZZA

SERVES 6

225g/8oz flour quantity brioche dough (see page 373)
450g/1lb ripe apricots
3 large nectarines
110g/4oz caster sugar
5 tablespoons white wine
1 vanilla pod
2–3 tablespoons vodka-macerated raisins (see page 612) (optional)
340g/12oz mascarpone
85g/3oz soft dark brown sugar

1. Preheat the oven to 190°C/375°F/gas mark 5.
2. Knock back the risen brioche dough and roll out to a circle about 28cm/11in in diameter. Place on a baking sheet. Refrigerate until ready to use.
3. Halve and stone the apricots. Halve and stone the nectarines.
4. Put the sugar, wine and vanilla pod into a saucepan. Dissolve the sugar over a low heat and bring to the boil. Add the apricots and nectarines and poach for 4–5 minutes, or until the fruit has softened slightly. Stir in the raisins. Turn into a bowl and cool.
5. Spread the mascarpone over the surface of the brioche, leaving a 2.5cm/1in border all the way around the edge.
6. Lightly drain the fruit mixture. Arrange on top of the mascarpone and sprinkle the brown sugar on top. Allow to stand at room temperature for 15 minutes.
7. Bake the pizza in the centre of the preheated oven for 30–40 minutes, or until a rich brown colour and cooked. Reduce the oven temperature if the pizza shows signs of becoming too dark. Serve warm.

 MUSCAT DE BEAUMES DE VENISE

CHOCOLATE HAZELNUT RAVIOLI WITH CANDIED ORANGE

SERVES 4

225g/8oz orange pasta (see page 653)
salt
1 tablespoon hazelnut or sunflower oil

For the filling
45ml/1½fl oz double cream
110g/4oz good-quality plain chocolate, chopped
55g/2oz toasted hazelnuts, finely chopped
2 tablespoons Grand Marnier or Cointreau

For the sauce
150ml/¼ pint water
225g/8oz granulated sugar
2 oranges
290ml/½ pint crème anglaise (see page 661), made with 150ml/¼ pint single cream and 150ml/¼ pint milk

1. Make the filling: bring the cream to the boil in a small saucepan and simmer, stirring gently, until reduced by half. Add the chocolate, hazelnuts and Grand Marnier. Stir until the chocolate has melted. Tip the mixture into a bowl and leave to set in a cool place (but not the refrigerator) until firm.
2. Make the syrup: put the water and sugar into a saucepan and leave over a low heat until the sugar has dissolved, stirring occasionally.
3. Peel strips of zest off the oranges, leaving behind any white pith. Cut the zest into julienne strips. Blanch the julienne in a saucepan of boiling water for 1 minute, then drain well.
4. Add the julienne to the (sugar) syrup and simmer for 5–10 minutes until it looks glassy and shiny and holds its shape well. Strain the candied orange zest on to the back of a sieve, separate out the individual strands and allow the excess syrup to drip off.
5. Roll out the pasta until it is very thin and cut out 20 × 10cm/4in circles. Brush one edge of each circle with a little water. Place a teaspoon

of chocolate filling in the centre and fold the edges together to form a crescent, making sure there are no air pockets inside the parcel. Allow the ravioli to dry out slightly on a lightly floured surface.
6. Bring a large saucepan of water to the boil with the salt and oil. Add the ravioli and simmer gently for 4–5 minutes. Drain well.
7. Divide the ravioli between 4 warmed soup plates and pour over the warmed crème anglaise. Sprinkle over the candied orange zest and serve immediately.

 CALIFORNIAN ORANGE MUSCAT

COFFEE, WALNUT AND WHITE CHOCOLATE BROWNIES

MAKES 24

450g/1lb soft light brown sugar
85g/3oz butter
2 tablespoons instant coffee granules
1 tablespoon boiling water
2 eggs
1 teaspoon vanilla essence
285g/10oz plain flour
2 teaspoons baking powder
½ teaspoon salt
170g/6oz walnuts, roughly chopped
170g/6oz white chocolate, roughly chopped into ½cm/¼in pieces

1. Preheat the oven to 180°C/350°F/gas mark 4. Grease a 27.5 × 20cm/11 × 8in deep baking tray.
2. Heat the sugar and butter in a medium saucepan over medium–low heat until the butter melts. Dissolve the coffee in the water and stir into the butter mixture. Allow to cool to room temperature, then beat in the eggs and vanilla essence.
3. Sift the flour with the baking powder and salt and stir into the butter mixture with the walnuts and chocolate.

4. Spread the mixture evenly in the prepared tin with a spatula. Bake in the preheated oven for 25–30 minutes, or until lightly browned, taking care not to overbake or the brownies will be hard and dry.

5. Transfer to a wire rack and leave to cook completely before cutting into squares for serving.

CHOCOLATE BRANDY SNAP CUPS

SERVES 8

110g/4oz butter
110g/4oz caster sugar
85g/3oz plain flour, sifted
30g/1oz cocoa powder, sifted
4–5 tablespoons golden syrup
2 tablespoons brandy or rum
butter for greasing

1. Preheat the oven to 190°C/375°F/gas mark 5.

2. Melt the butter in a small saucepan. Remove from the heat and stir in all the remaining ingredients.

3. Grease a large baking sheet with a little butter. Spread a large tablespoon of the mixture on to the sheet to form a 12cm/5in circle. Repeat with another spoonful.

4. Bake in the centre of the preheated oven for 5–7 minutes, or until golden-brown. Remove the tray from the oven and leave to cool for 1 minute.

5. Place 2 highball glasses or tall tumblers upside down on a work surface. Using a greased palette knife, carefully lift the chocolate snaps off the sheet and lay over the tops of the glasses, slightly off centre. Allow the snaps to cool for a few minutes until they have set into shape, then remove from the glasses and place on a cooling rack.

6. Wipe the baking sheet clean and repeat with the remaining mixture.

7. Store in an airtight container until ready to use.

NOTES: If the brandy snap cups are not to be served immediately, they must be put into an airtight container for storage once they are cool, or they will become soggy.

Similarly, brandy snaps should not be filled with moist mixtures like whipped cream or ice cream until shortly before serving, or they will quickly lose their crispness.

Do not bake too many snaps at one time as once they become cold, they are too brittle to shape. They can be made pliable again if returned to the oven.

MISCELLANEOUS

Drinks
Preserves
Breads
Sauces and Garnishes

DRINKS

ICED DARJEELING TEA WITH MINT AND ORANGE

SERVES 4

4 Darjeeling tea bags
1 bunch of fresh mint
1 orange, sliced
1 lemon, sliced
1.15 litres/2 pints boiling water
caster sugar
150ml/¼ pint freshly squeezed orange juice

To decorate
4 sprigs of fresh mint
orange and lemon slices
crushed ice

1. Put the tea bags, mint, orange and lemon slices into a heatproof jug and pour on the boiling water. Leave to infuse for 5 minutes. Add sugar to taste.
2. Remove the tea bags and allow the tea to get cold. Strain off the mint and fruit. Add the orange juice to the tea.
3. To serve: put plenty of ice into 4 large glasses. Pour over the tea. Decorate with the fresh mint and orange and lemon slices.

FRESH FRUIT PUNCH

SERVES 1

1 banana, peeled and roughly chopped
juice of 1 lime
100ml/3½fl oz freshly squeezed orange juice
4 ice cubes, crushed

1. Place all the ingredients in a blender and whizz until smooth. Serve immediately.

NOTE: For a protein punch add 1 egg and 4 tablespoons plain yoghurt.

GINGER BEER

This recipe has been taken from *Home-Made Wines, Syrups and Cordials*, first published by the National Federation of Women's Institutes in 1954 and subsequently frequently republished until 1966.

MAKES 4.5 LITRES/8 PINTS

5cm/2in piece of fresh ginger root, bruised
15g/½oz cream of tartar
450g/1lb caster sugar
thinly pared zest and juice of 1 lemon
4.5 litres/8 pints boiling water
15g/½oz fresh yeast or 7g/¼oz dried yeast

1. Put the ginger, cream of tartar, sugar and lemon zest into a large bowl and pour over the boiling water. Stir vigorously until the sugar is dissolved, then allow to cool to blood temperature.
2. Add the yeast and lemon juice. Cover with a

clean, heavy tea-towel and leave in a warm
place for 24 hours.

3. Skim off the scum carefully and pour or
syphon off the liquid without disturbing the
sediment.

4. Pour the liquid into special ginger beer
bottles. Cork and wire as quickly as possible.
Store in a cool, dark place. The ginger beer is
ready to drink in 2–3 days' time.

NOTES: It is essential to use the correct bottles
which are available from specialist wine- and
beer-making shops (ordinary wine bottles are
not strong enough to contain gas and may
explode).

The ginger beer must not be stored for longer
than 2 weeks before consumption.

PRESERVES

FRESH CUCUMBER AND MANGO CHUTNEY

SERVES 4

1 cucumber, peeled and de-seeded
1 large firm but ripe mango, peeled
1 small onion, very finely chopped
1 tablespoon sunflower oil
2.5cm/1in piece of fresh root ginger, peeled and
    finely chopped
1 large clove of garlic, crushed
½ teaspoon ground cumin
seeds from 2 cardamom pods
1 tablespoon Thai sweet chilli sauce
2 tablespoons chopped fresh coriander
salt and freshly ground black pepper

1. Cut the cucumber into 2.5cm/1in × 5mm/¼in batons. Cut the mango flesh into 1cm/½in cubes.
2. Fry the onion with the oil in a heavy-based frying pan over a medium heat until it just starts to brown. Add the ginger, garlic, cumin and cardamom seeds and fry for 1 further minute.
3. Tip the onion and seasonings into a large bowl and allow to cool.
4. Gently stir in the cucumber, mango, chilli sauce and coriander. Season to taste with salt and pepper.

RHUBARB, GOOSEBERRY AND ROSE-PETAL CONSERVE

MAKES 5 × 450G/1LB

2kg/4½ lb rhubarb, washed and trimmed into
    2.5cm/1in pieces
450g/1lb gooseberries, washed, topped and
    tailed
juice of 2 lemons
2.3kg/5lb granulated sugar
150ml/¼ pint rose-water
2 handfuls of rose petals, preferably red

1. Put the rhubarb and gooseberries into a large bowl, add the lemon juice, sugar and rose-water, cover and allow to stand for 24 hours in a cool, dark place.
2. The following day, sterilize and warm the jam jars (see page 277).
3. Put the fruit mixture and rose petals into a preserving pan and bring slowly to the boil, then lower the heat and allow to simmer for 10–15 minutes, or until setting point is reached (see page 103).
4. Remove the jam from the heat and allow to stand for 15 minutes.
5. Pour into warmed dry jars, cover and label.
6. Store in a cool, dark place. Use within 6–9 months.

NOTES: Rose-water can be bought from a pharmacy.
    See the notes on preserving on page 101.

SALTED LEMONS

This recipe is a good, less time-consuming version of the classic preserved lemon recipe.

2 lemons, washed
1 tablespoon coarse sea salt
1 teaspoon cayenne pepper
4 tablespoons extra virgin olive oil

1. Put the lemons into a saucepan and cover with water. Bring to the boil, then lower the heat and simmer for 10 minutes. Drain and allow to cool.

2. Slice the lemons very thinly with a serrated knife, removing any pips. Arrange on a plate, sprinkle with the salt and cayenne and allow to stand for 30 minutes.

3. Put into a bowl and pour over the oil. Cover and allow to macerate for 2–3 hours. Keep refrigerated and use within 7 days.

BREADS

FRESH MINT, GARLIC AND ONION NAAN BREAD

SERVES 4

7g/¼oz fresh yeast
150ml/¼ pint warm water
225g/8oz strong plain flour
1 teaspoon salt
strong plain flour for rolling

For the filling
30g/1oz butter
1 onion, finely chopped
2 large cloves of garlic, crushed
1 handful of fresh mint, roughly chopped
salt and freshly ground black pepper

1. Dissolve the yeast in the water.
2. Sift the flour and salt into a bowl, add the water and yeast and mix to a soft but not sticky dough, adding more water if needed. Knead for about 10 minutes, or until the dough is elastic, smooth and shiny.
3. Put the dough into an oiled bowl. Cover with greased clingfilm and leave to rise in a warm place until doubled in size (about 40 minutes).
4. Make the filling: melt the butter in a small saucepan and add the onion. Cover and cook over a low heat for 20 minutes, or until soft but not coloured. Add the garlic and cook for a further minute. Stir in the mint and season well with salt and pepper. Tip on to a plate and leave to cool.
5. Preheat the grill to its highest setting.
6. Punch the air out of the dough and sprinkle over some flour. Turn the dough on to a work surface and divide in half. Roll each piece into a large circle, using a little flour to prevent it from sticking to the work surface.
7. Spread the filling over half of each dough circle. Fold over the dough to form a semi-circle and press down the edges to seal them.
8. Roll out the naans a little to flatten them, then transfer to an oiled baking sheet. Grill for 2–3 minutes until golden-brown, lowering the grill pan if the naans darken too quickly. Turn them over and repeat on the second side.
9. Serve hot or leave to cool slightly on a wire rack and serve warm.

SESAME SORREL STICKS

MAKES 14

225g/8oz flour quantity Italian bread dough
   (see page 658)
450g/1lb fresh sorrel, blanched and refreshed
1 egg, beaten
110g/4oz strong Cheddar cheese, grated
salt and freshly ground black pepper
30g/1oz sesame seeds

To serve
1 quantity basil oil and garlic dip (see page 374)
   or sorrel and home-dried tomato
   mayonnaise (see page 239)

1. Preheat the oven to 200°C/400°F/gas mark 6.
2. Put the bread dough into a lightly oiled bowl and cover with clingfilm. Leave to rise in a warm place for 40 minutes.
3. Squeeze out excess water from the sorrel and chop it roughly.
4. Roll out the dough into a large rectangle

about 30 × 25cm/12 × 10in. Brush one half with beaten egg and sprinkle over the sorrel and Cheddar cheese. Season well with salt and pepper.

5. Fold the bread dough over and use the rolling pin to sandwich it firmly together. Brush the top with beaten egg and sprinkle all over with the sesame seeds.

6. Cut the dough into 1cm/½in strips. Grease 2 large baking sheets.

7. Place the strips on the baking sheets, twisting them several times to form spirals. Cover the sticks with oiled clingfilm and leave for 10 minutes in a warm place.

8. Bake the sticks near the top of the preheated oven for 10–15 minutes, or until firm to the touch and golden. Transfer to a wire rack to cool slightly before serving warm with the basil oil and garlic dip or sorrel and home-dried tomato mayonnaise.

SAUCES AND GARNISHES

SORREL AND HOME-DRIED TOMATO MAYONNAISE

MAKES 290ML/½ PINT

290ml/½ pint mayonnaise (see page 632)
225g/8oz sorrel leaves, stalks removed
85g/3oz home-dried tomatoes (see page 322),
 finely chopped
dry English mustard
salt and freshly ground black pepper

1. Put the mayonnaise into a food processor with the sorrel. Whizz until the sorrel is finely chopped.
2. Add the tomatoes and mustard and season with salt and pepper. Whizz again briefly and check the seasoning.

SHELLFISH BUTTER SAUCE

1 shallot, sliced
150ml/¼ pint dry white wine
½ bay leaf
100ml/3½fl oz double cream
55g/2oz roast shellfish butter, cubed (see
 following recipe)
a squeeze of lemon juice
salt and freshly ground white pepper

1. Simmer the shallot in the wine with the bay leaf in a small saucepan until reduced to 3 tablespoons.
2. Add the cream and simmer until reduced by half. Gradually whisk in the shellfish butter and season with lemon juice, salt and pepper. Strain into a sauce-boat to serve.

ROAST SHELLFISH BUTTER

225g/8oz prawn heads and shells
450g/1lb unsalted butter
1 bay leaf
a large pinch of ground mace
1 sprig of fresh thyme
12 black peppercorns

1. Preheat the oven to 200°C/400°F/gas mark 6.
2. Put the prawn heads and shells into a large roasting tin and bake in the preheated oven for 1 hour, or until golden-brown.
3. Transfer the shells to a heavy saucepan. Deglaze the roasting tin with a little cold water and add the water to the saucepan.
4. Add the butter to the pan with the bay leaf, mace, thyme and peppercorns. Gently melt the butter and simmer over a low heat for 15 minutes, or until the butter becomes clear. Leave to stand and infuse for an hour before straining through a clean J-cloth. Refrigerate.

WILD GARLIC PESTO

1 large handful of wild garlic leaves, washed
30g/1oz pinenuts, toasted
grated zest of 1 lemon
6 tablespoons extra virgin olive oil

55g/2oz Pecorino cheese, freshly grated
salt and freshly ground black pepper

1. Place the wild garlic, pinenuts, and lemon zest in a food processor or blender and whizz to a paste.
2. Add the oil slowly with the motor still running. Whizz in the cheese quickly. Season to taste with salt and pepper.
3. Keep in a covered jar in a cool place.

HARICOT AND BASIL DIP

SERVES 4

1 × 400g/14oz can of haricot beans, drained
5 tablespoons extra virgin olive oil
3 cloves of garlic, crushed
1 large bunch of fresh basil leaves
a squeeze of lemon juice
55g/2oz Parmesan cheese, freshly grated
salt and freshly ground black pepper

To serve
crudités

1. Rinse and drain the haricot beans.
2. Put all the ingredients into a food processor or blender and whizz to a smooth purée. Season to taste with salt and pepper.
3. Pile into a bowl and chill before serving with a selection of crudités.

SPRING ONION FLOWERS

Choose large cylindrical spring onions that do not have especially bulbous roots. Cut off a large part of the green tops and the roots. With a small, sharp knife, cut vertical lines halfway through the onions at both ends (see illustration). Leave in icy water for 2 hours, by which time they will have opened out.

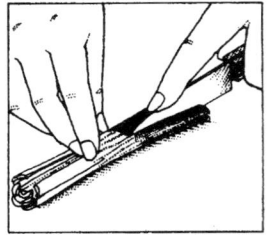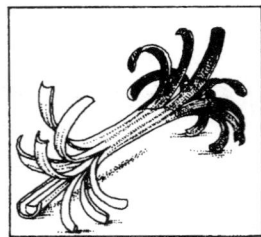

Slice from the ends towards the centre. Leave in iced water

DEEP-FRIED SAGE LEAVES

a handful of large fresh sage leaves
½ quantity tempura batter (see page 656)
salt and freshly ground black pepper
oil for deep-frying

1. Wash the sage leaves and pat them dry on kitchen paper.
2. Season the batter with salt and pepper.
3. Preheat 2.5cm/1in oil in a large heavy-based saucepan until a crumb of bread browns in 10–15 seconds.
4. Line a large roasting tin with kitchen paper.
5. Dip a few sage leaves at a time into the batter and drop them gently into the hot oil. Fry until just golden, then quickly remove them from the oil with a slotted spoon and tip them into the prepared roasting tin. Sprinkle the leaves with a little salt.
6. Continue frying the remaining leaves in the same way. Serve immediately.

PARSLEY POLENTA CROÛTONS

MAKES 8 WEDGES

1 litre/1¾ pints white stock, made with chicken
    bones (see page 625)
½ teaspoon salt
140g/5oz polenta (coarse cornmeal)
110g/4oz strong Cheddar cheese, grated
a large pinch of dry English mustard
a pinch of cayenne pepper
salt and freshly ground black pepper
2 tablespoons finely chopped fresh parsley
2 tablespoons olive oil
2 tablespoons freshly grated Parmesan cheese

1. Put the stock and salt into a large saucepan
and bring to the boil.
2. Remove the saucepan from the heat and
sprinkle on the polenta, whisking quickly to
prevent lumps from forming.
3. Return the saucepan to a low heat and
continue cooking until the polenta is very thick
(about 35–40 minutes unless using 'quick-cook'
polenta which will only take about 5 minutes),
stirring often to prevent sticking and burning.
Turn off the heat.
4. Stir in the Cheddar cheese, mustard, cayenne,
pepper and parsley. Check the seasoning.
5. Lightly oil a large round plate. Pour the
polenta on to the plate and spread it into a neat
round. Leave the polenta to cool, then
refrigerate for about 1 hour, or until set.
6. Preheat the grill to its highest setting.
7. Cut the polenta circle into 8 equal wedges
and transfer the wedges to a baking sheet.
Brush them with olive oil. Place the baking
sheet as high as possible under the grill until
golden.
8. Using a palette knife, carefully turn the
croûtons over. Brush with olive oil and sprinkle
with the Parmesan cheese. Grill the second side
until golden.

BITTER CHOCOLATE SAUCE

85g/3oz granulated sugar
150ml/¼ pint water
110g/4oz bitter or plain chocolate with
    minimum 70% cocoa solids, chopped

1. Put the sugar and water into a small
saucepan and heat gently until the sugar has
dissolved.
2. Remove from the heat and stir in the
chocolate until dissolved. Allow to cool before
serving.

WHITE CHOCOLATE GANACHE

This can be used for truffles or cake icing, or
melted as a rich sauce.

100ml/3½fl oz double cream
225g/8oz white chocolate, chopped
15g/½oz butter

1. Bring the cream to the boil in a small
saucepan. Lower the heat and simmer for 1
minute, then remove from the heat.
2. Stir in the chocolate and butter until melted.
Allow to cool, then chill for 2 hours, or until
set.

MENU IDEAS

SPRING MENUS

Ensuring that a menu is well balanced is one of the most important skills that a cook must learn.
Our suggested menus for spring entertaining are as follows:

Informal Supper (Late Spring)

Leek and olive beer bread tart
Wild garlic and mixed leaf salad
Chilli roast lamb with apricot salsa
Braised spring onions
Elderflower sorbet

Late Spring Barbecue

Rosemary lamb burgers with red onion and goat's cheese
Garlic and mint mash
Rhubarb and orange-flower water compote
Chocolate brandy snap cups

Formal Dinner Party

Spring lovage and Jerusalem artichoke soup
Citrus granita
Caul-wrapped chicken breasts with garlic herb stuffing
Hot asparagus and Jersey Royal new potatoes with mint butter sauce
Rhubarb strudel

Easter Day

Warm smoked cod's roe blinis
Chilli roast lamb with apricot salsa
Braised baby Jersey Royal potatoes with garlic butter
Rich lemon roulade

Late Spring Dinner Party

Asparagus with lemon sesame butter
Oriental filo parcels with spring greens and crisp carrots
Spring mint parfait

Buffet Party

Smoked haddock, watercress and grapefruit salad
Chicken and sage tart with wholemeal and Gruyère pastry
Baby beetroot and chickpea salad with sesame dressing
New potato and bacon gratin
Chocolate and strawberry pavlova

Informal Lunch or Supper

Roast chicken with leeks and yoghurt
Fresh cucumber and mango chutney
Fresh mint, onion and garlic naan
Caramelized pineapple and mascarpone tart

Vegetarian Menu

Swiss chard and Gruyère puff pastry tart
Lemon grass basmati rice with carrot ribbons
Blueberry and muscat sorbet

SUMMER
June – July – August

INTRODUCTION

When summertime comes, cooking is easy – choice is exceptional and with the huge variety of produce now available, we found our recipes flowing and flowing. Everywhere we looked, in the gardens, hedgerows and markets, there was a wealth of choice and it made us realize how flexible the seasons are, depending not only on the weather but what part of the country you happen to be in at the time. We were still able to pick elderflowers in August, for example. We urge you not to stick rigidly to the months specified in the seasonal chapters, but to use the index if you suddenly come across an ingredient we haven't used, because it is bound to be in another chapter.

Early summer brings all the soft fruits into our homes – raspberries, strawberries and currants. Gooseberries, especially when they are plump, golden and yellow, are wonderful eaten with sugar and cream. Young peas in the pod and broad beans blanched and popped out of their skins are worth the extra effort not only for their flavour, but their colour and texture. Keep an eye out for wild food – young nettles and samphire picked from the salt marshes around the coast. Peaches and nectarines make a picnic exciting and can be piled on top of shortbread with whipped cream for a quick dessert. All the tender herbs are growing profusely – keep picking them to prevent the flowers growing and they will last all summer long. A little later when courgettes and tomatoes are in full swing and there is an abundance of peppers and aubergines, use them to make summer stews for the cooler evenings.

We all want to spend the long summer days outside, so menus need to be flexible for spontaneous plans such as a barbecue or beach picnic. Marinating meats and vegetables in advance of cooking will give plenty of depth of flavour with minimum fuss. Use ingredients that are quick to cook – we found that in the summer months we automatically wrote lots of fish recipes and used tender fillets rather than slow-cooking joints of meat. Food served cold need never be dull – mix the vibrant summer colours together and use the best olive oils and vinegars for pestos and salsas to serve as accompaniments.

Pick-your-own produce farms are a wonderful way of making use of the abundance of fruit and vegetables available without the fuss of tending a large garden all year round. Now is the time to make use of the glut: every week there will be another fruit to add to your rumtopf (see page 369), but before you can blink the season will be over. Most soft fruits can be frozen very successfully for use later, whether in jams, jellies and vinegars or ice creams, mousses and crumbles. For some exciting and unusual menus try the following recipes: Blackened salmon with samphire, fresh pea tartlets with walnut and oat pastry, barbecued sweetcorn with hot and sweet butter, sweet raspberry vinegar bavarois or whitecurrant and gooseberry swirl frozen yoghurt.

Make the most of the summer sun and entertain with ease and style. Village fêtes and barn dances can be livened up with a spit-roast suckling pig, and sophisticated picnics put together for Glyndebourne, Ascot or Henley. We have thought of wedding breakfasts and summer balls with recipes such as smoked salmon parcels and wild strawberries with claret.

Most importantly for the summer season, try to give yourself the time to plan ahead for the coming months when the produce so abundant now is only available from abroad. Do not give all your excess produce away – preserve it for later and you will be thankful, whether enjoying it yourself or seeing the pleasure on friends' faces when they receive it as a present.

FRUIT AND VEGETABLES IN SEASON

TOP FRUIT	June	July	August
Apples		XXXXXXXX	XXXXXXXX
Apricots			XXXXXXXX
Cherries	XXXXXXXX	XXXXXXXX	XXXXXXXX
Figs	XXXXXXXX	XXXXXXXX	XXXXXXXX
Mulberries		XXXXX	XXXXXXXX
Peaches and Nectarines			XXXXXXXX
Pears	XXXXXXXX	XXXXXXXX	XXXXXXXX
Plums		XXXXXXXX	XXXXXXXX
Greengages			XXXXXXXX

BERRY FRUIT			
Bilberry			XXXXXXXX
Loganberries		XXXXXXXX	
Red, white and black Currants	XXXXXXXX	XXXXXXXX	XXXXX
Gooseberries	XXXXXXXX	XXXXXXXX	
Grapes		XXXXXXXX	XXXXXXXX
Raspberries	XXXXXXXX	XXXXXXXX	XXXXX
Strawberries	XXXXXXXX	XXXXXXXX	XXXXX

ALLIUMS			
Garlic			XXXXXXXX
Onions			XXXXXXXX
Spring and Welsh Onions	XXXXXXXX	XXXXXXXX	XXXXXXXX

BRASSICAS			
Cabbage		XXXXXXXX	XXXXXXXX
Kale	XXXXXXXX	XXXXXXXX	XXXXXXXX
Chinese cabbage		XXXXXXXX	XXXXXXXX
Cauliflowers		XXXXXXXX	XXXXXXXX
Calabrese		XXXXXXXX	XXXXXXXX
Broccoli		XXXXXXXX	XXXXXXXX

BEANS AND PODS			
Broad beans	XXXXXXXX	XXXXXXXX	XXXXXXXX
French beans		XXXXXXXX	XXXXXXXX
Runner beans		XXXXXXXX	XXXXXXXX
Sweetcorn			XXXXXXXX

LETTUCE/SPINACH			
Spinach	XXXXXXXX	XXXXXXXX	XXXXXXXX
Various lettuce types	XXXXXXXX	XXXXXXXX	XXXXXXXX

FRUIT AND VEGETABLES IN SEASON—*contd*

ROOTS AND TUBERS	June	July	August
Early potatoes	XXXXXXXXXXX	XXXXXXXXXXX	XXXXXXXXXXX
Jersey Royals	XXXXXXXXXXX	XXXXXXXXXXX	XXXXXXXXXXX
Maris bard	XXXXXXXXXXX	XXXXXXXXXXX	XXXXXXXXXXX
Pentland	XXXXXXXXXXX	XXXXXXXXXXX	XXXXXXXXXXX
Javelin	XXXXXXXXXXX	XXXXXXXXXXX	XXXXXXXXXXX
Second earlies		XXXXXXXXXXX	XXXXXXXXXXX
		XXXXXXXXXXX	XXXXXXXXXXX
Turnips	XXXXXXXXXXX	XXXXXXXXXXX	XXXXXXXXXXX
Beetroot	XXXXXXXXXXX	XXXXXXXXXXX	XXXXXXXXXXX
Horseradish	XXXXXXXXXXX	XXXXXXXXXXX	XXXXXXXXXXX
Carrots	XXXXXXXXXXX	XXXXXXXXXXX	XXXXXXXXXXX
Radishes	XXXXXXXXXXX	XXXXXXXXXXX	XXXXXXXXXXX

STALKS/SHOOTS			
Globe	XXXXXXXXXXX	XXXXXXXXXXX	XXXXXXXXXXX
Artichokes	XXXXXXXXXXX	XXXXXXXXXXX	XXXXXXXXXXX
Sea kale	XXXXXXXXXXX	XXXXXXXXXXX	XXXXXXXXXXX
Spinach beet	XXXXXXXXXXX	XXXXXXXXXXX	XXXXXXXXXXX
Asparagus	XXXXXXXXXXX		
Florence fennel	XXXXXXXXXXX	XXXXXXXXXXX	XXXXXXXXXXX
Rhubarb	XXXXXXXXXXX	XXXXXXXXXXX	XXXXXXXXXXX

VEGETABLE FRUITS			
Aubergine			XXXXXXXXXXX
Peppers			XXXXXXXXXXX
Chillies			XXXXXXXXXXX
Cucumbers	XXXXXXXXXXX		XXXXXXXXXXX
Courgettes		XXXXXXX	XXXXXXXXXXX
Marrows			XXXXXXXXXXX
Squashes			XXXXXXXXXXX
Tomatoes			XXXXXXXXXXX

HERBS			
Basil	XXXXXXXXXXX	XXXXXXXXXXX	XXXXXXXXXXX
Chervil	XXXXXXXXXXX	XXXXXXXXXXX	XXXXXXXXXXX
Chives	XXXXXXXXXXX	XXXXXXXXXXX	XXXXXXXXXXX
Coriander	XXXXXXXXXXX	XXXXXXXXXXX	XXXXXXXXXXX
All types	XXXXXXXXXXX	XXXXXXXXXXX	XXXXXXXXXXX
In abundance	XXXXXXXXXXX	XXXXXXXXXXX	XXXXXXXXXXX

FRUIT AND VEGETABLES IN SEASON—*contd*

WILD	June	July	August
Elderflowers	XXXXXXXXXXX		
Blackberry			XXXXXXXXXXX
Crab apple			XXXXXXXXXXX
Samphire		XXXXXXXXXXX	XXXXXXXXXXX

FISH IN SEASON

SALMON FAMILY
Farmed Atlantic and Pacific Salmon
Wild and farmed Trout and Char
Atlantic Salmon
Wild Brown Trout
Wild and farmed Rainbow Trout

SHELLFISH
Brown Crab
Spider Crab
Lobster
Dublin Bay Prawn
Crayfish
Prawns (various)
Shrimp
Whelk
Cockle
Clam
Mussel – farmed only
Native Oyster ⎫
Pacific Oyster ⎭ farmed only
Scallop (all species) – farmed only
Octopus
Squid

BEST FROM HOME
Monkfish
John Dory
Gurnard
Red Mullet
Sea Bass
Wrasse
Black Sea Bream
Red Sea Bream
Rockfish/Catfish

FLAT FISH
Plaice
Halibut
Lemon Sole
Flounder
Turbot
Brill
Megrim
Witch
Skate

MACKEREL FAMILY
Mackerel
Tuna
Bonito/Wahoo

HERRING FAMILY
Herring
Anchovy
Whitebait
Shad

COD FAMILY
Cod
Haddock
Whiting
Pollock
Coley/Saithe/Coalfish
Ling
Hake

FIRST COURSES AND SOUPS

FIRST COURSES

CHARENTAIS MELON WITH LEMON BALM AND PINEAU

SERVES 4

4 ripe charentais melons
1 small handful of fresh lemon balm leaves
290ml/½ pint Pineau (French aperitif wine from Pineau)

To garnish
4 sprigs of fresh variegated lemon balm

1. Cut the melons in half horizontally. Remove the seeds.
2. Scoop out neat chunks of melon using a melon baller and put them into a separate bowl. Scrape out the remains of the flesh and keep for another use. Reserve 4 of the tidiest melon halves for serving.
3. Layer the lemon balm leaves on top of each other, roll them up into a cigar shape, then thinly slice the leaves into julienne strips.
4. Gently toss the melon balls, lemon balm julienne and Pineau together. Chill for 1 hour.
5. Pile the melon balls up into the reserved melon halves and spoon over the juices. Garnish with sprigs of lemon balm before serving.

 *PINEAU DES CHARENTES*

BRAISED BABY GLOBE ARTICHOKES

SERVES 4

8 baby globe artichokes (see page 30)
salt
4 tablespoons extra virgin olive oil
2 red onions, thinly sliced
2 cloves of garlic, crushed
150ml/¼ pint dry white wine
200ml/7fl oz vegetable stock (see page 627)
1 bouquet garni
black pepper
1–2 tablespoons beurre manié (see page 108)

To serve
1 teaspoon finely chopped fresh sage
2–3 tablespoons freshly grated Parmesan cheese

1. Wash and halve the artichokes and trim off any excess stalk and tough outer leaves.
2. Soak the artichokes in water with 1 teaspoon salt for 15 minutes.
3. Heat the oil in a large flameproof casserole, add the onion and cook over a low heat for 25–30 minutes, or until completely soft. Add the garlic and continue to cook for 2–3 minutes.
4. Drain and rinse the artichokes and add to the casserole with the wine, stock and bouquet garni. Season with salt and pepper. Cover and cook over a very low heat for 50 minutes, or until the artichokes are tender.
5. Lift the artichokes from the casserole and set aside. Bring the cooking liquid to the boil, thicken with a little beurre manié and season to taste with salt and pepper.
6. Arrange the artichokes in a warmed serving

dish, pour the cooking liquid over the top and sprinkle with the sage and Parmesan cheese.

 YOUNG BEAUJOLAIS-VILLAGES

HOT CRISP ARTICHOKES WITH PARMA HAM

SERVES 4

6 baby globe artichokes
salt
2 lemons, halved
110g/4oz plain flour
freshly ground black pepper
oil for deep-frying
110g/4oz lamb's lettuce or mâche
150ml/¼ pint vinaigrette, made with extra
    virgin olive oil (see page 634)
110g/4oz thinly sliced Parma ham
2 tablespoons chopped fresh chives
½ yellow pepper, de-seeded, skinned and finely
    diced
12 cherry tomatoes, halved

To serve
hot crusty bread

1. Cook the artichokes for 15–20 minutes in a large pan of boiling salted water with one of the lemons, halved. When a blunt knife goes easily into the base of the stem, drain the artichokes upside-down on a wire rack until cool.
2. Squeeze the juice from the remaining lemon into a shallow non-metallic dish. Cut the artichokes in half from top to bottom and cut off the tips where the purple leaves start. Pull off and discard all the inedible outer leaves. Quickly place the artichoke hearts, cut side down, in the dish with the lemon juice.
3. Lift the artichoke hearts out of the lemon juice and pat dry on kitchen paper.
4. Season the flour with salt and pepper. Heat 2.5cm/1in oil in a large pan for deep-frying.
5. Toss the artichoke hearts in the seasoned flour, shaking off the excess. When the oil is very hot and a cube of bread will brown

immediately, fry them until golden-brown, then drain on kitchen paper. Sprinkle with a little salt which will help to absorb excess oil.
6. Toss the lamb's lettuce in 2 tablespoons of the vinaigrette and arrange a central pile on 4 individual plates. Arrange the Parma ham and artichokes around the salad, then arrange the chives, pepper and tomatoes around the outer edge of the plates. Drizzle the remaining dressing around the plates and serve immediately with the bread.

 *SAUVIGNON BLANC*

INDIVIDUAL AUBERGINE AND FETA TIMBALES

SERVES 4

2 medium aubergines, thinly sliced
1 teaspoon salt
olive oil

For the marinade
5 tablespoons sherry vinegar
grated zest of 1 lemon
1 clove of garlic, crushed
salt and freshly ground black pepper

For the filling
85g/3oz fresh white breadcrumbs, sieved
2 tablespoons extra virgin olive oil
4 sun-dried tomatoes, chopped
2 tablespoons chopped fresh basil
170g/6oz feta cheese, crumbled
1 teaspoon green peppercorns, rinsed
freshly ground black pepper

For the dressing
4 tablespoons extra virgin olive oil
1 tablespoon sherry vinegar
1 tablespoon capers, rinsed and chopped
1 tablespoon pinenuts, toasted

To garnish
4 sprigs of basil

1. Sprinkle the aubergine slices with the salt and leave to degorge for 30 minutes.

2. Mix together all the marinade ingredients in a shallow bowl. Rinse the aubergines, drain and dry well. Add them to the marinade and leave for 1 hour. Drain well.

3. Mix all the filling ingredients together and season with pepper.

4. Preheat the grill to its highest setting.

5. Brush the aubergines with a little oil and grill for about 3–4 minutes on each side, or until soft and lightly browned.

6. Line 4 timbale moulds or teacups with clingfilm and arrange the aubergine slices overlapping in the mould. Fill each with the filling. Cover with clingfilm, weight down and leave for 2–3 hours.

7. Turn the aubergine timbales on to 4 individual plates. Drizzle with the oil and vinegar and sprinkle the capers and pinenuts around the edges. Garnish each timbale with a sprig of basil. Serve chilled.

 *DRY ROSÉ*

AUBERGINE AND TAHINI PÂTÉ

SERVES 4

2 large aubergines
2 tablespoons extra virgin olive oil
6 cloves of garlic, unpeeled
3 tablespoons tahini (sesame seed paste)
1 tablespoon light soy sauce
2–3 tablespoons chopped fresh coriander
salt and freshly ground black pepper
lemon juice to taste

To serve
4 sprigs of fresh coriander
Italian bread with Parmesan and truffle oil (see page 615)

1. Preheat the oven to 190°C/375°F/gas mark 5.

2. Place the aubergines in a baking tray, brush with a little of the oil and bake them in the preheated oven for 40–50 minutes, or until soft. After 20 minutes add the whole cloves of garlic.

3. Remove from the oven and allow the aubergines and garlic to cool, then peel.

4. Put the garlic and tahini into a food processor with the aubergine flesh, soy sauce, coriander, salt and pepper. Whizz to a smooth purée.

5. Gradually beat in the remaining oil and when the mixture is smooth stir in the lemon juice and season to taste with salt and pepper.

6. Divide between 4 ramekins and garnish each with a sprig of coriander. Hand the Italian bread separately.

 *NEW WORLD CABERNET SAUVIGNON*

ASPARAGUS WITH RED SALSA

SERVES 4

675g/1½lb asparagus, prepared (see page 31)
salt

For the salsa
2 tablespoons walnut oil
1 quantity oven-dried baby plum tomatoes (see page 322) or sun-dried tomatoes soaked in oil, drained and sliced
1 red onion, finely chopped
1 tablespoon chopped fresh red basil
1 red pepper, grilled, peeled, de-seeded and sliced
1 tablespoon rice wine vinegar
salt and freshly ground black pepper

To garnish
shavings of Parmesan cheese

1. Cook the asparagus in boiling salted water until just tender. Drain well and refresh in cold water.

2. Mix together all the salsa ingredients and season to taste with salt and pepper.

3. Arrange the asparagus on a large serving

platter and spoon the salsa on top. Chill until required.

4. Sprinkle with shavings of Parmesan cheese before serving.

 *SANCERRE*

BARBECUED SWEETCORN WITH HOT AND SWEET BUTTER

SERVES 4

4 sweetcorn, preferably still in the husk
2 tablespoons olive oil

For the hot and sweet butter
110g/4oz butter
1 tablespoon wasabi paste (see page 161)
1 red chilli, finely chopped
1 green chilli, finely chopped
2 tablespoons finely chopped fresh coriander
2 teaspoons clear honey
grated zest and juice of 1 lime
salt and freshly ground black pepper

1. Preheat the barbecue.
2. Brush the sweetcorn with the oil and wrap in kitchen foil. Put on to the barbecue and cook for 20–25 minutes turning every few minutes.
3. Meanwhile, make the hot and sweet butter: put the butter into a food processor with all the remaining ingredients and season with salt and pepper. Process until well mixed.
4. When the sweetcorn is cooked, remove the foil, peel back the husk and brush generously with the butter. Serve warm.

 *ALSATIAN TOKAY/PINOT GRIS*

RED PEPPER AND GARLIC FRITTATA

SERVES 2

1 large onion, thinly sliced
3 tablespoons olive oil

1 clove of garlic, crushed
2 red peppers
3 eggs
30g/1oz Parmesan cheese, freshly grated
salt and freshly ground black pepper
20g/¾oz butter

1. Cook the onion slowly in the oil for 45–60 minutes, or until reduced in quantity, soft and a rich golden-brown. Add the garlic and continue to cook for a further 2–3 minutes. Tip into a sieve over a bowl, leave to cool.
2. Cut the peppers into quarters and remove the stalks, inner membranes and seeds. Preheat the grill to its highest setting.
3. Grill the peppers, skin side uppermost, until the skin is black and blistered. Using a small knife, scrape off all the skin. Cut the flesh into strips.
4. Beat the eggs until lightly mixed. Mix all but 3 tablespoons of the egg with the onion, peppers, cheese, salt and pepper. Mix well.
5. Melt the butter in a 20cm/8in frying pan over a medium heat. When foaming, add the egg and pepper mixture. Reduce the heat to *very* low.
6. Cook very slowly for 15 minutes. The eggs should be set and the surface runny. Pour over the reserved egg. Place under the hot grill until set but not brown. Loosen with a spatula and slide on to a round dish. Serve cut into wedges.

 *COUNTRY RED*

FRESH PEA TARTLETS WITH WALNUT AND OAT PASTRY

SERVES 4

1 quantity walnut and oat pastry (see page 648)
plain flour

For the filling
15g/½oz butter
12 small shallots, peeled
225g/8oz shelled fresh peas
salt

2 egg yolks
150ml/¼ pint single cream
1 tablespoon chopped fresh tarragon
freshly ground black pepper

1. Divide the pastry into 4 pieces. Roll each piece out into a circle and use to line 4 × 8.5cm/ 3½in flan rings. Chill for 30 minutes.
2. Preheat the oven to 190°C/375°F/gas mark 5.
3. Bake the pastry blind (see page 640). Reduce the oven temperature to 150°C/300°F/gas mark 2.
4. Make the filling: melt the butter in a small heavy-based frying pan. Add the shallots and season with salt and pepper. Cover and cook over a very low heat for 20 minutes, or until a skewer slides easily into the centre of the shallots, shaking the pan gently from time to time to prevent the shallots from burning. If the shallots are starting to caramelize a little too much, add a few drops of water and turn the heat down even lower.
5. Blanch the peas in boiling salted water for 2 minutes. Drain and refresh in cold water. Do not allow the peas to sit in the cold water for too long or they will lose flavour.
6. Put the egg yolks, cream and tarragon into another bowl and stir together. Add the peas and season to taste with salt and pepper.
7. Arrange 3 shallots in the centre of each pastry case. Using a slotted spoon, divide the peas between the tartlets and pile them around the shallots. Pour egg mixture over the peas, filling the tartlets up as much as possible.
8. Place the tartlets on a baking sheet and bake near the bottom of the oven for 20 minutes, or until the filling is just set but not brown.

 *SAUVIGNON BLANC/CRISP DRY WHITE*

MEDITERRANEAN MILLE-FEUILLE

SERVES 8–10

For the herb pancakes
8 eggs, beaten
4 tablespoons finely chopped fresh chives

salt and freshly ground black pepper
olive oil for frying

For the filling
olive oil
2 red peppers, de-seeded and finely diced
2 green peppers, de-seeded and finely diced
2 cloves of garlic, crushed
1 tablespoon dried herbes de Provence
salt and freshly ground black pepper
1 red onion, finely chopped
2 small courgettes, finely diced
1 small aubergine, finely diced
150ml/¼ pint tomato sauce (see page 635)
1 teaspoon Tabasco sauce
2 teaspoons tomato purée
a pinch of sugar
juice of ½ lemon

To serve
2 tablespoons walnut oil
1 tablespoon sesame seeds, toasted

1. Make the herb pancakes: put the eggs into a bowl and whisk together, then sieve, add the chives and season well with salt and pepper.
2. Heat a non-stick frying pan and wipe out with a very light coating of oil. Pour a ladleful of the egg mixture into the pan, tip it around and pour the excess back into the bowl. When the pancake is set and the edges are curling, remove from the pan. Repeat until you have used up all the egg mixture – you should have 12–14 pancakes.
3. Make the filling: heat the frying pan again with a little more oil, add the peppers with a little garlic, some herbes de Provence and plenty of seasoning and toss over a high heat for 1 minute. Transfer to a large bowl and leave to cool. Heat the frying pan again and repeat with each of the vegetables.
4. Mix all the vegetables together, add the tomato sauce, Tabasco, tomato purée, sugar and lemon juice, and season to taste with a little more salt and pepper if necessary.
5. Spread a little filling evenly over one pancake, place another pancake on top and continue layering until everything is used up, finishing with a pancake. Cover and chill for 1 hour.

6. Brush the stacked pancakes all over with walnut oil and sprinkle with sesame seeds.

7. Cut into 8–10 wedges and place a wedge on each individual plate.

 *CHILEAN PINOT NOIR*

BAKED MOZZARELLA IN PROSCIUTTO

SERVES 4

2 buffalo mozzarella cheeses
4 slices of prosciutto or Parma ham
8 large fresh basil leaves
salt and freshly ground black pepper
2 tablespoons extra virgin olive oil

For the salad
1 bunch of flat-leaf parsley
2 tomatoes, skinned, de-seeded and chopped
2 tablespoons chopped fresh basil
4 tablespoons extra virgin olive oil
1 tablespoon lemon juice
½ tablespoon Dijon mustard
a pinch of sugar

1. Preheat the oven to 200°C/400°F/gas mark 6.

2. Drain the mozzarella cheeses and cut each in half.

3. Lay out the slices of ham and arrange 2 basil leaves in the centre of each slice. Season with pepper.

4. Place a piece of mozzarella on the basil and wrap up into a parcel, making sure the mozzarella is completely covered. Repeat with the remaining mozzarella. Wrap each parcel in clingfilm and chill for 30 minutes.

5. Unwrap the parcels and place them seam side down on a baking sheet. Drizzle 1 teaspoon of the oil over each and season with pepper. Bake in the preheated oven for 5–10 minutes, or until the prosciutto is slightly crisp and the mozzarella warmed through.

6. Meanwhile, prepare the salad: put the parsley and tomato into a bowl. Mix the basil, oil, lemon juice, mustard and sugar together.

Season with salt and pepper and toss with the parsley and tomato.

7. Place a prosciutto parcel in the centre of each of 4 large plates and spoon the salad around. Serve immediately.

 *LIGHT RED*

GRILLED PROSCIUTTO AND TOMATO ON BRIOCHE

This very simple 'open sandwich' is perfect for a summer breakfast or brunch.

SERVES 4

1–2 tablespoons extra virgin olive oil
4 thick slices of brioche loaf (see page 373)
8 slices of prosciutto, fat removed
4 tomatoes, thickly sliced
1 handful of lettuce leaves
salt and freshly ground black pepper
caster sugar

1. Preheat the grill to its highest setting.

2. Sprinkle a little oil over each slice of brioche and toast lightly on each side. Keep warm.

3. Grill the prosciutto for 2–3 minutes on each side, or until lightly browned and crisp. Grill the tomato slices for 1 minute on each side.

4. Arrange some lettuce leaves on 4 individual plates. Top with the toasted brioche, followed by the tomato slices, and season with salt, pepper and sugar. Top the tomato with the grilled prosciutto and serve immediately.

 *BUCK'S FIZZ*

WARM GOAT'S CHEESE TIMBALES WITH RASPBERRIES

These unusual cheese timbales not only make a lovely first course, but are a perfect alternative to serve instead of a cheese course. The combination of cheese and lightly sweetened fruit is wonderful.

SERVES 4

170g/6oz mild-flavoured goat's cheese
225g/8oz ricotta cheese
55g/2oz Parmesan cheese, freshly grated
2 eggs, beaten
freshly ground black pepper
a pinch of grated nutmeg
110g/4oz raspberries
1 tablespoon caster sugar
1 tablespoon raspberry vinegar

For the dressing
4 tablespoons extra virgin olive oil
1 tablespoon raspberry vinegar
1 teaspoon sugar
salt and freshly ground black pepper

To garnish
4 sprigs of fresh flat-leaf parsley

1. Preheat the oven to 180°C/350°F/gas mark 4.
2. Put the goat's cheese, ricotta, Parmesan cheese and eggs into a food processor and whizz to form a paste. Season to taste with pepper and nutmeg. Set aside.
3. Put the raspberries and sugar into a small saucepan and bring to the boil, then lower the heat and allow to simmer until the mixture is jam-like in consistency. Remove from the heat, add the vinegar and season to taste with pepper. Allow to cool.
4. Divide half the cheese mixture between the timbales. Using a spoon, make a small hollow in each and spoon the raspberries into the hollow. Put the remaining cheese mixture on top to enclose the raspberries. Smooth the top

of each timbale and cover with a piece of buttered greaseproof paper.
5. Put the timbales into a roasting tin half filled with boiling water and bake in the preheated oven for 20–25 minutes, or until the timbales are completely firm.
6. Meanwhile, make the dressing: put all the ingredients into a small bowl and whisk together to form an emulsion.
7. When the timbales are cooked, turn out on to individual plates and spoon the dressing around the outside. Garnish each timbale with a sprig of flat-leaf parsley.

 CHAMPAGNE OR SPARKLING WINE

SAMPHIRE

A good source of samphire is the salt marshes on the north coast of Norfolk: namely Stiffkey, Morston and Blakeney. Samphire should be eaten simply boiled and then dipped into melted butter or vinegar before sucking the flesh off the stalks. In London you tend to be served only with individual strands of young samphire whereas when you gather it yourself, you can pick the largest stalks with plenty of flesh which are much more satisfying to eat.

SERVES 4

900g/2lb samphire on the stalk

To serve
melted butter
balsamic vinegar

1. Cut the roots off the samphire and wash it very thoroughly 3 or 4 times in cold water.
2. Boil the samphire in unsalted water for about 5 minutes, or until the green flesh slides off the stem.
3. Drain well and serve the samphire with bowls of melted butter and vinegar.

 *ALSACE PINOT BLANC*

SMOKED SALMON PARCELS

SERVES 4

8 large slices of smoked salmon, about
  17.5 × 5cm/7 × 2in

For the filling
2 smoked trout fillets, skinned and boned
½ cucumber, peeled, de-seeded and finely diced
½ ripe but still quite firm avocado
2 tablespoons crème fraîche
1 tablespoon lemon juice
1 tablespoon chopped fresh dill
cayenne pepper
salt and freshly ground black pepper

To garnish
1 tablespoon olive oil
4 lemon wedges
4 sprigs of fresh dill

1. Make the filling: flake the trout into a bowl.
Add the cucumber.
2. Peel the avocado, finely dice the flesh and tip
it into the bowl.
3. Add the crème fraîche, lemon juice and dill
and season with cayenne and salt and pepper to
taste.
4. Make up the parcels: lay a large piece of
clingfilm on a work surface. Place a piece of
smoked salmon on top and lay another piece
directly on top, at right angles to the first piece.
5. Pile a quarter of the filling into the centre of
the smoked salmon and carefully fold each
corner into the centre to create a parcel. Wrap
up in the clingfilm and place on a tray. Make
the remaining parcels up the same way, then
chill.
6. To serve: unwrap the clingfilm and place the
parcels, folded side down, on 4 plates. Brush the
oil on to the salmon to give the parcels a shine.
Arrange the lemon wedges and sprigs of dill
beside the parcels.

 *WHITE BURGUNDY/CHARDONNAY*

SMOKED SALMON AND FETA MOUSSE

SERVES 4

225g/8oz smoked salmon
140g/5oz feta cheese
juice of ½ lemon
1 teaspoon grated horseradish
freshly ground black pepper
2 teaspoons chopped fresh chives
1 teaspoon chopped capers

To garnish
4 sprigs of fresh dill

1. Mince or pound the salmon with the feta
cheese. Mix with the lemon juice, horseradish,
pepper, chives and capers.
2. Divide the mixture between 4 ramekins and
garnish each with a sprig of dill.

 SOUTH AFRICAN CHARDONNAY

NIÇOISE TERRINE WITH TUNA AND GREEK YOGHURT

SERVES 8

1 large aubergine, sliced lengthways
200ml/7fl oz basic vinaigrette (see page 634)
salt and freshly ground black pepper
3 courgettes, sliced lengthways
3 red onions, peeled and quartered
2 red peppers, quartered and de-seeded
2 yellow peppers, quartered and de-seeded
2 bulbs of fennel, cut in half and core removed
1 clove of garlic, crushed
1 tablespoon chopped fresh thyme
1 tablespoon chopped fresh basil
1 tablespoon good-quality olive oil
4 × 85g/3oz tuna fillet steaks

For the sauce
150ml/¼ pint Greek yoghurt
30g/1oz Greek black olives, pitted
1 tablespoon chopped fresh parsley
juice of ½ lemon
freshly ground black pepper

1. Preheat the grill to its highest setting.
2. Lay the aubergine slices on a baking sheet, brush with a little vinaigrette and season with salt and pepper. Place under the grill until golden-brown. Turn the aubergine over, brush with a little more vinaigrette, season again with salt and pepper and grill until golden-brown.
3. Repeat the process with the courgettes and red onions.
4. Place the peppers, skin side uppermost, on a baking sheet. Grill until the skin is blackened. Tip the peppers into a bowl, cover with clingfilm and leave for 15 minutes. Remove the clingfilm and peel the skins off the peppers.
5. Separate out the layers of fennel and blanch for 4 minutes in boiling salted water. Drain the fennel and refresh under cold running water for 1 minute. Dry the fennel on kitchen paper.
6. Lightly oil a 900g/2lb terrine tin and line with clingfilm, making sure there is enough to overlap the edges generously.
7. Mix the remaining vinaigrette together with the garlic, thyme and basil.
8. Line the bottom of the tin with the aubergine slices. Sprinkle over a little vinaigrette and some chopped herbs and season well with salt and pepper.
9. Continue layering up the vegetables in the following order: red pepper, courgette, red onion, yellow pepper and fennel, seasoning each layer as before with the vinaigrette, salt and pepper.
10. Fold over the overlapping edges of clingfilm and place another terrine tin of a similar size on top. Turn both terrine tins over on to a tray and place some heavy weights on the top (this will allow excess liquid to drain away and keep the layers stuck together). Refrigerate for 24 hours.
11. Heat the oil in a frying pan, season the tuna with salt and pepper and fry on both sides for 1 minute, or until brown.
12. Mix the yoghurt in a bowl with the olives, parsley, lemon juice and plenty of pepper.

13. Remove the weights and turn the terrine out on to a serving dish. Slice carefully with a sharp knife and arrange on a serving plate with the seared tuna steaks and Greek yoghurt.

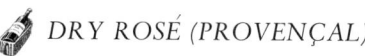 *DRY ROSÉ (PROVENÇAL)*

INDIVIDUAL ANCHOVY CHARLOTTES

SERVES 4

1 full quantity marinated anchovies (see
  following recipe)
4 tablespoons fresh white breadcrumbs
  (preferably Italian bread)
110g/4oz oven-dried baby plum tomatoes (see
  page 322) or sun-dried tomatoes soaked in
  oil, drained and chopped
2 teaspoons capers, rinsed and roughly chopped
2 teaspoons chopped fresh chives
1 tablespoon chopped fresh parsley

To serve
sprigs of fresh flat-leaf parsley
12 oven-dried baby plum tomatoes or 2
  tablespoons chopped sun-dried tomatoes
focaccia (see page 371)

1. Lift the anchovies from their dressing and pat dry with kitchen paper. Line 4 ramekins with the anchovy fillets.
2. Chop the remaining anchovies and mix with the breadcrumbs, tomatoes, capers and herbs. Season to taste with salt and pepper.
3. Fill the lined ramekins with the mixture and pack down firmly. Cover and chill for 1 hour.
4. To serve: turn each anchovy charlotte on to an individual plate and garnish with the parsley and tomatoes. Hand the bread separately.

 *ITALIAN WHITE*

MARINATED ANCHOVIES

This recipe originates from a traditional Spanish recipe. Fresh anchovies are in season throughout the summer and autumn, but are not always readily available in the UK. Fresh sardines can be used in their place.

SERVES 4

450g/1lb fresh anchovies, filleted (see page 132)
150ml/¼ pint rice wine vinegar
2 teaspoons salt
1 bay leaf
6 tablespoons extra virgin olive oil
grated zest and juice of 1 lemon
1 shallot, very finely chopped
2 cloves of garlic, crushed
salt and freshly ground black pepper
1 tablespoon chopped fresh parsley

To serve
Caesar dressed leaves (see page 574)

1. Open out the anchovy fillets and arrange in a flat dish, skin side uppermost.
2. Pour the vinegar over the anchovies, sprinkle with the salt and add the bay leaf. Cover and refrigerate for 24 hours.
3. Lift the anchovies from the vinegar and pat dry with kitchen paper. Discard the liquid. Put the anchovies into a shallow dish.
4. Put the oil, lemon zest and juice, shallot and garlic into a bowl and whisk together until well emulsified. Season with salt and pepper and mix in the parsley. Pour over the anchovies and leave to marinate for a further 30 minutes. Check the seasoning.
5. To serve: pile the Caesar dressed leaves into a bowl and toss the anchovies into the salad.

NOTE: Alternatively, serve the anchovies with bread as an hors d'oeuvre.

 *DRY SPANISH WHITE*

BROWN SHRIMP AND ASPARAGUS VOL-AU-VENTS

SERVES 4

12 asparagus spears
170g/6oz cooked and peeled brown shrimp
1 tablespoon chopped fresh dill
110g/4oz prawn butter, softened (see page 636)
salt and freshly ground black pepper
4 large vol-au-vent cases, about 10cm/4in in
    diameter (see page 644)

To garnish
4 large sprigs of fresh dill
4 lemon wedges

1. Preheat the oven to 180°C/350°F/gas mark 4.
2. Blanch the asparagus in boiling salted water for 5 minutes, or until just tender. Drain and refresh in cold water. Dry well on kitchen paper. Cut off the tips of the asparagus on the diagonal and slice the stalks into 1cm/½in pieces.
3. Mix the asparagus stalks with the shrimp, dill and prawn butter and season with salt and pepper.
4. Remove the lids from the vol-au-vent cases and set aside. Scrape any raw pastry out of the middle of the cases and discard. Place the cases on a baking sheet and pile the shrimp filling into the centre of each.
5. Arrange the asparagus tips on top and divide the remaining butter between the vol-au-vents. Bake them in the preheated oven for 20 minutes, or until just hot. Replace the pastry lids at a jaunty angle.
6. Serve on 4 warmed individual plates garnished with the dill and lemon wedges.

 *ALSACE MUSCAT (DRY)*

SMOKED EEL AND WARM BEETROOT SALAD

SERVES 4

4 raw beetroots
salt
450g/1lb pink fir apple potatoes or similar new
   potatoes
150ml/¼ pint Greek yoghurt
1 tablespoon chopped fresh chives
1 teaspoon chopped fresh mint
2 teaspoons red wine vinegar
grated zest of 1 lemon
freshly ground black pepper
1 handful of mixed bitter leaves such as
   radicchio, lollo rosso and curly endive
450g/1lb smoked eel fillets

1. Cook the beetroot in boiling salted water for
1–1½ hours, or until tender. Drain, peel and
slice.

2. Meanwhile, cook the potatoes in boiling
salted water for 7–10 minutes, or until tender.

3. Put the yoghurt, herbs, vinegar and lemon
zest into a large bowl and season to taste with
salt and pepper. Add the warm beetroot and
potatoes.

4. Tear the leaves into bite-sized pieces and
arrange on a serving dish. Pile the warm
beetroot salad on top and arrange the eel fillets
on top. Serve immediately.

 *MUSCADET DE SÈVRE ET MAINE SUR LIE*

SOUPS

SUMMER TOMATO BREAD SOUP WITH BASIL OIL AND MASCARPONE

SERVES 4

6 tablespoons extra virgin olive oil
1 Spanish onion, finely chopped
1 clove of garlic, crushed
1kg/2¼lb ripe tomatoes, skinned, quartered
    and de-seeded
1 teaspoon tomato purée
a pinch of sugar
1 × 4cm/1½in slice of ciabatta, torn into small
    pieces
570ml/1 pint vegetable stock (see page 627)
salt and freshly ground black pepper
1 handful of fresh basil leaves
4 tablespoons mascarpone

To serve
warm Italian bread (see page 658)

1. Heat 2 tablespoons of the oil in a heavy-based saucepan, add the onions and sweat over a low heat until soft but not coloured. Add the garlic and cook for a further minute.
2. Cut the tomato quarters in half and add to the pan with the tomato purée, sugar, bread and stock. Season with salt and pepper. Bring to the boil, then lower the heat and simmer gently for 20 minutes, or until you have a fairly thick, well-flavoured soup.
3. Whizz the basil and remaining oil together in a blender to form a smooth purée, adding extra oil if needed.
4. To serve: ladle the soup into 4 warmed deep soup bowls. Drizzle a tablespoon of basil oil in

a spiral around each serving and dollop a teaspoon of mascarpone into the centre. Serve immediately with warm Italian bread.

 WHITE LOIRE/SAUVIGNON BLANC

TARRAGON, CHERVIL AND YOUNG BEAN BROTH

SERVES 4

1 tablespoon extra virgin olive oil
1 large onion, finely chopped
1.7 litres/3 pints well-flavoured white stock,
    made with chicken bones (see page 625)
2 tablespoons chopped fresh tarragon leaves
    and stalks
1 tablespoon chopped fresh chervil leaves and
    stalks
1 clove of garlic, peeled
salt and freshly ground black pepper
1 egg white

To serve
110g/4oz shelled broad beans, blanched and
    refreshed
110g/4oz young mangetout, blanched and
    refreshed
110g/4oz dwarf French beans, blanched and
    refreshed

To garnish
4 small sprigs of fresh tarragon
4 small sprigs of fresh chervil

1. Heat the oil in a saucepan, add the onion and cook over a low heat until soft but not coloured. Add the stock, herbs and garlic and season with salt and pepper. Bring to the boil, then lower the heat and simmer for 30 minutes.
2. Strain the stock into a clean saucepan. Whisk the egg white until frothy. Pour into the warm stock and keep whisking steadily (preferably with a balloon whisk) until a crust begins to form. Allow the mixture to subside. Take care not to break the crust formed by the egg white. Cool for 2 minutes.
3. Fix a double layer of fine scalded muslin over a clean basin. Lift the egg white crust into the sieve and pour the stock through it. Do not try to hurry the process by squeezing the cloth, or the liquid will be murky.
4. To serve: add the blanched vegetables to the broth and heat through. Pour into warmed soup bowls and add the herb garnish just before serving.

 YOUNG MOSEL SPÄTLESE

SUMMER COURGETTE AND MINT SOUP

SERVES 4

1 tablespoon olive oil
1 onion, sliced
1 clove of garlic, crushed
1kg/2¼lb courgettes, sliced
1.1 litres/2 pints vegetable stock (see page 627)
salt and freshly ground black pepper
1 tablespoon chopped fresh mint

1. Heat the oil in a large saucepan, add the onion, garlic and courgettes, and soften over a low heat.
2. Add the stock and bring to the boil, then lower the heat and simmer for 10 minutes. Do not cook for longer as the courgettes will lose their colour. Season to taste with salt and pepper and allow to cool.
3. Add the mint and whizz in a blender until smooth.
4. Serve warm or chilled.

NOTE: Reheat the soup carefully over a low heat. Any bright green soup will lose its colour if left over heat for too long.

 NEW ZEALAND SAUVIGNON BLANC

CHILLED BABY COURGETTE SOUP

SERVES 4

55g/2oz unsalted butter
4 shallots, finely chopped
1 clove of garlic, crushed
1 teaspoon curry powder
450g/1lb baby courgettes or acorn squash, thinly sliced
1 litre/1¾ pints well-flavoured white stock, made with chicken bones (see page 625)
salt and freshly ground black pepper
150ml/¼ pint double cream (optional)

To garnish
2 teaspoons chopped fresh chives

1. Melt the butter in a saucepan, add the shallots and cook them over a low heat for 4–5 minutes or until soft but not coloured. Add the garlic and curry powder and cook for a further minute. Add the courgettes or squash, cover and cook over a very low heat for 2–3 minutes.
2. Add the stock and season with salt and pepper, then simmer for 8–10 minutes, or until the courgettes are soft.
3. Whizz in a food processor or blender until smooth and allow to cool. Stir in the cream, if using, and check the seasoning. Allow to cool, cover and chill for 2 hours.
4. To serve: pour into a chilled soup tureen and sprinkle with the chives.

 LANGUEDOC–ROUSSILLON VIOGNIER DE PAYS

CHILLED BLACK OLIVE AND ANCHOVY SOUP

SERVES 4

225g/8oz Kalamata olives, pitted
2 tablespoons capers, rinsed
6 anchovy fillets
1 clove of garlic, crushed
1 tablespoon chopped fresh parsley
freshly ground black pepper
juice of ½ lemon
150ml/¼ pint Greek yoghurt
150ml/¼ pint soured cream
150ml/¼ pint single cream

To garnish
1 tablespoon chopped fresh chives

1. Put the olives into a food processor with the capers, anchovies, garlic and parsley and pulse on and off until very well chopped.
2. Season with pepper. Add the lemon juice, yoghurt and soured and single creams and continue to pulse until well mixed. Check the seasoning.
3. Pour into a bowl and chill for 1 hour. Just before serving, sprinkle with the chives. Serve very well chilled.

 *DRY WHITE*

CHILLED RED PESTO SOUP

SERVES 4

2 red peppers, grilled, de-seeded and peeled
8 plum tomatoes, skinned and de-seeded
8 sun-dried tomatoes
2 cloves of garlic, crushed
55g/2oz pinenuts, toasted
30g/1oz Parmesan cheese, freshly grated
1 handful of fresh basil leaves
860ml/1½ pints tomato juice

6 tablespoons extra virgin olive oil
salt and freshly ground black pepper

To serve
sprigs of fresh basil
crushed ice
150ml/¼ pint Greek yoghurt (optional)

1. Put the peppers, tomatoes, sun-dried tomatoes, garlic and pinenuts into a food processor and whizz until well chopped. Add the Parmesan cheese and basil and continue to pulse on and off until well chopped. Add the tomato juice.
2. With the motor running, add the oil in a thin stream until well emulsified.
3. Pour into a bowl and season to taste with salt and pepper. Chill for 15 minutes.
4. To serve: pour into a chilled soup tureen, stir in the basil sprigs and add the crushed ice. Hand the Greek yoghurt separately.

 *WHITE BURGUNDY*

FENNEL AND DILL GAZPACHO

SERVES 4

2 large bulbs of Florence fennel
2 large cucumbers, peeled, de-seeded and diced
2 green chillies, de-seeded and chopped
2 tablespoons chopped fresh dill
2 cloves of garlic, crushed
3 handfuls of rocket
6 tablespoons rice wine vinegar
6 tablespoons extra virgin olive oil
6 tablespoons water
salt and freshly ground black pepper

To serve
ice cubes

1. Finely dice half of 1 fennel bulb and quarter of 1 cucumber. Reserve.
2. Chop the remaining vegetables roughly and put into a blender with the chillies, dill, garlic

and rocket. Whizz to a smooth paste and gradually blend in the vinegar, oil and water. Season to taste with salt and pepper. Chill until cold.

3. To serve: pour into a chilled soup tureen and garnish with the reserved fennel and cucumber. Just before serving, add some ice cubes.

 *FINO SHERRY*

CHILLED BEETROOT AND CARAWAY SOUP

SERVES 4

2 tablespoons extra virgin olive oil
1 Spanish onion, finely chopped
2 teaspoons caraway seeds
1 clove of garlic, crushed
450g/1lb raw beetroot, peeled and thinly sliced
1.7 litres/3 pints well-flavoured white stock,
    made with chicken bones, or vegetable stock
    (see page 625)
salt and freshly ground black pepper

To serve
150ml/¼ pint crème fraîche
2 teaspoons chopped fresh chives

1. Heat the oil in a saucepan, add the onion and cook over a low heat until soft but not coloured. Add the caraway seeds and garlic and cook for a further 5 minutes.
2. Add the beetroot to the onion with the stock and season with salt and pepper. Bring to the boil, then lower the heat and simmer for 40–50 minutes, or until the beetroot is tender.
3. Whizz in a blender or food processor, then push through a sieve. Allow to cool, then chill.
4. Stir in the crème fraîche and check for seasoning – this soup needs plenty of salt and pepper. Pour into a chilled soup tureen and sprinkle with the chives.

 *VODKA*

MAIN COURSES

Fish and Shellfish
Poultry and Game
Beef
Lamb
Pork
Veal
Offal
Vegetarian

FISH AND SHELLFISH

COD STEAKS WITH NEW PEAS, PARSLEY AND CHIVE BUTTER

SERVES 4

salt
4 × 170g/6oz cod steaks
1 tablespoon olive oil
juice of 1 lemon
freshly ground black pepper
340g/12oz shelled new peas, or frozen if fresh
*   peas are unavailable*

For the chive butter
110g/4oz unsalted butter, softened
1 tablespoon snipped fresh chives
2 tablespoons finely chopped fresh parsley

To garnish
4 sprigs of flat-leaf parsley

1. Preheat the grill to its highest setting. Bring a large pan of salted water to the boil.
2. Remove any scales from the cod steaks and place them on a wire rack over a shallow roasting tray. Brush with oil, spoon over half the lemon juice and season with salt and pepper.
3. Place the tray under the grill as close to the heat as possible and grill for 2 minutes. Turn the steaks over and brush again with oil, spoon over the remaining lemon juice and season again. Grill again until golden-brown and just firm to the touch (the fish is ready when a table knife will slip down beside the bone easily).
4. Tip the peas into boiling water and simmer for 2 minutes. Drain well.

5. Make the chive butter: mix the butter with the chives and parsley. Season to taste with salt and pepper. If you need to refrigerate the butter allow it to warm through to room temperature before serving or it will be too hard.
6. To serve: pile the peas on to a warmed serving dish and arrange the cod steaks on top, spooning any juices from the roasting tray over. Dollop a spoonful of the chive butter on to each cod steak and garnish with the parsley.

 WHITE LOIRE/SAUVIGNON BLANC

ROAST PEPPER-CRUST COD WITH TOMATO CONCASSE

SERVES 4

4 × 170g/6oz cod fillets, unskinned
1 tablespoon plain flour
1 teaspoon salt
2 tablespoons freshly ground black, pink or
*   white peppercorns*
150ml/¼ pint extra virgin olive oil
2–3 sprigs of fresh rosemary

For the concasse
4 tomatoes, skinned, de-seeded and diced
1 red chilli, de-seeded and chopped
1 teaspoon chopped fresh rosemary
10 black olives, pitted and chopped
salt and freshly ground black pepper

1. Preheat the oven to 240°C/475°F/gas mark 8.
2. Pinbone the cod fillets if necessary (see page 133) but do not skin them.
3. Mix together the flour, salt and peppercorns.

273

Dip the fish, skin side down, into the peppercorn mixture, pressing on as much as possible.

4. Put the oil and rosemary into a roasting tin, set over a direct heat and add the cod, skin side down. Let it sizzle for 2 minutes.

5. Turn the cod skin side uppermost and roast in the oven for 3 minutes, or until cooked (it should be opaque and firm).

6. Meanwhile, toss the concasse ingredients together and season to taste with salt and pepper. Divide between 4 individual plates.

7. To serve: lift the cod from the oil and arrange on top of the concasse. Drizzle a little of the cooking oil over the cod and serve immediately.

 NEW ZEALAND SAUVIGNON BLANC

ROAST COD WITH MARINATED AUBERGINES AND BLACK OLIVES

This recipe needs to be started a day in advance of serving.

SERVES 4

4 × 170g/6oz cod steaks, unskinned
2 aubergines
sea salt
1 lemon
290ml/½ pint extra virgin olive oil, plus 4
  tablespoons
10 sprigs of fresh thyme
2 cloves of garlic, chopped
½ teaspoon cayenne pepper
110g/4oz black olives, pitted

To serve
2 teaspoons balsamic vinegar
salad leaves

1. Preheat the oven to 190°C/375°F/gas mark 5.
2. Pinbone the cod steaks if necessary (see page 133) but do not skin them.

3. Slice the aubergines and sprinkle lightly with salt. Allow to stand for 10 minutes. Slice the lemon thinly, remove any pips and sprinkle with salt. Allow to stand for 10 minutes.

4. Heat 290ml/½ pint oil in a large roasting tin and add the thyme, garlic and cayenne. Remove from the heat.

5. Wipe the salt from the aubergines and put into the oil with the lemon slices. Bake in the preheated oven for 20 minutes, or until the aubergines are soft.

6. Transfer the contents of the roasting tin to a bowl and stir in the olives. Cool, cover and refrigerate overnight.

7. The next day, preheat the oven to 230°C/450°F/gas mark 8.

8. Cook the cod steaks: press a little salt on to the skin. Heat the oil in a roasting tin over direct heat and when hot add the cod, skin side down. Fry for 2–3 minutes, then remove from the heat, turn the cod over and roast in the preheated oven for 4–5 minutes, or until the fish is opaque and just cooked.

9. Meanwhile, lift the aubergine mixture from the oil and arrange on a large serving dish. Sprinkle with the vinegar. Put the hot fish on top of the aubergines and garnish with salad leaves. Serve immediately.

 ITALIAN CHARDONNAY

ROSEMARY-SCENTED COD WITH TOMATO AND CAPER VINAIGRETTE

SERVES 4

4 × 170g/6oz cod steaks
salt and freshly ground black pepper
6 tablespoons olive oil
4 sprigs of rosemary

For the vinaigrette
1 small red onion, very finely chopped
3 tablespoons olive oil

2 tomatoes, peeled, de-seeded and chopped
1 tablespoon good-quality capers, drained and
    rinsed
1 tablespoon lemon juice
salt and freshly ground black pepper
sugar (optional)

To serve
1 quantity Pommes Anna (see page 659)

To garnish
a few rosemary leaves

1. Preheat the oven to 200°C/400°F/gas mark 6.
2. Pinbone the cod steaks (see page 133) but do
not skin them. Season the cod skin with salt and
pepper.
3. Heat the oil in a roasting tin and add the cod
steaks, skin side down, with the sprigs of
rosemary. Fry for 2–3 minutes, or until the skin
is crisp.
4. Turn the cod over so that the skin side is
uppermost. Bake in the oven for 8–10 minutes
or until cooked (it should be opaque and firm).
5. Meanwhile, make the dressing: mix together
all the ingredients in a bowl and whisk well.
Leave to infuse while the fish continues to cook.
6. To serve: cut the Pommes Anna into 4
wedges and divide between 4 individual plates.
Place a cod steak on each wedge of potato and
spoon the dressing around the outside. Garnish
with a few rosemary leaves. Serve immediately.

NOTE: The Pommes Anna are superb made
using a little crushed garlic in the layers of
potato. Pommes Anna is traditionally served
with French roast chicken, as it absorbs the
juices given off by the bird. It does the same
with the rosemary-flavoured juices from the
cod.

 *LIGHT SPANISH WHITE*

MACKEREL WITH GOOSEBERRIES AND GRAPEFRUIT

SERVES 4

4 × 225g/8oz mackerel, gutted

For the gooseberry and grapefruit sauce
450g/1lb young gooseberries, topped and tailed
juice of 1 grapefruit
30g/1oz caster sugar
30g/1oz butter
2 grapefruit

To garnish
1 small grapefruit, cut into 8 wedges

1. Preheat the grill to its highest setting.
2. Rinse the mackerel under cold running water
and dry them with kitchen paper. Trim off the
fins and make 3 diagonal slashes into the flesh
on both sides, nearly to the bone.
3. Make the gooseberry and grapefruit sauce:
place 340g/12oz of the gooseberries into a
frying pan with the grapefruit juice and sugar.
Simmer until the gooseberries are tender and
the purée is quite thick.
4. Push the gooseberries through a sieve into a
saucepan. Beat in the butter and taste for
sweetness, adding more sugar if necessary.
5. Cut the remaining gooseberries in half and
add to the sauce. Stir over a very low heat for
3–5 minutes, or until the gooseberries are just
tender but still holding their shape.
6. Cut the tops and bottoms off the grapefruit
so that the flesh is exposed. Carve the skin and
pith away from the sides in 2.5cm/1in strips,
following the shape of the grapefruit. Cut out
the segments, leaving the core and membranes
behind. Squeeze the juice from the membranes
into the sauce.
7. Grill the mackerel for about 5 minutes on
each side, depending on size, or until cooked.
8. Arrange the mackerel on a warmed serving
dish and garnish with the grapefruit wedges.
Stir the grapefruit segments into the sauce and
hand it separately.

 *WHITE RIOJA*

ROAST MACKEREL WITH MELON AND CHILLI SALSA

SERVES 4

4 × 340g/12oz mackerel, gutted
1 quantity herb butter (see page 636)

For the salsa
½ small Galia melon or watermelon
2 green chillies, de-seeded and finely chopped
1 red chilli, de-seeded and finely chopped
2 tablespoons rice wine vinegar
3 tablespoons sunflower oil
salt and freshly ground black pepper

To garnish
sprigs of fresh dill

1. Preheat the oven to 200°C/400°F/gas mark 6.
2. Rinse the mackerel under cold running water and dry it with kitchen paper. Trim off the fins and make 3–4 diagonal slashes into the flesh on both sides, nearly through to the bone. Place in a roasting tin.
3. Melt the herb butter, pour over the mackerel and roast in the preheated oven for 12–15 minutes, or until cooked.
4. Make the salsa: remove the skin and seeds from the melon and cut into 2.5cm/1in pieces. Mix together with the chillies, vinegar and oil and season to taste with salt and pepper.
5. Lay the cooked mackerel on a serving dish and spoon the salsa over the top. Garnish with dill. Serve immediately.

 *WHITE RIOJA*

GRILLED MACKEREL WITH SWEET AND SOUR TOMATO CHUTNEY

The acidity of the chutney marries very well with the oily mackerel.

SERVES 4

4 × 225–285g/8–10oz mackerel, filleted and trimmed (see page 132)
2 tablespoons sesame oil
salt and freshly ground black pepper

For the chutney
1½ teaspoons tamarind pulp
5 tablespoons rice wine or white wine vinegar
2 tablespoons peanut oil
1 tablespoon sesame oil
10 plum tomatoes, skinned, de-seeded and diced
6 cloves of garlic, crushed
150ml/¼ pint malt vinegar
4 tablespoons peeled and finely grated fresh root ginger
3 tablespoons brown sugar
2 tablespoons light soy sauce
1 tablespoon clear honey
1 tablespoon dried chillies, mild if possible
1 tablespoon coarse sea salt
1½ teaspoons ground cardamom
1 teaspoon ground cumin

To serve
sprigs of fresh coriander

1. Pinbone the mackerel fillets (see page 133). Cover and refrigerate until required.
2. To make the chutney: put the tamarind pulp into a small bowl, pour over the rice or white wine vinegar and leave to infuse for 30 minutes.
3. Heat the oils together in a large saucepan, add the tomatoes and garlic and cook over a high heat for 5 minutes.
4. Add the soaked tamarind and rice vinegar, the malt vinegar, ginger, sugar, soy sauce, honey, chillies, salt, cardamom and cumin. Bring to the boil, reduce the heat and simmer

until the sauce has become thick and pulpy. Season to taste with salt and pepper if necessary. Set aside 8 tablespoons of the tomato chutney in a saucepan and keep warm. Pour the remainder into a clean, sterilized jar (see note), cover, cool and refrigerate. Use within 2 weeks.

5. Preheat the grill to its highest setting.

6. Brush the mackerel fillets with oil and season with salt and pepper. Grill for 2–3 minutes on each side or until the fish is cooked and lightly browned (it should be opaque and firm).

7. Arrange 2 mackerel fillets on each of 4 individual plates. Spoon 2 tablespoons of the chutney on one side of each plate and garnish with a few sprigs of coriander. Serve immediately.

NOTE: To sterilize a jam jar for preserving purposes: wash the jar thoroughly in hot soapy water and rinse well, but do not dry. Put the jar upside down to drain on a baking sheet. Put into a warm oven preheated to 150°C/300°F/ gas mark 2 and heat for 20 minutes. Fill the jar with the hot chutney when it is still hot, or the glass may shatter.

 *CHILEAN SAUVIGNON BLANC*

GRILLED MONKFISH WITH AÏOLI AND CITRUS BULGHAR WHEAT

SERVES 4

290ml/½ pint well-seasoned fish stock (see page 627)
grated zest of 2 limes
juice of 3 limes
juice of 2 lemons
225g/8oz bulghar wheat
2 red onions, cut into 6 wedges
3 tablespoons olive oil
salt and freshly ground black pepper
2 red peppers, grilled, peeled and de-seeded
1 teaspoon herbes de Provence
2 green peppers, grilled, peeled and de-seeded

675g/1½lb skinned monkfish fillet, cut into 2.5cm/1in chunks
½ quantity aïoli (see page 632)

To garnish
8 lemon wedges

1. Preheat the grill to its highest setting and the oven to 150°C/300°F/gas mark 2.

2. Bring the stock, lime zest and juice and lemon juice to the boil in a saucepan and add the bulghar wheat. Leave to stand for 15 minutes or until all the liquid has been absorbed.

3. Put the onions on to a baking sheet and toss with 2 tablespoons of the oil and the herbs and season with salt and pepper. Grill until golden-brown, turning once.

4. Cut the peppers into strips and toss with the onions. Put them into the oven to keep warm.

5. Toss the monkfish in the remaining oil and season well with salt and pepper. Grill for about 4 minutes, or until the flesh is opaque, turning once.

6. Put the bulghar wheat into the bottom of a shallow flameproof casserole and pour over any fish juices. Arrange the vegetables on top with the monkfish. Spoon over the aïoli and grill until golden-brown and sizzling. Serve immediately, garnished with the lemon wedges.

 *ALSATIAN WHITE*

WARM NAAN WITH ORIENTAL PESTO MONKFISH

SERVES 4

675g/1½lb monkfish, skinned and filleted
2 tablespoons sesame oil
2 tablespoons light soy sauce
1 teaspoon Sichuan peppercorns, roasted

For the oriental pesto
6 tablespoons chopped fresh coriander
1 clove of garlic, crushed

2.5cm/1in piece of fresh root ginger, peeled and
   grated
30g/1oz piece of creamed coconut
2 tablespoons sesame oil
1 teaspoon Sichuan peppercorns
salt and freshly ground black pepper
4 Sichuan-style naan breads (see page 372)

1. Put the monkfish into a shallow dish and
pour over the sesame oil, soy sauce and Sichuan
peppercorns. Cover and refrigerate for 30
minutes.

2. Meanwhile, prepare the oriental pesto: put
the coriander, garlic, ginger and coconut into a
food processor or blender and whizz until
smooth. With the motor running, pour in the
oil in a thin stream, add the Sichuan
peppercorns and season with salt and pepper.

3. Preheat the grill to its highest setting.

4. Lift the fish from the marinade and spread
with half of the pesto. Grill for 2–3 minutes,
then turn the monkfish over and spread the
second side with the remaining pesto. Grill for a
further 2–3 minutes, or until cooked and
browned. Slice the monkfish thickly.

5. Warm the naan under the grill and slit open
to make a pocket. Divide the salad leaves and
monkfish between the naan and serve.

 NEW ZEALAND SAUVIGNON BLANC

MONKFISH PESTO PANCAKES

SERVES 4

For the pancake batter
55g/2oz plain flour
salt and freshly ground black pepper
freshly grated nutmeg
1 egg
150ml/¼ pint milk
½ tablespoon oil
2 tablespoons chopped fresh parsley
oil for frying

For the filling
1 quantity basil pesto (see page 634)
4 × 170g/6oz pieces of monkfish fillet, skinned
   and boned

To serve
tomato and basil stew (see page 322)

To garnish
4 lemon wedges
1 tablespoon chopped fresh chives

1. Sift the flour into a large bowl with the salt,
pepper and nutmeg. Make a well in the centre
and add the egg with a little of the milk. Using a
wooden spoon or whisk, mix the egg and milk
and then gradually draw in the flour from the
sides as you mix.

2. When the mixture reaches the consistency of
thick cream, beat well and stir in the oil and
parsley. Add the remaining milk – the
consistency should be of thin cream. Cover the
bowl and refrigerate for 30 minutes.

3. Make 4 × 20cm/8in pancakes with the batter
(see page 654).

4. Lay the pancakes out on a flat surface, with
the lacy side on the underside. Spread 1–2
tablespoons of pesto over each pancake,
spreading it out to the edges. Season with
pepper.

5. Season the fish with a little salt and place one
fillet on each pancake. Fold over the ends and
roll the parcels up. Place the parcels in a
shallow ovenproof dish and chill for 30
minutes.

6. Meanwhile, preheat the oven to 180°C/
350°F/gas mark 4.

7. Brush the parcels with a little oil and bake in
the preheated oven for 20 minutes.

8. Serve the parcels on warmed individual plates
with the tomato and basil stew, garnished with
the lemon wedges and chives.

 NEW ZEALAND SAUVIGNON BLANC

RED MULLET WITH SUN-DRIED TOMATO AND BASIL POTATO GALETTE

SERVES 4

*8 × 85g/3oz red mullet fillets, pinboned (see
   page 133)*
4 tablespoons extra virgin olive oil
a pinch of saffron strands
freshly ground black pepper

For the galettes
450g/1lb potatoes, peeled and grated
1 teaspoon salt
55g/2oz sun-dried tomatoes, sliced
2 tablespoons thinly sliced fresh basil leaves

To garnish
4 sprigs of fresh basil
4 lemon wedges

1. Coat the mullet with 3 tablespoons of the oil
and saffron. Season with pepper, cover and
leave to marinate for 4 hours or overnight.
2. Make the galettes: mix the potatoes with the
salt and leave to stand in a sieve for 30 minutes,
then squeeze dry. Mix the potato with the sun-dried tomatoes and basil and season with
pepper.
3. Divide the mixture into 4 portions. Heat the
remaining oil in a non-stick pan and fry a
portion of the potato mixture, pressing it into a
12cm/5in round flat galette, until golden-brown. Turn over and gently brown the second
side. Repeat with the remaining potato to make
3 more galettes. Keep the galettes in a warming
oven while you cook the fish.
4. Wipe the pan clean and heat well. Sprinkle
the skin side of the mullet with salt and place
half the fillets skin side down in the pan. When
the skin is golden and crispy turn the fillets over
and cook for a further minute. Remove the
fillets from the pan and repeat with the
remaining fillets.
5. Put the galettes on to 4 individual plates and
arrange 2 mullet fillets on top of each. Garnish

with the basil and lemon wedges and serve
immediately.

 RULLY ROUGE – BURGUNDY

HOT WASABI COCONUT AND CHILLI CURED RED SNAPPER

SERVES 4

1 × 1.35kg/3lb red snapper, scaled and gutted
1 tablespoon wasabi paste (see page 161)
30g/1oz creamed coconut
1 green chilli, de-seeded and chopped
1 clove of garlic, crushed
1 stick of lemon grass
juice of ½ lime
*2.5cm/1in piece of galangal, peeled and
   chopped*
2 tablespoons chopped fresh coriander
salt and freshly ground black pepper

To serve
Thai sticky rice (see page 659)

1. Place the cleaned red snapper on a chopping
board. Make 2–3 diagonal slashes into both
sides of the fish, cutting right through to the
bone.
2. Put the wasabi paste, creamed coconut, chilli,
garlic, lemon grass, lime juice, galangal and
coriander into a spice grinder, and whizz to a
paste. Season with salt and pepper.
3. Rub half the paste on to one side of the red
snapper, turn it over and rub the remaining
paste on the second side.
4. Wrap the fish loosely in kitchen foil and chill
for 1 hour.
5. Preheat the oven to 180°C/350°F/gas mark 4.
6. Place the wrapped fish on a baking sheet and
bake in the preheated oven for 25–30 minutes,
or until the fish is cooked (the flesh should look
opaque and feel flaky to the touch).
7. Unwrap the red snapper and transfer to a
warmed serving dish with any cooking juices.
Hand the rice separately.

 ALSATIAN TOKAY/PINOT GRIS

HOT POACHED SALMON WITH SAUCE VIERGE

SERVES 4

675g/1½lb salmon fillet, skinned (see page 133)
juice of 1 lemon
4 tablespoons dry white wine
2 tablespoons olive oil
salt and freshly ground black pepper

For the sauce vierge
1 bulb of Florence fennel, very finely chopped
8 ripe tomatoes, skinned, de-seeded and
    chopped
juice of 2 lemons
1 clove of garlic, crushed
190ml/6½fl oz extra virgin olive oil
5 tablespoons dry white wine
1 teaspoon sugar
salt and freshly ground black pepper
1 bunch of fresh dill, chopped

1. Pinbone the salmon fillet if necessary (see page 133). Set aside.
2. Make the sauce: blanch the fennel in a pan of boiling water for 1 minute, drain and refresh under cold running water. Drain and pat dry on kitchen paper.
3. Mix the fennel, tomatoes, lemon juice, garlic, oil, wine, sugar, salt and pepper together and leave to infuse for 2 hours.
4. Preheat the oven to 180°C/350°F/gas mark 4.
5. Place the salmon fillet in a roasting tin and pour over the lemon juice, wine and olive oil. Season with salt and pepper. Bake in the centre of the preheated oven for 15 minutes, or until the fish is just firm and opaque. Transfer the salmon to a warmed serving dish.
6. Heat the sauce gently in a small saucepan and at the last moment stir in the dill and check the seasoning. Pour the sauce around the salmon fillet and serve immediately.

 *NEW ZEALAND CHARDONNAY*

BLACKENED SALMON WITH SAMPHIRE

The seasoning in this recipe is inspired by Paul Prudhomme in Louisiana who invented the 'blackened' way of cooking meat and fish.

SERVES 6

6 × 170g/6oz salmon steaks, unskinned
55g/2oz butter
2 tablespoons olive oil

For the seasoning
1 tablespoon paprika
2 teaspoons salt
1 teaspoon onion powder
1 teaspoon garlic powder
1 teaspoon cayenne pepper
¾ teaspoon freshly ground white pepper
¾ teaspoon freshly ground black pepper
½ teaspoon dried thyme
½ teaspoon dried oregano

For the samphire
675g/1½lb fresh young samphire shoots
30g/1oz butter
2 tablespoons malt vinegar
salt and freshly ground black pepper

To garnish
lemon wedges

1. Pinbone the salmon steaks if necessary (see page 133). Shape into noisettes: using a sharp knife, slice the skin away from the flesh round each steak. Fold the skinned piece of fish into the centre and wrap the rest of the steak round the outside. Tie with string. Place the noisettes between 2 plates, weight down, and chill for at least 1 hour.
2. Melt the butter. Mix all the seasoning ingredients together and put into a large bowl. Dip the salmon steaks into the butter and then into the seasoning mix, coating them evenly.
3. Heat a heavy-based frying pan over a high heat. When it is very hot arrange 3 salmon noisettes in the pan, pour in 1 tablespoon of the oil and fry for 2 minutes on each side until fairly

charred. Remove the salmon noisettes from the pan and wipe it out. Add the remaining oil and fry the remaining noisettes.

4. Boil the samphire in a saucepan of unsalted water for 5 minutes, or until tender. Drain well. Tip the samphire back into the pan, add the butter and vinegar and season well with salt and pepper.

5. Arrange a pile of samphire on 6 individual plates. Remove the string from the salmon noisettes and place on top of the samphire. Garnish with the lemon wedges. Serve immediately.

 CHILEAN RESERVE PINOT NOIR

SALMON EN CROÛTE WITH FENNEL AND SAMPHIRE

SERVES 8

450g/1lb flour quantity of puff pastry (see page 643)
2 bulbs of Florence fennel, thinly sliced
450g/1lb young samphire shoots
2 tablespoons fine semolina
salt and freshly ground black pepper
900g/2lb salmon fillet, skinned and pinboned (see page 133)
juice of 1 lemon
3 tablespoons vermouth or dry martini
1 egg, beaten

For the sauce
1 shallot, finely chopped
1 bay leaf
100ml/3½fl oz vermouth
225g/8oz unsalted chilled butter, diced
1 tablespoon double cream
1 tablespoon lemon juice
1 tablespoon chopped fresh dill or fennel weed

1. Preheat the oven to 220°C/425°F/gas mark 7.
2. Take one-third of the pastry and roll into a rectangle about 30 × 10cm/12 × 4in. Place on a baking sheet, prick the base well with a fork and chill for 30 minutes.

3. Bake the pastry in the top of the preheated oven for 20 minutes, or until risen and golden-brown all over. Cool on a wire rack.
4. Blanch the fennel in boiling salted water for 4 minutes. Drain and refresh under cold running water. Drain and dry well on kitchen paper.
5. Wash the samphire thoroughly. Boil in a large saucepan of unsalted water for 2 minutes. Drain and refresh under cold running water. Drain again and dry well.
6. Place the pastry carefully back on to the baking sheet and sprinkle over the fine semolina. Arrange the fennel on top and season with salt and pepper.
7. Lay the salmon fillet on top of the fennel and drizzle over the lemon juice. Season with salt and pepper.
8. Arrange the samphire on top, sprinkle over the vermouth and season with pepper.
9. Roll out the remaining pastry into a rectangle about 35 × 18cm/14 × 7in. Lay the pastry over the salmon and tuck the edges underneath. Brush the pastry with beaten egg and chill for 30 minutes. Brush with more beaten egg and make a pattern on the pastry with the back of a table knife.
10. Bake at the top of the oven for 20 minutes, or until the pastry is golden-brown all over.
11. Make the sauce: put the shallot, bay leaf and vermouth into a small saucepan and simmer over a low heat until reduced to 3 tablespoons.
12. Carefully whisk the butter into the liquid, piece by piece. The sauce should be gently simmering while the butter is added. If it starts to look oily at the edges, remove the pan from the heat and add a teaspoon of water before continuing. The sauce should be thick and glossy. Add the cream and lemon juice to taste. Stir in the dill or fennel and season with salt and pepper.
13. To serve: carefully transfer the salmon en croûte to a warmed serving dish and hand the sauce separately.

 FINE WHITE BURGUNDY OR NEW ZEALAND CHARDONNAY

HOME-SMOKED HICKORY SALMON

Hickory chips are used for barbecues and are therefore readily available at many supermarkets and hardware shops.

It is possible to smoke the salmon indoors: always have the extractor fan on full and make sure that there is very good ventilation.

SERVES 4

4 × 170g/6oz salmon fillets

For the cure
6 tablespoons soft light brown sugar
2 teaspoons wasabi paste (see page 161)
1 tablespoon salt
1 tablespoon whole white peppercorns

For smoking
2 large handfuls of hickory chips

To serve
sautéed enoki dake mushrooms (see following recipe)
soba noodles (see page 164)

1. Skin the salmon fillets and pinbone if necessary (see page 133).
2. Mix together the sugar, wasabi, salt and pepper and spread over the salmon. Cover and refrigerate for 8 hours.
3. Assemble the smoker: put the hickory chips into a large roasting tin and sit a small shallow cake tin directly on top. Put 5 tablespoons of water into the cake tin. Put a wire cooling rack across the top of the roasting tin and brush it lightly with oil.
4. Wipe off any excess cure from the salmon. Arrange the fillets on the cooling rack – they must not touch. Cover with a large sheet of kitchen foil and seal around the edges of the roasting tin.
5. Set over a low to medium heat and allow to smoke for 15–20 minutes. Do not be tempted to remove the foil too often as this will slow the smoking process. The salmon is cooked when it looks opaque.

6. To serve: place the salmon on a large serving platter and arrange the mushrooms around the outside. Hand the noodles separately.

 *WHITE BURGUNDY*

SAUTÉED ENOKI DAKE MUSHROOMS

SERVES 4

225g/8oz enoki dake, trimmed
30g/1oz butter
2 tablespoons sesame oil
freshly ground black pepper

1. Pick over the mushrooms, taking care any earth is wiped away. Break into clumps.
2. Melt the butter in a large sauté pan, add the oil and season with pepper. Add the mushrooms and fry over a brisk heat for 2–3 minutes, or until beginning to wilt.
3. Pile into a warmed serving dish and serve immediately.

WHOLE BONED SALMON WITH FENNEL AND WASABI

This salmon dish is a good summer buffet dish and a lighter alternative to traditional salmon mayonnaise.

SERVES 8

1 × 2.3kg/5lb salmon, filleted into 2 and skinned (see page 133)
oil for brushing
100ml/3½fl oz mirin (see page 164)
4 fronds of fresh herb fennel

For the filling
6 tablespoons roughly chopped herb fennel
1 teaspoon wasabi paste (see page 161)

1 green chilli, de-seeded and chopped
110g/4oz pinenuts, toasted
1 clove of garlic, crushed
2 tablespoons peanut oil
1 tablespoon rice wine vinegar
salt and freshly ground black pepper

To serve
fronds of fresh green or bronze herb fennel

1. Pinbone the salmon fillets if necessary (see page 133). Set aside.
2. Make the filling: put the fennel, wasabi paste, chilli, pinenuts and garlic into a food processor or blender and whizz until smooth. Add the oil and vinegar and season to taste with salt and pepper.
3. Preheat the oven to 180°C/350°F/gas mark 4.
4. Line a large roasting tin with oiled kitchen foil.
5. Assemble the salmon: put one fillet, skinned side down, into the roasting tin. Spread with the filling and put the second fillet on top, skinned side uppermost, to form a 'sandwich'. Brush with oil.
6. Pour the mirin over the salmon and place the fennel fronds on top.
7. Wrap the fish loosely in the foil (if it is wrapped too tightly it will not cook evenly). Bake in the preheated oven for 30–35 minutes, or until the fish is cooked (it should be opaque and firm).
8. To serve: cover a large serving dish with the fresh fennel fronds. Lift the cooked salmon on to the dish, discarding the cooked fennel fronds, serve hot or cold.

 *WHITE BURGUNDY*

NOISETTES OF SALMON WITH LIME BUTTER

SERVES 4

4 × 170g/6oz salmon cutlets, cut 4cm/1½in
   thick
grated zest of 2 limes
juice of 1 lime

85g/3oz butter, softened
2 teaspoons finely chopped fresh coriander
salt and freshly ground black pepper

To garnish
4 lime wedges
fresh coriander leaves

1. Prepare the salmon noisettes: carefully remove the bones from the cutlets. Using a sharp knife, slice the skin away from the flesh halfway round each cutlet. Fold the skinned piece of fish into the centre and wrap the rest of the cutlet round the outside. Tie with string. Place the noisettes between 2 plates, weight down, and chill for at least 1 hour.
2. Mix together the lime zest, juice, butter and coriander and season to taste with salt and pepper. Shape into a cylinder, roll up in kitchen foil or damp greaseproof paper and chill.
3. Preheat the oven to 180°C/350°F/gas mark 4.
4. Place the salmon noisettes on a baking sheet. Cut the butter into 4 thick slices and put one on each noisette. Cover with kitchen foil and bake in the preheated oven for 12–15 minutes, or until the fish is cooked.
5. To serve: remove the string from the noisettes and arrange on a warmed serving dish. Garnish with lime wedges and coriander leaves. Serve immediately.

 NEW WORLD CHARDONNAY

VODKA-MARINATED SALMON WITH HOT BEETROOT

SERVES 4

4 × 170–225g/6–8oz salmon steaks, skinned (see
   page 133)
150ml/¼ pint vodka
1 tablespoon chopped fresh dill
1 teaspoon coarse sea salt
freshly ground black pepper

For the beetroot
450g/1lb raw beetroot
55g/2oz butter
salt and freshly ground black pepper
a squeeze of lemon juice

1. Pinbone the salmon steaks if necessary (see page 133). Place in a shallow dish, pour over the vodka, sprinkle over the dill and season with salt and pepper. Cover and refrigerate for 30 minutes.
2. Preheat the oven to 180°C/350°F/gas mark 4.
3. Prepare the beetroot: peel and grate it on the coarse side of the grater. Set aside.
4. Arrange the salmon steaks and the marinade in a roasting tin and bake in the oven for 15–20 minutes or until the fish is just cooked (it should be opaque and firm).
5. Meanwhile, heat the butter in a frying pan until hot and foaming, add the beetroot and stir-fry for 1 minute or until very hot. Season with salt and pepper and add the lemon juice.
6. To serve: divide the beetroot between 4 individual plates and place a salmon steak on top of each. Serve very hot.

 *CHILLED VODKA OR VERY DRY WHITE*

SALMON AND CHILLI BURGERS

SERVES 6

675g/1½lb salmon fillet, skinned
1 teaspoon ground ginger
4 teaspoons light soy sauce
1 clove of garlic, crushed
2 spring onions, very finely chopped
1 red chilli, de-seeded and finely chopped
1 tablespoon cold water
1 tablespoon chopped fresh mint
salt and freshly ground black pepper

To serve
6 plain wholemeal baps (see page 657)
fennel, cucumber and chilli salad (see page 327)

1. Pinbone the salmon fillet if necessary (see page 133). Cut into chunks, put into a food processor and whizz until finely chopped. Turn the mixture into a bowl and add the ginger, soy sauce, garlic, spring onions, chilli, water, mint, salt and pepper. Mix together thoroughly.
2. Divide the mixture into 6 portions. Using wet hands, shape into burgers, about 7.5cm/3in across and 2.5cm/1in thick. Chill for 30 minutes.
3. Preheat the barbecue, or grill until very hot.
4. Warm the bread rolls, split in half and keep warm.
5. Barbecue or grill the salmon burgers for 4 minutes on each side, or until just cooked (they should be opaque and firm but still moist).
6. Sandwich the salmon burgers in the warm rolls and top each with a little fennel, cucumber and chilli salad. Serve warm.

 *LANGUEDOC*

GRILLED SARDINES WITH WARM GREEK SALAD

The idea for this recipe was given to us by Maxine Clark, a senior teacher at Leith's.

SERVES 4

8 × 110g/4oz sardines, scaled and gutted (see page 131)
2 tablespoons extra virgin olive oil
1 teaspoon coarse sea salt
freshly ground black pepper

For the salad
8 tomatoes, halved and de-seeded
2 courgettes, cut into 2.5cm/1in slices
1 large onion, very thickly sliced
4 cloves of garlic, unpeeled
3 tablespoons extra virgin olive oil
6 sprigs of fresh thyme

110g/4oz feta cheese, chopped
1 tablespoon balsamic vinegar
12 Kalamata olives, pitted
1 tablespoon chopped fresh basil

1. Preheat the oven to 200°C/400°F/gas mark 6.
2. Rinse and dry the sardines. Arrange on a baking sheet, drizzle with the oil and season with salt and pepper. Cover and set aside in the refrigerator.
3. Make the salad: put the tomatoes on to a baking sheet and add the courgettes, onion and garlic. Pour the oil over the vegetables and add the sprigs of thyme. Season with salt and pepper. Roast in the oven for 25 minutes, or until the vegetables are soft and lightly browned.
4. Meanwhile, preheat the grill to its highest setting.
5. Grill the sardines for 2–3 minutes on each side, or until cooked (they should be opaque and firm). Sprinkle the sardines with the crumbled feta cheese and grill for 1–2 further minutes, or until the cheese begins to brown.
6. Lift the vegetables into a large mixing bowl, discarding the thyme, and toss with the vinegar, olives and basil. Put on to a warmed serving dish and arrange the sardines on top. Serve with warm bread.

 RETSINA/DRY ITALIAN WHITE

BAKED SEA TROUT WITH FENNEL AÏOLI

SERVES 4

1 × 1.35kg/3lb whole sea trout
oil for brushing
100ml/3½fl oz dry white wine
sprigs of fresh fennel
1 bay leaf

For the fennel aïoli
1 quantity aïoli (see page 632)
1 bulb of Florence fennel, very finely diced
3 tablespoons chopped fresh herb fennel
2 teaspoons Pernod

To garnish
sprigs of fresh herb fennel

To serve
new potatoes (see page 26)

1. Preheat the oven to 180°C/350°F/gas mark 4.
2. Gut and trim the trout, removing the fins and gills, but leaving the dorsal fin intact. Rinse well.
3. Lay the trout on a sheet of lightly oiled kitchen foil, sprinkle with the wine and arrange the fennel and bay leaf on top of the fish. Wrap loosely in the foil and bake in the oven for 25–30 minutes, or until cooked (the dorsal fin should pull away easily).
4. Meanwhile, prepare the fennel aïoli: mix together the aïoli, fennel bulb and herb and Pernod.
5. To serve: unwrap the cooked trout and remove the skin, leaving the head and tail intact. Put the trout on to a serving dish and garnish with the sprigs of fennel. Serve hot with new potatoes. Hand the aïoli separately.

 WHITE BURGUNDY

SPICED SEA TROUT, GOUJONS WITH CHILLI AND MINTED YOGHURT

The oily texture of sea trout and other members of the salmon family such as trout and char lends itself well to spicy and oriental flavours.

SERVES 4

450g/1lb sea trout or salmon fillet, skinned (see page 133)
110g/4oz semolina
4 teaspoons ground coriander
4 teaspoons ground ginger
salt and freshly ground black pepper
2 egg whites, lightly beaten
oil for deep-frying

For the yoghurt sauce
2 green chillies, de-seeded and finely chopped
2 red chillies, de-seeded and finely chopped
4 tablespoons chopped fresh mint
150ml/¼ pint Greek yoghurt
salt and freshly ground black pepper

1. Pinbone the sea trout if necessary (see page 133). Cut into finger-length strips.

2. Mix the semolina with the spices and season with salt and pepper.

3. Dip the sea trout goujons into the egg white and then roll in the semolina. Arrange in a single layer on a plate and chill until required.

4. Heat the oil in a deep-fryer until a crumb sizzles in it. Fry the sea trout goujons until golden-brown, then drain on kitchen paper and sprinkle lightly with salt. Keep warm.

5. Mix together the ingredients for the yoghurt sauce and season with salt and pepper.

6. Arrange the sea trout goujons on a large warmed serving plate and serve very hot. Hand the yoghurt sauce separately.

 NEW WORLD CHARDONNAY

GRIDDLED SEA BASS WITH ROCKET AND ANCHOVY DRESSING

SERVES 4

4 × 170g/6oz sea bass fillets, skinned
1 tablespoon lemon juice
2 tablespoons olive oil
salt and freshly ground black pepper
oil for brushing

For the anchovy dressing
8 tinned anchovy fillets, soaked in milk for 15
*   minutes, drained and dried*
juice of 2 lemons
8 tablespoons olive oil
1 clove of garlic, crushed
1 handful of rocket leaves, washed, dried and
*   cut into julienne strips*

To serve
1 quantity rocket pasta I (see page 651)

To garnish
4 lemon wedges
a few fresh rocket leaves

1. Pinbone the sea bass fillets if necessary (see page 133) and cut them into 4cm/1½in strips on the diagonal. Place with the lemon juice and oil in a shallow dish and season well with salt and pepper. Leave to marinate for 15 minutes.

2. Make the anchovy dressing: whizz the anchovies, lemon juice, oil and garlic together in a food processor or blender, stir in the rocket and season to taste with pepper.

3. Preheat a griddle pan. Brush with a little oil, then place the sea bass strips on the pan and leave for 1 minute. Turn the strips over and cook for a further minute, or until the flesh is opaque.

4. Cook the rocket pasta and drain well.

5. Arrange the pasta on 4 warmed individual plates. Place the sea bass strips on top and spoon the dressing around. Garnish with the lemon wedges and rocket. Serve immediately.

 ITALIAN CHARDONNAY

ROAST TILAPIA WITH DEEP-FRIED BASIL AND THYME

SERVES 4

4 × 340g/12oz tilapia, gutted, scaled and fins
*   removed*
4 sprigs of fresh thyme
ground rock salt
freshly ground black pepper
2 tablespoons extra virgin olive oil
1 tablespoon chopped fresh thyme
1 tablespoon chopped fresh basil
juice of 1 large lemon

To garnish
12 large fresh basil leaves
4 large sprigs of fresh thyme
oil for deep-frying
4 lemon wedges

1. Preheat the oven to 220°C/425°F/gas mark 7. Preheat oil in a deep-fryer, if using, to its highest setting.

2. Make 3 diagonal slashes into both sides of each tilapia, cutting right through to the bone. Place a sprig of thyme in the belly of each fish. Season the tilapia with salt and pepper.

3. Heat the olive oil in a shallow roasting tray, large enough for all the fish (or 2 smaller ones if necessary). Fry the fish until golden-brown on both sides.

4. Sprinkle the thyme and basil on to the tilapia and bake in the preheated oven for 10 minutes, or until cooked (the flesh should be opaque).

5. Meanwhile, make the garnish: if you are not using a deep-fryer, heat 5cm/2in oil in a large heavy-based saucepan until a breadcrumb sizzles and browns within 20 seconds. Place the basil leaves in a metal basket, lower the basket carefully into the hot oil in the saucepan or deep-fryer, and fry for just a few seconds until the basil is crisp. Immediately remove the basil from the oil and drain on kitchen paper. Sprinkle with a little salt to absorb excess oil. Deep-fry the thyme sprigs in the same way.

6. When the tilapia are cooked, take the roasting tray out of the oven and place the fish on warmed individual plates. Pour the lemon juice into the fish juices in the roasting tray and stir over a high heat for a few seconds. Season the juices with salt and pepper before drizzling them over the tilapia.

7. Arrange the deep-fried herbs over the tilapia. Garnish with the lemon wedges. Serve immediately.

 *WHITE BURGUNDY*

RIVER TROUT STUFFED WITH TOMATO, MINT AND FETA

SERVES 4

4 × 340g/12oz pink river trout, ungutted

For the stuffing
110g/4oz feta, diced into ½cm/¼in cubes
1 tablespoon chopped fresh mint
4 ripe tomatoes, skinned, de-seeded and roughly chopped

55g/2oz fresh white breadcrumbs
juice of 1 lemon
a pinch of caster sugar
salt and freshly ground black pepper

To garnish
4 lemon wedges
4 sprigs of fresh mint

1. Preheat the oven to 200°C/400°F/gas mark 6.

2. Make a slit down the back bone of each trout, to one side of the dorsal fin. Remove the bones and guts from the fish (see page 131), leaving the head and tail intact.

3. Wash the inside of the fish thoroughly and dry well on kitchen paper.

4. Make the stuffing: mix together all the ingredients and season to taste with a little sugar, salt and pepper.

5. Lay the trout out on a board with the flesh exposed. Season well with salt and pepper. Divide the filling between the trout, piling it down one side of the fish. Fold each trout back together again, so it resembles its original shape, but with the stuffing showing.

6. Lay the trout on a lightly greased baking sheet and season the skin with salt and pepper. Bake near the top of the preheated oven for 15 minutes, or until the flesh is firm. Transfer to a warmed serving dish and garnish with the lemon wedges and sprigs of mint.

 SANCERRE OR POUILLY FUMÉ

GRILLED TURBOT WITH ROCKET SALSA

SERVES 4

4 × 170–225g/6–8oz turbot steaks, skinned (see page 133)
2 tablespoons hazelnut oil
salt and very finely ground white pepper

For the salsa
85g/3oz rocket, washed and de-stalked

287

1 clove of garlic, crushed
55g/2oz macadamia nuts, coarsely chopped
30g/1oz Gruyère cheese, finely grated
4 tablespoons hazelnut oil
1 tablespoon sherry vinegar
½ teaspoon grain mustard
salt and freshly ground black pepper

1. Preheat the grill to its highest setting.
2. Brush the turbot steaks with the oil and season lightly with salt and pepper. Set aside.
3. Make the salsa: chop the rocket finely, put into a bowl and mix with the garlic, macadamia nuts and Gruyère cheese.
4. Put the turbot steaks on to a baking sheet and grill for 2–3 minutes on each side, or until cooked (the flesh should be opaque, firm and lightly browned).
5. Add the oil, vinegar and mustard to the salsa ingredients. Whisk well and season to taste with salt and pepper.
6. Place a turbot steak on each of 4 individual plates and spoon a little of the salsa on one side. Serve immediately.

 *ITALIAN DRY WHITE*

BAKED CRAB AND SAMPHIRE RISOTTO

SERVES 4

1 large onion, sliced
1 yellow pepper, de-seeded and
    sliced
3 tablespoons olive oil
salt and freshly ground black pepper
225g/8oz risotto or short-grain rice
1 teaspoon saffron strands
½ bottle dry white wine
juice of 2 lemons
450g/1lb fresh samphire shoots
225g/8oz fresh white crabmeat
110g/4oz fresh brown crabmeat
225g/8oz shell-on prawns

To serve
8 lemon wedges

1. Preheat the oven to 200°C/400°F/gas mark 6.
2. Put the onion, pepper and oil into a large roasting tin and season with salt and pepper. Roast in the preheated oven for 30 minutes.
3. Add the rice and saffron with half the wine. Stir everything together and cover with kitchen foil. Return the roasting tin to the oven for 15 minutes.
4. Add the remaining wine, lemon juice and samphire. Replace the foil and cook in the oven for a further 10 minutes.
5. Stir the risotto again and add the crabmeat and prawns. Cover the roasting tin again and return to the oven for a further 5 minutes, or until the seafood is hot and all the liquid has been absorbed.
6. Serve garnished with the lemon wedges.

 SINGLE ESTATE MOSEL SPÄTLESE

GLAZED CRAB AND ARTICHOKE GRATIN

SERVES 4

4 globe artichokes
coarse sea salt
juice of ½ lemon
225g/8oz hand-picked crabmeat
a pinch of cayenne pepper
freshly ground black pepper
2-egg quantity hollandaise sauce (see page 633)
2 teaspoons chopped fresh tarragon

1. Remove the leaves and choke from the artichokes to reveal the bottom. Cook the bottoms in boiling salted water, with a splash of lemon juice, for 20–25 minutes, or until tender. Drain.
2. Preheat the grill to its highest setting.
3. Cut each artichoke into thick slices and arrange in the base of 4 individual ramekins or gratin dishes.
4. Heat the crabmeat with the cayenne and 1 teaspoon lemon juice in a small saucepan until it is very hot. Season to taste with salt and pepper and divide the mixture between the dishes.

5. Season the hollandaise sauce with a little lemon juice and stir in the tarragon. Spoon a couple of tablespoons over the top of the crab.
6. Grill for 20–30 seconds, or until the hollandaise begins to brown. Serve very hot.

 *DRY WHITE*

LOBSTER AND STRAWBERRY SALAD

SERVES 4

4 × 675g/1½lb live lobsters, poached (see page 134)
2 bunches of watercress, washed thoroughly and stalks removed
juice of 1 lemon

To garnish
225g/8oz ripe and full-flavoured strawberries, hulled and halved

For the dressing
170g/6oz ripe and full-flavoured strawberries, hulled
juice of 1 lemon
1–2 tablespoons champagne vinegar or white wine vinegar
8 tablespoons olive oil
salt and freshly ground black pepper

To serve
new potato, chive and sour cream salad (see page 328)

1. Remove the lobster meat from the tails and claws. Cut the tails into neat 1cm/½in slices.
2. Place a neat line of watercress leaves on 4 large individual plates. Arrange the lobster meat on the watercress, making sure the claws and tails are divided evenly. Sprinkle over a little lemon juice and season with salt and pepper.
3. Garnish the plates with the strawberries.
4. Make the dressing: whizz all the ingredients together in a blender and pass through a sieve. Season to taste with salt and pepper.

5. Spoon a little dressing over the lobster and serve the remainder in a sauce-boat. Hand the new potato, chive and sour cream salad separately.

 *CHAMPAGNE*

BARBECUED LOBSTER WITH THAI SPICE GLAZE

SERVES 2

2 small live lobsters

For the Thai spice glaze
2 green chillies, de-seeded and finely chopped
55g/2oz creamed coconut
1 stick of lemon grass, very finely chopped
5cm/2in piece of galangal, peeled and finely grated
1 tablespoon finely chopped fresh basil
1 tablespoon nam pla fish sauce (see page 180)

To garnish
2 sprigs of fresh basil

1. Prepare the lobsters: put them into the freezer for 2 hours. Push a sharp strong knife through the head of each lobster. There is a well-defined cross on the back of the head – when the middle of the cross is pierced the lobster will die instantly and painlessly, although it will still move alarmingly.
2. Lay the lobsters out flat and split in half lengthways. Remove the stomach sac from near the head and remove the threadlike intestine running the length of the body. Do not mistake the roe (or coral), which may or may not be present, for the intestine, which is tiny. The roe, when cooked, will be bright red and has an excellent flavour. Do not throw away the soft grey-green flesh near the head either – it is the liver (or tomalley) and quite delicious. Crack the claws of the lobster.
3. Preheat the barbecue.
4. Put all the Thai spice glaze ingredients together in a saucepan and heat until the creamed coconut has melted.

5. Arrange the lobster, shell side down, on the top shelf of the barbecue. Brush the flesh generously with the Thai spice glaze. Cover the lobsters with a piece of kitchen foil and barbecue for 12–15 minutes, or until the lobster is cooked.

6. Arrange the lobster on a serving platter and garnish with the sprigs of basil.

 AUSTRALIAN RHINE RIESLING

GRILLED BUTTERFLIED KING PRAWNS WITH PISTOU

SERVES 4

675g/1½lb raw, shell-on prawns, weighed
   without heads
1 teaspoon paprika
½ teaspoon ground coriander
½ teaspoon curry powder
salt and freshly ground black pepper
1 quantity pistou (see page 315)

To serve
a few bitter salad leaves

1. Using a sharp knife, slit the prawns along the backs, through the shell and halfway through the flesh. Remove the black vein. Trim off the legs, wash and dry on kitchen paper.
2. Mix together the paprika, coriander, curry powder, salt and pepper. Rub over the prawns and refrigerate for 30 minutes to allow to marinate.
3. Preheat the grill to its highest setting.
4. Arrange the prawns on the grill rack, cut side down, and brush the shell with half the pistou. Cook the prawns for 2 minutes, then turn them over and brush the second side with the remaining pistou. Grill for a further 2 minutes.
5. Arrange the salad leaves on a large serving platter and pile the prawns on top. Serve very hot.

 POUILLY FUMÉ OR CALIFORNIAN FUMÉ BLANC

ARTICHOKES STUFFED WITH GARLIC PRAWNS AND BROAD BEANS

SERVES 4

4 globe artichokes
salt
1 lemon, halved
225/8oz cooked, peeled prawns
225g/8oz shelled broad beans, blanched,
   refreshed and skins removed
4 ripe tomatoes, skinned, de-seeded and
   chopped
salt and freshly ground black pepper
juice of 1 lemon
55g/2oz butter
2 shallots, finely chopped
1 large clove of garlic, crushed
55g/2oz fresh white breadcrumbs
1 tablespoon chopped fresh parsley

To serve
1 × 2-egg quantity hollandaise sauce (see page
   633)

1. Prepare the artichokes: twist and pull the stalk off very close to the base so that the artichoke will stand without rolling. Cut the tips of the bottom few rows of leaves off straight if they are hard or cracked and the tip spines are prickly. Leave the smaller higher leaves.
2. Boil the artichokes in salted water for 45 minutes with the lemon halves. When an inner leaf will pull out easily, drain the artichokes upside down on a wire rack and leave until they are cool enough to handle.
3. Mix the prawns, broad beans and tomato together in a bowl and season with salt, pepper and lemon juice.
4. Melt the butter in a frying pan, add the shallot and cook over a low heat for 2 minutes. Add the garlic and breadcrumbs and stir gently together over a low heat until the butter is absorbed and you can smell the garlic. Remove from the heat, stir in the parsley and season to taste with salt and pepper.

5. Preheat the oven to 200°C/400°F/gas mark 6.
6. When the artichokes are cool enough to handle, prise open the middle leaves and lift out the central cluster of tiny leaves. Using a teaspoon, scrape out the fibrous choke and discard it. Open out the leaves a little further and pile a quarter of the prawn filling into the centre of each artichoke.
7. Spoon the breadcrumbs over the top of each artichoke, pressing some of the crumbs down inside the outer leaves. Place the stuffed artichokes on a baking sheet and bake in the preheated oven for 10–15 minutes, or until the crumb topping is sizzling and golden.
8. Serve on individual plates with the hollandaise sauce handed separately in a sauce-boat.

 WHITE BORDEAUX

BARBECUED SCAMPI WITH FRESH HERBS

SERVES 4

900g/2lb scampi, de-veined
2 tablespoons light soy sauce
grated zest and juice of 1 lime
freshly ground black pepper

For the herb dressing
2 tablespoons chopped fresh mint
2 tablespoons chopped fresh parsley
1 teaspoon chopped fresh tarragon
1 clove of garlic, crushed
2 spring onions, finely chopped
3 tablespoons extra virgin olive oil
2 teaspoons rice wine vinegar
salt and freshly ground black pepper

To serve
1 handful of rocket leaves
warm pitta bread

1. Preheat the barbecue.
2. Put the scampi into a bowl and add the soy sauce, lime zest and juice and pepper. Toss

together and allow to marinate for 10 minutes.
3. Arrange the scampi on a narrow-meshed wire rack and arrange on the barbecue. Cook the scampi for 1–2 minutes on each side, or until lightly browned.
4. Meanwhile, make the herb dressing: toss all the ingredients together and season to taste with salt and pepper. Toss the hot scampi into the dressing.
5. Put the rocket leaves into a salad bowl and add the warm scampi and dressing. Toss together and serve immediately with the pitta bread handed separately.

 *SOAVE CLASSICO OR AUSTRALIAN SÉMILLON*

POULTRY AND GAME

CHICKEN WITH GOLDEN GARLIC AND OLIVES

SERVES 4

4 × 170g/6oz boneless chicken breasts, skinned
1 corn on the cob or 170g/6oz frozen sweetcorn
    kernels
4 tablespoons olive oil (from the olives)
8 large cloves of garlic, thinly sliced
55g/2oz marinated olives in olive oil, pitted (see
    page 376)
4 ripe tomatoes, skinned and roughly chopped
a pinch of caster sugar
salt and freshly ground black pepper
1 tablespoon lemon juice

1. Cut each chicken breast into 5 thick strips
across the grain. Shave the sweetcorn kernels
off the cob with a sharp knife.
2. Heat the olive oil in a wok and add half the
garlic. Fry over a low heat until pale golden-
brown, then remove quickly and drain on
kitchen paper. Set aside.
3. Put the remaining garlic in the oil and when
just starting to turn golden, add the chicken
strips and fry until golden-brown on all sides.
4. Add the olives, tomatoes, corn and sugar to
the pan, season with salt and pepper and
simmer over a low heat until the chicken is firm
and the tomatoes reduced to a syrupy pulp.
5. Season with lemon juice, sprinkle over the
golden garlic flakes and serve immediately.

 *RED BURGUNDY OR PINOT NOIR*

CHICKEN AND OREGANO CIABATTAS

MAKES 4

4 large ciabatta rolls
450g/1lb poached chicken, skinned and boned
2 tablespoons chopped fresh oregano
½ red onion, very finely chopped
juice of ½ lemon
4 tablespoons basic vinaigrette (see page 634)
4 tablespoons mayonnaise (see page 632)
¼ cucumber, thinly sliced
2 tomatoes, skinned and sliced
1 handful of salad leaves
salt and freshly ground black pepper

1. Cut the ciabatta rolls in half horizontally,
leaving one side hinged together.
2. Cut the chicken into bite-sized pieces. Mix
the chicken in a large bowl with the oregano,
onion, lemon and vinaigrette and season well
with salt and pepper. Chill for 30 minutes.
3. Spread the mayonnaise on to the inside of the
rolls. Divide the chicken mixture, cucumber
and tomato between the rolls and top with
some salad leaves. Season well with salt and
pepper.

*NORTHERN ITALIAN CHARDONNAY
OR CHIANTI CLASSICO*

CHICKEN STUFFED WITH SPINACH, RICOTTA, PARMESAN AND PINENUTS

SERVES 4

4 × 170g/6oz chicken breasts, with skin and
*   wing attached*
salt and freshly ground black pepper
110g/4oz young spinach leaves, washed
85g/3oz ricotta cheese
15g/½oz Parmesan cheese, freshly grated
15g/½oz pinenuts, toasted
freshly grated nutmeg

To serve
1 quantity grilled red pepper salsa (see page
*   374)*

1. Remove the breastbone from the chicken
breasts, leaving the winglet intact. Trim away
any excess fat. Cut the first 2 joints off the
wing, and scrape the flesh and skin away from
the end of the bone, leaving 2.5cm/1in of clean
bone exposed.
2. Cut a horizontal pocket in the centre of each
breast, entering from the thickest side.
3. Open out the fillets and season well with salt
and pepper.
4. Blanch the spinach in boiling salted water for
a few seconds until it wilts. Drain and refresh in
cold water. Press the spinach between 2 plates
to remove excess water, then chop roughly.
5. Mix the spinach in a large bowl with the
ricotta, Parmesan cheese, pinenuts and nutmeg.
Season to taste with salt and pepper.
6. Preheat a griddle pan over a high heat for 5
minutes or preheat a grill to its highest setting.
Preheat the oven to 180°C/350°F/gas mark 4.
7. Divide the filling between the 4 chicken
breasts and push into the pockets so that it fills
the breasts evenly. Chill for 20 minutes.
8. Season the outside of the chicken breasts
with salt and pepper and place on the griddle
pan, skin side down (or on the grill, skin side
up). Leave for about 3–5 minutes, or until the

skin is marked with black griddle lines.
9. Transfer the chicken breasts to a shallow
roasting tin, skin side uppermost, and bake in
the centre of the preheated oven for 20 minutes,
or until the chicken is cooked through and hot
in the middle.
10. Serve the breasts whole or sliced into 3
pieces on the diagonal, arranging them on the
plate showing the green filling. Spoon the
grilled red pepper salsa around.

 ITALIAN PINOT GRIGIO

CHICKEN BREASTS WITH GRILLED RED PEPPER MOUSSELINE AND BLACK OLIVE TAPENADE

This recipe was devised by Fiona Burrell,
former Principal of Leith's School of Food and
Wine.

SERVES 4

5 × 170g/6oz boneless chicken breasts, skinned
1 red pepper
½ tablespoon chopped fresh basil
1 teaspoon finely chopped fresh parsley
1 egg white
75ml/2½fl oz double cream
1 teaspoon ground mace
salt and freshly ground black pepper
1 tablespoon tapenade (see page 633)
570ml/1 pint white stock, made with chicken
*   bones (see page 625)*

To serve
warm red salsa (see following recipe)

1. Remove the false fillets from 4 of the chicken
breasts, chop roughly and place in a food
processor with the remaining chicken breast.
2. Grill or roast the red pepper until the skin
blisters. Allow to cool and remove the seeds and
skin. Cut into medium dice. Add to the food
processor with the basil and parsley.

3. Whizz briefly, then add the egg white and cream with the motor running. Be careful not to over-process but the mixture should be smooth.
4. Season well with the mace, salt and pepper. Chill until ready to use.
5. Cut a small pocket in the side of each chicken breast and spread a little tapenade inside it. Put a spoonful of the red pepper mousseline mixture into the pocket and pull the pocket together to seal. Wrap the breasts in clingfilm.
6. Place the stuffed chicken breasts in a large shallow pan or roasting tin. Heat the stock to boiling point and pour over the chicken. Set the chicken over a low heat so that the stock barely simmers. Poach for about 15 minutes, or until firm to the touch. Remove the chicken breasts from the stock and allow to cool.
7. Slice the chicken breasts and serve with the warm red salsa.

 *NEW WORLD CABERNET SAUVIGNON*

WARM RED SALSA

SERVES 4

1 red pepper
1 large tomato, skinned, de-seeded and finely diced
½ tablespoon chopped fresh basil
½ tablespoon olive oil
juice of ½ small lemon
juice of ½ small orange
salt and freshly ground black pepper

1. Preheat the grill to its highest setting.
2. Grill the pepper, skin side uppermost, until the skin is black and blistered. Using a small knife, scrape off all the skin.
3. When the pepper is cold, cut it in half, remove and discard the seeds and inner membrane. Dice finely and mix with all the remaining ingredients. Season to taste with salt and pepper. Serve warm.

GALANTINE OF CHICKEN WITH TARRAGON

SERVES 6

1 × 1.35kg/3lb chicken
55g/2oz butter, melted

For the stuffing
170g/6oz chicken breast, boned and skinned
2 tablespoons fresh tarragon leaves, blanched and refreshed
1 egg white
2 tablespoons double cream
salt and freshly ground black pepper

For poaching
1.7 litres/3 pints white stock, made with chicken bones (see page 625)
1 bay leaf
2 sprigs of fresh tarragon

To serve
2–3 sprigs of fresh tarragon

1. Bone the chicken completely, including the legs and wings (see page 127).
2. Make the stuffing: briefly whizz the chicken breast and tarragon leaves in a food processor. Pass through a fine sieve. Stir in the egg white and cream and season to taste with salt and pepper.
3. Lay the chicken flat on a work surface, skin side down. Place the stuffing in the middle and draw up the sides.
4. Dip a clean J-cloth or 40cm/16in square piece of muslin in the melted butter. Wrap the chicken in the cloth and tie at either end to resemble a Christmas cracker.
5. Put the stock and herbs into a large saucepan and place over a low heat. Lower the chicken into the pan and bring to the boil, then lower the heat and poach for 1¼–1½ hours, or until the chicken is cooked.
6. Remove the chicken from the stock and remove and discard the cloth. Allow the chicken to cool.

7. When the chicken is cold, slice and serve garnished with the sprigs of tarragon.

 CRU BEAUJOLAIS OR ALSACE PINOT BLANC

SUMMER CHICKEN SALAD WITH CHERRIES AND TOASTED WALNUTS

SERVES 6

1 × 1.6kg/3½lb chicken, poached
85g/3oz walnut halves, roughly chopped
200ml/7fl oz Greek yoghurt
150ml/¼ pint soured cream
juice of 1 lemon
salt and freshly ground black pepper
225g/8oz fresh cherries, stoned
6 spring onions, thinly sliced on the diagonal

To garnish
4 spring onion flowers (see page 240)

1. Preheat the oven to 180°C/350°F/gas mark 4.
2. Remove the skin from the chicken and strip the flesh off the bones, which can be discarded. Cut the chicken flesh into bite-sized pieces.
3. Place the walnuts on a baking sheet and bake in the preheated oven for 10 minutes, or until just starting to brown at the edges – be careful as they burn easily. Tip on to a cold plate and allow to cool.
4. Mix the yoghurt with the soured cream and lemon juice. Season with salt and pepper.
5. Reserve a few cherries and walnuts for the garnish.
6. Stir half the sauce into the chicken with the remaining walnuts, cherries and spring onions and pile into a serving dish.
7. Using a large metal spoon, coat the chicken with the remaining sauce.
8. Sprinkle over the reserved cherries and walnuts and garnish with the spring onion flowers.

NOTE: The flavours of this dish develop if it is left for 1–2 hours in the refrigerator before eating.

 FRUITY ROSÉ/ROSÉ D'ANJOU (LOIRE)

WARM CHINESE CHICKEN SALAD

SERVES 4

4 × 170g/6oz chicken breasts, skinned and boned
2 tablespoons groundnut oil
1 tablespoon light soy sauce
1 tablespoon sesame oil

For the dry marinade
1 teaspoon salt
1 teaspoon freshly ground black pepper
1 teaspoon soft light brown sugar
1 teaspoon ground ginger
1 teaspoon ground coriander
½ teaspoon ground turmeric
1 teaspoon garam masala
2.5cm/1in piece of fresh root ginger, peeled and grated
2 cloves of garlic, crushed

For the salad
110g/4oz beansprouts
110g/4oz mangetout, blanched
1 red pepper, de-seeded and sliced
2 tablespoons chopped fresh coriander

1. Remove any fat or gristle from the chicken breasts and cut into 2.5cm/1in pieces.
2. Mix together all the marinade ingredients, add the chicken and marinate in the refrigerator for at least 4 hours.
3. Heat the groundnut oil in a frying pan and fry a few pieces of chicken at a time until lightly browned and cooked. Set aside.
4. Deglaze the frying pan with the soy sauce and pour over the chicken. Sprinkle the sesame oil over the chicken.
5. Add the beansprouts to the frying pan and

heat for 1 minute. Add the mangetout and red pepper and toss over a medium heat for a further minute.

6. Toss the hot vegetables, chicken and coriander together and serve hot or warm.

 *DRY WHITE*

SMOKED CHICKEN, WALNUT AND WILD RICE SALAD

SERVES 4–6

1 cooked smoked chicken
225g/8oz seedless black grapes, washed and halved
30g/1oz unsalted butter
110g/4oz walnuts, roughly chopped
170g/6oz basmati rice
55g/2oz wild rice
salt
110g/4oz chorizo sausage, diced
2 teaspoons chopped fresh tarragon

For the dressing
1 tablespoon lemon juice
1 teaspoon Dijon mustard
2 tablespoons sunflower oil
3 tablespoons walnut oil
salt and freshly ground black pepper

1. Skin and bone the chicken and pull the meat into bite-sized pieces. Put into a bowl with the grapes.
2. Melt the butter in a frying pan, add the walnuts and fry over a low heat until lightly browned. Remove from the heat and allow to cool.
3. Cook the basmati and wild rice in plenty of boiling salted water until *al dente*. Drain very thoroughly.
4. Make the dressing: combine all the ingredients in a bowl and whisk to emulsify. Stir the dressing into the rice, then stir in the walnuts.
5. Fork the chicken, grapes, walnuts, chorizo

and tarragon into the rice. Check the seasoning, then pile into a serving dish.

 *AUSTRALIAN CHARDONNAY*

PAELLA

This version of paella was inspired by both the fish market of St Tropez and the annual paella party on the Hunniwell estate outside Boston where Maine lobsters are the star attraction.

SERVES 8

olive oil for frying
8 chicken thighs
225g/8oz piece of smoked belly of pork, skin removed, cut into 2.5cm/1in pieces
225g/8oz chorizo sausage
2 red onions, thinly sliced
2 red peppers, de-seeded and sliced
110g/4oz field mushrooms, quartered
2 cloves of garlic, crushed
saffron
1 tablespoon ground turmeric
225g/8oz Spanish paella rice or risotto rice
55g/2oz Provençal black olives
juice of 2 large lemons
570ml/1 pint dry white wine
salt and freshly ground black pepper
150ml/¼ pint fish stock (see page 626)
55g/2oz frozen peas
570ml/1 pint fresh mussels, scrubbed clean
8 Mediterranean prawns
225g/8oz shell-on prawns

To garnish
2 tablespoons chopped fresh parsley

1. Heat 2 tablespoons oil in a large paella pan or large heavy-based roasting tin, add the chicken thighs, skin side down, and fry until browned. Tip them on to a plate and continue to brown the smoked belly of pork and chorizo in the same way. Tip them on to the plate, with the chicken thighs.
2. Heat a little more oil in the pan and fry the onions over a low heat until they start to soften.

Add the peppers and mushrooms and cook for a further 5 minutes. Return the chicken thighs, pork and chorizo to the pan and stir in the garlic, saffron, turmeric, rice, olives, lemon juice and half the wine. Bring to the boil, then lower the heat and simmer for 2 minutes. Season with plenty of pepper, then cover the pan closely with a sheet of kitchen foil and leave over a very low heat for 15 minutes.

3. Remove the foil and stir the paella gently, making sure that any rice lying on the top is put to the bottom. Add the remaining wine and the fish stock and bring back to the boil, then lower the heat and simmer for 2 minutes. Replace the foil and cook for a further 15 minutes.

4. Remove the foil and tip in the peas, mussels, Mediterranean prawns and shell-on prawns. Season well with salt and pepper and add a little water if the rice is looking dry and is not yet cooked. Return the paella to the heat, covered, for a final 5 minutes, or until all the mussels have opened up (discard any that do not).

5. Sprinkle with the parsley and serve immediately.

 SPANISH RED OR WHITE/BEER

GRIDDLED TURKEY BURGERS WITH SOURED CREAM RELISH

SERVES 4

675g/1½lb minced turkey
1 onion, very finely chopped
1 clove of garlic, crushed
1 egg
3 tablespoons chopped fresh coriander
3 tablespoons chopped fresh parsley
1–2 tablespoons hot sweet chilli sauce
salt and freshly ground black pepper
1 tablespoon sunflower or vegetable oil

To serve
1 quantity soured cream relish (see page 375)

1. Mix the turkey, onion, garlic, egg, coriander and parsley together and season to taste with the chilli sauce, salt and pepper. Chill for 30 minutes.

2. Preheat a griddle pan or the grill to its highest setting.

3. Brush the griddle pan with the oil (or if using a grill, brush the burgers with the oil) and place the burgers on the pan. Cook without moving for 4–5 minutes, or until there are pronounced black griddle marks on the underside of each burger. Turn the burgers over and continue cooking until they are cooked through: test by inserting a metal skewer into the centre of the burger and leaving it for 10 seconds – if the skewer is very hot when it comes out the burger is cooked.

4. Serve the burgers with the soured cream relish.

 DRY ROSÉ OR BEER

DUCK BREAST WITH SPICED APRICOT AND RED WINE SAUCE

SERVES 4

2 large duck breasts, boned
salt and freshly ground black pepper
30g/1oz caster sugar
12 firm fresh apricots, halved and stones removed

For the sauce
15g/½oz butter
4 shallots, finely chopped
1 clove of garlic, crushed
1 teaspoon ground mixed spice
150ml/¼ pint red wine
290ml/½ pint white stock, made with chicken bones (see page 625)
1 tablespoon redcurrant jelly

To garnish
1 bunch of watercress

1. Trim the duck breasts of any membranes or sinew. Score the skin side in a criss-cross pattern with a sharp knife and season well with salt and pepper.

2. Make the sauce: melt the butter in a heavy-based saucepan, add the shallots and fry until golden. Add the garlic and mixed spice and cook for a further minute. Pour in the wine and boil until reduced to 3 tablespoons. Add the stock.

3. Heat a heavy-based frying pan and place the duck breasts in it, skin side down. Fry over a high heat for at least 5–8 minutes, possibly longer depending on the size of the duck breasts, until the skin is well browned. As the duck skin browns it will release a lot of fat which should be tipped out of the frying pan at intervals or the skin will not become crispy.

4. Turn the duck breasts over in the pan, lower the heat and continue to cook for a further 2 minutes. If you do not like duck served pink, continue to cook for a further 5 minutes. Transfer the duck breasts to a plate and keep warm.

5. Tip the fat out of the frying pan and wipe out with kitchen paper. Strain the sauce into the pan and reduce by boiling rapidly, stirring to release any sediment from the bottom of the pan, until the sauce has a syrupy consistency. Meanwhile, skim off any scum that rises to the surface.

6. Pour 2 tablespoons of the duck fat into a separate frying pan. Add the sugar and heat until caramelized. Put the apricots into the pan and fry them, turning them over occasionally, until they caramelize and start to soften.

7. To serve: slice the duck breasts very thinly and arrange, overlapping, on a warmed serving dish with the apricots. Pour the red wine sauce around and garnish with the watercress.

 TOP ESTATE NEW ZEALAND PINOT NOIR

BARBECUED SPATCHCOCKED QUAIL

SERVES 4

8 small quail
freshly ground black pepper
4 tablespoons light soy sauce
1 clove of garlic, crushed
1 red chilli, de-seeded and chopped
1 tablespoon sesame oil
2 tablespoons dry sherry

To serve
sprigs of fresh coriander

1. Remove the trussing strings (if any) from the quail. Split each quail down one side of the backbone with a pair of poultry shears or kitchen scissors. Cut down the other side of the backbone to remove it. Open out the quail and flatten well on a board by pressing with the heel of your hand. Skewer the birds so that they are flat and open. Season with pepper.

2. Mix together all the remaining ingredients and pour over the quail. Cover and refrigerate for 4 hours to allow the birds to marinate.

3. Preheat a barbecue until very hot.

4. Lift the quail from the marinade and place, breast side down, on the barbecue. Cook for 3–4 minutes, then turn the birds over and brush with any remaining marinade. Continue to cook for a further 3–4 minutes. Turn the quail once more and cook for a further 2–3 minutes, or until cooked.

5. Arrange the quail on a warmed serving plate and garnish with the coriander.

 *LIGHT RED/CHINON OR RED LOIRE*

BEEF

MEATBALLS WITH GREEN TOMATO SAUCE

SERVES 4

1 red pepper, quartered and de-seeded
675g/1½lb lean minced beef
1 onion, finely chopped
1 red chilli, de-seeded and finely chopped
1 clove of garlic, crushed
1 tablespoon Worcestershire sauce
2 tablespoons tomato purée
salt and freshly ground black pepper
plain flour
oil for frying

For the sauce
2 large onions, finely chopped
2 tablespoons olive oil
1 large clove of garlic, crushed
1 teaspoon chopped fresh thyme
450g/1lb green tomatoes, or tomatoes that have
    not quite ripened, skinned and chopped
1 bay leaf
290ml/½ pint dry white wine
2 tablespoons white wine vinegar
1–2 tablespoons caster sugar

To serve
4 tablespoons soured cream
2 tablespoons chopped parsley
fresh crusty bread

1. Grill the pepper, skin side uppermost, until the skin is black and blistered. Using a small knife, scrape off all the skin. Dice the flesh finely.
2. Mix the minced beef, onion, chilli, garlic, Worcestershire sauce, tomato purée and grilled diced pepper together and season well with salt and pepper. With wet hands, shape the mixture into 12 balls.
3. Toss the meatballs in flour so they are completely covered, then shake off the excess.
4. Heat oil in a frying pan and fry, a few at a time, until browned on all sides. Arrange the meatballs in a single layer in an ovenproof dish.
5. Preheat the oven to 180°C/350°F/gas mark 4.
6. Make the sauce: cook the onions with the oil in a heavy-based saucepan for 5 minutes, then add the garlic and thyme and continue to cook for a further minute.
7. Stir in the tomatoes, bay leaf, wine, vinegar and sugar and season with salt and pepper. Bring to the boil, then pour the sauce over the meatballs.
8. Cover the dish with kitchen foil and bake in the preheated oven for 30–40 minutes, or until bubbling at the edges.
9. Drizzle over the soured cream, sprinkle with the parsley and serve immediately with fresh crusty bread.

 DOLCETTO D'ALBA

SUMMER BARBECUE BEEF FILLET

This recipe needs to be started a day in advance of serving.

SERVES 8

900g/2lb piece of mid-beef fillet, trimmed

For the marinade
4 large cloves of garlic, crushed
2 teaspoons dried chilli flakes
2 tablespoons demerara sugar

100ml/3½fl oz balsamic vinegar
2 tablespoons grain mustard
freshly ground black pepper

To serve
2 fresh ciabatta loaves, warmed and split in half
1 quantity parsley pesto (see page 635)
290ml/½ pint Greek yoghurt

1. Lay the beef fillet in a non-metallic dish. Add all the ingredients for the marinade and season with plenty of pepper. Cover the dish with clingfilm and leave to marinate for 24 hours, turning the beef in the marinade from time to time.
2. Light a barbecue and when the coals are white (after about 40 minutes), lift the beef out of the marinade.
3. Lay the fillet on the barbecue and leave to sear, turning it every few minutes until a good brown crust has formed on all sides, basting regularly with the remaining marinade.
4. Transfer the fillet to a cool part of the barbecue and continue to cook, turning it regularly until a metal skewer is just hot when inserted into the centre of the meat.
5. Wrap the beef in kitchen foil and allow to stand for 10 minutes in a warm place before carving.
6. Place the ciabattas on a coolish part of the barbecue until warm and crisp on the outside. Split them in half lengthways and spread each half generously with the pesto and yoghurt.
7. Carve the beef into ½cm/¼in slices and pile generously into the ciabattas. Cut each loaf into 4 and serve immediately.

NOTE: If the weather is not suitable for a barbecue, cook the beef in the following way. Preheat the oven to 230°C/450°F/gas mark 8. Heat a tablespoon of sunflower oil in a frying pan and when very hot add the beef. Brown the beef on all sides then add the marinade, turning the beef over in it, and simmer until the marinade has reduced to a thick syrupy consistency. Transfer the beef to an ovenproof dish with the marinade and bake in the preheated oven for 20 minutes. Allow to stand in a warm place for 10 minutes before carving.

 *FULL RED*

SESAME BEEF SALAD

This recipe needs to be started a day in advance of serving.

SERVES 6

450g/1lb sirloin steak, about 5cm/2in thick
oil for frying
225g/8oz button mushrooms, sliced
225g/8oz mangetout, topped, tailed and blanched

For the marinade
2 onions, thinly sliced
5 tablespoons dry sherry
5 tablespoons light soy sauce
3 tablespoons sesame oil
plenty of freshly ground black pepper

For the dressing
6 tablespoons grapeseed oil
3 tablespoons white wine vinegar
1 tablespoon Dijon mustard
1 teaspoon clear honey

1. Remove any fat or gristle from the steak.
2. Mix together the marinade ingredients, add the steak and leave to marinate overnight. Turn the steak occasionally if not completely submerged in the marinade.
3. Place the dressing ingredients in a bowl and whisk until well emulsified.
4. Remove the beef from the marinade. Strain the marinade (reserving the onions and marinade). Heat a little oil in a frying pan and brown the steak well on both sides. Turn the heat down to medium and cook for a further 4 minutes on each side (this timing assumes that you like rare steak – it can obviously be cooked for longer). Remove the steak, place on a wire rack and leave to get completely cold.
5. Add the onions from the marinade to the frying pan and cook over a high heat for about 4 minutes. Lift out and place in the dressing.
6. Add the mushrooms and the marinade to the frying pan and cook until the marinade has reduced to about 1 tablespoon. Add to the dressing and allow to get completely cold.
7. When all the ingredients are cold, cut the steak into very thin strips and add to the dressing with the mangetout. Toss together and pile on to a serving dish.

 *FULL RED*

LAMB

GRILLED BUTTERFLY LEG OF LAMB WITH WHITE WINE, HONEY AND ROSEMARY

This recipe needs to be started a day in advance of serving.

SERVES 6–8

1 × 2.3kg/5lb leg of lamb, butterfly boned (see
    page 121)
290ml/½ pint dry white wine
4 tablespoons clear honey
1 onion, sliced
2 cloves of garlic, crushed
2 tablespoons chopped fresh rosemary
salt and freshly ground black pepper
225g/8oz short-grain brown rice
570ml/1 pint water

To garnish
sprigs of fresh rosemary

1. Weigh the boned leg of lamb and calculate the cooking time at 8 minutes per 450g/1lb.
2. Trim any excess fat from the lamb and lay, boned side uppermost, in a shallow dish. Pour over the wine, honey, onion, garlic and rosemary. Season well with pepper. Fold the leg of lamb back together, cover and marinate for 24 hours, turning occasionally.
3. Preheat the grill to a medium setting.
4. Place the lamb, skin side down (reserving the marinade) on a wire rack over a roasting tin. Season well with salt and pepper. Grill for 20 minutes, checking from time to time that the

meat is not too close to the grill and is not burning. Turn the lamb over and continue to grill for about a further 20 minutes, depending on the size of the leg of lamb, covering the lamb with kitchen foil if it starts to get too dark. Test to see if the lamb is done by inserting a metal skewer into the thickest part of the meat and leaving it there for 10 seconds – if it is hot the lamb is done.
5. Turn off the grill and transfer the lamb to another roasting tin. Leave to rest in a warm place for 15 minutes before carving. Tip any excess fat out of the roasting tin and deglaze with a little water. Keep the deglazing liquid for cooking the rice.
6. Prepare the rice: put the rice with all the reserved marinade into a saucepan. Add the water and season with salt and pepper. Cook over a gentle heat, covered, for about 30 minutes, or until the rice is *al dente* and the liquid absorbed. Add the deglazing liquid and a little extra water if needed to prevent the rice from sticking to the bottom of the pan. Check the seasoning.
7. To serve: place the lamb on a board over a tray and carve. Pour the meat juices into the rice. Tip the rice on to a warmed serving dish and arrange the lamb in overlapping slices on top. Garnish with sprigs of rosemary before serving.

NOTE: This recipe would work well with a boned shoulder of lamb on a barbecue.

 *FRUITY RED – TOURAINE*

MINTED LAMB CASSEROLE WITH REDCURRANTS AND PORT

This recipe needs to be started a day in advance of serving.

SERVES 4

900g/2lb lamb neck fillet, trimmed
sunflower oil for frying
1 tablespoon plain flour
290ml/½ pint brown stock (see page 625)
salt and freshly ground black pepper
150ml/¼ pint port

For the marinade
2 onions, thinly sliced
1 clove of garlic, bruised
750ml/1 bottle red wine
1 bay leaf

To garnish
110g/4oz redcurrants
55g/2oz sugar
1 bunch of fresh mint, shredded

1. Cut the lamb into 4cm/1½in pieces and place in a bowl. Add the marinade ingredients, cover and leave overnight, turning the lamb from time to time.
2. Drain the lamb, reserving the marinade.
3. Preheat the oven to 150°C/300°F/gas mark 2.
4. Heat 1 tablespoon oil in a frying pan and brown the lamb, a few pieces at a time. Deglaze the pan with some water between batches if it starts to burn. Add a little more oil to the pan and fry the onions from the marinade until golden-brown. Crush the garlic from the marinade, add to the pan and cook for 1 further minute.
5. Stir the flour into the onions, then add the reserved marinade. Bring to the boil, then lower the heat and simmer for 2 minutes.
6. Tip into a casserole with the stock and any extra water needed to cover the lamb. Season well with salt and pepper, cover with a close-fitting lid and cook at the bottom of the preheated oven for 1½ hours, or until the lamb is tender.
7. Strain the juices into a frying pan, add the port and reduce by boiling rapidly until syrupy. Tip the sauce back into the casserole. Check the seasoning.
8. Put the redcurrants, sugar and 2 tablespoons of water into a small saucepan and heat gently. Sprinkle them on to the casserole with the mint and serve immediately.

 *RIOJA RESERVA*

SAUTÉ OF LAMB WITH RED PEPPER

SERVES 4

900g//2lb lamb neck fillets
3 teaspoons ground allspice
salt and freshly ground black pepper
30g/1oz butter
1 tablespoon olive oil
1 onion, finely chopped
2 cloves of garlic, crushed
1 red pepper, de-seeded and sliced
3 tablespoons brandy
570ml/1 pint demi-glace sauce (see page 630)
3 tablespoons chopped fresh coriander

To serve
sprigs of fresh coriander

1. Trim the lamb fillets of excess fat, rub with the allspice and season with pepper. Refrigerate for 4 hours.
2. Cut the lamb into 4cm/1½in pieces and season with salt.
3. Heat the butter and oil together in a sauté pan and fry the lamb, a few pieces at a time, until well browned. Lift on to a plate and set aside.
4. Add the onion to the pan and cook over a low heat for 15 minutes, or until soft. Add the garlic and red pepper and cook for a further 2 minutes.
5. Return the lamb to the pan. Heat the brandy

in a ladle, ignite and pour flaming over the meat. When the flames subside, add the demi-glace sauce and season lightly with salt and pepper. Bring to the boil, lower the heat and simmer very gently for 50 minutes, or until the lamb is tender.

6. Remove the lamb from the sauce and keep warm. Skim the sauce of any fat and reduce if necessary by boiling rapidly. Season to taste with salt and pepper and stir in the chopped coriander. Return the lamb to the pan and transfer to a warmed serving dish. Garnish with sprigs of coriander before serving.

 *RED RHÔNE*

ANDER'S LAMB AND NUT BURGERS

This recipe was given to us by Ander Cohen. They are his speciality for barbecues and other informal occasions. If it is inconvenient to barbecue, grill them instead.

MAKES 30 SMALL BURGERS

30g/1oz shelled pistachios, roughly chopped
30g/1oz pinenuts, roughly chopped
30g/1oz sunflower seeds, roughly chopped
5 tablespoons red wine vinegar
5 tablespoons red wine
2 tablespoons extra virgin olive oil
1kg/2¼lb minced lamb or pork
2 onions, finely chopped
225g/8oz flat mushrooms, finely chopped
55g/2oz fine white breadcrumbs
2 eggs, beaten
2 teaspoons chopped fresh mint
2 teaspoons chopped fresh sage
2 teaspoons chopped fresh parsley
2 teaspoons mustard
1 tablespoon Worcestershire sauce
salt and freshly ground black pepper

1. Put the nuts, sunflower seeds, vinegar, wine and oil into a small saucepan. Bring to the boil, then lower the heat and simmer for 3 minutes.

Remove from the heat and allow to get completely cold.

2. Preheat the grill or barbecue.

3. Add the nut and wine mixture to all the remaining ingredients in a bowl and mix together with a fork until very well combined.

4. With wet hands, shape the mixture into flattish rounds, making sure that they are equal in size. Make a slight dip in the centre of each. The burgers will shrink and thicken as they cook.

5. Grill steadily, turning once. Allow 3 minutes each side for rare burgers, 5 for well done.

6. Serve on a warmed serving dish or between halved warm soft buns.

 *NEW WORLD CABERNET SAUVIGNON*

PORK

ROAST SUCKLING PIG WITH CORIANDER AND LIME

This recipe has been adapted from *The Silver Palate Cook Book*. It needs to be started a day in advance of serving.

SERVES 10

1 × 6.8kg/15lb suckling pig, well cleaned
18 cloves of garlic, peeled
zest and juice of 3 limes
4 tablespoons chopped fresh oregano
2 tablespoons capers in brine
3 tablespoons brine from capers
4 tablespoons olive oil
1 teaspoon salt
1 teaspoon finely ground black pepper
1 teaspoon curry powder
1 bunch of coriander, stalks removed
2 tablespoons sunflower oil
salt

To garnish
1 small Cox's Orange Pippin apple
watercress

1. Using a small sharp knife, cut slits 1½cm/¾in deep all over the body of the pig (do not prick the head). Slice 5 cloves of garlic thinly and stuff the pieces into the slits.
2. Crush the remaining garlic and mix with the lime zest and juice, oregano, capers, brine, olive oil, salt, pepper and curry powder.
3. Rub half the mixture around the cavity of the pig and the remainder all over the outside. Place the coriander leaves inside the cavity, cover the

pig and leave to marinate for 24 hours.
4. Preheat the oven to 200°C/400°F/gas mark 6.
5. Place the pig on a rack in a large roasting tin, sitting upright. Cover the ears and snout with kitchen foil to prevent them from burning.
6. Brush the sunflower oil over the pig and rub salt all over the skin. Roast in the preheated oven for 30 minutes. Baste the pig with fat and continue to baste regularly during cooking to prevent the skin from cracking.
7. Reduce the oven temperature to 180°C/350°F/gas mark 4 and cook for a further 2½–3 hours, or until the juices run clear when the flesh is pierced with a metal skewer and the skewer comes out very hot.
8. Remove the pig from the oven and leave to rest for 20 minutes. Make the gravy: use a baster to remove the pan juices from the fat in the roasting tin. Heat the juices in a saucepan and reduce by boiling rapidly until syrupy. Season with salt and pepper.
9. Place the pig on a warmed serving dish. Put the apple in the pig's mouth and garnish with watercress. Hand the gravy separately.

 *RED BURGUNDY*

BRAISED PORK FILLET WITH PAPRIKA AND CRÈME FRAÎCHE

SERVES 4

675g/1½lb pork fillet, trimmed
salt and freshly ground black pepper
30g/1oz butter
1 tablespoon olive oil

1 large onion, thickly sliced
2 cloves of garlic, crushed
3 teaspoons paprika
1 teaspoon tomato purée
4 ripe tomatoes, de-seeded and chopped
1 glass of dry sherry
150ml/¼ pint white stock, made with chicken
*   bones (see page 625)*
1 bouquet garni
150ml/¼ pint crème fraîche

To garnish
2 teaspoons chopped fresh chives

1. Season the pork fillets with salt and pepper. Heat the butter and oil together in a flameproof casserole and brown the pork over a medium heat. Do not allow the butter to burn. Remove the pork to a plate and keep warm.
2. Add the onion to the casserole and cook over a low heat for 10 minutes, or until beginning to soften. Add the garlic and paprika and cook for a further 2–3 minutes. Do not allow the garlic to brown.
3. Add the tomato purée, tomatoes, sherry, stock and bouquet garni to the casserole and bring to the boil, then lower the heat and return the pork fillets to the casserole. Cover and cook over a low heat for 20–25 minutes, or until the pork is cooked (the juices should run clear when pierced with a skewer).
4. Lift the pork from the casserole, cover and keep warm. Remove the bouquet garni and whizz the remaining contents of the casserole in a food processor, then push through a sieve. Return to a clean saucepan. Bring to the boil, then reduce to a thick consistency by boiling rapidly. Slake the crème fraîche into the sauce and heat through. Do not allow to boil. Season to taste with salt and pepper.
5. Slice the pork fillets into 2.5cm/1in medallions and arrange, overlapping, on a warmed serving dish. Coat with the sauce and sprinkle with the chives. Serve immediately.

RED LOIRE

MARINATED SESAME SPARE RIBS

The ribs need to be marinated for at least 12 hours.

SERVES 8

2kg/4¼lb pork spare ribs

For the marinade
2 teaspoons sesame oil
2 tablespoons soft light brown sugar
2 tablespoons clear honey
4 tablespoons light soy sauce
2 cloves of garlic, crushed
2 teaspoons grain mustard
2 teaspoons ground coriander
1 teaspoon ground Sichuan peppercorns
juice of 1 lemon
freshly ground black pepper

To serve
30g/1oz sesame seeds, toasted

1. Cut the pork into individual ribs. Put into a polythene bag.
2. Mix together the ingredients for the marinade and add to the ribs in the bag. Secure and refrigerate for at least 12 hours.
3. Preheat the oven to 180°C/350°F/gas mark 4.
4. Put the ribs and marinade into a roasting tin, cover with damp greaseproof paper and bake in the preheated oven for 45 minutes. Remove the greaseproof paper and bake for a further 45 minutes, brushing the ribs frequently with the marinade. The ribs are cooked when they are tender and have a sticky brown glaze.
5. To serve: sprinkle the ribs with the sesame seeds, arrange on a large warmed serving dish and serve very hot.

 *BEER*

GAMMON STEAKS WITH BROAD BEANS IN A CREAMY PARSLEY SAUCE

SERVES 4

4 × 225g/8oz gammon steaks, cut 1cm/½in
    thick, trimmed of excess fat
freshly ground black pepper

For the sauce
450g/1lb broad beans
salt
290ml/½ pint béchamel sauce (see page 629)
2 tablespoons chopped fresh parsley
2 tablespoons double cream

To garnish
4 large sprigs of fresh flat-leaf parsley

1. Preheat the grill to its highest setting.
2. Season the gammon steaks with pepper on both sides.
3. Blanch the broad beans in boiling salted water for 2 minutes. Drain and refresh under cold running water. Remove the skins from the beans.
4. Grill the gammon steaks for 7–8 minutes on each side, or until tender and cooked.
5. Reheat the béchamel sauce. Stir in the parsley, cream and broad beans. Season to taste with salt and pepper.
6. Spoon the sauce on to 4 warmed individual plates and arrange the gammon steaks on top. Garnish with the sprigs of parsley and serve immediately.

 *CALIFORNIAN OR CHILEAN PINOT NOIR*

VEAL

GRILLED MEDALLIONS OF VEAL WITH GOAT'S CHEESE AND AUBERGINE PURÉE

SERVES 4

4 × 110g/4oz veal medallions
4 slices of goat's cheese
4 tablespoons fresh white breadcrumbs

For the purée
2 medium aubergines
1 clove of garlic
about 150ml/¼ pint olive oil
225g/8oz olives, pitted and finely chopped
freshly ground black pepper

To garnish
frisée lettuce tossed in a hazelnut oil French
    dressing

1. Preheat the oven to 200°C/400°F/gas mark 6.
2. Brush the aubergines lightly with oil and put into a roasting pan. Cook in the preheated oven for 30 minutes, then add the unpeeled garlic and cook for a further 30 minutes, until they are soft.
3. Remove the aubergines and garlic from the oven and allow to cool.
4. Peel the aubergines, put the flesh into a clean cloth and squeeze lightly to extract the bitter juices. Peel the garlic and chop the aubergines and garlic together. Add half the oil and the olives. Season with pepper and leave for at least 30 minutes for the flavour to develop.
5. Preheat the grill to its highest setting. Baste the veal medallions with some of the remaining oil and grill for 2 minutes on each side.
6. Put the goat's cheese slices on the veal medallions, brush lightly with oil and sprinkle with the breadcrumbs. Grill until lightly coloured.
7. Place the medallions of veal on 4 warmed dinner plates. Place a generous spoonful of the warm aubergine and olive purée on each plate.
8. Garnish with the frisée tossed in hazelnut dressing.

 MEDIUM RED/CHIANTI

OFFAL

CALVES' LIVER WITH MINT AND GINGER

SERVES 4

450g/1lb calves' liver
55g/2oz unsalted butter for frying
salt and freshly ground black pepper

For the sauce
150ml/¼ pint white stock, made with veal
bones (see page 625)
1 glass of red wine
2.5cm/1in piece of fresh root ginger, peeled and
chopped
1 small onion or shallot, chopped
1 tablespoon chopped fresh mint
30g/1oz button mushrooms, chopped
2 tablespoons soured cream

To garnish
1 bunch of watercress

1. Trim the liver (see notes) and cut into thin slices. Set aside.
2. Make the sauce: put the stock, wine, ginger and onion or shallot into a small saucepan. Raise the heat and boil rapidly until reduced by just under half. Strain into a clean saucepan. Add the mint and mushrooms and simmer slowly for 5 minutes.
3. Heat the butter in a frying pan until it stops foaming. Season the liver with salt and pepper and fry quickly in the hot butter until just firm to the touch, but by no means hard. Arrange on a warmed serving dish.
4. Pour the sauce into the frying pan and reheat, stirring. Remove from the heat, whisk in the

soured cream and pour over the liver. Garnish with the watercress and serve immediately.

Preparing calves' liver:
NOTES:
1. To prepare the liver, remove the fine membrane that covers the liver, using a small sharp knife. Hold the knife against the liver and gently pull away the skin.
2. Cut into very thin slices with a long, thin knife. Remove any tubes carefully – they are unpleasantly tough when cooked.

 *RED BURGUNDY*

Fresh Pea Tartlets with Walnut and Oat Pastry

Barbecued Scampi with Fresh Herbs and Barbecued Sweetcorn with Hot and Sour Butter

Spinach and Saffron Bread with Hot Crispy Artichokes, Parma Ham and Chive Salad

Grilled Monkfish with Aïoli and Citrus Bulghar Wheat

*Barbecued Spatchcocked Quail and Broad Beans, Roast Corn
and Plum Tomatoes in Saffron Oil*

Duck Breast with Spiced Apricot and Red Wine Sauce

Minted Lamb Casserole with Redcurrants and Port

Baked Nectarines with Mascarpone and Praline

Red, White and Blackcurrant Iced Terrine

Raspberry and Gooseberry Caramel Meringue

Cherry and Pecan Muffins with Cherry Jam

Elderflower Vinegar, Rose Petal Vinegar, Lavender and Rose Petal Vinegar and Sweet Raspberry Vinegar

VEGETARIAN

PEA, EGG AND POTATO CAKES

MAKES 8

4 large baking potatoes
salt
110g/4oz shelled peas
3 eggs, hardboiled, peeled and finely chopped
freshly ground black pepper
plain flour
2 eggs, beaten
110g/4oz fresh white breadcrumbs
oil for frying

1. Preheat the oven to 200°C/400°F/gas mark 6. Prick the potatoes all over with a skewer and bake in the preheated oven for 1½ hours, or until soft. Allow to cool a little, then cut in half and scoop out the flesh into a large bowl.
2. Bring a large saucepan of salted water to the boil, add the peas and simmer for 1 minute, strain and refresh in cold water. Strain again and dry well on kitchen paper.
3. Add the peas and egg to the potato and season with salt and pepper.
4. Divide the mixture into 8 balls and flatten slightly.
5. Put the flour, eggs and breadcrumbs into 3 separate shallow containers. Dip the potato cakes into the flour, shaking off the excess, then into the egg and finally the crumbs. Arrange the cakes on a tray in a single layer and chill for 30 minutes.
6. Pour 1cm/½in oil into a shallow frying pan and heat until a breadcrumb sizzles and turns brown immediately. Fry 4 cakes at a time in the oil until golden, then turn them over to brown the other side. Remove from the pan with a slotted spoon and drain on kitchen paper.

Sprinkle with salt. Fry the remaining cakes in the same way and serve immediately.

 MERLOT VIN DE PAYS D'OC

PENNE WITH COURGETTES AND CREAMY GORGONZOLA

SERVES 4

4 medium courgettes
15g/½oz butter
1 onion, finely chopped
15g/½oz plain flour
150ml/¼ pint milk
150ml/¼ pint double cream
110g/4oz Gorgonzola cheese, rind removed and
  cubed
salt and freshly ground black pepper
225g/8oz penne, fresh or dried

To serve
30g/1oz Parmesan cheese, freshly grated

1. Cut the ends off the courgettes. Cut each courgette in half lengthways, then cut each length into 1cm/½in slices on the diagonal so you end up with pieces of courgette looking like ovals cut in half.
2. Melt the butter in a heavy-based saucepan. Add the onion and cook over a low heat, preferably covered with a lid to create a steamy atmosphere. The onions should become very soft and transparent, but on no account allow them to brown. Stir in the flour and cook for 1 minute.

3. Add the milk and continue to stir over a medium heat until the sauce comes to the boil and thickens. It is essential to stir continuously. Add the cream and bring to the boil, then lower the heat and simmer for 2 minutes. Remove from the heat and stir in the Gorgonzola cheese. Season to taste with a little salt and plenty of pepper.

4. Boil the penne in plenty of salted water until just tender – the timing will depend on the make (follow the manufacturer's recommendation). Drain well.

5. Boil the courgettes in salted water for 2 minutes, then drain well. Stir them into the sauce with the penne. Check the seasoning.

6. Pile the pasta into a large warmed serving dish and serve immediately with the Parmesan cheese.

 *ITALIAN RED/CHIANTI*

HOT SWEETCORN, RICOTTA AND PARMESAN BAKE

SERVES 4

4 corn on the cob, husks removed
salt
225g/8oz runner beans, shredded
225g/8oz ricotta cheese
1 egg
3 tablespoons milk
freshly ground black pepper
2 teaspoons Tabasco or hot chilli sauce
85g/3oz Parmesan cheese, freshly grated

1. Preheat the oven to 200°C/400°F/gas mark 6.

2. Blanch the sweetcorn in boiling salted water for 5 minutes, then drain and allow to cool. When the corn is cool enough to handle, shave the kernels off the cob with a sharp knife.

3. Blanch the runner beans in boiling salted water for 3–4 minutes, or until just tender. Drain and refresh in cold water. Drain again.

4. Mix the sweetcorn kernels, beans, ricotta,

egg and milk together and season to taste with plenty of salt, pepper and Tabasco. Tip the mixture into an ovenproof dish and smooth the top with a knife.

5. Sprinkle the Parmesan cheese generously over the top and bake near the top of the preheated oven for 20 minutes, or until golden-brown and bubbling at the edges. Serve hot.

 *VALPOLICELLA*

ROAST TOMATO PIE

SERVES 8

900g/2lb ripe tomatoes, halved and de-seeded
4 tablespoons extra virgin olive oil
1 tablespoon caster sugar
1 tablespoon chopped fresh thyme
salt and freshly ground black pepper
450g/1lb flour quantity rough puff pastry (see page 644)
1 egg, lightly beaten

For the filling
170g/6oz Gruyère cheese, grated
85g/3oz Parmesan cheese, grated
55g/2oz butter, melted
110g/4oz fresh white breadcrumbs
2 tablespoons chopped fresh basil
2 tablespoons chopped fresh chives
2 large cloves of garlic, crushed
200ml/7fl oz soured cream
juice of 1 lemon

1. Preheat the oven to 180°C/350°F/gas mark 4.

2. Lay the tomatoes out on a large flat baking sheet, cut side up. Drizzle over a little oil, the sugar and thyme and season with salt and pepper. Bake in the preheated oven for about 1 hour, or until the tomatoes are half their original size. They should still be slightly fleshy and easy to eat.

3. Roll out one-third of the pastry into a 25cm/10in square and lay it on a baking sheet. Chill for 30 minutes. Roll out the remaining pastry into a 30cm/12in square and lay it on another baking sheet. Chill for 30 minutes. Increase the oven temperature to 200°C/400°F/gas mark 6.

4. Bake the smaller pastry square near the top of the hot oven for 25–30 minutes, or until risen and golden-brown all over. Brush the pastry with a little beaten egg and bake it for a few more minutes or until the egg has set. Transfer the pastry to a wire rack to cool, then return it to the baking sheet.

5. Make the filling: mix together all the ingredients and season with salt and pepper.

6. Spread half the filling mixture on to the cooked pastry. Arrange the tomatoes on top and spread the remaining filling mixture on top. Lay the remaining pastry over the top and tuck the edges under to seal.

7. Brush the pie with beaten egg and score the top with the back of a table knife. Make a small steam hole in the centre of the pie. Bake near the top of the hot oven for 30 minutes, or until golden-brown all over. Serve warm or cold.

 *CALIFORNIAN FUMÉ BLANC*

VEGETABLE AND BULGHAR WHEAT CRUMBLE

This is a delicious spicy vegetarian main course.

SERVES 4

For the crumble
110g/4oz bulghar wheat
3 tablespoons extra virgin olive oil
1 onion, finely chopped
2 cloves of garlic, crushed
1 green chilli, de-seeded and chopped
1 teaspoon ground cumin
1 teaspoon cayenne pepper
3 tablespoons chopped fresh coriander
salt and freshly ground black pepper

For the base
1 aubergine, thickly sliced
110g/4oz flat mushrooms
6 tomatoes, skinned, de-seeded and chopped

2 courgettes, sliced
225g/8oz French beans, topped and tailed
1 red pepper, de-seeded and sliced
2 teaspoons tomato purée

To serve
sprigs of fresh coriander

1. Preheat the oven to 180°C/350°F/gas mark 4.

2. Rinse the bulghar wheat under cold running water, then turn into a large saucepan. Cover with water and bring to the boil, then lower the heat and allow to simmer for 1 minute. Remove from the heat and allow to stand for 15 minutes. Drain away excess water and pat dry with kitchen paper.

3. Heat 1 tablespoon of the oil in a small saucepan, add the onion and cook over a low heat until soft and transparent. Add the garlic, chilli, cumin and cayenne and cook for a further 2 minutes. Put the onion mixture into a blender with the coriander and whizz to form a textured paste. Season with salt and pepper and set aside.

4. Heat the remaining oil in a frying pan, add the aubergine and sauté over a low heat for 2–3 minutes, or until beginning to soften. Add the mushrooms and tomatoes and cook for a further 10 minutes. Set aside.

5. Meanwhile, blanch the courgettes and French beans in boiling salted water for 1 minute. Drain and refresh under cold running water.

6. Transfer to a large bowl. Add the red pepper, tomato purée and aubergine mixture and season with salt and pepper. Put the mixture into a large casserole. Mix the drained bulghar wheat with the coriander paste and season with salt and pepper. Spoon this mixture over the vegetables, making sure that everything is well covered. Do not pack too tightly.

7. Bake in the preheated oven for 25–30 minutes, or until bubbling hot. Serve immediately.

 *NEW WORLD CABERNET SAUVIGNON*

AUBERGINE AND CHILLI CANNELLONI

SERVES 4

225g/8oz quantity green pasta (see page 653)
salt
4 plum tomatoes, sliced
1 teaspoon sugar
290ml/½ pint mornay sauce (see page 629)
55g/2oz Parmesan cheese, freshly grated

For the filling
2 tablespoons extra virgin olive oil
1 large aubergine, diced
1 red chilli, de-seeded and chopped
110g/4oz chickpeas, cooked
1 clove of garlic, crushed
2 teaspoons chopped fresh basil
salt and freshly ground black pepper

1. Cut the pasta into 10 × 6cm/4 × 2½in strips. Cook in a saucepan of boiling salted water for 2–3 minutes, then drain and pat dry with a tea-towel.
2. Preheat the oven to 190°C/375°F/gas mark 5 and the grill to its highest setting.
3. Make the filling: heat the oil in a frying pan and cook the aubergine until brown. Add the chilli and chickpeas and fry over a high heat until browned. Add the garlic and cook for a further minute. Add the basil and season to taste with salt and pepper.
4. Divide the aubergine mixture between the pasta strips and roll them up to form cannelloni. Place them in a greased ovenproof dish.
5. Arrange the tomato slices on top of the cannelloni and season with salt, pepper and sugar. Pour over the mornay sauce and sprinkle with the Parmesan cheese. Bake in the preheated oven for 15 minutes, then place under the grill until nicely browned.

NOTE: Commercially made cannelloni are usually tube-shaped, and the filling is inserted with a teaspoon.

 *CHILEAN SAUVIGNON BLANC*

GOAT'S CHEESE, ROCKET AND TRUFFLE OIL PIZZA

SERVES 2

15g/½oz fresh yeast
1 teaspoon caster sugar
150ml/¼ pint lukewarm water
225g/8oz plain flour
½ teaspoon salt
3 tablespoons olive oil
1 clove of garlic, crushed
55g/2oz black olives, pitted and roughly
    chopped
55g/2oz green olives, pitted and roughly
    chopped
grated zest of 1 lemon
1 quantity garlic butter (see page 636)
2 large handfuls of rocket
110g/4oz semi-hard goat's cheese, grated
a little truffle oil
freshly ground black pepper

1. Cream the yeast with the sugar and 2 tablespoons of the water.
2. Sift the flour with the salt in a bowl and make a well in the centre. Pour in the yeast mixture, the remaining water and the oil. Mix together to make a soft but not wet dough. Add more water or flour if necessary.
3. Turn out on to a floured surface and sprinkle over the garlic, olives, and lemon zest. Knead well for about 5 minutes until the dough is smooth. Place in a clean bowl and cover with greased clingfilm. Leave in a warm place until the dough has doubled in bulk.
4. Preheat the oven to 230°C/450°F/gas mark 8.
5. Divide the dough in half. Roll each piece into a 25cm/10in circle. Place on greased and floured baking sheets.
6. Bake in the preheated oven for 15–20 minutes, or until the dough is golden-brown.
7. Remove from the oven and spread with the garlic butter. Arrange the rocket on top and sprinkle with the goat's cheese and truffle oil. Season with pepper and serve immediately.

 *YOUNG BARDOLINO*

INDIVIDUAL GRILLED VEGETABLE TARTS

SERVES 4

170g/6oz polenta pastry (see page 645)
1 large raw beetroot
1 large potato
1 large carrot
1 aubergine

For the French dressing
1 tablespoon white wine vinegar
3 tablespoons extra virgin olive oil
1 teaspoon Dijon mustard
salt and freshly ground black pepper

To finish
3 tablespoons freshly grated Parmesan cheese
1 tablespoon fresh white breadcrumbs

1. Preheat the oven to 220°C/425°F/gas mark 7.
2. Roll out the pastry and divide into 4 equal pieces.
3. On a floured work surface, roll out each piece of pastry as thinly as possible. Cut each into a 12.5cm/5in circle, place on a baking sheet and refrigerate until required.
4. Peel the vegetables and, using a mandolin, slice very thinly.
5. Whisk together the French dressing ingredients, add the vegetables and leave to soak together for 30 minutes.
6. Lift the vegetables from the French dressing and drain on kitchen paper.
7. Arrange the vegetables in overlapping rows across each pastry circle. Bake in the preheated oven for 10 minutes.
8. Mix together the Parmesan cheese and breadcrumbs and sprinkle over the vegetables. Bake for a further 7–10 minutes, or until the pastry is golden-brown and the vegetables are tender. Serve warm or cold.

 YOUNG SYRAH VIN DE PAYS D'OC

CARAMELIZED ONION AND TOMATO TART

SERVES 4

170g/6oz flour quantity rich shortcrust pastry
  (see page 642)
8 tablespoons single cream
1 egg yolk
1 egg
30g/1oz Parmesan cheese, freshly grated
1 teaspoon chopped fresh chives
salt and freshly ground black pepper
450g/1lb button onions, peeled
30g/1oz butter
2 teaspoons caster sugar
4 ripe tomatoes, skinned, quartered and de-seeded
1-egg quantity hollandaise sauce (see page 633)

1. Roll out the pastry and use to line a 15cm/6in flan ring. Refrigerate for about 45 minutes to relax – this prevents shrinkage during baking.
2. Preheat the oven to 200°C/400°F/gas mark 6. Bake the pastry case blind (see page 640) and remove from the oven. Reduce the oven temperature to 150°C/300°F/gas mark 2.
3. Mix together the cream, egg yolk, egg, Parmesan cheese and chives and season to taste with salt and pepper.
4. Pour the mixture into the prepared flan case. Bake the flan in the centre of the preheated oven for about 30–40 minutes, or until the filling is set.
5. Meanwhile, prepare the onions: blanch in boiling salted water for 3 minutes, drain and dry on kitchen paper. Melt the butter with the sugar in a saucepan, add the onions and cook over a low heat until the onions are cooked through and caramelized. Tip into a sieve and allow the excess butter to drain away. Preheat the grill to its highest temperature.
6. Pile the onions on to the baked flan and arrange the tomato pieces on top. Spoon the hollandaise sauce on top and grill for 30 seconds to glaze the top. Serve warm.

 *DRY WHITE*

DEEP-FRIED ONIONS WITH SOURED CREAM AND LIME, TOMATO AND CHILLI SALSA

SERVES 4

4 large onions
seasoned plain flour
570ml/1 pint batter (see page 655)
oil for deep-frying

For the salsa
grated zest and juice of 2 limes
4 large ripe tomatoes, skinned and chopped
1 green chilli, de-seeded and finely chopped
1 clove of garlic, crushed
1 small red onion, chopped
4 tablespoons extra virgin olive oil
1 teaspoon caster sugar
salt and freshly ground black pepper

To serve
290ml/½ pint soured cream

1. Remove the skins from the onions, leaving the root intact. Trim away any excess straggly roots.
2. Slice the onions into 1cm/½in rings. Separate out the layers.
3. Preheat a deep-fryer to its highest setting.
4. Make the salsa: put the lime zest and juice, tomatoes, chilli, garlic, onion, olive oil and sugar into a pan. Season with salt and pepper. Bring to the boil, then lower the heat and simmer for 10 minutes, or until the salsa has the consistency of a thick purée.
5. Dip the onions in the seasoned flour and shake off the excess. Coat the floured rings with the batter, shake off the excess and carefully put a few into the oil and fry until golden brown (a crumb of bread should sizzle in 15 seconds). Repeat with the remaining onions and fry until golden-brown. Drain well on kitchen paper and sprinkle with salt. Serve hot with the salsa.

 ALSACE PINOT GRIS (TOKAY)

GREEN BEAN RISOTTO WITH PISTOU

SERVES 4

55g/2oz unsalted butter
1 large onion, finely chopped
400g/14oz risotto (arborio) rice
150ml/¼ pint dry white wine
1.5 litres/2½ pints well-flavoured white stock,
*   made with chicken bones or vegetable stock*
*   (see page 625)*
salt and freshly ground black pepper
225g/8oz French beans, sliced and blanched
675g/1½lb broad beans, shelled and blanched
225g/8oz young peas, blanched
55g/2oz Parmesan cheese, freshly grated
1 quantity peasant pistou (see following recipe)

1. Melt the butter in a large saucepan, add the onion and cook over a low heat until soft and lightly coloured. Add the rice and wine, bring to the boil and cook until the wine is absorbed (about 3 minutes), then lower the heat and stir gently and constantly.
2. Meanwhile, heat the stock in a second saucepan. Allow the stock to simmer very gently.
3. Start adding the hot stock to the rice a little at a time, stirring gently. Allow the stock to become absorbed after each addition. Keep stirring constantly. Season with salt and pepper, and keep adding the stock until the rice is cooked but still *al dente* (about 30–35 minutes).
4. Stir in the beans, peas and finally the Parmesan cheese. Remove from the heat.
5. Serve the risotto with the pistou handed separately.

NEW ZEALAND SAUVIGNON BLANC

PEASANT PISTOU

This Mediterranean herb paste resembles pesto, but is a lighter alternative.

SERVES 4

6 cloves of garlic, crushed
6 tablespoons chopped fresh basil
6 tablespoons extra virgin olive oil
salt and freshly ground black pepper

1. Put the garlic and basil into a mortar or blender and pound to a paste. Add the oil, drop by drop (as when making mayonnaise), mixing all the time, to form an emulsion. Cover and refrigerate until ready to use. The pistou will only keep for a day or so in the refrigerator.

VEGETABLES AND SALADS

VEGETABLES

BRAISED SUMMER BEANS

SERVES 4

2 tablespoons olive oil
1 large onion, finely chopped
110g/4oz cooked haricot beans
225g/8oz cherry tomatoes, halved
1 teaspoon tomato purée
1 head of garlic, broken into cloves
225g/8oz French beans, topped and tailed and
    cut into 5cm/2in pieces
225g/8oz runner beans, thinly sliced on the
    diagonal
150ml/¼ pint white stock, made with chicken
    bones (see page 625)
a pinch of sugar
salt and freshly ground black pepper

To serve
2 tablespoons roughly chopped fresh flat-leaf
    parsley

1. Preheat the oven to 200°C/400°F/gas mark 6.
2. Heat the oil in a heavy-based saucepan, add
the onion and cook over a low heat until soft
but not coloured.
3. Add all the remaining ingredients, season
with salt and pepper and toss everything
together. Tip into a casserole, cover with wet
greaseproof paper and a well-fitting lid and
bake in the preheated oven for 30–45 minutes,
or until the beans are tender.
4. Check the seasoning and stir in the parsley to
serve.

BROAD BEANS, ROAST CORN AND PLUM TOMATOES IN SAFFRON OIL

SERVES 4

450g/1lb broad beans in pod, shelled
225g/8oz baby corn
2 tablespoons extra virgin olive oil
sea salt and freshly ground black pepper
juice of ½ lemon
a pinch of saffron strands
4 ripe plum tomatoes, skinned, quartered and
    de-seeded

1. Preheat the grill to its highest setting.
2. Blanch the broad beans in boiling water for 1
minute, drain and refresh in cold water.
Remove the skins.
3. Brush the corn with 1 tablespoon of the oil
and season with salt and pepper. Place on a
baking sheet and grill as close as possible to the
top of the grill until golden on all sides.
(Alternatively, a griddle pan could be used,
which gives very effective markings.)
4. Put the remaining oil, lemon juice and
saffron into a very small saucepan and gently
warm through to release the flavour from the
saffron.
5. Toss all the ingredients together and season
to taste with salt and pepper. Serve
immediately.

NOTE: This salad should not be dressed in
advance because the beans lose their colour.

 *ALSATIAN TOKAY – PINOT GRIS*

ROAST COURGETTE SLIVERS

SERVES 4

2 large courgettes, preferably 1 golden and 1
    green
1 clove of garlic, crushed
2 tablespoons extra virgin olive oil
1 tablespoon chopped fresh thyme
½ tablespoon chopped fresh rosemary
½ tablespoon chopped fresh oregano
a pinch of sugar
salt and freshly ground black pepper

1. Preheat the oven to 230°C/450°F/gas mark 8.
2. Slice the courgettes into 1cm/½in large oval
slices, preferably using a mandolin.
3. Mix the courgettes with all the remaining
ingredients and plenty of salt and pepper in a
large bowl.
4. Arrange the courgettes, overlapping, in a
single layer on a large ovenproof serving dish.
5. Bake near the top of the oven for 15–20
minutes, or until the courgettes are tender and
starting to turn golden-brown.

BABY MARROW GRATIN

SERVES 4

1 baby marrow, about 30cm/12in long, or 2–3
    large courgettes
salt and freshly ground black pepper

For the topping
30g/1oz Parmesan cheese, freshly grated

1. Preheat the oven to 230°C/450°F/gas mark 8.
2. Cut the marrow or courgettes into fine
matchsticks, preferably using a mandolin.
3. Put the marrow into a large bowl and season
with salt and pepper. Toss the marrow so that
it is evenly coated with the seasoning. It is
important to be generous with the seasoning for
the flavours to come through.
4. Pile the marrow into a gratin dish and
sprinkle over the Parmesan cheese.

5. Bake the marrow at the top of the preheated
oven for 10 minutes. Preheat the grill to its
highest setting.
6. Place the gratin dish under the grill until the
cheese browns nicely into a golden crunchy
topping. Serve immediately.

BRAISED MINTED LETTUCE

SERVES 4

2 Cos lettuces
1 radicchio
30g/1oz butter
4 shallots, finely chopped
1 clove of garlic, crushed
150ml/¼ pint vegetable stock (see page 627)
5 tablespoons balsamic vinegar
2 tablespoons sherry
salt and freshly ground black pepper
2 sprigs of fresh mint

To finish
30g/1oz butter
1 tablespoon chopped fresh mint

1. Preheat the oven to 180°C/350°F/gas mark 4.
2. Cut the lettuces in half lengthways and cut
out the cores. Wash the lettuces well.
3. Melt the butter in a large flameproof
casserole, add the shallots and cook for 10–12
minutes, or until soft. Add the garlic and
continue to cook for a further 5 minutes.
4. Add the lettuces and pour over the stock,
vinegar and sherry. Season to taste with salt and
pepper. Add the sprigs of mint. Cover and cook
in the preheated oven for 25–30 minutes, or
until the lettuces are tender.
5. Lift the lettuces from the casserole and
arrange on a large warmed serving dish.
Remove the mint sprigs and discard. Keep the
lettuce warm. Bring the braising liquid to the
boil and reduce to 4 tablespoons by boiling
rapidly.
6. Whisk the butter and mint into the reduced
liquid and season to taste with salt and pepper.
Pour over the lettuce and serve immediately.

SLOW-ROASTED SUMMER MEDITERRANEAN VEGETABLES

SERVES 6

For roasting
8 tablespoons extra virgin olive oil
2 tablespoons fresh basil leaves
1 large aubergine
8 shallots
1 red pepper, quartered and de-seeded
1 yellow pepper, quartered and de-seeded
2 small bulbs of Florence fennel, halved
4 cloves of garlic, unpeeled
salt and freshly ground black pepper
4 plum tomatoes, halved and de-seeded

To serve
2 tablespoons sunflower seeds, toasted
a few sprigs of fresh basil

1. Heat the oil and basil together in a saucepan until the basil begins to sizzle, then remove from the heat and leave to infuse.
2. Cut the aubergine into 2.5cm/1in pieces, sprinkle with salt and allow to degorge for 20 minutes. Rinse and pat dry with kitchen paper.
3. Blanch the shallots in boiling water for 5 minutes, then drain and peel when cool enough to handle.
4. Preheat the oven to 170°C/325°F/gas mark 3.
5. Put the oil and basil into a roasting tin and add all the vegetables except the tomatoes. Season with salt and pepper. Roast in the preheated oven for 1½ hours, or until the vegetables are completely soft, basting frequently. Add the tomatoes 20 minutes before the end of cooking time. Check the seasoning.
6. Arrange the vegetables on a warmed serving dish. Sprinkle with the sunflower seeds and garnish with the basil leaves. Serve warm or cold.

SOY AND SESAME TOSSED GREEN BEANS

SERVES 4

450g/1lb fine French beans
salt
1 tablespoon sesame oil
2 tablespoons light soy sauce
1 tablespoon toasted sesame seeds
freshly ground black pepper

1. Top and tail the beans. Cook in boiling salted water for 2–3 minutes, until al dente.
2. Drain and refresh in cold water. Drain again.
3. Heat the sesame oil in the saucepan and add the beans, soy sauce and sesame seeds. Season to taste with pepper. Toss over the heat for 30 seconds or until very hot. Serve immediately.

STIR-FRIED SAMPHIRE AND FENNEL

SERVES 4

450g/1lb samphire
1 large bulb of Florence fennel
2 tablespoons extra virgin olive oil
1 clove of garlic, crushed
2 tablespoons sesame seeds, toasted
freshly ground black pepper

1. Wash the samphire in several changes of water and trim off any tough shoots.
2. Blanch the samphire in boiling water for 2–3 minutes. Drain and refresh under cold running water. Drain again.
3. Slice the fennel, discarding any tough outer leaves.
4. Heat the oil in a large frying pan, add the fennel and stir-fry for 1 minute, then add the samphire and garlic and cook for a further 1–2 minutes. Sprinkle with the sesame seeds and season with pepper. Serve very hot.

FRIED GREEN TOMATOES

SERVES 4

55g/2oz butter
900g/2lb green tomatoes, roughly chopped
1 tablespoon demerara sugar
salt and freshly ground black pepper
225g/8oz cherry tomatoes, cut in half
2 tablespoons chopped fresh basil

To serve
1 small stick of crusty French bread
4 sprigs of fresh basil

1. Preheat the oven to 180°C/350°F/gas mark 4.
2. Melt the butter in a large frying pan, add the tomatoes and fry over a high heat for 5 minutes. Add the sugar and season to taste with salt and pepper.
3. Warm the bread in the preheated oven for 5 minutes.
4. Continue to cook the tomatoes until you have a thick, rough-textured consistency. Stir in the cherry tomatoes and basil and cook for a further minute. Check the seasoning.
5. Cut 4 thick slices from the stick of bread and arrange them on 4 warmed individual plates. Pile the tomatoes on to the bread and garnish with the sprigs of basil.

BABY OVEN-DRIED PLUM TOMATOES

SERVES 4

450g/1lb baby plum tomatoes or cherry
*   tomatoes*
2 teaspoons caster sugar
2 teaspoons chopped fresh rosemary
salt and freshly ground black pepper

1. Preheat the oven to 100°C/200°F/gas mark ½.
2. Cut the tomatoes in half and arrange in a single layer, cut side up, in a large roasting tin.

3. Sprinkle with the sugar and rosemary, season with salt and pepper.
4. Bake, uncovered, in the oven for 5–6 hours, or until the tomatoes are dried out but not crisp. Allow to cool, then store in the refrigerator for up to 1 week. Use in salads such as warm pulse salad (see page 326).

TOMATO AND BASIL STEW

SERVES 4

900g/2lb mixed cherry, plum and round ripe
*   tomatoes, cores removed from the large ones*
1 large handful of fresh basil leaves, roughly
*   torn*
4 tablespoons extra virgin olive oil
1 teaspoon caster sugar
salt and freshly ground black pepper

To garnish
a few fresh basil leaves, roughly torn
30g/1oz pinenuts, toasted

To serve
1 stick of crusty French bread

1. Preheat the oven to 200°C/400°F/gas mark 6.
2. Prepare the tomatoes: halve the cherry tomatoes, quarter the plum tomatoes lengthways and slice the round tomatoes.
3. Put the tomatoes into a large bowl and add the basil, oil and sugar. Season well with salt and pepper. Tip the tomatoes into a large casserole and bake in the centre of the preheated oven for 30 minutes, or until the tomatoes have started to collapse.
4. Stir and garnish with the basil and pinenuts. Serve warm with French bread.

SWEET POTATO AND COURGETTE RÖSTI

SERVES 4

3 tablespoons sunflower oil
1 Spanish onion, very finely chopped
55g/2oz rindless streaky bacon, finely chopped
340g/12oz sweet potatoes, peeled and coarsely grated
170g/6oz potatoes, peeled and coarsely grated
225g/8oz courgettes, coarsely grated
salt and freshly ground black pepper
30g/1oz butter

1. Heat 1 tablespoon of the oil in a small saucepan, add the onion and cook over a low heat until transparent and soft but not coloured. Add the bacon and cook for a further 2 minutes.
2. Mix the sweet potato, potato and courgettes together in a bowl. Season with salt and pepper. Leave to stand for 20 minutes, then squeeze dry. Fork in the onion and bacon mixture.
3. Heat 1 tablespoon of the oil in a 23cm/9in non-stick frying pan and when hot add 15g/½oz butter. When the butter stops foaming, add the potato mixture. Pat it lightly into a flat cake with straight sides.
4. Fry over a low heat for about 10 minutes, or until the underside is crusty and golden-brown. Shake the pan from time to time to ensure that the cake does not stick.
5. Place a plate larger than the frying pan over the pan, turn both the plate and pan over and tip the rösti out on to the plate.
6. Heat the remaining oil in the frying pan and when hot add the remaining butter. Slip the rösti immediately back into the pan for 10 minutes to cook the other side.
7. To serve: cut into wedges with a sharp knife or kitchen scissors and serve on a warmed flat serving plate.

NOTE: These could be served as a starter with a tomato sauce such as salsa pizzaiola (see page 636).

ROAST GARLIC HALVES

This recipe can be cooked successfully on a barbecue.

SERVES 4

2 whole bulbs of garlic
2 tablespoons extra virgin olive oil
4 sprigs of fresh rosemary
salt and freshly ground black pepper

To serve
warm bread

1. Preheat the oven to 200°C/400°F/gas mark 6.
2. Cut the whole, unpeeled garlic bulbs in half crossways. Arrange them cut side up on a sheet of kitchen foil.
3. Drizzle the oil over the garlic and arrange the rosemary sprigs on top. Season with salt and pepper.
4. Wrap loosely in the foil and bake in the preheated oven for 35–40 minutes, or until the garlic is soft.
5. To serve: arrange the garlic and rosemary on a serving dish. Allow each guest to scoop their own garlic. Serve with warm bread.

RED ROOT LYONNAISE

SERVES 4

45g/1½oz butter
2 red onions, thinly sliced
4 large beetroots, uncooked
2 teaspoons chopped fresh dill
salt and freshly ground black pepper
1 tablespoon sunflower oil
5 tablespoons dry white wine
200ml/7fl oz vegetable stock (see page 627)

1. Preheat the oven to 170°C/325°F/gas mark 3.
2. Heat the butter in a frying pan, add the onions and cook until soft but not coloured.
3. Peel and slice the beetroot very thinly.
4. Butter a large pie dish and arrange the

beetroot in layers with the onion and dill, adding a little salt and pepper as you go.

5. Arrange the top layer of beetroot in overlapping slices.

6. Sprinkle the top with a little oil and pour around the wine and stock. Press the beetroot down firmly – the stock should come three-quarters of the way up the dish.

7. Bake in the preheated oven for about 2 hours, or until the beetroot is tender.

WILTED LETTUCE

SERVES 4

1 radicchio
1 punnet of lamb's lettuce (mâche)
1 handful of rocket
1 small frisée endive
4 tablespoons olive oil
1 clove of garlic, slivered
170g/6oz rindless smoked belly of pork, cut into
 lardons
sea salt and freshly ground black pepper

1. Tear the salad leaves into small pieces and wash thoroughly. Dry well.

2. Heat the oil with the garlic in a large wok, or similar pan over a low heat, until the garlic is golden. Remove it from the oil with a slotted spoon and discard.

3. Add the lardons to the pan and fry until golden. Remove with the slotted spoon and drain on kitchen paper.

4. Add the salad leaves to the pan, pushing it all in – it will soon wilt and become manageable. Use 2 spoons to turn the leaves over to cook evenly and increase the heat under the wok when the leaves have started to wilt.

5. Season with salt and pepper and add the pork lardons. Toss everything together and serve immediately.

SALADS

FRENCH BEAN AND SHALLOT SALAD

SERVES 4

450g/1lb fine French beans, topped and tailed
salt
2 shallots, very finely chopped
4 tablespoons basic vinaigrette (see page 634)
freshly ground black pepper

1. Boil the beans in salted water for about 5 minutes, or until tender. Drain and refresh in cold water.
2. Drain the beans, dry them on kitchen paper and cut them into 2.5cm/1in pieces.
3. Put the shallots into a bowl with the vinaigrette and season with salt and pepper. Leave the shallots to stand for 15 minutes.
4. Toss the beans with the shallots, check the seasoning and serve in a large bowl.

NOTE: Do not put the beans into the dressing too far in advance or they will lose their bright green colour.

BROCCOLI, BROWN RICE AND PARMESAN SALAD

SERVES 4

2 heads of broccoli
salt
225g/8oz short-grain brown rice
110g/4oz Parmesan cheese, shaved or grated
freshly ground black pepper

For the dressing
basic vinaigrette (see page 634)

1. Cut the broccoli into small florets. Peel the stalks and cut into discs. Blanch the broccoli for 2 minutes in boiling salted water. Drain and refresh in cold water. Drain the broccoli well and dry on kitchen paper.
2. Bring the rice to the boil in a large saucepan of salted water, then lower the heat and simmer gently until the rice is *al dente* (this can sometimes take up to 45 minutes). Pour the rice into a colander, make a few holes in the rice to allow steam to escape and leave to steam-dry and cool down.
3. Toss the broccoli, rice and three-quarters of the Parmesan cheese with enough basic vinaigrette dressing to coat the ingredients. Season to taste with salt and pepper.
4. To serve: pile into a serving dish and scatter over the remaining Parmesan cheese.

COOL RADISH, CUCUMBER AND FETA SALAD

SERVES 4

12 radishes with leaves, roots trimmed
1 cucumber, peeled
225g/8oz feta cheese, cut into 1cm/½in cubes

For the dressing
4 tablespoons Greek yoghurt
4 tablespoons olive oil
1 tablespoon chopped fresh mint
1 tablespoon chopped fresh chives

juice of ½ lemon
a pinch of sugar
salt and freshly ground black pepper

To garnish
4 sprigs of fresh mint

1. Trim the radish stalks down to 1cm/½in. Cut the radishes in half through the stalk and root.
2. Cut the cucumber in half lengthways and scoop out the seeds with a teaspoon. Cut the flesh into 1cm/½in boat shapes.
3. Mix together all the dressing ingredients and season to taste with salt and pepper.
4. Toss the radish, cucumber and feta together and arrange on 4 individual plates. Spoon over the dressing and garnish with the sprigs of mint.

STRAWBERRIES WITH AVOCADO AND LEMON DRESSING

SERVES 4

450g/1lb ripe strawberries, hulled
4 ripe but firm avocados
150ml/¼ pint basic vinaigrette (see page 634)
lemon juice
salt and freshly ground black pepper
2 tablespoons chopped fresh chives

To garnish
chopped fresh chives

1. Cut any large strawberries in half.
2. Cut the avocados in half and remove the stones. Using a dessert spoon, scoop out spoonfuls of the avocado flesh into a large bowl.
3. Pour over the vinaigrette with lemon juice to taste and season with salt and pepper.
4. Add the strawberries and chives and gently fold the salad together, taking care not to break up the avocado. Arrange on 4 individual plates and garnish with chives before serving.

WARM PULSE AND BEAN SALAD

SERVES 6–8

110g/4oz aduki beans, dry weight
110g/4oz chickpeas, dry weight
110g/4oz Puy lentils, dry weight
110g/4oz bulghar wheat, dry weight
3 tablespoons hazelnut oil
3 tablespoons extra virgin olive oil
1 tablespoon soy sauce
2–3 teaspoons rice wine vinegar
salt and freshly ground black pepper
2 tablespoons chopped mixed fresh herbs, such
*   as mint, chives and parsley*
4 tablespoons capers, rinsed
baby oven-dried tomatoes (see page 322) or
*   sun-dried tomatoes*

1. Soak and cook the aduki beans, chickpeas and Puy lentils until tender. Drain well and put into a bowl.
2. Rinse the bulghar wheat under cold running water and cook in plenty of boiling water for 5–8 minutes. Drain and allow to drip-dry in the strainer for a few minutes, then toss into the bowl with the beans.
3. Mix together the oils, soy sauce and rice wine vinegar and fold into the bean mixture. Season to taste with salt and pepper. Toss the herbs, capers and tomatoes into the salad, mix well and pile into a serving dish.

BEETROOT AND AUBERGINE SALAD WITH SHERRY VINEGAR DRESSING

SERVES 4

8 small, raw, even-sized beetroots, unpeeled
1 teaspoon salt
1 small aubergine
2 cloves of garlic, unpeeled
a little oil

For the dressing
1 tablespoon sherry vinegar
4 tablespoons extra virgin olive oil
2 teaspoons soft dark brown sugar
1 teaspoon Dijon mustard
2 teaspoons chopped fresh tarragon
salt and freshly ground black pepper

1. Cook the beetroots in boiling salted water until tender (1–2 hours), depending on size.
2. Preheat the oven to 190°C/375°F/gas mark 5.
3. Slice the aubergine and arrange in a single layer in a roasting tin. Add the unpeeled garlic and drizzle with a little oil. Bake in the preheated oven until tender. Remove the garlic after about 20 minutes. Peel and crush.
4. Meanwhile, make the dressing: whisk together all the ingredients and season to taste with salt and pepper. Add the crushed garlic.
5. When the aubergines are cooked, tip into a large bowl and pour over the dressing.
6. Drain and peel the beetroot and slice into the same thickness as the aubergine. Toss with the aubergine. Season again with salt and pepper. Serve warm or chilled.

FENNEL, CUCUMBER AND CHILLI SALAD

SERVES 4

1 large bulb of Florence fennel
salt
1 cucumber
2 green chillies, de-seeded and finely chopped

For the dressing
4 tablespoons light soy sauce
2 tablespoons sesame oil
2 tablespoons rice wine vinegar
2 teaspoons caster sugar
salt and freshly ground black pepper

1. Remove the feathery green fennel tops and set aside. Slice the fennel bulb thinly, discarding any tough outer leaves. Blanch in boiling salted water for 30 seconds. Refresh under cold

running water. Drain well.
2. Cut the cucumber in half and scoop out the seeds. Cut the cucumber into strips and pile into a bowl with the fennel. Add the chilli and toss together. Cover and refrigerate for 20 minutes.
3. Make the dressing: whisk together all the dressing ingredients in a bowl until well emulsified. Toss the dressing with all the other ingredients and season to taste with salt and pepper. Allow to marinate for 1 hour before serving.

NEW POTATO VINAIGRETTE

SERVES 4

675g/1½lb small new potatoes, scrubbed
salt
2 sprigs of fresh mint
150ml/¼ pint basic vinaigrette (see page 634)
freshly ground black pepper
1 red pepper, de-seeded and cut into 1cm/½in
  dice
1 yellow pepper, de-seeded and cut into 1cm/
  ½in dice
1 handful of fresh mint leaves, chopped

1. Boil the potatoes in salted water with the sprigs of mint for about 10 minutes, or until tender. Drain the potatoes in a colander and discard the sprigs of mint.
2. Put the potatoes and the vinaigrette into a large bowl and season with salt and pepper. Toss together and allow the potatoes to cool down in the vinaigrette so they pick up the flavour.
3. Stir in the red and yellow pepper with the mint and check the seasoning before serving.

NEW POTATO, SOURED CREAM AND CHIVE SALAD

SERVES 4

675g/1½lb baby new potatoes, scrubbed
salt
2 sprigs of fresh mint
1 small red onion, finely chopped
4 tablespoons finely chopped fresh chives
290ml/½ pint soured cream
freshly ground black pepper

To garnish
1 tablespoon finely chopped fresh chives

1. Boil the potatoes in salted water with the mint for 10 minutes, or until tender. Drain in a colander and allow to cool.
2. Put all the remaining ingredients into a large bowl and season well with salt and pepper. Add the potatoes and toss together. Pile into a bowl and sprinkle with the chives before serving.

PUDDINGS

Fruit Puddings
Mousses, Soufflés and Creams
Ice Creams and Sorbets
Meringues
Pastries, Pies and Tarts
Cakes and Pâtisserie

FRUIT PUDDINGS

BLACKCURRANT AND AMARETTI BISCUIT TRIFLE

SERVES 4

450g/1lb blackcurrants
170g/6oz granulated sugar
4 tablespoons crème de cassis
1 teaspoon chopped fresh mint
225g/8oz mascarpone
290ml/½ pint Greek yoghurt
icing sugar, to taste
340g/12oz amaretti biscuits
30g/1oz flaked almonds, toasted

1. Wash the blackcurrants and, using the prongs of a fork, remove the stalks.
2. Put the blackcurrants and sugar into a saucepan, heat slowly until the sugar has dissolved, then simmer until the blackcurrants are soft. Remove from the heat, add the crème de cassis and mint, and allow to cool completely.
3. Mix the mascarpone and yoghurt together and sweeten to taste with the icing sugar.
4. Break the amaretti biscuits into pieces.
5. Layer the blackcurrant mixture, mascarpone and yoghurt mixture and amaretti biscuits in a large glass bowl, finishing with a layer of mascarpone. Sprinkle with the almonds. Cover and chill for 30 minutes before serving.

 *ASTI SPUMANTE*

FLAMING CHERRY BRANDY PANCAKES

SERVES 4

12 French pancakes (see page 654)

For the cherry filling
900g/2lb cherries, stoned
3 tablespoons soft light brown sugar
2 tablespoons kirsch
30g/1oz butter
85g/3oz chopped almonds, browned

For the meringue
2 egg whites
110g/4oz caster sugar
2 tablespoons flaked almonds, browned

To flame
4 tablespoons cherry brandy

1. Put the cherries, sugar, kirsch and butter into a saucepan. Heat together until the cherries begin to soften, then remove from the heat and stir in the almonds.
2. Preheat the grill to its highest setting.
3. Arrange the pancakes on a large work surface. Divide the cherry mixture between the pancakes. Fold each into 4 to form a triangle and arrange in a large ovenproof dish.
4. Whisk the egg whites until they form stiff peaks, then whisk in 2 teaspoons of the sugar and continue to whisk until the mixture is stiff and shiny. Fold in the remaining sugar with a large metal spoon. Place the meringue in a piping bag fitted with a star nozzle and pipe it over the pancakes. Sprinkle the almonds on top.

5. Place under the grill for a few seconds, or until the meringue browns. Do not allow to burn.

6. Heat the brandy in a ladle over a medium heat and ignite. Pour the flaming brandy over the meringue and serve immediately.

 *MARSALA*

WARM GREENGAGE, APRICOT AND RASPBERRY COMPOTE

SERVES 4

290ml/½ pint water
5 tablespoons sloe gin (see page 495) or crème de cassis
110g/4oz granulated sugar
1 vanilla pod
1 tablespoon coriander seeds, crushed
6 cardamom pods, crushed
½ teaspoon Chinese five spice
2 teaspoons peeled and grated fresh ginger
thinly pared zest and juice of 1 lime
450g/1lb ripe greengages
450g/1lb ripe apricots
170g/6oz raspberries

To serve
290ml/½ pint Greek yoghurt

1. Put the water, sloe gin or crème de cassis and sugar into a heavy-based saucepan. Dissolve slowly over a low heat. When the sugar has completely dissolved, add the spices and lime zest and boil for 2–3 minutes. Remove from the heat and allow to infuse for 10 minutes. Strain into a clean saucepan.

2. Halve and stone the greengages and apricots, add to the syrup and poach gently for 8–10 minutes, or until tender but not broken up.

3. Remove the fruit and reduce the cooking liquor, by boiling rapidly, to 200ml/7fl oz.

4. Add the lime juice to the syrup and allow to cool for 1–2 minutes.

5. Arrange the greengages and apricots in a large shallow bowl and sprinkle over the raspberries. Pour the syrup over the top and serve warm, with the yoghurt handed separately.

 *LIGHT SWEET WHITE*

MULBERRY CLAFOUTIS

SERVES 4

4 tablespoons mulberry gin or kirsch
450g/1lb mulberries
100ml/3½fl oz milk
150ml/¼ pint whipping cream
½ vanilla pod
4 eggs
140g/5oz caster sugar
30g/1oz plain flour
a pinch of salt
butter and caster sugar for greasing and sprinkling

1. Preheat the oven to 200°C/400°F/gas mark 6.

2. Sprinkle the gin over the mulberries and leave to macerate for 30 minutes.

3. Put the milk, cream and vanilla pod into a small saucepan. Bring to the boil, then turn off the heat and leave to infuse.

4. Place the eggs and sugar in a mixing bowl. Whisk until creamy. Add the flour and salt and whisk until smooth. Strain in the infused milk and cream and beat until well mixed.

5. Generously butter an ovenproof dish about 25 × 23 × 5cm/10 × 9 × 2in and sprinkle with caster sugar.

6. Tip the mulberries into the dish and pour over the batter.

7. Bake in the preheated oven for 50–55 minutes. Remove and allow to cool before serving sprinkled with a little extra caster sugar.

 *SWEET VOUVRAY*

BAKED NECTARINES WITH MASCARPONE AND PRALINE

SERVES 4

4 small or 2 large ripe nectarines, halved and
  stoned
110g/4oz mascarpone or mild soft goat's cheese
4 teaspoons soft dark brown sugar
30g/1oz praline, not ground (see page 664)
8 × 17.5cm/7in square sheets of filo pastry (see
  page 647)
55g/2oz butter, melted

1. Preheat the oven to 200°C/400°F/gas mark 6.
2. Take a small slice off the bottom of one half
of each nectarine so it sits easily on the surface
without toppling over. If there isn't a very large
dip left from where the stone lay, enlarge the
hole a little by scraping out some of the flesh
with a teaspoon. Place a large spoonful of
mascarpone in the centre of each nectarine half,
pressing it into the hole left by the stone.
Sprinkle a teaspoon of the sugar over the
mascarpone in each nectarine.
3. Break up the praline a little by crushing it
with the end of a rolling pin and divide the
pieces into 4, pressing a quarter of the praline
into the mascarpone on each of the nectarine
halves. Replace the other nectarine halves back
on top. (If using large nectarines you won't
need to do this.)
4. Lay one sheet of filo flat on a clean, dry work
surface and brush quickly with melted butter.
Place another sheet of filo on top and brush
with more melted butter. Place a nectarine in
the centre, with the mascarpone layer
horizontal, and gather up the edges to form a
parcel like a Dick Whittington sack. Repeat
with the remaining nectarines.
5. Place the parcels on a greased baking sheet,
brush the outsides with more melted butter and
bake in the centre of the preheated oven for 20
minutes, or until golden-brown. Serve
immediately.

 *RECIATO DI SOAVE*

PINENUT CARAMEL AND PASSION FRUIT PUDDINGS

SERVES 4

4 ripe passion fruit
2 tablespoons clear honey
170g/6oz mascarpone
150ml/¼ pint Greek yoghurt
grated zest and juice of 1 orange
85g/3oz caster sugar
55g/2oz pinenuts, toasted
3 tablespoons Grand Marnier

1. Cut the passion fruit in half and scoop out
the seeds and juice into a bowl. Stir in the
honey, mascarpone, yoghurt, orange zest and
juice. Taste for sweetness, add more honey if
necessary and divide the mixture between 4
ramekins. Cover and chill.
2. Put the sugar into a heavy-based saucepan
and set over a medium heat until the sugar has
melted and begun to caramelize. Add the
pinenuts and Grand Marnier, taking care as the
caramel will hiss and splutter. Stir over a low
heat for a few seconds to allow any lumps of
caramel to dissolve. Remove from the heat and
allow to cool for 1 minute.
3. Pour the pinenut caramel over each ramekin
and allow to cool. Leave to stand for 30
minutes.

 *SAUTERNES*

PEACH, STRAWBERRY AND MANGO COMPOTE WITH CLOTTED CREAM

SERVES 4

6 ripe peaches
450g/1lb ripe strawberries
2 ripe mangoes
4 passion fruit

For the sauce
150ml//¼ pint sugar syrup (see page 661)
juice of 1 lemon

To decorate
a few sprigs of fresh mint

To serve
8 meringues (see page 666)
110g/4oz clotted cream

1. Blanch the peaches in boiling water for 8 seconds, then quickly refresh them in cold water. Peel off the skins.
2. Cut the peaches in half and remove the stones. Cut each half into 3–4 segments.
3. Cut the strawberries in half or into quarters if they are very large and put them into a large bowl with 12–16 peach segments.
4. Peel the mangoes and cut the flesh into large chunks, discarding the stone. Add the mango chunks to the bowl.
5. Cut the passion fruit in half and scrape the seeds into the bowl with the other fruit.
6. Make the sauce: whizz the syrup, the remaining peach segments and lemon juice together in a blender until smooth.
7. Pour the sauce over the fruit and stir gently together. Check for sweetness and add more lemon juice if necessary. Tip the compote into a large bowl and decorate with the sprigs of mint. Serve with the meringues and clotted cream.

NOTE: Nectarines may be substituted for the peaches.

 MUSCAT DE BEAUMES DE VENISE

PEACHES WITH HAZELNUT STUFFING AND RASPBERRY PURÉE

SERVES 4

4 large ripe peaches

For the syrup
85g/3oz granulated sugar
290ml/½ pint water
thinly pared zest and juice of 1 lemon

For the hazelnut stuffing
110g/4oz hazelnuts, toasted
30g/1oz caster sugar
¼ teaspoon ground cinnamon
½ egg white

To finish
225g/8oz fresh raspberries
juice of 1 lemon

To serve
amaretti biscuits

1. Simmer the peaches in boiling water for 1 minute, then lift into cold water and allow to cool. Peel off the skins.
2. Make the syrup: put the sugar, water and lemon zest into a saucepan and dissolve the sugar over a low heat. Bring to the boil, then lower the heat and simmer for 2 minutes. Remove from the heat and allow to cool.
3. Make the stuffing: grind the hazelnuts with the sugar and cinnamon in a blender. Remove from the blender and bind to a stiff paste with a little egg white. Form the mixture into 4 discs.
4. Cut the peaches in half and remove the stones. Replace with a disc of hazelnut stuffing, sandwiching the two halves together. Lower the stuffed peaches into the syrup and cover the pan with damp greaseproof paper and a lid. Bring to the boil, then lower the heat and poach for 10 minutes.
5. Lift the peaches onto a serving dish.
6. Put the raspberries and 2–3 tablespoons of the poaching liquid into the rinsed-out blender. Whizz to a purée, then strain. Taste the purée for sweetness and add the lemon juice or more syrup as required.
7. Spoon the raspberry purée over the peaches and serve at room temperature with the biscuits handed separately.

 MUSCAT DE BEAUMES DE VENISE

PEACH AND MELON SALAD

This recipe has been adapted from *The Josceline Dimbleby Collection.*

SERVES 4

juice of 2 lemons
110g/4oz granulated sugar
1 tablespoon orange-flower water
4 peaches or nectarines
1 small melon
450g/1lb strawberries

1. Make up the lemon juice to 150ml/¼ pint with water. Pour into a saucepan, add the sugar and set over a low heat. Dissolve the sugar carefully, then bring up to the boil. Lower the heat and simmer for 3–4 minutes. Remove from the heat, add the orange-flower water and allow to cool.
2. Prepare the fruit. If using peaches, place them for a few seconds in a pan of boiling water, then in a bowl of cold water. Peel off the skins. If using nectarines, leave the skins on. Slice the fruit into segments, away from the stone. Halve and peel the melon, scoop out the seeds and cut the flesh into chunks. Hull and halve the strawberries.
3. Mix the fruit together in a serving bowl. Pour over the cold syrup. Chill for about 20 minutes.

 *LIGHT SWEET WHITE*

RASPBERRY AND ROSE-WATER RISOTTO

SERVES 4

30g/1oz unsalted butter
400g/14oz risotto (arborio) rice
170g/6oz granulated sugar
1.1 litres/2 pints water
290ml/½ pint champagne
150ml/¼ pint rose-water
450g/1lb fresh raspberries

1. Heat the butter in a large saucepan, add the rice and cook for 4–5 minutes.
2. Meanwhile, heat the sugar and water together until the sugar has dissolved. Bring to the boil, then lower the heat and allow to simmer gently.
3. Add the champagne to the rice and boil until the liquid has been absorbed.
4. Start adding the hot syrup to the rice a little at a time, stirring gently. Allow the syrup to become absorbed after each addition. Keep stirring constantly. Continue to add the syrup until the rice is cooked but still *al dente* (about 30–40 minutes).
5. Add the rose-water and cook for a further 5 minutes until it has been absorbed. Stir in the raspberries and stir together for 2–3 minutes, or until the fruit is beginning to break up.
6. Check for sweetness and add a little icing sugar if necessary. Serve very hot.

 LIGHT SWEET WHITE

MACERATED RASPBERRY SALAD

SERVES 4

8 tablespoons crème de framboise (raspberry liqueur)
2–3 tablespoons icing sugar
450g/1lb small raspberries
1 tablespoon chopped fresh mint

1. Mix the liqueur and icing sugar together.
2. Pick over the raspberries and rinse under cold running water. Drain and pat dry on kitchen paper. Tip into a bowl.
3. Pour the sweetened liqueur over the raspberries and allow to macerate for 2 hours. Sprinkle with the mint and serve.

 YOUNG CHILEAN PINOT NOIR

FRUIT AND COCONUT SUSHI

MAKES 25

225g/8oz sushi rice
425ml/¾ pint water
1 cinnamon stick
2 star anise
100ml/3½fl oz coconut milk
45g/1½oz creamed coconut, grated
6–7 tablespoons icing sugar
1 tablespoon rum
1 kiwi fruit, peeled and sliced into strips
    lengthways
1 small papaya, halved, de-seeded and sliced
    into strips
1 banana, peeled and sliced into strips
55g/2oz strawberries, hulled and sliced
icing sugar for dusting

To serve
lime wedges
mango dipping sauce (see page 376)

1. Put the rice into a sieve and hold under cold running water for 2–3 minutes, or until the water runs clear.
2. Put the rice into a saucepan and cover with the water. Add the cinnamon stick and star anise, cover and allow to stand for 10 minutes.
3. Set the rice over a low heat. Bring to the boil, then lower the heat, cover and cook gently for 10 minutes, or until all the water has been absorbed.
4. Meanwhile, put the coconut milk, creamed coconut, icing sugar and rum into a small saucepan and heat gently, stirring constantly, until the coconut has melted.
5. When the rice is cooked, turn it on to a deep plate, remove the spices and pour over the coconut mixture. Stir with a fork until the rice has cooled. Sweeten to taste with icing sugar if necessary.
6. Divide the sushi into 25 portions. Shape each portion into a lozenge shape and arrange a slice of fruit on each piece.

7. Arrange on a large unpatterned plate and dust with icing sugar. Arrange the lime wedges around and hand the dipping sauce separately.

 MUSCAT DE BEAUMES DE VENISE

ROAST RHUBARB WITH ORANGE AND PERNOD CREAM

SERVES 4

900g/2lb young rhubarb
30g/1oz butter
85g/3oz demerara sugar
2 tablespoons pernod

For the orange and pernod cream
grated zest of 1 orange
2–3 tablespoons pernod
1 tablespoon icing sugar, sifted
150ml/¼ pint double cream

To decorate
4 sprigs of fresh mint

1. Preheat the oven to 220°C/425°F/gas mark 7.
2. Wash the rhubarb and cut it into 2.5cm/1in chunks, on a slight diagonal.
3. Melt the butter in a large, shallow roasting tin. Add the rhubarb, sugar and pernod and stir everything together to make sure the rhubarb is well coated with butter and sugar.
4. Roast the rhubarb near the top of the preheated oven for 15–20 minutes, or until just tender and starting to brown.
5. Make the orange and pernod cream: mix the orange zest with the pernod and icing sugar. Stir in the cream and whisk gently until it holds its shape.
6. Serve the rhubarb piled in the centre of 4 cold individual plates, with a spoonful of the orange and pernod cream to one side. Decorate each with a sprig of mint and serve immediately.

 CALIFORNIAN ORANGE MUSCAT

WILD STRAWBERRIES WITH CLARET

This is for the morning after . . . !

SERVES 4

450g/1lb strawberries, hulled
1–2 glasses of good claret
1 tablespoon soft light brown sugar
freshly ground black pepper

1. Place the strawberries in a glass bowl, pour over the claret and sprinkle over the brown sugar. Season with pepper.
2. Leave to macerate for 15 minutes before serving.

 *CLARET!*

GLAZED SKEWERED FRUIT

MAKES 12 SKEWERS

12 bamboo skewers
1 pineapple
2 ripe peaches
12 fresh apricots
1 small papaya
4 kiwi fruit
icing sugar to dust

To serve
mango dipping sauce (see page 376)

1. Soak the skewers in cold water for 30 minutes.
2. Preheat the grill to its highest setting.
3. Prepare the fruit: peel the pineapple and cut into 2.5cm/1in dice. Halve the peaches and apricots and remove the stones. Cut the peaches into 2.5cm/1in chunks and the apricots into quarters. Halve, de-seed and peel the papaya and cut into 2.5cm/1in chunks. Peel and quarter the kiwi fruit.
4. Drain the skewers and thread on the fruits, alternating the pineapple, peaches, apricots, papaya and kiwi fruit.
5. Arrange the skewers on a baking sheet and dust generously with icing sugar. Grill for 1–2 minutes, or until the icing sugar has caramelized. Turn the skewers over, dust the second side with icing sugar and grill for a further 1–2 minutes.
6. To serve: lift the skewers on to a large warmed serving dish and hand the dipping sauce separately.

 *SAUTERNES*

SUMMER STONE FRUIT CLAFOUTIS

SERVES 4

6 ripe apricots, halved and stoned
4 peaches, peeled and sliced
butter for greasing
85g/3oz caster sugar
2 tablespoons brandy
30g/1oz plain flour
4 eggs, beaten
200ml/7fl oz whipping cream

To serve
icing sugar for dusting

1. Preheat the oven to 200°C/400°F/gas mark 6.
2. Put the apricots and peaches into a lightly buttered shallow dish and sprinkle over half the sugar and all the brandy. Bake in the preheated oven for 5 minutes, or until the fruit is beginning to soften.
3. Meanwhile, beat the remaining sugar and flour with the eggs, stir in the cream and whisk to form a smooth batter. Pour the batter over the fruit and return to the oven for 20–25 minutes, or until set.
4. To serve: dust the top with icing sugar and serve warm.

NOTE: This batter cake was traditionally made with cherries and served to the grape harvesters.

 SWEET WHITE

MOUSSES, SOUFFLÉS AND CREAMS

SWEET RASPBERRY VINEGAR BAVAROIS

SERVES 4

6 tablespoons sweet raspberry vinegar (see page 365)
2 tablespoons water
7g/¼oz powdered gelatine
210ml/7½fl oz milk
3 egg yolks
85g/3oz caster sugar
150ml/¼ pint double cream

To decorate
110g/4oz raspberries
sprigs of fresh mint
icing sugar for dusting

1. Place the raspberry vinegar and water in a small saucepan and sprinkle over the gelatine. Leave for 5 minutes to become spongy.
2. Place the milk in a heavy-based saucepan and heat gently until the milk is at scalding point.
3. Mix the egg yolks and sugar together. Stir in the warm milk and return to the saucepan. Stir constantly with a wooden spoon, over a low heat, until the mixture will coat the back of the spoon. Be careful not to overheat or the mixture will curdle. Strain.
4. Dissolve the gelatine over a low heat without boiling, then stir into the cooling custard. Stir occasionally until on the point of setting. Whip the cream lightly and fold it into the raspberry mixture.
5. Turn into individual ramekins and leave in the refrigerator to set. Decorate with

raspberries and sprigs of mint lightly dusted with icing sugar.

 SWEET WHITE

COLD PASSION FRUIT SOUFFLÉ

SERVES 4

8 passion fruits
grated zest and juice of 1 lemon
1 tablespoon water
7g/¼oz powdered gelatine
3 eggs
110g/4oz caster sugar
150ml/¼ pint double cream
icing sugar (optional)

To decorate
1 passion fruit

1. Cut the passion fruits in half. Scoop out and sieve all the flesh.
2. Put the lemon juice and water into a small saucepan and sprinkle over the gelatine. Leave for 5 minutes to become spongy.
3. Separate the eggs. Place the yolks, lemon zest and sugar into a mixing bowl and whisk together with an electric mixer (or with a balloon whisk or rotary beater with the bowl set over a saucepan of simmering water). Whisk until very thick. If whisking by hand over hot water, remove from the heat and whisk for a few minutes longer, until the mixture is lukewarm. Gradually add the passion fruit pulp.
4. Dissolve the gelatine over a low heat without boiling until liquid and clear, then add to the

338

mousse mixture. Stir gently until the mixture is on the point of setting, then fold in the cream. Taste and if too tart sift in a little icing sugar; if too bland add a little more lemon juice.

5. Whisk the egg whites until stiff but not dry and fold them into the soufflé with a large metal spoon.

6. Pour the mixture into a soufflé dish and leave to set in the refrigerator for 2–3 hours. When set decorate with the seeds of 1 passion fruit.

 *SWEET WHITE*

CHERRY AND MASCARPONE BURNT CREAMS

SERVES 4

225g/8oz fresh ripe black cherries, stoned
225g/8oz strawberries, hulled and quartered
4 tablespoons kirsch
2 tablespoons caster sugar
200g/7oz mascarpone
8 tablespoons demerara sugar

1. Put the cherries, strawberries, kirsch and caster sugar into a bowl and gently toss together. Divide between 4 ramekins.

2. Divide the mascarpone into 4 equal portions and spread a portion over each ramekin, completely covering the fruit. Chill for 30 minutes.

3. Preheat the grill to its highest setting.

4. Place the ramekins on a baking sheet. Spread 2 tablespoons of demerara sugar over the top of each. Place the baking sheet as close as possible to the heat and grill until the sugar has melted and caramelized. Allow to cool and set before serving.

NOTE: Generally it is difficult to get an even caramelization of the sugar when using a domestic grill. Blow-torches are used in the catering trade for this purpose and give a wonderful even colour to brûlées. As an alternative you can use 110g/4oz caster sugar

and make a caramel (see page 661), which can be poured over the mascarpone instead.

 *MOSCATO D'ASTI*

ELDERBERRY CREAMS WITH ELDERFLOWER SORBET

SERVES 4

450g/1lb elderberries
110g/4oz granulated sugar
2 tablespoons water
1 tablespoon lemon juice
2 teaspoons powdered gelatine
290ml/½ pint double cream, lightly whipped
oil for greasing

To serve
1 quantity elderflower sorbet (see page 217)
4 sprigs of fresh mint

1. Put the elderberries and sugar into a saucepan and stir over a low heat until the sugar has dissolved and the berries have softened.

2. Whizz the berries in a food processor or blender, then pass through a nylon sieve. Allow to cool.

3. Put the water and lemon juice into a small saucepan. Sprinkle over the gelatine and allow to sponge for 5 minutes. Melt the gelatine over a low heat without boiling and stir into the elderberry syrup.

4. When the elderberry syrup has reached setting point, fold in the double cream and pour into 4 lightly oiled ramekins. Chill for 1 hour.

5. Turn the elderberry creams out on to chilled individual plates. Place a neat spoonful of elderflower sorbet on each plate and decorate each serving with a sprig of mint. Serve immediately.

NOTE: Blueberries may be substituted for elderberries if these are not available.

 ASTI SPUMANTE OR SWEET VOUVRAY

ICE CREAMS AND SORBETS

LAVENDER HONEY AND MASCARPONE ICE CREAM

SERVES 4

425ml/¾ pint milk
20 heads of lavender, crushed
4 egg yolks
5 tablespoons lavender honey
340g/12oz mascarpone

To serve
2 tablespoons clear honey
pepper and spice brandy snaps (see page 355)

1. Put the milk and lavender heads into a heavy-based saucepan and heat until the milk just comes to the boil. Remove from the heat and allow to infuse for 15 minutes.
2. Beat the egg yolks and honey together until creamy, add the milk and lavender flowers and pour back into the rinsed-out pan. Return the mixture to the heat and cook, stirring constantly with a wooden spoon, until the custard thickens and lightly coats the back of the spoon. Do not allow to boil. Remove from the heat, strain into a bowl and allow to cool.
3. Taste the custard for sweetness, adding more honey if necessary. Beat the custard into the mascarpone.
4. Turn into an ice tray and freeze. When the ice cream is half frozen, stir with a fork to break up any ice crystals and return to the freezer.
5. To serve: scoop a spoonful of the ice cream on to a plate and drizzle with honey. Hand the pepper and spice brandy snaps separately.

 *AUSTRALIAN LIQUEUR MUSCAT*

SUMMER BERRY RIPPLE ICE CREAM

SERVES 4

225g/8oz raspberries
110g/4oz strawberries, hulled and sliced
110g/4oz blackcurrants, de-stalked
85g/3oz icing sugar
4 tablespoons crème de framboise or cassis
85g/3oz granulated sugar
150ml/¼ pint water
3 egg yolks
290ml/½ pint double cream
290ml/½ pint single cream

1. Put the fruits into a bowl and stir in the icing sugar and liqueur. Break up slightly with a fork and leave to macerate for 1 hour.
2. Put the sugar and water into a small saucepan and dissolve over a low heat. When the sugar has completely dissolved, bring to the boil and simmer until the syrup reaches the short thread stage (when a little syrup is put between a wet finger and thumb and the fingers opened, it should form a sticky thread 2.5cm/1in long).
3. Remove from the heat and allow the syrup to cool for 1 minute. Start whisking the egg yolks and pour the syrup on to the yolks. Whisk until the mixture has become pale and mousse-like.
4. Stir the creams into the mixture. Add the macerated fruit and taste for sweetness, adding more icing sugar if necessary.
5. Freeze until half frozen, then stir well and return to the freezer until solid (at least 1 hour).

 *SWEET WHITE*

CASSATA

SERVES 8

1 quantity summer berry ripple ice cream (see page 340)
1 quantity chocolate ice cream (see page 665)
1 quantity rich vanilla ice cream (see page 665)

For the macerated fruit
2 tablespoons glacé cherries, roughly chopped
1 tablespoon raisins
1 tablespoon sultanas
1 tablespoon finely chopped candied fruit
2 tablespoons rum

To decorate
chocolate caraque (see page 664)
a few small strawberries and raspberries
sprigs of fresh mint
icing sugar for dusting

1. Line a 2 litre/3½ pint loaf tin with clingfilm or a strip of kitchen foil.
2. Take the summer berry ripple ice cream from the freezer and allow to stand at room temperature for 10 minutes, or until slightly softened.
3. Spread the ice cream around the base and sides of the tin, cover and return to the freezer for 30 minutes, or until solid.
4. Take the chocolate ice cream from the freezer and allow to stand at room temperature for 10 minutes. Spread a thick layer over the summer berry ripple ice cream and return to the freezer until solid.
5. Take the rich vanilla ice cream from the freezer and allow to stand at room temperature for 10 minutes.
6. Meanwhile, soak all the dried fruits in the rum and allow to macerate for a few minutes.
7. Spread half the rich vanilla ice cream over the chocolate, leaving a small well in the centre. Return to the freezer until solid.
8. Put a layer of the macerated fruits in the well, cover with the remaining rich vanilla ice cream and return to the freezer until solid, or for at least 1 hour.
9. To serve: turn the ice cream on to a plate and

remove the clingfilm. Cut into thick slices and arrange, overlapping, on a large chilled oval serving plate. Arrange chocolate caraque down the middle and clusters of strawberries and raspberries around the sides. Decorate the fruit with sprigs of mint and dust each cluster with a little icing sugar. Keep in the freezer until ready to serve.

 MUSCAT DE BEAUMES DE VENISE

PEACH AND RASPBERRY ICE CREAM BOMBE

SERVES 6

4 ripe peaches
450g/1lb raspberries
55g/2oz icing sugar, sifted
1 quantity Pavlova meringue (see page 666)
290ml/½ pint double cream

To serve
macerated raspberry salad (see page 335)

1. Simmer the peaches in boiling water for 1 minute. Lift into a bowl of cold water and allow to cool for 1 minute, then peel off the skins. Halve the peaches, remove the stones and dice. Set aside.
2. Liquidize or crush the raspberries and push through a nylon sieve. Sweeten with the icing sugar.
3. Break up the meringue into small pieces and stir into the raspberries. Add the peach slices.
4. Lightly whip the cream and stir into the raspberry mixture.
5. Turn into a lightly oiled loaf tin, cover with kitchen foil and freeze for 2 hours.
6. Turn the frozen bombe on to a plate and allow to stand in the refrigerator for 15 minutes before cutting into thick slices. Serve with macerated raspberry salad.

 *MOSCATO D'ASTI*

WHITE CHOCOLATE AND LOGANBERRY BOMBE

SERVES 8

oil for greasing
150ml/¼ pint double cream, whipped
150ml/¼ pint loganberry or raspberry coulis
  (see page 662)
½ quantity white chocolate mousse (see page
  213)

To serve
225g/8oz fresh loganberries or raspberries
a few sprigs of fresh mint
icing sugar

1. Lightly oil a round-based, 12–15cm/5–6in
bowl and line with clingfilm, leaving some
hanging over the edge.
2. Spread the cream in an even layer around the
inside of the bowl. Freeze for 1 hour.
3. Pour the coulis into the bowl and tip it
around so it coats all the cream. Pour out the
excess and reserve. Freeze for a further 15
minutes, then repeat the process with the coulis
until it has all been used. Freeze for 15 minutes.
4. Make the white chocolate mousse and pour it
into the bombe. Cover it with clingfilm and
freeze it for 2–3 hours, or until firm.
5. To serve: turn the bombe out on to a large
chilled plate and remove the clingfilm. Pile the
loganberries or raspberries around the edge and
decorate with the sprigs of mint. Sift a little
icing sugar over the berries.

 *LOUPIAC OR SAINTE-CROIX-DU-
MONT*

BLACKCURRANT LEAF ICE

SERVES 4

a large handful of blackcurrant leaves, washed
  and chopped
110g/4oz granulated sugar
570ml/1 pint water
juice of 2 large lemons
½ egg white

1. Place the blackcurrant leaves, sugar and
water in a heavy-based saucepan. Dissolve the
sugar over a low heat and, when completely
dissolved, boil rapidly to the short thread stage
(when a little syrup is put between a wet finger
and thumb and the fingers opened, it should
form a sticky thread 2.5cm/1in long).
2. Remove from the heat and allow to cool
completely. When the syrup is cold, add the
lemon juice and strain.
3. Freeze for 30 minutes, or until beginning to
solidify.
4. Whisk the egg white until stiff and fold into
the mixture.
5. Return to the freezer until firm.

NOTE: Roughly chopped fresh mint leaves can
be used in place of blackcurrant leaves, if
unavailable.

 *LIGHT SWEET WHITE*

RED, WHITE AND BLACKCURRANT ICED TERRINE

This recipe needs to be started a day in advance
of serving.

SERVES 10–12

oil for greasing
450g/1lb whitecurrants
450g/1lb redcurrants
450g/1lb blackcurrants

675g/1½lb caster sugar
290ml/½ pint water
1½ egg whites

To decorate
8 sprigs of fresh mint
1 egg white
caster sugar
150ml/¼ pint crème de cassis

To serve
290ml/½ pint double cream

1. Lightly oil a 1kg/2¼lb terrine tin, then carefully line with clingfilm.
2. Take 3 small saucepans and put the separate colour currants into each pan. Divide the sugar and water equally between the pans.
3. Put the saucepans over a low heat and stir until the sugar has dissolved. Bring to the boil, then lower the heat and simmer for 2 minutes, or until the currants have burst.
4. Whizz the whitecurrants in a food processor or blender, then push the fruit through a nylon sieve. Pour into a freezerproof dish.
5. Repeat with the redcurrants and blackcurrants in that order, keeping the colours well separated. Freeze the 3 purées overnight.
6. Transfer the frozen purées to the refrigerator for 20 minutes. Take out the whitecurrant purée and cut it up into cubes. Tip it into a food processor, add ½ egg white and whizz, using the pulse action, just long enough to break down the ice crystals and for the purée to become creamy in texture. Tip into the bottom of the prepared terrine tin, smooth the surface and freeze immediately.
7. Repeat with the redcurrant purée. When the sorbet has been whizzed, tip it back into its original container and freeze immediately.
8. Whizz the blackcurrant purée in the same way and freeze it immediately in its original container.
9. When the whitecurrant sorbet has been in the freezer for 20 minutes, carefully spoon the redcurrant sorbet over the top and smooth the surface. Freeze for 20 minutes, then spoon over the blackcurrant sorbet. Freeze the whole terrine for at least 3 hours, or overnight.

10. Prepare the decoration: take each sprig of mint and carefully brush each leaf with a very thin layer of egg white. Dip the leaves in caster sugar and lay out to dry on silicone paper for 30 minutes in a warm, dry atmosphere.
11. To serve: turn the terrine out on to a chopping board.
12. Dip a large, sharp knife into a jug of hot water and slice off 1cm/½in of the terrine. Transfer to a chilled serving plate. Clean the knife before cutting further slices.
13. Drizzle a little crème de cassis around each serving and decorate with the frosted mint sprigs. Serve immediately with the cream handed separately in a jug.

 *MOSEL RIESLING AUSLESE*

WHITECURRANT AND GOOSEBERRY SWIRL FROZEN YOGHURT

This recipe needs to be started a day in advance of serving.

SERVES 4

For the whitecurrant yoghurt
450g/1lb whitecurrants
170g/6oz caster sugar
1 tablespoon water
290ml/½ pint crème anglaise (see page 661)
290ml/½ pint Greek yoghurt
1 egg white

For the gooseberry purée
450g/1lb gooseberries
225g/8oz caster sugar
1 tablespoon water

1. Make the whitecurrant yoghurt: put the currants in a heavy-based saucepan with the sugar and water and cook over a low heat until the sugar has dissolved and the currants have burst.
2. Whizz the currants briefly in a food

processor, then press through a nylon sieve into a large bowl. Allow to cool.

3. Mix the crème anglaise and yoghurt into the whitecurrant purée. Pour into a freezerproof container and freeze overnight.

4. Make the gooseberry purée: put the gooseberries into a heavy-based saucepan with the sugar and water and cook over a low heat until the sugar has dissolved and the gooseberries have burst.

5. Whizz the gooseberries in a food processor for 1 minute, then press through a nylon sieve into a bowl. Allow to cool.

6. Take the frozen whitecurrant yoghurt out of the freezer and refrigerate for 15 minutes. Cut into cubes and place in a food processor with the egg white.

7. Whizz, using the pulse action, for 30 seconds, to make a smooth, thick creamy purée. Tip into a freezerproof container.

8. Immediately pour the gooseberry purée into the yoghurt, making large swirls with a large metal spoon – be sure not to mix it in too much. Freeze for 2 hours before serving.

NOTE: If the yoghurt has been frozen for longer than 2–3 hours and is very solid it must be transferred to a refrigerator for 30 minutes before serving.

 *SAINTE-CROIX-DU-MONT*

MERINGUES

RASPBERRY AND GOOSEBERRY CARAMEL MERINGUE

SERVES 8

For the meringue
4 egg whites
225g/8oz caster sugar

For the filling
450g/1lb fresh raspberries
450g/1lb very ripe golden gooseberries
570ml/1 pint double cream, whipped

For the caramel topping
170g/6oz granulated sugar
water

1. Preheat the oven to 70°C/150°F/gas mark ¼. Line 2 baking sheets with silicone paper.
2. Whisk the egg whites in a large, clean bowl until they form stiff peaks. Add a tablespoon of the sugar and whisk again until the mixture is stiff and shiny.
3. Fold the remaining sugar into the meringue with a large metal spoon. Drop tablespoonfuls of the meringue mixture set fairly far apart on to the lined baking sheets. Bake at the bottom of the preheated oven for 2 hours, or until the meringues are dry right through and will lift off the paper easily.
4. Put the meringues into the bottom of a large heatproof serving bowl and pile the fruit on top.
5. Pour over the cream, covering the fruit as much as possible.

6. Make the caramel topping: put the sugar into a heavy-based saucepan. Add just enough water to cover the sugar.
7. Dissolve the sugar slowly without stirring or allowing the water to boil.
8. Once all the sugar has dissolved, turn up the heat and boil until it is a good caramel colour.
9. Immediately tip the caramel all over the cream. Leave for a minute for the caramel to cool before serving.

NOTE: If you are unable to get the golden gooseberries you can use the green ones. However, they will need to be pre-cooked with a little sugar as they are very tart.

 ASTI SPUMANTE

CHOCOLATE MERINGUE CAKE WITH RASPBERRIES AND CHOCOLATE CARAQUE

This is a variation of Gâteau Diane, taken from the Cordon Bleu Good Housekeeping series.

SERVES 6

For the meringue
4 egg whites
a pinch of salt
225g/8oz caster sugar

For the filling
225g/8oz plain chocolate, chopped
425ml/¾ pint double cream, very lightly
  whipped
225g/8oz fresh raspberries

345

For the caraque
110g/4oz white or dark chocolate, melted
cocoa powder for dusting

1. Preheat the oven to 100°C/200°F/gas mark
½. Draw 3 × 15cm/6in circles on the underside
of silicone paper and then lay the paper on
baking sheets.
2. Whisk the egg whites with the salt until stiff
but not dry. Add 2 tablespoons of the sugar and
whisk again until very stiff and shiny.
3. Fold in the remaining sugar.
4. Divide the meringue between the 3 circles and
spread out evenly to make 3 thin meringue cakes.
Bake in the preheated oven for about 2 hours, or
until the meringues are dry right through and will
lift easily off the paper. Allow to cool.
5. Put the chocolate into a heatproof bowl set
over, not in, a saucepan of recently boiled
water. Stir occasionally until melted.
6. Quickly pour the chocolate into the cream and
whisk together to make a thick chocolate cream.
7. Put a spoonful of the chocolate cream on to a
serving plate and place one of the meringue
discs on top; this will prevent the meringue
from sliding. Spread a little of the chocolate
cream over the meringue and arrange half the
raspberries on top. Place the second layer of
meringue over the raspberries and spread with a
little more chocolate cream and top with the
remaining raspberries.
8. Place the final layer of meringue on top and use
the remaining chocolate cream to cover the top
and sides of the cake evenly. Chill for 2 hours.
9. Make the caraque: spread the melted
chocolate on to a flat baking sheet in a thick
layer. Allow the chocolate to set, unrefrigerated
(unless the weather is very hot).
10. When the chocolate has set, take a large
chopping knife or palette knife and scrape
across the top of the chocolate, forming long
cigarette-shaped rolls. If this does not appear to
work, the chocolate is either too warm or too
cold, and adjusting its temperature will make
all the difference.
11. Pile the caraque on top of the meringue and
dust with a little sifted cocoa powder before
serving.

 MUSCAT DE BEAUMES DE VENISE

PASTRIES, PIES AND TARTS

INDIVIDUAL POACHED STONE FRUIT KONAFA

SERVES 4

340g/12oz konafa pastry
110g/4oz unsalted butter, melted and cooled
a large pinch of ground cinnamon
oil for greasing
225g/8oz apricots
225g/8oz ripe plums
225g/8oz greengages
5 tablespoons Sauternes wine
icing sugar to taste

To serve
4 tablespoons mascarpone
icing sugar

1. Preheat the oven to 190°C/375°F/gas mark 5.
2. Put the pastry into a large bowl. Pull out and separate the strands as much as possible with your fingers so that they do not stick together too much. Pour in the melted butter and work it in very well. Add the cinnamon.
3. Divide the pastry into 12 equal pieces. Shape each into a thin round, using a large pastry cutter as a template. Arrange on a lightly oiled baking sheet. Bake in the preheated oven for 12–15 minutes, or until the pastry is crisp and golden-brown. Allow to cool.
4. Wash and halve the fruit. Put into a large saucepan with the wine and a little icing sugar, cover and poach for 7–10 minutes, or until the fruit is soft. Lift the fruit from the pan and reduce the poaching liquid to 1–2 tablespoons. Pour over the fruit and sweeten to taste with icing sugar. Allow to cool.

5. To assemble: put a konafa round on to each of 4 individual plates. Spoon a little of the mascarpone on each and arrange some of the fruit on top; cover with a second round of pastry, followed by more mascarpone and fruit. Top each with a third round of pastry and dust each serving generously with icing sugar. Serve warm.

NOTE: Konafa pastry is available in delicatessens.

 MUSCAT DE BEAUMES DE VENISE

HOT APRICOT GOUGÈRE

SERVES 4

For the gougère
55g/2oz no-soak dried apricots, chopped
55g/2oz strong Cheddar cheese, coarsely grated
1 tablespoon caster sugar
1 × 3-egg quantity choux pastry (see page 645)

For the filling
290ml/½ pint milk quantity crème pâtissière
   (see page 661)
450g/1lb fresh apricots, halved and stoned
4 tablespoons amaretto liqueur
15g/½oz butter, melted
30g/1oz nibbed almonds
1 tablespoon demerara sugar

To serve
icing sugar
crème fraîche

1. Preheat the oven to 200°C/400°F/gas mark 6.

2. Stir the dried apricots, Cheddar cheese and sugar into the choux pastry.

3. Grease a 25 × 20cm/10 × 8in deep ovenproof dish and spoon the choux pastry around the edges, spreading it evenly with a knife so that it comes right up the sides of the dish.

4. Bake in the preheated oven for 25–30 minutes, or until the pastry is well risen, golden and firm to the touch. Be careful not to take the gougère out of the oven before the pastry is set or it will collapse.

5. Spread the crème pâtissière over the bottom of the dish. Mix the apricots with the amaretto and pile on top with the juices, making sure the rounded sides of the apricots are uppermost.

6. Mix the butter, almonds and sugar together and sprinkle over the apricots.

7. Return the gougère to the oven for 15–20 minutes, or until the nuts are golden and the apricots are warmed through.

8. Dust with icing sugar and serve the crème fraîche separately.

 *MONBAZILLAC*

CHERRY AND ALMOND STRUDELS

MAKES 20

450g/1lb fresh cherries, stoned and halved
55g/2oz granulated sugar
2 teaspoons kirsch
110g/4oz ground almonds
2 tablespoons ground rice
55g/2oz butter, melted
4 sheets of filo pastry
1 egg, beaten, to glaze
30g/1oz blanched almonds, chopped
oil for greasing

1. Preheat the oven to 200°C/400°F/gas mark 6.

2. Place the cherries, sugar and kirsch together in a saucepan and cook over a very low heat until the sugar has dissolved and the cherries are soft. Remove the cherries with a slotted spoon and set aside.

3. Reduce the cooking liquid to 1–2 tablespoons

by boiling rapidly, then pour over the cherries. Allow to cool.

4. Sift the almonds and ground rice together into a bowl and stir in the cherries. Set aside.

5. Brush the melted butter over the sheets of filo pastry. Cut each sheet of pastry into strips 5cm/2in wide.

6. Place a spoonful of the cherry filling at one end of each strip. Form a triangle by folding the right-hand corner to the opposite side, and fold over and then across from the left-hand corner to the right edge. Continue folding until the strip of pastry is used up (see diagram).

7. Brush the strudels with beaten egg and sprinkle with the chopped almonds. Place on a greased baking sheet and bake in the preheated oven for about 10 minutes, or until golden-brown.

 *SWEET WHITE*

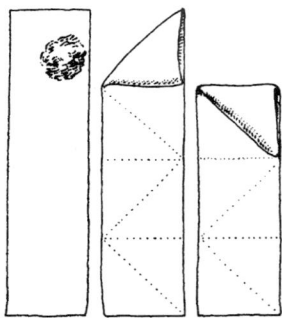

Put a spoonful of filling in the top right-hand corner and fold the pastry into successive triangles

CINNAMON FEUILLETÉ WITH CHERRY AND KIRSCH SABAYON

SERVES 4

225g/8oz cinnamon puff pastry (see page 646)
1 egg, lightly beaten

For the sabayon
450g/1lb ripe black cherries, washed and stoned
6 tablespoons kirsch or brandy
1 egg

3 large egg yolks
110g/4oz caster sugar
4 tablespoons double cream

To decorate
4 sprigs of fresh mint

1. Preheat the oven to 220°C/425°F/gas mark 7.
2. Put the cherries into a bowl with the kirsch or brandy, cover and leave to macerate for 1 hour.
3. Make the feuilleté cases: roll the pastry into a rectangle 1cm/½in thick and cut it into 4 diamonds, each side measuring 10cm/4in.
4. Place the pastry diamonds on a damp baking sheet and brush with the lightly beaten egg. Using a sharp knife, trace a line about 1cm/½in from the edge of each diamond, without cutting all the way through the pastry; this will form a 'hat' for the pastry case. Flour the blade of a knife and use this to knock up the sides of the pastry. Chill in the refrigerator for 15 minutes.
5. Bake the pastry cases in the preheated oven for 20 minutes, or until puffed up and brown. Using a knife, outline and remove the hats and scoop out any uncooked dough inside. Return to the oven for 2 minutes to dry out.
6. Transfer the pastry cases and hats to a wire rack and leave to cool. Reduce the oven temperature to 130°C/250°F/gas mark 1.
7. Place the feuilleté cases on a baking sheet and pile the cherries into the central cavities. Place the sheet in the oven for 15 minutes to allow the cherries and pastry to warm through.
8. Make the sauce: whisk the egg and egg yolks with the sugar in a large heatproof bowl until pale and creamy. Strain the kirsch from the cherries into the bowl and whisk the egg yolk, sugar and kirsch mixture over a saucepan of gently simmering water. Continue to whisk until the sauce becomes thick and holds a ribbon trail when the whisk is lifted out of the mixture. Fold in the cream.
9. To serve: place the feuilleté cases on 4 warmed individual plates and spoon over the sabayon. Replace the hats on top, decorate with the sprigs of mint and serve immediately.

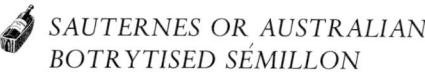 *SAUTERNES OR AUSTRALIAN BOTRYTISED SÉMILLON*

FRESH MORELLO CHERRY AND FRANGIPANE TART

SERVES 8

1 × 225g/8oz flour quantity pâte sucrée (see page 645)
560g/1¼lb fresh morello cherries, stoned
4 tablespoons kirsch or Poire William
200g/7oz butter, softened
200g/7oz caster sugar
2 eggs, beaten
2 egg yolks
1 teaspoon vanilla essence
200g/7oz blanched almonds, ground
85g/3oz plain flour, sifted
100ml/3½fl oz double cream

To serve
icing sugar
caramel cherries (see page 376)

1. Preheat the oven to 190°C/375°F/gas mark 5.
2. Roll out the pastry to the thickness of a £1 coin and use to line a 25cm/10in loose-based flan ring. Chill for 30 minutes.
3. Toss the cherries with the kirsch or Poire William and leave to macerate for 15 minutes.
4. Cream the butter in a bowl, gradually beat in the sugar and continue beating until pale and creamy. Mix the eggs and egg yolks together and gradually add to the butter mixture, beating after each addition to prevent curdling.
5. Stir in the vanilla essence, ground almonds, flour and cream.
6. Pile the frangipane into the chilled pastry case, spreading it evenly. Press the cherries into the frangipane and drizzle over the remaining juices.
7. Bake at the top of the preheated oven for 20 minutes. Reduce the oven temperature to 170°C/325°F/gas mark 3, transfer the tart to the bottom of the oven and continue baking for 40 minutes, or until golden-brown and firm to the touch.
8. To serve: remove the flan ring from the tart

and place on a serving dish. Sift some icing sugar over the tart and arrange the caramel cherries around the edge.

 *LOUPIAC*

FIG AND TOFFEE TART

SERVES 6

170g/6oz flour quantity pâte sucrée (see page 645)
8 fresh figs, wiped and quartered
5 tablespoons brandy
110g/4oz light soft brown sugar
grated zest of 1 orange
150ml/¼ pint water
3 tablespoons double cream
85g/3oz unsalted butter
110g/4oz cottage cheese, drained
55g/2oz flaked almonds, toasted

1. Roll out the pâte sucrée thinly and use to line a 22cm/9in flan ring. Bake blind (see page 640). Allow to cool, then remove the flan ring.
2. Put the figs into a saucepan with the brandy, sugar, orange zest and water. Stir over a low heat until the sugar has dissolved, then cover and cook for 5–7 minutes, or until the figs are very soft but not broken up. Lift the figs from the saucepan and allow to cool.
3. Bring the poaching liquid to the boil, then lower the heat and simmer until it has reduced to a syrupy consistency. Add the cream and butter, stir together until the butter has melted, then allow to cool.
4. Sieve the cottage cheese and spread over the base of the pastry case. Arrange the figs on top. Pour the cool toffee sauce over the top and sprinkle with the almonds.

NOTE: This tart may be assembled 1 hour in advance.

 *SAUTERNES*

INDIVIDUAL SEMI-DRIED FIG TARTS

SERVES 4

225g/8oz flour quantity pâte frollée (see page 646)

For the topping
16 semi-dried fig conserve (see page 367)
2 tablespoons chopped pinenuts, toasted
icing sugar

1. Preheat the oven to 200°C/400°F/gas mark 6.
2. Roll out the pastry and divide into 4 equal pieces.
3. On a floured work surface, roll out each piece of pastry as thinly as possible. Cut each into a 12.5cm/5in circle, place on a baking sheet and refrigerate for 20 minutes.
4. Bake the pastry at the top of the preheated oven for 15 minutes, or until golden-brown. Remove from the oven and cool for 1 minute, then lift on to a wire rack and leave to cool completely.
5. Lift the figs from their syrup and pat dry. Cut the figs in half and arrange on the pastry circles. Put 6 tablespoons of the syrup into a saucepan, bring to the boil and reduce to 3 tablespoons by boiling rapidly. Remove from the heat and brush the syrup over the figs. Sprinkle with the pinenuts and allow to set.
6. Dust with icing sugar and serve immediately.

 MUSCAT DE RIVESALTES

WILD (PINK) GOOSEBERRY TART

SERVES 6–8

For the pastry
170g/6oz flour quantity sweet pastry (see page 643)

For the filling
310g/11oz wild gooseberries, hulled (if only cultivated gooseberries are available, cut them in half lengthways)
55g/2oz caster sugar
2 tablespoons ground rice
1 egg
2 yolks
4 tablespoons double cream, lightly whipped

1. Preheat the oven to 180°C/350°F/gas mark 4.
2. Roll out the pastry and use to line a 20cm/8in loose-based flan ring.
3. Mix the gooseberries in a bowl with 2 tablespoons of the sugar.
4. Sprinkle the ground rice over the base of the flan case, then spread the gooseberries in a single layer on top.
5. Whisk the egg, egg yolks and remaining sugar together until thick, pale and creamy. Fold in the cream.
6. Coat the gooseberries evenly with the egg mixture, then bake the tart in the centre of the preheated oven for 20–30 minutes, or until pale golden and set. Allow to cool for 15 minutes before serving.

 *MONBAZILLAC OR LOUPIAC*

PEACH TORTE

SERVES 4

For the peach compote
4 ripe peaches
55g/2oz granulated sugar
5 tablespoons water
5 tablespoons white wine

For the pastry
110g/4oz butter
30g/1oz caster sugar
225g/8oz self-raising flour
vanilla essence
1 tablespoon olive oil
½ beaten egg

To finish
icing sugar

To serve
Greek yoghurt

1. Plunge the peaches into boiling water for 1 minute, then cool in a bowl of cold water. Peel off the skins and halve the peaches. Remove the stones, then slice.
2. Dissolve the sugar in the water and wine in a heavy-based saucepan over a low heat. Bring to the boil, then lower the heat and simmer for 5 minutes, or until the syrup has reduced by half. Add the peach slices and cook for 5–6 minutes, or until the peaches are very soft and beginning to break up. Remove from the syrup with a slotted spoon and set aside. Continue to boil the syrup until it is sticky, then pour over the peaches and allow to cool.
3. Cream the butter and sugar together in a bowl until light and fluffy, add the flour, vanilla essence and oil, and bind together with beaten egg. Wrap in clingfilm and chill in the refrigerator for 2–3 hours, or until very firm.
4. Preheat the oven to 190°C/375°F/gas mark 5.
5. Coarsely grate the pastry and put half in a shallow pie dish. Arrange the peaches and syrup on top, sprinkle with the remaining grated pastry and press lightly together.
6. Bake in the preheated oven for 30–35 minutes, or until golden-brown.
7. To serve: dust generously with icing sugar and serve warm. Hand the yoghurt separately.

 *MUSCAT DE BEAUMES DE VENISE*

PEACH SHORTBREAD

SERVES 10

For the shortbread
140g/5oz butter, softened
grated zest of 1 large orange
70g/2½oz caster sugar
225g/8oz plain flour, sifted
a pinch of salt

For the topping
10 ripe peaches
4 tablespoons soft dark brown sugar
290ml/½ pint double cream, whipped

To finish
55g/2oz shelled pistachios, roasted
a few sprigs of fresh mint

1. Make the shortbread: mix the butter together with the orange zest and sugar. Add the flour and salt and mix to a stiff dough.
2. Press the dough into the bottom of a 28cm/11in loose-based fluted flan ring. Flatten the surface with a palette knife and prick holes all over the pastry with a fork, making sure you press the fork right down to the base of the dough. Take a large knife and cut right through the shortbread, making 10 even slices. Chill for 30 minutes.
3. Cut the peaches in half and remove the stones. Cut each half into 3 wedges. Place the wedges in a large bowl and sprinkle over the sugar. Stir the peaches gently together until they are all coated with the sugar. Set side for 30 minutes.
4. Meanwhile, preheat the oven to 170°C/325°F/gas mark 3.
5. Bake the shortbread in the preheated oven for 30 minutes, or until pale golden. Re-cut along the dividing lines marked earlier. Leave the shortbread to cool for 5 minutes before transferring to a wire rack to cool completely.
6. When the shortbread is cold, transfer it carefully to a large flat serving dish, arranging it back into the original circle. Spread the cream over the base, leaving a 2.5cm/1in gap all around the edge and piling the cream up around the edge a little.
7. Toss the peaches together again and pile them neatly into the centre of the cream. Scatter over the pistachios and arrange the sprigs of mint around the edge before serving.

NOTE: The shortbread should be assembled at the last moment or it will go soft. Alternatively, once the shortbread is cold, a layer of melted white chocolate could be spread over and allowed to set. The pudding can then be assembled before the meal begins.

 *MONBAZILLAC*

PLUM AND HAZELNUT FRANGIPANE TARTLETS

SERVES 4

170g/6oz flour quantity pâte sucrée (see page 645)

For the hazelnut frangipane
125g/4½oz butter, softened
125g/4½oz caster sugar
1 egg
1 egg yolk
125g/4½oz ground hazelnuts, browned
1 tablespoon plain flour
1 tablespoon brandy
4 ripe plums, stoned and thickly sliced
4 tablespoons redcurrant jelly, warmed

To serve
crème fraîche

1. Preheat the oven to 190°C/375°F/gas mark 5.
2. Roll out the pastry thinly and use to line 4 × 10cm/4in tartlet tins. Chill for 30 minutes.
3. Make the hazelnut frangipane: cream the butter in a bowl, gradually beat in the sugar and continue beating until the mixture is light and fluffy. Gradually add the egg and egg yolk, beating well after each addition. Stir in the ground hazelnuts, flour and brandy.

4. Divide the mixture between the tart cases and spread flat.

5. Bake in the preheated oven for 15–20 minutes, or until the pastry is lightly browned and the frangipane firm to the touch.

6. Transfer to a wire rack to cool. A short time before serving arrange slices of plum on the top of each tart and brush with warm redcurrant jelly. Serve at room temperature with crème fraîche.

 *AUSTRALIAN BOTRYTISED SÉMILLON*

TARTELETTES COEUR À LA CRÈME

SERVES 8

2-egg quantity pâte sucrée (see page 645)
6 tablespoons Petit Suisse cream cheese or
  mascarpone
2–3 teaspoons caster sugar
alpine strawberries
redcurrant jelly

1. Roll out the pastry and use to line 8 tartlet tins or bateau moulds. Chill for 30 minutes, then bake blind (see page 640). Allow to cool.

2. Put the cream cheese into a bowl and beat to a smooth paste, adding sugar to taste.

3. Fill the cold pastry cases with the cheese and cover generously with the strawberries.

4. Warm the redcurrant jelly and brush over the fruit. Allow to set.

 *ROSÉ*

PEACH, RICOTTA AND CINNAMON LASAGNE

SERVES 4

½ quantity cinnamon and almond pasta (see
  page 653)
225g/8oz ricotta cheese

110g/4oz mascarpone
1 tablespoon Curaçao liqueur or peach brandy
2 tablespoons caster sugar
1 teaspoon ground cinnamon
4 ripe peaches or nectarines
1 litre/1¾ pints apple juice
570ml/1 pint water
butter for greasing

For the custard
425ml/¾ pint milk
55g/2oz sugar
3 eggs
1 egg yolk

To finish
110g/4oz flaked almonds, toasted

1. Roll the pasta into a long, very thin strip and cut into 10 × 7.5cm/4 × 3in rectangles. Lay out individually on a floured surface.

2. Mix together the ricotta, mascarpone, liqueur, caster sugar and cinnamon.

3. Halve the peaches, remove the stones and slice. Set aside.

4. Heat the apple juice and water in a large sauté pan, add the lasagne sheets and cook for 2–3 minutes, or until *al dente*.

5. Preheat the oven to 170°C/325°F/gas mark 3.

6. Line a 25cm/10in oval buttered ovenproof dish with 2–3 rectangles of the cooked pasta, spoon on a quarter of the ricotta mixture and arrange over a few slices of peach. Cover with pasta and continue to layer the lasagne finishing with a layer of pasta.

7. Make the custard: bring the milk and sugar to scalding point in a saucepan, then remove from the heat and allow to cool. Beat the eggs in a bowl, pour on the milk, mix well and strain on to the pasta.

8. Bake the lasagne in the preheated oven for 1 hour, or until the custard is just set. Remove from the oven, sprinkle the almonds on top and serve.

 *BUAL MADEIRA*

CAKES AND PÂTISSERIE

STICKY CHOCOLATE AND RUM CAKE WITH POACHED MULBERRIES

SERVES 6

170g/6oz good-quality plain chocolate
85g/3oz butter
55g/2oz caster sugar
3 eggs, separated
55g/2oz ground almonds
3 tablespoons fresh white breadcrumbs,
    preferably brioche
2 tablespoons rum

For the mulberries
170g/6oz caster sugar
2 tablespoons crème de cassis
225g/8oz mulberries

To serve
Greek yoghurt

1. Preheat the oven to 190°C/375°F/gas mark 5.
2. Prepare a 20cm/8in moule-à-manqué tin (see page 57).
3. Put the chocolate and butter into a heatproof bowl set over, not in, a saucepan of simmering water. Stir until melted, then remove from the heat and allow to cool for 2 minutes.
4. Stir half the sugar and the egg yolks into the chocolate mixture and set aside.
5. Whisk the egg whites until stiff but not dry, and whisk in the remaining sugar.
6. Add the ground almonds, breadcrumbs, egg white and rum to the chocolate mixture and fold swiftly together.
7. Pile the mixture into the prepared tin and smooth the top with a spatula. Bake in the middle of the preheated oven for 25–30 minutes, or until the cake is just cooked, it should be slightly sticky in the middle.
8. Transfer the cake to a wire rack and leave to cool completely. Peel off the lining paper.
9. Meanwhile, cook the mulberries: put the sugar, crème de cassis and mulberries into a saucepan and bring to the boil, stirring occasionally. Lower the heat and allow to poach for 25–30 minutes, or until the mulberries are very soft.
10. Lift the mulberries from the cooking liquid and set aside. Reduce the cooking liquid to a syrupy consistency by boiling rapidly, then pour over the mulberries and allow to cool.
11. To serve: cut the cake into wedges and hand the mulberries and yoghurt separately.

 *FORTIFIED SWEET WHITE*

DATE AND GOOSEBERRY CAKE

SERVES 8

170g/6oz gooseberries
3 tablespoons caster sugar
2 tablespoons water
170g/6oz medjool dates
170g/6oz self-raising flour
a pinch of salt
1 teaspoon baking powder
170g/6oz butter, softened
170g/6oz soft light brown sugar
3 eggs, lightly beaten

To serve
double cream, whipped

1. Grease and line the bottom of a 20cm/8in deep spring-form cake tin. Preheat the oven to 180°C/350°F/gas mark 4.
2. Reserve 10 gooseberries. Put the remainder with half the caster sugar and the water into a heavy-based saucepan. Cook over a low heat, stirring gently, until the gooseberries are reduced to a pulp. Pass through a nylon sieve and allow to cool.
3. Cut the dates in half lengthways, remove the stones and chop roughly.
4. Sift the flour with the salt and baking powder.
5. Cream the butter with the sugar until light and fluffy. Gradually beat the eggs into the mixture a little at a time, adding 1 tablespoon of flour if the mixture begins to curdle.
6. Fold in the flour, adding enough water to bring the mixture to dropping consistency.
7. Spread half the mixture over the bottom of the prepared cake tin. Spread over the gooseberry purée and two-thirds of the dates. Spread over the remaining cake mixture.
8. Put the remaining dates and the reserved gooseberries on top and sprinkle with the remaining caster sugar. Bake in the lower half of the preheated oven for 40 minutes, or until the cake is golden-brown and is starting to come away from the edges of the tin.
9. Allow to cool on a wire rack for 15 minutes before removing the tin. Serve warm or cold with the cream.

 ELDERFLOWER SPARKLER (see page 362)

CIGARETTES RUSSES

MAKES APPROX 15

2 egg whites
110g/4oz caster sugar
55g/2oz butter, melted and cooled
55g/2oz plain flour
2–3 drops of vanilla essence

1. Preheat the oven to 190°C/375°F/gas mark 5. Grease a baking sheet or line it with silicone paper.

2. Whisk the egg whites and sugar to a smooth paste in a bowl.
3. Gradually add the butter to the egg whites, alternately with the flour. Stir in the vanilla essence.
4. Spread out teaspoonfuls of the mixture very thinly into oblongs on the prepared baking sheet, keeping them well apart to allow for spreading during baking. Bake in the preheated oven for 5–6 minutes, or until golden-brown.
5. Loosen the cigarettes russes from the baking sheet while still hot. While they are still warm and pliable, curl them round wooden skewers. When they are quite firm slip them off. Leave to cool completely on a wire rack.

PEPPER AND SPICE BRANDY SNAPS

These spiced wafers are an unusual accompaniment to ice cream such as nutmeg and bay leaf (see page 588).

MAKES 24

110g/4oz unsalted butter
110g/4oz demerara sugar
4 tablespoons golden syrup
grated zest and juice of 1 lime
110g/4oz plain flour
1 teaspoon ground ginger
1 teaspoon freshly ground black pepper
1 teaspoon freshly ground coriander seeds
1 dried red chilli, finely chopped

1. Preheat the oven to 180°C/350°F/gas mark 4. Line a baking sheet with silicone paper.
2. Melt the butter, sugar and syrup together in a saucepan. Remove from the heat and add the lime zest and juice.
3. Sift the flour and spices together and stir into melted mixture.
4. Put small teaspoons of the mixture on to the prepared baking sheet, keeping them well apart to allow for spreading during baking, and spread out thinly. Bake in the preheated oven

for 10–12 minutes. Do not allow the mixture to brown too much.

5. Remove from the oven and allow to cool for 1–2 minutes, then transfer to a cooling rack or shape over a lightly oiled rolling pin.

WHITE CHOCOLATE AND MACADAMIA NUT COOKIES

MAKES 8

110g/4oz butter
55g/2oz caster sugar
170g/6oz self-raising flour
a pinch of salt
110g/4oz white chocolate, roughly chopped
110g/4oz unsalted macadamia nuts, roughly
    chopped

1. Preheat the oven to 180°C/350°F/gas mark 4. Line a baking sheet with silicone paper.
2. Put the butter and sugar into a bowl and beat together until pale and creamy.
3. Sift the flour and salt together into the bowl. Add the chocolate and macadamia nuts and mix together until the mixture comes together to form a dough.
4. Divide the mixture into 8 equal portions and shape into balls. Arrange on the prepared baking sheet, keeping them well apart to allow for spreading during baking. Press each ball into a flat round or oval, using lightly floured fingers.
5. Bake in the preheated oven for 10–12 minutes, or until the cookies are a light golden-brown. Allow to cool on the baking sheet for 5 minutes, then transfer to a cooling rack.
6. When cold, store in an airtight container.

BROWN SUGAR SCONES WITH CREAM AND BLACKCURRANT CURD

MAKES 6

225g/8oz self-raising flour
½ teaspoon salt
55g/2oz butter
55g/2oz dark brown Muscovado sugar
150ml/¼ pint milk
1 egg, beaten, to glaze
½ quantity blackcurrant curd (see page 366)
150ml/¼ pint double cream, whipped
    (optional)
55g/2oz fresh blackcurrants

1. Preheat the oven to 200°C/400°F/gas mark 6. Flour a baking sheet.
2. Sift the flour with the salt into a large bowl. Rub in the butter until the mixture resembles breadcrumbs. Stir in half the sugar. Make a deep well in the flour, pour in the milk and mix to a soft, spongy dough with a knife.
3. On a floured surface, knead the dough very lightly until it is just smooth. Roll or press out to about 2.5cm/1in thick and stamp into rounds with a small pastry cutter. Brush with beaten egg and sprinkle over the remaining sugar.
4. Bake at the top of the preheated oven for 7 minutes, or until the scones are well risen and brown. Remove from the oven and leave to cool on a wire rack.
5. To serve: split the scones in half horizontally and place a teaspoonful of blackcurrant curd on the lower half. Put a teaspoonful of cream, if using, on to the curd and garnish with a few blackcurrants. Replace the top half of the scone.

CHERRY AND PECAN MUFFINS

MAKES 12

110g/4oz pecan nuts, halved
125g/4½oz unsalted butter, melted and cooled
225g/8oz self-raising flour
1 teaspoon baking powder
55g/2oz caster sugar
55g/2oz soft dark brown sugar
a pinch of salt
1 teaspoon ground mixed spice
1 egg, lightly beaten
190ml/⅓ pint milk, plus a little extra if
  necessary
225g/8oz fresh cherries, stoned and halved

1. Preheat the oven to 200°C/400°F/gas mark 6.
Line a muffin tray with paper cases.
2. Mix the pecan nuts with 1 tablespoon of the
melted butter and spread them out on to a
baking sheet. Bake in the preheated oven for 8
minutes, then remove from the oven and allow
to cool. Reduce the oven temperature to 180°C/
350°F/gas mark 4.
3. Sift together the flour, baking powder,
sugars, salt and mixed spice in a large bowl.
Make a well in the centre.
4. Put the egg and the remaining butter into the
well and mix with a wooden spoon, gradually
drawing in the flour from the sides as you stir.
Gradually add the milk as you stir, adding a
little extra if necessary to achieve a loose
dropping consistency. Quickly fold in the pecan
nuts and cherries.
5. Fill each muffin case three-quarters full with
the batter. Bake in the middle of the preheated
oven for 30–35 minutes, or until just firm and
golden. Transfer the muffins to a wire rack and
allow to cool before serving.

MISCELLANEOUS

Drinks
Preserves
Breads
Sauces and Garnishes

DRINKS

BLOODY MARY

SERVES 2

12 ripe tomatoes, washed
4 sticks of celery, washed
2.5cm/1in piece of fresh horseradish, peeled
a few drops of Tabasco sauce
juice of 1 lemon
1 teaspoon chopped fresh oregano
2 large dashes of vodka (optional)
salt and freshly ground black pepper

To serve
a few ice cubes
2 small sticks of celery, with leaves

1. Whizz the tomatoes, celery and horseradish in an electric vegetable juice extractor.
2. Add the Tabasco, lemon juice, oregano and vodka and season to taste with salt and pepper.
3. Place a few ice cubes in 2 large glasses and pour over the juice. Garnish with the sticks of celery and serve immediately.

CASSIS

This tried and trusted recipe was taken from *Country Wines, Beers and Beverages* by Brian Leverett, published in 1988.

MAKES 570ML/1 PINT

340g/12oz blackcurrants
about 425ml/¾ pint vodka
200g/7oz caster sugar

1. Put the blackcurrants into a large bowl and crush them with the end of a rolling pin. Add half the vodka.

2. Pour the mixture into a large sterilized jar, cover and leave to macerate for 1 month.
3. Pour the caster sugar through a funnel into a clean wine bottle.
4. Line a fine sieve with muslin or a clean J-cloth. Strain the macerated blackcurrants. If the liquor is not clear, strain it again through a strong filter paper (e.g. for a coffee filter machine).
5. Pour the liquor through the funnel on to the sugar in the bottle, and top up with extra vodka if necessary. Seal the bottle.
6. Store the bottle in a cool, dry place away from sunlight. Shake at regular intervals until all the sugar has dissolved. Store for 6 months before drinking.

ELDERFLOWER CORDIAL

This recipe was given to us by Caroline Yates, a teacher at Leith's School. The cordial makes a refreshing summer drink which needs to be diluted, with sparkling mineral water and ice added to taste.

MAKES 2.8 LITRES/5 PINTS

20 elderflower heads
900g/2lb soft light brown sugar
900g/2lb caster sugar
85g/3oz citric acid
thinly pared zest and juice of 3 lemons
1.7 litres/3 pints water, boiled and cooled to
*   room temperature*

1. Put all the ingredients into a large bowl, stir well, cover and leave in a cool place for 5 days.
2. Strain through a piece of muslin and pour into sterilized, dry bottles. Seal and allow to stand for 3–4 weeks before use.

ELDERFLOWER SPARKLER

This recipe is taken from *Home-made Wines, Syrups and Cordials*, published by the National Federation Women's Institutes.

MAKES 4.5 LITRES/8 PINTS

2 elderflower heads, in full bloom and
    unblemished
thinly pared zest and juice of 1 lemon
675g/1½lb caster sugar
2 tablespoons white wine vinegar
4.5 litres/8 pints water

1. Put the elderflower heads into a large bowl with the lemon zest and juice, sugar and vinegar.
2. Add the water, cover with a clean tea-towel and leave to soak for 24 hours, stirring occasionally, until the sugar has dissolved.
3. Strain the liquid and pour through a funnel into sterilized screwtop or wire-top bottles. Seal the bottles immediately and store in a cool, dark place for 2 weeks.
4. Serve chilled.

ELDERFLOWER MUSCAT SYRUP

The flavour of this syrup is reminiscent of the muscat grape. It is a perfect addition when making gooseberry fool.

MAKES 2 LITRES

10 elderflower heads (umbels)
1 litre/1¾ pints water
225g/8oz granulated sugar
thinly pared zest of 1 lemon

1. Rinse the elderflowers and shake well.
2. Put the water and sugar into a saucepan and heat gently until the sugar has completely dissolved. Bring to the boil, then lower the heat and simmer for 3–4 minutes.

3. Add the elderflowers and lemon zest and bring back to the boil, then lower the heat and simmer for 2–3 minutes. Remove the syrup from the heat and allow to cool for 30 minutes.
4. Strain the syrup through muslin or a fine sieve, cool and pour into a sterilized jar (see page 277), cover and store in the refrigerator or freezer. If stored in the refrigerator, it should be used within 1 month.

LAVENDER AND ROSE CHAMPAGNE COCKTAIL

This makes a refreshing summer cocktail as an alternative to Kir Royale. The lavender cordial is also perfect for teetotallers, as it can be made with sparkling water instead of champagne. Rose-water is available from good chemists.

SERVES 4

2 handfuls of lavender flowers and leaves
290ml/½ pint water
150ml/¼ pint rose-water
85g/3oz caster sugar
1 bottle of champagne or sparkling Saumur,
    chilled

To decorate
a few lavender heads or rose petals

1. Wash the lavender and allow to drain and dry for 10 minutes.
2. Put the water, rose-water and sugar into a saucepan and heat gently until the sugar has dissolved. Bring to the boil, then lower the heat and simmer for 1 minute. Remove the pan from the heat, add the lavender and leave to infuse for 30 minutes.
3. Strain the syrup, bring back to the boil, then lower the heat and simmer for a further 5 minutes. Allow to cool, cover and chill.
4. To serve: put 2 tablespoons of the cordial into the bottom of the champagne flute and top up with the champagne. Sprinkle the lavender or rose petals on top.

LIME, GINGER AND LEMON GRASS SYRUP

When diluted with mineral water and plenty of ice added, this makes a cooling summer drink and a perfect accompaniment to a spicy meal.

MAKES 1 LITRE

570ml/1 pint water
140g/5oz granulated sugar
grated zest and juice of 3 limes
5cm/2in piece of root ginger, peeled and grated
2 sticks of lemon grass, sliced
a pinch of salt

1. Put the water, sugar, lime zest, ginger, lemon grass and salt into a saucepan. Place over a low heat until the sugar has completely dissolved. Bring to the boil, then lower the heat and simmer for 5 minutes.
2. Remove from the heat and allow the syrup to infuse for 30 minutes. Add the lime juice, strain and refrigerate.

MARROW RUM

This recipe came from Viv Pidgeon who tested many of the recipes in the book. She comes from a family with a reputation for fine home-made wines and her grandfather used to make this whenever there was a glut of marrows. Apparently it works in the same way with pineapples

MAKES APPROX 570ML/1 PINT

1 medium marrow
1.1kg/2¼lb granulated sugar
450g/1lb demerara sugar
juice of 2 lemons

1. Cut the marrow in half horizontally, about two-thirds of the way up from the base. Remove the seeds and the pith surrounding them.
2. Mix the granulated and demerara sugar together and pack 900g/2lb into the centre of the marrow with the lemon juice.
3. Replace the marrow lid and secure with string or sellotape. Bore a hole in the base of the marrow. Slide the marrow into a clean stocking and tie the end.
4. Tie each end of the stocking with string and suspend the marrow in a cool place over a demi-john (wine-making vessel) on a table. Make sure the bore hole is about 5–10cm/2–4in directly above the funnel so it catches the drips.
5. Allow the liquid that forms to drop on to the funnel leading into the demi-john. When the liquid has finished dripping into the vessel top it up with water and the remaining 110g/4oz of the sugar.
6. Place the air lock in the top of the demi-john and allow fermentation to proceed until the bubbles cease to escape from the air lock.
7. As the rum ferments there will be a collection of sediment on the bottom of the demi-john. It is important to syphon the rum into a clean demi-john, leaving the sediment behind, or the rum may begin to taste musty.
8. Leave the rum to stand in the clean demi-john for a week or so until you are sure that there is no more sediment. Bottle the rum and store in a cool place – it will keep almost indefinitely.

ROSE BLOSSOM PUNCH

SERVES 4

2 litres/3½ pints dry white wine, chilled
120ml/4fl oz kirsch
2 tablespoons rose-water

To decorate
small pink unsprayed rose petals, rinsed and
*   patted dry*

1. Put the wine, kirsch and rose-water into a large punch bowl.
2. Serve sprinkled with the rose petals.

SPARKLING BERRY COOLER

SERVES 6

170g/6oz soft fruit, such as strawberries,
raspberries, mulberries, blueberries,
blackberries, chilled
1 tablespoon caster sugar
1 bottle of sparkling dry white wine, well
chilled

To serve
a few fresh berries, halved if large
a few sprigs of fresh mint

1. Whizz the fruit and sugar in a food processor and pass through a fine nylon sieve. Pour the juice into a large glass jug.
2. Pour the sparkling wine on to the juice.
3. Put a few of the fresh berries into 6 large wine or champagne glasses. Pour in the juice and decorate with sprigs of mint. Serve immediately.

PRESERVES

BLACKBERRY VINEGAR

MAKES 1 LITRE/1¾ PINTS

1.1 litres/2 pints cider vinegar or white wine vinegar
1kg/2¼lb ripe blackberries, washed if necessary

1. Bring the vinegar to the boil in a saucepan and simmer for 2 minutes. Set aside to cool to 40°C/104°F.
2. Roughly chop the blackberries and transfer them to a large glass bowl or jar.
3. Pour over the warm vinegar and mix together. Cover the bowl or jar with a clean tea-towel and leave to stand in a warm room or on a sunny windowsill for 2 weeks, stirring occasionally.
4. Strain the vinegar through a jelly bag and pour the liquid into sterilized bottles (see page 277).

NOTE: The vinegar can be used straight away but the flavour will improve with keeping.

ELDERFLOWER VINEGAR

This vinegar captures the delicate fragrance of elderflowers beautifully and is an easy and effective way of using the heads or 'umbels' as they are in season for such a short period of time in the early summer.

MAKES 1 LITRE/1¾ PINTS

10 elderflower heads (umbels)
1 litre/1¾ pints white wine vinegar

1. Wash the elderflowers, shake well to remove excess liquid and allow to dry for 30 minutes.
2. Put the vinegar into a bowl with the elderflowers, cover and allow to infuse for 5 days. Strain through muslin or a fine cloth and store in sterilized bottles.

NOTE: For best results use within 6 months.

SWEET RASPBERRY VINEGAR

This traditional recipe was given to us by Ann Jackson. It is time-consuming to make but the end-result is delicious and bears little resemblance to bottles of shop-bought 'infused' raspberry vinegar. The vinegar is very sweet and can be used as a sauce for ice creams. At Leith's it is also used for raspberry vinegar bavarois.

MAKES 1 LITRE/1¾ PINTS

1.6kg/3½lb fresh raspberries
1.1 litres/2 pints white wine vinegar
450g/1lb preserving sugar to each 570ml/1 pint flavoured vinegar

1. Put 450g/1lb of the raspberries into a nylon sieve and rinse under cold running water. Stir well and crush the raspberries lightly with a fork. Put the raspberries into a bowl with the vinegar, cover and refrigerate for 24 hours.
2. Strain the raspberries and vinegar into a bowl, pressing well to extract as much moisture as possible, without pushing any of the pulp through the sieve.

3. Add another 450g/1lb of the raspberries to the strained raspberry vinegar. Crush with a fork, cover and refrigerate for a further 24 hours.

4. Strain and repeat the same process with the remaining raspberries.

5. On the fourth day, strain the vinegar from the raspberries and filter through a clean J-cloth or piece of muslin. Measure the raspberry vinegar and add 450g/1lb of preserving sugar to each 570ml/1 pint vinegar. Place both the sugar and vinegar in a heavy-based saucepan. Heat gently until the sugar has completely dissolved, then bring to the boil and boil for 4–5 minutes. Skim if necessary, remove from the heat and allow to cool.

6. Pour into screwtop sterilized bottles (see page 277), seal and label.

NOTE: This vinegar will keep for about 6 months in a cool, dark cupboard.

ROSE PETAL VINEGAR

This vinegar is time-consuming to make, but makes an unusual dressing.

MAKES 1 LITRE/1¾ PINTS

225g/8oz fresh unbruised rose petals, preferably red
55g/2oz caster sugar
1 litre/1¾ pints white wine vinegar

1. Arrange the rose petals in a single layer on a clean tea-towel and leave to dry for 2–3 days in a cool place, away from direct sunlight.

2. Put the shrunken petals into a bowl, sprinkle with the sugar and pound with a rolling pin or in a pestle and mortar.

3. Pour over the vinegar and allow to infuse for 4–5 days.

4. Strain the vinegar through muslin and store in sterilized bottles.

NOTE: The vinegar will keep its flavour well for 5–6 months.

BLACKCURRANT CURD

MAKES 450G/1LB

200g/7oz blackcurrants, fresh or frozen
85g/3oz butter, diced
225g/8oz granulated sugar
3 eggs, lightly beaten

1. Whizz the currants in a food processor for 30 seconds.

2. Put the blackcurrants, butter, sugar and eggs into a heavy-based saucepan or double boiler and heat gently, stirring constantly, until the mixture is thick.

3. Strain through a fine sieve into warmed, dry, sterilized jars and cover.

NOTES: The curd will keep in the refrigerator for about 3 weeks.

If the curd is boiled, no great harm is done, as the acid and sugar prevent the eggs from scrambling.

CHERRY JAM

MAKES 2 × 225G/8OZ

450g/1lb under-ripe cherries, washed and stoned
450g/1lb preserving sugar

1. Put the cherries and sugar together in a non-metallic bowl and leave to stand overnight.

2. The following day, tip the cherries and sugar into a preserving pan or large saucepan and heat gently until the sugar has dissolved. Bring to the boil and boil the jam rapidly, skimming off any scum that rises to the surface, until it reaches setting point (see page 103). This takes about 5 minutes.

3. Allow the jam to stand for 15 minutes, which will prevent the cherries rising to the top in the jars.

4. Pour the jam into warmed, dry, sterilized jars (see page 277).

5. Cover and label the jars.

6. Leave undisturbed overnight, then store in a cool, dark, airy place.

SEMI-DRIED FIG CONSERVE

MAKES 1KG/2¼LB

20 figs, washed and dried
2 tablespoons granulated sugar
a pinch of ground ginger
a pinch of ground coriander

For the syrup
150ml/¼ pint crème de mûr (blackberry liqueur)
150ml/¼ pint water
55g/2oz granulated sugar
1 tablespoon black peppercorns
1 cinnamon stick

1. Preheat the oven to 80°C/175°F/gas mark ¼.
2. Halve the figs and lay them in a single layer on a baking sheet.
3. Mix together the sugar, ginger and coriander and sprinkle over the figs. Bake in the preheated oven for 4 hours, or until shrivelled but still soft.
4. Meanwhile, make the syrup: put all the ingredients into a saucepan. Set over a low heat until the sugar has dissolved, then bring to the boil. Lower the heat and simmer for 10 minutes, then strain into a clean saucepan.
5. Add the semi-dried figs, bring back to the boil and pack into warmed, dry, sterilized jars (see page 277). Store in the refrigerator until required.

NOTE: As this conserve has a low sugar content it will not store in the same way as a conventional jam or preserve. Use within 1 week.

ALPINE STRAWBERRY AND GOOSEBERRY CONSERVE

MAKES 2 × 450G/1LB

450g/1lb alpine strawberries
450g/1lb gooseberries, washed and dried
900g/2lb warmed preserving sugar
150ml/¼ pint Grand Marnier

1. Hull the strawberries and top, tail and halve the gooseberries.
2. Layer the fruit and sugar together in a non-metallic bowl and leave to stand for 8 hours.
3. Transfer the mixture to a preserving pan or a large saucepan. Heat gently until the sugar has dissolved, then bring to the boil and boil rapidly for 5 minutes. Allow to cool, transfer into a non-metallic container and add the Grand Marnier. Allow to stand overnight.
4. The following day, transfer to a preserving pan, bring to the boil and cook until setting point is reached. Allow to stand for 15 minutes.
5. Pour into warmed, dry, sterilized jars (see page 277).
6. Cover and label the jars and leave undisturbed overnight. Store in a cool, dark, airy place.

RED SUMMER FRUIT AND PICKLED GINGER JAM

MAKES 900G/2LB

900g/2lb strawberries
900g/2lb raspberries
450g/1lb redcurrants
1 tablespoon water
3 tablespoons peeled and grated fresh root ginger
5 tablespoons rice wine vinegar
1.8kg/4lb preserving sugar
juice of 2 lemons

1. Hull the strawberries and raspberries and remove the stalks from the redcurrants, using the prongs of a fork.
2. Put the redcurrants into a preserving pan or large saucepan with the water. Cook to form a pulp (about 5 minutes).
3. Add the strawberries and raspberries and bring to the boil.
4. Put the ginger and vinegar into a small saucepan and simmer for 5–7 minutes. Remove from the heat and set aside.
5. Add the sugar to the fruit and when

dissolved, boil rapidly for 20–25 minutes, or until the jam reaches setting point. Stir in the ginger mixture. Remove from the heat and allow to cool for 15 minutes. This will prevent the berries from rising to the top in the jars. Allow to stand for 10 minutes.

6. Pour into warmed, dry, sterilized jars (see page 277).

7. Cover and label the jars. Leave undisturbed overnight.

8. Store in a cool, dark, airy place.

STONE FRUIT JAM WITH SAUTERNES AND PASSION FRUIT

MAKES 2KG

450g/1lb plums
450g/1lb nectarines
450g/1lb peaches
450g/1lb apricots
290ml/½ pint Sauternes wine
grated zest and juice of 4 limes
1.3kg/3lb warmed preserving sugar
pulp of 10 ripe passion fruit

1. Wash, halve, stone and slice the plums, nectarines, peaches and apricots.

2. Put the fruit into a preserving pan or large saucepan with the wine and lime zest and juice. Simmer for 12–15 minutes, or until the fruit is soft.

3. Add the sugar and passion fruit and allow the sugar to dissolve, then boil rapidly until setting point is reached. Allow to stand for 10 minutes.

4. Pour into warmed, dry, sterilized jars (see page 277), cover and label.

5. Store in a cool, dark, airy place.

HOT PRESERVED PEACHES AND NECTARINES

MAKES 4KG/8½LB

900g/2lb peaches
900g/2lb nectarines
675g/1½lb soft light brown sugar
425ml/¾ pint rice wine vinegar
½ teaspoon ground mixed spice
1 teaspoon wasabi paste
grated zest and juice of 2 limes
1 cinnamon stick
1 bay leaf
2.5cm/1in piece of fresh root ginger, peeled and grated

1. Peel the fruit by plunging first into boiling water for 1 minute, then into cold water. Peel off the skins. Halve the fruit and remove the stones, then slice thickly.

2. Place the sugar, vinegar, spice, wasabi, lime zest and juice, cinnamon stick, bay leaf and ginger in a large saucepan or preserving pan. Heat gently until the sugar has dissolved, then bring to the boil and simmer for 5 minutes.

3. Add the prepared fruit and simmer for 12–15 minutes, or until the fruit is soft but not breaking up. Remove the cinnamon stick and bay leaf.

4. Remove from the heat and allow to cool for 10 minutes. Pack into warmed, dry, sterilized jars (see page 277), cover and label. Store in a cool, dark, airy place for 1 month before using.

NOTE: This unusual stone fruit preserve is delightful with crumpets or scones for tea, or as an accompaniment to ice cream.

GOOSEBERRY AND TOMATO CHUTNEY

MAKES 8 × 225G/8OZ

900g/2lb gooseberries, topped and tailed
900g/2lb ripe tomatoes, roughly chopped
450g/1lb red onions, chopped
4 large cloves of garlic, finely chopped
5cm/2in stem ginger, peeled and finely chopped
225g/8oz sultanas
1 tablespoon salt
900g/2lb soft light brown sugar
1.1 litres/2 pints cider vinegar

1. Put all the ingredients into a large heavy-based saucepan and stir gently over a low heat until the sugar has dissolved.
2. Bring the chutney to the boil, then lower the heat and simmer gently for about 2 hours, until the vegetables are soft and the chutney has a good thick consistency.
3. Pour the chutney into warmed, dry, sterilized jars (see page 277) and seal. Store in a cool, dark, airy place for 1 month before using.

RASPBERRY AND SULTANA CHUTNEY

MAKES 4 × 225G/8OZ

900g/2lb raspberries
2 large onions, thinly sliced
2 large Bramley apples, peeled, cored and cut
 into 2.5cm/1in cubes
4 cloves of garlic, finely chopped
225g/8oz sultanas
1 tablespoon mustard seeds
450g/1lb soft light brown sugar
1 litre/1¾ pints raspberry or white wine vinegar
1 teaspoon salt

1. Put all the ingredients into a large heavy-based saucepan. Stir over a low heat until the sugar has dissolved. Bring to the boil, then lower the heat and simmer gently for 1 hour,

until very soft and a good thick consistency.
2. Pour into warmed, dry, sterilized jars (see page 277) and seal. Store in a cool, dark, airy place for at least 1 month before using.

RUMTOPF

Rumtopf is fun to make over the summer as the different fruits come into season, and can then be enjoyed as a warming influence over the cold winter months.

450G/1LB FRUIT SERVES 4 PEOPLE

fresh summer fruits, such as strawberries,
 raspberries, blackberries, plums, cherries,
 redcurrants and blackcurrants, unbruised
 and in good condition
225g/8oz caster sugar to each 450g/1lb fruit
dark rum

1. Weigh the fruit to calculate the amount of sugar needed.
2. Put the fruit into a large bowl and sprinkle over the weighed sugar. Leave the fruit for at least 1 hour, or until the juices begin to seep out and the sugar begins to dissolve.
3. Carefully transfer the fruit to a rumtopf pot (or large ceramic pot with lid) and pour in enough rum to cover the fruit by 2.5cm/1in. Put a layer of clingfilm directly over the fruit and a small saucer or plate if necessary to keep the fruit submerged in the rum.
4. Cover the top of the jar with another piece of clingfilm, which will prevent the alcohol from evaporating, and place the rumtopf jar lid on top. Store the jar in a cool, dark place.
5. Continue to add fruit to the pot as it comes into season over the summer following the same method.
6. The rumtopf is ready to use 3 months after the last fruit has been added.

NOTE: Rumtopf can be served on its own or with ice cream, or you can add the fruit to crumbles and other fruit puddings to make them more exciting. The rum syrup can be served on its own as a liqueur after a meal.

BREADS

CHERRY TOMATO AND ARTICHOKE PICNIC BREAD

MAKES 8 ROLLS

For the bread
20g/¾oz fresh yeast
290ml/½ pint warm milk
1 teaspoon soft dark brown sugar
225g/8oz granary or wholemeal flour
225g/8oz strong plain white flour
2 teaspoons salt
2 teaspoons dried herbes de Provence
3 tablespoons extra virgin olive oil
1 egg, beaten

For the filling
675g/1½lb cherry tomatoes, halved
8 artichoke hearts, canned or fresh, cooked and
    quartered
8 anchovies, chopped
4 tablespoons extra virgin olive oil
2 tablespoons chopped fresh thyme
1 tablespoon chopped fresh rosemary
1 teaspoon caster sugar
freshly ground black pepper

For the glaze
extra virgin olive oil
2 tablespoons freshly grated Parmesan cheese

1. Dissolve the yeast with a little of the milk and the sugar in a tea cup.
2. Sift the flours with the salt into a mixing bowl and add the bran from the sieve and the herbes de Provence.

3. Pour in the yeast mixture, oil, egg and three-quarters of the remaining milk and mix to a fairly slack dough, adding more milk if necessary. When the dough will leave the sides of the bowl, press it into a ball and tip it out on to a floured board. Knead until elastic, smooth and shiny (about 15 minutes).
4. Put the dough back into the bowl and cover it with a piece of lightly greased clingfilm. Put it into a warm place (on a shelf above a radiator, in the airing cupboard or a draughtproof corner of the kitchen). Leave it until the dough has doubled in bulk (at least 1 hour).
5. Make the filling: mix all the ingredients together and season with pepper.
6. Preheat the oven to 200°C/400°F/gas mark 6.
7. Take the dough out of the bowl, knock down and knead for 2 minutes. Divide the dough into 8 equal pieces and shape them into ovals about 10cm/4in long.
8. Using a sharp knife, slash a deep cut down the centre of each roll, three-quarters of the way through the dough. Open out the edges of the cut, making a pocket, and pile a large spoonful of the filling into the centre. Place on a baking sheet. Fill the remaining rolls in the same way, using up all the filling.
9. Glaze the edges of the rolls with the olive oil.
10. Cover the rolls with lightly greased clingfilm and leave in a warm place for 10 minutes.
11. Remove the clingfilm, sprinkle the rolls with the Parmesan cheese and bake at the top of the preheated oven for 10 minutes. Reduce the oven temperature to 180°C/350°F/gas mark 4 and bake for a further 15–20 minutes, or until the bread is golden-brown on both the top and the bottom.
12. Transfer the rolls to a wire rack and allow to cool a little before serving.

FOCACCIA WITH CHEESE

This recipe was given to us by Ursula Ferrigno.

SERVES 4

370g/13oz unbleached strong white flour
2 teaspoons coarse sea salt, plus a little extra for
*   sprinkling*
7g/¼oz fresh yeast
200ml/7fl oz lukewarm water
3 tablespoons olive oil
140g/5oz mozzarella, sliced
140g/5oz Gorgonzola
salt and freshly ground black pepper
2 tablespoons chopped fresh basil or sage

To garnish
a few sprigs of fresh rosemary
extra virgin olive oil

1. Sift the flour and salt into a large mixing bowl. Make a well in the centre.
2. Dissolve the yeast in a little of the water, add the oil and pour the liquid into the well.
3. Gradually stir the liquid with a wooden spoon, slowly incorporating the flour. When it is all incorporated the dough should be of a very soft consistency. Turn the dough out on to a clean work surface and knead for 10 minutes or until the dough is smooth, soft and springy, adding a little extra flour if the dough is a little too sticky to handle.
4. Put the dough into a lightly oiled bowl, cover with clingfilm and leave to rise in a warm, draught-free place for about 1 hour, or until doubled in bulk.
5. Punch the air out of the dough and knead again for a few minutes to get rid of any large pockets of air. Divide the dough into 2 equal portions.
6. Roll each portion of dough into a 30cm/12in diameter circle. Place one circle on a greased baking sheet. Spread the cheeses over the dough and season with salt and pepper. Sprinkle over the basil or sage leaves and place the remaining circle of dough directly on top. Press the edges together.
7. Cover with a lightly greased piece of clingfilm and leave to prove (rise) in a warm, draught-free place for 20 minutes.

8. Preheat the oven to 200°C/400°F/gas mark 6.
9. Remove the clingfilm and make dimples in the top of the dough with your fingertips. Sprinkle with a little sea salt, rosemary and oil.
10. Bake near the top of the oven for about 35–40 minutes or until golden-brown. Cool on a wire rack for 30 minutes to set the cheese before serving.

NOTE: The bread will keep fresh for 18 hours.

SPINACH AND SAFFRON BREAD

This is a delicious loaf which is exciting to look at and excellent for sophisticated sandwiches and dramatic dinner parties.

MAKES 2 LOAVES

For the spinach dough
15g/½oz fresh yeast
45ml/1½fl oz warm water
1 egg, beaten
450g/1lb fresh spinach, blanched, refreshed and
*   finely chopped*
450g/1lb strong plain flour
2 teaspoons salt
½ teaspoon freshly grated nutmeg
freshly ground black pepper
30g/1oz butter

For the saffron dough
1 large pinch of saffron strands or 1 heaped
*   teaspoon ground turmeric*
150ml/¼ pint boiling water
15g/½oz fresh yeast
150ml/¼ pint lukewarm milk
450g/1lb strong plain flour
2 teaspoons salt
30g/1oz butter
1 egg, lightly beaten

1. Make the spinach dough: dissolve the yeast with a little of the water in a cup. Mix together with the remaining water, egg and spinach.
2. Sift the flour with the salt, nutmeg and

pepper into a large mixing bowl and rub in the butter with the fingertips.

3. Pour in the yeast mixture and mix to a softish dough, adding more water if necessary. When the dough will leave the sides of the bowl, press it into a ball and tip it out on to a floured board. Knead until it is elastic, smooth and shiny (about 15 minutes). Put the dough back into the bowl and cover it with a piece of lightly greased clingfilm.

4. Make the saffron dough: put the saffron strands into the boiling water in a small bowl and leave to infuse until the water is lukewarm.

5. Dissolve the yeast with a little of the milk in a cup.

6. Sift the flour with the salt into a warmed large bowl and rub in the butter. Pour in the saffron liquid, the yeast mixture and the egg and mix to a softish dough with the remaining water. Knead, then place in a bowl, covered, as for the spinach bread.

7. Put both bowls in a warm, draught-free place and leave them to rise until the doughs have doubled in bulk (at least 1 hour).

8. Preheat the oven to 200°C/400°F/gas mark 6. Lightly grease 2 baking sheets.

9. Punch the doughs back down into the bowls and cut each in half. Take one piece of spinach dough and place on top of a piece of saffron dough. Roll out to form a rectangle about 40 × 22.5cm/16 × 9in.

10. Roll the sheet of dough up from the narrow end and place on a greased baking sheet, seam side down. Repeat with the remaining pieces of dough.

11. Cover the loaves with oiled clingfilm and prove (allow to rise again) in a warm, draught-free place (10–15 minutes).

12. Using a sharp knife, cut 5 slashes 1cm/½in deep in the top of each loaf and sprinkle with flour. Bake at the top of the preheated oven for about 25 minutes, or until the loaves are golden and sound hollow when tapped on the underside.

13. Transfer to a wire rack to cool before serving.

SICHUAN-STYLE NAAN BREAD

MAKES 8

450g/1lb strong plain flour
1 teaspoon salt
15g/½oz fresh yeast
1 teaspoon sugar
90–150ml/3–5fl oz warm milk
2 tablespoons sesame oil
150ml/¼ pint fromage frais or plain yoghurt
1 egg, beaten
1 tablespoon Sichuan peppercorns, dry-roasted
*   and crushed*

1. Sift the flour and salt into a bowl.

2. Cream the yeast with the sugar, then mix with the milk, oil, fromage frais or yoghurt and the egg.

3. Mix the yeast mixture into the flour to form a soft but not sticky dough. Knead for 5 minutes or until smooth.

4. Put the dough into an oiled bowl. Cover with greased clingfilm and leave to rise in a warm, draught-free place until doubled in bulk.

5. Turn the dough on to a floured board and knead for a further 5 minutes. Knead the peppercorns into the bread.

6. Divide the dough into 8 equal pieces and roll each piece into an oval measuring about 12.5 × 20cm/5 × 8in. Place on a greased baking sheet, cover with clingfilm and leave to rise for about 15 minutes, or until 1½ times the original bulk.

7. Preheat the grill.

8. Brush the bread with water and grill on each side for 3 minutes or until well browned. Serve warm.

BRIOCHE

MAKES 1 LARGE OR 12 SMALL BRIOCHES

7g/¼oz fresh yeast
5 teaspoons caster sugar
2 tablespoons warm water
225g/8oz plain white flour
½ teaspoon salt
2 eggs, beaten
55g/2oz melted butter, cool

For the glaze
1 egg, mixed with 1 tablespoon water and 1
  teaspoon sugar

1. Grease a large brioche mould or 12 small
brioche tins.
2. Mix the yeast with 1 teaspoon of the sugar
and the water. Leave to dissolve.
3. Sift the flour with the salt into a mixing
bowl. Sprinkle over the remaining sugar. Make
a well in the centre. Drop in the eggs, yeast
mixture and melted butter and mix with the
fingers of one hand to a soft but not sloppy
paste. Knead on an unfloured board for 5
minutes or until smooth. Put into a clean bowl,
cover with a damp cloth or lightly oiled
clingfilm and leave to rise in a warm, draught-
free place until doubled in bulk (about 1 hour).
4. Turn out and knead again on an unfloured
board for 2 minutes.
5. Place the dough in the brioche mould (it
should not come more than halfway up the
mould). If making individual brioches, divide
the dough into 12 pieces. Using three-quarters
of each piece roll them into small balls and put
them in the brioche tins. Make a dip on top of
each brioche. Roll the remaining paste into 12
tiny balls and press them into the prepared
holes. Push a pencil, or thin spoon handle,
right through each small ball into the brioche
base as this will anchor the balls in place when
baking.
6. Cover with lightly oiled clingfilm and leave in
a warm place to prove (rise again) until risen to
the top of the mould or tin (about 30 minutes
for the large brioche, 15 minutes for individual
ones).

7. Preheat the oven to 200°C/400°F/gas mark 6.
8. Brush the brioches with the egg glaze. Bake
the large one in the preheated oven for 20–25
minutes, the small ones for 10 minutes.

SAUCES AND GARNISHES

BASIL OIL AND GARLIC DIP

SERVES 4

4 large heads of garlic
2 tablespoons water
150ml/¼ pint extra virgin olive oil
1 large handful of fresh basil leaves
sea salt and freshly ground black pepper

1. Preheat the oven to 200°C/400°F/gas mark 6.
2. Place the garlic with the water in a small roasting tin. Cover closely with kitchen foil and bake in the preheated oven for 20 minutes, or until the garlic cloves are really soft. Allow the garlic to cool.
3. Peel off the outer casings of the heads of garlic and press the cloves through a sieve with a wooden spoon.
4. Place the garlic, oil and basil in a blender and whizz to make a smooth purée. Season the dip with a little salt and plenty of pepper.

GRILLED RED PEPPER SALSA

SERVES 4

4 red peppers, quartered and de-seeded
1 red onion, finely chopped
1 clove of garlic, crushed
4 tablespoons extra virgin olive oil
2 tablespoons sherry vinegar
juice of 1 lemon
a pinch of sugar
salt and freshly ground black pepper

1. Preheat the grill to its highest setting.
2. Grill the peppers, skin side uppermost, until the skin is black and blistered. Place the peppers in a bowl and cover with a plate or clingfilm, allowing them to steam for 10 minutes.
3. Peel the blackened skins off the peppers and cut the flesh into strips.
4. Mix the pepper strips with all the remaining ingredients, seasoning to taste with salt and pepper. Cover and leave to stand for 30 minutes.
5. Gently heat the salsa in a small heavy-based saucepan and check the seasoning.

NOTE: This salsa can be served hot or cold.

HERB-SMOKED TOMATO SAUCE

SERVES 4

900g/2lb plum tomatoes
6 sprigs of fresh rosemary
4 sprigs of fresh thyme
1 onion, finely chopped
2 tablespoons extra virgin olive oil
2 cloves of garlic, crushed
5 tablespoons crème fraîche
salt and freshly ground black pepper
1 teaspoon soft light brown sugar
3 tablespoons chopped sun-dried tomatoes

1. Cut the tomatoes in half, scoop out the seeds and rub through a sieve to extract the juice. Discard the seeds and reserve the flesh and juice.
2. Put the herb sprigs into a roasting tin and place a wire rack over the top. Arrange the tomato halves on the rack and cover generously with kitchen foil.

3. Set the roasting tin over a low to medium heat and cook for 10–12 minutes, or until the herbs have burnt away and the tomatoes are lightly smoked.

4. Meanwhile, cook the onion in the oil until soft but not coloured. Add the garlic and cook for a further 3 minutes. Stir in the tomatoes and reserved juice, bring to the boil and stir over a medium heat until the tomatoes begin to break up.

5. Put the tomato mixture into a food processor and whizz until well chopped. Push through a sieve. Return to the rinsed-out saucepan.

6. Stir in the crème fraîche, bring back to the boil and season with salt, pepper and sugar. Stir in the sun-dried tomatoes and serve.

NOTE: This unusual sauce is wonderful with pasta sprinkled with freshly grated Parmesan cheese.

SAFFRON, BASIL AND TOMATO HOLLANDAISE

SERVES 4

3 tablespoons white wine vinegar
6 black peppercorns
1 bay leaf
1 blade of mace
2 egg yolks
salt
110g/4oz cold unsalted butter, diced
1 teaspoon saffron strands
2 tablespoons shredded fresh basil leaves
2 ripe tomatoes, skinned, de-seeded and cut into
*   strips*
freshly ground black pepper

1. Place the vinegar, peppercorns, bay leaf and mace in a small heavy saucepan and reduce by simmering to 1 tablespoon. Strain.

2. Cream the egg yolks with a pinch of salt and a nut of butter in a small bowl. Set in a bain-marie (see page 55) over a low heat. Using a wooden spoon, beat the mixture until slightly thickened, taking care that the water immediately around the bowl does not boil. Mix well.

3. Add the reduced vinegar. Mix well. Stir over the heat until slightly thickened. Beat in the diced butter piece by piece until the sauce thickens and all the butter is incorporated.

4. Add the remaining ingredients and season to taste.

SOURED CREAM RELISH

This recipe would be good served with grilled turkey burgers (see page 297).

SERVES 4

1 corn on the cob, boiled and refreshed in cold
*   water*
¼ cucumber
salt
8 radishes, washed and roots removed
½ red onion, very finely chopped
150ml/¼ pint soured cream
freshly ground black pepper

1. Scrape the sweetcorn kernels off the husk.

2. Cut the cucumber in half lengthways and scrape out the seeds. Cut the flesh into ½cm/¼in cubes.

3. Put the cucumber into a colander and sprinkle over ½ teaspoon salt. Stir together and leave for 15 minutes. Rinse off the excess salt and dry well on kitchen paper.

4. Trim the radish stalks down to 1cm/½in and cut the radishes into quarters.

5. Mix the corn, cucumber, radish, onion and soured cream together and season to taste with salt and pepper. Serve immediately.

REDCURRANT SAUCE

This sauce is to serve with the venison and oyster steamed pudding on page 432. It would also be good with roast game or cold roast meats.

SERVES 4

150ml/¼ pint port
2 tablespoons redcurrant jelly
110g/4oz redcurrants, fresh or frozen
salt and freshly ground black pepper

1. Heat the port with the redcurrant jelly over a low heat until the jelly has melted. Simmer gently for 5 minutes.
2. Stir in the redcurrants and cook gently for 2 minutes, until the redcurrants are tender but still holding their shape. Season to taste with salt and pepper.

MANGO DIPPING SAUCE

SERVES 4

1 large mango, peeled and stoned
grated zest and juice of 1 lime
icing sugar to taste

1. Process the mango flesh, lime zest and juice together until smooth.
2. Sieve into a bowl and add sugar to taste. Chill before serving.

NOTE: Other fruit dipping sauces can be made in the same way. Fruits that also work well include strawberry, raspberry and papaya.

TOMATO CRISPS

SERVES 4

4 sun-ripened beef tomatoes
salt
extra virgin olive oil

1. Preheat the oven (preferably fan-assisted) to 100°C/200°F/gas mark ½.
2. Slice the tomatoes horizontally into ½cm/ ¼in rounds.
3. Lay the tomato slices in a single layer on wire racks placed over baking sheets. Season with a little salt and brush over a little oil.
4. Bake the tomato slices in the preheated oven for about 4–5 hours, turning them once.
5. When the tomatoes have lost all their moisture and are almost crisp, take out of the oven and allow to cool before storing in an airtight container.

MARINATED OLIVES IN OLIVE OIL

SERVES 8

225g/8oz good-quality black and green olives
6 tablespoons olive oil
2 cloves of garlic, peeled and sliced
1 bay leaf
2 lemon slices
1 tablespoon dried herbes de Provence, rubbed

1. Put all the ingredients into a bowl and mix well together.
2. Pack the olives into a jar and refrigerate for a few days.
3. To serve: leave the olives to stand at room temperature for an hour, to allow the flavours to develop.

CHERRIES IN CARAMEL

SERVES 4

225g/8oz granulated sugar
water
170g/6oz ripe but firm cherries, stalks intact

1. Put the sugar into a heavy-based saucepan and add water to cover.
2. Dissolve the sugar in the water over a low heat.
3. Boil the syrup rapidly until the bubbles start to turn over more slowly and the syrup turns a pale golden colour. Turn off the heat and allow the bubbles to subside.
4. Line a baking sheet with silicone paper.
5. Tip the pan slightly to one side so that the pale caramel collects in a deep puddle on one side of the pan. Take one cherry at a time, holding it by the tip of the stalk, and carefully dip it into the caramel until it is completely covered. Remove and allow the excess caramel to drain off. Place on the baking sheet to set and continue in the same way with the remaining cherries.
6. If the caramel becomes too thick, return it to a low heat for a while before continuing.

SEMI-DRIED STONE FRUIT

When there is a glut of stone fruit in the garden, a useful way of preserving the fruit is to semi-dry them. The semi-dried fruit is delicious for snacks or in cakes and biscuits (see page 649). If you cook them for a while longer and dry them out completely, they will last a lot longer, and can be used in place of dried fruit for rich cake recipes.

ripe stone fruit, such as plums, damsons,
    greengages

1. Preheat the oven to 140°C/275°F/gas mark 1. Line several baking sheets with silicone paper.
2. Cut the fruit in half and remove the stones. Lay the fruit, cut side uppermost, in a single layer on the prepared baking sheets.
3. Bake in the preheated oven for 2–3 hours, or until the fruit has shrunk to about half its original size. (If you want to dry the fruit completely, continue to cook it for a further few hours until it is one-quarter its original size.)

MENU IDEAS

SUMMER MENUS

Ensuring that a menu is well balanced is one of the most important skills that a cook must learn.
Our suggested menus for summer entertaining are as follows:

Mid-summer Barbecue

Marinated sesame spare ribs
Barbecued scampi with fresh herbs
Barbecued spatchcocked quail
Peach torte
Summer berry ripple ice cream

Formal Dinner Party

Chilled baby courgette soup
Roast pepper-crust cod with tomato concasse
Braised minted lettuce
Warm goat's cheese timbales with raspberries
Blackcurrant leaf ice

Light Lunch

Salmon and chilli burgers in wholemeal rolls
Fennel, cucumber and chilli salad
or
Warm naan with oriental pesto monkfish
Macerated raspberry salad

Wedding Reception or Sophisticated Dinner Party

Mediterranean mille-feuille
Hot poached salmon with sauce vierge
French bean and shallot salad
New potatoes with fresh mint
Red, white and blackcurrant iced terrine

Glyndebourne/Ascot/Henley Picnic

Rocket ravioli with garlic and goat's cheese
Spinach and saffron bread
Lobster and strawberry salad
New potato, soured cream and chive salad
Cherry and mascarpone burnt creams

Beach Picnic

Chicken and oregano ciabattas
Roast tomato pie
Cool radish, cucumber and feta salad
Date and gooseberry cake

Barbecue

Griddled turkey burgers with soured cream relish
Broad beans, roast corn and plum tomatoes in saffron oil
New potato vinaigrette
Cherry tomato and artichoke picnic bread
Peach shortbread

Vegetarian Menu

Fresh pea tartlets with walnut and oat pastry
Hot sweetcorn, ricotta and Parmesan bake
Tomato and basil stew
Sweet potato and courgette rösti
Peach, strawberry and mango compote with clotted cream

AUTUMN
September – October – November

INTRODUCTION

Suddenly it's a little chillier, but as the leaves turn golden so the produce changes to the warm colours of autumn – bright orange pumpkins and squash. Suddenly the pace in the garden slows a little – now is the time to put up your feet and see how last year's mulberry gin has matured.

The game season, having started on the 'Glorious 12th' of August with grouse, is under way and we can eat shellfish again as there is now an 'R' in the month. Root vegetables such as celeriac and parsnips, the classic winter warmers, become available – they tend to be large and thick-skinned, full of flavour from spending so much time underground. Cook them slowly and gently for the best results. Swede and celeriac can be baked like potatoes for wonderful vegetable suppers. The autumnal fruits are around now – blackberries, damsons and quince, and still a few mulberries in early September. These fruits go very well with the rich, dark meat of venison, boar and game birds, and are often cooked together; meats will need longer cooking now as the animals will have matured over the season.

With autumn leaves falling, and warm fires lit indoors, you can indulge in hearty soups, steamed puddings, and tea-time treats such as doughnuts with apples and blackberries. Be prepared for the orchard fruits – apples, pears and plums – in order to make the most of them in their season. In autumn it is natural to feel the need for filling ingredients to stock up the body for the harsh and lean winter ahead. Some of our favourite recipes for this season include rich mussel bourride, full of garlic; roast tomato soup; braised oxtail with port and autumn berries; and something lighter but refreshing – quince and poire William sorbet.

Enjoy the next phase of preserving – chutneys come into their own now with all the plums, apples and green tomatoes. Damson cheese, a thick sweet jam, can be made and stored away for the rest of the year, and sloe gin needs to be laid down for the Christmas festivities ahead. These preserves are so simple to make – the worst part is cleaning the jars of their former labels – and they are immensely satisfying to have at the ready for delicious sandwiches and quick meals.

Often there are simply too many apples and plums to cook, in which case a wonderful way to use them up is with a vegetable and fruit juice extractor attachment to your food processor – drink the fresh juice chilled, or warmed, as in spiced pear juice or simply freeze it for another occasion.

Autumn is a time of fun festivities, particularly for children – Hallowe'en and Guy Fawkes – and for adults, these are often the first excuse of the year for mulled wine and some interesting nibbles. We have an exciting recipe for a pumpkin pancake pie, using a whole pumpkin, scraped of seeds and filled with layered pancakes, mince and seasonal vegetables. It takes a while to prepare but will feed a crowd and captures the seasonal spirit. Bonfire potatoes can be tossed into the embers at the bottom of the fire so that they are ready when the fireworks are over and can keep children's fingers warm until you return indoors. Roasting chestnuts at the fireside is rewarding too – if there are too many to eat, use them up in a chestnut and wild mushroom carbonnade.

Some families follow the American traditional celebration of Thanksgiving at the end of November, another excuse for a family gathering – sweet potatoes creep in with turkeys and cranberries, a sure sign that winter is really on its way.

FRUIT AND VEGETABLES IN SEASON

TOP FRUIT	September	October	November
Apples	XXXXXXXXX	XXXXXXXXX	XXXXXXXXX
Pears	XXXXXXXXX	XXXXXXXXX	XXXXXXXXX
Quinces	XXXXXXXXX	XXXXXXXXX	XXXXXXXXX
Medlars	XXXXXXXXX	XXXXXXXXX	XXXXXXXXX
Figs	XXXXXXXXX	XXXXXXXXX	
Mulberries	XXXXXXXXX	XXXXXXXXX	
Pomegranates			XXXXXXXXX
Plums	XXXXXXXXX	XXXXXXXXX	XXXXXXXXX
Damsons	XXXXXXXXX	XXXXXXXXX	XXXXXXXXX
Greengages	XXXXXXXXX	XXXXXXXXX	XXXXXXXXX

BERRY FRUIT	September	October	November
Raspberries	XXXXXXXXX	XXXXXXXXX	
Blackberries	XXXXXXXXX		

ALLIUMS	September	October	November
Onions (new and store)	XXXXXXXXX	XXXXXXXXX	XXXXXXXXX
Garlic (new and store)	XXXXXXXXX	XXXXXXXXX	XXXXXXXXX
Leeks		XXXXXXXXX	XXXXXXXXX
Shallots (new and store)	XXXXXXXXX	XXXXXXXXX	XXXXXXXXX

BRASSICAS	September	October	November
Broccoli	XXXXXXXXX	XXXXXXXXX	XXXXXXXXX
Calabrese	XXXXXXXXX	XXXXXXXXX	
Cauliflower	XXXXXXXXX	XXXXXXXXX	XXXXXXXXX
Kohlrabi		XXXXXXXXX	XXXXXXXXX
Cabbage	XXXXXXXXX	XXXXXXXXX	XXXXXXXXX
Brussels sprouts			XXXXXXXXX

BEANS AND PODS	September	October	November
French beans	XXXXXXXXX	XXXXXXXXX	
Runner beans	XXXXXXXXX	XXXXXXXXX	
Peas	XXXXXXXXX	XXXXXXXXX	
Sweetcorn	XXXXXXXXX	XXXXXXXXX	

LETTUCE/SPINACH	September	October	November
Spinach	XXXXXXXXX	XXXXXXXXX	XXXXXXXXX
Late-sowing summer lettuces	XXXXXXXXX	XXXXXXXXX	
Radicchio and some chicorys	XXXXXXXXX	XXXXXXXXX	XXXXXXXXX

FRUIT AND VEGETABLES IN SEASON—*contd*

ROOTS AND TUBERS	September	October	November
Main crop potatoes for			
winter storage	XXXXXXXX	XXXXXXXX	XXXXXXXX
Beetroot	XXXXXXXX	XXXXXXXX	XXXXXXXX
Radishes	XXXXXXXX	XXXXXXXX	XXXXXXXX
Turnips	XXXXXXXX	XXXXXXXX	XXXXXXXX
Carrots	XXXXXXXX	XXXXXXXX	XXXXXXXX
Celeriac		XXXXXXXX	XXXXXXXX
Swedes		XXXXXXXX	XXXXXXXX

STALKS/SHOOTS			
Globe Artichokes	XXXXXXXX	XXXXXXXX	
Rhubarb	XXXXXXXX	XXXXXXXX	
Florence fennel	XXXXXXXX	XXXXXXXX	

VEGETABLE FRUITS			
Tomatoes	XXXXXXXX	XXXXXXXX	XXXXXXXX
Marrows	XXXXXXXX	XXXXXXXX	XXXXXXXX
Pumpkins and Squashes	XXXXXXXX	XXXXXXXX	XXXXXXXX
Ridge Cucumbers	XXXXXXXX	XXXXXXXX	XXXXXXXX

HERBS			
Thyme	XXXXXXXX	XXXXXXXX	XXXXXXXX
Rosemary	XXXXXXXX	XXXXXXXX	XXXXXXXX
Sage	XXXXXXXX	XXXXXXXX	XXXXXXXX
Basil	XXXXXXXX	XXXXXXXX	XXXXXXXX
Late-sowing herbs, die after frosts	XXXXXXXX	XXXXXXXX	XXXXXXXX

WILD			
Samphire	XXXXXXXX		
Elderberries	XXXXXXXX	XXXXXXXX	
Blackberries	XXXXXXXX		
Hips and haws	XXXXXXXX	XXXXXXXX	XXXXXXXX
Sloes (after frost)	XXXXXXXX	XXXXXXXX	XXXXXXXX
Wild Mushrooms	XXXXXXXX	XXXXXXXX	XXXXXXXX
Nuts: Walnuts	XXXXXXXX	XXXXXXXX	XXXXXXXX

FISH IN SEASON

SALMON FAMILY
Farmed Atlantic and Pacific Salmon
Wild and farmed Trout and Char
Atlantic Salmon
Wild Brown Trout
Wild Rainbow Trout

SHELLFISH
Brown Crab
Spider Crab
Lobster
Dublin Bay Prawn
Crayfish
Prawns (various)
Shrimp
Winkle
Cockle
Clam
Mussel
Native Oyster
Pacific Oyster
Scallop (all species)
Octopus
Squid

BEST FROM HOME
Monkfish
John Dory
Gurnard
Red Mullet
Grey Mullet
Wrasse
Black Sea Bream
Red Sea Bream

FLAT FISH
Plaice
Halibut
Lemon Sole
Dab
Flounder
Turbot
Brill
Megrim
Witch
Skate

MACKEREL FAMILY
Mackerel
Tuna
Bonito/Wahoo

HERRING FAMILY
Herring
Pilchard/Sardine
Anchovy
Sprat

COD FAMILY
Cod
Haddock
Whiting
Pollock
Coley/Saithe/Coalfish
Ling
Hake

FIRST COURSES AND
SOUPS

FIRST COURSES

CÈPES, GARLIC AND PARSLEY BRIOCHE

SERVES 4

450g/1lb fresh cèpes
85g/3oz butter
2 large cloves of garlic, crushed
salt and freshly ground black pepper
4 thick slices of brioche, toasted
2 tablespoons chopped fresh parsley

To garnish
chopped fresh parsley

1. Preheat the oven to 130°C/250°F/gas mark 1.
2. Wipe the cèpes with damp kitchen paper to remove any dirt. If they are particularly gritty, wash them very quickly in a large bowl of cold water, then lift them out with your hands or a slotted spoon, leaving the water and grit behind. Pat dry on kitchen paper and slice thickly.
3. Fry the cèpes with 55g/2oz of the butter in a heavy-based frying pan over a very low heat to prevent them from burning. When their juices start to flow, add the garlic and cook for a few more minutes. Season to taste with salt and pepper.
4. Spread the brioche toast with the remaining butter, place on a baking sheet and keep warm in the oven.
5. Stir the parsley into the cèpes and check the seasoning.
6. Pile the cèpes on to the 4 slices of brioche, sprinkle over a little more parsley and serve immediately.

 *CRU BOURGEOIS CLARET*

CROTTIN IN FILO WITH PRUNES AND ARMAGNAC

SERVES 4

4 ready-to-eat pitted prunes
4 tablespoons Armagnac
½ packet of filo pastry
30g/1oz butter, melted
4 crottins (individual goat's cheese)
1 teaspoon chopped fresh thyme
freshly ground black pepper
1 egg, beaten, to glaze

To garnish
½ small frisée endive, washed and dried
6 tablespoons walnut oil
1 tablespoon balsamic vinegar

1. Put the prunes and Armagnac into a small saucepan. Bring to the boil and cover, then remove from the heat and set aside for 30 minutes.
2. Preheat the oven to 190°C/375°F/gas mark 5.
3. Cut out 8 × 20cm/8in squares of filo pastry. For each parcel take one sheet, brush with melted butter and lay another sheet on top at an angle.
4. Place a crottin on the filo with 2 prunes, sprinkle with thyme and pepper, then draw up the edges to form a parcel. Repeat with the remaining crottins.
5. Brush the pastry with beaten egg and bake in the middle of the preheated oven for 15 minutes, or until golden-brown all over.

6. Toss the frisée, walnut oil and vinegar together, use to garnish the parcels and serve immediately.

 ROBUST FULL-BODIED CABERNET SAUVIGNON – PÉCHARMANT

GRILLED GOAT'S CHEESE AND FIG BRUSCHETTA

SERVES 4

*1 French stick, cut diagonally into slices 2.5cm/
   1in thick*
2 tablespoons extra virgin olive oil
4 figs, washed and dried
2 × 55g/2oz crottin goat's cheese
salt and freshly ground black pepper
1 teaspoon chopped fresh rosemary

To garnish
sprigs of flat-leaf parsley

1. Preheat the oven to 180°C/350°F/gas mark 4.
2. Brush the slices of French stick with some of the oil and bake in the oven until golden-brown. Set aside.
3. Preheat the grill to its highest setting.
4. Thickly slice the figs and cheese and arrange overlapping on the pieces of bread.
5. Season each bruschetta with salt and pepper and drizzle with the remaining oil. Sprinkle with the rosemary and grill for 2–3 minutes. Garnish with the parsley and serve very hot.

 SAUVIGNON DE TOURAINE OR ITALIAN PINOT GRIGIO

FIG AND ROQUEFORT TOASTIE CASES

MAKES 20

20 toastie cases (see following recipe)
4 ripe figs
salt and freshly ground black pepper
1 tablespoon port
110g/4oz Roquefort cheese, finely diced

1. Preheat the grill to its highest setting.
2. Dice the figs evenly and put into a bowl. Season with salt and pepper, add the port and allow to stand for 15 minutes.
3. Divide the figs between the toastie cases. Sprinkle the Roquefort cheese on top. Grill for 1–2 minutes, or until the cheese has just begun to melt. Take care not to allow the toastie cases to burn.

 MOSCATO D'ASTI

TOASTIE CASES

MAKES 20

5 thin slices of bread
butter, melted

1. Preheat the oven to 180°C/350°F/gas mark 4. Stamp out rounds of bread, using a small fluted cutter.
2. Dip into the melted butter and mould into tiny patty tins. Press an empty patty tin on top and bake in the preheated oven until golden-brown and crisp.

STEAMED PIGEON DUMPLINGS

SERVES 4

For the filling
2 pigeon breasts, skinned
1 teaspoon Chinese five spice
salt and freshly ground black pepper
2 tablespoons sunflower oil
1 tablespoon soy sauce
1 tablespoon clear honey
1 clove of garlic, crushed
2 spring onions, thinly sliced

For the dough
225g/8oz self-raising flour
salt
110g/4oz shredded beef suet
about 8 tablespoons cold water

To serve
1 quantity soy, honey and red wine sauce (see
page 502)
1 quantity sweet and sour cabbage (see page
458)

1. Make the filling: trim the pigeon breasts of any sinew. Sprinkle over the Chinese five spice and season with salt and pepper.
2. Heat the oil in a heavy-based frying pan. Fry the pigeon breasts for 2 minutes on each side. Transfer to a plate and allow to cool.
3. Cut the pigeon breasts into 1cm/½in cubes and place in a bowl with the soy sauce, honey, garlic and spring onions. Season with salt and pepper.
4. Bring a large saucepan of water to the boil. Line a steamer with 4 × 7.5cm/3in squares of silicone paper.
5. Make the dough: sift the flour with the salt into a large bowl. Stir in the suet and using a knife, mix to a soft dough with the cold water.
6. Divide the dough into 4 equal pieces and press each out into a circle about 10cm/4in wide. Place a quarter of the filling in the centre of each circle. Brush the edges of the circles with a little water and draw the edges up to the centre to form a parcel. Place each parcel on a piece of silicone paper in the steamer, place over the boiling water and cover with a lid.
7. Steam the dumplings for 15–20 minutes, or until risen and firm on the outside. Serve immediately with the soy, honey and red wine sauce and sweet and sour cabbage.

 *ALSATIAN WHITE/RIESLING*

GAME SAUSAGE ROLLS

MAKES 12

15g/½oz butter
1 small onion, very finely chopped
285g/10oz minced lean boned game, such as
venison, pheasant, grouse
85g/3oz minced belly of pork
2 tablespoons very finely chopped fresh parsley
salt and freshly ground black pepper
225g/8oz flour quantity shortcrust pastry (see
page 642)
1 egg, beaten, to glaze

1. Preheat the oven to 200°C/400°F/gas mark 6.
2. Melt the butter in a heavy-based saucepan, add the onion and cook until soft but not coloured.
3. Mix together the minced game, belly of pork, parsley and onion and season to taste with salt and pepper.
4. Roll out the pastry to a large rectangle about 2mm/⅛in thick and cut in half lengthways.
5. With wet hands, roll the game mixture into 2 long sausages the same length as the pastry and place one down the centre of each piece.
6. Damp one long edge of each piece of pastry and roll the pastry over the filling, pressing the edges together and making sure that the join is underneath the roll, Chill for 30 minutes.
7. Brush the pastry with a little beaten egg. Cut the rolls into 5cm/2in lengths and using kitchen scissors, snip a small 'V' in the top of each sausage roll to allow steam to escape during cooking. Or make a couple of small diagonal slashes with a sharp knife.
8. Place the rolls on a baking sheet and bake in

the preheated oven for 25–30 minutes, or until the pastry is golden-brown.

 LATE AUTUMN – BEAUJOLAIS NOUVEAU; EARLY AUTUMN – AUSTRALIAN SHIRAZ-CABERNET

WILD BOAR AND STILTON SAUSAGES

SERVES 4

450g/1lb minced wild boar or pork
55g/2oz minced pork fat
1 medium onion, very finely chopped
55g/2oz fresh white breadcrumbs
110g/4oz Stilton cheese, finely diced
1 egg
2 tablespoons chopped fresh sage
salt and freshly ground black pepper
oil for frying
2m/6½ft sausage skins, washed (available from good butchers)

To serve
1 quantity crab apple and redcurrant compote (see page 504)

1. Mix together the minced wild boar or pork, pork fat, onion, breadcrumbs, Stilton cheese, egg and sage and season well with salt and pepper.
2. Fry a small amount of the mixture in a little hot oil and taste for seasoning before filling the skins.
3. Fill the sausages: put a 2cm/¾in plain nozzle into a large piping bag and fill with the sausage mixture. Tie one end of the sausage skin, insert the nozzle into the open end and feed the skin on to the nozzle.
4. Squeeze the piping bag and allow the mixture to fill the sausage skins evenly, forming a loose rope 2.5cm/1in thick. Twist the rope every 10cm/4in to form sausages.
5. Cut the sausage skins where the sausages divide. Grill or fry the sausages in a little hot oil

and serve with the crab apple and redcurrant compote.

 MOSEL AUSLESE

PUFF-BALL, BACON AND GARLIC STIR-FRY

SERVES 2

1 medium puff-ball
55g/2oz butter
110g/4oz rindless rashers of streaky bacon, thinly sliced
1 large clove of garlic, crushed
1 tablespoon chopped fresh parsley
salt and freshly ground black pepper

1. Wipe the puff-ball with damp kitchen paper. Cut off the root end if it is muddy and gritty. Cut the puff-ball into 2.5cm/1in cubes.
2. Melt the butter in a large frying pan, add the bacon and fry until golden-brown. Remove the bacon with a slotted spoon and set aside.
3. Add the puff-ball to the frying pan and fry over a medium heat until golden-brown. Stir in the garlic, bacon and parsley and season to taste with salt and pepper. Serve immediately.

 PINOT NOIR

PORK, PIGEON AND PRUNE TERRINE WITH BRANDY

SERVES 6

450g/1lb rindless belly of pork, minced
2 shallots, finely chopped
1 clove of garlic, crushed
1 tablespoon chopped fresh thyme
2 tablespoons chopped fresh parsley
3 tablespoons brandy
salt and freshly ground black pepper

225g/8oz rindless rashers of streaky bacon
110g/4oz pitted prunes
2 pigeon breasts, skinned
1 bay leaf

1. Preheat the oven to 170°C/325°F/gas mark 3.
2. Mix together the pork, shallots, garlic,
thyme, parsley and 2 tablespoons of the brandy
and season with plenty of salt and pepper.
3. Stretch the bacon rashers and use to line a
450g/1lb terrine tin, leaving them overlapping
the top. Spread half the pork mixture over the
bottom of the tin. Arrange the prunes in a line
down the centre of the terrine and place the
pigeon breasts on top. Season with salt and
pepper and sprinkle over the remaining brandy.
4. Spread over the remaining pork mixture and
press down well to make sure there are no air
pockets and all the corners are well filled. Fold
the bacon rashers over the top of the terrine.
Place the bay leaf on top.
5. Cover the terrine with a piece of greased
greaseproof paper. Stand the tin in a roasting
tin half filled with hot water (a bain-marie) and
bake in the preheated oven for 45 minutes – 1
hour, or until the mixture feels firm to the
touch and a metal skewer inserted into the
centre comes out hot.
6. Remove from the roasting tin, place a weight
on the terrine (a can of fruit or a second terrine
with a weight in it will do). Leave overnight to
cool, then refrigerate for a further 24 hours.
7. Turn out the terrine and cut into 1cm/½in
slices to serve.

 *AUSTRALIAN OR CHILEAN
CABERNET SAUVIGNON*

COARSE COUNTRY
GAME PÂTÉ

SERVES 8

225g/8oz wild boar
450g/1lb boneless rabbit
2 pheasant breasts
225g/8oz pork tenderloin
110g/4oz belly pork

110g/4oz chicken livers, roughly chopped
5 tablespoons brandy
1 tablespoon olive oil
4 cloves of garlic, crushed
½ onion, very finely chopped
1 teaspoon chopped fresh thyme
½ teaspoon each ground mace, ground ginger,
   cinnamon and allspice
1 egg
salt and freshly ground black pepper
12 rashers of rindless streaky bacon
2 bay leaves

1. Whizz the wild boar, rabbit, pheasant, pork
tenderloin, belly pork and chicken livers
together in a food processor until roughly
chopped. Do not overwork. Pour over the
brandy and allow to marinate for 1 hour.
2. Heat the oil in a frying pan, add the garlic
and onion and cook until soft. Add the thyme
and spices and cook for a further 2–3 minutes
over a medium heat. Turn into a bowl and
allow to cool completely.
3. Preheat the oven to 170°C/325°F/gas mark 3.
4. Mix the onion mixture into the meat mixture
and work together well. Beat in the egg and
season to taste with salt and pepper.
5. Stretch the bacon rashers and use to line a 1.5
litre/2.5 pint capacity loaf tin or terrine, leaving
them overlapping at the top.
6. With wet hands, pack the meat mixture into
the lined terrine. Smooth the top and fold over
the bacon rashers. Place the bay leaves on top.
7. Cover the loaf tin or terrine with a well-
fitting lid or a double sheet of kitchen foil. Place
in a roasting tin half filled with hot water (a
bain-marie) and bake in the preheated oven for
1½–1¾ hours, or until the meat juices run clear
when a skewer is inserted.
8. Remove from the roasting tin and press the
top of the pâté down lightly with a small weight.
Leave to cool, then refrigerate overnight. Turn
out and cut into thick slices to serve.

NOTE: This terrine is excellent served with a
fruit pickle or quince or medlar jelly.

 *VIN DE PAYS D'OC – CHARDONNAY
OR VIOGNIER*

BAKED AUBERGINE, MOZZARELLA AND PARMESAN

SERVES 4

2 medium aubergines
1 teaspoon salt
2 beef tomatoes, thickly sliced
salt and freshly ground black pepper
1 teaspoon sugar
2 tablespoons extra virgin olive oil
225g/8oz mozzarella cheese, grated
2 teaspoons chopped fresh marjoram
570ml/1 pint hot tomato and pepper sauce (see
    page 502)
2 tablespoons freshly grated Parmesan cheese

1. Cut the aubergines into 1cm/½in slices, place in a colander, sprinkle with the salt and leave for 30 minutes to extract any bitter juices.
2. Preheat the oven to 190°C/375°F/gas mark 5.
3. Arrange the tomatoes in the bottom of a large ovenproof dish and season with salt, pepper and sugar. Set aside.
4. Rinse the aubergines well and pat dry. Heat the oil in a frying pan, add the aubergines and fry until golden-brown. Drain on kitchen paper.
5. Arrange the aubergine slices on top of the tomatoes and sprinkle with mozzarella cheese and marjoram. Cover with the hot tomato and pepper sauce and sprinkle with the Parmesan cheese. Bake in the preheated oven for 25 minutes. Serve hot.

 *DRY WHITE*

PARMESAN AND GARLIC FIELD MUSHROOMS

SERVES 4

8 large cup field mushrooms
110g/4oz button mushrooms
30g/1oz fine fresh breadcrumbs
2 cloves of garlic, crushed
85g/3oz Parmesan cheese, freshly grated
55g/2oz cooked ham, diced
salt and freshly ground black pepper

For the sauce
15g/½oz butter
15g/½oz plain flour
290ml/½ pint milk
1 tablespoon grain mustard
a pinch of cayenne pepper
30g/1oz Parmesan cheese, freshly grated

1. Prepare the cup mushrooms: wipe with damp kitchen paper, remove the centre stalk and peel. Reserve. Put the mushrooms, gill side up, into a large ovenproof dish. Set aside.
2. Wipe the button mushrooms and put into a food processor with the cup mushroom trimmings. Add the breadcrumbs, garlic, Parmesan cheese and ham and whizz until smooth. Season to taste with salt and pepper.
3. Spoon the mixture into the cup mushrooms, dividing it equally between them, and set aside.
4. Preheat the oven to 200°C/400°F/gas mark 6.
5. Make the sauce: melt the butter in a saucepan, add the flour and cook over a low heat for 30 seconds. Remove the pan from the heat and gradually whisk in the milk. Replace over a low heat and stir continuously until the mixture comes to the boil. Allow the sauce to simmer for 3 minutes. Remove the saucepan from the heat and allow to cool for 1 minute.
6. Add the mustard to the sauce and season with salt, pepper and cayenne. Coat the mushrooms sparingly with the sauce and sprinkle with the Parmesan cheese.
7. Bake the mushrooms in the preheated oven for 15–20 minutes, or until they are hot and sizzling and the top is golden-brown. Continue to brown under a hot grill if necessary. Serve hot or warm.

 *PINOT NOIR*

MIXED ROAST ONIONS

SERVES 4

16 shallots, peeled
4 red onions, peeled and quartered
4 small leeks, very thickly sliced and washed
4 cloves of garlic, peeled
5 tablespoons extra virgin olive oil
2 sprigs of fresh rosemary
salt and freshly ground black pepper
2 tablespoons balsamic vinegar

To serve
sprigs of fresh rosemary
focaccia (see page 371)

1. Preheat the oven to 190°C/375°F/gas mark 5.
2. Put the shallots, red onions, leeks and garlic into a large saucepan and cover with cold water. Bring to the boil, then lower the heat and blanch the vegetables for 2–3 minutes. Do not allow to boil vigorously or they will begin to disintegrate. Drain and pat dry with kitchen paper.
3. Arrange the vegetables in a single layer in a large roasting tin, brush with oil and sprinkle the rosemary over the top. Season well with salt and pepper.
4. Roast in the preheated oven for 15 minutes. Turn the vegetables and roast for a further 15 minutes, or until soft right through.
5. Pile the vegetables into a large warmed serving dish and drizzle with the vinegar. Serve garnished with rosemary sprigs and slices of warm focaccia.

TOMATO AND AUBERGINE RAVIOLI WITH BLACK BUTTER AND CAPER DRESSING

SERVES 4

225g/8oz quantity green pasta (see page 653)

For the filling
½ aubergine
salt
1 tablespoon olive oil
1 red onion, finely chopped
1 clove of garlic, crushed
4 tomatoes, skinned and chopped
1 tablespoon chopped fresh basil
freshly ground black pepper

For the black butter
30g/1oz butter
salt and freshly ground black pepper
a pinch of freshly grated nutmeg
juice of ½ lemon
2 tablespoons capers, rinsed

To serve
sprigs of fresh flat-leaf parsley

1. Make the pasta, wrap and allow to stand for 30 minutes.
2. Make the filling: cut the aubergine into 1cm/½in dice. Place in a colander, sprinkle lightly with salt and allow to degorge for 15 minutes, then rinse and drain.
3. Heat the oil in a large frying pan, add the aubergine and fry for 4–5 minutes, or until soft. Add the onion and cook over a low heat for a further 2–3 minutes. Add the garlic and the tomatoes and cook for 10–12 minutes, or until the mixture is very thick and pulpy.
4. Add the basil to the mixture and season with salt and pepper. Remove from the heat and allow to cool.
5. Roll out the pasta as thinly as possible. Stamp out 24 × 7.5cm/3in discs. Divide the aubergine mixture between 12 of the discs, lightly dampen the edges and press a second disc on top. Place in a single layer on a floured board until ready to cook.
6. Bring a large saucepan half filled with water to the boil, add 1 teaspoon salt and cook the ravioli for 4–5 minutes, or until *al dente*. Drain well and arrange in 4 warmed individual dishes.
7. Melt the butter in a large frying pan and season lightly with salt, pepper and nutmeg. Allow the butter to begin to brown. Add the

lemon juice and capers and pour over the ravioli while still sizzling. Garnish with the parsley and serve immediately.

 *PINOT GRIGIO*

RED RICE, PUMPKIN AND PANCETTA PILAF

SERVES 4

450g/1lb red Camargue rice
4 tablespoons extra virgin olive oil
2 red onions
2 cloves of garlic, crushed
110g/4oz pancetta, diced
1 litre/1¾ pints white stock, made with chicken bones (see page 625)
salt and freshly ground black pepper
1 butternut squash or pumpkin, peeled and diced

To serve
1 handful of fresh purple basil leaves, shredded

1. Put the rice into a bowl, cover with water and leave to soak for 2 hours.
2. Heat the oil in a large flameproof casserole, add the onions and cook over a low heat for 20–25 minutes, or until completely soft. Add the garlic and continue to cook for a further 2–3 minutes.
3. Add the pancetta to the casserole and cook over a medium heat for a further 2–3 minutes. Remove from the heat.
4. Drain the rice and stir into the onion mixture. Cook over a low heat for 1–2 minutes to soften the rice.
5. Add the stock to the casserole, season lightly with salt and pepper and cook over a very low heat for 20–25 minutes, or until the rice is nearly soft. If the stock evaporates before the rice is cooked, add a little water to prevent the rice from boiling dry.
6. Add the squash or pumpkin to the casserole and cook, covered, for a further 5–7 minutes, or until the squash or pumpkin is soft. Remove the

lid and stir briefly over the heat until any extra liquid has evaporated.
7. Season with salt and pepper and add the basil. Turn into a warmed serving dish and serve very hot.

 *NEW WORLD CABERNET SAUVIGNON*

WARM PINTO BEANS WITH RED CHILLI AND LEMON DRESSING

SERVES 4

1 × 400g/14oz can of pinto beans, drained
2 tablespoons extra virgin olive oil
1 Spanish onion, finely chopped
2 cloves of garlic, crushed
2 red chillies, de-seeded and chopped
grated zest and juice of 2 lemons
salt and freshly ground black pepper
1 tablespoon chopped fresh rosemary

1. Rinse the beans and allow to drain thoroughly.
2. Heat the oil in a frying pan, add the onion and cook until soft, then add the garlic and chillies and cook for a further 2 minutes. Add the beans, lemon zest and juice and toss over a high heat for 2–3 minutes, or until the beans are hot.
3. Season to taste with salt and pepper and add the rosemary. Pile into a warmed serving dish and serve warm.

 *BARBERA D'ASTI*

FIELD MUSHROOM AND RED LEICESTER FLAN

SERVES 6

*170g/6oz flour quantity rich shortcrust pastry
(see page 642)*

For the filling
*1 tablespoon sunflower oil
1 onion, finely chopped
1 clove of garlic, crushed
5 tablespoons milk
5 tablespoons single cream
2 eggs, lightly beaten
110g/4oz red Leicester cheese, finely grated
2 tablespoons chopped fresh chives
salt and freshly ground black pepper
6–8 small cup field mushrooms*

1. Preheat the oven to 200°C/400°F/gas mark 6.
2. Line a 20cm/8in flan ring with the pastry and chill for 15 minutes. Bake the pastry case blind (see page 640) for 15–18 minutes. Allow to cool. Reduce the oven temperature to 180°C/350°F/gas mark 4.
3. Meanwhile, heat the oil in a frying pan, add the onion and cook until transparent, then add the garlic and continue to cook for a further minute. Remove from the heat and allow to cool.
4. Mix together the milk, cream, eggs and red Leicester cheese, stir in the onion and chives and season to taste with salt and pepper.
5. Wipe the mushrooms and remove the stalks. Place the mushrooms, gill side up, in the baked flan case. Pour the cheese mixture over the top and bake in the preheated oven for 35–45 minutes, or until the filling is set. Serve warm or cold.

 *BEAUJOLAIS*

RED ONION POLENTA TATIN

This recipe was given to us by Puff Fairclough, a senior teacher at Leith's School.

SERVES 6–8

170g/6oz flour quantity polenta pastry (see page 645)

For the topping
*55g/2oz butter
900g/2lb red onions, thinly sliced
2 tablespoons white wine
2 cloves of garlic, crushed
1 tablespoon soft light brown sugar
2 large red peppers
1 tablespoon capers, rinsed and drained
3 anchovy fillets, slivered
¼ tablespoon chopped fresh rosemary*

1. Preheat the oven to 190°C/375°F/gas mark 5.
2. To make the topping: melt 30g/1oz of the butter in a heavy, ovenproof frying pan. Add the onions and cook, covered, for 15 minutes, until they begin to soften. Add the wine, garlic and half the sugar and cook for 20 minutes. Turn up the heat and reduce by boiling rapidly, until the liquid coats the onions. Transfer the mixture to a bowl.
3. Preheat the grill to its highest setting. Cut the peppers into quarters, then remove the stalks, membrane and seeds. Grill the peppers, skin side uppermost, until the skin is black and blistered. Scrape off the skin with a small knife.
4. Melt the remaining butter in the pan, stir in the remaining sugar and remove from the heat. Arrange the red pepper pieces in the pan in a daisy pattern. Place the capers and anchovies between the peppers and cover with the cooked onions, taking care not to dislodge the peppers. Sprinkle over the fresh rosemary.
5. Place the pan over a high heat until the butter and sugar start to caramelize, which may take 5 minutes. Remove the pan from the heat and place it on a baking sheet.
6. Lay the polenta pastry on top of the onions and press down lightly. Bake for 25 minutes.

Allow to cool slightly, then invert the pan over a serving plate and serve warm.

 LIGHT RED

PROSCIUTTO AND AUBERGINE GOUGÈRE

SERVES 4

butter for greasing
55g/2oz Parmesan or Gruyère cheese, grated
½ teaspoon dry English mustard
2-egg quantity choux pastry (see page 645)
1 small aubergine, cut into small dice
1 tablespoon olive oil
85g/3oz prosciutto, cut into shreds
1 teaspoon chopped fresh basil
4 tablespoons double cream
salt and freshly ground black pepper
1 tablespoon freshly grated Parmesan cheese

1. Lightly butter 4 ramekins.
2. Preheat the oven to 200°C/400°F/gas mark 6.
3. Beat the 55g/2oz cheese and the mustard into the choux pastry. Fit a piping bag with a 1cm/½in plain nozzle and fill with the cheese mixture. Pipe round the bottom and sides of the ramekins, leaving a small well in the centre.
4. Fry the aubergine lightly in the oil until soft.
5. Mix together the prosciutto, basil, aubergine and cream. Season to taste with salt and pepper.
6. Spoon the filling into the centre of the ramekins. Sprinkle with the Parmesan cheese. Bake in the preheated oven for 15–20 minutes, or until well risen and brown. Serve very hot.

 MEDIUM RED

THREE-CHEESE CROQUE MONSIEUR

SERVES 4

55g/2oz unsalted butter, softened
55g/2oz Roquefort cheese
8 thin slices of wholemeal bread

45g/1½oz Gruyère cheese, grated
45g/1½oz Parmesan cheese, freshly grated
freshly ground black pepper
4 slices of Parma ham, fat removed
8 dried apple crisps (see page 505)

1. Mix the butter with the Roquefort cheese and use to butter the bread. Mix together the Gruyère and Parmesan cheeses and season with pepper.
2. Divide the cheese mixture between 4 of the slices of bread, put a slice of ham on top and place under the grill until the ham begins to cook and the cheese to melt. Place 2 apple crisps on top of each slice and sandwich with the remaining slices of bread. Continue to grill on the lowest shelf, turn the sandwiches over when they are golden-brown and grill the other side. Cut the sandwiches in half and serve immediately.

 CÔTES DU RHÔNE

AUBERGINE SALAD WITH PARMESAN AND CHIVE CRISPS

This recipe was given to us by Sue Spaull, a senior teacher at Leith's School.

SERVES 4

340g/12oz aubergine, cut into 1.5cm/¾in cubes
salt
a pinch of ground Sichuan pepper
2 tablespoons olive oil
3 sun-dried tomatoes, drained and shredded
2 tablespoons olive oil
3 large fresh basil leaves, cut into thin strips

For the dressing
3 tablespoons extra virgin olive oil
1 teaspoon balsamic vinegar
1 teaspoon lemon juice
1 teaspoon white wine vinegar
salt and freshly ground black pepper

To garnish
4 Parmesan and chive crisps (see following recipe)

fresh rocket leaves
1 tablespoon pinenuts, toasted

1. Place the aubergine in a colander and sprinkle lightly with salt and the Sichuan pepper. Leave to degorge for 30 minutes.
2. Heat the oil in a frying pan and fry the aubergine until tender and golden-brown. Drain on kitchen paper.
3. Make the dressing: whisk all the ingredients together until well emulsified. Season to taste with salt and pepper.
4. Toss the aubergine in the dressing with the sun-dried tomatoes and basil.
5. Pile the aubergine salad into the centre of 4 individual plates. Arrange a Parmesan and chive crisp on top of each serving and surround with a garland of rocket leaves and pinenuts.

 *ITALIAN CHARDONNAY*

PARMESAN AND CHIVE CRISPS

These crisps make an excellent garnish for salads.

SERVES 4

oil for greasing
4 tablespoons finely grated fresh Parmesan cheese
1 tablespoon very finely chopped fresh chives

1. Preheat the oven to 200°C/400°F/gas mark 6. Grease a baking sheet lightly with oil. Heat it in the oven until very hot.
2. Sprinkle the cheese into 4 × 7.5cm/3in rounds on the flat baking sheet. Flatten the rounds slightly.
3. Bake in the preheated oven for 2 minutes. Sprinkle with the chives. Bake for a further minute, or until very lightly browned at the edges.
4. Remove the crisps to a wire rack and leave to cool.

WARM MUSHROOM, GARLIC AND CAPER SALAD

SERVES 4

225g/8oz large flat mushrooms
110g/4oz shiitake mushrooms
170g/6oz oyster mushrooms
55g/2oz butter
2 cloves of garlic, crushed
3 tablespoons rice wine vinegar
2 teaspoons capers, rinsed
1 teaspoon chopped fresh marjoram
salt and freshly ground black pepper
a selection of salad leaves such as rocket, radicchio, frisée, watercress, washed and dried
2 tablespoons hazelnut oil

1. Wipe all the mushrooms carefully. Leave the small ones whole and slice the larger ones thickly.
2. Melt the butter in a large sauté pan, add the garlic and cook over a low heat for 1–2 minutes. Add the mushrooms, increase the heat and sauté for 2–3 minutes, or until just cooked. Tip into a bowl and keep warm.
3. Add the vinegar and capers to the pan and bring to the boil. Remove from the heat, return the mushrooms to the pan and season to taste with salt and pepper.
4. Put the salad leaves into a large bowl and toss with the hazelnut oil, season with salt and pepper. Add the mushrooms and toss together. Pile into a serving dish and serve immediately.

 *SAUVIGNON DE TOURAINE*

RICH MUSSEL BOURRIDE

SERVES 4

30g/1oz butter
1 teaspoon curry powder (see page 637)
½ teaspoon cayenne pepper

a large pinch of saffron strands
100ml/3½fl oz dry white wine
150ml/5fl oz fish stock (see page 626)
1 clove of garlic, chopped
grated zest of 1 orange
1 sprig of fresh thyme
1 sprig of fresh parsley
salt and freshly ground black pepper
900g/2lb live mussels, prepared (see page 135)
1 quantity aïoli (see page 632)
2 tablespoons chopped fresh parsley

1. Melt the butter in a large saucepan, add the curry powder, cayenne and saffron and fry over a gentle heat for 2 minutes. Add the wine, stock, garlic, orange zest and herbs. Season with a little salt and pepper. Bring to the boil, then reduce the heat and simmer for 5 minutes.
2. Put the mussels into the pan, cover and return to the boil. Cook for 3–4 minutes or until the mussels are cooked and all the shells have opened.
3. Lift the mussels from the liquid, discarding any that have remained closed. Pile into a soup tureen and keep warm.
4. Return the poaching liquid to the heat and reduce if necessary by boiling rapidly to 290ml/ ½ pint.
5. Remove the saucepan from the heat and leave to cool for 2 minutes, then strain the liquid on to the aïoli and stir to mix well. Return the mixture to the rinsed-out saucepan and cook over a gentle heat, stirring continuously, for 2–3 minutes or until the liquid has just thickened. Do not allow to boil. Add the parsley and season to taste with more salt and pepper if necessary. Pour over the mussels and serve very hot.

 *DRY ROSÉ*

SOUPS

PHEASANT CONSOMMÉ

This recipe is only worth cooking if you have really well-hung, gamey pheasants, otherwise the flavours do not come through. If pheasants are unavailable you could use stronger-tasting game birds such as grouse.

SERVES 4

2 well-hung pheasants, plucked and drawn
4 tablespoons sunflower oil
2 onions, chopped
1 large carrot, chopped
2 sticks of celery, chopped
2 leeks, cut into 2.5cm/1in pieces
4 tomatoes, chopped
1 teaspoon tomato purée
4 cloves of garlic, halved
1 bouquet garni
salt and freshly ground black pepper
1.1 litres/2 pints white stock, made with
    chicken bones (see page 625)
570ml/1 pint dry white wine
5 tablespoons medium sherry or Madeira
3 egg whites and shells, crushed

To serve
game sausage rolls (see page 393) or parsley
    polenta croûtons (see page 241)

1. Preheat the oven to 150°C/300°F/gas mark 2. Joint each pheasant into 4 pieces.
2. Heat a little of the oil in a frying pan and fry the pheasant pieces until well browned on all sides. Remove from the pan and set aside on a plate.
3. Fry the onions, carrot, celery and leeks in a little oil in the pan, a few at a time, until they are a good russet-brown.

4. Add the tomatoes, tomato purée and garlic and cook for a further few minutes.
5. Tip all the vegetables into a large flameproof casserole, add the pheasant and bouquet garni and season well with salt and pepper. Pour in the stock and wine and enough water to cover by about 2.5cm/1in.
6. Bring to the boil and skim off any scum or fat that rises to the surface. Boil for 1 minute, then turn off the heat and skim off any more scum. Cover the casserole with a well-fitting lid, transfer to the bottom of the oven and cook for 3–4 hours, or until the pheasant flesh is falling off the bones.
7. Carefully strain the pheasant stock through a sieve lined with muslin or a clean J-cloth. If the liquid is very fatty, allow it to cool and then refrigerate it so that the fat solidifies and can be removed easily. It is important that the stock is now completely fat-free. Taste the liquid for strength of flavour – if it is a little watery boil rapidly and reduce until the flavour is strong enough.
8. If the liquid is beautifully clear at this point, add the sherry and season with salt before serving, otherwise the liquid must be clarified as follows.
9. Allow the stock to cool, then pour with the sherry into a large clean saucepan. Season very well with salt and pepper.
10. Put the egg whites and crushed shells into the stock. Place over the heat and whisk steadily with a balloon whisk until the mixture boils. Stop whisking immediately and remove the pan from the heat. Allow the mixture to subside. Take care not to break the crust formed by the egg white.
11. Bring up the consommé just to the boil again, then allow to subside. Repeat this procedure once more. The egg white will trap

the sediment in the stock and clear the consommé. Allow to cool for 2 minutes.

12. Place a double layer of fine muslin (or kitchen paper) in a clean sieve over a clean bowl and carefully strain the consommé through it, taking care to hold the egg white crust back. When all the liquid is through (or almost all of it), allow the egg white to slip into the muslin. Then strain the consommé again, this time through both egg white crust and cloth. Do not try to hurry the process by squeezing the cloth as this will produce murky soup: it must be allowed to drip through at its own pace. The consommé is now ready for serving.

NOTE: All equipment for clarifying the consommé should be scalded before use.

 *MADEIRA – SERCIAL*

ROAST TOMATO SOUP

SERVES 4

1kg/2¼lb plum tomatoes, halved and de-seeded
2 cloves of garlic, peeled
1 red pepper, de-seeded and sliced
3 tablespoons extra virgin olive oil
1 teaspoon caster sugar
1 teaspoon ground coriander
salt and freshly ground black pepper
150–190ml/¼–⅓ pint white stock, made with
   chicken bones (see page 625)
150ml/¼ pint crème fraîche
1 tablespoon chopped fresh coriander

1. Preheat the oven to 180°C/350°F/gas mark 4.
2. Put the tomatoes, garlic and red pepper into a roasting tin, brush generously with the oil and season with the sugar, coriander, salt and pepper.
3. Roast in the preheated oven for 1–1½ hours, or until the tomatoes, garlic and pepper are very soft. If the garlic begins to colour during the cooking, remove and set aside.
4. Once the vegetables are cooked, whizz in a blender to form a smooth purée. Sieve if necessary.

5. Put the purée into a clean saucepan, add the stock and bring to the boil. Remove from the heat and stir in the crème fraîche, then continue to heat until the soup comes to just below boiling point – do not allow it to boil. Check the seasoning and add the coriander.
6. Pour the soup into a warmed soup tureen and serve very hot.

 *DRY WHITE*

ROAST BUTTERNUT SQUASH AND GARLIC SOUP

SERVES 4

900g/2lb butternut squash, peeled and diced
2 cloves of garlic, peeled
1 red chilli, de-seeded and chopped
4 tablespoons extra virgin olive oil
salt and freshly ground black pepper
290ml/½ pint milk
290ml/½ pint vegetable stock (see page 627)
½ teaspoon freshly grated nutmeg
2–3 tablespoons chopped fresh coriander

1. Preheat the oven to 190°C/375°F/gas mark 5.
2. Put the squash, garlic and chilli into a roasting tin, brush with the oil and season with salt and pepper. Roast in the preheated oven for 25–30 minutes, or until the squash is soft.
3. Whizz the vegetables with the milk and stock in a blender and pour into a saucepan. Bring to just below boiling point, then season with the nutmeg and add the coriander. Check the seasoning. Do not allow the soup to boil. Serve in a warmed soup tureen.

 *CHABLIS*

SCALLOP VICHYSSOISE

SERVES 4

8 large scallops, prepared (see page 136)
55g/2oz butter
3 large leeks, thinly sliced
1 large potato, weighing about 340g/12oz,
    peeled and cut into small dice
1 litre/1¾ pints fish stock (see page 626)
salt and freshly ground black pepper
290ml/½ pint crème fraîche

To garnish
chopped fresh chives

1. Cut the white meat of the scallops into thin slices horizontally. Leave the coral whole. Cover and set aside in the refrigerator.
2. Melt the butter in a large saucepan, add the leeks and cook over a very gentle heat until completely soft but not coloured. Add the diced potato and stock to the saucepan and season well with salt and pepper. Bring the soup to the boil, then reduce the heat and cook for 15–20 minutes or until the potato is very soft.
3. Whizz the soup to a fine purée in a blender, then sieve into a clean saucepan. Add the crème fraîche and reheat until the liquid is just coming to the boil. Season to taste.
4. Add the prepared scallops to the saucepan and cook over a low heat for 2–3 minutes or until the scallop meat is cooked (it should be completely opaque). Take care not to overcook the scallops, or they will be rubbery.
5. Serve in a warmed soup tureen, garnished with chives.

 PINOT BLANC D'ALSACE

MANHATTAN CLAM CHOWDER

Both Manhattan and New England are famous for clam chowder. The New England version is a pale, creamy soup, always made with salt pork belly or bacon as an important ingredient. The Manhattan chowder does not include this but uses tomatoes. On many menus in the USA the two are sold as White (New England) and Red (Manhattan) chowders. New England or Boston clam chowder usually calls for soft-shelled clams, and the New York or Coney Island version usually uses hard-shell clams, which are more readily available in this country.

SERVES 4

24 hard-shell clams, such as cherrystone
2 tablespoons olive oil
2 large onions, finely chopped
white part of 1 large leek, thinly sliced
1 clove of garlic, crushed
225g/8oz potato, peeled and diced
2 sticks of celery, chopped
1 green pepper, de-seeded and diced
4 tomatoes, skinned, de-seeded and diced
1.7 litres/3 pints fish stock (see page 626)
sprigs of fresh thyme
1 tablespoon chopped fresh marjoram
1 bay leaf
1 teaspoon cayenne pepper
salt and freshly ground black pepper

To serve
Italian bread (see page 658)

1. Open the clams with a shucking knife. Lift the clams from the shell and collect any juice. Set aside.
2. Heat the oil in a large flameproof casserole, add the onions and leeks and cook over a low heat until soft.
3. Add the garlic, potato, celery and green pepper to the casserole and cook for 3–4 further minutes.
4. Add the tomatoes, stock, any clam juice and the herbs to the pan. Bring to the boil, then reduce the heat and simmer slowly until the potatoes are cooked.
5. Stir the clams into the soup, bring back to the boil and simmer for 1 minute or until the clams are cooked. Remove the sprigs of thyme and the bay leaf.
6. Season the soup to taste with cayenne, salt and pepper.
7. To serve: pour into a tureen and serve very hot with Italian bread.

 CHARDONNAY

MEDITERRANEAN FISH AND SAFFRON SOUP

SERVES 4

1 × 225g/8oz John Dory fillet
1 × 225g/8oz monkfish tail
2 small squid, prepared (see page 135)
5 tablespoons extra virgin olive oil
1 bulb of Florence fennel, sliced
4 shallots, chopped
2 cloves of garlic, crushed
1 red chilli, de-seeded and chopped
4 tomatoes, skinned and chopped
1 red pepper, de-seeded and chopped
a large pinch of saffron
1 litre/1¾ pints well-flavoured white fish stock
    (see page 626)
salt and freshly ground black pepper
4 tablespoons seasoned plain flour (see page
    637)

To garnish
1 tablespoon chopped fresh basil

To serve
1 quantity aïoli (see page 632)

1. Skin the John Dory and monkfish and cut into 5cm/2in chunks. Slice the squid, leaving the tentacles whole. Cover and refrigerate.
2. Heat 3 tablespoons of the oil in a large saucepan, add the fennel and shallots and cook over a low heat for 12–15 minutes, or until soft. Add the garlic, chilli, tomatoes, red pepper and saffron and cook for a further 5 minutes.
3. Add the stock and bring to the boil, then lower the heat and simmer for 8–10 minutes, or until the vegetables are soft. Season to taste with salt and pepper.
4. Meanwhile, toss all the fish in the seasoned flour and shake off any excess. Heat the remaining oil in a sauté pan, add the fish and fry for 1–2 minutes, or until lightly browned.
5. Add the fish to the stock and continue to cook over a very low heat for 2–3 minutes, or until cooked through. Season to taste with salt and pepper.

6. Serve the soup in a warmed tureen, garnished with basil. Hand the aïoli separately.

 *DRY WHITE*

MAIN COURSES

Fish and Shellfish
Poultry and Game
Beef
Lamb
Pork
Veal
Offal
Vegetarian

FISH AND SHELLFISH

BRILL WITH DEEP-FRIED VEGETABLE RIBBONS

SERVES 4

4 × 170g/6oz brill fillets, skinned (see page 133)
30g/1oz butter
1 teaspoon chopped fresh sage
1 clove of garlic, crushed
salt and freshly ground black pepper
1 large courgette
1 large carrot
1 leek
oil for deep-frying

1. Fold each brill fillet into 3, skinned side inside, and arrange, seam side down, on an oiled baking sheet. Set aside.
2. Melt the butter in a small saucepan and add the sage and garlic. Cook over a low heat for 1 minute, or until the garlic begins to sizzle. Remove from the heat and leave to infuse for a few minutes.
3. Peel the courgette and carrot into ribbons about 2.5cm/1in wide, using a peeler. Put the strips into a colander, sprinkle with salt and leave to stand for 10 minutes.
4. Cut the leek in half lengthways and remove the outer leaves. Wash well, then cut the leek into long strips 2.5cm/1in wide.
5. Preheat the oven to 180°C/350°F/gas mark 4.
6. Heat the oil in a deep-fryer or large saucepan until a crumb browns within 25 seconds.
7. Rinse the courgette and carrot ribbons, then dry with kitchen paper.
8. Deep-fry a few vegetable ribbons at a time (do not allow to become too brown or they will taste bitter). Lift from the oil and drain on kitchen paper. Sprinkle with a little salt. Keep warm.

9. Brush the brill fillets with the infused butter and grill for 4–5 minutes, or until the fish is cooked (it should be opaque and firm).
10. To serve: lift the fish from the baking sheet, arrange on a serving dish and spoon over any cooking juices. Arrange the deep-fried vegetable ribbons around the fish and serve.

 AUSTRALIAN CHARDONNAY

PAN-FRIED JOHN DORY WITH ROASTED PUMPKIN

SERVES 4

4 × 170g/6oz John Dory, skinned (see page 132)
900g/2lb pumpkin
6 tablespoons extra virgin olive oil
1 onion, thinly sliced
1 teaspoon ground ginger
1 teaspoon garam masala
110g/4oz pumpkin or sunflower seeds
salt and freshly ground black pepper
seasoned flour (see page 637)
30g/1oz butter

To garnish
1 tablespoon chopped fresh thyme
lemon wedges

1. Pinbone the John Dory fillets if necessary (see page 133). Cover the fillets and set aside in the refrigerator.
2. Preheat the oven to 200°C/400°F/gas mark 6.
3. Cut the pumpkin in half and peel away the skin. Remove the seeds and set aside. Cut the

pumpkin into 3.5cm/1½in chunks.

4. Heat the oil in a large roasting tin. Add the pumpkin, baste with the hot oil and sprinkle over the onion. Roast in the oven for 40 minutes, basting occasionally, until the pumpkin is soft and golden-brown.

5. Sprinkle the spices and pumpkin seeds over the pumpkin, season with salt and pepper and cook in the oven for 10 further minutes. Remove the roasting tin from the oven, lift the pumpkin from the oil and pat dry on kitchen paper. Keep warm.

6. Toss the John Dory in the seasoned flour and put on to a plate. Do not stack the fillets or they will become soggy.

7. Heat the butter in a large frying pan until hot and foaming. Fry the fillets on each side for 3–4 minutes, or until lightly browned, opaque and firm to the touch.

8. To serve: pile the pumpkin on to a serving dish and sprinkle with the thyme. Arrange the John Dory fillets on top and garnish with the lemon wedges.

 *ST-VÉRAN*

BAKED HALIBUT WITH RED RATATOUILLE

SERVES 4

4 × 170g/6oz halibut steaks
1 tablespoon olive oil
salt and freshly ground black pepper

For the red ratatouille
1 large aubergine
olive oil
2 red onions, sliced
2 cloves of garlic, crushed
1 large red pepper, de-seeded and sliced
6 tomatoes, quartered and de-seeded
1 tablespoon tomato purée
75ml/2½fl oz tomato juice
salt and freshly ground black pepper
10 fresh purple basil leaves, chopped
10 Kalamata olives, pitted and halved

To garnish
a few fresh purple basil leaves

1. Preheat the oven to 180°C/350°F/gas mark 4.

2. Wipe the aubergine, cut into bite-sized pieces, sprinkle with salt and leave to drain for about 30 minutes. Rinse away the salt and dry the aubergine well.

3. Heat a little oil in a sauté pan, add the onions and garlic and fry until soft but not brown. Add the aubergine and fry until light brown. Add the red pepper and fry over a low heat for 2–3 further minutes, until the pepper softens a little.

4. Add the tomatoes, tomato purée and juice, cover with a lid and simmer gently for 20 minutes. Remove the lid and reduce the juices if necessary by boiling rapidly. Season with salt and pepper.

5. Mix the chopped basil and olives into the ratatouille and keep warm.

6. Brush the halibut with the oil and season with salt and pepper. Bake for 12 minutes, or until cooked (it should be opaque and firm).

7. To serve: spoon the ratatouille on to a warmed serving dish and arrange the halibut steaks on top. Garnish with the purple basil leaves.

 *CHINON – LOIRE*

NORFOLK SOUSED HERRINGS IN BLACKBERRY VINEGAR

SERVES 4

8 mackerel fillets
1 onion, thinly sliced
1 small carrot, thinly sliced
a few parsley stalks
3 bay leaves
12 black peppercorns, lightly crushed
1 blade of mace
1 teaspoon salt
290ml/½ pint blackberry vinegar
290ml/½ pint white wine
juice of 1 lemon

To serve
blackberry vinegar
fresh blackberries
new potato, chive and soured cream salad (see
page 328)

1. Pinbone the mackerel fillets if necessary (see page 133) and lay them flat in a baking dish.
2. Put all the remaining ingredients into a saucepan. Bring to the boil, then lower the heat and simmer gently for 20 minutes. Allow to cool.
3. Preheat the oven to 130°C/250°F/gas mark 1.
4. Strain the liquor on to the mackerel fillets (they should just be covered). Cover with damp greaseproof paper and bake near the bottom of the preheated oven for 45 minutes–1 hour, or until the fillets are opaque.
5. Allow the fillets to cool in the liquor. Chill for 1 hour before serving.
6. To serve: arrange the fillets on individual plates and spoon a little blackberry vinegar over each. Garnish with blackberries and serve with new potato, chive and soured cream salad.

 *WHITE RIOJA*

BAKED MACKEREL WITH LIME, BULGHAR AND ROAST GARLIC

SERVES 4

4 mackerel, ungutted
2 large heads of garlic
1 tablespoon olive oil
1 tablespoon water
85g/3oz bulghar wheat
grated zest and juice of 2 limes
salt and freshly ground black pepper
extra olive oil for brushing

To serve
4 lime wedges
crisp green salad
warm crusty bread

1. Preheat the oven to 200°C/400°F/gas mark 6.
2. Bone the mackerel out from the back, removing the guts at the same time (see page 131). Cut off the heads and fins. Wash the mackerel thoroughly and dry on kitchen paper.
3. Place the garlic in a piece of kitchen foil with the oil and water. Wrap tightly to form a parcel. Place the parcel in a small roasting tin and bake in the preheated oven for 20 minutes, or until tender. Remove from the oven and allow to cool.
4. Put the bulghar wheat into a bowl, cover with water and leave to soak for 15 minutes, then tip into a sieve and press out excess water.
5. Remove the garlic from the foil and with a blunt knife press the garlic flesh out of the skins which can be discarded.
6. Mix together the garlic, bulghar wheat, lime zest and juice and season to taste with salt and pepper.
7. Lay the mackerel out flat on a baking sheet, skin side down. Season with salt and pepper. Divide the bulghar mixture equally between the fish, then fold them back over to resemble their original shape.
8. Place the mackerel on a baking sheet, brush with oil and sprinkle with a little salt. Bake in the preheated oven for 15 minutes.
9. Serve immediately with lime wedges, a crisp green salad and warm crusty bread.

 *AUSTRALIAN SÉMILLON–CHARDONNAY*

MACKEREL WITH MANGO AND HORSERADISH

SERVES 2

4 mackerel fillets
seasoned plain flour
olive oil for frying
2 small ripe mangoes or 1 large mango, peeled and cut into matchsticks
2 teaspoons freshly grated horseradish or 3–4 teaspoons horseradish sauce

411

juice of 1 lemon
salt and freshly ground black pepper

To garnish
2 sprigs fresh flat-leaf parsley

1. Preheat the oven to 140°C/275°F/gas mark 1.
2. Pinbone the mackerel fillets if necessary (see page 133), dip them in the seasoned flour and shake off the excess.
3. Heat a large heavy-based frying pan. Add 2 tablespoons oil to the pan and when it is very hot place 2 mackerel fillets, skin side down, in the pan. Fry for a minute, or until the skin is golden-brown. Turn the fillets over and cook for a further minute or until the second side is also brown. Keep warm in the oven while cooking the remaining fillets in the same way.
4. Transfer the cooked fillets to the oven and toss the mango and horseradish into the pan. Season with salt and pepper and cook over a high heat for a minute until the mango has warmed through.
5. Pile a spoonful of the mango mixture on to 2 warmed individual plates and arrange the mackerel fillets on top. Garnish each with a sprig of flat-leaf parsley and serve immediately.

 *WHITE RIOJA*

SEA BASS WITH CONFIT OF LEEKS AND FRESH TOMATO SAUCE

SERVES 4

4 × 170g/6oz sea bass fillets, skinned
30g/1oz butter
450g/1lb trimmed leeks, thinly sliced
4 tablespoons double cream
salt and freshly ground black pepper
4 tablespoons dry white wine
juice of 1 lemon

For the sauce
30g/1oz butter

2 tablespoons extra virgin olive oil
1 clove of garlic, crushed
4 large sun-ripened tomatoes, skinned, de-seeded and chopped
1 tablespoon chopped fresh basil
1 tablespoon chopped fresh parsley
salt and freshly ground black pepper
a pinch of caster sugar

1. Preheat the oven to 170°C/325°F/gas mark 3.
2. Pinbone the sea bass fillets if necessary (see page 133). Cut each fillet into 2 diamond shapes and make a horizontal cut in the side of each fillet to form a pocket.
3. Melt the butter in a saucepan and add the leeks. Cook them gently over a low heat, covered, for 10 minutes, or until soft. Add the cream and simmer, uncovered, until all the juices have evaporated. Season with salt and plenty of pepper. Set aside to cool.
4. Take one-quarter of the leek mixture and place in the pocket in each sea bass fillet.
5. Grease a large, shallow casserole dish and lay the fillets in a single layer on the bottom. Sprinkle over the wine and lemon juice and season with salt and pepper. Cover with damp greaseproof paper and the lid. Bake in the middle of the oven for 10–15 minutes, or until the fish is just firm and opaque. Drain the fillets well and place in a warmed serving dish.
6. Make the sauce: melt the butter with the oil in a large frying pan, add the garlic and cook for 10 seconds over a high heat. Add the tomatoes, herbs, salt, pepper and sugar and toss over a high heat for 30 seconds, or until the tomatoes are just starting to lose their shape. Check the seasoning and spoon around the sea bass. Serve immediately.

 *CHABLIS*

LEMON SOLE KIEV

SERVES 4

110g/4oz butter, softened
1 clove of garlic, crushed
1 tablespoon chopped fresh parsley

2 teaspoons chopped fresh chives
a squeeze of lemon juice
salt and freshly ground black pepper
8 lemon sole fillets, skinned
seasoned plain flour
1 egg, beaten
dried white breadcrumbs
oil for deep-frying

1. Mix the butter with the garlic, parsley, chives, lemon juice, salt and pepper. Divide into 4 equal portions, shape each into a rectangle and chill well.
2. Bat the sole fillets between 2 sheets of clingfilm until they are double their original size.
3. Cut each butter rectangle in half and divide between the fish fillets. Roll up, ensuring that the butter is completely enclosed.
4. Dust each sole fillet lightly with seasoned flour. Dip into the beaten egg, then roll carefully in breadcrumbs. Chill for 30 minutes.
5. Brush with more beaten egg and roll again in breadcrumbs. Leave to chill for a further 30 minutes.
6. Heat the oil in a deep-fryer until a crumb will sizzle vigorously in it. Fry the sole fillets for 4–5 minutes, or until golden-brown. Drain well on kitchen paper and serve immediately.

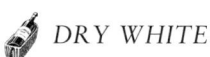 *DRY WHITE*

NOISETTES OF SALMON WITH ARTICHOKE BOTTOMS

SERVES 4

4 × 170g/6oz salmon cutlets, cut 3.5cm/1½in
    thick
salt and freshly ground black pepper
1 × 400g/14oz can of artichoke bottoms,
    drained
225g/8oz oyster mushrooms
30g/1oz butter
75ml/2½fl oz dry white vermouth

150ml/¼ pint double cream
2 teaspoons chopped fresh sage
juice of ½ lemon

1. Prepare the salmon noisettes (see page 283). Press the noisettes between 2 plates, cover and refrigerate for at least 1 hour. Season the noisettes on both sides with salt and pepper.
2. Preheat the grill to its highest setting.
3. Slice the artichokes and mushrooms thickly. Heat the butter in a frying pan and sauté the artichokes and mushrooms over a gentle heat until the mushrooms are soft.
4. Add the vermouth to the pan and reduce by boiling rapidly to half the original quantity. Add the cream and continue to boil until the mixture is syrupy. Stir from time to time to prevent the cream from catching on the bottom of the pan.
5. Add the sage to the mixture, season to taste with lemon juice, salt and pepper and keep warm.
6. Grill the salmon noisettes for 3 minutes on each side or until cooked (they should be opaque and firm). Remove the string and slice.
7. To serve: divide the artichoke and mushroom sauce between 4 individual plates. Place a salmon noisette on each and serve immediately.

 FULL-BODIED CHARDONNAY

SALT COD RAGOÛT

SERVES 4

450g/1lb salt cod
150ml/¼ pint olive oil
2 onions, thinly sliced
5 cloves of garlic, crushed
2 yellow peppers, grilled, de-seeded and peeled
2 red peppers, grilled, de-seeded and peeled
6 tomatoes, skinned, de-seeded and chopped
1 tablespoon chopped fresh thyme
450g/1lb potatoes, peeled and thinly sliced
150ml/¼ pint fish stock (see page 626)

To garnish
12 olives, pitted and halved
1 tablespoon capers, rinsed

413

1. Soak the salt cod in cold water for 24 hours. Change the water several times to extract as much salt as possible.

2. Drain the salt cod on kitchen paper. Remove the skin and bones and break the flesh into large flakes. Lay on a flat serving dish and pour over the oil. Cover and refrigerate for 2 hours.

3. Preheat the oven to 180°C/350°F/gas mark 4.

4. Heat 2 tablespoons of the cod-soaking oil in a saucepan. Add the onions and cook over a very low heat until soft. Add the garlic and cook for 2 further minutes.

5. Cut the peppers into strips and add to the onions and garlic with the tomatoes and thyme.

6. Arrange the potato slices in the bottom of a large casserole and pour over the stock.

7. Lift the salt cod from the oil, mix with the tomato and pepper mixture and spoon on to the potatoes. Cover and cook in the oven for 50 minutes, or until the cod and potatoes are tender.

8. Sprinkle over the olives and capers and serve hot.

 DRY ROSÉ BORDEAUX

SHARK, OKRA AND AUBERGINE CASSEROLE

SERVES 4

1 large aubergine
2 teaspoons salt
225g/8oz okra
675g/1½lb shark steak, skinned
2 tablespoons plain flour, seasoned with
  paprika and salt
4 tablespoons extra virgin olive oil
2 onions, finely chopped
2 cloves of garlic, crushed
1 teaspoon ground cumin
4 tomatoes, peeled, de-seeded and chopped
150ml/¼ pint fish stock (see page 626)
2 tablespoons tahini (see page 139)
30g/1oz sultanas
salt and freshly ground black pepper
fresh coriander leaves

1. Cut the aubergine into 2.5cm/1in chunks. Put into a colander, sprinkle over the salt and leave to degorge for 15 minutes. Wipe off the excess salt and pat dry on kitchen paper.

2. Trim the tops off the okra and blanch in plenty of boiling salted water for 5 minutes. Drain and refresh under cold running water.

3. Cut the shark into 2.5cm/1in chunks. Roll in the seasoned flour and place on a plate. Do not stack them or they will become soggy.

4. Heat the oil in a large flameproof casserole and brown the shark a few pieces at a time. Lift out and set aside.

5. Add the onions and aubergine and fry over a low heat until the onions are beginning to brown and the aubergine is soft. Add the garlic and cumin with the okra and fry for 3 further minutes.

6. Add the tomatoes to the casserole with the stock and tahini. Bring to the boil, then lower the heat, cover and cook over a low heat for about 20 minutes, or until the okra are soft.

7. When all the vegetables are nearly cooked and tender, remove the lid and replace the shark in the casserole. Sprinkle over the sultanas and season lightly with salt and pepper.

8. Cover again and cook over a low heat for 10 further minutes, or until the shark is cooked (it should be opaque and firm).

9. To serve: transfer the shark and vegetables to a clean casserole. Reduce the cooking liquid if necessary by boiling rapidly. Add the coriander leaves and season to taste with salt and pepper. Pour over the shark and serve very hot, straight from the casserole.

 *DRY ROSÉ*

SKATE WITH SPINACH AND BACON

SERVES 2

55g/2oz button mushrooms
15g/½oz fresh flat-leaf parsley, chopped
15g/½oz butter
juice of ½ lemon

salt and freshly ground black pepper
1 skate wing, filleted into 2
4 rindless rashers of streaky bacon
1 small piece of pig's caul, about 30cm/12in
square
oil
2 cloves of garlic
2 tablespoons balsamic vinegar
150ml/¼ pint white stock, made with chicken
bones (see page 625)

For the spinach
450g/1lb fresh spinach, cooked and chopped
30g/1oz butter
1 clove of garlic, crushed

1. Preheat the oven to 200°C/400°F/gas mark 6.
2. Sauté the mushrooms and half the parsley in the butter. Add the lemon juice and season to taste with salt and pepper.
3. Divide the mushroom mixture between the 2 fillets and roll each up into a ball. Wrap in the bacon and then in the caul. Secure, if necessary, with a cocktail stick.
4. Heat a little oil in a flameproof casserole and add the skate balls and the garlic. Sauté until the bacon is golden.
5. Cover and cook in the preheated oven for 15–20 minutes. Remove the cocktail sticks, if used.
6. Put the casserole back on the heat. Add the vinegar and reduce by half. Then add the chicken stock and reduce by half again. Add the remaining parsley.
7. Sauté the spinach in the butter and garlic.
8. Put the spinach on 2 plates, arrange the skate on top and pour over the reduced vinegar and stock.

 *CRISP DRY WHITE*

GRILLED SWORDFISH BROCHETTES WITH PANCETTA AND FIGS

SERVES 4

4 × 110g/4oz swordfish steaks, skinned
2 tablespoons extra virgin olive oil
salt and freshly ground black pepper
110g/4oz pancetta
4 ripe figs, quartered
4 bay leaves
2 teaspoons chopped fresh rosemary

1. Preheat the grill or barbecue to its highest setting.
2. Cut the swordfish into 4cm/1½in cubes. Put into a bowl, add the oil and season generously with salt and pepper. Leave to marinate for 15 minutes.
3. Cut the pancetta into 2.5cm/1in pieces and add to the swordfish.
4. Lightly oil 4 large skewers. Thread a piece of fig on to each skewer and thread on a bay leaf. Skewer pieces of swordfish and pancetta on to each skewer alternately with pieces of fig.
5. Brush each brochette generously with the marinade oil and sprinkle with the rosemary.
6. Grill the skewers for 1 minute, then turn and continue to grill, turning frequently, until the swordfish is just cooked and the pancetta browned. Do not overcook. Serve immediately.

 *AUSTRALIAN SÉMILLON–CHARDONNAY*

SMOKED HADDOCK SAUSAGES WITH TARRAGON BUTTER SAUCE

SERVES 4

75ml/2½fl oz double cream
55g/2oz fresh white breadcrumbs
340g/12oz undyed smoked haddock fillet,
  skinned
1 egg, beaten
a pinch of freshly grated nutmeg
1 tablespoon lemon juice
salt and freshly ground black pepper

For the tarragon butter sauce
150ml/¼ pint fish stock (see page 626)
2 tablespoons rice wine vinegar
110g/4oz unsalted butter, chilled
2 teaspoons chopped fresh tarragon
salt and freshly ground black pepper

To serve
crushed butternut squash (see page 461)

1. Scald the cream by bringing it just to the boil. Pour it over the breadcrumbs and leave to cool.
2. Pinbone the haddock fillet if necessary (see page 133). Put the haddock into a food processor and whizz to a smooth paste.
3. Transfer the fish paste to a bowl and stir in the egg, nutmeg and the cold cream mixture. Beat together well, then season with lemon juice, salt and pepper.
4. Divide the mixture into 8 equal portions and shape each into a ball. Wrap each ball in clingfilm and roll to a sausage shape.
5. Bring 1 litre/1¾ pints water to the boil in a large saucepan. Add the fish sausages, lower the heat and poach for 10–15 minutes, or until firm to the touch.
6. Meanwhile, make the tarragon butter sauce: put the stock and vinegar into a saucepan and bring to the boil, then reduce by boiling rapidly to 3 tablespoons. Lower the heat and gradually add the butter in small pieces, whisking vigorously after each addition. Add the tarragon and season to taste with salt and pepper.
7. To serve: unwrap the fish sausages and arrange 2 on each of 4 warmed individual plates. Spoon over a little of the tarragon butter sauce. Hand the crushed butternut squash separately.

 NEW ZEALAND CHARDONNAY

GRILLED TUNA FISH STEAKS WITH GREEN CHILLI PESTO

Tuna is wonderful if carefully cooked. If overdone it becomes very dry and rather cardboard-like in texture.

SERVES 4

4 × 170g/6oz tuna steaks, skinned (see page 133)

For the marinade
6 tablespoons olive oil
2 tablespoons balsamic vinegar
freshly ground black pepper

For the chilli pesto
2 green chillies
1 bunch of fresh coriander
55g/2oz pinenuts
2 cloves of garlic, crushed
55g/2oz Parmesan cheese, freshly grated
6 tablespoons olive oil
salt and freshly ground black pepper

To garnish
sprigs of fresh coriander

1. Put the tuna steaks into a flat dish and pour over the marinade ingredients. Cover and refrigerate for 2 hours.
2. Preheat the grill to its highest setting.
3. Make the chilli pesto: slit the chillies carefully and remove the seeds. Put the chillies,

coriander, pinenuts and garlic into a liquidizer. Blend well, add the Parmesan cheese and with the motor still running pour on the oil in a thin stream until well emulsified. Season to taste with salt and pepper.

4. Lift the tuna steaks from the marinade, place on the grill rack and grill for about 3 minutes on each side, until cooked (they should be opaque, lightly browned and firm but still moist).

5. To serve: place the tuna steaks on a serving dish, spoon the chilli pesto on top and garnish with coriander.

NOTE: Take care when handling chillies; the volatile oil contained in the juice can burn sensitive skin badly. It is a good idea to wear rubber gloves when chopping chillies.

 CALIFORNIAN CHARDONNAY

ROOT VEGETABLE AND FISH PIE

SERVES 6

900g/2lb haddock fillets, unskinned
290ml/½ pint milk
1 slice of onion
1 bay leaf
1 blade of mace
6 black peppercorns
20g/¾oz butter
20g/¾oz flour
1 tablespoon chopped fresh parsley
salt and freshly ground white pepper
340g/12oz sweet potato, peeled
340g/12oz swede, peeled
340g/12oz celeriac, peeled
340g/12oz parsnips, peeled
55g/2oz butter
a pinch of freshly grated nutmeg
15g/½oz Parmesan cheese, freshly grated

1. Poach the haddock in the milk with the onion, bay leaf, mace and peppercorns until cooked (the flesh should be opaque and flake easily).

2. Lift the fish out of the milk, skin and remove any bones. Break the flesh into large flakes and set aside. Strain the milk.

3. Melt the butter in a saucepan, add the flour and cook for 30 seconds. Remove from the heat and blend in the milk. Return to the heat and cook, stirring constantly, until the sauce boils. Simmer for 3 minutes, remove from the heat and cool.

4. Stir the haddock and parsley into the sauce, and season to taste with salt and pepper. Spoon into a pie dish.

5. Preheat the oven to 180°C/350°F/gas mark 4.

6. Cut the root vegetables into chunks. Boil the sweet potato and swede together in salted water until tender. Drain and mash.

7. Boil the celeriac and parsnip together in salted water, until tender. Drain and mash.

8. Stir 30g/1oz butter into each purée, and season to taste with nutmeg, salt and pepper.

9. Spoon the puréed vegetables in alternate lines across the top of the fish to give a striped effect. Sprinkle the top with Parmesan cheese.

10. Bake the pie in the preheated oven for 30 minutes, or until very hot. If necessary, brown the top under the grill.

 NEW WORLD SÉMILLON

BAKED SHRIMP WITH RICOTTA AND PARMESAN

SERVES 4

675g/1½lb raw tiger prawns, peeled and de-veined
1 large clove of garlic, crushed
340g/12oz ricotta cheese
1 egg, lightly beaten
150ml/¼ pint double cream
2 tablespoons chopped fresh chives
Tabasco sauce
freshly ground black pepper
85g/3oz Parmesan cheese, freshly grated

To serve
1 lemon, cut into wedges
½ quantity spinach and saffron bread (see page 371)

1. Preheat the oven to 180°C/350°F/gas mark 4.
2. Mix the prawns, garlic, ricotta, egg, cream and chives together in a large bowl and season to taste with Tabasco and pepper.
3. Tip into a shallow gratin dish, sprinkle with the Parmesan cheese and place on a baking sheet. Bake at the top of the oven for 20–25 minutes, or until bubbling at the edges and golden-brown on top.
4. Serve immediately with the lemon wedges and spinach and saffron bread.

 *MUSCADET*

TIGER PRAWN AND AUBERGINE PASTA GRATIN

SERVES 6

1 large aubergine, sliced
2 teaspoons salt
2 tablespoons extra virgin olive oil
6 tomatoes
15g/½oz butter
1 clove of garlic, crushed
salt and freshly ground black pepper
2 teaspoons sugar
340g/12oz cooked tiger prawns, peeled
juice of ½ lemon
340g/12oz tricolour penne or fusilli pasta, cooked
570ml/1 pint Cheddar and grain mustard sauce (see page 502)
3–4 tablespoons freshly grated Parmesan cheese

1. Slice the aubergine thickly, sprinkle with salt and allow to stand for 30 minutes to degorge. Rinse with water and pat dry.
2. Preheat the grill to its highest setting. Arrange the aubergine on a baking sheet, brush

with the oil and grill for 3–4 minutes on each side, or until cooked. Arrange the aubergine slices in a large gratin dish or casserole.
3. Preheat the oven to 190°C/375°F/gas mark 5.
4. Slice the tomatoes thickly. Melt the butter in a large frying pan, add the garlic and cook for 30 seconds. Add the tomatoes, turn them over in the pan, season with salt, pepper and sugar and arrange on top of the aubergine slices.
5. Toss the prawns in the lemon juice and sprinkle on top of the tomato.
6. Toss the pasta and Cheddar and grain mustard sauce together and pour over the prawns. Sprinkle with the Parmesan cheese and bake in the preheated oven for 15–20 minutes, or until very hot.

 ALSATIAN WHITE

RED-HOT SHELLFISH CURRY

SERVES 6

450g/1lb squid, prepared (see page 135)
2 tablespoons groundnut oil
12 raw tiger prawns, peeled and de-veined (see page 136)
6 large scallops, prepared (see page 136)
4 tablespoons red curry paste (see page 638)
10 large tomatoes, skinned, de-seeded and chopped
150ml/¼ pint coconut milk
55g/2oz creamed coconut
1 tablespoon nam pla/fish sauce
salt and freshly ground black pepper
12 green-lipped mussels, shelled
4 tablespoons chopped fresh coriander

To serve
Thai sticky rice

1. Cut the squid into 1cm/½in slices, keeping the tentacles whole. Set aside.
2. Heat the oil in a large sauté pan. Add the prawns and scallops and fry over a low heat for 1–2 minutes, or until firm to the touch and

lightly browned. Lift from the pan and set aside.

3. Add the red curry paste to the pan and fry over a low heat for 1–2 minutes. Add the tomatoes, coconut milk, creamed coconut and nam pla to the paste, bring to the boil and season to taste with salt and pepper. Reduce the heat and simmer for 4–5 minutes, or until the sauce is thick and pulpy.

4. Add the squid to the pan and cook for 30 seconds. Add the prawns, scallops and mussels to the pan, bring to the boil, then remove from the heat. Season to taste with more salt and pepper.

5. To serve: stir in the coriander and pile into a warmed serving dish. Serve with Thai sticky rice.

 CHILEAN SAUVIGNON BLANC

SMOKED GAME FISH RAISED PIE

SERVES 6

340g/12oz quantity pâte à pâté (see page 645)
1 onion, finely chopped
30g/1oz butter
110g/4oz cooked basmati rice
salt and freshly ground black pepper
225g/8oz smoked salmon fillet or slices
225g/8oz smoked trout fillet
2 tablespoons chopped fresh tarragon
1 egg white, beaten
1 beaten egg, to glaze

1. Roll out two-thirds of the pastry and use to line a 1 litre/1¾ pint raised pie mould or a 20cm/8in spring-form mould. Roll out the remaining pastry to fit as a lid. Chill.

2. Preheat the oven to 190°C/375°F/gas mark 5.

3. Cook the onion in the butter until soft and transparent, then allow to cool. Mix with the cooked rice and season well with salt and pepper.

4. Pinbone the fish fillets if necessary (see page 133). Cut into finger-sized strips.

5. Mix the tarragon with the egg white and season with salt and pepper. Toss with the fish strips until well coated.

6. Place half the rice mixture at the bottom of the pastry-lined mould and arrange the fish strips on top, followed by the remaining rice mixture.

7. Brush the edge of the pastry with beaten egg and place the lid on top. Use the pastry trimmings to make leaves, fishes, etc. and use to decorate the pie. Chill well. Glaze with more beaten egg, then bake on the top shelf of the preheated oven for 35 minutes, or until the pastry is golden-brown. Serve warm.

 *CHABLIS*

POULTRY AND GAME

TERRINE OF CORN-FED CHICKEN AND FENNEL WITH TRUFFLE VINAIGRETTE

This recipe works well with an additional layer of quickly pan-fried foie gras in the middle, though this has been left out here because of the extra expense.

SERVES 8

1.35kg/3lb corn-fed chicken, poached
salt
½ lemon, sliced
2 large bulbs of Florence fennel, halved
8 large spinach leaves
290ml/½ pint truffle vinaigrette (see page 502)
freshly ground black pepper

To garnish
a few sprigs of fresh chervil

1. Skin the chicken and remove the meat from the bones.
2. Bring a saucepan of salted water to the boil with the lemon, then add the fennel. Simmer for 10 minutes, or until tender. Drain on a wire rack until cool.
3. Bring another saucepan of water to the boil. Wash the spinach well. Take one leaf by the stalk and dip into the boiling water for 5 seconds. Remove and immediately refresh in cold water. Leave to dry on kitchen paper. Repeat with the remaining leaves.
4. Line a 1kg/2¼lb terrine tin with clingfilm, leaving some hanging over the edge of the tin.

Remove the thick stalks from the blanched spinach leaves and use to line the tin, overlapping the sides.
5. Separate the layers of fennel. Lay a quarter of the fennel over the bottom of the terrine. Drizzle 3–4 tablespoons of the truffle vinaigrette over the top and season well with salt and pepper. Lay one-third of the chicken in an even layer on top and drizzle over a a further 3–4 tablespoons of the vinaigrette. Season well with salt and pepper. Repeat the layers until all the chicken has been used up, finishing with the fennel.
6. Cover with the overlapping spinach leaves and clingfilm.
7. Place another terrine tin of a similar size on top with a 900g/2lb weight inside. Refrigerate for 24 hours.
8. To serve: remove the weights and the second terrine tin and turn the terrine out on to a chopping board. Using a very sharp knife and a fish slice, cut 1.5cm/½in slices from the terrine. Use the fish slice to prevent the slices from falling and breaking apart.
9. Arrange the slices on individual plates, and garnish with sprigs of chervil and drizzle some of the remaining vinaigrette around.

 *RED BORDEAUX*

POT-ROASTED POUSSINS WITH PARMESAN

SERVES 4

2 double poussins
salt and freshly ground black pepper
2 tablespoons olive oil
30g/1oz butter, clarified (see page 637)

1 large onion, finely chopped
2 cloves of garlic, crushed
2 sprigs of fresh tarragon, bruised
5 tablespoons fino sherry
150ml/¼ pint well-flavoured white stock, made
  with chicken bones (see page 625)

For the sauce
15g/½oz butter
15g/½oz plain flour
150ml/¼ pint milk
55g/2oz Parmesan cheese, freshly grated

To garnish
sprigs of fresh tarragon

1. Preheat the oven to 180°C/350°F/gas mark 4.
2. Wipe the poussins and season with salt and
pepper.
3. Heat the oil and butter together in a large
flameproof casserole. Brown the poussins
slowly all over, turning them so that they are
evenly coloured.
4. Lift the poussins out of the casserole and set
aside. Add the onion to the casserole and cook
over a low heat until soft and transparent. Add
the garlic, tarragon, sherry and stock. Return the
poussins to the casserole, cover with a tight-
fitting lid and cook in the preheated oven for 30–
40 minutes, or until the poussins are cooked (the
juices should run clear when the thigh is pierced).
5. Meanwhile, make the sauce: melt the butter
in a small saucepan, stir in the flour and cook
for 30 seconds, then remove the pan from the
heat and blend in the milk until smooth. Set
aside until the poussins are cooked.
6. Lift the poussins from the casserole and keep
warm. Strain the contents of the casserole into a
bowl and skim off excess fat.
7. Add the fat-free liquid to the sauce and cook
over a low heat, stirring continuously until the
mixture comes to the boil, then lower the heat
and simmer for 2–3 minutes. Remove from the
heat and stir in the Parmesan cheese; the sauce
should be of a syrupy consistency. Season to
taste with salt and pepper.
8. Trim the poussins and cut in half. Arrange on
a serving dish and coat with the sauce. Garnish
with sprigs of tarragon.

 *PINOT NOIR*

LAPSANG AND SPICE SMOKED DUCK BREAST WITH PLUM GLAZE

SERVES 4

4 duck breasts, skinned
1 teaspoon ground coriander
salt and freshly ground black pepper
a little olive oil

For smoking
4 tablespoons lapsang souchong tea
1 tablespoon coriander seeds, crushed
2 teaspoons cumin seeds
1 teaspoon cardamom pods, crushed

For the plum glaze
2 tablespoons sesame oil
225g/8oz ripe plums, halved and stoned
2 tablespoons hoisin sauce
1 tablespoon dark soy sauce
2.5cm/1in piece of fresh root ginger, peeled and
  grated
1 clove of garlic, crushed

To garnish
fresh coriander leaves

1. Season the duck breasts with the coriander,
salt and pepper. Fry the duck breasts in a little
hot oil in a frying pan for 2 minutes on each
side, or until lightly browned.
2. Smoke the duck: if a home-smoker is
available, smoke it for 15 minutes over the tea
leaves and spices (see page 72). Alternatively,
use a large roasting tin: sprinkle the tea and
spices on the bottom and put a shallow cake tin
half filled with water on top. Place a wire rack
on top of the tin and arrange the prepared duck
breasts on this.
3. Cover the roasting tin with a large piece of
kitchen foil and set the tin over a low to
medium heat. Smoke the duck for 15 minutes,
or until still pink in the middle. Avoid removing
the foil or the smoke will escape and the
smoking time will be greatly increased.

4. Preheat the grill to its highest setting.

5. Meanwhile, make the plum glaze: heat the oil in a frying pan, add the plums and fry briskly for 2–3 minutes, then add the hoisin sauce, soy sauce, ginger and garlic and stir over a low heat until the plums are soft. Push the mixture through a sieve and season with salt and pepper.

6. Brush the duck breasts with the plum glaze and grill for 1–2 minutes on each side, or until caramelized and sticky.

7. Arrange the duck breasts on a large warmed serving dish and garnish with the coriander leaves. Serve immediately.

 ALSACE GEWÜRZTRAMINER

SLOW-ROAST DUCK WITH THAI MARINADE

SERVES 3

1 × 1.35kg/3lb oven-ready duckling

For the marinade
3 tablespoons chopped galangal (see page 137)
2 green chillies, de-seeded and finely chopped
2 sticks of lemon grass, finely chopped
5 tablespoons light soy sauce
1 tablespoon nam pla (see page 138)
2 tablespoons chopped fresh coriander
freshly ground black pepper

To garnish
sprigs of fresh coriander

1. Prick the duck all over with a fork and remove the parson's nose. Place on a wire rack over a roasting tin.

2. Mix together all the marinade ingredients and rub over the duck skin and inside the body cavity. Cover and refrigerate for 8 hours, preferably overnight.

3. Preheat the oven to 200°C/400°F/gas mark 6.

4. Roast the duck in the preheated oven for 30 minutes, then reduce the oven temperature to 170°C/325°F/gas mark 3. Cover with kitchen

foil and roast for a further 1–1½ hours, or until the duck is cooked, basting frequently.

5. Remove the duck from the oven and allow to stand for 10 minutes. Joint and garnish with the coriander.

 *CHILEAN PINOT NOIR*

BAKED GUINEA FOWL WITH FRESH CORN AND PARSNIPS

SERVES 4

1 × 1.6kg/3½lb guinea fowl or corn-fed chicken
30g/1oz butter, softened
1 Spanish onion, thinly sliced
3 corn on the cob, kernels scraped off and husks removed
4 small parsnips, peeled and quartered lengthways
2 tablespoons chopped fresh parsley
2 tablespoons chopped fresh thyme
2 cloves of garlic, crushed
salt and freshly ground black pepper
juice of 2 lemons
290ml/½ pint strong white stock, made with chicken bones (see page 625)
150ml/¼ pint double cream

To garnish
1 tablespoon chopped fresh parsley

1. Preheat the oven to 180°C/350°F/gas mark 4.

2. Place the guinea fowl or chicken in a large roasting tin, breast side uppermost, and smear the skin with the butter.

3. In a large bowl mix together the onion, corn kernels, parsnips, parsley, thyme and garlic. Season well with salt and pepper, then tip into the roasting tin around the guinea fowl or chicken.

4. Pour the lemon juice over the guinea fowl or chicken, then pour the stock and cream over the parsnips and corn.

5. Cover the roasting tin with kitchen foil and

bake in the centre of the preheated oven for 1 hour. Increase the oven temperature to 200°C/400°F/gas mark 6.

6. Remove the foil. Baste the guinea fowl or chicken and the parsnips with the juices and return the tin to the top of the oven for a further 20–30 minutes, or until the parsnips are pale golden and tender and the juices of the guinea fowl or chicken run clear when the thigh is pierced with a skewer.

7. Transfer the guinea fowl or chicken to a large warmed serving dish and arrange the vegetables around. Scatter over the parsley and carve at the table.

 TOP-QUALITY CLARET OR BAROLO

POT-ROAST GROUSE WITH BLACK AND WHITE GRAPES

SERVES 2

2 grouse
salt and freshly ground black pepper
30g/1oz butter
1 tablespoon olive oil
2 shallots, finely chopped
1 clove of garlic, crushed
5 tablespoons dry sherry
2 sprigs of fresh rosemary

For the sauce
150ml/¼ pint double cream
55g/2oz black grapes, halved and de-seeded
55g/2oz white grapes, halved and de-seeded
1 teaspoon finely chopped fresh rosemary

1. Preheat the oven to 180°C/350°F/gas mark 4.
2. Wipe the grouse and season with salt and pepper.
3. Heat the butter and oil together in a flameproof casserole, add the grouse and brown slowly all over, then remove to a plate.
4. Add the shallots and garlic to the casserole and cook over a low heat for 2–3 minutes. Add

the sherry and rosemary, return the grouse to the casserole and season lightly with salt and pepper. Cover with a close-fitting lid and cook in the preheated oven for 25–30 minutes, or until the grouse are just cooked.

5. Lift the grouse from the casserole and keep warm. Strain the cooking liquid into a saucepan and skim off the excess fat.

6. Make the sauce: add the cream to the casserole and bring to the boil, then lower the heat and simmer for 6–10 minutes, or until of a syrupy consistency. Add the grapes and rosemary and season to taste with salt and pepper.

7. Trim the grouse and split in half. Arrange on a large warmed serving plate and pour the sauce over the top. Serve very hot.

 NORTHERN RHÔNE OR MATURE CLARET

ROAST PARTRIDGE WITH CRAB APPLE GRAVY

SERVES 4

4 small partridges
salt and freshly ground black pepper
225g/8oz crab apples, washed and finely diced
2 shallots, finely chopped
150ml/¼ pint game stock (see page 626)
5 tablespoons red wine
1 tablespoon soft dark brown sugar

To serve
chestnuts with pancetta (see page 459)

1. Preheat the oven to 190°C/375°F/gas mark 5.
2. Clean the partridges and season inside and out with salt and pepper. Put the crab apples, shallots, stock, wine and sugar into a roasting tin and season with salt and pepper.
3. Place the partridges on a wire rack and place in the roasting tin. Roast in the preheated oven, basting occasionally with the liquid in the tin, for 35–40 minutes.
4. Remove from the oven and transfer the

partridges to a warmed serving platter. Keep warm. Leave the crab apples and any cooking juices from the partridges in the roasting tin. Bring to the boil and stir vigorously to reduce the crab apples to a pulp. Lower the heat and simmer for 2–3 minutes.

5. Push the contents of the tin through a sieve, pressing well to extract all the flavour, into a saucepan. The sauce should be the required syrupy consistency: if it is too thin, boil rapidly to reduce. Season to taste with salt and pepper.

6. Serve the partridges with the sauce handed separately in a sauce-boat. Hand the chestnuts with pancetta separately.

 *BAROLO*

POT-ROAST PARTRIDGE WITH MULBERRIES AND SHALLOTS

SERVES 4

4 partridges, plucked and drawn
225g/8oz mulberries
salt and freshly ground black pepper
55g/2oz clarified butter (see page 637)
225g/8oz small shallots
110g/4oz rindless belly of pork, cut into lardons
4 tablespoons mulberry gin (see page 495) or
    crème de cassis
150ml/¼ pint double cream
juice of ½ lemon

To garnish
55g/2oz mulberries
4 sprigs of fresh flat-leaf parsley
1 quantity root vegetable chips (see page 7)

1. Preheat the oven to 180°C/350°F/gas mark 4.
2. Singe the partridges over a flame to remove any remaining feathers. Fill the central cavity of the birds with the mulberries. Season the birds with salt and pepper on all sides.
3. Heat some of the clarified butter in a large flameproof casserole. Brown the partridges all

over, using 2 wooden spoons to prevent the skin from tearing. Transfer the birds to a plate. Deglaze the casserole with a little water if necessary.

4. Add a little more clarified butter to the casserole with the shallots and cook, stirring occasionally, over a low heat for 10 minutes, then add the bacon and continue to cook until golden-brown all over.

5. Return the partridges to the casserole. Heat the mulberry gin in a small pan or ladle. When hot, pour over the partridges and set alight with a match. When the flames subside, scrape the casserole with a wooden spoon to loosen any sediment stuck to the bottom.

6. Cover the casserole with a well-fitting lid and cook in the bottom of the oven for 10–15 minutes, or until the partridge leg joints feel loose to the touch.

7. Transfer the partridges to a warmed serving dish, strain the juices into a saucepan and arrange the shallots and lardons on the dish with the partridges.

8. Add the cream to the casserole and reduce by boiling rapidly until the sauce is syrupy in consistency. Season with the lemon juice.

9. Garnish the partridges with the mulberries, parsley and root vegetable chips. Hand the sauce separately in a sauce-boat.

 *AUSTRALIAN COONAWARRA CABERNET SAUVIGNON*

BRAISED PHEASANT WITH QUINCES

SERVES 4

30g/1oz butter
1 tablespoon olive oil
2 plump oven-ready pheasants
1 large onion, finely chopped
2 large quinces, peeled and diced
2 glasses of port
1 bouquet garni
thinly pared zest and juice of 1 orange
190ml/⅓ pint double cream
salt and freshly ground black pepper

1. Preheat the oven to 190°C/375°F/gas mark 5.
2. Melt the butter in a large flameproof casserole, add the oil and brown the pheasants on all sides. Remove from the casserole and set aside. Add the onion and quinces to the casserole and soften for 10 minutes over a low heat. Return the pheasants to the casserole. Pour over the port and add the bouquet garni, orange zest and juice. Season with salt and pepper, then cover the casserole closely and cook in the oven for 30–40 minutes, or until the pheasants are tender.
3. Remove and joint the pheasants. Keep warm.
4. Sieve the cooking juices and quinces into a saucepan. Boil the juices over a high heat, stirring all the time, until reduced to 5–7 tablespoons, then gradually add the cream, boiling until you have a syrupy sauce. Season with salt and pepper and pour over the pheasant. Serve very hot.

 *PINOT NOIR*

AROMATIC PHEASANT WITH CUMIN MASH

SERVES 4

4 pheasant breasts
1 teaspoon ground cardamom
1 teaspoon ground coriander
1 teaspoon plain flour
salt and freshly ground black pepper
2 tablespoons grapeseed oil

For the sauce
1 teaspoon sunflower oil
1 leek, sliced and washed
1 clove of garlic, bruised
570ml/1 pint game stock (see page 626)
150ml/¼ pint red wine
5 tablespoons port
1 bouquet garni
salt and freshly ground black pepper
85g/3oz unsalted butter

For the cumin mash
55g/2oz butter
1 large onion, finely chopped
2 teaspoons ground cumin
675g/1½lb celeriac, peeled, diced and cooked until tender
salt and freshly ground black pepper

To garnish
sprigs of fresh sage

1. Trim the pheasant breasts and remove any membrane.
2. Mix the spices, flour and salt and pepper together. Toss the pheasant breasts in the mixture. Cover and refrigerate for 30 minutes.
3. Meanwhile, make the sauce: heat the oil in a saucepan, add the leeks and cook for 5 minutes until softened, then add the garlic, stock, wine, port and bouquet garni. Simmer for 15–20 minutes, or until reduced to 290ml/½ pint. Strain and discard the leeks. Set the sauce aside.
4. Meanwhile, make the cumin mash: melt the butter in a saucepan, add the onion and cook until very soft. Add the cumin and fry over a medium heat for 1–2 minutes.
5. Mash the celeriac, stir into the onion and season to taste with salt and pepper. Keep warm.
6. To serve: heat the oil in a frying pan, add the pheasant breasts and fry for 2–3 minutes, or until just cooked through. Lift on to a warmed serving dish. Add the sauce to the pan, bring to the boil and reduce to 150ml/¼ pint. Remove the pan from the heat and add the butter a piece at a time, whisking vigorously after each addition. Season to taste with salt and pepper.
7. Divide the mash between 4 warmed individual plates and place a pheasant breast on top of each. Pour over the sauce and garnish with the sage.

 *CLARET*

MARTINMAS PHEASANT

St Martin's Day is 11 November, when you might have a pheasant nicely hung and ready for the pot. This sealed-pot cooking method is one of the few ways of keeping a pheasant (or chicken) really succulent. So kick the roast pheasant habit and try it.

This recipe has been taken from *Country Cooking from Farthinghoe* by Nicola Cox.

SERVES 3–4

2 apples, peeled, cored and thickly sliced, cores reserved
salt and freshly ground black pepper
1 plump oven-ready pheasant
55g/2oz butter
1 onion, thickly sliced
1–2 sprigs of fresh rosemary
¼ teaspoon ground cinnamon
2–3 rashers of streaky bacon
30g/1oz raisins or sultanas
225ml/8fl oz cider
¼ chicken stock cube
150ml/¼ pint double or whipping cream
½–1 teaspoon potato flour, or arrowroot or cornflour
2–3 tablespoons cold water
extra 55g/2oz butter (optional)

For the huff paste
225g/8oz plain flour
½ teaspoon salt
150ml/¼ pint cold water

1. Preheat the oven to 220°C/425°F/gas mark 7. Make the huff paste: mix the flour, salt and water to a stiff paste in a bowl, then knead until smooth.
2. Place the apple cores, salt and pepper inside the pheasant and wipe dry. Melt the butter in a frying pan and use a little to rub the pheasant all over.
3. Add the onion to the pan and fry until golden. Remove and fry the apple slices until golden on both sides.
4. Place the onions and apples with any remaining frying butter in a large casserole and add the rosemary and cinnamon. Lay the buttered pheasant on its side on top. Season with salt and pepper, then cover with the rashers of bacon. Cover with the lid and seal in place with the huff paste.
5. Cook in the preheated oven for 50 minutes–1 hour, or until the pheasant is cooked (when a skewer is inserted through to the middle of the bird and left for 15 seconds, it should be very hot when removed).
6. Meanwhile, simmer the raisins or sultanas in the cider with the stock cube, until the liquid has reduced by half and the fruit is well plumped. Remove from the heat and set aside.
7. Boil the cream for several minutes to reduce, then remove from the heat and set aside, covered. Mix the potato flour, arrowroot or cornflour with a little cold water.
8. When the pheasant is ready, break off the huff paste and discard. Remove the pheasant, being careful not to spike or prod it with a knife or fork, which would let the juices out, and keep warm.
9. Remove and discard the rosemary. Tip the remaining contents of the casserole into a food processor or blender and whizz until very smooth. Sieve into a small saucepan, then add the cider and raisins, the cream and the slaked potato flour. Bring to the boil to thicken the potato flour, then check the seasoning. If liked, whisk in the extra butter piece by piece just as you take the sauce off the stove; once the butter is added the sauce must be served immediately.
10. Carve the pheasant, which improves for resting in a warm place for 20–30 minutes before carving, so that the flesh relaxes and re-absorbs the juices, and cover with the sauce, or hand it separately in a sauce-boat.

 CLARET

POTTED PHEASANT

SERVES 4

340g/12oz skinned and boned pheasant, cubed
110g/4oz rindless rashers of streaky bacon, chopped
55g/2oz butter, diced

1 large clove of garlic, crushed
150ml/¼ pint port
1 blade of mace
1 bouquet garni
2 strips of thinly pared orange zest
salt and freshly ground black pepper

For the seal
110g/4oz clarified butter (see page 637)
4 bay leaves
12 cranberries

To serve
melba toast (see page 658) or warm crusty French bread

1. Preheat the oven to 170°C/325°F/gas mark 3.
2. Mix together all the ingredients, except those for the seal, in a deep casserole. Cover with a well-fitting lid and bake in the preheated oven for 1–1½ hours, or until the pheasant is tender.
3. Remove the bouquet garni, mace and orange zest. Put the remaining contents of the casserole into a food processor and whizz to a smooth paste. Pour the mixture into a serving dish, leaving a 5mm/¼in gap at the top for the seal. Allow to cool completely, then cover and refrigerate for 2 hours.
4. Melt the clarified butter gently and pour over the potted pheasant to seal. Arrange the bay leaves and cranberries on top and chill for 15 minutes, or until the butter has set, before serving.
5. Serve with melba toast or warm crusty French bread.

NOTE: The potted pheasant will keep for up to a month in the refrigerator while the seal is left unbroken. Once cut, it must be used within 2–3 days.

 *PINOT NOIR*

ROAST PHEASANT PASTA WITH MADEIRA

SERVES 4

900g/2lb pheasant joints
salt and freshly ground black pepper
1 onion, sliced
2 medium parsnips, peeled and cut into 5cm/2in sticks
15g/½oz butter
100ml/3½fl oz Madeira or medium sherry
225g/8oz tagliatelle or pappardelle
225g/8oz sugarsnap peas, topped and tailed
290ml/½ pint double cream

To garnish
1 tablespoon chopped fresh parsley

1. Preheat the oven to 180°C/350°F/gas mark 4.
2. Remove any feathers or shot from the pheasant joints and season with salt and pepper. Place the joints in a single layer, skin side up, in a shallow roasting tin. Cover the tin with kitchen foil.
3. Roast the pheasant in the preheated oven for 45 minutes–1 hour – the timing will depend on the age of the bird and the type of joints: breast joints will cook faster than leg joints. The pheasant is cooked when the meat starts to shrink away from the bones, a knife can be inserted easily into the flesh and there are no bloody juices.
4. Increase the oven temperature to 200°C/400°F/gas mark 6.
5. Allow the pheasant to cool a little before removing the fat and separating the meat from the bones. Cut the meat into 2.5cm/1in pieces. Pour any juices that have collected in the roasting tin into a glass bowl, to allow the fat to rise to the top.
6. Pour 2 tablespoons of the pheasant fat back into the roasting tin. Add the onions and parsnips and roast them in the oven for 30 minutes, or until golden, turning them over half-way through cooking.
7. Transfer the onion and parsnips to another roasting tin and keep warm while finishing the

427

sauce. Add the Madeira to the roasting tin and stir with a wooden spoon over the heat to release any sediment stuck to the bottom of the pan. Boil until the liquid has reduced to 2 tablespoons. Use a baster to remove any pheasant juices from the bottom of the bowl, leaving the fat behind. Add the juices to the roasting tin.

8. Cook the pasta in boiling salted water until tender (timing will depend on the type of pasta).

9. Boil the sugarsnap peas in salted water for 1 minute, then drain.

10. Add the cream to the roasting tin and bring to the boil, then reduce to 150ml/¼ pint by boiling rapidly. Stir in the pheasant until just heated through.

11. Add the pasta to the roasting tin with the parsnips, onions and sugarsnap peas. Toss everything gently together and season to taste with salt and pepper.

12. Pile into a large warmed serving dish and sprinkle with the parsley before serving.

 MONTEPULCIANO D'ABRUZZO

BALLOTINE OF PHEASANT WITH WILD MUSHROOMS AND PANCETTA

This recipe can be made with many different types of feathered game.

SERVES 6

2 plump oven-ready pheasants, boned (see page 127)
salt and freshly ground black pepper

For the stuffing
340g/12oz minced pork
55g/2oz fine fresh white breadcrumbs
2 shallots, very finely chopped
1 teaspoon chopped fresh tarragon
55g/2oz pancetta, diced
30g/1oz dried porcini mushrooms, soaked, drained and chopped

1 beaten egg, to bind
55g/2oz unsalted butter, melted

For the gravy
15g/½oz butter
170g/6oz wild mushrooms, wiped and sliced if large
2 glasses of port
290ml/½ pint game stock (see page 626)
1 teaspoon arrowroot

To garnish
1 bunch of fresh tarragon

1. Lay the pheasants, skinned side down, on a chopping board and season lightly with salt and pepper.

2. Make the stuffing: put the minced pork, breadcrumbs, shallots, tarragon, pancetta and porcini mushrooms into a bowl. Mix thoroughly and add just enough beaten egg to bind, but do not allow it to become too wet. Season with salt and pepper.

3. Preheat the oven to 190°C/375°F/gas mark 5.

4. Divide the stuffing between the pheasants. Draw the skin and flesh around the stuffing to reshape the birds, trying to avoid allowing the skin to overlap.

5. Cut a piece of muslin into large squares big enough to enclose the birds. Dip the muslin squares into the melted butter, making sure that they are well soaked. Wring the muslin lightly to remove excess butter.

6. Wrap each pheasant in a square of muslin, tying the ends to form a cracker shape.

7. Arrange the birds on a wire rack over a roasting tin. Roast in the preheated oven for 45 minutes, or until cooked (when a skewer is inserted through to the middle of the bird and left for 15 seconds, it should be very hot when removed). Remove the muslin immediately, transfer the pheasants to a warmed serving dish and keep warm.

8. Make the gravy: melt the butter in the roasting tin, add the mushrooms and sauté for 1 minute, or until beginning to soften. Add the port and bring to the boil over a medium heat, then lower the heat and simmer for 1–2 minutes, or until reduced by half. Remove the mushrooms with a slotted spoon and set aside. Add the stock and bring back to the boil, then lower the heat and simmer for 5 minutes. Slake the arrowroot with a little water and add to the gravy. Bring back to the boil, then lower the heat and simmer for 1 minute. Season to taste with salt and pepper and return the mushrooms to the gravy.

9. Garnish the pheasants with the tarragon and hand the sauce separately in a sauce-boat.

NOTE: Dried porcini mushrooms can be gritty, so strain the soaked mushrooms carefully.

 NEW ZEALAND PINOT NOIR

STIR-FRIED PIGEON AND CHORIZO

SERVES 4

8 pigeon breasts, skinned
3 tablespoons grapeseed oil
110g/4oz chorizo sausage, thinly sliced
5 tablespoons dark soy sauce
freshly ground black pepper

To serve
warm red cabbage coleslaw (see page 465)

1. Cut the pigeon breasts into strips and set aside.
2. Heat the oil in a frying pan, add the chorizo and fry over a brisk heat until crisp. Remove with a slotted spoon and keep warm.
3. Season the pigeon strips with soy sauce and pepper. Add to the pan and stir-fry for 1–2 minutes. Return the chorizo to the pan and toss together.
4. Pile on to a warmed serving dish and hand the warm red cabbage coleslaw separately.

 *NAVARRA TEMPRANILLO*

BONED STUFFED QUAIL WITH MUSHROOMS

SERVES 4

8 quail, boned (see page 127)
salt and freshly ground black pepper

For the stuffing
1 × 170g/6oz chicken breast, skinned and
  minced
3 tablespoons chopped fresh parsley, mint and
  sage
grated zest of 1 lemon
55g/2oz fine fresh white breadcrumbs
1 egg, beaten
3 tablespoons olive oil
1 leek, thinly sliced
1 small carrot, peeled and thinly sliced
2 cloves of garlic, crushed
150ml/¼ pint white stock, made with chicken
  bones (see page 625)
55g/2oz button mushrooms
5 tablespoons double cream

To garnish
1 teaspoon chopped fresh parsley

1. Lay the boned quail, skin side down, on a chopping board and season with salt and pepper. Set aside.
2. Make the stuffing: put the minced chicken, herbs, lemon zest and breadcrumbs into a bowl. Mix together and add enough egg to bind the mixture, which should not be too wet. Season with salt and pepper.
3. Divide the stuffing between the quail and sew up with fine string. Season the outside of the birds with salt and pepper.
4. Heat 2 tablespoons of the oil in a large flameproof casserole. Brown the quail, 4 at a time, first on the breast side, then on the underside.
5. When all the quail are browned, set aside. Add the leek and carrot to the casserole and sweat over a low heat until soft. Add the garlic and cook for a further minute.
6. Return the quail to the casserole and pour

over the stock. Bring to the boil, cover the casserole and cook over a very low heat for 20 minutes, or until the quail are cooked.

7. Lift the quail from the casserole and keep warm (do not remove the string).

8. Strain the contents of the casserole into a small saucepan. Skim to remove any fat. Bring to the boil and reduce by boiling rapidly to 5 tablespoons.

9. Meanwhile, sauté the mushrooms in the remaining oil and add to the pan. Stir in the cream and bring back to the boil, then lower the heat and simmer for 2–3 minutes, or until the sauce is of a syrupy consistency. Season to taste with salt and pepper.

10. Remove the string from the quail and arrange in a warmed serving dish. Pour the cream sauce and mushrooms over the top, sprinkle with the parsley and serve immediately.

 *PINOT NOIR*

BONED GAME WITH DRIED CHERRY AND WALNUT STUFFING

This recipe can be made with many different types of feathered game and the stuffing is also delicious with roast goose.

SERVES 4

*2 plump oven-ready pheasants or 4 partridges,
    boned (see page 127)*
salt and freshly ground black pepper
55g/2oz unsalted butter, melted

For the stuffing
340g/12oz minced veal or pork
55g/2oz fine fresh white breadcrumbs
2 shallots, very finely chopped
55g/2oz dried cherries or blueberries
55g/2oz walnuts, chopped
2 teaspoons chopped fresh sage
1 beaten egg, to bind
salt and freshly ground black pepper

For the gravy
2 glasses of port
290ml/½ pint game stock (see page 626)
1 teaspoon arrowroot

To garnish
1 small bunch of fresh sage

1. Lay the birds, skinned side down, on a chopping board and season lightly with salt and pepper.

2. Make the stuffing: put the minced veal or pork, breadcrumbs, shallots, cherries or blueberries, walnuts and sage into a bowl. Mix thoroughly, adding just enough beaten egg to bind the mixture, which should not be too wet. Season with salt and pepper.

3. Preheat the oven to 190°C/375°F/gas mark 5.

4. Divide the stuffing between the birds. Draw the skin and flesh around the stuffing to reshape the birds, trying to avoid allowing the skin to overlap.

5. Cut a piece of muslin into large squares big enough to enclose the birds. Dip the muslin squares into the melted butter, making sure that they are well soaked. Wring the muslin lightly to remove excess butter.

6. Wrap each bird in the muslin, tying the ends to form a cracker shape.

7. Arrange the birds on a wire rack over a roasting tin. Roast in the preheated oven for 45 minutes if using pheasants, or 35 minutes for partridges, or until cooked (a skewer inserted through to the middle of the bird and left for 15 seconds should be very hot when removed). Remove the muslin immediately, put the birds on to a warmed serving dish and keep warm.

8. Make the gravy: add the port to the roasting tin and bring to the boil over a medium heat, then lower the heat and simmer for 1–2 minutes, or until reduced by half. Add the stock and bring back to the boil, then lower the heat and simmer for 5 minutes. Slake the arrowroot with a little water, add to the reducing gravy and bring back to the boil, then lower the heat and simmer for 1 minute. Season to taste with salt and pepper.

9. Garnish the birds with the sage and hand the sauce separately in a sauce-boat.

 *CLARET*

JUGGED HARE

SERVES 6

1 hare, skinned and jointed, with its blood
2 tablespoons oil
225g/8oz mirepoix of carrot, onion and celery
1 bouquet garni
570ml/1 pint brown stock (see page 625)
salt and freshly ground black pepper
1 tablespoon redcurrant jelly
3 tablespoons port

1. Wash and wipe dry the pieces of hare, removing any membranes. Heat the oil in a large saucepan and fry the joints until well browned, adding more dripping if the pan becomes dry. Lift out the joints and brown the mirepoix.
2. Return the hare to the pan. Add the bouquet garni, stock, salt and pepper. Cover and simmer for 2 hours, or until the hare is very tender.
3. Arrange the joints in a casserole.
4. Strain the stock into a saucepan. Add the redcurrant jelly and port and simmer for 5 minutes. Remove the pan from the heat.
5. Mix the blood with a cupful of the hot stock. Pour back into the pan without allowing the sauce to boil. The blood will thicken the sauce slightly.
6. Taste the sauce, adding salt and pepper if necessary. Pour over the hare joints in the casserole and serve.

NOTE: The sauce depends on the hare's blood to thicken it. If very little blood (less than 150ml/¼ pint) comes with the hare, the basic stock must be thickened with a little beurre manié – flour and butter kneaded together in equal quantities – and whisked in small pieces into the boiling stock. This must be done before the addition of the blood, which would curdle if boiled.

 *CLARET*

VENISON CASSEROLE

SERVES 4

675g/1½lb venison

For the marinade
5 tablespoons sunflower oil
1 onion, sliced
1 carrot, sliced
1 stick of celery, sliced
1 clove of garlic, crushed
6 juniper berries
1 slice of lemon
1 bay leaf
290ml/½ pint red wine
2 tablespoons red wine vinegar
6 black peppercorns

For the casserole
1 tablespoon sunflower oil
30g/1oz butter
110g/4oz onions, peeled
1 clove of garlic, crushed
110g/4oz button mushrooms
2 teaspoons plain flour
150ml/¼ pint brown stock (see page 625)
1 tablespoon cranberry jelly
salt and freshly ground black pepper
55g/2oz fresh cranberries
15g/½oz sugar
110g/4oz cooked whole chestnuts

To garnish
chopped fresh parsley

1. Cut the venison into 5cm/2in cubes, trimming away any tough membrane or sinew.
2. Mix the ingredients for the marinade together in a bowl and add the venison. Mix well, cover and leave in a cool place or in the refrigerator overnight.
3. Preheat the oven to 170°C/325°F/gas mark 3.
4. Lift out the venison cubes and pat dry with kitchen paper. Strain the marinade, reserving the liquid for cooking.
5. Heat half the oil in a heavy saucepan and brown the venison cubes a few at a time. Place

them in a casserole. If the bottom of the pan becomes brown or too dry, pour in a little of the strained marinade, swish it about, scraping off the sediment stuck to the bottom, and pour over the venison cubes. Then heat a little more oil and continue browning the meat.

6. When all the venison has been browned, repeat the déglaçage (boiling up with a little marinade and scraping the bottom of the pan).

7. Now melt the butter in a saucepan and fry the onions and garlic until the onions are pale brown all over. Add the mushrooms and continue cooking for 2 minutes.

8. Stir in the flour and cook for 1 minute. Remove from the heat, add the remaining marinade and the brown stock, return to the heat and stir until boiling, again scraping the bottom of the pan. When boiling, pour over the venison.

9. Add the cranberry jelly. Season with salt and pepper.

10. Cover the casserole and cook in the heated oven for about 2 hours, or until the venison is very tender.

11. Meanwhile, cook the cranberries briefly with the sugar in 2–3 tablespoons water until just soft but not crushed. Strain off the liquor. Lift the venison, mushrooms and onions with a slotted spoon into a serving dish.

12. Boil the sauce fast until reduced to a shiny, almost syrupy consistency. Add the chestnuts and cranberries and simmer gently for 5 minutes.

13. Pour the sauce over the venison and serve garnished with parsley.

 *FULL RED*

STEAMED VENISON AND SMOKED OYSTER PUDDING

SERVES 4

*675g/1½lb stewing venison, trimmed of fat and
   sinew and cut into 2.5cm/1in pieces*
110g/4oz smoked oysters
1 tablespoon plain flour
1 small onion, chopped
1 clove of garlic, crushed
1 tablespoon redcurrant jelly
1 tablespoon chopped fresh parsley
½ tablespoon chopped fresh thyme
salt and freshly ground black pepper
butter for greasing
*340g/12oz flour quantity suet pastry (see page
   643)*
150ml/¼ pint red wine

To serve
1 small bunch of watercress
1 quantity redcurrant sauce (see page 375)

1. Mix the venison with the smoked oysters and flour in a large bowl. Add the onion, garlic, redcurrant jelly, parsley and thyme and season with salt and pepper.

2. Grease a 1kg/2¼lb pudding basin lightly with butter.

3. On a floured surface, roll out the pastry into a round 1cm/½in thick. Cut a wedge of pastry out of the circle (not cutting the point of the wedge quite as far in as the middle of the circle) and set this piece of pastry aside for the lid. Line the bowl with the remaining pastry and seal the cut edges together with a little water.

4. Fill the lined basin with the meat. Pour in the wine and add a little extra water so that the liquid comes three-quarters of the way up the meat.

5. Wet the top edge of the pastry lining the bowl. Shape the pastry for the lid into a round to fit the top of the basin. Put the lid in place and press the edges together securely. Trim off the excess pastry.

6. Cover the pudding with a double piece of greased greaseproof paper, pleated down the centre to allow room for the pastry to expand, and a similarly pleated piece of kitchen foil. Tie down with string, making a handle at the top to lift the pudding in and out of the pan.

7. Place the pudding in a saucepan of boiling water with a close-fitting lid, or in a steamer, for 4–5 hours, taking care to top up with boiling water occasionally to prevent the pudding from boiling dry.

8. Remove the foil and paper and turn the pudding out on to a warmed serving dish. Garnish with watercress and serve with the redcurrant sauce.

 *AUSTRALIAN SHIRAZ*

ROAST SADDLE OF VENISON WITH JUNIPER AND ORANGE

SERVES 6–8

1.8–2.7kg/4–6lb saddle of venison (roe, fallow or farmed)
2 teaspoons juniper berries, crushed
grated zest of 2 large oranges
2 cloves of garlic, crushed
150ml/¼ pint red wine
1 tablespoon redcurrant jelly
4 tablespoons olive oil
salt and freshly ground black pepper
1 large sheet of pig's caul, washed

For the mirepoix
2 tablespoons olive oil
1 carrot, diced
1 stick of celery, diced
1 large onion, diced
55g/2oz mushrooms, quartered
1 bouquet garni
juice of 2 oranges
290ml/½ pint brown stock (see page 625)

For the sauce
150ml/¼ pint double cream
4 tablespoons port

To garnish
watercress

1. Carefully remove all the fat from the saddle of venison and discard. Trim away all the membrane from the saddle, leaving exposed flesh. Weigh the saddle to calculate the cooking time, allowing 8 minutes per 450g/1lb.

2. Mix together the juniper berries, orange zest, garlic, wine, redcurrant jelly and oil. Season with pepper. Pour over the exposed flesh on either side of the saddle, cover and leave to marinate overnight.

3. Preheat the oven to 240°C/475°F/gas mark 8.

4. Remove the saddle from the marinade and season with salt and pepper. Cover with the caul and tuck any excess underneath.

5. Make the mirepoix: heat the oil in a large roasting tin, add the remaining vegetables and cook until well browned all over. Add the bouquet garni, orange juice, marinade and stock and bring to the boil, then lower the heat and simmer for 2 minutes. Place the venison on the mirepoix, season with salt and cook at the top of the oven for 15 minutes.

6. Reduce the oven temperature to 180°C/350°F/gas mark 4 and continue to cook the saddle for the calculated time.

7. Transfer the saddle to a warmed carving dish and allow to stand for 20 minutes before carving.

8. Meanwhile, make the sauce: strain the mirepoix and cooking juices into a shallow saucepan, pressing out the juices with a wooden spoon. Reduce by boiling rapidly to a syrupy consistency. Add the cream and port and reduce again until syrupy. Season with salt and pepper. Strain into a sauce-boat.

9. Remove the caul and carve the saddle. (It may be easier to remove the meat completely and then carve into long thin slices.)

10. Garnish with watercress and hand the sauce separately.

 *CLARET*

GAME AND WILD MUSHROOM SAUSAGES

MAKES 20

450g/1lb pheasant breast, skinned and boned
450g/1lb wild boar, fat and sinew removed
225g/8oz pork fat
55g/2oz dried porcini mushrooms, soaked
110g/4oz shiitake mushrooms
2 cloves of garlic, crushed
85g/3oz fresh white breadcrumbs
1 teaspoon finely chopped juniper berries
1 tablespoon chopped fresh rosemary
1 teaspoon chopped fresh sage
½ teaspoon freshly grated nutmeg
1 teaspoon ground coriander
1 teaspoon cayenne pepper
salt and freshly ground black pepper
2 tablespoons whisky
4 tablespoons red wine
sausage skins, soaked (available from good
butchers)

1. Mince the pheasant, wild boar, pork fat and mushrooms together. Mix with all the remaining ingredients, beating well. Season to taste with salt and pepper. Test the seasoning by frying a small amount of the mixture in a little oil first.
2. Put the mixture into a piping bag fitted with a 2.5cm/1in plain nozzle. Fit the sausage skin over the nozzle and fill with the mixture, taking care not to fill the skins too tightly or leave any air pockets.
3. Twist the length of sausage into links and chill before cooking. Cut into individual sausages with kitchen scissors.
4. Grill or fry the sausages for 8–10 minutes, or until brown all over.

 *CLARET*

BEEF

PUMPKIN PANCAKE PIE

SERVES 12

4.5kg/10lb pumpkin, about 30cm/12in in
  diameter
salt and freshly ground black pepper
290ml/½ pint water
8 × 20cm/8in pancakes (see page 654)
olive oil for brushing

For the filling
900g/2lb minced beef
2 large onions, chopped
2 sticks of celery, chopped
170g/6oz rindless rashers of streaky bacon,
  diced
2 cloves of garlic, crushed
1 tablespoon plain flour
1 litre/1¾ pints brown stock (see page 625)
2 tablespoons Madeira
1 tablespoon tomato purée
1 teaspoon chopped fresh thyme
olive oil for frying
450g/1lb courgettes, cut into 1cm/½in chunks
2 aubergines, cut into 1cm/½in chunks

For the topping
570ml/1 pint béchamel sauce (see page 629)
110g/4oz Cheddar cheese, grated
55g/2oz dry white breadcrumbs
1 tablespoon chopped fresh parsley

1. Preheat the oven to 200°C/400°F/gas mark 6.
2. Cut the top off the pumpkin neatly and scoop out the seeds. Season the inside of the pumpkin generously with salt and pepper. Place in a large roasting tin. Pour the water around the pumpkin, replace the lid and cover with kitchen foil. Bake in the middle of the preheated oven for 1½ hours, or until the pumpkin is just tender but still holding its shape well. Remove from the oven and allow to cool.
3. Make the filling: fry one-quarter of the mince in a hot frying pan. Lift out with a slotted spoon and place in a large saucepan.
4. Fry the remaining mince and transfer this to the saucepan too.
5. When all the mince has been fried, fry the onion, celery, bacon and garlic, until just turning brown. Pour off the fat and tip all the vegetables into the saucepan with the mince.
6. Add the flour and cook over a low heat, stirring, for 1 minute. Stir in the stock and Madeira and bring to the boil, stirring continuously. Add the tomato purée and thyme and season with salt and pepper. Simmer gently for about 1 hour, or until thick and syrupy.
7. Heat a little oil in the frying pan and fry half the courgettes over a high heat for a minute, until just starting to turn golden-brown at the edges. Tip them into a large bowl before frying the remaining courgettes.
8. Fry the aubergines in batches with more olive oil over a medium heat. Cover the frying pan with a lid, which will help the aubergines to sweat a little and will prevent them absorbing too much oil before they start to brown.
9. Season the courgettes and aubergines with salt and pepper, stir them into the meat sauce and cook together for a further 30 minutes. Check the seasoning.
10. Layer the meat sauce and pancakes inside the pumpkin, finishing with a pancake layer.
11. Spoon the béchamel sauce over the top. Mix the Cheddar cheese with the breadcrumbs and sprinkle over the top.
12. Brush the outside of the pumpkin with oil and season with salt and pepper. Bake in the

preheated oven for 45 minutes, or until thoroughly reheated, golden on top and bubbling. Reheat the pumpkin lid for 10 minutes. Sprinkle the filled pumpkin with the parsley and replace the lid to serve.

 *MONTEPULCIANO D'ABRUZZO*

Warm Mushroom, Garlic and Caper Salad

Grilled Swordfish Brochettes with Pancetta and Figs

Pot-Roasted Poussins with Parmesan and Sorrel Leaves

Pork, Prune and Armagnac Sausages

Chestnut and Wild Mushroom Carbonnade with Red Pesto Root Mash

Mediterranean Fish and Saffron Soup with Aïoli

Cajun Honey Roast Squash with Pumpkin Seeds

Individual Steamed Autumn Puddings

Baked Stuffed Quinces

Continental Plum Streusel

*Molasses Bread, Quince Cheese, Roast Plums with Brie, Fig
and Goat's Cheese Brushetta*

Toffee Apple Danish

LAMB

CELERIAC, SWEET POTATO AND LAMB PASTIES

MAKES 8

450g/1lb flour quantity shortcrust pastry (see
    page 642)
beaten egg, to glaze

For the filling
225g/8oz minced lamb
1 large onion, very finely chopped
1 celeriac, peeled and cut into 1cm/½in dice
1 large sweet potato, peeled and cut into 1cm/
    ½in dice
4 tablespoons water
salt and freshly ground black pepper

1. Chill the pastry.
2. Make the filling: mix together the lamb,
onion, celeriac and potato. Add the water, salt
and pepper and mix thoroughly.
3. Preheat the oven to 200°C/400°F/gas mark 6.
4. Divide the pastry into 8 equal pieces and roll
each piece out to the thickness of a £1 coin.
Using a 20cm/8in plate as a template, cut each
piece of pastry into a circle.
5. Spoon the lamb and vegetable mixture into
the centre of each pastry circle. Brush around
the edges with water. Carefully bring the sides
up over the filling so that the pasties look like
closed purses. Using floured fingers, crimp the
edges.
6. Place the pasties on 2 baking sheets, brush
with beaten egg and chill for 10 minutes. Brush
again with egg, then bake near the top of the
preheated oven for 10–15 minutes.

7. Reduce the oven temperature down to
180°C/350°F/gas mark 4 and bake for a further
45–50 minutes. Check occasionally, and if the
pasties show signs of over-browning, move to a
lower shelf. Serve hot or warm.

 *RIOJA RESERVA OR CRU BOURGEOIS
CLARET*

ROAST LAMB WITH APRICOTS, ROSEMARY AND PINENUTS

SERVES 6

1 × 1.6–1.8kg/3½–4lb shoulder of lamb, boned

For the stuffing
30g/1oz butter
1 onion, finely chopped
1 clove of garlic, crushed
2 tablespoons chopped fresh rosemary
55g/2oz fresh white breadcrumbs
85g/3oz no-soak dried apricots, chopped
55g/2oz pinenuts
juice of 1 lemon
1 egg
salt and freshly ground black pepper

For the gravy
1 tablespoon plain flour
290ml/½ pint lamb stock (see page 625)
150ml/¼ pint port
1 tablespoon redcurrant jelly

1. Preheat the oven to 180°C/350°F/gas mark 4.
2. Melt the butter in a heavy-based saucepan,

add the onion and cook over a low heat until soft. Add the garlic and rosemary and cook for a further minute.

3. Add the breadcrumbs, apricots, pinenuts, lemon juice and egg and season with plenty of salt and pepper.

4. Remove any excess fat or gristle from the lamb and season inside with salt and pepper. Fill with the stuffing and secure with a skewer or string. Calculate the cooking time at 20 minutes per 450g/1lb.

5. Place the lamb in a roasting tin, season well with salt and pepper and roast in the preheated oven for the calculated time, basting frequently. The lamb is cooked when a metal skewer inserted into the thickest part comes out hot. Remove from the oven and allow to rest in a warm place for 20 minutes before carving.

6. Make the gravy: pour the cooking juices into a bowl and let the fat rise to the top. Put 1 tablespoon of fat back into the roasting tin with the flour and stir over the heat until the flour browns. Add the stock, port and redcurrant jelly and bring to the boil, stirring constantly, then lower the heat and simmer for 2 minutes. Check the seasoning.

7. Remove the string from the lamb and carve.

 AUSTRALIAN CABERNET-SHIRAZ

SPICED LAMB AND ROSEMARY NAVARIN WITH COUSCOUS CRUMBLE

SERVES 4

1.35kg/3lb middle neck of lamb
4 tablespoons plain flour
1 teaspoon ground allspice
½ teaspoon cayenne pepper
salt and freshly ground black pepper
2 tablespoons olive oil
30g/1oz butter
450g/1lb button onions, peeled
4 cloves of garlic, crushed

110g/4oz button mushrooms
570ml/1 pint brown stock (see page 625)
4 large sprigs of fresh rosemary
1 teaspoon redcurrant jelly
1 teaspoon red wine vinegar

For the couscous crumble topping
225g/8oz couscous
45g/1½oz butter
1 onion, finely chopped
1 teaspoon ground allspice
1 tablespoon chopped fresh rosemary
salt and freshly ground black pepper

1. Preheat the oven to 170°C/325°F/gas mark 3.
2. Trim the lamb of any excess fat or gristle. Cut the lamb into pieces.
3. Sift the flour, allspice, cayenne, salt and pepper together on to a plate. Roll the lamb pieces in the seasoned flour, making sure that they are thoroughly coated.
4. Heat the oil and butter together in a large flameproof casserole and brown the lamb pieces a few at a time in the hot fat. Lift out and set aside. When all the lamb is browned, add the onions and cook over a low heat until lightly coloured. Add the garlic and mushrooms and cook for a further 1–2 minutes.
5. Return the lamb to the casserole, pour over the stock, bring to the boil and season very lightly with salt and pepper. Arrange the sprigs of rosemary on top of the meat. Cover the casserole and cook in the preheated oven for 50 minutes–1 hour, or until the meat is tender.
6. Meanwhile, prepare the couscous crumble topping. Put the couscous into a bowl, cover with boiling water and allow to stand for 15 minutes.
7. Drain the couscous and pat dry with kitchen paper.
8. Melt the butter in a frying pan, add the onion and cook over a very low heat until soft. Add the allspice and cook for a further 1–2 minutes. Add the rosemary, stir in the couscous and season with salt and pepper.
9. When the lamb is tender, remove the rosemary and discard. Lift the lamb and vegetables out of the casserole and set aside. Skim off the fat from the cooking liquid. Bring

the liquid to the boil, then add the redcurrant jelly and vinegar, lower the heat and simmer until the liquid is of a syrupy consistency. Continue to skim as required.

10. Return the lamb and vegetables to the casserole and sprinkle the couscous crumble mixture over the top. Return to the oven and bake for a further 15 minutes, or until the couscous has begun to toast. Serve very hot.

 *PINOT NOIR*

PORK

ROAST HAM WITH SEAWEED AND PUY LENTILS

SERVES 4

900g/2lb corner or middle gammon, soaked (see page 555)
1 onion
2 cloves
1 bay leaf

For the glaze
1 teaspoon cayenne pepper
3 tablespoons clear honey
grated zest and juice of 1 orange
2 tablespoons medium sherry

For the lentils
170g/6oz Puy lentils
15g/½oz nori seaweed, shredded (see page 161)

For the dressing
1 red chilli, de-seeded and chopped
1 tablespoon chopped mixed fresh herbs
1 tablespoon sesame oil
1 tablespoon soy sauce
1 tablespoon medium sherry
freshly ground black pepper

1. Soak the ham in cold water for 24 hours.
2. Put the ham into a large saucepan, cover with fresh water and add the onion, cloves and bay leaf. Bring to the boil, then lower the heat and simmer for 1¼ hours, or until the ham skin pulls away easily. Lift the ham from the liquid and set aside. Strain and reserve the cooking liquid.

3. Preheat the oven to 180°C/350°F/gas mark 4.
4. Make the glaze: mix together the cayenne, honey, orange zest and juice and the sherry. Carefully strip the skin from the gammon and score the layer of fat underneath. Smear the glaze over the top and place the ham in a roasting tin. Roast in the preheated oven for 30 minutes, basting every 10 minutes. Do not allow the ham to burn.
5. Meanwhile, rinse the lentils in cold water, put into a saucepan and add the reserved cooking liquid from the ham. Bring to the boil, then lower the heat and simmer for 20–25 minutes, or until the lentils are soft. Add the seaweed, then remove the pan from the heat. Strain the lentils and allow to drain in the strainer.
6. Whisk all the dressing ingredients together in a small bowl and season well with pepper.
7. Toss the lentils and seaweed in the dressing and pile down the centre of a warmed large oval serving dish.
8. Remove the ham from the oven and carve. Arrange the slices over the lentils and serve hot.

 *NEW WORLD CABERNET SAUVIGNON*

ROAST LOIN OF PORK WITH HARISSA JACKET

SERVES 4

1 × 1.35kg/3lb loin of pork
oil and salt for the crackling
30g/1oz butter, softened
55g/2oz fresh white breadcrumbs

440

3 tablespoons harissa paste (see page 634)
salt and freshly ground black pepper
150ml/¼ pint white stock, made with chicken
    bones (see page 625)

To garnish
sprigs of fresh coriander

1. Preheat the oven to 200°C/400°F/gas mark 6.
2. Remove the pork skin carefully and trim off excess fat.
3. Mark the skin into strips, brush with oil and rub with salt. Place in a roasting tin and bake on the top shelf of the oven for 20–30 minutes, or until the skin is beginning to blister and therefore crackle. Transfer to the bottom shelf of the oven.
4. Meanwhile, mix together the butter, breadcrumbs and harissa paste and season with salt and pepper. Spread the mixture over the fatty side of the pork. Place in a roasting tin, fat side up, and pour around the stock. Roast in the preheated oven for 1½ hours, or until the pork is cooked.
5. Lift the pork on to a warmed serving dish and keep warm. Strain the cooking juices and remove as much fat as possible. Pour the juices into a saucepan, bring to the boil and reduce to a syrupy consistency by boiling rapidly. Season to taste with salt and pepper.
6. Cut the crackling into pieces and arrange around the pork. Garnish with the coriander and hand the gravy separately in a sauce-boat.

 *CÔTES DU RHÔNE*

PORK, PRUNE AND ARMAGNAC SAUSAGES

SERVES 4

450g/1lb belly of pork, minced
4 shallots, finely chopped
110g/4oz fresh white breadcrumbs
110g/4oz stoned prunes, finely chopped
4 tablespoons Armagnac
1 egg

salt and freshly ground black pepper
2 × 1m/40in sausage skins, washed thoroughly

To garnish
deep-fried sage leaves (see page 240)

To serve
parsnip and crème fraîche purée (see page 460)

1. Mix together the minced pork, shallots, breadcrumbs, prunes, Armagnac and egg in a bowl. Season well with salt and pepper, cover and leave overnight to marinate.
2. Fit a large piping bag with a 2cm/¾in plain nozzle and fill the bag with half the pork mixture. Tie a knot in one end of a sausage skin and push the open end over the nozzle until the knot is up to the nozzle. Pipe the pork mixture into the sausage skin to form a long sausage 2.5cm/1in thick. Fill the other sausage skin with the remaining pork mixture in the same way.
3. Twist the filled sausage skin at 10cm/4in intervals to form a chain of sausages. If there are any air pockets, use a pin to pierce the sausage skin gently and press out the air. Chill the sausages for an hour.
4. Preheat the grill to a medium setting.
5. Cut the filled sausage skins into individual sausages and place on a wire rack over a baking sheet. Grill the sausages until well browned on all sides.
6. Reheat the parsnip and crème fraîche purée and pile it on to a warmed serving dish. Cover with the sausages and garnish with the fried sage leaves.

 *FRENCH COUNTRY RED*

ROAST CHESTNUT, PORK, APPLE AND APRICOT PIE

SERVES 6

110g/4oz no-soak dried apricots
4 tablespoons brandy
340g/12oz whole chestnuts
340g/12oz flour quantity rich shortcrust pastry
    (see page 642)
675g/1½lb boneless pork, cut into 1cm/½in
    cubes
1 onion, finely chopped
1 large Bramley apple, peeled and diced
1 tablespoon chopped fresh sage
2 tablespoons chopped fresh parsley
1 tablespoon plain flour
salt and freshly ground black pepper
beaten egg, to glaze

To serve
warm damson sauce (see page 503)

1. Chop the apricots roughly. Put them into a small bowl with the brandy, cover and leave to soak overnight.
2. Preheat the oven to 220°C/425°F/gas mark 7.
3. Place the chestnuts in a baking tray and roast in the preheated oven for 10–15 minutes, or until the skins are crisp. When the chestnuts are cool enough to handle, peel off the skins and chop roughly.
4. Reduce the oven temperature to 200°C/400°F/gas mark 6. Place a baking sheet in the oven.
5. Divide the pastry in half. Roll out one half to the thickness of a £1 coin and use to line a 20 × 2.5cm/8 × 1in deep flan ring. Roll out the remaining pastry into a large circle and lay it on a baking sheet. Chill all the pastry for 30 minutes.
6. Mix together the pork, onion, apple, sage, parsley, chestnuts, apricots, brandy and flour and season with salt and pepper. Pile the mixture into the flan ring, keeping some height in the centre.

7. Brush the edges of the pastry with a little water and lay the circle of pastry over the top, easing the pastry over the filling and taking care not to stretch it. Press the edges together and crimp them with your fingers to make a neat pattern. Make a small hole in the top of the pie and use any pastry trimmings to make a decoration on the top.
8. Glaze the pie carefully with beaten egg and chill for 15 minutes.
9. Glaze the pie again with beaten egg. Place it on the hot baking sheet and bake at the top of the oven for 20 minutes, or until the pastry is a pale golden-brown. Reduce the oven temperature to 170°C/325°F/gas mark 3, transfer the pie to the bottom of the oven and bake for a further 15–20 minutes.
10. Remove the pie from the flan ring and serve with the warm damson sauce.

 *CALIFORNIA RED ZINFANDEL*

PARSNIP, PUMPKIN, CHEDDAR AND BACON PASTIES

MAKES 8

450g/1lb flour quantity shortcrust pastry (see
    page 642)
beaten egg, to glaze

For the filling
225g/8oz rindless smoked streaky bacon, finely
    diced
110g/4oz mature Cheddar cheese, finely diced
1 large onion, very finely chopped
1 parsnip, peeled and cut into 1cm/½in cubes
340g/12oz pumpkin or butternut squash, cut
    into 1cm/½in cubes
4 tablespoons water
salt and freshly ground black pepper

1. Chill the pastry.
2. Make the filling: mix together the bacon, Cheddar cheese, onion, parsnip and pumpkin

or squash. Add the water, a little salt and plenty of pepper and mix thoroughly.

3. Preheat the oven to 200°C/400°F/gas mark 6.

4. Divide the pastry into 8 equal pieces and roll each piece out to the thickness of a £1 coin. Using a 20cm/8in plate as a template, cut each piece of pastry into a circle.

5. Spoon the lamb and vegetable mixture into the centre of each pastry circle. Brush around the edges with water. Carefully bring the sides up over the filling so that the pasties look like closed purses. Using floured fingers, crimp the edges.

6. Place the pasties on 2 baking sheets, brush with beaten egg and chill for 10 minutes. Brush again with egg, then bake near the top of the preheated oven for 10–15 minutes.

7. Reduce the oven temperature to 180°C/350°F/gas mark 4 and bake for a further 45–50 minutes. Check occasionally, and if the pasties show signs of over-browning, move to a lower shelf. Serve hot or warm.

 CRU BOURGEOIS CLARET

VEAL

VEAL KNUCKLE AND BLACK-EYED BEAN STEW

SERVES 4

225g/8oz black-eyed beans
4 × 170g/6oz veal knuckles (osso bucco), left
     untrimmed
salt and freshly ground black pepper
2 tablespoons extra virgin olive oil
30g/1oz butter
2 red onions, finely chopped
4 cloves of garlic, crushed
55g/2oz prosciutto, diced
5 tablespoons red wine
290ml/½ pint good-flavoured white stock, made
     with veal or chicken bones (see page 625)
10 plum tomatoes, skinned, de-seeded and
     chopped
1 tablespoon chopped fresh parsley
1 tablespoon chopped fresh basil
3 tablespoons fresh white breadcrumbs
2 tablespoons freshly grated Parmesan cheese

1. Soak the beans in cold water overnight. The following day, drain and cover with fresh water. Bring to the boil, then lower the heat and simmer for 1–1½ hours, or until tender. Drain the beans and set aside.
2. Preheat the oven to 150°C/300°F/gas mark 2.
3. Season the veal knuckles with salt and pepper.
4. Heat the oil and butter together in a flameproof casserole. Brown the veal knuckles well on all sides, then remove and keep warm.
5. Add the onion to the casserole and cook for 10–12 minutes, or until very soft. Add the garlic and prosciutto and cook for a further 2–3 minutes.

6. Add the wine and stock and bring to the boil, then add the beans, tomatoes and herbs. Return the veal to the casserole, cover and cook in the oven for 1–1½ hours, or until the veal is tender. Add more water if the beans begin to dry out.
7. When the veal is cooked, lift on to a plate and keep warm. Reduce the liquid in the casserole if necessary by boiling rapidly. Return the veal to the casserole, sprinkle the top with the breadcrumbs and Parmesan cheese, and cook, uncovered, in the oven for a further 10 minutes. Serve very hot.

 *PINOT NOIR*

OFFAL

SKEWERED LAMB'S KIDNEYS WITH PARSLEY BUTTER

SERVES 4

8 lamb's kidneys
55g/2oz unsalted butter
1 tablespoon very finely chopped fresh parsley
2 shallots, very finely chopped
1–2 teaspoons lemon juice
salt and freshly ground black pepper
cayenne pepper

To serve
red pesto root mash (see page 206)

1. Soak 4 bamboo skewers in cold water for 10 minutes. Skin the kidneys, quarter them and remove the cores with kitchen scissors.
2. Thread the kidneys on to the skewers and refrigerate.
3. Meanwhile, melt the butter in a saucepan, add the parsley, shallots and lemon juice and season with salt and pepper.
4. Preheat the grill to its highest setting.
5. Season the kidneys with salt and cayenne, arrange on the grill rack and grill for 1–2 minutes. Turn the kidneys and grill for a further 1–2 minutes, or until just cooked through but still pink in the middle.
6. Brush the kidneys generously with the parsley butter and arrange on a warmed serving dish. Serve immediately with the red pesto root mash handed separately.

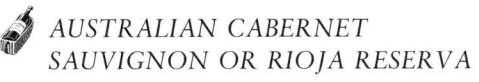 *AUSTRALIAN CABERNET SAUVIGNON OR RIOJA RESERVA*

SAUTÉ OF VEAL SWEET-BREADS AND MORELS WITH ROSEMARY

SERVES 4

675g/1½lb veal sweetbreads
1 slice of lemon
570ml/1 pint white stock, made with veal bones (see page 625)
4 sprigs of fresh rosemary
85g/3oz unsalted butter
2 cloves of garlic, chopped
170g/6oz morel mushrooms
2 teaspoons white truffle butter (optional)
salt and freshly ground black pepper
a squeeze of lemon juice

1. Soak the sweetbreads in cold water for 4–6 hours.
2. Drain the sweetbreads, place in a saucepan and cover with clean water. Add the slice of lemon, cover the saucepan and bring to the boil, then lower the heat and simmer for 2–3 minutes. Drain, refresh under cold running water and press between 2 plates. Allow to cool for 15 minutes.
3. Peel any membrane from the sweetbreads. Return to the rinsed-out pan, add the stock and rosemary and poach for 10 minutes. Strain the sweetbreads, reserving the liquid.
4. Melt 30g/1oz of the butter in a sauté pan. Fry the sweetbreads until brown on both sides, then lift out of the pan and set aside. Add the garlic to the pan, lower the heat and cook for 1 minute. Add the morels and sauté briskly for 2–3 minutes, then remove with a slotted spoon, add to the sweetbreads and keep warm.
5. Add the reserved stock to the pan and bring to the boil, then lower the heat and simmer until the liquid has reduced to 5–6 tablespoons.
6. Add the remaining butter piece by piece,

445

whisking vigorously after each addition. Stir in the truffle butter, if using, and season with salt, pepper and lemon juice. Return the sweetbreads and morels to the pan and heat through until very hot. Serve immediately.

NOTE: White truffle butter is a paste available from specialist grocers.

 ALSACE PINOT GRIS

BRAISED OXTAIL WITH PORT AND AUTUMN BERRIES

SERVES 4

2 oxtails, total weight about 1.35kg/3lb, cut
*   into 2.5cm/1in lengths*
seasoned plain flour
30g/1oz beef dripping or oil
1 large onion, sliced
2 cloves of garlic, crushed
2 tomatoes, halved and de-seeded
150ml/¼ pint port
290ml/½ pint brown stock (see page 625)
5 tablespoons sloe gin (optional)
110g/4oz blackberries
110g/4oz elderberries
55g/2oz sloes
1 bay leaf
1 sprig of fresh thyme
2 teaspoons bramble or sloe jelly or 2 teaspoons
*   soft light brown sugar*
1 tablespoon white wine vinegar
salt and freshly ground black pepper

To serve
fresh herb dumplings (see page 650)
110g/4oz blackberries
55g/2oz caster sugar
1 tablespoon chopped fresh parsley

1. Preheat the oven to 150°C/300°F/gas mark 2.
2. Wash and dry the oxtails. Trim off any excess fat and toss in the seasoned flour.
3. Melt the dripping or heat the oil in a large flameproof casserole. Add the oxtail, a few pieces at a time, and brown evenly and well on all sides. Remove to a plate as they are done.

4. Add the onion to the casserole and cook until nearly soft, then add the garlic and tomatoes and cook for a further 2–3 minutes.
5. Return the oxtail to the casserole. Pour over the port, stock and the sloe gin, if using. Add the blackberries, elderberries and sloes, the herbs, jelly or sugar and the vinegar. Season with a little salt and pepper. Cover and cook in the preheated oven for 1½ hours.
6. Remove the pieces of oxtail and place in a clean casserole. Strain the cooking liquid over the top, pressing well to extract the fruit purée. Discard any remaining pulp. Cover the oxtail with the strained liquid and return to the oven for a further 2–2½ hours, or until the oxtail is very tender and almost falling off the bone. Forty-five minutes before the end of cooking, add the dumplings to the casserole and continue to cook in the oven.
7. Meanwhile, put the blackberries and sugar into a small saucepan and bring to the boil, then lower the heat and simmer for 3–4 minutes, or until the fruit is beginning to break up.
8. To serve: sprinkle the blackberries on top of the casserole and sprinkle with the parsley.

 BAROLO OR SOUTH AFRICAN CABERNET SAUVIGNON

OXTAIL AND DAMSON STEW WITH HERB DUMPLINGS

SERVES 4

2 oxtails, cut into 2.5cm/1in lengths, total
*   weight about 1.35kg/3lb*
seasoned plain flour
2–4 tablespoons sunflower oil
2 large onions, sliced
2 sticks of celery, sliced into 1cm/½in pieces
2 large cloves of garlic, crushed
450g/1lb damsons, cut in half and stoned
290ml/½ pint red wine
570ml/1 pint brown stock (see page 625)
1 tablespoon tomato purée
2 tablespoons redcurrant jelly or damson jam
1 bouquet garni

salt and freshly ground black pepper
1 quantity of fresh herb dumplings (see page 650)

To garnish
2 tablespoons chopped fresh parsley

1. Preheat the oven to 150°C/300°F/gas mark 2.
2. Wash and dry the oxtails. Trim off any excess fat and toss in seasoned flour, shaking off the excess.
3. Heat 2 tablespoons of oil in a frying pan. Add the oxtail, a few pieces at a time, and brown on all sides evenly and well. Remove to a plate as they are done.
4. Brown the onion and celery in the remaining oil. Add the garlic and cook for a few seconds.
5. Place the oxtail in a large oven-proof heavy bottomed casserole dish (e.g. Le creuset) with a well fitting lid. Tip over the onion, celery and garlic. Add the damsons, wine, stock, tomato purée, redcurrant jelly or jam and bouquet garni and add enough water to cover the meat completely. Season well with salt and pepper.
6. Place the casserole on the direct heat and bring to the boil. Replace the lid and bake in the lower half of the oven for approximately 4½ hours or until the oxtail flesh is just starting to fall away from the bone.
7. Remove the lid and add the dumplings to the casserole. Return the casserole to the oven for a further 30 minutes or until the dumplings are cooked.
8. Sprinkle over the parsley before serving.

 *BURGUNDY*

CALVES' LIVER WITH SAUTERNES AND JERUSALEM ARTICHOKES

SERVES 4

4 × 170g/6oz slices of calves' liver
675/1½lb Jerusalem artichokes, washed
55g/2oz butter
seasoned plain flour

150ml/¼ pint brown stock (see page 625)
150ml/¼ pint Sauternes or other sweet dessert wine
salt and freshly ground black pepper
450g/1lb fresh spinach, washed and stalks removed

1. Preheat the oven to 150°C/300°F/gas mark 2. Remove the membrane and any large veins from the liver. Bring a large saucepan of salted water to the boil.
2. Cut the artichokes into 5mm/¼in slices.
3. Heat half the butter in a large frying pan, add the artichokes and fry until golden-brown and tender. Tip on to a baking sheet and keep warm in the oven.
4. Heat the remaining butter in the frying pan. Dip the liver into the seasoned flour and shake off the excess. Fry the liver, 2 slices at a time, over a high heat on one side, just until it starts to brown. Quickly turn it over and fry briefly on the second side. Keep the cooked liver in the warming oven while you fry the remaining slices.
5. Deglaze the pan with the stock, stirring with a wooden spoon over a high heat to release any sediment stuck on the bottom.
6. When the stock has reduced to 4 tablespoons, add the wine and reduce again by boiling rapidly until the sauce is of a syrupy consistency. Season with salt and pepper.
7. Plunge the spinach into the boiling water and when it goes limp, immediately strain in a colander and press out the excess water.
8. Arrange the spinach on 4 warmed individual plates, scatter the artichokes around and place the liver on top.
9. Strain the sauce through a fine sieve over the liver. Serve immediately.

 *SYRAH VIN DE PAYS D'OC OR CHIANTI CLASSICO*

VEGETARIAN

STUFFED BAKED CELERIAC WITH TOMATO AND CHEDDAR

SERVES 4

4 medium celeriac, scrubbed
55g/2oz butter, softened
4 tablespoons double cream
4 ripe tomatoes, roughly chopped
110g/4oz strong Cheddar cheese, grated
1 teaspoon Dijon mustard
2 tablespoons chopped fresh parsley
salt and freshly ground black pepper

1. Preheat the oven to 200°C/400°F/gas mark 6.
2. Pierce the celeriac several times all over with a skewer. Place in an ovenproof dish and bake in the middle of the oven for 1½ hours, or until soft.
3. Cut a large slice off the top of each celeriac and scrape the flesh from the middle into a bowl. Mash with a fork or a potato masher.
4. Mix in the butter, cream, tomatoes, half the Cheddar cheese, the mustard and parsley. Season to taste with salt and pepper.
5. Pile the filling back into the centre of each celeriac and sprinkle with the remaining Cheddar cheese.
6. Place the lids back on top of the celeriac. Bake at the top of the oven for 20 minutes, or until the cheese is brown and bubbling.

NEW ZEALAND SAUVIGNON BLANC

WILD MUSHROOM, TOMATO AND POTATO GNOCCHI

SERVES 4

450g/1lb mixed wild mushrooms, such as cèpes, chanterelles, girolles, pleurottes, wood blewitts
2 tablespoons olive oil
2 large cloves of garlic, crushed
butter for greasing
570ml/1 pint tomato sauce (see page 635)
1 quantity potato gnocchi (see page 571)
2 tablespoons chopped fresh parsley
salt and freshly ground black pepper
110g/4oz mozzarella cheese, cut into cubes

1. Preheat the oven to 200°C/400°F/gas mark 6.
2. Plunge the mushrooms very briefly into a large bowl of cold water, swirl them around and lift them out of the water, leaving grit and any twigs, etc. behind. Dry them well on kitchen paper. Cut any very large mushrooms into 2.5cm/1in pieces.
3. Heat the oil in a large heavy-based frying pan, add the mushrooms and fry over a low heat until they start to sweat. Add the garlic and cook gently for a further minute.
4. Lightly butter a shallow ovenproof dish. Spread half the tomato sauce over the bottom.
5. Arrange the gnocchi over the sauce and spread the mushrooms on top with 1 tablespoon of the parsley. Season well with salt and pepper.
6. Spread the remaining tomato sauce over the top and sprinkle over the mozzarella cubes.
7. Bake the gnocchi at the top of the preheated

oven for 20–30 minutes, or until golden-brown and bubbling at the edges. Sprinkle with the remaining parsley before serving.

 *CHIANTI CLASSICO*

PUMPKIN AND PINENUT CANNELLONI

SERVES 4

1 small pumpkin or large butternut squash,
    peeled
2 tablespoons olive oil
1 teaspoon caster sugar
salt and freshly ground black pepper
55g/2oz pinenuts
225g/8oz egg pasta dough (see page 652)
flour for rolling
1 tablespoon sunflower oil
225g/8oz ricotta cheese
1 tablespoon chopped fresh thyme
juice of 1 lemon
2 tablespoons freshly grated Parmesan cheese

To serve
570ml/1 pint tomato sauce (see page 635)

1. Preheat the oven to 230°C/450°F/gas mark 8.
2. Cut the pumpkin or squash in half and remove the seeds. Cut the flesh into 2.5cm/1in chunks and place in a shallow roasting tray with the oil and sugar. Season with salt and pepper. Toss the pumpkin or squash until well coated with the oil and seasoning. Roast at the top of the preheated oven for 20 minutes, or until it starts to caramelize. Remove from the oven and allow to cool.
3. Place the pinenuts on a baking sheet and roast them in the hot oven for a couple of minutes, until they begin to brown – be very careful not to leave them too long or they will burn. When they are a pale golden-brown, remove them from the oven and tip them on to a cold plate, which will prevent them from browning further.
4. Cut the pasta in half and roll each half out,

using a pasta machine, in a long strip about 10cm/4in wide. Coat the strips with enough flour to prevent them from sticking to the work surface, then leave them to dry for 15–20 minutes, or until a slight crust has formed on the outside, turning them once. (If it is a very hot, dry day this may take less time.)
5. Cut each pasta strip into 4 equal squares. Blanch the pasta squares in a large saucepan of boiling salted water, with the oil, for 2 minutes, then refresh them in cold water. Drain the pasta squares and pat dry with kitchen paper.
6. Mix the pumpkin or squash with the pinenuts, ricotta, thyme and lemon juice. Season to taste with salt and pepper.
7. Lay the pasta squares out on a large flat work surface. Divide the filling between the squares, arranging it in a line to one side. Roll up the pasta to form the cannelloni.
8. To serve: pour the tomato sauce into the bottom of a large shallow gratin dish. Arrange the cannelloni on top, seam side down. Sprinkle over the Parmesan cheese and bake in the preheated oven for 20 minutes, or until the tomato sauce is bubbling and the Parmesan is lightly browned.

 *ITALIAN RED*

PUMPKIN GNOCCHI WITH FRESH SAGE AND FONTINA

SERVES 4

1 large baking potato
85g/3oz butter
1 small pumpkin or 1 medium butternut
    squash, peeled, de-seeded and cubed
110g/4oz ricotta cheese
1 egg
salt and freshly ground black pepper
freshly grated nutmeg
plain flour
2 tablespoons chopped fresh sage
110g/4oz Fontina cheese, grated

1. Preheat the oven to 200°C/400°F/gas mark 6.
2. Bake the potato in the preheated oven for 1 hour, or until soft. Cut the potato in half and when it is cool enough to handle, scrape the flesh out of the skin and press it through a sieve, using a wooden spoon.
3. Melt 30g/1oz of the butter in a saucepan, add the pumpkin or squash, cover and cook over a low heat until tender. Remove the lid, increase the heat and allow any juices to evaporate. Push the pumpkin through a sieve.
4. Mix the potato and pumpkin or squash in a large bowl with the ricotta and egg. Season to taste with salt, pepper and nutmeg.
5. Bring a large saucepan of salted water to a simmer.
6. Meanwhile, shape the pumpkin or squash mixture into egg shapes, using a tablespoon and the palm of your hand. Roll the gnocchi lightly in flour. Place them in the simmering water a few at a time and poach gently until they rise to the surface (about 2–3 minutes).
7. Remove the gnocchi from the pan with a slotted spoon, allowing excess liquid to drain off. Place the gnocchi in the bottom of an ovenproof dish.
8. Melt the remaining butter, add the sage and cook gently for 1 minute. Drizzle the sage butter over the gnocchi and sprinkle with the Fontina cheese.
9. Place the dish on a baking sheet and bake at the top of the preheated oven for 20 minutes, or until the cheese is golden-brown and bubbling. Serve immediately.

 *AUSTRALIAN SÉMILLON-CHARDONNAY*

HONEY PUMPKIN SKEWERS

SERVES 4

450g/1lb pumpkin, peeled and de-seeded
8 shallots
8 bay leaves
2 tablespoons hazelnut oil

2 tablespoons clear honey
1 tablespoon rice wine vinegar
salt and freshly ground black pepper

1. Preheat the oven to 200°C/400°F/gas mark 6. Soak 4 bamboo skewers in cold water for 10 minutes.
2. Cut the pumpkin into 5cm/2in chunks.
3. Blanch the shallots for 5 minutes then refresh under cold running water and peel.
4. Thread the pumpkin and shallots on to the skewers. Thread 2 bay leaves on to each skewer. Arrange on a baking sheet.
5. Mix together the oil, honey and vinegar. Season with salt and pepper. Brush a little of the honey dressing on to the pumpkin, then bake in the preheated oven for 10 minutes.
6. Turn the skewers over and brush the skewered vegetables again with more dressing. Cook for a further 35–40 minutes, turning and brushing the pumpkin every 10 minutes, until the pumpkin and shallots are soft.
7. Arrange the skewers on a warmed serving plate and serve very hot.

 *CHILEAN RED*

PUFF-BALL WITH PARMESAN

SERVES 4

1 large puff-ball
2 eggs, lightly beaten
salt and freshly ground black pepper
55g/2oz dry white breadcrumbs
30g/1oz Parmesan cheese, freshly grated
1 tablespoon chopped fresh parsley
30–55g/1–2oz butter

To serve
4 lemon wedges

1. Preheat the oven to 180°C/350°F/gas mark 4.
2. Wipe the outside of the puff-ball with damp kitchen paper. Cut away the root end if it is gritty and muddy. Cut the puff-ball into 1cm/½in slices.

3. Tip the eggs into a shallow tray or roasting tin and season with salt and pepper.

4. Mix together the breadcrumbs, Parmesan cheese and parsley in a separate shallow tray.

5. Dip the puff-ball slices one at a time into the egg, shake off the excess and then dip them into the breadcrumb and Parmesan cheese mixture. Shake off any excess and put the slices in a single layer on a large board.

6. Melt half the butter in a large heavy-based frying pan. When the foam starts to subside, place one or two slices of puff-ball (depending on their size) in the pan in a single layer. Fry until golden on one side, then turn the slices over and fry until golden on the other side.

7. Place the fried puff-ball on a baking sheet in the oven to keep warm while frying the remaining slices in the same way with the remaining butter.

8. Serve immediately on a warmed serving dish with the lemon wedges.

 *PINOT NOIR*

CHESTNUT AND WILD MUSHROOM CARBONNADE

SERVES 4

55g/2oz butter
1 large onion, finely chopped
1 clove of garlic, crushed
1 teaspoon chopped fresh thyme
1 teaspoon soft light brown sugar
450g/1lb peeled chestnuts
290ml/½ pint vegetable stock (see page 627)
150ml/¼ pint brown ale
450g/1lb mixed mushrooms, such as pied de mouton, chanterelles and oyster
salt and freshly ground black pepper

To serve
1 tablespoon chopped mixed fresh herbs
red pesto root mash (see page 463)

1. Melt half the butter in a large saucepan, add the onion and cook over a very low heat for 45 minutes–1 hour, or until very soft and golden-brown. Add the garlic, thyme and sugar and cook for a further 3–4 minutes.

2. Add the chestnuts, stock and brown ale to the pan. Bring to the boil, then lower the heat and cook for 10–15 minutes, or until the chestnuts are tender.

3. Pick over and trim the mushrooms. Heat the remaining butter in a frying pan, add the mushrooms and sauté briefly. Add the mushrooms to the chestnut mixture and continue to cook for 5 minutes.

4. Lift the chestnuts and mushrooms from the liquid with a slotted spoon and arrange in a warmed casserole dish. Bring the cooking liquid in the pan to a rapid boil and reduce to a syrupy consistency.

5. Season to taste with salt and pepper and pour over the chestnuts and mushrooms. Sprinkle with the herbs and serve with the red pesto mash handed separately.

 CRU BOURGEOIS CLARET

BAKED SPAGHETTI SQUASH WITH FARMHOUSE CHEDDAR

SERVES 2

1 spaghetti squash
150ml/¼ pint water
30g/1oz butter
freshly grated nutmeg (optional)
salt and freshly ground black pepper
85g/3oz strong farmhouse Cheddar cheese, grated

1. Preheat the oven to 200°C/400°F/gas mark 6.

2. Cut the spaghetti squash in half lengthways and scoop out all the seeds. Place the squash, cut side uppermost, in a large roasting tin.

3. Pour the water around the squash, put half the butter into each squash and season with the nutmeg, if using, salt and pepper. Cover with kitchen foil and bake in the preheated oven for 30 minutes, or until the flesh is just tender. (Be careful not to overcook the squash or the spaghetti strands will turn into a pulp.)

4. Place the squash on 2 warmed individual plates, ruck up the flesh with a fork so that it looks like spaghetti, sprinkle over the Cheddar cheese and serve immediately.

 CABERNET SAUVIGNON VIN DE PAYS D'OC

SPAGHETTI SQUASH, LEEK AND CAULIFLOWER CHEESE

SERVES 4

1 spaghetti squash, halved and de-seeded
salt and freshly ground black pepper
4 leeks, washed and cut into 2.5cm/1in chunks
1 small cauliflower
570ml/1 pint mornay sauce (see page 629)
55g/2oz strong Cheddar cheese, grated
2 tablespoons dry white breadcrumbs

1. Preheat the oven to 200°C/400°F/gas mark 6.
2. Season the inside of the spaghetti squash with salt and pepper. Place the squash in a roasting tin, cut side down. Pour in 1cm/½in of water and bake in the middle of the preheated oven for 40 minutes, or until the squash is just tender. (Be careful not to overcook or the spaghetti strands will turn to a pulp.)
3. Blanch the leeks in a large saucepan of boiling salted water for 3 minutes. Add the cauliflower florets and cook for a further 3 minutes. Drain and allow to steam-dry in the pan.
4. Scrape the flesh of the spaghetti squash out of the skins, using a fork to separate out the strands. Spread over the bottom of a shallow casserole dish. Season with salt and pepper. Arrange the leeks and cauliflower over the squash, making sure the rounded side of the

cauliflower florets are uppermost. Season with pepper.
5. Spoon the mornay sauce over the vegetables, making sure they are all completely coated. Mix the Cheddar cheese with the breadcrumbs and sprinkle over the top.
6. Return the dish to the top of the oven for 15–20 minutes, or until the top is golden-brown. (If this is taking too long, finish the dish off under a hot grill before the vegetables overcook.)

 ALSACE MUSCAT

BAKED SWEDE WITH SOURED CREAM AND CHIVES

SERVES 4

4 medium swedes, scrubbed and trimmed
85g/3oz butter
salt and freshly ground black pepper

For the topping
290ml/½ pint soured cream or crème fraîche
4 tablespoons chopped fresh chives

1. Preheat the oven to 200°C/400°F/gas mark 6.
2. Pierce the swedes several times all over with a skewer. Bake in the middle of the preheated oven for 1½ hours, or until soft in the middle.
3. Cut a large slice off the top of the swedes and lightly mash up the soft flesh inside with a fork. Mix a quarter of the butter into the centre of each swede and season well with salt and pepper.
4. Make the topping: mix the soured cream or crème fraîche with the chives, reserving a few for the garnish, and season to taste with salt and pepper.
5. To serve: place the swedes on individual serving dishes and pile the soured cream and chives on top of each one. Replace the lids and serve immediately, garnished with the reserved chives.

 SOUTH AFRICAN CHENIN BLANC

SHIITAKE DUXELLES AND RHUBARB CHARD DOLMADES

SERVES 4

340g/12oz shiitake mushrooms, finely chopped
2 tablespoons olive oil
1 clove of garlic, crushed
2 teaspoons chopped fresh thyme
grated zest of 1 lemon
110g/4oz cooked basmati rice
salt and freshly ground black pepper
12 large rhubarb chard leaves
1 quantity basic vinaigrette, made with extra
    virgin olive oil (see page 634)

1. Finely chop the mushrooms. Heat the oil in a frying pan, add the mushrooms and sauté for 4–5 minutes, or until dry. Add the garlic, thyme and lemon zest. Stir in the cooked rice and season with salt and pepper.
2. Wash the rhubarb chard leaves. Blanch each leaf in boiling salted water until soft. Refresh in cold water and dry thoroughly on kitchen paper.
3. Divide the mushroom mixture between each rhubarb chard leaf. Fold the leaf around the mushroom mixture. Secure with a cocktail stick if necessary. Arrange in a serving dish and pour over the dressing. Chill for 30 minutes before serving.

 *PINOT NOIR*

BAKED MARROW WITH ADUKI BEAN AND WILD MUSHROOM STUFFING

SERVES 4

1 × 675g/1½lb marrow, peeled
1 bay leaf
½ teaspoon salt
1 × 400g/14oz can of aduki beans, drained
3 shallots, finely chopped
3 tablespoons walnut oil
1 clove of garlic, chopped
170g/6oz mixed wild mushrooms, such as
    morels, chanterelles and pied de mouton
55g/2oz chopped walnuts, toasted
salt and freshly ground black pepper
110g/4oz feta cheese, crumbled

1. Preheat the oven to 200°C/400°F/gas mark 6.
2. Cut the marrow into 2.5cm/1in rings and remove the seeds. Cook in boiling salted water with the bay leaf for 3–4 minutes, or until tender. Drain and dry on kitchen paper, then arrange in a shallow ovenproof dish.
3. Drain and rinse the aduki beans and set aside.
4. Cook the shallots in the oil in a frying pan until soft, then add the garlic and continue to cook for a further minute. Add the mushrooms and walnuts and fry over a high heat until the mushrooms are just cooked. Stir into the aduki beans and season to taste with salt and pepper.
5. Divide the bean mixture between the marrow rings and sprinkle over the feta cheese. Bake in the preheated oven for 12–15 minutes, or until very hot and golden-brown. Serve immediately.

 *CLARET*

ROAST ONIONS STUFFED WITH SPICED LENTILS

SERVES 6

6 large Spanish onions
1 tablespoon olive oil

For the filling
2–3 tablespoons olive oil
170g/6oz onion cores, finely chopped
2 cloves of garlic, crushed
1 teaspoon ground cinnamon
3 whole cloves, ground
¼ nutmeg, grated
1 × 400g/14oz can of tomatoes
3–4 tablespoons tomato purée

110g/4oz brown lentils, cooked
55g/2oz toasted almonds, chopped
55g/2oz raisins
2 tablespoons chopped fresh marjoram
grated zest of 1 lemon
salt and freshly ground black pepper

To garnish
3 tablespoons finely chopped fresh marjoram

1. Preheat the oven to 180°C/350°F/gas mark 4.
2. Trim the onion roots but do not cut them off.
Keeping the knife parallel with the roots, cut off
the tops of the onions and remove the skin.
Leave 3 layers of each onion intact and scrape
away the insides with a teaspoon. Reserve the
cores for the filling.
3. Blanch the onions in boiling water for 3–4
minutes. Drain and pat dry with kitchen paper.
Allow to cool.
4. Meanwhile, make the filling: heat the oil in a
sauté pan, add the onion cores and garlic and
cook over a low heat until soft. Add the
cinnamon, cloves and nutmeg. Cook for 1
minute.
5. Add all the remaining ingredients and cook
until the mixture is dry. Check the seasoning.
6. Fill the onions with the lentil mixture,
packing it in well. Brush with oil. Place together
closely in a roasting tin or baking dish. Cover
the stuffing with a little kitchen foil.
7. Bake in the preheated oven for 1½–2 hours,
or until the onion flesh is soft and brown.
Remove the foil for the last 15 minutes to allow
the onions to caramelize.
8. Serve the onions in their own juices and
garnish generously with marjoram.

 *PINOT NOIR*

VEGETABLES AND SALADS

VEGETABLES

SZECHUAN-STYLE AUBERGINE

olive oil and sesame oil for frying
2 teaspoons peeled and chopped fresh root
  ginger
2 cloves of garlic, chopped
2 spring onions, finely chopped
2 medium aubergines, cut into 5cm/2in cubes
2 tablespoons black bean sauce
1 tablespoon dark soy sauce
75ml/2½fl oz stock or water
2 tablespoons dry sherry

1. Heat about 2 tablespoons olive oil plus a few drops of sesame oil in a wok or frying pan.
2. Add the ginger, garlic and spring onions and stir-fry. Add the aubergine and continue to stir-fry, then add the remaining ingredients. Cook for 8–10 minutes, then pile into a warmed serving dish and serve immediately.

STEAMED CABBAGE, RICE AND SULTANA PARCEL

SERVES 8

butter for greasing
salt and freshly ground black pepper
4 Savoy cabbage leaves, washed
225g/8oz short-grain brown rice
30g/1oz sultanas
4 tablespoons extra virgin olive oil
1 tablespoon chopped fresh thyme
1 tablespoon chopped fresh oregano
½ teaspoon ground cinnamon

290ml/½ pint dry white wine
290ml/½ pint white stock, made with chicken
  bones (see page 625)

1. Butter a 1 litre/1¾ pint pudding basin and sprinkle some salt and pepper around the inside.
2. Blanch the cabbage leaves in a large saucepan of boiling salted water for 1 minute. Drain and refresh in cold water. Trim the thick stalks away from the cabbage leaves and cut each leaf in half. Arrange the leaves around the inside of the basin, overlapping, with the underside of the cabbage leaves facing uppermost.
3. Put the rice, sultanas, oil, thyme, oregano and cinnamon into a heavy-based saucepan and season well with salt and pepper. Add the wine and stock and bring to the boil. Cover the pan and simmer the rice gently for 30–40 minutes, or until all the liquid is absorbed (you may need to add a little more hot water, depending on the type of rice) and the rice is cooked. Check the seasoning. Pack the rice mixture firmly into the bowl lined with cabbage leaves.
4. Fold the tops of the cabbage leaves over the top of the rice. Bring water to the boil in a large saucepan or steamer.
5. To cover the basin: lay 2 sheets of greased greaseproof paper on 1 sheet of kitchen foil. Invert the covering on to the basin and secure well with string. Trim off the excess paper, leaving 2.5cm/1in. Tuck the remaining inch of foil and paper under the lip of the basin to create a good seal.
6. Steam for 30 minutes.
7. Uncover the basin and turn out the cabbage parcel. Serve as a vegetable accompaniment to lamb.

SMOKY SAVOY CABBAGE

SERVES 8

1 Savoy cabbage
110g/4oz smoked belly of pork
55g/2oz duck fat
2 onions, thinly sliced
150ml/¼ pint white wine
290ml/½ pint strong white stock, made with
*   chicken bones, or game stock (see page 625)*
1 bouquet garni
salt and freshly ground black pepper

1. Preheat the oven to 180°C/350°F/gas mark 4.
2. Remove the tough outer leaves from the cabbage. Cut the cabbage into 8 wedges through the core so that they remain held together.
3. Cut the rind off the belly of pork and cut the meat across the grain into 2.5cm/1in strips.
4. Heat the duck fat in a large heavy-based saucepan, add the pork and fry over a high heat until golden-brown. Remove the pork from the pan with a slotted spoon and lower the heat. Add the onions to the pan and cook very gently over a low heat for 5 minutes. Pour the wine into the pan, increase the heat and boil rapidly for 3 minutes.
5. Arrange the cabbage in a single layer in a large ovenproof dish. Pour over the onions, wine, pork and stock. Add the bouquet garni and season well with salt and pepper.
6. Cover with a large sheet of kitchen foil or a well-fitting lid and bake in the preheated oven for 1 hour. Check the seasoning before serving.

SWEET AND SOUR CABBAGE

SERVES 4

120ml/4fl oz rice wine vinegar
150ml/¼ pint pineapple juice
¼ large green cabbage, core removed and finely
*   shredded*
2 tablespoons demerara sugar
freshly ground black pepper

1. Bring the vinegar and pineapple juice to the boil in a large saucepan. Add the cabbage and sugar and cover with a close-fitting lid. Cook the cabbage, stirring frequently, for 5–10 minutes, or until almost cooked.
2. Remove the lid, turn up the heat and allow the liquid to almost boil dry. Season with pepper before serving.

CRISP CAULIFLOWER WITH HOT PEANUTS

SERVES 4

1 large head of cauliflower, cut into 2.5cm/1in
*   florets*
55g/2oz butter, melted
salt and freshly ground black pepper
1 tablespoon sunflower oil
1 onion, very finely chopped
1 clove of garlic, crushed
1 small red chilli, de-seeded and finely chopped
110g/4oz roasted salted peanuts, roughly
*   chopped*

1. Preheat the oven to 230°C/450°F/gas mark 8.
2. Toss the cauliflower in the melted butter and season with salt and pepper. Tip it on to a shallow roasting tray. Roast at the top of the preheated oven for 20 minutes, or until crisp and golden-brown, turning the cauliflower over from time to time so that it browns on all sides.
3. Heat the oil in a frying pan, add the onion and fry until golden-brown. Add the garlic and chilli and fry for a further minute. Stir in the peanuts and season to taste with salt and pepper.
4. Pile the cauliflower into a warmed serving dish and sprinkle over the hot peanut mixture.

CHESTNUTS WITH PANCETTA

SERVES 4

450g/1lb peeled chestnuts (see page 569)
290ml/½ pint white stock, made with chicken
bones (see page 625)
2 cloves of garlic, peeled
1 tablespoon oil
170g/6oz piece of pancetta, diced
freshly ground black pepper
1 teaspoon finely chopped fresh sage

1. Cook the chestnuts in the stock with the garlic in a saucepan for 15–20 minutes, or until tender. Lift the chestnuts and garlic into a bowl with a slotted spoon. Reduce the stock to 5 tablespoons by boiling rapidly, add the chestnuts and set aside. Crush the garlic and add to the chestnuts.
2. Heat the oil in a frying pan, add the pancetta and fry briskly until browned. Stir into the chestnuts. Season with pepper and add the sage. Serve very hot as an accompaniment to roast game.

CORIANDER AND CHILLI PESTO MASH

SERVES 4

675g/1½lb potatoes, peeled
1 teaspoon rock salt
2 cloves of garlic
55g/2oz butter
1 quantity coriander and chilli pesto (see page
416)
finely ground rock salt and freshly ground
black pepper

1. Cut the potatoes into large pieces, put them into a large saucepan, cover with cold water and add 1 teaspoon rock salt. Cover the pan and bring to the boil, then lower the heat and simmer until the potatoes are tender.

2. Drain the potatoes and push through a sieve, then return to the saucepan. Stir in the butter and coriander and chilli pesto and season to taste with salt and pepper.

BONFIRE POTATOES

SERVES 4

4 baking potatoes, scrubbed and halved
55g/2oz butter
salt and freshly ground black pepper

1. Light a good bonfire at the end of the garden! (It needs to burn for 2 hours.)
2. Cut 8 × 30cm/12in squares of kitchen foil. Fold each square in half and lay them out on a flat surface. Prick the potatoes all over with a fork.
3. Spread the butter on one half of the potatoes and sandwich them back together with the remaining halves. Place each potato on a double piece of kitchen foil and season them well with salt and pepper.
4. Wrap the potatoes up tightly and place them in the glowing embers of the fire, not on a direct flame. Turn them occasionally, leaving them for about 1 hour, or until they feel soft to the touch.
5. Unwrap the potatoes with gloves and nibble them as the fire subsides.

PARSNIP AND HORSERADISH PURÉE

SERVES 4

675g/1½lb parsnips
salt and freshly ground black pepper
30–55g/1–2oz butter
3–4 teaspoons freshly grated horseradish
5 tablespoons buttermilk

1. Peel the parsnips and cut them into chunks.
2. Boil the parsnips in salted water until tender, then drain very well.

3. Mash with a potato masher or in a mouli. Beat in the butter, salt, pepper, horseradish and buttermilk. Check the seasoning. Serve very hot.

PARSNIP AND CRÈME FRAÎCHE PURÉE

SERVES 4

450g/1lb floury potatoes, peeled and cut into
    quarters
salt and freshly ground black pepper
450g/1lb parsnips, peeled
200g/7oz crème fraîche
1 clove of garlic, crushed

1. Boil the potatoes in salted water for 5 minutes. Add the parsnips and simmer until tender (a table knife should easily press into them).
2. Push the parsnips and potatoes through a sieve or mouli. Return them to the dry saucepan. Heat carefully, stirring, to allow the potatoes and parsnips to steam-dry.
3. In a separate saucepan bring the crème fraîche to the boil with the garlic and simmer gently for 5 minutes until reduced by half. Pour the cream into the parsnip and potato pan and season with salt and pepper.
4. Beat the cream into the purée and check the seasoning.

DEEP-FRIED BABY PARSNIPS IN A SAGE DERBY JACKET

These make a pleasant change from the traditional roast parsnips. They are a great accompaniment to roast game, pork or duck, or can be served as a canapé with a dip.

SERVES 4

450g/1lb baby parsnips
1 teaspoon coarse sea salt
2 tablespoons seasoned plain flour
1 egg, beaten
85g/3oz fresh white breadcrumbs
85g/3oz sage Derby cheese, finely grated
a pinch of dry English mustard
salt and freshly ground black pepper
oil for deep-frying

1. Scrape the parsnips with a knife to remove the thin outer skin. Blanch in a saucepan of boiling water with the salt for 5 minutes, or until just tender. Drain and dry.
2. Roll the parsnips in the seasoned flour and brush with the beaten egg.
3. Mix together the breadcrumbs, sage Derby cheese, mustard, salt and pepper and toss the parsnips in this until completely coated. Place in a single layer on a plate and chill until required. Do not stack or they will become soggy.
4. Heat oil in a deep-fryer or half filled saucepan with oil and heat until a cube of bread colours golden-brown in 20 seconds.
5. Fry 4–5 parsnips at a time until the crust is a deep golden-brown. Lift out of the oil and drain on kitchen paper. Sprinkle with salt and serve very hot.

SESAME AND SOY MUSHROOMS

SERVES 4

450g/1lb chestnut mushrooms
2 tablespoons sesame oil
2 cloves of garlic, crushed
1 teaspoon Sichuan peppercorns, crushed
freshly ground black pepper
2 tablespoons dry sherry
3 tablespoons light soy sauce

1. Wipe the mushrooms and if large, cut into quarters.
2. Heat the oil in a large frying pan, add the mushrooms and sauté over a medium heat for 2–3 minutes. Add the garlic and Sichuan pepper and cook for a further 2 minutes.
3. Season the mushrooms with pepper, add the sherry and soy sauce, bring to the boil and boil for 1 minute. Tip into a bowl and serve hot or cold.

GOLDEN JERUSALEM ARTICHOKES AND CELERIAC

SERVES 6

675g/1½lb Jerusalem artichokes, scrubbed
2 celeriac, peeled and cut into 1cm/½in
*   segments*
salt and freshly ground black pepper
2 tablespoons plain flour
4 tablespoons freshly grated Parmesan cheese
6–8 tablespoons olive oil

1. Preheat the oven to 200°C/400°F/gas mark 6.
2. Cut the artichokes into roughly 2.5cm/1in pieces.
3. Blanch the celeriac in boiling salted water for 2 minutes, then drain and allow to steam-dry in a colander for 5 minutes.
4. Mix the flour and Parmesan cheese together in a large bowl and add the artichokes and celeriac. Season with salt and pepper and toss everything together.
5. Heat the oil in a large shallow roasting tin.
6. Tip in the artichokes and celeriac, spreading them in a single layer, and spoon the oil over so they are well coated.
7. Roast the vegetables for 20 minutes near the top of the preheated oven. When they are starting to brown, turn them over and continue to roast for a further 30 minutes, or until they are golden-brown all over and a blunt knife can be pushed into them easily.
8. Drain off the excess oil and pile the vegetables into a warmed serving dish.

CAJUN HONEY ROAST SQUASH WITH PUMPKIN SEEDS

SERVES 4

1 large butternut squash
45g/1½oz butter
1 tablespoon clear honey
salt and freshly ground black pepper
55g/2oz pumpkin seeds
1 teaspoon Cajun seasoning

1. Preheat the oven to 220°C/425°F/gas mark 7.
2. Peel the squash and cut it in half lengthways. Scoop out the seeds and cut each half into 4 strips lengthways.
3. Heat the butter and honey in a roasting tin, add the squash and season with salt and pepper. Baste well. Roast at the top of the preheated oven for 30 minutes, or until golden-brown. If the squash is not browning, put the roasting tin back over direct heat and fry quickly in the roasting tin until coloured.
4. Add the pumpkin seeds and Cajun seasoning. Baste with the pan juices and return to the oven for 10 minutes.

CRUSHED BUTTERNUT SQUASH

SERVES 4

450g/1lb butternut squash, peeled, de-seeded
*   and cut in chunks*
salt and freshly ground black pepper
55g/2oz butter
4 shallots, finely chopped
5 tablespoons crème fraîche

1. Cook the butternut squash in boiling salted water until tender. Drain and set aside.
2. Melt the butter in a large saucepan, add the shallots and cook over a low heat until completely soft.

3. Break up the squash lightly with a fork and add to the shallots, season to taste with salt and pepper and add the crème fraîche. Stir over a medium heat until very hot. Serve immediately.

WILTED SORREL LEAVES

Sorrel is a hardy herb that grows all year round. It has a strong citrus taste, but discolours on cooking. In the absence of sorrel, spinach can be used, but add a little grated lemon zest to enhance the flavour.

SERVES 2

4 large handfuls of sorrel leaves
2 tablespoons extra virgin olive oil
a pinch of cayenne pepper
salt and freshly ground black pepper

1. Remove the stalks from the sorrel and wash thoroughly. Dry and shred into thin strips.
2. Heat the oil, cayenne and salt and pepper in a frying pan until very hot but not smoking. Add half the sorrel and stir over a brisk heat for 30–40 seconds, or until wilted. Lift on to a plate and cook the remaining leaves. Do not overcook or it will become slimy.
3. Serve immediately.

SORREL AND SPINACH SQUEAK

SERVES 8

225g/8oz sorrel, washed and stalks removed
225g/8oz spinach, washed and stalks removed
salt
900g/2lb potatoes, peeled and cut into large
  pieces
freshly ground black pepper
freshly grated nutmeg
beef dripping

1. Preheat the oven to 150°C/300°F/gas mark 2.
2. Blanch the sorrel and spinach in a large saucepan of boiling salted water for a few seconds until they become limp. Quickly refresh the leaves in cold water, reserving the cooking liquor. Drain the leaves in a colander, squeeze out the excess liquid with your hands, then roughly chop the leaves.
3. Boil the potatoes in the blanching liquid until tender. Drain, then press the potatoes, a few pieces at a time, through a sieve with a wooden spoon.
4. Mix the sorrel and spinach with the potato and season to taste with salt, pepper and nutmeg. Using your hands, shape the potato mixture into 8 round, even-sized patties.
5. Heat 2 tablespoons of dripping in a large, heavy-based frying pan. Fry 4 patties at a time over a low heat for about 5 minutes, or until golden-brown and a good thick crust is formed. Turn the patties over and fry until golden and crusty on the second side. Place the cooked patties on a baking sheet and keep warm in the oven while cooking the remaining patties in the same way.

SWEET POTATO WEDGES

SERVES 4

4 sweet potatoes, scrubbed
4 tablespoons olive oil
1 tablespoon Cajun seasoning
salt and freshly ground black pepper

1. Preheat the oven to 220°C/425°F/gas mark 7.
2. Cut the potatoes in half lengthways. Cut each half into 4 long wedges.
3. Heat the oil in a large roasting tin and add the potatoes, Cajun seasoning and salt and pepper. Toss everything together so that the potato is well coated with oil and seasoning.
4. Roast the potatoes near the top of the oven for 30–40 minutes, turning them over half-way through the cooking time. The potatoes are ready to serve when they are golden-brown and tender.

RED PESTO ROOT MASH

SERVES 4

225g/8oz swede
225g/8oz celeriac
225g/8oz potatoes
salt and freshly ground black pepper
5 tablespoons warm milk
freshly grated nutmeg
1 quantity red pesto (see page 634)

1. Peel the vegetables and cut them into chunks.
2. Boil all the vegetables in salted water until tender. Drain very well.
3. Mash with a potato masher or ricer and beat in the warm milk. Season with nutmeg. Stir in the red pesto to taste, and season to taste with salt and pepper. Serve very hot.

SALADS

BARLEY, APPLE, SMOKED CHEDDAR AND ONION SALAD

SERVES 4

225g/8oz pearl barley, rinsed in cold water to
    remove excess starch
salt and freshly ground black pepper
1 red onion, finely chopped
75ml/2½fl oz basic vinaigrette (see page 634)
juice of 1–2 lemons
2 dessert apples, quartered, cored and thinly
    sliced
1 small bunch of spring onions, thinly sliced
110g/4oz smoked Cheddar cheese, coarsely
    grated

To garnish
1 punnet of mustard and cress, snipped and
    washed

1. Boil the barley in plenty of salted water for
45–60 minutes, or until just cooked. Drain and
leave to steam-dry in the sieve for 10 minutes.
2. Tip the barley into a bowl with the onion,
dressing and lemon juice and set aside for the
flavours to infuse for 30 minutes.
3. Stir in the apple slices, spring onions and
smoked Cheddar cheese and season to taste
with plenty of black pepper.
4. To serve: tip the salad into a serving bowl
and scatter the cress on top.

HOT PARSNIP AND PECAN SALAD

SERVES 4

85g/3oz pecan nuts, roughly chopped
salt
450g/1lb parsnips, peeled and cut into batons
450g/1lb carrots, peeled and cut into batons
450g/1lb leeks, washed and cut into 2.5cm/1in
    lengths

For the dressing
1 tablespoon grain mustard
2 tablespoons cider vinegar
6 tablespoons extra virgin olive oil
2 tablespoons plain yoghurt
1 teaspoon soft light brown sugar
55g/2oz walnuts, ground
freshly ground black pepper

1. Preheat the oven to 180°C/350°F/gas mark 4.
2. Place the pecan nuts on a baking sheet and
roast in the preheated oven for 10–15 minutes,
or until golden-brown.
3. Bring a large saucepan of salted water to the
boil.
4. Put the vegetables into the pan and simmer
gently for 5 minutes, or until they are just
tender. Drain well.
5. Whisk together the dressing ingredients and
season to taste with salt and pepper.
6. Put the vegetables and pecan nuts into a large
warmed serving bowl, pour over the dressing
and toss everything together.

OKRA AND TOMATO SALAD

SERVES 4

450g/1lb okra, trimmed
6 tablespoons extra virgin olive oil
4 large tomatoes, skinned and chopped
1 tablespoon finely chopped fresh parsley
1 tablespoon chopped fresh mint
grated zest and juice of 1 lemon
salt and freshly ground black pepper

1. Cook the okra in boiling salted water for 1 minute, then drain and refresh under cold running water. Heat 2 tablespoons of oil in a frying pan, add the okra and sauté over a low heat for 5–6 minutes, or until the okra is soft.
2. Mix the tomatoes, herbs, the remaining oil and lemon zest and juice together in a bowl and season to taste with salt and pepper.
3. Arrange the okra in a serving dish, spoon over the tomato dressing and serve warm or chilled.

WARM RED CABBAGE COLESLAW

SERVES 4

340g/12oz red cabbage
4 tablespoons extra virgin olive oil
2 red onions, finely chopped
1 clove of garlic, crushed
salt and freshly ground black pepper
2 tablespoons chopped dried apple
1 tablespoon sultanas

For the dressing
2 egg yolks
3 tablespoons red wine vinegar
1 teaspoon caster sugar
150ml/¼ pint vegetable stock (see page 627)
2 tablespoons double cream (optional)
salt and freshly ground black pepper

1. Shred the cabbage very finely and set aside.
2. Heat the oil in a wok or frying pan, add the onion and cook until golden-brown. Add the garlic and cook for a further minute.
3. Meanwhile, make the dressing: put the egg yolks, vinegar, sugar and stock into a saucepan. Stir over a low heat with a wooden spoon until the mixture coats the back of the spoon, then season to taste with salt and pepper and set aside.
4. When the onion and garlic are cooked, increase the heat and add the red cabbage. Stir-fry over a brisk heat for 2–3 minutes, or until hot. Season to taste with salt and pepper and add the apple and sultanas. Pour over the dressing, heat gently for 1 minute and toss together. Pile into a warmed serving dish and serve warm.

AUBERGINE, CHILLI AND CHICKPEA SALAD

SERVES 4

1 large aubergine
2 teaspoons salt
6 tablespoons extra virgin olive oil
3 red chillies, de-seeded and finely chopped
1 clove of garlic, sliced
grated zest and juice of 1 lemon
225g/8oz chickpeas, cooked and drained
salt and freshly ground black pepper
1 tablespoon chopped fresh mint

1. Wipe the aubergine and cut into bite-sized chunks. Place in a colander, sprinkle with salt and leave to degorge for about 30 minutes. Rinse away the salt and dry the aubergine well with kitchen paper.
2. Meanwhile, make the chilli oil: heat the oil in a small saucepan with the chillies, garlic and lemon zest over a low heat for 4–5 minutes, then remove from the heat and allow to infuse for 10 minutes. Strain the oil into a clean frying pan and reserve the chillies and garlic.
3. Heat the strained chilli oil in a frying pan, add the aubergines and fry until lightly browned and soft. Add the chillies and garlic, lemon juice, chickpeas and fresh mint and season to taste with salt and pepper. Pile into a warmed serving dish and serve warm.

PUDDINGS

Fruit Puddings
Mousses, Soufflés and Creams
Ice Creams and Sorbets
Meringues
Pastries, Pies and Tarts
Cakes and Pâtisserie

FRUIT PUDDINGS

EARLY AUTUMN FRUIT SOUPS

This light pudding is a simple low-fat pudding and perfectly suited to end a rich game dinner.

SERVES 4

For the blackberry soup
450g/1lb blackberries
55g/2oz granulated sugar
4 tablespoons apple juice
2 tablespoons crème de mûre (blackberry liqueur)

For the pear soup
450g/1lb ripe pears
55g/2oz granulated sugar
150ml/¼ pint apple juice
3 tablespoons Poire William liqueur

For the melon soup
1 medium Galia melon
juice of 1 lemon
icing sugar
2 teaspoons white port (optional)

To decorate
2 teaspoons chopped fresh mint

1. Make the blackberry soup: put the blackberries into a saucepan with the sugar and apple juice. Bring to the boil, then lower the heat and simmer for 5 minutes, or until the fruit begins to break up.
2. Liquidize the blackberries and cooking liquid in a blender and sieve the purée into a bowl. Taste for sweetness and add the crème de mûre. Cover and chill until required.

3. Make the pear soup: peel, quarter and core the pears. Put into a saucepan with the sugar and apple juice and cook over a very low heat for 20–25 minutes, or until the fruit is soft and translucent.
4. Liquidize the pears and syrup in a blender and sieve the purée into a bowl. Taste for sweetness and add the Poire William. Cover and chill until required.
5. Halve, de-seed, peel and dice the melon. Liquidize in a blender and flavour the purée with lemon juice and icing sugar to taste. Add the white port, if using, and chill until required.
6. To serve: chill 4 individual soup bowls. Spoon a ladleful of each soup into the bowls and swirl lightly together. Sprinkle with the mint and serve.

 AUSTRALIAN LIQUEUR MUSCAT

GINGERED APPLES AND ORANGES

SERVES 4

85g/3oz granulated sugar
290ml/½ pint water
6 large Cox's Orange Pippin apples
2 navel oranges
5cm/2in piece of fresh root ginger, peeled and chopped
1 cinnamon stick
2 star anise
grated zest and juice of 1 lemon
2–3 sprigs of fresh mint

For the caramel
85g/3oz caster sugar

To serve
*ginger and brown sugar meringues (see page
  592)*

1. Put the sugar into a large saucepan, add the water and dissolve over a low heat. Bring to the boil, then lower the heat and simmer for 2 minutes. Remove from the heat and set aside.
2. Peel, quarter and core the apples and put into the sugar syrup. Thinly pare the zest from the oranges and add to the syrup. Peel and segment the oranges, removing all the pith, and set aside.
3. Add the spices and lemon zest to the apples in the syrup, cover and cook over a very low heat for 12–20 minutes, or until the apples are transparent, then remove from the heat. Add the mint and lemon juice to the pan and allow to cool.
4. Lift the cooled apples from the syrup and arrange on a shallow serving dish with the orange segments. Strain the syrup over the top, cover and chill.
5. Make the caramel: put the sugar into a small saucepan and cook over a low heat until the sugar turns to a dark caramel. Pour the caramelized sugar on to an oiled baking sheet and allow to cool until set. Crush the caramel with the end of a rolling pin and sprinkle over the apples and oranges.
6. Allow the apples and oranges to stand for a further 30 minutes, or until the caramel has begun to dissolve. Serve with the meringues handed separately.

 *AUSTRALIAN ORANGE MUSCAT*

WARM WILD BERRY COMPOTE

SERVES 4

450g/1lb blackberries
225g/8oz elderberries
150ml/¼ pint water
140g/5oz caster sugar
1 cinnamon stick

grated zest and juice of 1 orange
2 teaspoons arrowroot
5 tablespoons crème de cassis

1. Rinse the blackberries and elderberries and allow to drain.
2. Put the water, sugar, cinnamon stick, orange zest and juice into a saucepan and heat until the sugar has dissolved. Add the berries and bring to the boil, then lower the heat and poach for 7–10 minutes, or until the fruit is soft.
3. Slake the arrowroot with the crème de cassis and add to the berries. Bring back to the boil, stirring continuously. Immediately remove from the heat. Serve the compote warm.

 *BANYULS*

BLACKBERRY AND LIME COMPOTE

SERVES 4

For the sauce
225g/8oz blackberries, fresh or frozen
grated zest and juice of 1 lime
*55–110g/2–4oz caster sugar, depending on the
  sweetness of the blackberries*
2 tablespoons water

For the fruit
340g/12oz blackberries
225g/8oz blueberries
2 tablespoons crème de cassis

To decorate
a few sprigs of fresh mint

To serve
1 quantity shortbread (see page 648)
150ml/¼ pint double cream, lightly whipped

1. Make the sauce: put the blackberries into a heavy-based saucepan with the lime zest and juice, sugar and water. Heat gently together until the blackberries have just collapsed and the sugar has dissolved. Remove from the heat and allow to cool.

2. Put the remaining blackberries and the blueberries into a bowl and stir in the sauce with the cassis.

3. Pile the compote into a glass bowl and serve decorated with the sprigs of mint. Hand the shortbread and cream separately.

 *MUSCAT DE RIVESALTES*

QUINCE AND HERB COMPOTE

The Moscatel wine of the Valencia region of Spain makes the perfect accompaniment to the bitter flavour of the quince, which are used for making *membrillo*, the classic quince preserve.

SERVES 4

4 large quinces
570ml/1 pint Moscatel or dry white wine
1 cinnamon stick
3 bay leaves
2 sprigs of fresh mint
2 sprigs of fresh sage
2 sprigs of fresh rosemary

To serve
150ml/¼ pint Greek yoghurt

1. Preheat the oven to 100°C/200°F/gas mark ½.
2. Peel, quarter and core the quinces. Arrange them in a single layer in a flameproof casserole dish.
3. Pour the wine over the quinces, add the cinnamon and herbs and bring to the boil. Cover the quinces with a piece of damp greaseproof paper and a lid. Bake in the preheated oven for 1½ hours, or until the quinces are tender.
4. Lift the quinces from the liquid, remove the cinnamon and herbs and discard. Strain the liquid into a saucepan and bring to the boil, then

lower the heat and simmer for 5–7 minutes, or until reduced to about 150ml/¼ pint.
5. Arrange the quinces in a serving dish and pour the reduced liquid over the top. Serve warm with the yoghurt handed separately.

 *MOSCATEL*

BAKED STUFFED QUINCES

SERVES 4

4 large quinces
30g/1oz butter, melted
110g/4oz dried apricots, roughly chopped
4 dried figs, chopped
30g/1oz ground almonds
2 tablespoons soft light brown sugar
2 tablespoons clear honey
½ teaspoon ground cardamom
5 tablespoons water
5 tablespoons brandy or Calvados

To serve
mascarpone
amaretti biscuits (optional)

1. Preheat the oven to 190°C/375°F/gas mark 5.
2. Wash the quinces. Remove the cores with an apple corer. Using a sharp knife, cut a ring just through the skin around the middle of each quince. Place in an ovenproof dish.
3. Mix together the butter, chopped dried fruit, ground almonds, sugar, honey and cardamom. Pack this stuffing into the centre of each quince and pour over the water and brandy or Calvados. Cover with kitchen foil and bake in the preheated oven for 1–1¼ hours, or until the quinces are soft all the way through when tested with a skewer.
4. Arrange the quinces in a serving dish and spoon around the cooking juices. Serve warm or chilled with the mascarpone and amaretti biscuits, if using, handed separately.

 *MONBAZILLAC*

BAKED BLACKBERRY CHEESECAKE

SERVES 8

For the crust
225g/8oz digestive biscuits, crushed
110g/4oz butter, melted

For the filling
450g/1lb soft cream cheese
3 eggs, beaten
1 teaspoon vanilla essence
150ml/¼ pint double cream, lightly whipped
225g/8oz blackberries
110g/4oz caster sugar

For the topping
340g/12oz blackberries
7g/¼oz powdered gelatine
1–2 tablespoons sugar

1. Preheat the oven to 150°C/300°F/gas mark 2.
2. Mix the biscuits with the melted butter and use to line the base and sides of a 20cm/8in loose-based deep flan ring. Chill for 15 minutes.
3. Put the cream cheese into a large bowl and gradually stir in the eggs. Fold in the vanilla essence and the cream.
4. Using a fork, lightly crush the blackberries in a bowl with the caster sugar. Fold into the cream cheese mixture.
5. Pour the cheesecake filling into the prepared base, place on a baking sheet and bake on a low shelf in the preheated oven for 1–1½ hours, or until just set. Remove from the oven, transfer to a wire rack and leave until cool.
6. Make the topping: whizz 225g/8oz of the blackberries in a blender, then push through a sieve, reserving the juice. Put 3 tablespoons of the juice into a small saucepan, sprinkle over the gelatine and leave to sponge for 5 minutes.
7. Warm the remaining blackberry juice in a small saucepan and add 1–2 tablespoons of caster sugar, depending on the tartness of the juice. Stir until the sugar has dissolved.
8. Place the gelatine over a very low heat until melted, then stir into the sweetened blackberry

juice. Allow to cool. Carefully stir in the remaining whole blackberries and pour over the top of the cheesecake. Chill for at least 2 hours before removing from the tin to serve.

 BARSAC OR MONBAZILLAC

GREENGAGE AND ALMOND SPONGE PUDDING WITH RED PLUM SAUCE

SERVES 6

For the almond sponge
butter for greasing
170g/6oz butter, softened
170g/6oz caster sugar
3 eggs, lightly beaten
3 tablespoons dark rum
85g/3oz self-raising flour
a pinch of salt
85g/3oz ground almonds

For the topping
12 ripe greengages, halved and stoned
2 tablespoons demerara sugar
icing sugar

To serve
1 quantity red plum sauce (see page 503)

1. Preheat the oven to 180°C/350°F/gas mark 4. Butter a 20cm/8in ovenproof dish.
2. Cream the butter in a bowl, add the sugar and beat until light and fluffy. Beat in one egg at a time, beating well after each addition to prevent curdling. (If the mixture does curdle, add 1 tablespoon of the flour.) Stir in the rum.
3. Sift the flour with the salt and fold into the egg mixture with the ground almonds. Spread the mixture over the bottom of the prepared dish.
4. Arrange the greengages over the top in a circular pattern, cut side uppermost, and sprinkle with the demerara sugar.
5. Bake in the middle of the preheated oven for

40–45 minutes, or until the cake has risen and feels firm underneath the greengages.

6. Dust with icing sugar and serve with the red plum sauce.

NOTE: If greengages are unavailable, small plums may be used instead.

 SWEET WHITE OR SWEET SPARKLING SUCH AS ASTI SPUMANTE

INDIVIDUAL STEAMED AUTUMN PUDDINGS

SERVES 6

170g/6oz blackberries
1 cooking apple, peeled and diced
2 pears, peeled and diced
1 quince or medlar, peeled and diced
85g/3oz soft light brown sugar
5 tablespoons brandy or sloe gin
170g/6oz unsalted butter, softened
110g/4oz caster sugar, plus extra for dusting
grated zest of 1 orange
2 eggs, beaten
110g/4oz self-raising flour
a pinch of salt
1 teaspoon ground cinnamon
5 tablespoons milk

To serve
cinnamon crème anglaise (see page 505)

1. Make the topping: put all the fruit together into a saucepan with the sugar and brandy or sloe gin. Bring to the boil, then lower the heat and poach for 15–20 minutes, or until all the fruit is soft. Lift the fruit into a bowl with a slotted spoon and if necessary reduce the cooking liquid to a syrupy consistency, then stir into the fruit.

2. Meanwhile, generously grease 6 dariole or timbale moulds with 55g/2oz of the butter and sprinkle with caster sugar. Put a generous tablespoon of the fruit mixture at the bottom of each mould and set aside.

3. In a mixing bowl, cream the remaining butter and when very soft, add the sugar. Beat until light and fluffy. Add the orange zest.

4. Gradually add the eggs, beating very well after each addition.

5. Sift the flour with the salt and cinnamon and fold into the mixture.

6. Add enough milk to give a dropping consistency (the mixture should be just loose enough to drop from a spoon).

7. Divide the mixture between the moulds, cover with greaseproof paper and then with kitchen foil and tie securely with string, to prevent moisture entering the puddings.

8. Steam over continuously boiling water for 45 minutes, keeping a close eye on the water, so that it does not boil dry.

9. Turn out the moulds and serve with chilled cinnamon crème anglaise.

 *SAUTERNES*

PLUM, ORANGE AND BRANDY STEAMED PUDDING

SERVES 4

butter for greasing
110g/4oz butter, softened
110g/4oz soft light brown sugar
grated zest of 1 large orange
2 eggs, beaten
110g/4oz self-raising flour
a pinch of salt
2 tablespoons milk

For the filling
4 ripe plums, each stoned and cut into eighths
2 tablespoons brandy
2–3 tablespoons soft light brown sugar
½ teaspoon ground cinnamon

To serve
150ml/¼ pint extra thick double cream

1. Pour 5cm/2in water into a large saucepan, cover and bring to the boil. Grease an 860ml/1½ pint pudding basin with butter.

2. Cream the butter and sugar together in a bowl until light and fluffy. Add the orange zest.

3. Gradually add the eggs, beating very well after each addition.

4. Sift the flour with the salt into the bowl, add the milk and carefully fold the mixture together.

5. Mix together all the filling ingredients.

6. Spoon two-thirds of the cake mixture into the prepared pudding basin, making a well in the centre. Tip in the filling and cover with the remaining cake mixture.

7. To cover the pudding basin: lay 2 sheets of greaseproof paper on 1 sheet of kitchen foil. Grease the top layer of greaseproof paper. Make a large pleat in the centre of the layers. Invert the covering on to the basin and secure well with string. Trim off the excess paper, leaving 3.5cm/1½in which can be tucked under the lip of the bowl to create a good seal. Place the basin over the boiling water in the pan and cover with a lid.

8. Steam for 1¼–1½ hours, making sure the pan is regularly topped up with boiling water from a kettle.

9. Remove the string and paper and invert the pudding on to a plate. Serve immediately with the cream handed separately.

 MUSCAT DE BEAUMES DE VENISE

VICTORIA PLUM AND BANANA CRUMBLE

If the plums are not very ripe they should be cooked in a little sugar syrup before they are baked.

SERVES 4

For the filling
675g/1½lb ripe Victoria plums, halved and
  stoned
2 large bananas, cut into 2.5cm/1in chunks
1–2 tablespoons soft light brown sugar

1 teaspoon ground mixed spice
4 tablespoons water

For the crumble topping
170g/6oz plain flour
a pinch of salt
1 teaspoon ground mixed spice
110g/4oz butter, diced
55g/2oz soft dark brown sugar

To serve
200ml/7fl oz crème fraîche or mascarpone

1. Preheat the oven to 180°C/350°F/gas mark 4.

2. Make the filling: mix the plums, bananas, sugar and spice together in a bowl. Transfer to a pie dish, making sure the fruit is piled up a little in the centre. Pour over the water.

3. Make the crumble: sift the flour, salt and spice into a large bowl. Rub in the butter with the fingertips until the mixture resembles coarse breadcrumbs. Stir in the sugar.

4. Tip the mixture over the fruit, making sure it is completely covered. Put the dish on to a baking sheet and bake in the preheated oven for 40 minutes, or until golden-brown and bubbling at the edges.

5. Serve with the crème fraîche or mascarpone handed separately.

 SAINTE-CROIX-DU-MONT

INDIVIDUAL PEAR AND RAISIN CRUMBLES

SERVES 4

4 ripe pears
55g/2oz raisins
4 teaspoons Poire William liqueur
170g/6oz plain flour
110g/4oz butter
55g/2oz soft light brown sugar
2 tablespoons pinhead oatmeal

To serve
150ml/¼ pint Greek yoghurt

1. Preheat the oven to 180°C/350°F/gas mark 4.
2. Wash and peel the pears, remove the cores and cut the flesh into small chunks. Mix with the raisins, then divide between 4 ramekins. Sprinkle the fruit with the liqueur.
3. Sift the flour into a bowl, cut the butter into small pieces and rub into the flour with the fingertips until it resembles coarse breadcrumbs. Add the sugar and oatmeal and stir together, but do not allow to become sticky.
4. Divide the crumble topping between the ramekins and press lightly on to the fruit. Bake in the preheated oven for 25 minutes, or until the fruit is soft, testing with a knife.
5. Serve hot or warm, with the yoghurt handed separately.

 *SAUTERNES*

CARDAMOM, PEAR AND BREAD PUDDING

SERVES 4

150ml/¼ pint milk
150ml/¼ pint single cream
6 cardamom pods, crushed
3 slices of white bread
30g/1oz butter, softened
grated zest of 1 orange
1 ripe pear, peeled and diced
2 eggs
1 egg yolk
2 rounded tablespoons caster sugar
ground cardamom
demerara sugar

1. Put the milk and cream into a saucepan with the cardamom pods and heat to scalding point. Remove from the heat and allow to infuse for 30 minutes.
2. Spread the bread with the butter, cut the slices into quarters and arrange in a shallow ovenproof dish, layering the bread with the orange zest and diced pear.
3. Make the custard: mix the eggs and egg yolk with the caster sugar and strain over the cream mixture in the pan.

4. Strain the custard carefully over the bread and leave to soak for 10 minutes. Sprinkle with the ground cardamom and demerara sugar.
5. Preheat the oven to 180°C/350°F/gas mark 4.
6. Place the pudding dish in a roasting tin half filled with hot water (a bain-marie) and bake in the middle of the preheated oven for about 45 minutes, or until the custard is set and the top is brown and crusty.

 *SAUTERNES*

ROAST PLUMS WITH BRIE

This is good as part of a buffet or can be served instead of a dessert.

SERVES 4

450g/1lb ripe plums, halved and stoned
55g/2oz butter, melted
55g/2oz soft light brown sugar
salt
225g/8oz ripe Brie

1. Preheat the oven to 150°C/300°F/gas mark 2. Line 2 baking sheets with silicone paper.
2. Place the plums, cut side uppermost, in a single layer on the baking sheets.
3. Drizzle the butter on to the plums and sprinkle over the sugar. Season with salt before putting in the oven.
4. Bake in the preheated oven for 1–1½ hours, or until the plums are beginning to caramelize at the edges and are about half their original size. Remove from the oven and leave to cool for 5 minutes.
5. Arrange the plum halves on 4 warmed individual plates. Cut the Brie into wedges and serve with the plums immediately.

 *SWEET VOUVRAY*

BARBECUED FIG PARCELS WITH CORIANDER AND HONEY

SERVES 4

8 ripe figs
4 tablespoons clear honey
1 teaspoon ground coriander
4 tablespoons whisky
1 tablespoon chopped fresh coriander

To serve
Greek yoghurt

1. Preheat the barbecue (see page 72). Cut
4 × 20cm/8in squares of kitchen foil.
2. Wash the figs and make 2–3 slits in each. Put
2 figs on each square of kitchen foil.
3. Mix together the honey, ground coriander,
whisky and chopped coriander and divide
between each parcel. Wrap each parcel loosely.
Allow to macerate for 30 minutes.
4. Arrange the parcels on the top shelf of the
barbecue and cook for 10 minutes. Open each
parcel, turn the figs, re-seal and cook for a
further 10 minutes.
5. Serve the parcels for diners to open
themselves, with the yoghurt handed separately.

NOTE: In the absence of whisky a liqueur such
as crème de cassis can be used instead.

 *AUSTRALIAN ORANGE MUSCAT*

MOUSSES, SOUFFLÉS AND CREAMS

CHESTNUT, CHOCOLATE AND ORANGE TIMBALES

SERVES 6

1 × 400g/14oz can of unsweetened chestnut purée
170g/6oz dark chocolate, chopped
3 tablespoons water
1 tablespoon rum
grated zest of 2 oranges
110g/4oz unsalted butter
110g/4oz caster sugar

To serve
orange marmalade crème anglaise

1. Line 6 timbale moulds with lightly oiled clingfilm.
2. Sieve the chestnut purée into a bowl and set aside.
3. Place the chocolate in a heatproof bowl with the water, rum and orange zest. Set over, not in, a saucepan of simmering water and stir until the chocolate has melted. Remove from the heat and allow to cool.
4. Cream the butter and sugar together in a bowl until light and fluffy, then stir into the chestnut purée with the melted cooled chocolate.
5. Divide the mixture between the timbale moulds, filling them two-thirds full. Cover with clingfilm and chill for 2 hours.
6. To serve: turn the moulds on to individual plates and remove the clingfilm. Smooth the surface of each timbale and pour the crème anglaise around the edge.

 *AUSTRALIAN LIQUEUR MUSCAT*

ARMAGNAC CRÊPE SOUFFLÉ WITH CARAMELIZED APPLES

SERVES 4

3 Granny Smith apples, peeled, quartered and cored
55g/2oz butter
55g/2oz caster sugar
4 large pancakes (see page 654)

For the soufflé
1 quantity crème pâtissière (see page 661)
4 tablespoons Armagnac
4 egg whites
1 tablespoon caster sugar

To serve
icing sugar
sweet orange butter (see page 504)

1. Preheat the oven to 200°C/400°F/gas mark 6.
2. Put the apples, butter and sugar into a large frying pan and cook over a medium heat for 4–5 minutes, or until the apples are tender and well caramelized. Tip on to a plate to cool.
3. Lay the pancakes out on to 2 baking sheets and place 3 pieces of apple on one half of each pancake.
4. Put the crème pâtissière into a large bowl and stir in the Armagnac. Place the egg whites in a separate large bowl and whisk until they form stiff peaks. Add the sugar and whisk again until stiff and shiny.
5. Quickly stir a large spoonful of the meringue mixture into the crème pâtissière, then carefully

fold in the remainder. Divide the soufflé mixture between the pancakes, spooning it on to the apples. Fold over the free half of the pancakes and bake in the preheated oven for 5 minutes.
6. Transfer the pancakes quickly to warmed individual plates, dust with icing sugar and serve immediately with the orange butter.

 *ARMAGNAC*

STEAMED CHOCOLATE SOUFFLÉ WITH POACHED PEARS AND HOT CHOCOLATE SAUCE

SERVES 4

For the pears
4 ripe Comice pears, peeled and sliced
290ml/½ pint water
55g/2oz granulated sugar
5 tablespoons Poire William liqueur

For the soufflé
butter for greasing
290ml/½ pint milk
55g/2oz plain chocolate, chopped
45g/1½oz butter
15g/½oz plain flour
30g/1oz cornflour
30g/1oz caster sugar
2 eggs, separated

For the chocolate sauce
170g/6oz plain chocolate
85g/3oz butter
5 tablespoons strong black coffee

1. Butter a 20cm/8in soufflé dish.
2. Poach the pears in the water, sugar and liqueur in a saucepan over a very low heat for 15–20 minutes, or until translucent.
3. Make the soufflé: heat half the milk slowly with the chocolate in a saucepan, stirring constantly. When the chocolate has dissolved,

add the remaining milk, remove from the heat and set aside.
4. Melt the butter in a saucepan, add the flour and cornflour and blend in the chocolate milk. Return to the boil, stirring constantly, and cook for 1–2 minutes. Remove from the heat and sprinkle the sugar over.
5. Whisk the egg whites until they form medium peaks, then fold into the chocolate mixture with the egg yolks.
6. Pour the mixture into the prepared soufflé dish and cover with a piece of kitchen foil. Tie securely with string. Trim off the excess foil.
7. Steam over a saucepan of boiling water for 30–35 minutes, or until just firm to the touch.
8. Meanwhile, make the chocolate sauce: melt the chocolate, butter and coffee together in a heatproof bowl set over, not in, a saucepan of simmering water. Keep warm.
9. Turn the soufflé on to a warmed serving plate. Arrange the pears around the edge and drizzle the hot chocolate sauce over the fruit. Serve very hot.

 *ASTI SPUMANTE*

HOT BLACKBERRY SOUFFLÉ

SERVES 6

450g/1lb blackberries
85g/3oz caster sugar
5 tablespoons crème de mûre (blackberry liqueur)
butter for greasing
110g/4oz caster sugar
6 egg whites

To decorate
30g/1oz flaked almonds, toasted
1 tablespoon icing sugar

1. Put the blackberries, sugar and crème de mûre into a saucepan and bring to the boil, then lower the heat and simmer for 6–8 minutes, or until the fruit is soft. Purée in a liquidizer, then sieve and set aside.

2. Preheat the oven to 190°C/375°F/gas mark 5. Put a baking sheet into the oven on the top shelf.

3. Lightly butter 6 ramekins and sprinkle with a little of the caster sugar.

4. Whisk the egg whites until they form stiff peaks. Add the sugar 1 tablespoon at a time, whisking until the whites are stiff and glossy.

5. Fold the blackberry purée into the egg whites and divide between the ramekins. Bake on the hot baking sheet in the preheated oven for 8 minutes, then sprinkle the top of each soufflé with the almonds and dust generously with icing sugar. Bake for a further 2–3 minutes. Test by giving the ramekins a slight shake or push. If the soufflés wobble alarmingly, they need further cooking. If they wobble slightly, they are ready. Serve immediately.

 *SAUTERNES*

BAKED BLACKBERRY AND SLOE GIN CREAMS

SERVES 4

225g/8oz blackberries, washed
4 tablespoons sloe gin (see page 495)
30g/1oz caster sugar, plus 4 teaspoons
290ml/½ pint milk
150ml/¼ pint single cream
grated zest of 1 orange
4 egg yolks
1 egg

To serve
icing sugar

1. Preheat the oven to 150°C/300°F/gas mark 2.

2. Divide the blackberries between 4 ramekins. Sprinkle 1 tablespoon of the sloe gin and 1 teaspoon of the sugar over each and allow to stand for 10 minutes.

3. Place the milk, cream, the remaining sugar and the orange zest in a saucepan and scald by bringing to just below boiling point.

4. Beat the egg yolks with the whole egg and

pour on to the scalded milk. Strain and divide between the ramekins.

5. Stand the ramekins in a roasting tin half filled with hot water (a bain-marie).

6. Cover with a piece of kitchen foil and bake in the preheated oven for 35–40 minutes. Remove the foil and allow to cool. Serve warm or chilled. Dust with icing sugar just before serving.

 *MONBAZILLAC*

GREENGAGE SYLLABUB

SERVES 4

450g/1lb ripe greengages, halved and stoned
2 tablespoons water
55g/2oz granulated sugar
grated zest of ½ lemon
juice of 1 lemon
3 tablespoons dry white wine
2 tablespoons sweet ginger wine
a little icing sugar (optional)
290ml/½ pint double cream, lightly whipped

To decorate
a few sprigs of fresh mint

1. Put the greengages, water, sugar and lemon zest into a heavy-based saucepan. Cover and cook over a low heat until the greengages have softened and the sugar has dissolved. Push through a nylon sieve into a large bowl and allow to cool.

2. Add the lemon juice, white wine and ginger wine and taste the mixture, which should be fairly strong in flavour. Add a little icing sugar if it seems too tart, remembering that when the cream is added the flavour will become less pronounced.

3. Add the cream and gently fold together until the mixture just holds its shape.

4. Spoon into individual glasses and decorate with the mint before serving.

 *ASTI SPUMANTE*

ICE CREAMS AND SORBETS

BANANA AND RUM ICE CREAM

SERVES 4

3 ripe bananas, roughly chopped
55g/2oz soft light brown sugar
290ml/½ pint double cream
290ml/½ pint crème anglaise (see page 661)
3 tablespoons dark rum

1. Put the bananas into a sauté pan with the sugar and half the cream. Cook over a low heat until the bananas are soft. Remove from the heat and set aside to cool.
2. Mix the bananas with the remaining cream, the crème anglaise and the rum. Taste and add more sugar or rum if the flavour is not strong enough.
3. Churn in an ice-cream machine for 20 minutes, then transfer to a freezerproof container and freeze for 30 minutes before serving.

NOTE: If the ice cream is made in advance, it should be transferred to a refrigerator 30 minutes before serving.

 *AUSTRALIAN LIQUEUR MUSCAT*

QUINCE AND MULBERRY PARFAIT

SERVES 8

6 quinces, peeled and diced
450g/1lb mulberries
4 tablespoons mulberry gin (see page 495) or
*   sloe gin*
290ml/½ pint water
170g/6oz granulated sugar
3 egg yolks
55g/2oz icing sugar
290ml/½ pint double cream

To serve
quince and herb compote (see page 471)
vanilla crème anglaise (see page 661)

1. Lightly oil 8 ramekins.
2. Put the fruit, gin, water and sugar into a saucepan and heat together until the sugar has completely dissolved. Simmer over a low heat until the quinces are tender.
3. Purée the fruit and liquid in a food processor, then push through a sieve.
4. Whisk the egg yolks with the icing sugar until very thick and light.
5. Lightly whip the double cream.
6. Fold the fruit purée and cream into the yolk mixture, taste and add more icing sugar if required.
7. Pour the mixture into the prepared ramekins, cover with clingfilm and freeze for at least 4 hours.
8. To serve: turn the parfaits out on to 8 individual plates. Arrange the quince and herb compote around the side and spoon over a little crème anglaise.

 *ASTI SPUMANTE*

PEAR AND QUINCE SORBET WITH POIRE WILLIAM

SERVES 4

450g/1lb quinces
450g/1lb ripe pears
450g/1lb granulated sugar
290ml/½ pint water
juice of 1–2 lemons
4 tablespoons Poire William liqueur
1 egg white

1. Peel and core the quinces and pears. Cut into small pieces. Put into a saucepan and add just enough water to cover the fruit.
2. Bring to the boil, then poach over a very low heat for 40–45 minutes, or until the fruit is very soft. Remove from the heat and allow to cool. Liquidize the fruit and liquid together in a blender.
3. Meanwhile, dissolve the sugar in the water in a saucepan over a low heat. Bring to the boil, then lower the heat and simmer for 5 minutes.
4. Mix the fruit purée with the sugar syrup and taste for sweetness. Add lemon juice to taste and stir in the liqueur.
5. Pour the mixture into a freezerproof container and freeze. When nearly frozen, place the sorbet in a food processor and whizz briefly. Gradually add the unwhisked egg white with the motor running. The mixture will fluff up tremendously. Return to the container and freeze until firm.

 *ASTI SPUMANTE*

HERB WATER ICE

This refreshing water ice is a good palate cleanser, particularly after a rich game dinner.

SERVES 4

110g/4oz granulated sugar
290ml/½ pint water
thinly pared zest and juice of 1 lemon
4 tablespoons roughly chopped fresh mint leaves
150ml/¼ pint dry champagne

1. Put the sugar, water and lemon zest into a heavy-based saucepan. Dissolve slowly over a low heat.
2. When the sugar has completely dissolved, increase the heat and boil rapidly to the short thread stage: when a little syrup is placed between a wet finger and thumb and the fingers opened, it should form a thread 2.5cm/1in long.
3. Add the lemon juice, mint and champagne to the warm sugar syrup. Allow to cool for 30 minutes, then strain.
4. Pour into a freezerproof container and freeze overnight. Whisk until smooth, then return to the freezer until firm. Transfer to the refrigerator for 15 minutes before serving. Serve in well-chilled goblets.

 *SAUTERNES*

MERINGUES

MOCHA AND CHESTNUT VACHERIN

SERVES 6

4 egg whites
170g/6oz caster sugar
55g/2oz soft light brown sugar, sifted
2 teaspoons coffee essence
1 × 310g/11oz can of unsweetened chestnut
*   purée*
140g/5oz plain chocolate
30g/1oz butter
1 tablespoon rum
290ml/½ pint double cream, lightly whipped

To serve
marrons glacés (see page 605)
icing sugar

1. Preheat the oven to 110°C/225°F/gas mark ½. Line 2 baking sheets with silicone paper.
2. Whisk the egg whites until stiff but not dry, then add 2 tablespoons of the caster sugar. Whisk again until very stiff and shiny. Fold in the remaining caster and brown sugar and the coffee essence with a large metal spoon.
3. Fill a piping bag fitted with a medium plain nozzle with the meringue. Pipe into a round the size of a dessert plate on each prepared baking sheet.
4. Cook in the oven to dry out for 2–3 hours. The meringue is ready when light and dry and the paper will peel off the underside easily.
5. Sieve the chestnut purée into a bowl.
6. Cut the chocolate into pieces and put into a heatproof bowl set over, not in, a saucepan of simmering water. Add the butter and rum and stir until the chocolate has melted. Stir into the chestnut purée and allow to cool.
7. Spread three-quarters of the cream over one of the meringue rounds and pile on the cool chocolate and chestnut mixture. Place the second meringue on top of this. Using the remaining cream, pipe rosettes or a rope around the top. Decorate each rosette with a marron glacé. Allow to stand for 1 hour before serving. Just before serving, dust with icing sugar.

 *AUSTRALIAN LIQUEUR MUSCAT*

PASTRIES, PIES AND TARTS

PEAR DUMPLINGS

SERVES 4

*4 ripe Williams or short, round pears, peeled
   and cored, but kept whole*
grated zest of 1 orange
2 tablespoons Poire William liqueur
*340g/12oz flour quantity sweet rich shortcrust
   pastry (see page 642)*
2 tablespoons soft light brown sugar
30g/1oz nibbed almonds, toasted
1 teaspoon ground mixed spice
1 egg, lightly beaten

To serve
290ml/½ pint custard (see page 505) or cream

1. Put the pears into a bowl with the orange zest
and liqueur. Cover and leave to macerate for 30
minutes.
2. Divide the pastry into 4 equal pieces and roll
out each piece into a rough triangle the
thickness of a £1 coin.
3. Mix the sugar, almonds and mixed spice
together. Push a quarter of the nut mixture into
the cavity of each pear.
4. Lay a pear on each piece of pastry, with the
stalk end towards the point of the triangle. Roll
the pastry over the pear and when the two sides
meet, seal them together with a little water.
Wrap the pastry over each end neatly and trim
off any excess pastry.
5. Place the pear dumplings on a baking sheet
and lightly brush the pastry with beaten egg.
Roll out any pastry trimmings and use to
decorate the top of the dumplings with leaves
and stalks. Glaze with a little more beaten egg
and chill for 45 minutes.

6. Preheat the oven to 200°C/400°F/gas mark 6.
7. Glaze the dumplings again with the beaten
egg. Bake the dumplings near the top of the
preheated oven for 30 minutes or until golden-
brown all over.
8. Serve warm with the custard or cream.

 MUSCAT DE BEAUMES DE VENISE

STICKY GREENGAGE TART

SERVES 6

*170g/6oz sweet rich shortcrust pastry (see page
   642)*
125g/4½oz ground almonds
*450g/1lb very ripe greengages, halved and
   stoned*
110g/4oz soft light brown sugar
85g/3oz butter, melted and cooled

To serve
290ml/½ pint double cream

1. Preheat the oven to 190°C/375°F/gas mark 5.
2. Roll out the pastry to the thickness of a £1
coin and use to line a 20cm/8in loose-based flan
ring. Chill the pastry case for 30 minutes.
3. Sprinkle the almonds over the bottom of the
pastry case and arrange the greengages, cut side
uppermost, in a single layer over the almonds.
Sprinkle over the sugar and melted butter.
4. Bake the tart near the top of the oven for 15
minutes, then reduce the oven temperature to
170°C/325°F/gas mark 3 and transfer the tart to
a shelf near the bottom of the oven. Bake for a

further 30–45 minutes, or until the greengages are starting to caramelize and the pastry is golden-brown.

5. Allow the tart to cool slightly before removing the flan ring. Serve with the cream handed separately.

 *SAUTERNES*

PUMPKIN PIE

SERVES 8

225g/8oz sweet shortcrust pastry (see page 642)
450g/1lb cooked pumpkin purée, made from about 675g/1½lb pumpkin
1 × 375ml/14fl oz can of evaporated milk
55g/2oz soft light brown sugar
55g/2oz caster sugar
½ teaspoon salt
1 teaspoon ground cinnamon
½ teaspoon ground ginger
½ teaspoon freshly grated nutmeg
½ teaspoon ground cloves
¼ teaspoon ground allspice
2 eggs, lightly beaten

To serve
450g/1lb fresh blueberries
crème fraîche
a few sprigs of fresh mint

1. Preheat the oven to 190°C/375°F/gas mark 5.
2. Roll out the pastry to the thickness of a £1 coin and use to line a 25cm/10in loose-based flan ring. Chill the pastry for 30 minutes, then bake blind (see page 640). Allow the baked flan case to cool on a wire rack.
3. Reduce the oven temperature to 180°C/350°F/gas mark 4.
4. Mix all the remaining ingredients together in a bowl.
5. Place the pastry case on a baking sheet and pour in the mixture. Bake in the middle of the preheated oven for 30 minutes, or until set. Allow to cool slightly.
6. To serve: remove the flan ring and serve the pumpkin pie with a bowl of fresh blueberries

and the crème fraîche decorated with the sprigs of mint.

 *SAUTERNES*

CARAMELIZED APPLE, CIDER AND CHEESE CRUST PIE

SERVES 4

900g/2lb cooking apples
110g/4oz demerara sugar
150ml/¼ pint dry cider
1 teaspoon ground cinnamon
30g/1oz butter, melted

For the pastry
170g/6oz plain flour
55g/2oz semolina
55g/2oz unsalted butter, diced
55g/2oz mature Cheddar cheese, grated
55g/2oz caster sugar
1 egg, beaten with 1 tablespoon water
a little extra caster sugar for sprinkling

To serve
nutmeg and bay leaf ice cream (see page 588)

1. Peel, quarter and core the apples, then cut each quarter in half.
2. Meanwhile, put the sugar and half the cider into a saucepan and place over a low heat until the sugar has completely dissolved. Increase the heat and bring to the boil, then cook until the sugar has become a caramel colour. Remove from the heat and immediately pour over the remaining cider. Bring back to the boil and add the cinnamon.
3. Add the apples and poach over a low heat for 2–3 minutes, then remove the apples with a slotted spoon and allow to cool. Bring the poaching liquid to the boil, then lower the heat and simmer until reduced to 3–4 tablespoons. Remove from the heat, stir in the melted butter and allow to cool.

4. Meanwhile, make the pastry: sift the flour and semolina into a bowl. Rub the butter into the flour until the mixture resembles fine breadcrumbs. Stir in the Cheddar cheese and sugar and add just enough beaten egg to bind together to a dough.

5. Roll the pastry into a 20cm/8in round to fit the top of a 1 litre/1¾ pint round pie dish. Put the cold apples and cooking liquor into the pie dish. Dampen the edge of the pie dish and put the pastry on top. Make a hole in the centre to allow the steam to escape and crimp the edge of the pie attractively. Chill for 30 minutes.

6. Preheat the oven to 190°C/375°F/gas mark 5.

7. Just before baking, brush the pastry with water and sprinkle with a little caster sugar. Place the pie dish on a baking sheet and bake on the top shelf of the preheated oven for 25–30 minutes, or until the pie crust is golden-brown. Serve warm or cold with scoops of nutmeg and bay leaf ice cream.

 *MONBAZILLAC*

INDIVIDUAL APPLE AND BLACKBERRY GOUGÈRES

SERVES 4

butter for greasing
2-egg quantity choux pastry (see page 645)
15g/½oz Parmesan cheese, freshly grated
¼ teaspoon ground mixed spice
2 eating apples
225g/8oz blackberries
55g/2oz soft light brown sugar
2 tablespoons Calvados
30g/1oz chopped almonds

To serve
1 quantity crème anglaise (see page 661)

1. Lightly butter 4 ramekins.

2. Preheat the oven to 200°C/400°F/gas mark 6.

3. Beat the Parmesan cheese and mixed spice into the choux pastry. Fit a piping bag with a 1cm/½in plain nozzle and fill with the choux

mixture. Pipe round the bottom and sides of the ramekins, leaving a small well in the centre.

4. Peel, core and dice the apples and place in a small saucepan with the blackberries, sugar and Calvados. Bring to the boil, then lower the heat and simmer gently for 8–10 minutes, or until the apples are soft and the blackberries are breaking up. Remove from the heat and allow to cool for 5 minutes.

5. Spoon the filling into the centre of the ramekins and sprinkle with the almonds. Bake in the preheated oven for 15–20 minutes, or until well risen and brown. Serve very hot with the crème anglaise handed separately.

 RHINE RIESLING AUSLESE

MAPLE SYRUP, WALNUT AND PLUM PARCELS

SERVES 4

16 ripe Victoria plums
8 tablespoons maple syrup
4 tablespoons chopped walnuts

To serve
150ml/¼ pint fromage frais
peanut brownies (see page 602)

1. Preheat the oven to 190°C/375°F/gas mark 5. Cut 4 × 20cm/8in squares of kitchen foil.

2. Wash, halve and stone the plums. Divide them equally between the foil squares.

3. Spoon the maple syrup over the plums and sprinkle with the walnuts.

4. Wrap the parcels loosely. Place on a baking sheet and bake in the preheated oven for 20–25 minutes, or until the plums are soft.

5. To serve: open the parcels and put a couple of spoonfuls of the fromage frais on top of the plums. Hand the peanut brownies separately.

 AUSTRALIAN LIQUEUR MUSCAT

STILTON AND PEAR SABLÉS WITH FROMAGE FRAIS

SERVES 8

For the sablé
225g/8oz plain flour
a pinch of salt
a pinch of dry English mustard
225g/8oz butter, chilled
225g/8oz mature Stilton cheese, chilled and
    crumbled
freshly ground black pepper
1 egg, beaten

For the pears
110g/4oz granulated sugar
thinly pared zest of ½ lemon
juice of 1 lemon
570ml/1 pint water
4 large, ripe pears, peeled, quartered and cored

To decorate
icing sugar
4 sprigs of fresh mint
4 tablespoons fromage frais

1. Line 2 baking sheets with silicone paper.
2. Sift the flour with the salt and mustard into a bowl. Rub in the butter with the fingertips until the mixture resembles coarse breadcrumbs.
3. Add the Stilton cheese and egg and stir with a knife to form a stiff paste. Do not over-handle or the pastry will become greasy and be tough. Place between 2 sheets of clingfilm, flatten into a rectangle and chill for 30 minutes.
4. Put the sugar, lemon zest, juice and water into a saucepan and stir gently over a low heat until the sugar has dissolved. Add the pears and poach them for 40 minutes or until they look glassy. Remove the pears with a slotted spoon and place them in a shallow dish. Reduce the poaching liquid by boiling rapidly until syrupy. Slice the pears lengthways, then pour over the syrup and leave to cool.
5. Preheat the oven to 190°C/375°F/gas mark 5.

6. Roll out the pastry on a floured board to the thickness of a £1 coin. Using a template, cut out 12 diamond shapes with sides of about 6cm/2½in. Place on the prepared baking sheets and chill for 1 hour.
7. Bake the pastry diamonds near the top of the preheated oven for about 15 minutes, or until golden-brown. Allow the sablés to cool for a few minutes on the baking sheets before transferring them to a wire rack and leaving to cool completely.
8. To assemble: place 6 pastry diamonds on a board and arrange half the pears neatly on top. Arrange the remaining sablés on top of the pears.
9. Place each pear sablé on an individual plate, dust with icing sugar and decorate with a sprig of mint, a quenelle of fromage frais and a little of the pear syrup.

 SINGLE ESTATE MOSEL AUSLESE

RASPBERRY AND CASHEW TORTE

SERVES 8

For the pastry
170g/6oz plain flour
a pinch of salt
85g/3oz butter, softened
3 egg yolks
85g/3oz caster sugar
3 drops of vanilla essence

For the filling
170g/6oz butter, softened
170g/6oz caster sugar
2 egg yolks
1 tablespoon raspberry liqueur, kirsch or
    brandy
170g/6oz cashew nuts, ground
85g/3oz plain flour, sifted
a pinch of salt
170g/6oz frozen raspberries, defrosted, puréed
    and sieved

For the topping
450g/1lb fresh raspberries
110g/4oz whole cashews, lightly roasted
icing sugar

To serve
290ml/½ pint thick double cream

1. Make the pastry: sift the flour with the salt on to a board. Make a large well in the centre and put the butter in it. Place the egg yolks and the sugar on the butter with the vanilla essence.
2. Using the fingertips of one hand, mix the butter, yolks and sugar together. When mixed to a soft paste, draw in the flour and knead just until the pastry is smooth.
3. If the pastry is very soft, wrap and chill before rolling.
4. Roll out the pastry and use to line a 20cm/8in loose-based flan ring. Chill until firm.
5. Preheat the oven to 200°C/400°F/gas mark 6. Bake the pastry blind (see page 640). Reduce the oven temperature to 170°C/325°F/gas mark 3.
6. Make the filling: cream the butter in a bowl, gradually beat in the sugar and continue beating until the mixture is light and soft.
7. Fold in the yolks, alcohol, cashew nuts, flour and salt, then carefully stir in the raspberry purée until almost incorporated, giving a marbled effect. Tip into the flan case and spread out evenly.
8. Bake the flan in the lower half of the preheated oven for 30 minutes, or until the filling is golden-brown and set.
9. Allow the tart to cool slightly before transferring to a wire rack. Leave to cool completely.
10. To serve: arrange the fresh raspberries and cashew nuts on top of the tart and dust with icing sugar. Serve with the cream handed separately.

 *AUSTRALIAN ORANGE MUSCAT AND FLORA*

CONTINENTAL PLUM STREUSEL

SERVES 6

1 quantity foundation bread dough (see page 613)
450g/1lb ripe plums, halved and stoned
110g/4oz soft dark brown sugar
110g/4oz hazelnuts, browned and roughly chopped
55g/2oz unsalted butter, melted

1. Preheat the oven to 200°C/400°F/gas mark 6.
2. Roll the dough to a rectangle about 30 × 20cm/12 × 8in on a lightly floured board. Lift on to a baking sheet.
3. Arrange the plums, cut sides down, on top of the dough.
4. Mix together the sugar, hazelnuts and butter and sprinkle over the plums. Cover with lightly oiled clingfilm and allow to stand at room temperature for 10 minutes to allow the dough to prove.
5. Remove the clingfilm and bake at the top of the preheated oven for 10 minutes, then reduce the oven temperature to 180°C/350°F/gas mark 4 and bake for a further 20–25 minutes, or until the plums are soft and the top is golden-brown. Serve warm.

 AUSTRALIAN ORANGE MUSCAT

AUTUMN FRUIT AND ROQUEFORT JALOUSIE

SERVES 4

225g/8oz flour quantity puff pastry (see page 643)
1 × 450g/1lb jar apple, pear and Calvados Marmelade (see page 498)
110g/4oz Roquefort or other blue cheese, crumbled
plain flour for dusting
1 egg, beaten
55g/2oz blanched almonds
caster sugar for sprinkling

1. Preheat the oven to 230°C/450°F/gas mark 8.
2. Roll the pastry into 2 thin rectangles, about 13 × 20cm/5 × 8in and 18 × 25cm/7 × 10in. Leave to relax for 20 minutes.
3. Place the smaller rectangle on a baking sheet and prick all over with a fork. Bake in the preheated oven for 15–20 minutes, or until crisp and brown. Remove from the oven and turn over on to another baking sheet. Allow to cool. Spread the marmelade all over the cooked pastry and sprinkle with the Roquefort cheese.
4. Lay the larger pastry rectangle on a board and dust it lightly with flour. Fold it gently, so that the pastry does not stick, in half lengthways. Using a sharp knife, cut through the folded side of the pastry, at right angles to the edge, in parallel lines, as though you were cutting between the teeth of a comb. Leave an uncut margin about 2.5cm/1in wide all round the other edges and open the pastry up.
5. Now lay the cut pastry on top of the pastry covered with marmelade and cheese and tuck the edges underneath. Brush the top carefully all over with egg. Sprinkle with the almonds and sugar.
6. Bake in the preheated oven for about 20 minutes, or until well browned. If the almonds begin to burn, cover with a sheet of kitchen foil. Serve warm or cold.

NOTE: Jalousie is French for shutters, which the pie resembles.

 *SAUTERNES*

CAKES AND PÂTISSERIE

CARROT AND SULTANA CAKE

MAKES 1 × 20CM/8IN CAKE

170g/6oz sultanas (soaked overnight in the
    sherry)
6 tablespoons medium sherry
450g/1lb fresh carrots, peeled and grated
225g/8oz butter, softened
1 teaspoon ground cumin
225g/8oz soft light brown sugar
3 eggs, lightly beaten
225g/8oz self-raising flour
55g/2oz wholemeal flour
1 teaspoon baking powder
85g/3oz ground almonds
a little milk

To serve
icing sugar for dusting or 1 quantity cream
    cheese icing (see page 664)
85g/3oz almond paste (see page 663) or fondant
    icing (optional)
green and orange food dye (optional)

1. Preheat the oven to 170°C/325°F/gas mark 3.
Grease and line a 20cm/8in deep round cake tin.
2. Cook the carrots with 55g/2oz of the butter
and the cumin in a heavy-based saucepan over a
low heat until the carrots start to collapse. Tip
them on to a plate and leave to cool.
3. Cream the remaining butter in a bowl, add
the sugar and beat until light and fluffy. Beat in
the eggs, a little at a time, to prevent curdling.
(If the mixture starts to curdle, add 1
tablespoon of the flour.)
4. Sift the flours, baking powder and ground

almonds on to the egg mixture.
5. Spoon the cool carrot and sultana mixture
around the edge of the bowl and fold everything
together with a large metal spoon, adding a
little milk to the bowl to bring the mixture to a
dropping consistency.
6. Tip the mixture into the prepared tin,
spreading it out evenly. Bake in the middle of the
oven for 1 hour, or until golden, firm to the touch
and coming away from the sides of the tin. Allow
to cool completely in the tin before removing.
7. Serve simply dusted with icing sugar or
spread with the cream cheese icing.
8. If liked, make a marzipan carrot garnish:
colour one-third of the almond paste or fondant
with green food dye, and the remainder with
orange food dye. Shape the paste into baby
carrots with stalks and leaves and arrange them
around the top of the cake.

MALTED BRAMLEY APPLE CAKE

MAKES I × 20CM/8IN CAKE

For the purée
450g/1lb Bramley apples, peeled and cored
30g/1oz butter
grated zest of 1 lemon
1 tablespoon water

For the cake
225g/8oz butter, softened
170g/6oz soft light brown sugar
3 eggs, beaten
4 tablespoons malt syrup
225g/8oz self-raising flour

1 teaspoon baking powder
a pinch of salt
55g/2oz rolled oats
55g/2oz ground almonds

For the topping
1 medium Bramley apple, peeled, cored and
    evenly sliced into thin segments
15g/½oz butter, melted
4 tablespoons malt syrup

1. Preheat the oven to 170°C/325°F/gas mark 3.
Grease and line a 20cm/8in deep cake tin.
2. Make the purée: cut the apples into small
chunks. Melt the butter in a small saucepan and
add the apple chunks, lemon zest and water.
Cover and cook over a low heat until the apples
have collapsed. Remove the lid and stir the
purée over a medium heat until thick and dry.
Tip it on to a plate and leave to cool.
3. Beat the butter with the sugar in a large bowl
until pale and creamy. Gradually beat in the
eggs, adding a tablespoonful of flour if the
mixture begins to look curdled.
4. Mix the malt syrup with the cold apple
purée. Stir it into the creamed egg mixture.
5. Sift the flour with the baking powder and salt
on to the mixture. Add the oats and almonds
and fold everything together with a large metal
spoon until all the ingredients are incorporated,
then tip the mixture into the prepared cake tin.
6. Make the topping: mix the apple segments
with the butter and arrange them on top of the
cake in a circular pattern. Drizzle the malt
syrup over the apples.
7. Bake the cake in the middle of the preheated
oven for 1¼–1½ hours, or until golden-brown
on top, firm to the touch and starting to come
away from the edges of the tin. Allow to cool
completely in the tin before turning out to
serve.

NOTE: Malt syrup is available from chemists.

TOFFEE APPLE DANISH

SERVES 8

1 quantity Danish pastry dough (see page 647)
2 large Bramley apples, peeled and cored
grated zest of 1 lemon
2 tablespoons caster sugar
1 tablespoon water
3 Granny Smith apples
4 tablespoons demerara sugar
1 egg, lightly beaten

For the toffee sauce
110g/4oz granulated sugar
water
150ml/¼ pint double cream

1. Preheat the oven to 200°C/400°F/gas mark 6.
2. Cut the Bramley apples into small chunks
and cook them, covered, with the lemon zest,
caster sugar and water in a heavy-based
saucepan over a low heat. When the apples
have broken down to a pulp, remove the lid and
stir them over a medium heat until you have a
thick, dry purée. Tip on to a plate and leave to
cool.
3. Peel, core and quarter the Granny Smith
apples. Cut each quarter into 3 equal slices.
4. Roll out the Danish pastry dough into a
square about 30cm/12in. Place on a baking
sheet.
5. Spread the apple purée in an even line down
the centre third of the pastry. Arrange the apple
slices on top and sprinkle them with the
demerara sugar.
6. Using a sharp knife, make cuts in the dough
2.5cm/1in apart down each side of the purée at
a 60-degree angle to the purée. Brush the
exposed dough with the beaten egg, then take
one strip of dough at a time from each side and
overlap the strips until the apples are
completely covered. Brush the top carefully
with more beaten egg.
7. Prove the cake for 15 minutes (put into a
warm, draught-free place to allow the dough to
rise), then brush the top with beaten egg. Bake
in the centre of the preheated oven for 20–30
minutes, or until risen and golden. Remove

from the oven and transfer to a wire rack. Leave to cool.

8. Make the toffee sauce: put the sugar into a small, heavy-based saucepan and pour over enough water to cover. Dissolve the sugar over a low heat without stirring or allowing the water to boil.

9. Once all the sugar has dissolved, turn up the heat and boil until it is a good caramel colour.

10. Immediately tip in the double cream (it will splutter dangerously, so stand well back). Stir until any lumps have dissolved, then simmer the sauce for 2 minutes. Remove from the heat and allow to cool.

11. Once the cake is cool, drizzle the toffee sauce all over. Serve immediately.

DOUGHNUTS WITH BLACKBERRY AND APPLE CREAM

MAKES 6

225g/8oz plain flour
a pinch of salt
7g/¼oz fresh yeast
45g/1½oz sugar
30g/1oz butter
2 egg yolks
150ml/¼ pint warm milk
oil for deep-frying
caster sugar flavoured with ground cinnamon,
*   for coating*

For the filling
15g/½oz butter
2 dessert apples, peeled, cored and cut into
*   1cm/½in pieces*
225g/8oz blackberries
85g/3oz soft light brown sugar
2 tablespoons crème de cassis (optional)
¼ pint quantity crème pâtissière (see page 661)
150ml/¼ pint double cream, lightly whipped

1. Sift the flour with the salt into a warmed bowl. Cream the yeast with 1 teaspoon of the sugar.

2. Rub the butter into the flour. Make a well in the centre.

3. Mix together the egg yolks, yeast mixture, remaining sugar and the milk. Pour the mixture into the well in the flour.

4. Using the fingertips of one hand, mix the wet ingredients together, gradually drawing in the surrounding flour. Mix to a smooth, soft dough.

5. Cover the bowl with a piece of greased clingfilm and leave to rise in a warm, draught-free place for 45 minutes.

6. Knead the dough well for at least 10 minutes. Roll out on a floured board to 1cm/½in thick. With a 7.5cm/3in plain cutter, press into rounds. Place on a greased tray and cover with greased clingfilm. Leave to prove (rise again) until doubled in size.

7. Heat the oil in a deep-fryer until a crumb will sizzle vigorously in it. Put 3 doughnuts into the fryer basket and lower into the fat. Fry until golden-brown, then drain on kitchen paper. Fry the remaining doughnuts in the same way.

8. Toss the hot doughnuts in caster sugar and cinnamon. Cool on a wire rack.

9. Make the filling: melt the butter in a frying pan, add the apple, blackberries, sugar and the crème de cassis, if using, and stir over a high heat until the apples are just tender and the juices are syrupy. Tip on to a large plate and leave to cool.

10. Put the crème pâtissière into a bowl and beat well. Fold in the cream.

11. To serve: cut the doughnuts in half. Spoon the blackberry and apple on to the bottom halves and dollop the cream filling on top. Replace the lids at a slight angle and serve immediately.

491

MISCELLANEOUS

Drinks
Preserves
Breads
Sauces and Garnishes

DRINKS

SLOE GIN

This recipe is taken from *Country Wines, Beers and Beverages* by Brian Leverett.

MAKES 570ML/1 PINT

225g/8oz ripe sloes
200g/7oz caster sugar
570ml/1 pint gin

1. Place all the ingredients in a sterilized wide-necked jar (see page 277).
2. Leave for 4 months, shaking daily, then strain through fine muslin and transfer to a sterilized wine bottle. If necessary, top up with extra gin.

NOTE: The liqueur may be drunk after 4 months but it does benefit from at least a year to mature.

MULBERRY GIN

MAKES 570ML/1 PINT

225g/8oz mulberries
425ml/¾ pint gin
55–85g/2–3oz caster sugar

1. Put the mulberries into a wide-rimmed sterilized jar (see page 277) with the gin and sugar. Make sure the fruit is covered by the alcohol. Place a layer of clingfilm on top if necessary to keep the mulberries submerged.
2. Seal the jar with a close-fitting lid and leave for 3 months, shaking the bottle gently from side to side during the first week to ensure the sugar dissolves.

3. Strain the liquor through muslin or a clean J-cloth and pour into small bottles for storage.

NOTE: The mulberry gin can be drunk immediately but is best if left for at least a year to mature. Do not throw away the macerated mulberries after bottling – a few added to a crumble or mulberry clafoutis (see page 332) will add an exciting touch to the pudding.

SPICED AUTUMN BERRY LIQUEUR

This liqueur makes a perfect Christmas drink. Served warm, it makes a delicious alternative to mulled wine.

MAKES 570ML/1 PINT

2kg/4½lb mixed autumn berries, including
*   elderberries, blackberries, sloes, hips and haws*
290ml/½ pint water
900g/2lb granulated sugar
1 tablespoonful freshly grated nutmeg
2 tablespoons whole cloves
2 cinnamon sticks
1 teaspoon whole cardamom pods
570ml/1 pint brandy

1. Wash the fruit and put into a saucepan with the water. Bring to the boil, then lower the heat and simmer for 15–20 minutes, or until the fruit is soft. Strain through a jelly bag and leave to drip overnight; there should be about 2.5 litres/ 4 pints of juice.
2. The following day, put the fruit juice back into a saucepan with the sugar and heat slowly until the sugar has dissolved.

3. Add the spices to the juice and bring to the boil, then lower the heat and simmer for 15 minutes, skimming the liquid if necessary.

4. Remove the pan from the heat and add the brandy. Allow to cool, then pour into a jug, cover and leave to stand in a cool, dark place for 2–3 days, stirring occasionally.

5. Strain the liquid through a piece of muslin and pour into dry, sterilized bottles. Seal tightly with a cork or screwtop.

6. Allow the liqueur to mature for at least 1 month before serving.

HOT SPICED PEAR JUICE

MAKES 1 LITRE/1¾ PINTS

2kg/4½lb ripe pears
10 whole cloves
1 small orange
570ml/1 pint dry cider
1 cinnamon stick
2 tablespoons Poire William liqueur

1. Preheat the oven to 200°C/400°F/gas mark 6.

2. Cut the pears into quarters and remove the cores. Whizz them in a juice extractor and collect the juice.

3. Press the cloves into the skin of the orange, then slice the orange.

4. Put the pear juice, cider, orange and cinnamon stick into a heavy-based saucepan. Bring to the boil, then lower the heat until the liquid is barely moving and leave to infuse for 30 minutes.

5. Stir in the liqueur and serve in warmed mulled wine glasses.

FRESH PRESSED APPLE JUICE

MAKES 425ML/¾ PINT

6 dessert apples such as Cox's Orange Pippin, Braeburn, washed
55g/2oz blackberries, washed (optional)
2 sprigs of fresh mint

To serve
a few ice cubes
1 sprig of fresh mint

1. Cut the apples into quarters and remove the cores.

2. Whizz the apples, blackberries, if using, and mint in a juice extractor and collect the juice.

3. Put a few ice cubes in a large glass and pour over the apple juice. Top with a sprig of fresh mint.

PRESERVES

WARM BLACKBERRY AND PEAR PICKLE

MAKES 675G/1½LB

225g/8oz blackberries
1 large pear, not too ripe
225g/½lb granulated sugar
150ml/¼ pint cider vinegar
grated zest and juice of 1 orange
2.5cm/1in piece of fresh root ginger, cut into
    julienne strips
3 teaspoons yellow mustard seeds
6 cloves
1 cinnamon stick

1. Wash the blackberries briefly if necessary and
dry on kitchen paper. Peel and core the pear
and cut it into 2.5 × 1cm/1 × ½in pieces.
2. Dissolve the sugar in the vinegar in a
saucepan over a low heat. Add the orange zest
and juice, ginger, mustard seeds, cloves and
cinnamon stick.
3. Bring to the boil, then lower the heat and
simmer for 10 minutes. Add the fruit and
simmer gently for a further 5 minutes.
4. Strain the fruit and reduce the liquid by
boiling until syrupy. Mix it with the fruit.
5. Serve the pickle warm or cold.

NOTE: This pickle will keep for a week in the
refrigerator, but if stored in sterilized jars (see
page 277), sealed with jam seals, it will keep for
a month in a cool, dark, airy place.

GARLIC PICKLED ONIONS

1kg/2¼lb baby onions
brine (70g/2½oz salt per 2 litres/3½ pints
    water)

For the vinegar
2 litres/3½ pints white wine vinegar
1 tablespoon black peppercorns
1 tablespoon pink peppercorns
1 tablespoon mustard seeds
1 teaspoon allspice berries
2 blades of mace
3 bay leaves
1 tablespoon salt
12 cloves of garlic

1. Blanch the onions in boiling water for 1
minute. Refresh under cold running water and
drain. Peel off the skins and cut off the hairy
ends of the root, but not too much or the
onions will fall apart.
2. Put the onions into a bowl and cover
completely with water. Strain out the water and
measure it. Add enough salt to make a brine
solution and pour it back over the onions. Place
a small plate or saucer on the onions to weight
them down under the brine. Leave, covered, for
24 hours.
3. Put all the vinegar ingredients, except the
garlic, into a large saucepan. Bring to the boil,
then lower the heat and simmer for 10 minutes,
adding the garlic for the last minute. Remove
from the heat and leave to cool.
4. Pour away the brine and rinse the onions
well.
5. Pour the vinegar over the onions and mix
together. Pour the onions into sterilized jars (see

page 277) with vinegar-proof tops, with the
vinegar and flavourings, making sure the onions
are completely submerged in the vinegar. (If
they float you can use a sterilized pebble or
something similar to press them down.)
6. Seal the jars and store them in a cool, dark,
airy place for 3–4 weeks.

SWEET PICKLED SHALLOTS

MAKES 2 × 450G/1LB

225g/8oz salt
2 litres/3½ pints water
1.35kg/3lb shallots
2 litres/3½ pints cider vinegar
5cm/2in cinnamon stick
1 teaspoon cloves
4 teaspoons allspice berries
2 teaspoons black peppercorns
2 teaspoons mustard seeds
2–3 bay leaves
3–4 blades of mace
110g/4oz soft light brown sugar

1. Dissolve the salt in the water over a low heat
and allow to go cold.
2. Peel the shallots carefully. Do not remove too
much root or the shallots will fall apart. The
skin comes away easily if they are allowed to
stand in boiling water for 5 minutes first.
3. Put the shallots into a large bowl, cover with
the salt solution (brine) and allow to stand,
covered, for 12 hours and no more than 24 hours.
4. Meanwhile, put all the remaining ingredients
into a large saucepan and heat gently until the
sugar has dissolved. Increase the heat until the
vinegar just comes to the boil. Do not allow to
bubble. Remove from the heat and allow to
infuse for 3 hours. Strain the vinegar and set
aside.
5. Drain the shallots from the brine and pack
tightly into clean sterilized jars (see page 277).
Pour over the cold spiced vinegar to cover the
shallots. Cover the jars, seal with screwtop lids
and label. Allow to stand in a cool, dark, airy
place for 6 weeks before using.

HOT ONION MUSTARD CHUTNEY

MAKES 2 × 450G/1LB

450g/1lb large onions, thinly sliced
1 red chilli, or 2 if they are quite mild, de-seeded
    and thinly sliced
30g/1oz yellow mustard seeds
290ml/½ pint cider vinegar
thinly pared zest of 1 orange, cut into julienne
    strips
juice of 1 orange
½ teaspoon salt
225g/8oz soft light brown sugar

1. Put the onions, chilli, mustard seeds, vinegar,
orange zest and juice and salt into a large,
heavy-based saucepan. Bring to the boil, then
lower the heat and simmer for 10–15 minutes,
or until the onions start to soften.
2. Add the sugar and continue to simmer until
most of the moisture has evaporated and the
mixture is thick.
3. Ladle the mixture into hot sterilized jars (see
page 277), then seal with lids or jam pot covers.
Leave the chutney to cool and store in a cool,
dark, airy place for at least 1 month before
eating.

APPLE, PEAR AND CALVADOS MARMELADE

MAKES 2 × 450G/1LB

4 cooking apples, peeled, cored and diced
4 ripe pears, peeled, cored and diced
2 dried pears, chopped
2 dried figs, chopped
grated zest of 2 lemons
2 onions, very finely chopped
450g/1lb soft dark brown sugar
2 teaspoons rock salt
570ml/1 pint cider vinegar
1 tablespoon mustard seeds
150ml/¼ pint Calvados

1. Put all the ingredients, except the Calvados, into a large saucepan. Bring to the boil, then lower the heat and cook over a very low heat for 25–30 minutes, or until the fruit is soft, pulpy and the mixture very thick. Add the Calvados and boil briefly.

2. Pour immediately into warmed, sterilized jars (see page 277) and cover with jam covers if to be eaten within a few months or more securely with non-metallic lids or stoppers if to be kept longer. Store in a cool, dark, airy place.

QUINCE CHEESE

This aromatic paste resembles *membrillo*, the quince preserve so popular in Portugal and Spain.

2kg/4½lb quinces
1 litre/1¾ pints water
20 juniper berries
2 teaspoons allspice berries
4 star anise
2 sprigs of fresh rosemary
4 sprigs of fresh thyme
preserving sugar

1. Wash and chop the quinces, place in a large saucepan with the water, herbs and spices, and stew until soft.

2. Sieve and measure the pulp.

3. Return the pulp to a clean saucepan. To every 570ml/1 pint of quince pulp, add 450g/1lb preserving sugar. Bring to the boil, then cook, stirring, until a spoon will stand upright in the paste. It will spit and splutter furiously, so take care. Do not allow the paste to stick and burn.

4. Turn on to shallow baking trays lined with silicone paper. Spread flat and allow to cool completely.

5. Cut the quince cheese into squares to serve.

BREADS

CARAWAY AND DULSE SODA BREAD

MAKES 900G/2LB LOAF

butter for greasing
225g/8oz plain white flour
225g/8oz wholemeal flour
1 teaspoon salt
2 teaspoons bicarbonate of soda
85g/3oz butter
15g/½oz dulse or similar seaweed, soaked in
* cold water*
425ml/¾ pint smetana or buttermilk
2 teaspoons caraway seeds

1. Preheat the oven to 190°C/375°F/gas mark 5. Grease a 900g/2lb loaf tin.
2. Sift the flours, salt and soda into a large mixing bowl.
3. Rub in the butter with the fingertips until the mixture resembles fine breadcrumbs.
4. Dry the dulse well on kitchen paper and chop finely. Stir into the flour with the smetana and caraway seeds to form a soft but not sticky dough.
5. Shape with a minimum of kneading to fit into the prepared loaf tin.
6. Bake on the top shelf of the preheated oven for 30–35 minutes, or until the bread feels firm to the touch and is lightly browned. Remove from the tin and allow to cool on a wire rack.

WALNUT AND MOLASSES BREAD

SERVES 4

225g/8oz strong plain flour
225g/8oz wholemeal flour
1 teaspoon salt
20g/¾oz fresh yeast
290ml/½ pint warm milk
2 tablespoons molasses or black treacle
225g/8oz walnuts, roughly chopped
extra flour for sprinkling

To serve
quince cheese (see page 499)
wedges of mature farmhouse Cheddar cheese

1. Sift the flours and salt into a large mixing bowl and make a well in the centre.
2. Mix the yeast with 1 tablespoon of the milk. Pour into the well with the remaining milk and the molasses or treacle.
3. Mix with a knife, then draw together with the fingers of one hand to make a soft but not sticky dough.
4. Knead until smooth and elastic (about 5 minutes by hand), using more flour if necessary.
5. Put the dough into a large, clean bowl and cover with a piece of lightly greased clingfilm. Put in a warm, draught-free place to rise until the dough has doubled in bulk (about 1 hour).
6. Preheat the oven to 190°C/375°F/gas mark 5.
7. Knock back the dough and knead the walnuts into it. Shape into a long bloomer-style loaf. Make diagonal slashes in the top with a sharp knife.
8. Cover the loaf with lightly greased clingfilm

and leave in a warm place until 1½ times the original size.

9. Sprinkle the top of the loaf with a little flour and bake in the preheated oven for 30 minutes, or until the loaf sounds hollow when tapped on the underside.

10. Place on a wire rack and leave to cool.

11. Serve with the quince cheese and Cheddar cheese.

SAUCES AND GARNISHES

TRUFFLE VINAIGRETTE

MAKES 290ML/½ PINT

1 tablespoon Dijon mustard
3 tablespoons white wine vinegar
2 tablespoons strong chicken glace (see page
 625)
2 tablespoons Madeira
juice of 1 lemon
150ml/¼ pint extra virgin olive oil
2 tablespoons truffle oil
1 black truffle, finely chopped
salt and freshly ground black pepper

1. Put the mustard, vinegar, chicken glace, Madeira and lemon juice into a blender. With the motor running, gradually pour the olive oil and truffle oil through the lid until the oils are incorporated.
2. Pour the vinaigrette into a bowl and whisk in the chopped truffle. Season to taste with salt and pepper.

SOY, HONEY AND RED WINE SAUCE

SERVES 4

150ml/¼ pint red wine
30ml/1fl oz dark soy sauce
3 tablespoons clear honey

1. Put all the ingredients into a heavy-based saucepan. Bring to the boil, then lower the heat and simmer for 5 minutes. Serve with steamed pigeon dumplings (see page 393).

CHEDDAR CHEESE AND GRAIN MUSTARD SAUCE

MAKES 290ML/½ PINT

20g/¾oz butter
20g/¾oz flour
a pinch of cayenne pepper
290ml/½ pint milk
45g/1½oz mature Cheddar cheese, grated
1 tablespoon grain mustard
salt and freshly ground black pepper

1. Melt the butter in a heavy-based saucepan. Add the flour and cayenne and stir over a medium heat for 1 minute. Remove the pan from the heat, pour in the milk and mix well.
2. Return the sauce to the heat and stir continuously until boiling. Lower the heat and simmer for 2–3 minutes, then remove from the heat and stir in the cheese and mustard. Season to taste with salt and pepper.

HOT TOMATO AND PEPPER SAUCE

MAKES 2 × 450G/1LB

1 tablespoon sunflower oil
1 Spanish onion, finely chopped
2 cloves of garlic, crushed
2 red chillies, de-seeded and finely chopped
6 tomatoes, skinned, de-seeded and roughly
 chopped
1 red pepper, de-seeded, grilled and peeled
5 tablespoons dry white wine

salt and freshly ground black pepper
1 teaspoon caster sugar

1. Heat the oil in a saucepan, add the onion and cook until just beginning to soften. Add the garlic and chillies and cook for a further 2–3 minutes.
2. Add the tomatoes, pepper and wine. Season with salt, pepper and sugar, then cover and cook over a low heat for 20 minutes.
3. Whizz in a blender until smooth, then push through a sieve, season to taste with salt and pepper and use as required.

FRESH HORSERADISH AND MUSTARD SAUCE

MAKES 2 × 225G/½LB

7.5cm/3in piece of fresh horseradish, peeled and
*   finely grated*
150ml/¼ pint white wine or cider vinegar
110g/4oz yellow mustard seeds, ground in a
*   blender*
55g/2oz whole yellow mustard seeds
1 tablespoon soft light brown sugar
2 teaspoons salt
2 tablespoons brandy

1. Preheat the oven to 170°C/325°F/gas mark 3. Place 2 × 225g/8oz glass jars with lids on a baking sheet and heat them in the oven for 20 minutes. Allow the jars to cool.
2. Put the horseradish and vinegar together in a small saucepan. Bring to the boil, then lower the heat and simmer for 5 minutes.
3. Tip the horseradish and vinegar into a bowl with all the remaining ingredients and stir well. Allow to cool completely.
4. Pack the mustard sauce into the sterilized jars and place discs of waxed greaseproof directly on to the surface. Screw on the lids. Store in a cool, dark, airy place for 2 weeks.

NOTE: If you wish to keep the mustard for longer than 2 weeks it will be necessary to sterilize the filled and sealed jars in boiling water (see page 105).

RED PLUM SAUCE

Serve with greengage and almond sponge pudding (see page 472).

SERVES 4

450g/1lb ripe red plums, halved and stoned
110g/4oz caster sugar
4 tablespoons dark rum

1. Cut the plums into quarters. Cook in a heavy-based saucepan with the sugar and rum, stirring over a low heat until the sugar has dissolved.
2. Cover the pan and simmer for 5–10 minutes, or until the plums have completely collapsed.
3. Whizz the plums in a blender to make a very smooth purée, then pass through a fine nylon sieve.
4. Return the sauce to the pan and stir over a low heat until it is thick and shiny.
5. Serve warm with greengage and almond sponge pudding (see page 472).

WARM DAMSON SAUCE

This is a savoury dish which is best served with meat pies or roast meats.

MAKES 290ML/½ PINT

225g/8oz damsons, washed
15g/½oz butter
1 onion, finely chopped
1 tablespoon redcurrant jelly
150ml/¼ pint dessert wine
salt and freshly ground black pepper

1. Cut the damsons in half, remove the stones and roughly chop the fruit.
2. Melt the butter in a small heavy-based saucepan, add the onion and cook over a very low heat until soft but not coloured.
3. Add the damsons, redcurrant jelly and wine to the pan. Season with salt and pepper, cover the pan and simmer gently for 30 minutes, or until the damsons are completely cooked and have broken down into a purée – you may need

to add a little water if the sauce starts to dry out before the damsons are cooked.

4. Whizz the sauce in a blender until completely smooth, then pass it through a nylon sieve into the rinsed-out pan.

5. Gently warm the sauce through and check the seasoning.

ORANGE, PLUM AND MUSTARD COMPOTE

This is delicious served with a raised game pie.

SERVES 8

1 orange, preferably thin-skinned, washed
6 ripe but firm red plums, washed
2 tablespoons caster sugar
2 tablespoons grain mustard

1. Cut the unpeeled orange into 8 segments and remove the pips.

2. Cut the plums in half and remove the stones.

3. Put the orange segments, plums, sugar and mustard into a food processor and whizz, using the pulse action, until everything is coarsely chopped.

4. Taste and season with more sugar if necessary.

CRAB APPLE AND REDCURRANT COMPOTE

This recipe is to be served warm or cold as an accompaniment to cold meats and pies.

SERVES 4

1 large onion, finely chopped
30g/1oz butter
225g/8oz crab apples, quartered and cored
110g/4oz redcurrants, fresh or frozen
4 tablespoons redcurrant jelly
salt and freshly ground black pepper

1. Sweat the onion with the butter in a shallow saucepan until soft. Increase the heat and add

the crab apples, redcurrants and jelly.

2. Cook, stirring gently, until the apples are just tender and coated with a syrupy redcurrant glaze. Add a little extra water if necessary.

3. Season to taste with salt and pepper.

SAUTERNES JELLY

MAKES 570ML/1 PINT

150ml/¼ pint white stock, made from chicken
    bones, fat free (see page 625)
salt and freshly ground black pepper
2 egg shells, crushed
1 egg white
3 leaves of gelatine, soaked in cold water
150ml/¼ pint Sauternes wine

1. Season the stock well with salt and pepper.

2. Put the stock into a saucepan, add the crushed egg shells and egg white, place over the heat and whisk steadily with a balloon whisk until the mixture begins to boil. Stop whisking immediately and remove the pan from the heat. Bring back to the boil, then remove from the heat. Do not stir.

3. Fix a double layer of fine muslin over a clean saucepan and carefully strain the stock into it. Add the gelatine leaves and allow to dissolve completely. Stir in the wine.

4. Pour into a clean shallow tray and allow to set. Serve, carefully diced, as a garnish for terrines and pâtés.

SWEET ORANGE BUTTER

SERVES 4

110g/4oz unsalted butter, softened
110g/4oz caster sugar
grated zest of 2 oranges
2–3 tablespoons orange liqueur

1. Cream the butter and sugar together in a bowl until light and fluffy. Beat in the orange zest and the liqueur to taste.

2. Spoon into a bowl and chill.

HOME-MADE CUSTARD

MAKES 570ML/1 PINT

570ml/1 pint milk
30g/1oz cornflour
4 egg yolks
55g/2oz caster sugar
a few drops of vanilla essence

1. Mix 3 tablespoons of the milk with the cornflour. Heat the remaining milk to scalding point in a heavy-based saucepan.
2. Stir the slaked cornflour again to make sure there are no lumps. Pour it into the hot milk, whisking continuously, and stir over a medium heat until the milk boils and thickens.
3. Mix the egg yolks with the sugar. Pour the hot thickened milk on to the yolks from a height, stirring continuously. Return the custard to the pan and stir again over a low heat until the mixture thickens again. When the custard starts to bubble at the edges, immediately turn off the heat and stir in the vanilla essence.
4. Check the seasoning and add a little more sugar or vanilla essence if necessary.

ORANGE MARMALADE CRÈME ANGLAISE

SERVES 4

150ml/¼ pint milk
150ml/¼ pint whipping cream
2 egg yolks
3 tablespoons Seville orange marmalade,
  chopped
1 tablespoon Cointreau

1. Heat the milk with the cream in a heavy-based saucepan and bring slowly to the boil.
2. Beat the egg yolks and marmalade together until pale.
3. Pour the milk and cream mixture on to the egg yolks, stirring steadily.
4. Return the mixture to the pan and cook over a low heat, stirring well with a wooden spoon, for about 5 minutes, or until the custard is thick

enough to coat the back of the spoon. Do not allow to boil.
5. Pour into a chilled bowl and add the Cointreau. Allow to cool before using.

CINNAMON CRÈME ANGLAISE

SERVES 4

290ml/½ pint milk
290ml/½ pint whipping cream
2 cinnamon sticks
3 egg yolks
4 tablespoons caster sugar

1. Put the milk, cream and cinnamon sticks into a heavy-based saucepan and bring to scalding point. Remove from the heat and allow to infuse for 30 minutes.
2. Beat the egg yolks and sugar together in a bowl until light and frothy. Strain the infused milk mixture on top and stir together.
3. Return to the rinsed-out pan and bring back to scalding point over a low heat, stirring constantly with a wooden spoon, until the custard is slightly thickened and will just coat the back of the spoon. Do not allow the mixture to boil or it will curdle. Strain into a clean bowl and serve hot, warm or chilled.

DRIED APPLE CRISPS

MAKES 20

2 Cox's Orange Pippin apples, washed and
  cored
2–3 teaspoons icing sugar, sifted
a pinch of ground cinnamon

1. Preheat the oven to 70°C/150°F/gas mark ¼.
2. Using a very sharp knife or mandolin, slice the apples very thinly. Arrange the slices on a baking sheet and sprinkle with the icing sugar and cinnamon.
3. Bake in the preheated oven for 3–4 hours, or until completely dry and crisp. Transfer to a wire rack and allow to cool completely, then store in an airtight container.

MENU IDEAS

AUTUMN MENUS

Ensuring that a menu is well balanced is one of the most important
skills that a cook must learn.
Our suggested menus for autumn entertaining are as follows:

Informal Supper

Mixed roast onions
Caraway and dulse soda bread
Game and wild mushroom sausages
Red pesto root mash
Mixed leaf salad
Pear and quince sorbet with Poire William
Cigarettes russes

Light Lunch

Field mushroom and red Leicester flan
Warm wild berry compote
Savoury damson biscuits

Formal Dinner Party

Blackened scallops with squid ink butter
Boned pheasant with dried cherry and walnut stuffing
Sweet potato and nutmeg purée
Seasonal green vegetable
Individual cardamom pear and bread puddings

Hallowe'en Party

Hot spiced pear juice
Cèpes, garlic and parsley brioche
Game sausage rolls
Pumpkin pancake pie or pumpkin gnocchi with fresh sage and Fontina
Hot parsnip and pecan salad
Warm red cabbage coleslaw
Bonfire potatoes
Banana and rum ice cream
Greengage and almond sponge pudding with red plum sauce

Dinner Party/Thanksgiving

Crottin in filo with prunes in Armagnac
Pot-roast partridge with mulberries and shallots
Sweet potato wedges
Pumpkin pie with blueberries, mint and crème fraîche
Sloe gin

Informal Lunch or Supper

Steamed venison and smoked oyster pudding
Smoky Savoy cabbage
Cajun honey roast squash with pumpkin seeds
Blackberry and lime compote

WINTER
December – January – February

INTRODUCTION

Winter is a time for wrapping up warm and marching across crunchy grass with the trees frosted over and glistening in the sun. The days are short, a wonderful excuse for lazy morning lie-ins, but more importantly long evenings in front of the fire – essential for planning the forthcoming festivities in fine detail. With the arrival of the New Year, hopes are high and resolutions are strong – many feel the need to shed a few pounds before having to release the forgiving extra layers of jumpers and jackets which hide a multitude of sins.

Winter goodies come in the form of cranberries with their appealing bright red colour – turkey wouldn't be the same without them. Make the most of the truffle season; they are an acquired taste, but if you have a good excuse, team them up with foie gras for the ultimate gourmet delight. The game season continues in full swing, and many of our recipes can be used for exciting dinner-party menus as an alternative to chicken. Wild mushrooms are ready to pick and are often best served simply fried with butter, parsley and garlic. Brussels sprouts have arrived, and the rich colour of red cabbage blends well with the stark winter reds and whites outside. Look out for satsumas and clementines, pomegranates and Seville oranges – the essential ingredient for marmalade, though we also use them for ice creams and syllabubs.

The style of food changes with our mood over the winter months. At this time of the year we can feel tired and need feeding up, looking forward to the excesses and treats available over Christmas. Winter is a 'foodie' time of year, with plenty of occasions to enjoy all our favourite things. Many hands make light work, so rather than be a martyr, get friends and family to help with the more humdrum chores

so that you have time to concentrate on preparing your favourite recipes. When the festivities are over, but the weather is still cold, we often start to plan summer holidays, and for this reason we have tended towards the use of tropical fruits in our recipes – bright and full of colour and flavour. An exotic fruit salad can be livened up further with the addition of a little alcohol. Inexpensive but delicious meals, such as baked celeriac rarebit, can be made using the more exciting winter vegetables, or if the butcher has some game on offer, make a broth with mushrooms and pearl barley. If you are feeling short of change after buying lots of Christmas presents, there is no need for your tastebuds to be left feeling neglected!

Some of our favourite recipes for this time of year include: warm pheasant mousse with port essence, venison steaks with Seville orange rösti, or for the vegetarian, Jerusalem artichoke and Parmesan tart followed by nutmeg and bay leaf ice cream and chocolate shortbread torte with sticky cranberry glaze. Raised pies and terrines are excellent for festive buffet lunches, and again, this is the perfect time to bring out the preserves and pickles made and stored away in summer and autumn to accompany them.

Make Christmas and the New Year celebrations to remember. Keep your spirits high with prunes in port or a little mulberry gin. Impress your friends with a galantine of duck with foie gras, or marinated oysters with a garlic and potato mousse, or a cappuccino of white truffles. To refresh the palate, or for a welcome break from alcohol, try cranberry and orange crush, or make up some lemon and orange cordial. Remember that January will be a time for detoxifying yourself – so make the most of it while you have the perfect excuse.

FRUIT AND VEGETABLES IN SEASON

TOP FRUIT	December	January	February
Apples in store	XXXXXXXXX	XXXXXXXXX	XXXXXXXXX
Pears in store	XXXXXXXXX	XXXXXXXXX	XXXXXXXXX
Plums	XXXXXXXXX		

BERRY FRUIT			
Grapes	XXXXXXXXX		
Cranberries	XXXXXXXXX	XXXXXXXXX	

MOST CITRUS			
Oranges	XXXXXXXXX	XXXXXXXXX	XXXXXXXXX
Seville oranges		XXXXXXXXX	XXXXXXXXX
Kumquats		XXXXXXXXX	XXXXXXXXX
Mandarin family	XXXXXXXXX	XXXXXXXXX	XXXXXXXXX

EXOTIC FRUITS			
Bananas	XXXXXXXXX	XXXXXXXXX	XXXXXXXXX
Mango	XXXXXXXXX	XXXXXXXXX	XXXXXXXXX
Pineapple	XXXXXXXXX	XXXXXXXXX	XXXXXXXXX
Passion fruit	XXXXXXXXX	XXXXXXXXX	XXXXXXXXX
Kiwi	XXXXXXXXX	XXXXXXXXX	XXXXXXXXX

ALLIUMS			
Onions in store	XXXXXXXXX	XXXXXXXXX	XXXXXXXXX
Garlic in store	XXXXXXXXX	XXXXXXXXX	XXXXXXXXX
Shallots in store	XXXXXXXXX	XXXXXXXXX	XXXXXXXXX
Leeks	XXXXXXXXX	XXXXXXXXX	XXXXXXXXX

BRASSICAS			
Cabbages:	XXXXXXXXX	XXXXXXXXX	XXXXXXXXX
Dutch, savoy	XXXXXXXXX	XXXXXXXXX	XXXXXXXXX
Broccoli	XXXXXXXXX	XXXXXXXXX	XXXXXXXXX
Cauliflowers	XXXXXXXXX	XXXXXXXXX	XXXXXXXXX
Brussels sprouts	XXXXXXXXX	XXXXXXXXX	XXXXXXXXX
Kohlrabi	XXXXXXXXX	XXXXXXXXX	XXXXXXXXX

BEANS AND PODS			
Bean shoots, indoors (alfalfa)	XXXXXXXXX	XXXXXXXXX	XXXXXXXXX
Use dried beans			

FRUIT AND VEGETABLES IN SEASON–*contd*

LETTUCE/SPINACH	December	January	February
Winter varieties of lettuce:	XXXXXXXXX	XXXXXXXXX	XXXXXXXXX
Webb's Wonder	XXXXXXXXX	XXXXXXXXX	XXXXXXXXX
Iceberg	XXXXXXXXX	XXXXXXXXX	XXXXXXXXX
Some varieties under cloche	XXXXXXXXX	XXXXXXXXX	XXXXXXXXX
Lamb's lettuce	XXXXXXXXX	XXXXXXXXX	XXXXXXXXX
All the chicory family	XXXXXXXXX	XXXXXXXXX	XXXXXXXXX
Spinach	XXXXXXXXX	XXXXXXXXX	

ROOTS AND TUBERS			
Main crop potatoes in store:	XXXXXXXXX	XXXXXXXXX	XXXXXXXXX
Maris piper	XXXXXXXXX	XXXXXXXXX	XXXXXXXXX
Cara	XXXXXXXXX	XXXXXXXXX	XXXXXXXXX
Pentland	XXXXXXXXX	XXXXXXXXX	XXXXXXXXX
Romano	XXXXXXXXX	XXXXXXXXX	XXXXXXXXX
King Edward	XXXXXXXXX	XXXXXXXXX	XXXXXXXXX
Sante	XXXXXXXXX	XXXXXXXXX	XXXXXXXXX
Parsnips	XXXXXXXXX	XXXXXXXXX	XXXXXXXXX
Swedes	XXXXXXXXX	XXXXXXXXX	XXXXXXXXX
Carrots (in store)	XXXXXXXXX	XXXXXXXXX	XXXXXXXXX
Celeriac	XXXXXXXXX	XXXXXXXXX	XXXXXXXXX
Salsify	XXXXXXXXX	XXXXXXXXX	XXXXXXXXX
Turnips	XXXXXXXXX	XXXXXXXXX	XXXXXXXXX
Beetroot	XXXXXXXXX		
Jerusalem artichokes	XXXXXXXXX	XXXXXXXXX	XXXXXXXXX

STALKS/SHOOTS			
Celery	XXXXXXXXX	XXXXXXXXX	XXXXXXXXX
Sea kale	XXXXXXXXX	XXXXXXXXX	XXXXXXXXX
Kale	XXXXXXXXX	XXXXXXXXX	XXXXXXXXX

VEGETABLE FRUITS			
Marrows	XXXXXXXXX		
Pumpkins	XXXXXXXXX		

HERBS			
Rosemary	XXXXXXXXX		
Sage	XXXXXXXXX		
Thyme	XXXXXXXXX		

WILD MUSHROOMS			
	XXXXXXXXX		

FISH IN SEASON

SALMON FAMILY
Farmed Atlantic and Pacific Salmon
Farmed Trout and Char

SHELLFISH
Brown Crab
Prawns (various)
Shrimp
Whelk
Cockle
Clam
Mussel
Native Oyster
Pacific Oyster
Scallop
Octopus

BEST FROM HOME
Monkfish
John Dory
Gurnard
Grey Mullet
Wrasse
Black Sea Bream
Red Sea Bream
Rockfish/Catfish

FLAT FISH
Plaice
Halibut
Lemon Sole
Dab
Brill
Megrim
Witch
Skate

MACKEREL FAMILY
Mackerel
Tuna
Bonito/Wahoo

HERRING FAMILY
Herring
Pilchard/Sardine
Anchovy
Whitebait
Sprat

COD FAMILY
Cod
Haddock
Whiting
Coley/Saithe/Coalfish
Ling
Hake

FIRST COURSES AND SOUPS

FIRST COURSES

FETA AND GREEN OLIVE STRUDELS

MAKES 20

85g/3oz feta cheese, crumbled
85g/3oz ricotta cheese
4 tablespoons fresh white breadcrumbs
1 egg yolk
55g/2oz large green olives, pitted and chopped
2 teaspoons chopped fresh sage
freshly ground black pepper
4 sheets of filo pastry
4 tablespoons extra virgin olive oil
1 egg, beaten, to glaze
2–3 teaspoons caraway seeds

1. Preheat the oven to 200°C/400°F/gas mark 6.
2. Mix together the feta cheese, ricotta, breadcrumbs, egg yolk, olives and sage and season to taste with pepper and salt if necessary (the feta cheese may be salty).
3. Brush the sheets of filo with the oil and cut each sheet of pastry into strips 4cm/1½in wide.
4. Place a spoonful of filling at one end of each strip. Form a triangle by folding the right-hand corner to the opposite side and fold over and then across from the left-hand corner to the right edge. Continue folding until the strip of pastry is used up.
5. Brush the strudels with beaten egg and sprinkle with the caraway seeds. Place on a greased baking sheet and bake in the preheated oven for about 10 minutes, or until golden-brown.

 *RED RIOJA*

MARINATED FRESH TUNA WITH SOY AND LIME

SERVES 4

450g/1lb fresh tuna fillet, skinned
juice of 6 limes
juice of 2 lemons
75ml/2½fl oz light soy sauce
freshly ground black pepper

To garnish
2 limes, segmented
sprigs of fresh dill

1. Trim the tuna fillet of any dark flesh and slice very thinly across the grain. Arrange in a single layer on a large platter.
2. Mix the lime and lemon juice with the soy sauce.
3. Spoon half the marinade over the fish, season with pepper and refrigerate for 1½–2 hours.
4. Remove the fish from the marinade, arrange on 4 individual plates, garnish with lime segments and sprigs of dill and serve immediately with the remaining marinade spooned over.

 *DRY AUSTRALIAN RIESLING*

MARINATED OYSTERS WITH GARLIC AND POTATO MOUSSE

SERVES 8

150ml/¼ pint aspic (see page 631)
8 sprigs of fresh chervil or dill
675g/1½lb baking potatoes, baked and kept
    warm
1 clove of garlic, crushed
290ml/½ pint double cream
2 leaves of gelatine, soaked in cold water until
    soft (about 3–4 minutes)
1 tablespoon chopped fresh chives
salt and freshly ground white pepper
3 egg whites
½ green pepper, de-seeded and very finely diced
½ red pepper, de-seeded and very finely diced
½ stick of celery, very finely diced
¼ bulb of Florence fennel, very finely diced
1 shallot, very finely chopped
18 fresh oysters, shucked (see page 136)
juice of 1–2 lemons
150ml/¼ pint dry white wine
1 tablespoon chopped fresh dill

To garnish
chopped fresh chives

1. Spoon the aspic into the bottom of 8 small
ramekins, dividing it equally among them. Chill
until set. Place a sprig of chervil on the centre of
the aspic and chill again until required.
2. Remove the hot potato flesh from the potato
skins. Weigh out 255g/9oz and keep the
remainder for another use. Press the weighed
potato through a sieve into a warmed heavy-
based saucepan and stir in the garlic and
enough cream to give a very loose dropping
consistency. Add the pre-soaked gelatine and
stir over a low heat without boiling until
dissolved. Sieve the potato mixture again into a
large bowl. Add the chives and season to taste
with salt and pepper.
3. Whisk the egg whites until they form medium
peaks, then fold into the potato. Divide the

mixture equally between the ramekins and chill
for 1 hour, or until set.
4. Blanch the peppers, celery, fennel and shallot
in boiling water for 1 minute, then drain and
refresh in cold water. Dry well on kitchen
paper.
5. Mix the blanched vegetables with the oysters,
oyster juice, lemon juice, wine and dill. Season
with salt and pepper and leave to marinate in
the refrigerator for 15 minutes.
6. Dip the base of each ramekin briefly into a
bowl of hot water, run a small sharp knife
around the edge and turn the mousses out on to
8 individual plates. Arrange the marinated
oyster mixture around the mousses and garnish
with a few chives.

 *SOUTH AFRICAN OR AUSTRALIAN
CHARDONNAY*

BLACKENED SCALLOPS WITH SQUID INK BUTTER

SERVES 4

12 scallops in their shells
1 tablespoon oil
salt and freshly ground black pepper

For the squid ink butter sauce
140g/5oz cold unsalted butter
2 shallots, finely chopped
150ml/¼ pint fish stock (see page 626)
3 tablespoons white wine vinegar
1 × 7g/¼oz packet of squid ink
salt and freshly ground black pepper

To serve
sprigs of fresh seasonal herbs

1. Open the scallops with a strong knife and
detach the scallop from the lower shell. Pull
away the hard muscle opposite the coral or roe
and discard (see page 136). Cut the scallops in
half horizontally.
2. Brush the scallops with the oil, season with
salt and pepper and set aside.

3. Make the squid ink butter sauce: melt 30g/1oz of the butter in a saucepan, add the shallots and cook over a low heat until soft and transparent. Add the stock and vinegar and bring to the boil, then lower the heat and simmer until the liquid has reduced to 4 tablespoonfuls.

4. Meanwhile, cut the remaining butter into small pieces. Remove the reduced liquid from the heat and whisk in the butter a small piece at a time. Add the squid ink and season to taste with salt and pepper. Keep warm over a very low heat.

5. Heat a griddle pan over a high heat until very hot. Griddle the scallops for 20–30 seconds on each side.

6. Divide the squid ink butter sauce between 4 warmed individual plates and put the scallops on each. Garnish with the herbs and serve immediately.

 NEW WORLD SAUVIGNON BLANC

SMOKED FISH COUSCOUS

SERVES 6

450g/1lb pre-cooked couscous
570ml/1 pint fish stock (see page 626)
2 tablespoons olive oil
1 large onion, finely chopped
2 cloves of garlic, crushed
½ teaspoon cayenne pepper
1 teaspoon ground cumin
a few saffron strands
110g/4oz cooked chickpeas
450g/1lb smoked fish and shellfish selection, such as smoked mussels, prawns, oysters, halibut, monkfish, trout
2 tablespoons finely chopped fresh coriander
2 teaspoons paprika
45g/1½oz butter, melted
salt and freshly ground black pepper

1. Put the couscous and stock into a large saucepan. Bring to the boil, then remove from the heat and allow to stand for 20 minutes so that the couscous can swell.

2. Meanwhile, heat the oil in a large frying pan, add the onion and cook over a low heat until soft and transparent.

3. Add the garlic and spices and cook for 2 minutes.

4. Drain the soft, swollen couscous and add to the onion mixture with the chickpeas. Cook until the couscous is very hot.

5. Stir in the smoked fish, coriander, paprika and butter. Heat until the butter has melted. Season to taste with salt and pepper.

NOTE: Most couscous available in this country is pre-cooked.

 RIESLING D'ALSACE

WARM PHEASANT MOUSSE WITH PORT ESSENCE

SERVES 6

225g/8oz boned and skinned pheasant, all fat removed
1 egg white
570ml/1 pint strong pheasant or white stock, made with chicken bones (see page 625)
8 tablespoons tawny port
290ml/½ pint double cream, chilled
salt and freshly ground white pepper
30g/1oz butter, melted
oil for brushing

For the sauce
1 shallot, finely chopped
150ml/¼ pint white stock, made with chicken bones (see page 625)
100ml/3½fl oz dry white wine
110g/4oz chilled unsalted butter, diced
1 tablespoon double cream

To garnish
6 sprigs of fresh chervil

1. Preheat the oven to 170°C/325°F/gas mark 3.

2. Whizz the pheasant with the egg white in a food processor until smooth. Pass through a fine tammy sieve, then chill for 30 minutes.

3. Reduce the stock by boiling rapidly to 6 tablespoons. Remove 2 tablespoons and set aside to cool.

4. Make the port essence: add the port to the remaining reduced stock and continue to reduce by boiling rapidly until only 3 tablespoons remain. Pour into a small container and chill until set.

5. Put the puréed pheasant into a large bowl and set over ice. Stir in the reserved 2 tablespoons reduced stock. Gradually beat in half the cream, then carefully add the remainder and season with salt and pepper.

6. Brush 6 ramekins with melted butter. Chill and repeat with more butter.

7. Spoon half the pheasant mousse into the bottom of the ramekins. Cut the port essence into equal cubes and place a cube in the centre of each mousse. Spoon over the remaining mousse. Cover each mousse with a disc of oiled greaseproof paper and stand the ramekins in a roasting tin half filled with hot water (a bain-marie). Bake in the lower part of the preheated oven for 15 minutes, or until firm and coming away from the edges.

8. Make the sauce: put the shallot, stock and wine into a saucepan and simmer until reduced to 3 tablespoons.

9. Add the butter, piece by piece, whisking all the time. Add the cream and season with salt and pepper, then strain.

10. Turn each mousse out on to a fish slice, drain on kitchen paper, then transfer to the serving plates and pour around the sauce. Garnish with sprigs of chervil.

 *NEW ZEALAND OR OREGON PINOT NOIR*

FOIE GRAS MOUSSE WITH GREEN PEPPERCORNS AND PORT JELLY

SERVES 6

1 × 225g/8oz tin of foie gras
4 tablespoons sweet white wine
7g/¼oz powdered gelatine
225ml/8fl oz double cream, lightly whipped
1 teaspoon green peppercorns, rinsed and
*   mashed*
salt

For the port jelly
290ml/½ pint port
1 teaspoon powdered gelatine

To garnish
a few sprigs of fresh chervil

1. Put the foie gras into a bowl and beat with a wooden spoon until smooth.

2. Pour the wine into a small saucepan and sprinkle over the gelatine. Leave to stand for 5 minutes. Gently melt the gelatine over a low heat without boiling.

3. Stir the gelatine quickly into the foie gras, then fold in the cream with the green peppercorns. Season to taste with salt.

4. Make the port jelly: pour the port into a small saucepan and sprinkle over the gelatine. Leave to stand for 5 minutes. Gently melt the gelatine over a low heat without boiling.

5. Divide the jelly between the ramekins. Chill the ramekins for 15 minutes, or until the jelly has set.

6. Spoon the foie gras mousse into the ramekins and gently tap each ramekin on a work surface to release any air bubbles. Chill for 2 hours.

7. Fill a large bowl with hot water. Dip the base of each ramekin into the water for 5 seconds to release the mousse. Dip a small sharp knife into the hot water for a few seconds, then run it around the edge of each mousse. Turn the mousses out on to 6 individual plates and garnish with the sprigs of chervil.

 SWEET WHITE BORDEAUX

GRILLED AUBERGINE ROULADES WITH GOAT'S CHEESE, LEEK, SWEET PEPPERS AND ROUILLE

SERVES 4
1 large aubergine
olive oil
salt and freshly ground black pepper
2 red peppers, quartered and de-seeded
2 leeks
170g/6oz soft goat's cheese
4 tablespoons rouille (see page 635)

To serve
Italian bread with rosemary (see page 658)

1. Preheat the grill to its highest setting. Preheat the oven to 200°C/400°F/gas mark 6.
2. Slice the aubergine lengthways into 4 even slices about 1cm/½in thick, discarding the end pieces.
3. Lay the 4 aubergine slices on a baking sheet. Brush them with oil and season with salt and pepper. Grill the aubergine until golden-brown. Turn the slices over, season with salt and pepper and grill again until golden-brown.
4. Place the peppers, skin side up, on a baking sheet. Grill them until the skins are black and charred. Tip them into a bowl and cover with clingfilm. Leave them to steam for 10 minutes, then peel off the charred skins.
5. Bring a large saucepan of salted water to the boil. Cut the leeks in half lengthways and separate the layers. Wash them thoroughly to remove any mud and grit. Boil the leeks for 4–5 minutes, or until just tender, then drain and refresh in cold water. Drain again and dry well on kitchen paper.
6. Beat the goat's cheese in a bowl to spreading consistency.
7. To assemble: lay the aubergine slices out flat on a board and season with salt and pepper. Divide the cheese into 4 equal portions and spread evenly over each slice of aubergine. Arrange a layer of red pepper and a layer of leek over the cheese, seasoning each with salt

and pepper. Roll up the aubergines and place on a baking sheet, seam side down, securing with a wooden cocktail stick if necessary.
8. Coat each roulade with a tablespoon of rouille and bake in the preheated oven for 10 minutes, or until hot and bubbling on top.
9. Serve the roulades on warmed individual plates with the bread.

 ALSACE GEWÜRZTRAMINER

HOT SALSIFY, PUMPKIN AND BACON STIR-FRY

SERVES 4

450g/1lb salsify, unpeeled
salt and freshly ground black pepper
450g/1lb pumpkin, de-seeded and peeled
4 tablespoons sunflower oil
1 × 225g/8oz piece of bacon, cut into lardons
1 tablespoon chopped fresh parsley

1. Cook the salsify in boiling salted water for 12–15 minutes, or until tender. Drain, peel and cut into 2.5cm/1in lengths. Set aside.
2. Cut the pumpkin into 2.5cm/1in chunks. Cook in boiling salted water for 5–6 minutes, or until just tender. Drain and set aside.
3. Heat the oil in a wok, add the bacon and cook briskly for 5–7 minutes, or until brown and crisp. Add the salsify and pumpkin and continue to toss over the heat until everything is hot. Season with salt and pepper and sprinkle with the parsley.
4. Pile into a large warmed serving bowl and serve immediately.

NOTE: If parsley is kept under a cloche it will last well into winter.

 NEW WORLD CABERNET SAUVIGNON

SALSIFY GRATIN WITH THREE CHEESES

SERVES 4

900g/2lb salsify, unpeeled
1 teaspoon salt
170g/6oz ricotta cheese
2 teaspoons finely chopped fresh sage
salt and freshly ground black pepper
290ml/½ pint quantity mornay sauce (see page 629), made with 85g/3oz Gruyère cheese
55g/2oz Pecorino or Parmesan cheese, freshly grated
1 tablespoon fresh white breadcrumbs

1. Wash the salsify. Cook in boiling salted water for 12–15 minutes, or until tender. Drain and peel. Rinse and pat dry with kitchen paper. Cut into 5cm/2in pieces.
2. Preheat the oven to 190°C/375°F/gas mark 5.
3. Sieve the ricotta, add the sage and season to taste with salt and pepper. Mix with the salsify and arrange in 4 individual gratin dishes.
4. Reheat the mornay sauce and use to coat the salsify. Sprinkle with the Pecorino or Parmesan cheese and the breadcrumbs. Bake in the preheated oven for 12–15 minutes, or until hot and golden-brown on top. Serve very hot.

 *AUSTRALIAN CHARDONNAY*

PENNE WITH SCALLOPS, CHORIZO AND LEEKS

SERVES 4

340g/12oz penne
1 teaspoon salt
30g/1oz butter
2 leeks, thinly sliced
salt and freshly ground black pepper
5 tablespoons double cream
110g/4oz chorizo sausage, diced
8 large scallops, prepared (see page 136)
30g/1oz Parmesan cheese, freshly grated

1. Cook the penne in boiling salted water until *al dente*, drain and refresh under cold running water, then drain again. Set aside.
2. Meanwhile, melt the butter in a sauté pan, add the leeks and cook over a very low heat until soft. Season with salt and pepper and add the cream. Stir into the penne and keep warm.
3. Dry-fry the chorizo in a frying pan until crisp and lightly browned. Add the scallops and fry for 1 minute over a high heat until lightly browned.
4. Toss the scallops and chorizo into the penne and leeks, season with salt and pepper and sprinkle with the Parmesan cheese. Serve very hot.

 *ALSACE GEWÜRZTRAMINER*

SOUPS

ROASTED GAME SOUP WITH HARICOTS BLANCS

SERVES 4

450g/1lb pheasant, grouse or pigeon leg and
   wing joints
55g/2oz haricot or cannellini beans, soaked in
   cold water overnight
1 litre/1¾ pints white stock, made with chicken
   bones, or game stock (see page 625)
4 tablespoons sunflower oil
1 large onion, chopped
1 carrot, finely diced
2 sticks of celery, finely diced
1 tablespoon plain flour
2 cloves of garlic, crushed
1 bouquet garni
150ml/¼ pint red wine
salt and freshly ground black pepper
2–3 tablespoons tawny port

1. Preheat the oven to 200°C/400°F/gas mark 6.
Remove any feathers from the game joints.
2. Drain the haricot beans and put them into a
saucepan. Cover with water and bring to the
boil. Strain the beans and discard the water.
Put the beans back into the saucepan and
cover with the stock. Bring to the boil, then
lower the heat and simmer for 1–2 hours, or
until tender.
3. Put the game joints into a shallow roasting tin,
coat with 1 tablespoon of the oil and cook at the
top of the oven for 30 minutes, or until well
browned. Tip away any excess fat. Reduce the
oven temperature to 170°C/325°F/gas mark 3.
4. Heat the remaining oil in a large frying pan
and fry the onion, carrot and celery until pale
golden. Add the flour and continue to fry until

the vegetables are a good russet-brown. Stir in
the garlic.
5. Add the bouquet garni and wine. Bring to the
boil and reduce by boiling rapidly to half the
original quantity. Tip the vegetables and wine
into a large casserole.
6. Add the game joints, haricot beans and stock
and season with salt and pepper. Bring to the
boil, cover and cook in the oven for 1 hour, or
until the meat starts falling from the bone.
7. Place a large colander over a bowl and strain
the cooking liquid. Discard the bouquet garni.
Transfer the game joints to a plate and allow to
cool a little before separating the flesh from the
bones. Discard the bones and chop up the flesh
neatly.
8. Return the vegetables, beans and strained
liquid to the casserole and add the game meat
with the port. Season with salt and pepper
before serving in warmed deep soup bowls.

NOTE: This makes a more filling winter lunch
dish if served with cranberry and thyme
dumplings (see page 650).

 *AUSTRALIAN SHIRAZ OR
CHÂTEAUNEUF DU PAPE*

GAME BROTH WITH MUSHROOMS AND PEARL BARLEY

SERVES 4

1 large onion, thinly sliced
2 cloves of garlic
45g/1½oz butter

55g/2oz pearl barley
1.5 litres/2½ pints game stock (see page 626)
450g/1lb cup mushrooms, wiped and sliced
1 teaspoon finely chopped fresh sage
salt and freshly ground black pepper
2 teaspoons Worcestershire sauce

To garnish
1 tablespoon finely chopped fresh parsley

1. Sweat the onion and garlic in 30g/1oz of the butter in a saucepan over a low heat for 5–7 minutes, or until nearly soft.
2. Add the barley and sweat for a further 2–3 minutes.
3. Add the stock and bring to the boil, then lower the heat and simmer gently for 1–1¼ hours, or until the barley is cooked.
4. Heat the remaining butter in a frying pan, add the mushrooms and sage and sauté briskly for 2–3 minutes. Add the cooked mushrooms to the broth, bring to the boil and season to taste with salt, pepper and Worcestershire sauce.
5. Pour into a warmed soup tureen, sprinkle with the parsley and serve.

 *PINOT NOIR*

CAPPUCCINO OF WHITE TRUFFLE

SERVES 4

55g/2oz dried haricots blancs, soaked in cold
*   water overnight*
570ml/1 pint strong white stock, made with
*   chicken bones (see page 625)*
2 onions
1 stick of celery
1 carrot, peeled
1 bouquet garni
30g/1oz butter
1 white truffle, grated
15g/½oz plain flour
290ml/½ pint milk
salt and freshly ground black pepper
1 tablespoon double cream

1. Drain the haricots blancs and put them into a saucepan. Cover with water and bring to the boil. Drain and return the beans to the pan. Pour over the stock.
2. Cut 1 onion in half and add to the stock with the celery, carrot and bouquet garni. Bring to the boil, then lower the heat and simmer for 2 hours, or until the beans are tender. Strain the haricots, discarding the vegetables and bouquet garni, but reserving the liquor.
3. Finely chop the remaining onion and cook gently in the butter in a saucepan for 30 minutes, until very soft but not coloured. Add half the white truffle with the flour and cook for 30 seconds, then gradually add the milk and bring to the boil, stirring continuously.
4. Reduce the bean liquor by boiling rapidly to 290ml/½ pint, then add to the white sauce. Season to taste with salt and pepper.
5. Place a spoonful of haricots blancs into each of 4 warmed cups or deep soup bowls. Whizz the soup in a blender for a minute until very smooth, then pass through a fine sieve into a saucepan and reheat with the cream. Return the soup to the blender and whizz until frothy. Pour immediately into the cups, sprinkle with the remaining white truffle and serve immediately.

NOTE: The truffle may be omitted for a plain bean soup.

 *CHAMPAGNE*

CHESTNUT SOUP

SERVES 4

1 onion, finely chopped
1 carrot, finely chopped
30g/1oz butter
675g/1½lb fresh chestnuts, peeled
1 bouquet garni
860ml–1 litre/1½–1¾ pints white stock, made
*   with chicken bones (see page 625)*
150ml/¼ pint single cream
salt and freshly ground black pepper

To garnish
1 Cox's Orange Pippin apple, diced
15g/½oz butter
1 teaspoon caster sugar
1 tablespoon finely chopped fresh parsley

1. Sweat the onion and carrot in the butter in a saucepan until tender. Add the chestnuts and sweat for a further 5 minutes.
2. Add the bouquet garni and stock. Bring to the boil, then lower the heat and simmer for 20–30 minutes, or until the chestnuts are tender.
3. Whizz the soup in a food processor or blender and strain into a clean saucepan. Add the cream, bring just to the boil and season to taste with salt and pepper.
4. Meanwhile, prepare the garnish: fry the apple pieces in the butter in a small saucepan, add the sugar and let the apples caramelize. Add the parsley.
5. Tip the soup into a warmed soup tureen and sprinkle over the apple garnish.

NOTE: If fresh chestnuts are not available, use 1 × 400g/14oz can of whole, peeled chestnuts.

 AUSTRALIAN SÉMILLON

HAM AND BLACK BEAN CHILLI SOUP

SERVES 4

225g/8oz dried black beans, soaked in cold
    water overnight
2 tablespoons sunflower oil
1 large onion, finely chopped
2 green chillies, finely chopped
3 cloves of garlic, crushed
1–2 tablespoons mild chilli powder
2 teaspoons ground cumin
2 teaspoons dried oregano
570ml/1 pint white stock, made with chicken
    bones, or ham stock (see page 625)
520–570ml/18fl oz–1 pint water
225g/8oz smoked gammon steak, diced

salt and freshly ground black pepper
1 tablespoon chopped fresh coriander

To serve
150ml/¼ pint soured cream or plain yoghurt

1. Drain the beans and rinse well.
2. Heat the oil in a saucepan, add the onion and cook until soft and transparent. Add the chillies and garlic and cook over a low heat for a further 1–2 minutes. Add the chilli powder, cumin and oregano and cook for a further 2–3 minutes.
3. Add the stock, water and diced gammon. Bring to the boil, then cover, lower the heat and cook over a very low heat for 2–2½ hours, or until the beans are very soft and the soup very thick. Top up with water from time to time if necessary.
4. Season the soup to taste with salt and pepper. Stir in the coriander and serve in a warmed soup tureen, with the soured cream or yoghurt handed separately.

BEER

MAIN COURSES

Fish and Shellfish
Poultry and Game
Beef
Lamb
Pork
Veal
Offal
Vegetarian

FISH AND SHELLFISH

SALT COD AND PURÉED VEGETABLE PIE

This rustic combination of salt fish and mashed parsnip is a traditional English recipe that dates back several centuries. It is a delicious idea and here it is updated slightly by using a selection of root vegetables. It makes a good supper dish.

SERVES 4

450g/1lb salt cod
290ml/½ pint milk
290ml/½ pint water
1 bay leaf
6 black peppercorns
1 large parsnip, peeled and thickly sliced
1 small celeriac, peeled and thickly sliced
2 small potatoes, peeled and thickly sliced
1 carrot, peeled and thickly sliced
55g/2oz unsalted butter
1 egg, beaten
freshly ground white pepper

1. Soak the salt cod in cold water for 24 hours. Change the water several times to extract as much salt as possible.
2. Rinse the soaked cod well. Put it into a saucepan and add the milk, water, bay leaf and peppercorns. Bring to the boil, then lower the heat and poach for 30–40 minutes, or until the fish will flake. Lift the fish from the liquid and set aside. Strain and reserve the poaching liquid.
3. Preheat the oven to 180°C/350°F/gas mark 4.
4. Meanwhile, simmer the vegetables in the cod poaching liquid until tender. The parsnip, celeriac and potatoes should take about 15–20 minutes, the carrots about 5–7 minutes. When all the vegetables are cooked, drain and push

through a sieve while still hot to form a purée.
5. Beat the butter and egg into the puréed vegetables.
6. Remove the skin and bones from the salt cod and break the flesh into large flakes. Fork the fish into the vegetable mixture. If it is a little stiff, add some of the cod poaching liquid. Season to taste with pepper.
7. Pile into an ovenproof serving dish and bake in the oven for 15 minutes, or until the pie is hot and has formed a crust. Serve very hot.

 LIGHT FRENCH RED

DEEP-FRIED EEL WITH HOT TOMATO SAUCE AND AÏOLI

SERVES 4

oil for deep-frying
8 × 85g/3oz pieces of eel fillet
seasoned plain flour
1 quantity fish batter (see page 655)
salt

To serve
290ml/½ pint tomato sauce (see page 635)
about ½ teaspoon Tabasco sauce
½ quantity aïoli (see page 632)

To garnish
4 lemon wedges
a few sprigs of fresh flat-leaf parsley

1. Preheat the oven to 150°C/300°F/gas mark 2.
2. Heat the oil in a deep-fryer, making sure the

pan is no more than one-third full of oil, until a crumb of bread sizzles and turns brown in 15 seconds.

3. Dip the eel fillets in the seasoned flour and shake off the excess. Dip 2 fillets at a time into the batter, using metal tongs, and lower them carefully into the hot oil. Fry the fillets until golden-brown on both sides. Lift them out of the oil and put them on to a baking sheet lined with kitchen paper. Sprinkle with a little salt to absorb excess oil and keep warm in the oven while frying the remaining fillets in the same way.

4. Heat the tomato sauce and add a little Tabasco.

5. Arrange the eel fillets on warmed individual plates and spoon around a little tomato sauce. Garnish with the lemon wedges and parsley and serve with the aïoli handed separately.

 *CHILEAN SAUVIGNON BLANC*

GRILLED WASABI HALIBUT WITH LIME MAYONNAISE

SERVES 4

4 × 170g/6oz halibut steaks
1–2 tablespoons wasabi paste
juice of 1 lemon

For the mayonnaise
150ml/¼ pint mayonnaise (see page 632)
grated zest and juice of 2 limes
a pinch of sugar
freshly ground black pepper

To garnish
4 lime wedges

1. Spread the halibut steaks with a little wasabi on both sides. Place in a shallow dish and sprinkle over the lemon juice. Cover the dish with clingfilm and refrigerate for 15 minutes.

2. Preheat the grill to its highest setting.

3. Make the lime mayonnaise: mix the

mayonnaise with the lime zest and juice and season to taste with the sugar and pepper.

4. Place the halibut steaks on a wire rack over a baking sheet and place them under the grill, as close to the heat as possible. Grill for 4 minutes, or until golden-brown. Turn the steaks over and grill for a further 1–2 minutes, or until golden-brown and firm to the touch.

5. To serve: arrange the halibut steaks on 4 warmed individual plates and dollop a spoonful of the mayonnaise on to one side of each steak. Garnish with the lime wedges and serve immediately.

 *AUSTRALIAN RHINE RIESLING*

RARE ROAST TUNA WITH GLAZED ROOT VEGETABLES

SERVES 4

4 × 170g/6oz tuna steaks, skinned (see page 133)
2 tablespoons coarsely ground black pepper
salt
5 tablespoons grapeseed oil

For the vegetables
225g/8oz button onions
225g/8oz turnip, peeled
225g/8oz carrots, peeled
225g/8oz sweet potato, peeled
55g/2oz butter
2 teaspoons sugar
½ teaspoon ground coriander
salt and freshly ground black pepper

1. Pinbone the tuna steaks (see page 133). Press the pepper on to both sides of the steaks and season with salt. Cover and refrigerate until required.

2. Prepare the vegetables: blanch the onions in boiling water for 2–3 minutes, drain and peel.

3. Cut the turnip, carrots and sweet potato into even chunks of about 2.5cm/1in. Parboil in boiling salted water for 2 minutes. Drain and dry on kitchen paper.

4. Preheat the oven to 200°C/400°F/gas mark 6.
5. Melt the butter in a large saucepan and when hot add the sugar and coriander. Continue to cook until the sugar has dissolved. Add the vegetables, and season with salt and pepper. Cover the pan with a lid and cook over a medium heat for 3–4 minutes. Shake the pan from time to time to prevent the vegetables from burning or sticking, and avoid removing the lid too often. Continue to cook until the vegetables have a sticky brown glaze but are not burnt.
6. Meanwhile, heat the oil in a roasting tin. Add the tuna steaks and baste with the oil. Roast in the oven for 2–3 minutes, then turn the tuna over and roast for a further 2 minutes, or until the tuna is firm but still pink (it may be cooked for up to 8 minutes on each side if you prefer it well done).
7. To serve: pile the glazed vegetables on one side of a serving dish and arrange the tuna steaks, overlapping, on the other side. Serve immediately.

 CALIFORNIAN CHARDONNAY

TURBOT WITH WATERCRESS AND LEMON ROUILLE

SERVES 4

4 × 170g/6oz turbot steaks
grated zest of 1 lemon
salt and freshly ground black pepper
450g/1lb watercress, washed and stalks removed
1 small bunch of spring onions, thinly sliced

For the sauce
juice of 2 lemons
1 quantity rouille (see page 635)

To garnish
1 small bunch of watercress

1. Preheat the oven to 200°C/400°F/gas mark 6.
2. Put the turbot steaks into a shallow dish and sprinkle with the lemon zest, salt and pepper. Make sure the fillets are evenly coated. Cover the dish with clingfilm and refrigerate for 30 minutes.
3. Blanch the watercress in boiling salted water for a few seconds, or until just limp. Drain and refresh immediately in cold water. Squeeze the excess water out of the watercress and chop it roughly.
4. Make the sauce: mix the lemon juice with the rouille and check the seasoning.
5. Transfer the turbot steaks to a large baking sheet. Pile the chopped watercress over the top of the steaks, then sprinkle over the spring onions. Season well with salt and pepper and coat the watercress and spring onions with 2–3 tablespoons of the lemon rouille.
6. Bake at the top of the preheated oven for 10 minutes, or until the fish is just cooked and the rouille is starting to brown slightly on top.
7. Serve the turbot steaks on a large warmed platter garnished with the watercress.

 CHABLIS PREMIER CRU OR TOP-CLASS NEW ZEALAND SAUVIGNON BLANC

HOT LOBSTER PIZZA

MAKES 2 × 25CM/10IN PIZZAS

10g/⅓oz fresh yeast
a pinch of sugar
150ml/¼ pint lukewarm water
200g/7oz plain flour
½ teaspoon salt
3 tablespoons extra virgin olive oil
oil for greasing
1 quantity salsa pizzaiola (see page 636)
225g/8oz cooked lobster meat (see page 158), roughly chopped
1 green chilli, de-seeded and thinly sliced
2 buffalo mozzarella cheeses, sliced
freshly ground black pepper
55g/2oz Parmesan cheese, freshly grated
a little olive oil for drizzling

1. Cream the yeast with the sugar and 2 tablespoons of the water in a large bowl.

2. Sift the flour with the salt and make a well in the centre. Pour in the yeast mixture, the remaining water and the oil. Mix together to form a soft but not wet dough. Add more water or flour if necessary.

3. Turn out on to a floured surface and knead well for about 5 minutes, or until the dough is smooth. Place in a clean bowl and cover with greased clingfilm. Leave in a warm, draught-free place for 45 minutes, or until the dough has doubled in bulk.

4. Preheat the oven to 230°C/450°F/gas mark 8. Divide the dough in half. Roll each piece into a 25cm/10in circle. Place on greased and floured baking trays.

5. Crimp or flute the edges of the dough slightly to help keep in the filling. Spread with the pizzaiola sauce. Scatter with the lobster meat and chilli and arrange the mozzarella cheese on top. Season with plenty of pepper and sprinkle with the Parmesan cheese. Drizzle over a little olive oil. (The pizza can be left for up to 30 minutes before baking.)

6. Bake the pizzas near the bottom of the preheated oven for 5 minutes, then reduce the oven temperature to 200°C/400°F/gas mark 6 and bake for a further 15 minutes.

 *AUSTRALIAN RHINE RIESLING*

BRAISED OCTOPUS WITH GLAZED ONIONS AND AÏOLI

SERVES 4

900g/2lb octopus, cleaned
1 tablespoon oil
30g/1oz butter
1 onion, thinly sliced
1 carrot, thinly sliced
2 cloves of garlic, crushed
2 tablespoons brandy
100ml/3½fl oz red wine

150ml/¼ pint fish stock (see page 626)
salt and freshly ground black pepper
450g/1lb button onions
55g/2oz butter
1 tablespoon sugar

To serve
1 quantity aïoli (see page 632)

1. Blanch the octopus in boiling water for 2 minutes, then drain. Peel the dark skin off the main body of the octopus and scrape the skin off the tentacles with a knife. Beat thoroughly with a rolling pin. Cut the tentacles and body into 5cm/2in pieces. Set aside.

2. Preheat the oven to 170°C/325°F/gas mark 3.

3. Heat the oil and butter in a large flameproof casserole. When the butter is foaming, brown the octopus pieces a few at a time. Lift on to a plate.

4. Add the onion and carrot to the casserole, reduce the heat and cook slowly until soft. Add the garlic and cook for a further 2 minutes. Put the octopus on top of the vegetables. Add the ink, if any.

5. Heat the brandy in a ladle or small saucepan, ignite and pour, flaming, over the octopus and vegetables. When the flames have subsided, pour over the wine and stock and season lightly with salt and pepper. Bring to the boil and cover with a lid. Cook in the oven for 2 hours or until the octopus is completely tender.

6. Meanwhile, blanch the onions in boiling water for 3 minutes, then drain and peel. Take care when removing the skin not to cut too much of the top off, or the onion will disintegrate during cooking.

7. Heat the butter and sugar in a second large flameproof casserole, add the onions, cover, and set over a low heat. Shake the pan from time to time, but avoid removing the lid too often. When the onions are well browned all over, put into the oven and cook for 30 minutes, or until tender.

8. When the octopus is cooked, lift out of the casserole and stir into the glazed onions. Keep warm. Strain the remaining contents of the octopus casserole into a saucepan, bring to the boil and reduce by boiling rapidly if necessary until syrupy. Season to taste with salt and pepper.

9. Pour the reduced cooking liquid on to the octopus and onions.

10. To serve: divide the octopus, onions and sauce between 4 individual plates. Put a spoonful of aïoli on top of each and serve immediately.

 *CHILEAN CHARDONNAY*

SEARED SCALLOPS WITH HAZELNUTS

SERVES 4

12 fresh scallops, cleaned (see page 136)
salt and freshly ground black pepper
1 tablespoon hazelnut oil
1 small frisée endive, washed and dried
55g/2oz hazelnuts, toasted and roughly
   chopped

For the dressing
6 tablespoons hazelnut oil
1 teaspoon grain mustard
1 tablespoon lemon juice
1 tablespoon balsamic vinegar

1. Rinse the scallops and pat dry on kitchen paper, keeping the corals separate.

2. Whisk all the dressing ingredients together in a large bowl and season well with salt and pepper. Add the endive and hazelnuts and toss together. Arrange the salad on 4 individual plates.

3. Heat the oil in a frying pan until very hot. Season the scallops with salt and pepper, add 6 to the hot oil and fry on one side for 1 minute, turning when golden-brown. Remove from the pan and fry the remaining scallops in the same way.

4. Arrange 3 scallops around each salad and serve immediately.

 *ALSACE TOKAY*

SCALLOP AND SALSIFY GRATIN

SERVES 4

8 large fresh scallops, cleaned (see page 136)
4 heads of salsify, scrubbed
salt
1 lemon
a pinch of cayenne pepper
1 tablespoon finely chopped fresh parsley
freshly ground black pepper
150ml/¼ pint double cream
55g/2oz Gruyère cheese, finely grated
30g/1oz fresh white breadcrumbs

To garnish
1 tablespoon finely chopped fresh parsley

To serve
4 large scallop shells
hot French bread

1. Preheat the oven to 230°C/450°F/gas mark 8.

2. Cut the scallops in half horizontally, keeping the corals separate.

3. Boil the salsify in a saucepan of salted water with ½ the lemon for 10 minutes, or until just tender. Refresh the salsify under cold running water, then peel off the black skin. Cut the salsify into 2.5cm/1in sticks.

4. Put the scallops and salsify into a bowl with the juice of the remaining ½ lemon, a pinch of cayenne and the parsley and season with pepper.

5. Season the cream with salt and pepper.

6. Divide the scallops and salsify between the 4 scallop shells on a baking tray and spoon over the cream. Mix the Gruyère cheese with the breadcrumbs and sprinkle them over the top.

7. Bake at the top of the preheated oven for 10–15 minutes, or until the top is brown and the cream is bubbling at the edges (if there is no colour, finish off under a hot grill). Garnish with the chopped parsley and serve immediately with hot French bread.

 AUSTRALIAN CHARDONNAY

WINTER SEAFOOD STEW WITH SAFFRON

SERVES 4

16 live mussels
4 large scallops
16 live clams
4 Pacific oysters, shucked (see page 136)
225g/8oz brill fillet, skinned (see page 133)
225g/8oz sea bass fillet, skinned (see page 133)
2 shallots, finely chopped
30g/1oz butter
570ml/1 pint well-flavoured fish stock (see page 626)
5 tablespoons vermouth
a large pinch of saffron strands
grated zest of 1 orange
salt and freshly ground black pepper
150ml/¼ pint double cream
juice of ½ lemon

To garnish
finely chopped fresh parsley

1. Prepare the shellfish: scrub the mussels well under cold running water. Pull away the 'beards' (seaweed-like threads). Throw away any mussels that are cracked or that remain open when tapped.
2. Remove the tough muscle (found opposite the roe) from the scallops. Scrub the clams under cold running water. Remove the oysters from their shells and set aside.
3. Cut each brill and sea bass fillet into 4 pieces. Refrigerate until required.
4. Soften the shallots in the butter in a saucepan for 10 minutes, or until soft. Add the stock, vermouth, saffron and orange zest and season to taste with salt and pepper.
5. Poach the fish and the shellfish in the flavoured stock for 2–3 minutes, or until opaque: do not overcook. Lift out and keep warm.
6. Reduce the poaching liquid by boiling rapidly to 190ml/⅓ pint. Add the cream and bring back to the boil, then lower the heat and simmer until the sauce is of a syrupy consistency.
7. Return the fish and shellfish to the pan,

season with lemon juice, salt and pepper and heat through. Pile into a warmed serving dish and garnish with the parsley.

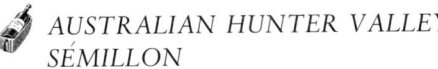

AUSTRALIAN HUNTER VALLEY SÉMILLON

SHELLFISH GRATIN

SERVES 6

30g/1oz butter
12 scallops, cleaned (see page 136)
12 raw tiger prawns, de-veined (see page 136)
6 oysters, shucked (see page 136)
225g/8oz smoked mussels (optional)
a pinch of cayenne pepper

For the sabayon
3 tablespoons white wine vinegar
2 egg yolks
1 egg
5 tablespoons double cream
salt and freshly ground black pepper
1 tablespoon grated Cheddar cheese

1. Preheat the grill to its highest setting.
2. Melt the butter in a large frying pan and fry the scallops over a high heat for 1 minute, until lightly browned. Put into a gratin dish. Fry the prawns in the same pan until nearly cooked through, then add the oysters and cook for a further minute. Pile into the gratin dish with the scallops, add the mussels, if using, and season with the cayenne.
3. Make the sabayon: put the vinegar into a small saucepan and simmer until reduced to about 1 tablespoon.
4. Put the egg yolks, egg and cream into a heatproof bowl set over, not in, a saucepan of simmering water, add the reduced vinegar and whisk until light and mousse-like. Season to taste with salt and pepper.
5. Spoon the mixture over the shellfish and sprinkle with the cheese. Grill for 1 minute, or until lightly browned. Serve very hot.

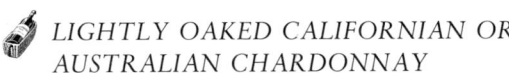

LIGHTLY OAKED CALIFORNIAN OR AUSTRALIAN CHARDONNAY

POULTRY AND GAME

COCONUT CHICKEN WITH MANGO

SERVES 4

4 chicken breasts, skinned
30g/1oz butter
1 large onion, finely chopped
1 clove of garlic, crushed
1 tablespoon curry powder
2 teaspoons garam masala
425ml/¾ pint white stock, made with chicken
    bones (see page 625)
110g/4oz creamed coconut
salt and freshly ground black pepper
150ml/¼ pint Greek yoghurt
1 large mango, halved, peeled and sliced
55g/2oz blanched almonds, toasted
3 tablespoons roughly chopped fresh coriander
    leaves

To serve
Thai sticky rice (see page 659)

1. Trim the chicken breasts of any fat. Cover
and refrigerate.
2. Melt the butter in a large sauté pan, add the
onion and cook over a very low heat until
golden-brown (this may take up to 1 hour). Add
the garlic, curry powder and garam masala and
cook for a further 3 minutes.
3. Add the stock and creamed coconut to the
pan and season to taste with salt and pepper.
Bring to the boil, then lower the heat so that the
liquid barely simmers. Add the chicken breasts,
cover the pan and cook over a very low heat for
20–25 minutes, or until the chicken is cooked
and feels firm to the touch.

4. Lift the chicken from the sauce and keep
warm. Reduce the liquid to a syrupy
consistency if necessary by boiling rapidly, then
add the yoghurt, mango and almonds and
season to taste with salt and pepper. Return the
chicken to the pan and add the coriander leaves.
Pile into a warmed serving dish and serve with
the rice handed separately.

 GERMAN FRUITY WHITE

CHICKEN AND RED PEPPER PIE

SERVES 4

225g/8oz flour quantity rough puff pastry (see
    page 644)
1 egg, beaten, to glaze

For the filling
450g/1lb boneless cooked chicken
45g/1½oz butter
1 small onion, finely chopped
110g/4oz button mushrooms, wiped and
    trimmed
30g/1oz plain flour
290ml/½ pint well-flavoured white stock, made
    with chicken bones (see page 625)
2 red peppers, grilled, de-seeded and peeled
5 tablespoons double cream
salt and freshly ground black pepper

1. Roll the pastry into a rectangle and cut out a
lid and strip for the lip to fit a 1.35 litre/3 pint
oval or round pie dish. Cut out leaves or other
decorations from the pastry trimmings. Put the

pastry on to a baking sheet, cover and refrigerate.

2. Remove any fat, skin, gristle and bone from the chicken. Cut the chicken into large bite-sized pieces, cover and refrigerate.

3. Melt the butter in a saucepan, add the onion, cover and cook for 7–10 minutes, or until soft and transparent. Add the mushrooms and cook for a further 5–7 minutes.

4. Add the flour and cook over a low heat for 1–2 minutes. Add the stock and bring to the boil, stirring continuously. Once the sauce comes to the boil, lower the heat and simmer for 3–4 minutes.

5. Meanwhile, cut the peppers into strips and add to the sauce. Stir in the cream and season to taste with salt and pepper. Turn into a bowl and allow to cool.

6. Preheat the oven to 190°C/375°F/gas mark 5.

7. Add the chicken to the cold sauce and put into the pie dish.

8. Dampen the edge of the dish, press the pastry strip on to the dish and brush with a little beaten egg. Put the pastry lid on top, press to seal the edges and trim off the excess.

9. Make a hole in the top of the pie and arrange the pastry leaves or other decorations on top. Brush the pastry with beaten egg and knock up the edges. Place the dish on a baking sheet and chill for 10 minutes.

10. Brush the pastry with a second light coating of the beaten egg and bake on the top shelf of the preheated oven for 25–30 minutes, or until the pastry is golden-brown and the filling piping hot.

11. Serve very hot.

 *PINOT NOIR*

TURKEY, HAM AND STILTON RAISED PIE

SERVES 4

For the hot watercrust pastry
450g/1lb plain flour
1 teaspoon salt

2 eggs, beaten
75ml/2½fl oz water
110g/4oz butter
55g/2oz lard

For the filling
450g/1lb cooked turkey leg meat
110g/4oz cooked ham
110g/4oz Stilton cheese, cubed
1 onion, finely chopped
2 tablespoons chopped fresh parsley
salt and freshly ground black pepper
1 egg, beaten

For the aspic
3 tablespoons tarragon vinegar
10g/⅓oz powdered gelatine
290ml/½ pint white stock, made with turkey bones (see page 625)

1. Wrap a piece of clingfilm around the outside of a 1 litre/1¾ pint soufflé dish, tucking the overlapping edge inside. Place the dish, upturned, on a baking sheet.

2. Sift the flour with the salt into a bowl. Make a dip in the middle, break the eggs into it and toss a liberal covering of flour over the eggs.

3. Put the water, butter and lard into a saucepan and bring slowly to the boil.

4. Once the liquid is boiling, pour it on to the flour, mixing with a knife as you do so. Knead until all the egg streaks have gone and the dough is smooth.

5. Wrap the dough in clingfilm and chill for 15 minutes.

6. Reserve one-third of the pastry for the lid, wrap in clingfilm and set aside. Roll out the remaining dough into a circle and drape it over the upturned soufflé dish. Working fast, shape the pastry to cover the dish to a depth of about 6cm/2.5in. Refrigerate for 4 hours or overnight.

7. When the pastry is hard, carefully remove the soufflé dish and the clingfilm and place the pastry case on the baking sheet ready to fill.

8. Preheat the oven to 190°C/375°F/gas mark 5. Roll out the reserved pastry for the pie lid.

9. Cut the turkey and ham into large cubes. Trim away most of the fat and all of the skin and gristle. Mix with the Stilton cheese, onion and parsley and season with salt and plenty of pepper.

10. Pile the filling into the pastry case, pressing it firmly into the corners, and cover with the pastry lid. Press the edges together to seal. Use any pastry trimmings to cut out leaves or other decorations for the top of the pie. Make a neat hole in the middle of the lid. Secure a sheet of silicone paper around the pie with a paper clip. Brush the lid with beaten egg, arrange the pastry decorations on top and brush with more beaten egg.

11. Bake the pie in the preheated oven for 30 minutes. Reduce the oven temperature to 170°C/325°F/gas mark 3. Remove the silicone paper and brush the pastry evenly all over with beaten egg. Bake for a further 30 minutes. Remove the pie from the oven and leave to cool completely.

12. Make the aspic: put the vinegar into a small saucepan and sprinkle over the gelatine. Leave to sponge for 5 minutes, then melt over a low heat without boiling and stir into the stock.

13. Using a funnel, fill up the pie with the aspic, allow to set slightly and then add more aspic until the pie is completely full. Chill for 2 hours to allow the jelly to set before serving.

 *CRU BOURGEOIS RED BORDEAUX*

GALANTINE OF DUCK WITH FOIE GRAS

SERVES 10

1.8kg/4lb duck, boned (see page 127)
2 tablespoons cognac
2 tablespoons tawny port
110g/4oz pork fat, cubed
2 shallots, finely chopped
1 clove of garlic, crushed
2 tablespoons chopped fresh thyme
1 bay leaf
salt and freshly ground black pepper
melted butter
1.7 litres/3 pints well-seasoned duck stock (see page 626)

For the stuffing
340g/12oz foie gras, at room temperature
2 tablespoons cognac
55g/2oz fresh cèpes
30g/1oz butter, unsalted
1 clove of garlic, crushed
1 fresh truffle, finely chopped

To garnish
Sauternes jelly (see page 504)
sprigs of fresh chervil

1. Remove any feathers from the duck. Remove the skin, then put both the skin and the meat into a bowl with the cognac, port, pork fat, shallots, garlic, thyme, bay leaf and plenty of pepper. Cover and refrigerate overnight. Remove the skin and bay leaf, reserving the skin, and pass the duck meat and its flavourings through a mincer or whizz in a food processor using the pulse action.

2. Begin to make the stuffing: separate the lobes of the foie gras and remove any blood vessels. (If it is at all bloody it must be soaked in salty milk for 1 hour.) Sprinkle with the cognac and leave at room temperature for 2 hours.

3. Wipe the cèpes with damp kitchen paper and cut into slices. Melt the butter in a frying pan, add the cèpes and cook over a low heat until soft. Stir in the garlic, season with salt and pepper and cook for 1 further minute. Tip out of the pan and leave on a plate until cold.

4. To assemble: dip a large piece of muslin in the melted butter and lay on a work surface. Season well with salt and pepper.

5. Lay the skin, inside uppermost, on the muslin and season with salt and pepper.

6. Season the minced duck meat well with salt and spread over the skin in a large rectangle, leaving a 2.5cm/1in gap at the edges. Sprinkle over the cèpes and truffle. Season with salt and pepper.

7. Roll the foie gras into a cylinder and lay over the centre of the duck. Roll up the duck to form a cylinder, making sure that the foie gras is in the middle. Sew the edges of the skin together with fine string, using large loose stitches.

8. Roll the muslin around the duck and tie each end securely with string. Tie 3 lengths of string

loosely along the middle for extra support.
9. Place the duck in a large saucepan and cover with the stock. Gently heat the stock. Cook for 1½–1¾ hours, or until the duck is cooked through (it is essential that the temperature of the stock does not exceed 80°C/175°F throughout the cooking process, so it must be checked regularly).
10. Turn off the heat and leave to cool in the stock. For hygiene reasons it is better to put the duck pan into a sink of cold water to speed up the cooling process.
11. Remove the duck from the stock and refrigerate overnight. Remove the muslin and string carefully. Serve cut into thin slices, garnished with chopped Sauternes jelly and sprigs of chervil.

 TOP-QUALITY ALSACE PINOT GRIS

ROAST MALLARD WITH GLAZED LIMEQUATS

SERVES 4

2 × 675g/1½lb oven-ready mallards
salt and freshly ground black pepper

For the glaze
225g/8oz limequats, thinly sliced
150ml/¼ pint water
1 teaspoon mustard seeds
2 tablespoons demerara sugar
2 tablespoons brandy
1 tablespoon sesame seeds, toasted

For the gravy
290ml/½ pint white stock, made with chicken
*   bones (see page 625)*
2 teaspoons arrowroot

1. Preheat the oven to 200°C/400°F/gas mark 6.
2. Pick over the duck, removing any remaining feathers, and cut off the parson's nose, including the fat gland which is just underneath. Prick the duck all over with a fork and season well with salt and a little pepper.

Put the duck into a roasting tin and roast in the preheated oven for 30–35 minutes.
3. Meanwhile, make the glaze: put the limequats into a saucepan with the water and bring to the boil, then lower the heat and simmer for 5–7 minutes, or until the limequats are soft. Add the mustard seeds and cook for a further minute, then stir in the sugar and continue to cook over a low heat until the liquid has evaporated and the limequats are glazed. Add the brandy and sesame seeds and set aside.
4. When the duck is nearly cooked and the juices are still a little red, remove from the roasting tin. Strain any cooking juices, removing the fat, and set aside. Joint the duck and return to the roasting tin, skin side uppermost. Spoon the glazed limequats over the top of each duck joint and return to the oven for a further 10 minutes.
5. Meanwhile, make the gravy: put the reserved cooking juices into a saucepan, add the stock and bring to the boil, then lower the heat and simmer for 5–6 minutes. Slake in the arrowroot, bring back to the boil and season to taste with salt and pepper, then lower the heat and continue to simmer until of a syrupy consistency. Strain into a warmed sauce-boat.
6. Lift the duck joints on to a warmed serving dish. Hand the sauce separately.

NOTE: Limequats are a cross between a Mexican lime and the little bitter-orange kumquat. They are grown commercially in Israel and are in season during the winter months. In their absence use kumquats instead.

 *PINOT NOIR*

ROAST DUCKLING WITH WHITE PORT AND CHUNKY MARMALADE SAUCE

SERVES 3

1 large oven-ready duckling
salt and freshly ground black pepper
½ orange, halved
½ onion, halved

For the sauce
225g/8oz chunky bitter orange marmalade
150ml/¼ pint white port
290ml/½ pint white stock, made with chicken
  bones (see page 625)

To garnish
2 oranges, segmented
1 bunch of watercress

1. Preheat the oven to 220°C/425°F/gas mark 7.
2. Prepare the duckling: cut off the parson's nose, including the fat gland which is just underneath. Using a fork, prick the skin all over, concentrating particularly on the fatty areas and trying not to stab the flesh below the skin. Season the cavity well with salt and pepper. Place the orange and onion inside the duckling and rub salt all over the skin.
3. Place the duckling, breast side down, on a wire rack in a roasting tin and roast near the top of the preheated oven for 20 minutes.
4. Make the sauce: put the marmalade, port and stock into a saucepan and heat gently until the marmalade has melted. Simmer for 5 minutes.
5. Pour off the fat from the roasting tin and reserve for roast potatoes. Turn the duckling over and continue roasting until cooked – about 25–30 minutes if you like the duckling a little pink, or 40 minutes if you like it cooked through completely. Test by piercing the thigh with a skewer; if the skewer comes out hot to the touch the duckling is ready. The juices will run pink; if you like the duckling well done, return it to the oven until they run clear.

6. Tip the juices from the duckling cavity into a glass jug or bowl together with any juices in the roasting tin. Allow the fat to rise to the top. Using a baster remove all the juices from the bottom of the jug or bowl, leaving all the fat behind, and add to the marmalade sauce.
7. Place the duckling on a board over a tray, to collect any further juices to add to the sauce, and joint it into 6 pieces. Arrange on a warmed serving dish and keep warm, without covering, so as not to spoil the crisp skin.
8. Bring the sauce back to the boil, then lower the heat and simmer for 2 minutes or until it is of a good, syrupy consistency. Season to taste with salt and pepper and pour into a warmed sauce-boat.
9. Garnish the duck with the orange segments and watercress. Hand the sauce separately.

 RED CÔTES DU RHÔNE

CARAMELIZED BREAST OF DUCK WITH HONEY, LIME AND GINGER SAUCE

This recipe was given to us by Alex Floyd, head chef of Leith's restaurant.

SERVES 4

4 × 200g/7oz duck breasts
salt and freshly ground black pepper
caster sugar
2 limes
2 tablespoons olive oil
30g/1oz unsalted butter
3 tablespoons clear honey
180ml/6fl oz dry white wine
225ml/8fl oz good brown stock (see page 625)
30g/1oz fresh root ginger, peeled and cut into
  fine slivers

1. Preheat the oven to 230°C/450°F/gas mark 8.
2. Score the duck skin in a lattice pattern with a sharp knife. Rub salt, pepper and sugar into the skin.

3. Using a potato peeler, pare the zest of the limes very thinly, so there is no pith. Cut into julienne strips. Blanch the lime zest in boiling water for 15 seconds, then refresh in cold water and drain.

4. Peel the limes with a knife, removing all the pith. Save any juice. Cut into neat segments, discarding the membrane.

5. Heat the oil in a large, heavy-based frying pan, add the butter and when sizzling place the duck breasts, fat side down, in the pan and fry for 1 minute. Turn the breasts over and place them, fat side up, on a wire rack over a roasting tin. Brush with half the honey and bake in the preheated oven for 7 minutes.

6. Meanwhile, pour all but 1 tablespoon of the fat from the frying pan. Add the wine, reserved lime juice and the remaining honey and boil until the liquid has reduced by half.

7. Add the stock and ginger and return to the boil. Lower the heat and simmer until the sauce starts to thicken.

8. Remove the duck breasts from the oven, slice and arrange on 4 individual plates. Add any meat juices to the sauce and simmer for a further 1–2 minutes. Strain and pour over the duck.

9. Garnish with the lime segments and sprinkle with the lime zest.

 *ALSACE TOKAY*

BONED GOOSE WITH DUCK, VEAL AND CHESTNUT STUFFING

SERVES 10

1 medium oven-ready goose, boned (see page 127), bones reserved
salt and freshly ground black pepper

For the stock
2 tablespoons sunflower oil
1 carrot, diced
2 leeks, sliced
1 stick of celery, diced
2 cloves of garlic, bruised
1 bouquet garni
1 teaspoon tomato purée
2 glasses of white wine
2 glasses of red wine
1 glass of dry sherry

For the stuffing
30g/1oz butter
1 red onion, finely chopped
2 × 340g/12oz duck breasts, skin removed
340g/12oz minced veal or pork
1 × 400g/14oz can of unsweetened chestnut
*   purée*
85g/3oz fresh white breadcrumbs
1 egg, beaten
55g/2oz dried apples, chopped
55g/2oz dried pears, chopped
1 tablespoon chopped fresh sage
3 tablespoons Calvados
salt and freshly ground black pepper

1. Preheat the oven to 190°C/375°F/gas mark 5.

2. Make the stock: brown the goose bones in the oil in a large flameproof casserole, add the vegetables and cook until well browned. Add the garlic, bouquet garni, tomato purée, wines and sherry, then bring to the boil and boil until the liquid is reduced by half.

3. Cover the bones with cold water and bring to the boil, then skim. Lower the heat and allow to simmer very gently for 2–3 hours. Skim frequently.

4. Make the stuffing: melt the butter in a saucepan, add the onion and cook over a low heat until soft but not coloured. Remove from the heat and allow to cool completely.

5. Chop the duck breasts finely in a food processor. Mix with the cooled onion and all the remaining ingredients except the Calvados, and season to taste with salt and pepper.

6. Lay the goose, skin side down, on a board. Remove any excess fat. Pile on the stuffing and roll the goose up into a neat roll, making sure that all the untidy ends are tucked in. Sew up neatly, using a needle and fine string. Calculate the cooking time, allowing 15 minutes per 450g/1lb plus an extra 15 minutes.

7. Prick the goose all over with a fork and season well with salt and pepper. Place on a wire rack over a roasting tin and roast in the preheated oven, basting occasionally.

8. When the goose is cooked, remove the string, and transfer to a serving dish. Return to the turned-off oven.

9. Tip all the fat and juices from the roasting tin into a large glass bowl. Allow the fat to rise to the top. Using a baster, remove the juices from the bottom of the bowl, leaving all the fat behind, and return the juices to a clean saucepan.

10. Strain the goose stock, add 1.1 litres/2 pints to the roasting juices and bring to the boil, then lower the heat and allow to simmer for 8–10 minutes, or until well reduced, skimming frequently. Add the Calvados and continue to simmer for a further 2–3 minutes. Strain into a warmed sauce-boat.

11. Carve the goose and hand the sauce separately.

 *RED BURGUNDY*

FESTIVE ROAST GOOSE

SERVES 6

1 × 4.5kg/10lb oven-ready goose
salt and freshly ground black pepper
½ lemon

For the stuffing
30g/1oz butter
1 onion, finely chopped
1 clove of garlic, crushed
1 large baking potato, peeled and cut into 1cm/
* ½in cubes*
225g/8oz fresh chestnuts
285g/10oz minced pork
1 dessert apple, peeled, cored and roughly
* chopped*
2 tablespoons chopped fresh sage
55g/2oz good-quality candied orange peel,
* finely chopped*
1 egg
salt and freshly ground black pepper

To finish
1 tablespoon clear honey

For the gravy
1 tablespoon plain flour
570ml/1 pint potato water or white stock, made
* with chicken bones (see page 625)*
2 tablespoons Calvados

To garnish
1 bunch of watercress

1. Wipe the goose all over. Season the inside with salt and pepper and rub with the cut lemon.

2. Preheat the oven to 190°C/375°F/gas mark 5.

3. Make the stuffing: melt the butter in a saucepan, add the onion and cook for about 10 minutes until soft but not coloured. Add the garlic to the onion and cook for a further minute. Tip on to a plate and cool. Cook the potato in boiling salted water for about 5 minutes, or until just tender. Drain and cool.

4. Pierce the flat side of the chestnuts with a sharp knife. Place them on a baking sheet and roast them at the top of the preheated oven for 10–15 minutes, or until they smell roasted. Remove from the oven and when they are cool enough to handle, peel off the skins and chop the nuts roughly.

5. Put all the stuffing ingredients into a large bowl and mix well together. Season to taste with salt and pepper.

6. Fill the goose cavity with the stuffing. Weigh the stuffed goose to calculate the cooking time, allowing 15 minutes per 450g/1lb plus an extra 15 minutes.

7. Prick the goose all over with a fork and sprinkle with salt. Place on a wire rack over a roasting tin. Roast in the preheated oven, removing the fat from the roasting tin with a baster from time to time. Reserve for use in cooking. If the goose gets too dark, cover it with kitchen foil.

8. Ten minutes before the bird is cooked, brush the honey evenly over the skin. When the goose is cooked (a metal skewer inserted into the centre of the stuffing for 10 seconds should come out hot), place on a serving plate and return to the turned-off oven to keep warm.

9. Make the gravy: tip all the fat and juices out of the roasting tin into a glass jug or bowl, leaving 1 tablespoon of fat behind. Add the flour to the roasting tin and stir with a whisk over a direct heat until the flour starts to brown gently. Using a baster, remove the juices from the bottom of the bowl, leaving all the fat behind, and add them to the roasting tin. Whisk well to prevent lumps forming. Gradually add the potato water or stock and bring to the boil. Skim off any scum that rises to the surface with a basting spoon. Increase the heat and boil until of a syrupy consistency, then add the Calvados and season to taste with salt and pepper. Check the seasoning and strain into a warmed sauce-boat.

10. Garnish the goose with the watercress and hand the gravy separately.

 *RED BURGUNDY*

BRAISED GROUSE WITH SPROUTS, BACON AND SHERRY

SERVES 4

4 grouse, plucked and drawn
1 apple, quartered and cored
salt and freshly ground black pepper
30g/1oz clarified butter
110g/4oz rindless rashers of smoked streaky bacon, thinly sliced
1 large onion, finely chopped
340g/12oz Brussels sprouts, trimmed and halved
1 bay leaf
150ml/¼ pint sweet sherry
150ml/¼ pint game stock or brown stock (see pages 625, 626)
110g/4oz plain flour
water

1. Preheat the oven to 150°C/300°F/gas mark 2.
2. Remove any stray feathers and shot from the grouse. Place a piece of apple inside the cavity of each bird and season the outside with salt and pepper.

3. Heat half the butter in a deep flameproof casserole. Fry the grouse until browned on all sides. Transfer them to a plate.

4. Heat the remaining butter in the casserole, add the bacon and fry until golden-brown. Remove the bacon with a slotted spoon and fry the onion in the bacon fat until starting to brown at the edges. Add the Brussels sprouts and continue to fry until the onion is golden-brown. Add the bay leaf and sherry. Bring to the boil, then lower the heat and simmer for 5 minutes, or until the liquid has almost evaporated. Sprinkle the bacon on top of the sprouts and arrange the grouse on top of the vegetables.

5. Pour the stock into the casserole around the grouse, bring to the boil and cover with a close-fitting lid. Turn off the heat.

6. Mix the flour with enough water to make a thick paste. Spread the paste around the lid to prevent the steam from escaping.

7. Bake the grouse in the middle of the preheated oven for 45 minutes.

8. Break off the huff paste and serve the grouse with the vegetables and their juices.

 NEW ZEALAND PINOT NOIR OR CRU CLASSÉ CLARET

PARTRIDGE STUFFED WITH CRANBERRIES AND PISTACHIOS WITH A RICH GAME SAUCE

SERVES 4

4 oven-ready partridges
1 small onion, finely chopped
45g/1½oz unsalted butter
55g/2oz rindless streaky bacon, finely chopped
85g/3oz cranberries
15g/½oz sugar
1 tablespoon water

375g/12oz boneless pheasant or chicken meat,
  skin removed and minced
1 egg
30g/1oz fresh white breadcrumbs
30g/1oz shelled pistachios, roughly chopped
salt and freshly ground black pepper

For the gravy
2 teaspoons plain flour
570ml/1 pint game stock (see page 626)
55ml/2fl oz port

To garnish
1 bunch of watercress, washed and trimmed

To serve
braised red cabbage with raspberry vinegar (see
  page 568)

1. Preheat the oven to 180°C/350°F/gas mark 4.
2. Remove any remaining feathers from the
partridges. Bone out the central cavity of the
birds (see page 127), starting from the back,
leaving the wing and leg/thigh joints intact.
3. Sweat the onion slowly in 15g/½oz of the
butter in a small saucepan.
4. Fry the bacon in its own fat until golden-
brown, drain off any excess fat and tip on to a
plate to cool.
5. Put the cranberries, sugar and water into a
small heavy-based saucepan and cook over a
low heat until the cranberries have softened.
Tip on to a plate to cool.
6. Mix together the onion, bacon, pheasant or
chicken, egg, breadcrumbs, cranberries and
pistachios and season to taste with salt and
pepper.
7. Open out the partridges, flesh side
uppermost, and season well with salt and
pepper. Divide the stuffing between the birds,
then sew them up carefully with thin string,
using large, loose stitches.
8. Heat the remaining butter in a sauté pan and
when foaming add the partridges. Brown
carefully on all sides, using wooden spoons to
turn the birds over. Put the sauté pan into the
middle of the oven and cook for 25 minutes.
The partridges are cooked when a skewer
inserted into the central cavity comes out hot.

9. Transfer the partridges to a warming oven to
rest for 15 minutes.
10. Make the gravy: tip the excess fat out of the
pan, then add the flour. Stir over a medium heat
until lightly browned, then add the stock and
port. Bring to the boil, stirring, then allow to
reduce by boiling rapidly to a syrupy
consistency.
11. Remove the string carefully from the
partridges. Arrange on a warmed serving dish
and garnish with the watercress. Strain the
gravy into a warmed sauce-boat and serve with
braised red cabbage with raspberry vinegar.

 RED CÔTES DU RHÔNE

PHEASANT EN PAPILLOTE

SERVES 4

4 × 170g/6oz pheasant breasts, skin removed
freshly ground black pepper
8 rindless rashers of streaky bacon
2 tablespoons chopped fresh rosemary
oil for brushing
4 teaspoons redcurrant jelly

To serve
bread sauce (see page 631)

1. Preheat the oven to 200°C/400°F/gas mark 6.
Preheat the grill to its highest setting.
2. Season the pheasant breasts well with pepper.
3. Lay 2 rashers of bacon side by side on a
board and stretch them out with the back of a
knife. Sprinkle over ½ tablespoon of the
rosemary. Lay a pheasant breast at one end and
roll up, securing the bacon with a wooden
cocktail stick. Repeat with the remaining
pheasant breasts.
4. Lay the pheasant breasts on a baking sheet
and grill for 3 minutes on each side until the
bacon is golden-brown. Set aside to cool.
5. Cut out 4 × 30cm/12in greaseproof paper
circles. Take a circle and brush with oil. Lay a
pheasant breast on one side of the paper.

545

Spread with 1 teaspoon of redcurrant jelly. Fold over the greaseproof paper to enclose the pheasant breast and twist the edges of the paper together so it is completely sealed.

6. Repeat with the remaining pheasant breasts.

7. Place the parcels on a baking sheet and bake at the top of the preheated oven for 10 minutes.

8. Place the parcels on individual plates and leave for the diners to open. Hand the bread sauce separately.

 *CLARET*

DRY-SPICED PIGEON BREASTS WITH CELERIAC RÖSTI

SERVES 4

4 pigeon breasts, skinned
55g/2oz clarified butter
2 teaspoons garam masala
1 teaspoon curry powder
2 teaspoons ground ginger
1 teaspoon dry English mustard
2 teaspoons caster sugar
2 teaspoons ground coriander
salt and freshly ground black pepper

For the rösti
1 onion, finely chopped
55g/2oz butter, melted
340g/12oz celeriac
salt and freshly ground black pepper
freshly grated nutmeg

To serve
sprigs of fresh coriander

1. Preheat the oven to 180°C/350°F/gas mark 4.

2. Make the rösti: sweat the onion in half the butter until soft, then allow to cool.

3. Peel the celeriac and grate on the coarse side of the grater. Mix with the softened onion and season to taste with salt, pepper and nutmeg.

4. Brush 8 patty tins with the remaining butter. Pack each tin generously with the celeriac mixture. Bake on the middle shelf of the preheated oven for 20–25 minutes, or until the celeriac is soft. Keep warm.

5. Meanwhile, prepare the pigeon: brush each pigeon breast with a little of the clarified butter and set aside.

6. Mix together the spices, mustard and sugar and season lightly with salt and pepper.

7. Roll each pigeon breast in the spices mixture. Heat the remaining butter in a frying pan. Fry the pigeon breasts over a medium heat for 1 minute on each side, or until browned. Lower the heat and cook gently for a further 1–2 minutes on each side, or until the pigeon is just cooked. Remove from the heat.

8. To serve: arrange the celeriac rösti on a large warmed serving dish and put the pigeon breasts on top. Garnish with the coriander and serve immediately.

 RED CÔTES DU RHÔNE

POT-ROASTED QUAIL WITH SHALLOTS, MUSHROOMS AND CAPERS

SERVES 4

8 quail
15g/½oz butter
2 tablespoons olive oil
450g/1lb button onions, peeled
2 cloves of garlic, crushed
2 teaspoons ground coriander
5 tablespoons dry sherry
5 tablespoons chicken stock
225g/8oz chestnut mushrooms, quartered
salt and freshly ground black pepper
4 tablespoons crème fraîche
2 tablespoons capers, rinsed

1. Preheat the oven to 180°C/350°F/gas mark 4.

2. Wipe the quail and remove the trussing

strings. Singe and remove any feathers if necessary.

3. Heat the butter and oil in a flameproof casserole, add the quail and brown all over. Remove from the casserole and set aside.

4. Lower the heat, add the onions to the casserole and cook for 4–5 minutes. Add the garlic and coriander and cook for a further 2–3 minutes. Add the sherry, stock and mushrooms and season well with salt and pepper. Return the quail to the casserole and bring the cooking liquor to the boil.

5. Cover the casserole and pot-roast for 25 minutes.

6. Remove the quail and split them in half. Arrange on a warmed serving plate. Lift out the onions and mushrooms with a slotted spoon and pile on top of the quail. Skim as much fat as possible from the cooking liquor. Strain into a clean saucepan and bring to the boil, then lower the heat and simmer until reduced by half.

7. Add the crème fraîche and bring back to the boil. Stir in the capers and season to taste with salt and pepper.

8. Pour over the quail and serve immediately.

 *PINOT NOIR*

MARINATED ROAST WILD BOAR

This recipe was given to us by Fiona Burrell, former Principal of Leith's School. You need to start this at least 36 hours before serving.

SERVES 8–10

1 × 2.7kg/6lb haunch of wild boar
2 tablespoons olive oil
30g/1oz butter
salt and freshly ground black pepper
a large piece of pork fat to cover the boar

For the marinade
4 tablespoons olive oil
1 medium onion, sliced
1 small carrot, chopped

1 small stick of celery, chopped
2 cloves of garlic, crushed
1 bay leaf
2 tablespoons chopped fresh rosemary
1 tablespoon coriander seeds, crushed
6 cloves
freshly ground black pepper
290ml/½ pint red wine

For the gravy
2 tablespoons plain flour
570ml/1 pint brown stock (see page 625)
salt and freshly ground black pepper

To garnish
2–3 sprigs of fresh rosemary

1. Trim the wild boar, removing any membranes.

2. Make the marinade: heat the oil in a sauté pan over a low heat and add the onion, carrot and celery. Cook over a low heat for 5 minutes. Add the garlic and cook for a further 2 minutes. Add the bay leaf, rosemary, coriander seeds, cloves, a little pepper and the wine. Bring to the boil, then lower the heat and simmer for 5 minutes. Remove from the heat and allow to cool completely.

3. Put the boar into a non-metallic bowl, pour over the cold marinade and turn the meat over to ensure it is completely coated. Leave to marinate for 36 hours, turning occasionally.

4. Preheat the oven to 180°C/350°F/gas mark 4. Lift the meat out of the marinade and remove any vegetables sticking to it. Reserve the marinade. Heat the oil and butter in a roasting tin. Put in the boar and season with salt and pepper, then cover with pork fat and a greased piece of kitchen foil to cover the whole tin. Roast in the middle of the preheated oven for 3 hours.

5. Meanwhile, begin to make the gravy: strain the marinade into a saucepan and reduce by half by boiling rapidly.

6. When the wild boar is cooked, allow to stand on a warmed serving dish for 15 minutes while finishing the gravy.

7. Strain the cooking juices from the roasting tin into a jug. Spoon 3 tablespoons of the fat back into the tin, stir in the flour and cook over a medium heat for 2–3 minutes to allow the flour to brown. Stir in the reduced marinade, stock and any reserved cooking juices and bring to the boil, then lower the heat and simmer for 7–10 minutes, or until of a syrupy consistency. Season to taste with salt and pepper and strain into a warmed sauce-boat. Carve the boar and garnish with the sprigs of rosemary. Hand the sauce separately.

 NEW WORLD CABERNET SAUVIGNON

VENISON FILLET WITH RASPBERRY VINEGAR AND BITTER CHOCOLATE SAUCE

SERVES 4

900g/2lb venison fillet, trimmed
salt and freshly ground black pepper
1 tablespoon sunflower oil
2 shallots, finely chopped
4 tablespoons raspberry vinegar
4 tablespoons port
425ml/¾ pint strong brown stock (see page 625)
30g/1oz unsalted butter, diced
15g/½oz bitter chocolate

To garnish
110g/4oz fresh raspberries

To serve
Winter game chip baskets (see page 570)

1. Preheat the oven to 200°C/400°F/gas mark 6.
2. Tie string around the venison fillet to give it a cylindrical shape. Season on all sides with salt and pepper. Chill for 30 minutes.
3. Heat the oil in a heavy-based frying pan and brown the venison evenly all over. Transfer to a small roasting tin and roast in the oven for 10–15 minutes, or until a skewer inserted into the

centre comes out hot. Remove from the oven and allow to rest for 5 minutes.
4. Add the shallots to the frying pan and cook over a medium heat until golden. Add the vinegar and reduce by boiling rapidly to 1 tablespoon. Add the port and reduce again. Add the stock and reduce by half.
5. Add the butter, whisking well, then remove from the heat and add the chocolate. Stir until smooth.
6. Remove the string from the venison and cut into 4 medallions. Add any juices in the roasting pan to the sauce.
7. Arrange the venison medallions on 4 warmed individual plates. Strain the sauce into a jug, taste and adjust the seasoning if necessary and pour around the venison.
8. Garnish with the raspberries and serve with the Winter game chip baskets.

 FULL-BODIED RED

VENISON TOAD-IN-THE-HOLE WITH RED WINE AND ONION GRAVY

SERVES 4

30g/1oz beef dripping or 4 tablespoons sunflower oil
8 venison sausages

For the batter
110g/4oz plain flour
½ teaspoon salt
1 tablespoon chopped fresh parsley
1 tablespoon chopped fresh chives
2 eggs
150ml/¼ pint milk mixed with 150ml/¼ pint water

For the gravy
2 Spanish onions, very thinly sliced
15g/½oz butter
1 teaspoon plain flour
150ml/¼ pint red wine

290ml/½ pint brown stock, preferably made
   with game bones (see page 625)
150ml/¼ pint port
1 tablespoon redcurrant jelly
salt and freshly ground black pepper

To serve
green salad

1. Make the batter: sift the flour and salt into a large bowl. Add the parsley and chives. Make a well or hollow in the centre of the flour and break the eggs into it.
2. Using a whisk or wooden spoon, mix the eggs to a paste and very gradually draw in the surrounding flour, adding just enough milk and water to the eggs to keep the central mixture a fairly thin paste. When all the flour is incorporated, stir in the remaining milk and water. The batter can be made more speedily by putting all the ingredients into a blender or food processor for a few seconds, but take care not to overwork or the mixture will be bubbly. Leave to rest at room temperature for 30 minutes before use. This allows the starch grains to swell, giving a lighter, less doughy result.
3. Preheat the oven to 220°C/425°F/gas mark 7.
4. Heat 1 tablespoon of the dripping or oil in a frying pan and fry the sausages until evenly browned all over, but do not cook them through.
5. Heat the remaining dripping or oil until smoking hot in an ovenproof shallow metal dish or roasting tin about 27.5 × 22.5cm/ 11 × 9in either in the oven or over direct heat. Add the sausages and pour in the batter.
6. Bake in the preheated oven for 40 minutes, or until the toad-in-the-hole is risen and brown.
7. Make the gravy: cook the onions in the butter in a heavy-based frying pan over a low heat until soft and golden-brown. Stir in the flour.
8. Add the wine and stir over a high heat until the wine thickens and there are no lumps. Boil the wine until reduced by two-thirds. Add the stock, port and redcurrant jelly and reduce by boiling rapidly until the sauce is of a syrupy consistency. Season to taste with salt and

pepper. Strain into a warmed sauce-boat and hand separately with the toad-in-the-hole.

 TOP-QUALITY AUSTRALIAN OR CALIFORNIAN CABERNET SAUVIGNON

PAN-FRIED VENISON STEAKS WITH SEVILLE ORANGE POTATO RÖSTI

SERVES 4

4 × 5cm/2in venison leg or loin steaks
salt and freshly ground black pepper
1 tablespoon juniper berries, crushed
2 tablespoons olive oil
2 tablespoons brandy
150ml/¼ pint brown stock (see page 625)
2 teaspoons arrowroot
1 tablespoon water

For the rösti
1 Seville orange
1 Spanish onion, finely chopped
1 tablespoon sunflower oil
900g/2lb waxy potatoes
salt and freshly ground black pepper
45g/1½oz butter

To garnish
sprigs of watercress

1. Make the rösti: cut the orange into quarters and cook in boiling water for 1 hour, or until soft. Drain and remove any pips and membrane from the orange, chop very finely and set aside.
2. Meanwhile, cook the onion in the oil until soft but not coloured.
3. Peel the potatoes and grate them coarsely. Place in a bowl and season with salt. Leave to stand for 20 minutes, then squeeze dry. Season with pepper. Fork in the orange and onion.
4. Heat the butter in the frying pan. Add the potato mixture and pat it lightly into a flat cake with straight sides.

5. Fry over a very low heat for about 15 minutes, or until the underside is crusty and golden-brown. Shake the pan from time to time to ensure that the cake does not stick.

6. Place a plate larger than the frying pan over the pan. Turn both plate and pan over and tip the rösti out on to the plate. Slip it immediately back into the pan and cook the other side for 10 minutes. Place in a warming oven for 15 minutes while cooking the venison steaks.

7. Trim the venison steaks of any tough membrane and season them with salt, pepper and juniper berries.

8. Heat the oil in a heavy frying pan, add the steaks and cook over a high heat to brown on both sides. Lower the heat and fry for about 4 minutes, depending on size, until cooked.

9. Remove the venison steaks to a warmed serving dish. Pour the fat out of the frying pan, add the brandy and ignite. When the flames subside, add the stock. Mix the arrowroot with the water and gradually add to the boiling liquid. Bring to the boil and reduce to a syrupy consistency. Season to taste with salt and pepper.

10. To serve: cut the rösti into 4 wedges and arrange on warmed individual plates. Put a venison steak on top of each, pour over a little of the sauce and garnish with a sprig of watercress.

 *CLARET*

BEEF

BEEF AND PICKLED WALNUT CARBONNADE

SERVES 4

675g/1½lb chuck steak
3 tablespoons olive oil
2 onions, thinly sliced
2 cloves of garlic, crushed
1 tablespoon soft dark brown sugar
2 teaspoons plain flour
290ml/½ pint Guinness
290ml/½ pint brown stock (see page 625)
10 pickled walnuts, halved
1 bay leaf
a pinch of freshly grated nutmeg
salt and freshly ground black pepper

To serve
beurre manié (optional, see page 108)

To garnish
1 tablespoon chopped fresh parsley

1. Preheat the oven to 150°C/300°F/gas mark 2.
2. Cut the beef into 5cm/2in steaks, cutting across the grain of the meat. Heat 1 tablespoon of the oil in a large frying pan and fry the meat a few pieces at a time until browned all over, transferring them to a flameproof casserole as they are done. If the bottom of the casserole becomes very dark or too dry, pour in a little water and swish it about, scraping off the sediment stuck to the bottom, then pour over the meat. Continue to brown the meat in the same way, adding a little more of the oil if necessary. When it is all browned, repeat the déglaçage (adding water and scraping the bottom of the casserole.

3. Heat the remaining oil in the casserole, add the onions and fry very slowly until they begin to brown, then add the garlic and sugar. Cook for a further minute, or until nicely brown.
4. Stir in the flour and cook, stirring, for 1 minute. Remove from the heat and pour in the Guinness and stock. Add the pickled walnuts, bay leaf and nutmeg and season lightly with salt and pepper.
5. Return to the heat and bring slowly to the boil, then simmer for 2 minutes, stirring continuously. Return the meat to the casserole, cover and cook in the preheated oven for 1½–2 hours, or until the meat is completely tender.
6. Using a slotted spoon, lift the meat, onion and walnuts into a clean casserole. Remove the bay leaf, check the seasoning and boil the sauce fast to reduce to a syrupy consistency. If the sauce is too salty do not reduce it, but thicken with a little beurre manié.
7. Pour the sauce over the beef, sprinkle with the parsley and serve immediately.

 *RED BORDEAUX*

SPICED BEEF WITH TROPICAL FRUITS

SERVES 4

675g/1½lb chuck or skirt steak
2 tablespoons olive oil
30g/1oz butter
2 large onions, thinly sliced
4 cloves of garlic, crushed
5cm/2in piece of fresh root ginger, peeled and
*   finely chopped*
2 teaspoons cumin seeds

8 dried chillies
1 teaspoon coriander seeds
1 teaspoon ground turmeric
1 teaspoon garam masala
30g/1oz creamed coconut
30g/1oz sweet tamarind
5 tablespoons boiling water
290ml/½ pint brown stock (see page 625)
salt and freshly ground black pepper

To serve
1 papaya
1 large plantain or 2 small unripe bananas
3 tablespoons chopped fresh coriander

To garnish
a few sprigs of fresh coriander

1. Preheat the oven to 170°C/325°F/gas mark 3.
2. Trim the meat of excess fat and gristle and cut across the grain into 5cm/2in steaks.
3. Heat the oil in a large flameproof casserole and brown the meat a few pieces at a time. Lift out and set aside and continue in the same way until all the meat is browned.
4. Add the butter to the casserole, lower the heat and add the onions. Cover and cook over a very low heat until the onions are very soft and golden-brown (this may take up to 45 minutes).
5. Meanwhile, put the garlic, ginger, cumin seeds, chillies, coriander seeds and 2 tablespoons of the stock into a blender and whizz to form a paste.
6. When the onions are cooked, add the chilli paste, increase the heat and cook for 5 minutes. Add the turmeric, garam masala and creamed coconut and continue to cook for a further minute.
7. Put the tamarind into a bowl and cover with the boiling water. Stir well and strain the liquid into the contents of the casserole. Discard the remaining pulp.
8. Add the remaining stock to the casserole, season lightly with salt and pepper and bring to the boil. Cover and cook in the preheated oven for 1½–2 hours, or until the meat is tender.
9. Prepare the fruit: peel the papaya and cut into thick slices and peel and slice the plantain or bananas.

10. When the meat is cooked, lift from the casserole and boil the sauce rapidly until it is of a syrupy consistency. Return the meat to the casserole, add the fruit and heat until the fruit is hot. Season to taste with salt and pepper and stir in the coriander. Arrange in a warmed serving dish and garnish with the sprigs of coriander. Serve very hot.

 *BEER*

FILLET OF BEEF WITH SMOKED OYSTERS AND MADEIRA SAUCE

SERVES 6

2 tablespoons oil
900g/2lb fillet of beef
salt and freshly ground black pepper
4 shallots, finely chopped
1 small bunch of fresh thyme
150ml/¼ pint brown stock (see page 625)
1 small tin of smoked oysters
1 bunch of fresh parsley
4 rashers of streaky bacon

To serve
double quantity Madeira sauce (see page 630)

1. Preheat the oven to 200°C/400°F/gas mark 6.
2. Heat the oil in a heavy-based frying pan, add the beef fillet and brown all over, seasoning with salt and pepper. Remove from the pan and cool.
3. Add the shallots to the pan and sweat with 4 sprigs of the thyme, until soft and lightly coloured. Add the stock, scraping the bottom of the pan to loosen any sediment. Reduce the liquid by boiling rapidly to a syrupy consistency. Drain the smoked oysters very well and add to the shallot mixture. Set aside to cool.
4. Chop the remaining thyme leaves and the parsley finely. Make a pocket in the beef by slicing horizontally along one long side. Stuff

first with the shallot mixture, then cover with
the parsley and thyme. Tie the meat, quite
loosely, with string. Cover with the bacon.
Roast in the preheated oven for 35 minutes.

5. Leave the fillet to rest for 5 minutes, then
remove the string and bacon, carve and serve
with the Madeira sauce.

 *CHÂTEAUNEUF DU PAPE*

LAMB

LAMB CURRY

SERVES 4

30g/1oz clarified butter (see page 637) or ghee
1 small onion, finely chopped
675g/1½lb boneless lamb, preferably shoulder,
    cut into 4cm/1½in cubes
2 teaspoons ground turmeric
½ teaspoon ground ginger
1 clove of garlic, crushed
1½ teaspoons ground coriander
¼ teaspoon salt
¼ teaspoon cayenne pepper
425ml/¾ pint brown stock (see page 625) or
    vegetable stock (see page 627)
1 tablespoon chopped fresh parsley
½ tablespoon chopped fresh mint

1. Melt the butter in a large saucepan and
brown the onion in it. Remove to a plate.
2. Put the lamb into the pan and brown all over.
Add the turmeric, ginger, garlic and coriander.
Return the onions to the pan and stir and cook
over a low heat for 1 minute.
3. Season with salt and cayenne and add enough
stock to come 1cm/½in below the top of the
lamb. This level should be kept constant. Bring
to the boil, then cover and simmer gently for
about 1½ hours, or until the lamb is tender,
adding more stock as necessary.
4. When the lamb is tender, remove it from the
pan and keep warm. Reduce the liquid by rapid
boiling. Add the parsley and mint and pour
over the lamb.

NOTES: More (or fewer) spices may be added
according to taste.
  Ghee is clarified fat sold in tins in Indian
stores.

 *LAGER OR FULL SPICY RED*

ACCOMPANIMENTS FOR CURRIES
BANANA AND COCONUT: Chop 2 bananas and
squeeze the juice of 1 lemon over them. Mix in
2 tablespoons freshly grated coconut.

TOMATO AND ONION: Chop 1 large onion and 3
peeled tomatoes finely. Mix together with salt
and pepper, 1 tablespoon olive oil and a squeeze
of lemon juice.

CHUTNEY AND CUCUMBER: Mix 1 cupful
chopped cucumber into the same quantity of
sweet chutney (such as mango or apple).

GREEN PEPPER, APPLE AND RAISIN: Chop equal
quantities of apple and green pepper finely, or
mince them. Add 1 tablespoon raisins or
sultanas and salt, pepper, lemon juice, cayenne
and sugar to taste.

POPPADOMS: These are large flat wafers,
available in most supermarkets. They are
heated in the oven or under the grill, or fried in
hot fat until crisp. They can be bought spiced or
plain.

PORK

GINGER GLAZED HAM OR GAMMON JOINT

SERVES 4–6

1 ham or gammon joint
1 onion
1 carrot
1 bay leaf
fresh parsley stalks
black peppercorns
3 tablespoons finely chopped stem ginger
1 teaspoon stem ginger syrup
3 tablespoons soft dark brown sugar
2 tablespoons brandy

1. Soak the joint overnight in cold water to remove excess salt. Weigh the joint and calculate the cooking time at 25 minutes per 450g/1lb. For large joints (i.e. 3.6kg/8lb upwards), allow 20 minutes per 450g/1lb.
2. Place the joint in a large saucepan of cold water and add the onion, carrot, bay leaf, parsley stalks and peppercorns. Bring slowly to the boil, then lower the heat, cover and simmer for the calculated cooking time.
3. Remove from the heat and leave the joint to cool slightly in the stock. Then lift out and carefully pull off the skin without removing any of the fat. Place in a roasting tin. Reserve the cooking liquor as ham stock.
4. Preheat the oven to 200°C/400°F/gas mark 6.
5. Mix together the ginger, syrup, sugar and brandy and spread all over the joint to form an even coating.
6. Using a sharp knife, cut a lattice pattern across the joint through the sugar and fat. Press back any coating that falls off. Stick a clove into each diamond segment, or into the cuts where the lines cross.
7. Bake the joint in the preheated oven for about 20 minutes, basting frequently, until brown and slightly caramelized.

 BEAUJOLAIS NOUVEAU

OLD-FASHIONED BOSTON BAKED BEANS

SERVES 6

450g/1lb black-eyed beans
170g/6oz piece of salt belly pork
1 large onion, finely chopped
5 tablespoons tomato chutney
5 tablespoons Worcestershire sauce
1 teaspoon Tabasco sauce
½ teaspoon chilli powder
3 tablespoons soft dark brown sugar
1 tablespoon grain mustard
salt and freshly ground black pepper

1. Put the beans into a large bowl, cover generously with water and allow to stand for at least 8 hours, preferably overnight.
2. Drain the beans and put them into a large saucepan. Cover with water, bring to the boil and cook for 5 minutes, then drain and return to the saucepan.
3. Cover the beans with fresh water and add the belly pork. Bring to the boil over a medium heat, then simmer for 1½ hours, or until the beans are tender. On no account allow the beans to boil dry.
4. Drain the beans, reserving the cooking liquor. Discard the belly pork.

5. Preheat the oven to 150°C/300°F/gas mark 2.
6. Mix the onion with all the remaining ingredients and season very generously with salt and pepper. Mix into the beans and pile into an earthenware casserole. Add enough of the bean liquid to come half-way up the beans. Cover and bake in the preheated oven for 4–5 hours, or until the beans are very soft, adding more bean liquid, salt and pepper as necessary. Serve very hot.

 *CALIFORNIAN ZINFANDEL*

ROAST LOIN OF PORK WITH HONEY KUMQUAT GLAZE

This recipe has been adapted from a recipe by Steven Wheeler in *BBC Gourmet*.

SERVES 4

85g/3oz kumquats, sliced
1 tablespoon clear honey
110g/4oz soft light brown sugar
2 teaspoons made English mustard
1.13kg/2½lb loin of pork, on the bone, chined and skin removed
5 tablespoons water

For the sauce
290ml/½ pint white stock, made with chicken bones (see page 625)
15g/½oz cornflour (optional)
1 tablespoon white wine vinegar
salt and freshly ground black pepper

1. Preheat the oven to 200°C/400°F/gas mark 6.
2. Cover the kumquats with cold water in a saucepan and bring to the boil, then lower the heat and simmer for 3 minutes. Drain and return the kumquats to the pan.
3. Put the honey, sugar and mustard into the saucepan. Stir well and allow the sugar to dissolve. Boil very briefly until the kumquats are lightly glazed.
4. Place the pork, fatty side up, in a roasting tin. Add the water.

5. Score the pork fat in a lattice pattern with a sharp knife. Spoon over the glaze, leaving the kumquats in the bottom of the saucepan. Roast the pork in the preheated oven for 1½ hours.
6. Transfer to a serving dish and keep warm in the turned-off oven.
7. Make the sauce: add the stock to the roasting tin. Bring gradually to the boil, stirring well to collect any sediment from the bottom of the tin. Taste and reduce to a syrupy consistency. If it needs to be thickened, mix the cornflour with 2 tablespoons of water. Add to the gravy and boil briefly. Add the vinegar and reserved kumquats and season to taste with salt and pepper.
8. Spoon a little of the sauce and as many of the kumquats as possible over the pork and hand the remainder in a warmed sauce-boat.

 CALIFORNIAN PINOT NOIR

LEEKS STUFFED WITH RICOTTA AND HAM

SERVES 4

8 large fat leeks, trimmed to 10cm/4in lengths
salt
30g/1oz butter
20g/¾oz plain flour
200ml/7fl oz milk
225g/8oz ricotta cheese
225g/8oz sliced baked ham, cut into shreds
freshly ground black pepper
55g/2oz Cheddar cheese, grated
30g/1oz fresh white breadcrumbs

1. Preheat the oven to 200°C/400°F/gas mark 6.
2. Boil the leeks in salted water for 8–10 minutes, or until tender. Drain and refresh in cold water. Drain well again.
3. Make a cut along the length of the leeks, about 1cm/½in into the centre. Carefully pull out the middle layers, leaving an outer shell of 4 layers intact. Lay the leek 'shells' in a large greased baking dish. Roughly chop the leek centres.
4. Melt the butter in a heavy-based saucepan

and add the chopped leeks and the flour. Stir over a low heat for a minute. Pour in the milk and continue stirring until the mixture boils and thickens.

5. Remove from the heat, add the ricotta and ham and season to taste with salt and pepper. Set aside to cool.

6. Divide the mixture between the leek shells and press them back into shape, with the filling bulging out of the top. Mix the Cheddar cheese with the breadcrumbs and sprinkle over the leeks.

7. Bake the stuffed leeks near the top of the preheated oven for 20 minutes, or until golden and bubbling.

 *VALPOLICELLA*

OFFAL

PRESSED TONGUE WITH HOT MUSTARD CHUTNEY

SERVES 8–10

1 salted ox tongue
2 bay leaves
6 whole black peppercorns
1 onion, peeled
1 carrot, peeled
½ small turnip, peeled
2 sticks of celery
salt

To garnish
1 small bunch of watercress

To serve
1 quantity hot mustard chutney (see page 498)

1. Wash the tongue thoroughly and soak in plenty of cold water overnight.
2. Rinse the tongue in fresh water and place in a saucepan just large enough to take it with the vegetables. Cover the tongue with cold water and bring to the boil. Lower the heat and simmer for 5 minutes, then drain.
3. Add fresh water to cover the tongue and add the remaining ingredients. Bring to the boil and skim off any scum that rises to the surface. Reduce the heat to a gentle simmer and cook the tongue for 1–2 hours, or until tender (a metal skewer can be inserted easily into the centre).
4. Remove the tongue from the pan, reserving the cooking liquid, and refresh briefly in cold water. While the tongue is still warm, remove the skin, any bones, gristle and excess fat from the root end.
5. Put the tongue into a mould, cake tin or large soufflé dish, just big enough to hold it. Add a little of the tongue cooking liquid to fill any crevices. Put a flat plate or slightly smaller tin on top with a heavy weight, so that the tongue will set in a flat, even shape. Allow to cool, then refrigerate overnight.
6. Turn out the tongue and cut it horizontally into thin slices. Arrange the slices, overlapping, on a serving platter. Garnish with the watercress and hand the hot mustard chutney separately.

NOTE: A tongue press may be used if available.

 *CHIANTI CLASSICO*

PEPPERED CALVES' LIVER SALADE TIÈDE

SERVES 4

340g/12oz calves' liver, skinned and sliced
2 tablespoons freshly ground black and white
    peppercorns
salt
30g/1oz butter
2 tablespoons walnut oil
4 tablespoons raspberry or sherry vinegar
4 handfuls of salad leaves: rocket, chicory,
    radicchio, frisée
30g/1oz pinenuts, toasted

1. Remove any large tubes from the slices of liver. Cut into finger-length pieces.

558

2. Put the peppercorns on to a plate and season with salt. Roll the liver in the peppercorns to give a light crust.

3. Heat the butter in a large frying pan and fry the liver a few pieces at a time for about 1 minute, or until lightly browned on the outside but still pink in the middle. Lift the liver on to a plate and continue frying until all the liver is cooked.

4. When the liver is cooked, add the oil and vinegar to the frying pan. Bring to the boil, scraping any sediment from the bottom of the pan, then remove from the heat.

5. Put the salad leaves into a large bowl, add the liver, pour over the dressing, toss together lightly and sprinkle with the pinenuts. Serve immediately.

NOTE: As liver toughens on standing, this dish is best cooked at the very last minute.

 FRENCH COUNTRY WHITE OR RED

VEGETARIAN

BAKED CELERIAC RAREBIT

SERVES 4

4 small celeriac, scrubbed and any whiskers or
    side roots removed

For the filling
110g/4oz Gruyère cheese, grated
110g/4oz Cheddar cheese, grated
2 tablespoons French mustard
1 egg, beaten
2 tablespoons brown ale
salt and freshly ground black pepper
cayenne pepper

To garnish
1 tablespoon chopped fresh parsley

1. Preheat the oven to 200°C/400°F/gas mark 6.
2. Prick the celeriac all over with a skewer,
place on a baking sheet and bake in the
preheated oven for 1½–2 hours, or until soft in
the centre.
3. Make the filling: mix all the ingredients
together and season to taste with salt, pepper
and cayenne.
4. Cut a large slice off the top of each celeriac
and set the lids aside. Scrape the flesh into a
bowl and mash it with a fork or potato masher.
Stir in the filling and check the seasoning.
5. Spoon the filling back into the celeriac skins
and replace the lids at a jaunty angle.
6. Return the stuffed celeriac to the oven for 15
minutes, or until the filling is bubbling. Sprinkle
with the parsley and serve immediately.

 *ZINFANDEL*

CHAMPAGNE AND WHITE TRUFFLE RISOTTO

SERVES 4

30g/1oz butter
2 shallots, finely chopped
1 clove of garlic, crushed
1–2 white truffles, thinly sliced
340g/12oz arborio risotto rice
½ bottle champagne
425ml/¾ pint vegetable or white stock, made
    with chicken bones (see pages 625, 627)
85g/3oz Parmesan cheese, freshly grated
salt and freshly ground black pepper

1. Melt the butter in a saucepan, add the
shallots and cook over a low heat for 5 minutes,
or until soft but not coloured. Add the garlic,
three-quarters of the truffle, and the rice.
2. Stir over a low heat for 2 minutes. Gradually
add a little champagne, stirring continuously
until it is all absorbed before adding the next
amount.
3. When all the champagne has been absorbed,
continue adding the stock gradually until the
rice is *al dente* and the risotto is of a creamy
consistency.
4. Remove from the heat and stir in three-
quarters of the Parmesan cheese. Season to taste
with salt and pepper. Tip the risotto into a
warmed serving bowl and sprinkle with the
remaining Parmesan cheese and truffle.

 *CHAMPAGNE*

SALSIFY, LEEK AND BLUE CHEESE FILO PIE

SERVES 4

450g/1lb salsify, washed thoroughly
salt
450g/1lb trimmed leeks, washed thoroughly
juice of 1 lemon
170g/6oz blue cheese
290ml/½ pint cold béchamel sauce (see page 629)
freshly ground black pepper
7 large sheets of filo pastry
85g/3oz butter, melted
1 egg, lightly beaten
1 tablespoon sesame seeds

1. Preheat the oven to 200°C/400°F/gas mark 6.
2. Bring 2 large saucepans of salted water to the boil. Put the salsify in one and simmer very gently for 10 minutes, or until tender, then strain. When the salsify is cool enough to handle, carefully peel off the black skin.
3. Simmer the whole leeks gently in the other saucepan of water for 10 minutes, or until tender. Strain and allow to steam-dry.
4. Stir the lemon juice and cheese into the béchamel sauce and season to taste with salt and pepper. Spread half the sauce over the bottom of an ovenproof dish 5cm/2in deep. Arrange the salsify and leeks on top and season to taste with salt and pepper. Spread the remaining sauce evenly over the top.
5. Lay a sheet of filo pastry out on a work surface and quickly brush all over with melted butter. Place another sheet directly on top and brush again with melted butter. Continue adding layers of the pastry in the same way until all the sheets are used up. Do not brush the top layer with melted butter.
6. Lay the pastry over the top of the dish and trim off the excess pastry, leaving a 2.5cm/1in overlapping edge. Brush a little beaten egg over the top of the pie and sprinkle with the sesame seeds. Make 6 criss-cross diagonal slashes through the pastry with a sharp knife.
7. Place the pie on a baking sheet and bake at the top of the preheated oven for 20–30 minutes, or until the pastry is golden-brown and crisp.

 AUSTRALIAN RHINE RIESLING

BAKED SWEDE WITH FIELD MUSHROOMS AND GOAT'S CHEESE

SERVES 4

4 medium swedes, scrubbed
4 large field mushrooms, wiped with damp kitchen paper and sliced
55ml/2fl oz olive oil
1 large clove of garlic, crushed
340g/12oz mature goat's cheese log, thinly sliced
2 tablespoons chopped fresh parsley
salt and freshly ground black pepper

1. Preheat the oven to 200°C/400°F/gas mark 6.
2. Cut a thin slice off the top and bottom of each swede and pierce them all over several times with a skewer. Place them on a baking sheet and bake in the preheated oven for 1½ hours, or until soft.
3. Fry the mushrooms in the oil in a frying pan until they start to sweat slightly. Season with salt and pepper. Add the garlic and cook for a further 5 minutes.
4. Scoop the swede flesh out into a bowl. Add all but 4 slices of the goat's cheese to the bowl with the mushrooms and the parsley. Mix together and season to taste with salt and pepper.
5. Pile the filling back into the swedes and place the remaining slices of goat's cheese on top. Replace the lids at a jaunty angle.
6. Return the swedes to the oven for 15 minutes, or until the cheese starts to bubble and is golden-brown on top.

 AUSTRALIAN SHIRAZ

JERUSALEM ARTICHOKE AND PARMESAN TART

SERVES 6

170g/6oz quantity polenta pastry (see next recipe)
450g/1lb Jerusalem artichokes, peeled and thinly sliced
1 teaspoon vinegar
1 teaspoon salt
1 red onion, thinly sliced
30g/1oz butter
1 clove of garlic, crushed
5 tablespoons single cream
5 tablespoons soured cream
55g/2oz finely grated fresh Parmesan cheese
1 egg
2 egg yolks
salt and freshly ground black pepper
freshly grated nutmeg

1. Roll out the pastry and use to line a 20cm/8in flan ring. Refrigerate for about 45 minutes to relax – this prevents shrinkage during baking.
2. Preheat the oven to 200°C/400°F/gas mark 6. Bake the pastry case blind (see page 640), then remove from the oven. Reduce the oven temperature to 150°C/300°F/gas mark 2.
3. Put the Jerusalem artichokes, vinegar and salt into a large saucepan and cover with water. Bring to the boil, then lower the heat and simmer slowly for 15–20 minutes, or until tender. Do not allow the artichokes to break up. Strain and pat dry with kitchen paper.
4. Cook the onion in the butter in a frying pan until soft, add the garlic and cook for a further minute. When soft but not coloured, drain well.
5. Mix together the creams, Parmesan cheese, egg and egg yolks. Add the onion mixture. Season to taste with salt, pepper and nutmeg.
6. Arrange the artichoke slices, overlapping, in the baked pastry case. Pour over the cream mixture. Bake the tart in the preheated oven for 40–45 minutes, or until the filling is set.
7. Serve warm or cold.

 *NEW ZEALAND SAUVIGNON BLANC*

BUTTON ONION AND THYME TATIN

SERVES 4

For the pastry
225g/8oz plain flour
55g/2oz coarse polenta (cornmeal)
a pinch of salt
110g/4oz butter, diced
55g/2oz Parmesan cheese, freshly grated
1 tablespoon chopped fresh thyme
1 egg, beaten

For the topping
900g/2lb button onions
55g/2oz butter
2 tablespoons soft dark brown sugar
2 cloves of garlic, crushed

1. Make the pastry: sift the flour into a bowl and stir in the polenta and salt.
2. Rub the butter into the flour with the fingertips until the mixture resembles coarse breadcrumbs. Stir in the Parmesan cheese and thyme and add just enough beaten egg to bind.
3. Put the pastry between 2 sheets of clingfilm and roll out to a round to fit a 22.5cm/9in ovenproof frying pan. Chill for 30 minutes.
4. Preheat the oven to 200°C/400°F/gas mark 6.
5. Make the topping: put the onions into a large saucepan and cover with cold water. Bring to the boil, then lower the heat and simmer for 5 minutes. Strain, then peel the onions, shaving off the root and trimming a little off the top.
6. Melt the butter in the frying pan, add the sugar and cook over a low heat for 2–3 minutes. Add the onions and the garlic, place over a low heat and cook for 4–5 minutes, or until the onions begin to brown. Put the pastry on top of the onions in the pan, trimming off any excess. Bake in the preheated oven for 25–30 minutes, or until the pastry is golden-brown.
7. Allow the tatin to cool for a minute before turning out on to a serving plate.

BEAUJOLAIS

WINTER VEGETABLES BOURGUIGNONNE

SERVES 4

225g/8oz celeriac
225g/8oz sweet potato
2 large leeks
225g/8oz cup mushrooms
225g/8oz peeled chestnuts
225g/8oz stoned prunes
seasoned plain flour
30g/1oz butter
2 tablespoons olive oil
3 cloves of garlic, crushed
1 bottle young red Burgundy
1 bouquet garni
salt and freshly ground black pepper
beurre manié (see page 108)

To garnish
chopped fresh thyme

To serve
buttered noodles or red pesto root mash

1. Preheat the oven to 150°C/300°F/gas mark 2.
2. Wash and peel the celeriac and sweet potato and cut into 5cm/2in chunks.
3. Cut the leeks into 5cm/2in pieces and wash well. Wipe the mushrooms, leave whole.
4. Roll all the vegetables and the chestnuts and prunes in the seasoned flour.
5. Heat the butter and oil together in a large flameproof casserole. Brown the vegetables, a few at a time, and lift on to a plate. When all the vegetables are browned, add the garlic to the casserole and cook for a minute. Replace the vegetables and pour over the wine.
6. Add the bouquet garni and season with salt and pepper. Bring to the boil, then cook in the preheated oven for 35–40 minutes, or until the vegetables are tender.
7. Using a slotted spoon, transfer the vegetables to a clean flameproof casserole. Remove the bouquet garni, check the seasoning and boil the sauce fast to reduce to a syrupy consistency. If the sauce is too salty, do not reduce it but thicken with a little beurre manié.

8. Pour the sauce over the vegetables and sprinkle the thyme on top. Serve with buttered noodles or red pesto root mash (see page 463).

 *RED BURGUNDY*

WHOLE BRIE WITH TRUFFLES AND MASCARPONE

1 small whole ripe Brie, about 20cm/8in in
    diameter, chilled
about 340g/12oz mascarpone, depending on the
    exact size of the Brie
1 fresh black truffle, grated
salt and freshly ground black pepper

To serve
fresh French bread or plain cheese biscuits

1. Cut the Brie in half horizontally and lay the two halves, skin side down, on a clean surface.
2. Beat the mascarpone in a bowl until soft and stir in the grated truffle. Season the mixture with a little salt and pepper.
3. Spread the mascarpone over one half of the Brie in an even layer about ¾cm/⅓in thick. Sandwich the two halves of the Brie back together again. Wrap the Brie in its waxed paper or a piece of silicone paper and leave in a cool place or the refrigerator for 24 hours.
4. To serve: allow the Brie to come to room temperature before serving with fresh French bread or plain cheese biscuits.

 *CLARET*

Cappuccino of White Truffle with Haricot Blancs

Marinated Oysters with Garlic and Potato Mousse

Griddled Scallops with Black Butter Sauce

Warm Pheasant Mousse with Port Essence

Shellfish Gratin

Peppered Calves' Liver Salade Tiède

Pheasant en Papillote and Winter Game Chip Baskets

Spiced Beef with Tropical Fruits

Baked Celeriac Rarebit

Seville Orange Syllabub with Nougatine

Chocolate Shortbread Torte with Sticky Cranberry Glaze

Cappuccino Brûlé

VEGETABLES AND SALADS

VEGETABLES

AUBERGINE AND RED PEPPER SAMBAL

SERVES 4

1 large aubergine
1 teaspoon salt
2 potatoes, unpeeled
2 red peppers
4 tablespoons groundnut oil
2 teaspoons mustard seeds
2 teaspoons cumin seeds
2 teaspoons black onion seeds
1 teaspoon ground coriander
½ teaspoon ground turmeric
salt and freshly ground black pepper

1. Cut the aubergine into 5cm/2in dice. Place in a colander, sprinkle with the salt and leave to degorge for 15 minutes.
2. Boil the potatoes in salted water for 12–15 minutes, or until nearly tender. When cooked, strain and peel, then cut into 5cm/2in chunks and set aside.
3. Cut the red peppers into 2.5cm/1in pieces, discarding the membrane and seeds, and set aside.
4. Drain and dry the aubergines. Heat the oil in a frying pan, add the aubergines and fry over a low to medium heat for 4–5 minutes, or until they are cooked and browned. Add the mustard, cumin and black onion seeds and fry over a low heat, stirring occasionally, for 5 minutes.
5. Add the remaining spices with the red peppers and fry for a further 7–10 minutes, then add the potatoes and heat through for a further 5 minutes, or until everything is very hot. Season to taste with salt and pepper. Pile into a warmed serving dish and serve very hot.

BRAISED RED CABBAGE WITH OLIVES AND GARLIC CRISPS

SERVES 4

30g/1oz butter
1 Spanish onion, thinly sliced
1 small red cabbage, core removed and thinly sliced
290ml/½ pint red wine vinegar
3 tablespoons soft dark brown sugar
salt and freshly ground black pepper
85g/3oz Kalamata olives in olive oil, pitted
2 large cloves of garlic, peeled and thinly sliced

For the garlic crisps
6 large cloves of garlic, thinly sliced
oil for frying

1. Preheat the oven to 180°C/350°F/gas mark 4.
2. Melt the butter in a large flameproof casserole, add the onion, cabbage, vinegar and sugar and season with salt and pepper. Cover and cook in the preheated oven for 1 hour, stirring from time to time.
3. Add the olives and the garlic and cook for a further 30 minutes.
4. Meanwhile, make the garlic crisps: heat 1cm/½in oil in a large frying pan, add the garlic and fry until pale golden. Remove with a slotted spoon and drain on kitchen paper. Sprinkle with salt.
5. When the cabbage is tender, season again with salt and pepper. Pile into a warmed serving dish and scatter over the garlic crisps before serving.

BRAISED RED CABBAGE WITH RASPBERRY VINEGAR

SERVES 8

1 small red cabbage
30g/1oz butter
1 large onion, thinly sliced
55g/2oz dried apricots, thinly sliced
1 teaspoon ground allspice
1 teaspoon ground cloves
55g/2oz soft dark brown sugar
150ml/¼ pint raspberry vinegar
salt and freshly ground black pepper

1. Preheat the oven to 180°C/350°F/gas mark 4.
2. Shred the cabbage and discard the core and hard stalks. Rinse well.
3. Melt the butter in a large flameproof casserole. Add the cabbage and onion, cover and cook over a low heat for 10 minutes.
4. Add all the remaining ingredients, stir together and season well with salt and pepper. Transfer to the oven and cook, covered, for about 1¼ hours, or until tender. Check the cabbage after 30 minutes and add a little water if it is becoming too dry.
5. Season to taste with salt and pepper before serving.

ORANGE-GLAZED BABY CARROTS

SERVES 4

675g/1½lb baby carrots, washed and trimmed, leaving 1cm/½in stalk
15g/½oz butter
15g/½oz soft light brown sugar
290ml/½ pint orange juice
salt and freshly ground black pepper

1. Put the carrots, butter, sugar and orange juice into a large sauté pan and season with salt and pepper.

2. Bring the orange juice to the boil and simmer, stirring frequently, until the liquid has evaporated, leaving a shiny, syrupy glaze.

CELERIAC RÖSTI

SERVES 4

1 large onion, finely chopped
55g/2oz butter, melted
450g/1lb celeriac
salt and freshly ground black pepper
ground mace

1. Preheat the oven to 180°C/350°F/gas mark 4.
2. Sweat the onion in half the butter in a frying pan until soft, then remove from the heat and allow to cool.
3. Peel and grate the celeriac on the coarse side of the grater. Mix with the softened onion and season to taste with salt, pepper and mace.
4. Brush 12 patty tins with the remaining butter. Pack each tin with a generous amount of the celeriac mixture. Bake in the middle of the preheated oven for 25–30 minutes, or until the celeriac is soft.

BRAISED CELERIAC AND APPLES IN CIDER

SERVES 4

450g/1lb peeled celeriac
1 Bramley apple
1 Cox's Orange Pippin apple
30g/1oz butter
3 shallots, finely chopped
salt and freshly ground black pepper
290ml/½ pint dry cider
2 bay leaves
1 large sprig of fresh rosemary
55g/2oz unsalted butter, diced
1 teaspoon finely chopped fresh rosemary

1. Preheat the oven to 170°C/325°F/gas mark 3.
2. Peel the celeriac and cut into 5cm/2in chunks. Peel and core the apples and slice thickly.

3. Melt the butter in a large flameproof casserole, add the shallots and fry for 1–2 minutes. Add the celeriac and apples and toss over the heat for 2–3 minutes. Season to taste with salt and pepper.

4. Pour over the cider and add the herbs. Bring to the boil, then cover and bake in the preheated oven for 40–45 minutes, or until the celeriac is tender and the apples are beginning to break up.

5. Using a slotted spoon, transfer the celeriac and apples to a clean casserole.

6. Bring the cooking liquid to the boil and reduce by boiling rapidly to 150ml/¼ pint. Remove the casserole from the direct heat and whisk the butter into the liquid, piece by piece. Season to taste with salt and pepper. Add the rosemary and pour over the celeriac and apples.

CHRISTMAS CRACKED WHEAT

SERVES 4

110g/4oz cracked wheat
570ml/1 pint white stock, made from chicken or
*   turkey bones (see page 625)*
55g/2oz butter
1 large onion, very finely chopped
225g/8oz Brussels sprouts, trimmed
85g/3oz whole chestnuts, peeled (see note)
55g/2oz fresh or frozen cranberries
salt and freshly ground black pepper
juice of ½ lemon

1. Preheat the oven to 180°C/350°F/gas mark 4.
2. Put the cracked wheat into a bowl, pour over the stock and leave to stand for 15 minutes. Drain, reserving any stock that has not been absorbed.
3. Melt the butter in a heavy-based saucepan, add the onion and cook over a low heat for 20 minutes, or until soft but not coloured.
4. Meanwhile, blanch the Brussels sprouts in boiling salted water for 4–5 minutes, or until just tender. Drain and refresh under cold running water and drain again.

5. Add the chestnuts to the onion and cook over a medium heat until the onion starts to caramelize. Add the cranberries and reserved stock, season with salt and pepper and cook over a low heat until the cranberries start to soften.

6. Tip the cranberry mixture and the sprouts into the bowl of cracked wheat, toss together and season with salt, pepper and lemon juice. Transfer to an ovenproof dish, cover with buttered kitchen foil and bake for 20 minutes in the preheated oven until hot. Serve immediately.

NOTES: To peel a chestnut: make a slit in the skin of each chestnut and put them into a saucepan of cold water. Bring to the boil, then simmer for 15 minutes and remove from the heat. Remove 1–2 chestnuts at a time and peel. The skins come off easily if the chestnuts are hot but not well cooked.

Cracked wheat is another name for bulghar wheat.

GLAZED LEEK AND CELERIAC SABAYON

SERVES 4

4 small leeks
1 medium celeriac
425ml/¾ pint vegetable stock (see page 627)
salt and freshly ground black pepper
1 teaspoon chopped fresh rosemary

For the sabayon
1 egg
2 egg yolks
2 teaspoons rice wine vinegar
5 tablespoons double cream
salt and freshly ground white pepper
4 teaspoons freshly grated Parmesan cheese

1. Prepare the vegetables: cut the leeks into 2.5cm/1in pieces and wash thoroughly. Peel the celeriac and cut into 1cm/½in slices.
2. Put the celeriac into a saucepan, add the stock, salt, pepper and rosemary and simmer

over a low heat until the celeriac is just tender. Add the leeks and cook for a further 5 minutes or until tender. Using a slotted spoon, lift the vegetables from the cooking liquid and arrange in a large shallow gratin dish. Keep warm.

3. Preheat the grill to its highest setting.

4. Make the sabayon: bring the vegetable cooking liquid to the boil and reduce to 5–6 tablespoons by boiling rapidly.

5. Put the egg and egg yolks into a heatproof bowl with the vinegar and reduced vegetable liquid. Set the bowl over, not in, a pan of simmering water and whisk until thick and creamy. Stir in the cream and season to taste with salt and pepper.

6. Spoon the sabayon over the vegetables and sprinkle with the Parmesan cheese.

7. Grill for 40–50 seconds, or until the top is lightly browned. Serve immediately.

PARSNIP AND CRÈME FRAÎCHE PURÉE

SERVES 4

450g/1lb floury potatoes, peeled and quartered
salt and freshly ground white pepper
450g/1lb parsnips, peeled
200ml/7fl oz crème fraîche
1 clove of garlic, crushed

1. Boil the potatoes in salted water for 5 minutes. Add the parsnips and simmer until tender (a table knife will pierce them easily).

2. Push the potatoes and parsnips through a sieve or mouli. Return them to the dry saucepan. Heat carefully, stirring to allow the potato to steam-dry.

3. Bring the crème fraîche and garlic to the boil in a separate saucepan, then lower the heat and simmer gently for 5 minutes until reduced by half. Pour the cream into the potato and parsnip mixture and season to taste with salt and pepper.

4. Beat the cream into the purée and check the seasoning. Serve hot.

PARSNIP AND MATURE CHEDDAR BAKE

SERVES 4

675g/1½lb parsnips, peeled
salt and freshly ground black pepper
30g/1oz butter
150ml/¼ pint soured cream
85g/3oz mature farmhouse Cheddar cheese, grated
freshly grated nutmeg

1. Preheat the oven to 180°C/350°F/gas mark 4.

2. Cook the parsnips in boiling salted water until tender.

3. Drain well, put back into the saucepan and mash until smooth over a low heat.

4. Add the butter, soured cream and farmhouse Cheddar cheese. Season to taste with salt, pepper and nutmeg.

5. Pile into a large ovenproof dish and bake in the preheated oven for 20 minutes, or until the top is golden-brown and has formed a light crust. Serve very hot.

WINTER GAME CHIP BASKETS

SERVES 4

For the baskets
2 litres/3½ pints sunflower oil
2 large potatoes, peeled and thinly sliced with a mandolin

For the filling
55g/2oz butter
225g/8oz pumpkin flesh, cut into 5 × 1cm/ 2 × ½in batons
225g/8oz small Brussels sprouts, trimmed, blanched and refreshed
55g/2oz cranberries
1 teaspoon caster sugar
225g/8oz whole chestnuts, peeled (see page 569) or 110g/4oz peeled chestnuts
salt and freshly ground black pepper

1. Heat the oil in a deep-fryer until a crumb will sizzle in it.

2. Dip a small wire strainer or sieve into the oil to get it well greased. Remove and line the strainer with overlapping potato slices. Using a small ladle to press the chips into the strainer and prevent them from floating away during cooking, deep-fry the baskets until golden and crisp.

3. Drain well on kitchen paper.

4. Make the filling: melt the butter in a saucepan and add the pumpkin. Cover and cook over a medium heat until the pumpkin is starting to caramelize and is just tender. Tip the pumpkin on to a plate. Add the sprouts to the pan with a little more butter if necessary and cook over a medium heat for 2 minutes.

5. Add the cranberries, sugar and chestnuts and season to taste with salt and pepper. Stir gently over a low heat until the cranberries start to soften. Carefully return the pumpkin to the pan and toss everything together over the heat.

6. Carefully spoon the vegetable mixture into the baskets. Serve immediately.

NOTE: A gadget for making deep-fried baskets is available in shops selling to the catering trade, but the sieve and ladle method works perfectly well.

POLENTA POTATO CAKES

SERVES 4

450g/1lb floury potatoes, peeled and halved
salt and freshly ground black pepper
55g/2oz sweetcorn kernels
1 egg yolk
85g/3oz butter, melted
1 tablespoon chopped fresh chives
seasoned plain flour
1 egg, beaten
55g/2oz coarse polenta

1. Preheat the oven to 200°C/400°F/gas mark 6.

2. Cook the potatoes in boiling salted water until just tender. Drain and press a few at a time

through a coarse sieve with a wooden spoon. Return the mashed potato to the rinsed-out and dry pan and stir over a low heat until the potato is really firm and dry, making sure it does not catch on the bottom of the pan.

3. Add the sweetcorn to the potato with the egg yolk, 15g/½oz of the butter and the chives. Stir until mixed well and season to taste with salt and pepper.

4. Divide the mixture into 4 equal portions and with floured hands shape each into a flattish circle about 9cm/3½in in diameter. Chill for 1 hour.

5. Coat the potato cakes evenly with the seasoned flour, then dip into the beaten egg and finally coat with the polenta. Place on a baking sheet.

6. Brush half the remaining butter over the cakes. Bake at the top of the preheated oven for 20 minutes. Turn the cakes over, brush with a little more butter and cook for a further 20 minutes, or until golden-brown all over.

POTATO GNOCCHI

SERVES 4

4 large floury baking potatoes
salt
100g/3½oz plain flour
freshly grated nutmeg
freshly ground white pepper
extra plain flour for rolling out

1. Preheat the oven to 200°C/400°F/gas mark 6. Prick the potatoes with a skewer, place them on a baking sheet and bake in the preheated oven for 1½ hours, or until soft. Remove from the oven and allow to cool slightly.

2. Bring a large saucepan of salted water to the boil. Fill a bowl with cold water.

3. Cut the potatoes in half and scoop out the flesh. Gently press the potato through a sieve with a wooden spoon, a little at a time, into a large bowl.

4. Sift the flour on to the potato. Sprinkle over some nutmeg and pepper and carefully fold the mixture together. (If you beat the potato too hard it will become heavy and glutinous.)

5. Sprinkle a little flour on to a work surface. Take half the potato mixture and roll it into a long sausage shape about 2cm/¾in thick. Cut the sausage into 2.5cm/1in lengths.

6. Using a slotted spoon, drop a few of the gnocchi at a time into the boiling water. When they rise to the top again, after 1–2 minutes, remove them with a slotted spoon and drop them into the cold water for a minute, then drain immediately in a single layer in a large colander. Continue until all the potato mixture is used up. The gnocchi are now ready to use.

SWEET POTATO PURÉE

SERVES 4

900g/2lb red sweet potato
1 bay leaf
1 teaspoon salt
30g/1oz butter
5 tablespoons crème fraîche
1 teaspoon freshly grated nutmeg
coarse sea salt and freshly ground black pepper

1. Peel the sweet potato and cut into 5cm/2in chunks. Put into a large saucepan and cover with cold water. Add the bay leaf and salt.

2. Cover the pan and bring to the boil, then lower the heat and simmer for 10–12 minutes, or until the sweet potato is soft, but not breaking up.

3. Drain the sweet potato and discard the bay leaf.

4. Sieve the sweet potato and return to the rinsed-out pan. Set over a low heat and beat in the butter, crème fraîche and nutmeg. Season to taste with salt and pepper. Serve very hot.

NOTE: If the sweet potato purée is a little wet once it has been sieved, stir it over a low heat, before the butter is added, to help evaporation.

HOT LEMON AND OLIVE OIL DRESSED SPINACH

SERVES 4

salt and freshly ground black pepper
900g/2lb fresh spinach, washed and stalks removed
2 tablespoons extra virgin olive oil
grated zest of 1 lemon
juice of ½ lemon

1. Bring a large saucepan half filled with salted water to the boil. Add the spinach and bring back to the boil, then lower the heat and simmer for 30 seconds.

2. Drain the spinach and refresh with a little cold water. Drain again.

3. Put the spinach between 2 plates and press well to remove as much excess moisture as possible.

4. Put the oil and lemon zest into the saucepan. Set over a low heat for 3–4 minutes, to allow the lemon zest to infuse with the oil. Increase the heat, add the spinach and toss over the heat for 30 seconds, or until the spinach is thoroughly reheated. Add the lemon juice and season to taste with salt and pepper.

5. Transfer to a warmed serving dish and serve very hot.

WINTER ROOT LYONNAISE

SERVES 6

450g/1lb celeriac
1 medium swede
8 small turnips
2 medium parsnips
2 tablespoons sunflower oil
2 large onions, thinly sliced
55g/2oz unsalted butter
salt and freshly ground black pepper

1. Peel the vegetables and cut into even 3.5cm/

1½in chunks. Parboil in a large saucepan of boiling salted water for 6–8 minutes, or until just tender. Drain well.

2. Heat the oil in a large frying pan, add the onions and cook until very soft, then transfer to a plate, using a slotted spoon.

3. Melt the butter in the frying pan, add the vegetables and fry over a low to medium heat until beginning to break up. Add the onions and stir into the vegetables. Season to taste with salt and pepper and serve very hot.

WINTER VEGETABLES EN PAPILLOTE

SERVES 4

1 large parsnip
½ small swede
½ small celeriac
1 large leek
4 tablespoons extra virgin olive oil
½ teaspoon grated nutmeg
4 cloves of garlic, unpeeled
4 sprigs of fresh rosemary
2 teaspoons coarse sea salt
freshly ground black pepper

1. Preheat the oven to 200°C/400°F/gas mark 6.
2. Peel the parsnip, swede and celeriac and cut into even 5cm/2in pieces. Cook in boiling salted water for 8–10 minutes, or until nearly tender. Drain and allow to dry.
3. Slice the leek thinly and blanch in boiling water for 1 minute. Drain and allow to dry.
4. Put the vegetables on to a large piece of greaseproof paper. Turn them lightly in the oil and sprinkle the nutmeg over the top.
5. Add the garlic and rosemary and season with salt and pepper. Wrap the vegetables in the greaseproof paper, sealing the parcel tightly to prevent the steam from escaping.
6. Bake in the preheated oven for about 25–30 minutes, or until the vegetables are completely tender.

LIME-GLAZED WINTER VEGETABLES

SERVES 8

340g/12oz potatoes, peeled
340g/12oz celeriac, peeled
340g/12oz pumpkin, peeled
340g/12oz parsnips, peeled
340g/12oz swede, peeled
salt

For the glaze
2 tablespoons sunflower oil
grated zest and juice of 3 limes
1 tablespoon soft dark brown sugar
salt and freshly ground black pepper
1 teaspoon ground coriander

1. Preheat the oven to 200°C/400°F/gas mark 6.
2. Cook all the vegetables in boiling salted water until tender, then drain and refresh under cold running water. Drain and pat dry. Transfer to a roasting tin.
3. Mix together the ingredients for the glaze, pour over the vegetables and toss together.
4. Roast in the preheated oven for 30–35 minutes, basting frequently, until golden-brown and sticky. Serve very hot.

SALADS

POMEGRANATE, SPINACH AND BACON SALAD

This recipe would work well as either a starter or a main course salad at Christmastime.

SERVES 4

2 pomegranates
340g/12oz rindless rashers of smoked bacon
450g/1lb baby spinach leaves, washed thoroughly and stalks removed

For the dressing
1 clove of garlic, crushed
2 tablespoons mayonnaise (see page 632)
4 tablespoons low-fat plain yoghurt
1 tablespoon lemon juice
salt and freshly ground black pepper

1. Preheat the grill to its highest setting.
2. Peel the skin off the pomegranate and separate out the red seeds from the membranes. Discard the membranes.
3. Grill the bacon until brown and crisp. Chop into small pieces.
4. Make the dressing: mix all the ingredients together in a bowl and season well with salt and pepper.
5. Put all the salad ingredients together in a large bowl and toss together with the dressing. Check the seasoning before piling on to 4 individual plates.

CAESAR DRESSED LEAVES

SERVES 4

2 cloves of garlic, crushed
6 tablespoons extra virgin olive oil
3 anchovy fillets
2 tablespoons lemon juice
1 teaspoon Dijon mustard
freshly ground black pepper
1 egg
1 head of Cos lettuce
55g/2oz Parmesan cheese, freshly grated

1. Make the dressing: put the garlic, oil, anchovy fillets, lemon juice, mustard, pepper and egg into a blender and whizz to form a thick emulsion.
2. Wash and dry the lettuce and tear into bite-sized pieces. Toss together with the dressing and sprinkle the Parmesan cheese on top. Serve immediately.

PUDDINGS

Fruit Puddings
Mousses, Soufflés and Creams
Ice Creams and Sorbets
Meringues
Pastries, Pies and Tarts
Cakes and Pâtisserie

FRUIT PUDDINGS

HOT CITRUS SALAD

SERVES 4

*4 large oranges, segmented with some zest
reserved*
*4 pink grapefruits, segmented with some zest
reserved*
*8 kumquats, washed, cut in half horizontally
and finely sliced*
*1 medium pineapple, peeled and cut into 2.5cm/
1in chunks*

For the syrup
285g/10oz demerara sugar
425ml/¾ pint water
290ml/½ pint medium sherry
1 cinnamon stick
10 cloves
4 strips of thinly pared lemon zest
4 strips of thinly pared orange zest

To serve
macadamia and chocolate biscuits (see page 356)

1. Cut 4 pieces of the reserved orange and
grapefruit zest into julienne strips 5cm/2in long.
2. Blanch the julienne in boiling water for 2
minutes, then drain and refresh in cold water.
3. Make the syrup: dissolve the sugar in the
water and sherry in a saucepan over a low heat.
Add the cinnamon stick, cloves and lemon and
orange zest. Bring to the boil, then lower the
heat and simmer for 15 minutes. Remove from
the heat and leave to stand for a further 30
minutes.
4. Strain the syrup into a clean saucepan and
bring to the boil. Lower the heat and stir in the
orange and grapefruit segments, kumquats and

pineapple. Cook for 1–2 minutes, or until the
fruit is hot but not breaking up. Pour into a
warmed serving bowl and serve immediately
with macadamia and vanilla biscuits.

 *SOUTH AFRICAN SAUVIGNON
BLANC*

WARM WINTER FRUIT SALAD

SERVES 4

*450g/1lb mixed fruits, such as prunes, apricots,
figs and apples*
1 tablespoon Calvados
cold Earl Grey tea
4 tablespoons fresh orange juice
3–4 cloves
5cm/2in cinnamon stick
¼ teaspoon ground mixed spice
thinly pared zest of 1 lemon
1 star anise

1. Soak the mixed dried fruits in the Calvados
and enough tea just to cover. Leave overnight to
macerate.
2. Pour the fruit into a saucepan and add the
orange juice, cloves, cinnamon, mixed spice,
lemon zest and star anise. Bring to the boil, then
lower the heat and simmer gently for about 20
minutes, or until the fruit is soft.
3. Discard the cloves, cinnamon, lemon zest and
star anise. Turn the fruit into a serving bowl
and serve hot or cold.

 MUSCAT DE BEAUMES DE VENISE

CARAMELIZED CLEMENTINES

SERVES 4

8 clementines
170g/6oz granulated sugar
290ml/½ pint water
a pinch of ground ginger
a pinch of ground cinnamon
1 tablespoon finely chopped candied orange
    peel
1 tablespoon Grand Marnier

1. Carefully grate the zest from the clementines and set aside. Peel the clementines and remove as much pith as possible from around the segments. Leave the clementines whole.
2. Place the sugar in a heavy-based saucepan with half the water.
3. Dissolve the sugar slowly without stirring it or allowing the water to boil. Add the ginger and cinnamon.
4. Once all the sugar has dissolved, turn up the heat and boil until it is a good caramel colour.
5. Immediately tip in the remaining water (it will splutter dangerously, so stand back).
6. Stir until any lumps have dissolved, then remove from the heat and add the clementine zest, candied orange peel and Grand Marnier. Allow to cool.
7. Arrange the clementines in a large glass bowl, pour over the cold caramel sauce and chill for 1 hour before serving.

 AUSTRALIAN ORANGE MUSCAT

RICH DATE AND CHESTNUT POTS

SERVES 4

12 fresh dates, pitted and roughly chopped
6 tablespoons Madeira
1 × 200g/7oz can of unsweetened chestnut purée
55g/2oz caster sugar

290ml/½ pint double cream, lightly whipped
4 whole Medjool dates, cut in half and pitted
icing sugar

1. Put the dates and 4 tablespoons of the Madeira into a small heavy-based saucepan. Cover and simmer gently for 5–10 minutes, or until the dates are reduced to a pulp. Remove from the heat and allow to cool.
2. Put the chestnut purée into a large bowl with the caster sugar and the remaining Madeira. Mix to a smooth paste and gradually stir in half the cream with a wooden spoon. Fold in the remaining cream.
3. Divide half the date pulp between 4 ramekins. Divide half the chestnut cream between the 4 ramekins, then continue layering with the remaining date pulp, finishing with the chestnut cream. Spread the tops flat with a palette knife. Chill for 30 minutes.
4. To serve: arrange the dates on top of the ramekins and dust with icing sugar just before serving.

 MADEIRA

ROAST FIGS IN PORT

SERVES 4

8 ripe fresh figs, washed and dried well
30g/1oz butter, melted
55g/2oz soft light brown sugar
150ml/¼ pint tawny port

To serve
1 quantity iced vanilla sauce (see page 617)

1. Preheat the oven to 220°C/425°F/gas mark 7.
2. Cut the tips of the stalks off the figs and then cut the figs in half lengthways.
3. Place the figs in a bowl and coat them with the melted butter. Arrange them, cut side uppermost, in a small roasting tin.
4. Sprinkle the sugar over the figs and pour the port around them, taking care not to dislodge the sugar.
5. Roast the figs near the top of the oven for 15

minutes, basting them with the port after 10 minutes. They are ready to serve when the port has reduced to a syrupy consistency. Serve immediately with the iced vanilla sauce.

 *PORT*

LIME AND GINGER SABAYON WITH PEARS

SERVES 4

2 limes
15 lumps of sugar
4 tablespoons water
4 egg yolks
5 tablespoons Poire William liqueur
2 pieces of stem ginger, chopped
290ml/½ pint double cream
4 ripe pears

To serve
55g/2oz flaked almonds, toasted

1. Wash and dry the limes. Rub half the sugar lumps over the skin of the limes, removing as much zest as possible. Put the sugar into a bowl. Halve and squeeze the limes, pour the juice on to the sugar and stir until dissolved.
2. Dissolve the remaining sugar in the water, then boil rapidly to the short thread stage (when a little syrup is put between a wet finger and thumb and the fingers opened, it should form a sticky thread 2.5cm/1in long). Remove from the heat and cool for 1 minute.
3. Whisk the egg yolks with the Poire William in a heatproof bowl and gradually pour in the sugar syrup. Set the bowl over, not in, a pan of simmering water and continue to whisk until the mixture is thick. Remove from the heat and continue to whisk until the mixture is cold. Stir in the lime syrup and ginger and set aside.
4. Whisk the cream until it leaves a trail, then fold into the cooled sabayon mixture.
5. Peel, core and slice the pears and arrange half

the slices on the bottom of a large glass dish. Spoon half the sabayon over the top, then add the remaining pear slices and sabayon. Sprinkle the top with the toasted almonds and serve.

 MUSCAT DE BEAUMES DE VENISE

CHOCOLATE, PEAR AND KUMQUAT STEAMED PUDDING

SERVES 4

For the pastry
170g/6oz self-raising flour
30g/1oz cocoa powder
a pinch of salt
15g/½oz baking powder
100g/3½oz shredded beef suet
290ml/½ pint milk and water, mixed
butter for greasing

For the filling
85g/3oz kumquats, pricked all over
85g/3oz dried pears, quartered
110g/4oz butter, diced
110g/4oz soft dark brown sugar
100ml/3½fl oz orange juice

1. Sift the flour, cocoa powder, salt and baking powder into a large bowl. Stir in the suet. Add three-quarters of the milk and water and mix to a soft but not sticky dough with a knife, adding the remaining liquid if needed. Roll out the pastry into a circle 5mm/¼in thick. Cut out a wedge from the circle, about one-third, and set aside for the lid.
2. Butter a 1.5 litre/2½ pint pudding basin generously. Line the basin with the circle of pastry, pressing the seam together.
3. Mix the kumquats, pears, butter and sugar together in a bowl and pile into the basin. Pour over the orange juice.
4. Reshape the remaining pastry to form a circle the size of the top of the basin and brush the edge with water. Lay over the fruit and press

the pastry edges together to seal firmly. Make sure there is some room at the top of the basin for the pastry to rise.

5. Put a piece of oiled greaseproof paper and a piece of kitchen foil over the top of the basin and make a pleat in the middle. Tie it in place with string and tuck the excess paper and foil up underneath the string to prevent the water from getting in.

6. Bring a large saucepan of water to the boil and lower the pudding into it. The water must be boiling and must come half-way up the sides of the basin. Cover and leave to steam for 3–4 hours, topping up regularly with boiling water. (If you have a steamer, you can use this instead.)

7. To serve: remove the greaseproof and foil and put a dish over the top of the basin. Quickly invert and remove the basin. Serve immediately.

 AUSTRALIAN LIQUEUR MUSCAT

SETE AL LIQUORE
(Macerated Pomegranates)

This recipe was given to us by Fiona Burrell, former Principal of Leith's School.

SERVES 6

3 medium ripe pomegranates
juice of 1 lemon
85g/3oz granulated sugar
85ml/3fl oz Grand Marnier or brandy

1. Cut the pomegranates in half and scoop out the seeds into a bowl.
2. Add the lemon juice, sugar and liqueur to the bowl and mix carefully.
3. Cover the bowl and chill for at least 1 hour before serving.

NOTE: The marinated pomegranate seeds may be served with whipped cream, vanilla ice cream or Panna Cotta.

 *MONBAZILLAC*

MOUSSES, SOUFFLÉS AND CREAMS

DARK CHOCOLATE AND ORANGE MOUSSE

SERVES 4

110g/4oz plain, sweetened chocolate, roughly
  chopped
1 tablespoon brandy
2 eggs, separated
55g/2oz caster sugar
grated zest of 1 orange
190ml/⅓ pint double cream, very lightly
  whipped

1. Melt the chocolate with the brandy in a non-metallic bowl set over, not in, a saucepan of simmering water.
2. Whisk the egg yolks with the sugar until pale and creamy. Beat in the orange zest.
3. Put the egg whites in a very clean bowl and whisk them until they form medium peaks.
4. Stir the melted chocolate into the egg yolk mixture and quickly fold in the cream.
5. Stir a spoonful of the whisked egg white into the chocolate mixture, then fold in the remainder. Tip into a serving dish and chill for 2 hours before serving.

 *BUAL MADEIRA*

CHOCOLATE TIMBALES WITH ORANGES IN BRANDY SYRUP

SERVES 4

oil for brushing
1 quantity chocolate and orange mousse (see
  previous recipe)
8 large oranges

For the syrup
85g/3oz granulated sugar
150ml/¼ pint water
grated zest of 1 orange
2–3 tablespoons brandy

To decorate
white chocolate caraque (see page 664)
a little cocoa powder

1. Line the base of 4 timbale moulds or ramekins with greaseproof paper. Lightly oil the insides of the moulds and turn them upside down on kitchen paper to drain.
2. Divide the mousse between the ramekins and chill for 2–3 hours, or until set.
3. Make the syrup: dissolve the sugar in the water over a low heat. Add the orange zest and simmer for 5 minutes. Turn off the heat and leave the syrup to cool. Strain the syrup through a fine sieve into a bowl and add the brandy to taste.
4. Segment the oranges and tip them into a sieve to drain off any extra juice. Add the orange

segments to the cold syrup and leave to stand for 5 minutes.

5. To serve: turn the chocolate timbales out on to individual plates. Pile some white chocolate caraque on top and sift a little cocoa powder over. Arrange the orange segments around the mousses with a little syrup poured over.

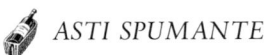 *ASTI SPUMANTE*

TAMARILLO SUÉDOISE AND VANILLA BAVAROIS TERRINE

SERVES 6

For the tamarillos
4 tamarillos
170g/6oz granulated sugar
290ml/½ pint water
15g/½oz powdered gelatine
oil for greasing

For the vanilla bavarois
2 tablespoons water
7g/¼oz powdered gelatine
210ml/7½fl oz warm milk
1 vanilla pod
3 egg yolks
55g/2oz caster sugar
150ml/¼ pint double cream

1. Blanch the tamarillos in boiling water for 20 seconds, then drain, refresh in cold water and remove the skins.
2. Put the sugar and water into a heavy-based saucepan and dissolve over a low heat. Bring to the boil, then lower the heat and add the tamarillos. Poach gently for 12–15 minutes, or until the tamarillos are tender.
3. Using a slotted spoon, lift the tamarillos from the syrup, slice and set aside.
4. Soak the gelatine in 2 tablespoons water for 5 minutes until spongy. Dissolve the gelatine over a very low heat without boiling and stir into the

tamarillo syrup. Allow to cool to the point of setting.
5. Pour half the syrup into the bottom of a lightly oiled 1.1 litre/2 pint terrine and chill until set.
6. Arrange the tamarillos, overlapping, on top of the set syrup and pour the remaining syrup over the top. Chill until set.
7. Meanwhile, make the vanilla bavarois: place the water in a small saucepan and sprinkle over the gelatine. Leave for 5 minutes until spongy.
8. Place the milk and vanilla pod in a heavy-based saucepan and heat gently to scalding point. Remove from the heat and leave to infuse for 15 minutes, then strain.
9. Mix the egg yolks and sugar together. Stir in the warm milk and return to the saucepan. Stir continuously with a wooden spoon for 3–5 minutes, or until the custard is thick enough to coat the back of the spoon. Be careful not to overheat or the mixture will curdle. Strain the custard into a bowl and leave to cool to room temperature.
10. Dissolve the gelatine over a very low heat without boiling, then stir into the cooling custard. Stir occasionally until on the point of setting. Whip the cream lightly and fold it into the vanilla custard.
11. Pour the mixture on top of the tamarillo mixture. Cover and chill for 2 hours, until set.
12. To serve, run a knife round the edges of the terrine, dip briefly in hot water and turn on to a serving plate. Cut into slices to serve.

 *SAUTERNES*

HOT VANILLA AND PISTACHIO SOUFFLÉ

SERVES 4

15g/½oz butter, melted
1 teaspoon caster sugar
290ml/½ pint milk
1 vanilla pod
55g/2oz caster sugar
5 eggs

15g/½oz plain flour
15g/½oz cornflour
½ teaspoon vanilla essence
55g/2oz pistachio nuts, chopped

To finish
icing sugar

1. Preheat the oven to 200°C/400°F/gas mark 6. Put a baking sheet to heat on the top shelf of the oven.

2. Prepare a 15cm/6in soufflé dish: brush the inside of the dish with the melted butter and sprinkle with the sugar.

3. Put the milk and vanilla pod into a heavy-based saucepan. Bring to scalding point, then remove from the heat and leave to infuse for 10 minutes before removing the vanilla pod.

4. Cream the sugar with 1 egg yolk and 1 egg until light. Stir in the flour and cornflour to form a smooth paste.

5. Blend in the infused milk. Return the mixture to the clean pan. Bring the mixture to the boil over a low heat, stirring constantly. As it begins to thicken the custard will become very lumpy; as it comes to the boil the lumps will disappear. Boil for 1 minute.

6. Remove the saucepan from the heat and allow to cool for a minute, then mix with the vanilla essence and 3 egg yolks.

7. Whisk the 4 egg whites until they form soft peaks. Fold into the custard with the pistachio nuts.

8. Pour into the prepared soufflé dish, filling it two-thirds full.

9. Place on the preheated baking sheet and bake in the preheated oven for 15 minutes, until well risen.

10. Remove from the oven and quickly dredge the top of the soufflé with icing sugar. Return the soufflé to the oven for a further minute. Serve immediately.

 *MUSCAT DE BEAUMES DE VENISE*

PANNA COTTA
(Cooked Cream Moulds)

This recipe was given to us by Fiona Burrell, former Principal of Leith's School.

SERVES 6

570ml/1 pint double cream
55g/2oz caster sugar
1 vanilla pod
1 thinly pared strip of lemon zest
10g/⅓oz powdered gelatine
55ml/2fl oz milk
55ml/2fl oz light rum
oil for greasing
1 tablespoon caster sugar

To serve
Sete al Liquore (see page 580)

1. Heat half the cream with the 55g/2oz caster sugar, vanilla pod and lemon zest in a heavy-based saucepan over a medium heat.

2. Meanwhile, soak the gelatine in the milk.

3. When the cream reaches the boil, remove the vanilla pod and lemon zest. Add the softened gelatine and the rum. Stir well to dissolve the gelatine, then strain into a large bowl and leave to cool.

4. Meanwhile, oil 6 dariole moulds or ramekins.

5. When the cooked cream has reached setting point, whip the remaining cream with the 1 tablespoon caster sugar until it just holds its shape.

6. Carefully fold the cooked and whipped creams together, folding whichever is thinner into the thicker mixture. Pour into the prepared moulds. Tap them on a work surface to release any air pockets and chill until set.

7. Dip the moulds quickly into very hot water and turn out on to individual dishes. Serve immediately with Sete al Liquore.

 *MONBAZILLAC*

SEVILLE ORANGE SYLLABUB WITH NOUGATINE

SERVES 4

For the syllabub
3 tablespoons Grand Marnier
3 tablespoons Seville orange marmalade
grated zest and juice of 2 Seville oranges
150ml/¼ pint double cream
290ml/½ pint mascarpone

For the nougatine
55g/2oz caster sugar
55g/2oz hazelnuts, toasted and skinned
oil for greasing

1. Mix together the Grand Marnier, marmalade, orange zest and juice.
2. Mix the cream with the mascarpone in a bowl and add the marmalade mixture. Pour into individual dishes and chill.
3. Meanwhile, make the nougatine: put the sugar into a small saucepan and heat gently, stirring occasionally, until a rich dark caramel colour. Add the hazelnuts and stir together. Turn on to a lightly oiled baking sheet and leave for 15 minutes to set.
4. When the nougatine has cooled, grind coarsely in a food processor or chop finely. Just before serving, sprinkle over the syllabubs.

 *AUSTRALIAN LIQUEUR MUSCAT*

CAPPUCCINO BRÛLÉ

SERVES 4

570ml/1 pint double cream
1 vanilla pod, split
30g/1oz medium-ground coffee
8 egg yolks
55–85g/2–3oz caster sugar

For the topping
4 heaped teaspoons drinking chocolate powder
caster sugar, or icing sugar if you have a blow-torch

1. Preheat the oven to 170°C/325°F/gas mark 3.
2. Put the cream, vanilla pod and coffee into a heavy-based saucepan and heat to scalding point. Turn off the heat, cover the pan with a lid and leave to infuse for 15 minutes.
3. Beat the yolks with the sugar and pour in the warm cream.
4. Place the pan over a very low heat and stir continuously with a wooden spoon until the mixture thickens sufficiently to coat the back of the spoon. Be very careful that the custard does not boil, or it will curdle and cannot be corrected.
5. Immediately strain the custard through a fine sieve into a bowl. This will ensure that the custard stops cooking and will also prevent curdling. Taste the custard and add extra sugar if needed. Divide the custard between 4 ramekins.
6. Sprinkle 1 heaped teaspoon of the drinking chocolate powder over each custard.
7. Place the ramekins in a large roasting tin half filled with hot water (a bain-marie) and bake on a low shelf in the preheated oven for 5–8 minutes, to create a good skin on top. Remove from the roasting tin and allow to cool, then refrigerate overnight.
8. Preheat the grill to its highest setting.
9. Sprinkle a 5mm/¼in layer of caster sugar (or icing sugar if you have a blow-torch) on top.
10. When the grill is blazing hot, put the custards under it, as close to the heat as possible, until the sugar caramelizes. If using icing sugar, caramelize it with a blow-torch. Allow the custards to cool completely, then chill for 6 hours before serving.

 *MUSCAT DE RIVESALTES*

WARM DRIED FRUIT YOGHURT BRÛLÉE

SERVES 4

8 dried pears, sliced
55g/2oz dried mango slices, diced
55g/2oz dried apricots, diced
55g/2oz dried prunes, stoned and diced
30g/1oz sultanas
55g/2oz dried pineapple, diced
150ml/¼ pint orange juice
1 tea bag
2 tablespoons brandy
5 tablespoons plain yoghurt
5 tablespoons Greek yoghurt
8 tablespoons soft light brown sugar

1. Put the dried fruit into a large saucepan and add the fruit juice and the tea bag. Bring to the boil, then lower the heat and simmer for 2–3 minutes. Remove from the heat, **add** the brandy and allow to stand for 30 minutes.
2. Preheat the grill to its highest setting.
3. Remove the tea bag from the saucepan and discard. Divide the fruit and juice between four small ovenproof dishes.
4. Mix the yoghurts together in a bowl and spoon over the fruit, so that it is evenly covered.
5. Sprinkle the top of each dish with a couple of spoonfuls of the sugar and press it flat. Place the dishes on a baking sheet and grill on the top shelf until the sugar has melted and is bubbling. Allow to cool for 2–3 minutes and serve warm.

 *MUSCAT DE RIVESALTES*

ICE CREAMS AND SORBETS

WHITE AND MILK CHOCOLATE CHUNK DARK CHOCOLATE ICE CREAM

SERVES 4

110g/4oz dark chocolate, chopped
1 teaspoon instant coffee powder
150ml/¼ pint milk
570ml/1 pint double or whipping cream
4 egg yolks
55g/2oz caster sugar
3 tablespoons rum
110g/4oz white chocolate, roughly chopped
110g/4oz milk chocolate, roughly chopped

1. Put the dark chocolate and the coffee into a small saucepan with half the milk and stir continuously over a low heat until the chocolate has just melted. Remove from the heat, stir in the remaining milk and allow to cool for 2–3 minutes.
2. Scald the cream in a separate saucepan and blend into the chocolate milk.
3. Beat the egg yolks and sugar in a bowl until light, stir in the chocolate cream and return the mixture to the rinsed-out pan. Cook over a medium heat, stirring constantly with a wooden spoon, until the custard is sufficiently thickened to coat the back of the spoon. On no account allow the custard to boil. Strain and allow to cool.
4. When the custard is cool, stir in the rum and taste for sweetness, adding a little more sugar if necessary. Transfer to a freezerproof container.
5. Freeze until the mixture has begun to

thicken, then stir in the white and milk chocolate. Freeze again until firm. Allow at least 1 further hour in the freezer for the flavours to ripen.
6. To serve: transfer the ice cream to the refrigerator for 15 minutes, then scoop into chilled bowls.

 *SAUTERNES*

CHOCOLATE CHRISTMAS BOMBES

This recipe was given to us by Eithne Neame, teacher at Leith's School.

SERVES 6

85g/3oz plain chocolate, chopped
2 tablespoons rum
1 tablespoon water
170g/6oz unsweetened chestnut purée
30g/1oz raisins
30g/1oz sultanas
30g/1oz candied peel
55g/2oz glacé cherries
290ml/½ pint double cream
2 egg whites
45g/1½oz caster sugar

1. Line 6 dariole moulds or ramekins with clingfilm.
2. Put the chocolate, 1 tablespoon of the rum and the water into a heatproof bowl set over, not in, a pan of simmering water and leave until the chocolate has just melted. Remove from the heat and stir into the chestnut purée. Set aside.
3. Sprinkle the remaining rum over the dried

586

fruits and leave to macerate for 5 minutes.

4. Whip the cream lightly. Whisk the egg whites until they form stiff peaks, then gradually add the sugar, a teaspoon at a time, whisking well after each addition.

5. Carefully fold the macerated fruit into the chocolate and chestnut mixture, then add the cream and finally the whisked egg whites.

6. Divide the mixture between the prepared moulds, cover and freeze for at least 3 hours.

7. To serve: remove the moulds from the freezer 10 minutes before serving. Turn on to individual plates, remove the clingfilm and serve immediately.

 *SAUTERNES*

THAI INFUSED ICE CREAM

SERVES 4

570ml/1 pint whipping cream
5cm/2in piece of galangal (see page 137), peeled and finely chopped
2 sticks of lemon grass, chopped
4 kaffir lime leaves, crushed
grated zest of 1 lime
10 whole black peppercorns
1 teaspoon ground cumin
85g/3oz granulated sugar
150ml/¼ pint water
4 egg yolks
2 pieces of stem ginger, chopped
1 teaspoon ground ginger

1. Put the cream, galangal, lemon grass, lime leaves, lime zest, peppercorns and cumin into a saucepan and heat gently until the cream comes to scalding point. Remove from the heat and allow to infuse for 30 minutes. Strain and set aside.

2. Meanwhile, put the sugar and water into a small heavy-based saucepan. Dissolve over a low heat, then boil for 3 minutes. Remove from the heat and allow to cool for a minute.

3. Put the egg yolks into a large bowl with the

stem and ground ginger. Whisk lightly, then pour on the warm sugar syrup (do not allow the syrup to touch the whisk if doing this in a machine as it cools fast against the cold metal and can harden and stick to the beaters). Fold in the cream and pour into an ice tray.

4. Freeze until half frozen, then whisk again to break up any large ice crystals. Freeze again.

5. Remove the ice cream from the freezer 20 minutes before it is to be eaten and scoop into a chilled glass bowl.

NOTE: In the absence of galangal, fresh root ginger may be used.

 *SAUTERNES*

SEVILLE ORANGE AND COINTREAU ICE CREAM

SERVES 4

170g/6oz Seville or bitter orange marmalade, warmed
290ml/½ pint crème anglaise (see page 661)
290ml/½ pint double cream
3 tablespoons Cointreau

1. Mix the marmalade with the crème anglaise, then add the cream and Cointreau.

2. Transfer the mixture to a freezerproof container and freeze overnight.

3. Transfer the ice cream to the refrigerator for 15 minutes. Cut it into cubes and whizz in a food processor, using the pulse action, until the ice crystals have broken up. Return quickly to the freezer and freeze for 2 hours before serving.

NOTE: If you have an ice-cream machine, churn it at stage 2.

 AUSTRALIAN ORANGE MUSCAT AND FLORA

NUTMEG AND BAY LEAF ICE CREAM

SERVES 4

290ml/½ pint milk
1–1½ large nutmegs, freshly grated
2 bay leaves
3 egg yolks
85g/3oz caster sugar
150ml/¼ pint crème fraîche

To serve
white chocolate and macadamia nut biscuits
    (see page 356)

1. Put the milk, nutmeg and bay leaves into a saucepan and bring to scalding point. Remove from the heat and allow to infuse for 30 minutes.
2. Put the egg yolks and sugar into a bowl and beat together until pale and creamy. Pour the cooled milk over and stir well.
3. Return the mixture to the rinsed-out pan and cook over a low to medium heat, stirring constantly with a wooden spoon, until the custard is sufficiently thickened to coat the back of the spoon. On no account allow the custard to boil.
4. Remove the pan from the heat and pour into a clean bowl. Remove the bay leaves and allow to cool.
5. Mix the custard thoroughly with the crème fraîche and churn in an ice-cream maker. Transfer to a freezerproof container and freeze until firm. Allow at least 1 further hour in the freezer for the flavours to 'ripen'.
6. To serve: transfer the ice cream to the refrigerator for 30 minutes before serving in scoops in chilled bowls, with the biscuits handed separately.

 AUSTRALIAN LIQUEUR MUSCAT

PINK GRAPEFRUIT CURD ICE CREAM

SERVES 6

1 quantity pink grapefruit curd (see page 221)
290ml/½ pint Greek yoghurt
290ml/½ pint crème fraîche

1. Mix together the pink grapefruit curd, yoghurt and crème fraîche. Transfer to a freezerproof container, cover closely and freeze.
2. Transfer the ice cream to the refrigerator about 1 hour before serving.

NOTE: This ice cream is also delicious made with good-quality shop-bought lemon curd.

 SAUTERNES

LYCHEE AND STAR ANISE SORBET WITH TOASTED COCONUT

SERVES 4

2 × 340g/12oz cans of peeled lychees in syrup
6 whole star anise, crushed
1 vanilla pod
grated zest and juice of 2 limes
2.5cm/1in piece of fresh root ginger, peeled and
    chopped
1–2 sprigs of fresh mint
icing sugar (optional)
1 egg white

To serve
55g/2oz coconut flakes, toasted

1. Strain the lychees, put the syrup into a saucepan and set the lychees aside.
2. Put the star anise, vanilla pod, lime zest, ginger and mint into the syrup. Bring to the boil, then lower the heat and simmer for 5

minutes. Remove from the heat and allow to cool completely, then strain.

3. Reserve 4 lychees and liquidize the remainder in a blender. Add the cold syrup and the lime juice. Taste for sweetness and flavour, adding a little icing sugar if necessary. Transfer to a freezerproof container.

4. Freeze the mixture until slushy, then break up with a fork. Dice the reserved lychees and fold in with the egg white. Freeze again until solid.

5. To serve: spoon the lychee sorbet into 4 chilled individual serving dishes and sprinkle with the toasted coconut.

 AUSTRALIAN ORANGE MUSCAT

MANGO AND PINEAPPLE SORBET

SERVES 4

1 small ripe mango
½ small pineapple

For the syrup
120ml/4fl oz water
85g/3oz granulated sugar
juice of 1 lemon
1 egg white

1. Peel the mango and pineapple and purée the flesh in a food processor.

2. Heat the water and sugar in a saucepan until dissolved. Bring to the boil, then lower the heat and simmer for 2–3 minutes. Remove from the heat and allow to cool. Add the lemon juice and fruit pulp and pour into an ice tray.

3. Freeze until just set. Break up the mixture with a fork and stir in the egg white. Freeze again until set.

4. Transfer to the refrigerator for 30 minutes before serving.

 *SAUTERNES*

POMEGRANATE GRANITA

SERVES 4

570ml/1 pint water
110g/4oz caster sugar
thinly pared zest of 1 orange
3 pomegranates
2 tablespoons gin
juice of 1 lemon

1. Heat the water and sugar in a heavy-based saucepan until the sugar is completely dissolved. Add the orange zest and boil rapidly for 5 minutes, or until the syrup is tacky. Remove from the heat and allow to cool, then strain.

2. Halve the pomegranates and remove the seeds and juice with a teaspoon, taking care to remove any pith. Stir the seeds and juice into the syrup with the gin and lemon juice.

3. Transfer to an ice tray and freeze until solid.

4. To serve: remove from the freezer 10 minutes before serving, break up the granita with a fork and pile into chilled ramekins.

 *ASTI SPUMANTE*

VANILLA, CINNAMON AND GINGER SORBET

SERVES 8

450g/1lb granulated sugar
720ml/1¼ pints water
1 vanilla pod, split lengthways
2 cinnamon sticks
5cm/2in piece of fresh root ginger, peeled and chopped
grated zest and juice of 1 lime
juice of 1 lemon
1 egg white
1 piece of stem ginger, finely chopped

1. Heat the sugar and water in a heavy-based

saucepan until the sugar is completely dissolved. Add the vanilla pod, cinnamon sticks, ginger, lime zest and juice and the lemon juice.

2. Bring to the boil, then lower the heat and simmer for 5 minutes. Remove from the heat and leave to infuse for 30 minutes.

3. When the syrup is cold, strain into a freezerproof container and freeze overnight.

4. Transfer the sorbet to the refrigerator for 15 minutes, then turn out on to a board and cut up into cubes. Place half the cubes in a food processor with half the egg white and whizz, using the pulse action, until smooth and white. Return quickly to the freezer and continue in the same way with the remaining cubes. (It is important not to allow the ice crystals to melt in the food processor by whizzing for too long.)

5. Stir the stem ginger into the sorbet and freeze for 2–3 hours before serving.

 *AUSTRALIAN BOTRYTISED SÉMILLON*

GRAPEFRUIT AND MINT SPOOM

A spoom is an old-fashioned sorbet, which has a slightly granular texture and sharp flavour.

SERVES 4

170g/6oz granulated sugar
425ml/¾ pint water
thinly pared zest and juice of 1 large grapefruit
thinly pared zest and juice of 1 lime
1 handful of fresh mint leaves

To decorate
fresh mint leaves
½ egg white, beaten until frothy
caster sugar

1. Put the sugar, water and grapefruit and lime zest into a heavy-based saucepan. Dissolve the sugar over a low heat, then boil rapidly for 3 minutes. Remove from the heat, add the mint

leaves and allow to cool completely.

2. When the syrup is cold, add the grapefruit and lime juice and strain. Pour into a freezerproof container.

3. Freeze for 1 hour, or until beginning to solidify, then break up with a fork and refreeze until firm. The spoom should be slightly granular.

4. Dip the mint leaves in the egg white. Dredge with caster sugar, shake well to remove excess and leave to dry on a wire rack.

5. Serve the spoom decorated with the frosted mint leaves.

SAUTERNES

MERINGUES

HOT WINTER FRUIT MERINGUE

This recipe was given to us by Janey Orr, former teacher at Leith's School.

SERVES 8

85g/3oz sultanas
6 tablespoons port
6 large red plums, halved and stoned
½ cinnamon stick
110g/4oz seedless red grapes
110g/4oz seedless white grapes
4 egg whites
225g/8oz caster sugar
255g/9oz mascarpone
16 amaretti biscuits, roughly crushed

1. Soak the sultanas in the port for at least 3 hours, or overnight.
2. Preheat the oven to 170°C/325°F/gas mark 3.
3. Put the plums and cinnamon stick into a heavy-based saucepan, cover and cook over a low heat until the plums soften. Add the grapes and the sultanas and port and cook for a further 2–3 minutes.
4. Strain the fruit through a sieve and reduce the liquid by boiling rapidly to a very syrupy consistency. Put the fruit and syrup into a large pie dish and leave to cool.
5. Meanwhile, make the meringue: whisk the egg whites until they form stiff peaks.
6. Add 2 tablespoons of the sugar and whisk again until stiff and shiny. Fold in the remaining sugar.
7. Beat the mascarpone lightly and spread it over the fruit. Sprinkle on the crushed amaretti biscuits and pile the meringue on top.

8. Bake in the preheated oven for 15–20 minutes, or until the meringue is cooked and a pale golden-brown.

 AUSTRALIAN ORANGE MUSCAT

GINGER MERINGUE BOMBE

SERVES 6

1 quantity ginger and brown sugar meringues
   (see following recipe)
2 tablespoons chopped stem ginger
2 tablespoons stem ginger syrup
290ml/½ pint double cream

1. Put the meringues into a bowl and break into pieces.
2. Add the stem ginger and the syrup.
3. Whip the cream lightly and fold into the meringues.
4. Put the mixture into a bombe mould or a loaf tin lined with silicone paper. Cover with kitchen foil and freeze until firm.
5. To serve: transfer the bombe to the refrigerator for 1 hour, then turn out on to a serving plate. Cut into slices to serve.

 AUSTRALIAN LIQUEUR MUSCAT

GINGER AND BROWN SUGAR MERINGUES

MAKES 16

4 egg whites
30g/1oz caster sugar
200g/7oz soft light brown sugar, sifted
2 teaspoons ground ginger

To serve
150ml/¼ pint double cream
2 pieces of stem ginger, chopped
2 tablespoons stem ginger syrup

1. Preheat the oven to 150°C/300°F/gas mark 2.
2. Line 2 baking sheets with silicone paper.
3. Whisk the egg whites until stiff but not dry, then add the caster sugar. Whisk again until very stiff and shiny. Fold in the brown sugar and ginger with a large metal spoon. (Do not overfold or the mixture will become runny.)
4. Fill a piping bag fitted with a medium plain nozzle with the meringue and pipe small pyramids on to the prepared baking sheets.
5. Bake in the preheated oven for 1 hour. Remove from the oven, carefully peel off the lining paper and transfer to a wire rack to cool completely.
6. Whip the cream to soft peaks, fold in the stem ginger and sweeten with the syrup. Use to sandwich the meringues together. Pile on to a serving dish and serve within 1 hour.

NOTE: Spices such as ground coriander, cinnamon or nutmeg can be used to flavour the meringues instead of the ginger.

 *AUSTRALIAN LIQUEUR MUSCAT*

CARAMEL MERINGUE BASKETS

SERVES 6

170g/6oz granulated sugar
150ml/¼ pint water
3 egg whites

For the filling
150ml/¼ pint double cream, lightly whipped
caramelized clementines (see page 578)

1. Preheat the oven to 110°C/225°F/gas mark ½. Line 2 baking sheets with silicone paper.
2. Put the sugar into a heavy-based saucepan with half the water.
3. Dissolve the sugar slowly without stirring it or allowing the water to boil.
4. Once all the sugar has dissolved, turn up the heat and boil until it is a good caramel colour.
5. Immediately tip in the remaining water (it will splutter dangerously, so stand back).
6. Stir until any lumps have dissolved, then remove from the heat and allow to cool for a minute.
7. Whisk the egg whites until they form stiff peaks. Pour the caramelized sugar syrup steadily on to the egg whites, whisking all the time, but taking care that the syrup does not strike the whisk wires, or it will harden. Continue to whisk until the meringue is thick and glossy.
8. Put the meringue mixture into a piping bag fitted with a rose nozzle and pipe on to the prepared baking sheets to form little baskets.
9. Place in the preheated oven for 2 hours to dry out. Remove from the oven, carefully peel off the lining paper and transfer the meringues to a wire rack. Leave to cool completely.
10. Place a little cream in each basket. Break the caramelized clementines into individual segments and pile on top of the cream. Drizzle some of the syrup on top. Serve within 30 minutes.

 *MUSCAT DE BEAUMES DE VENISE*

INDIVIDUAL RUMTOPF ALASKAS

SERVES 8

55g/2oz butter
170g/6oz ratafia biscuits, crushed
1 quantity rich vanilla ice cream (see page 665)
8 tablespoons rumtopf fruit (see page 369),
  strained with the liquor reserved
4 egg whites
a pinch of salt
225g/8oz caster sugar

1. Melt the butter in a saucepan and stir in the ratafias.
2. Using a 7.5cm/3in plain biscuit cutter, make 8 circular ratafia bases on 2 baking sheets, keeping them well spaced and pressing the crumbs firmly together inside the biscuit cutter. Chill for 20 minutes.
3. Place a scoop of the ice cream on to each base, then pile 1 tablespoon of the rumtopf fruit on top of the ice cream. Put the trays into the freezer.
4. Preheat the oven to 230°C/450°F/gas mark 8.
5. Whisk the egg whites with the salt until they form stiff peaks. Whisk in 2 tablespoons of the sugar and continue to whisk until the mixture is stiff and shiny. Fold in the remaining sugar with a large metal spoon.
6. Remove the bases from the freezer and spread the meringue evenly over the fruit and ice cream, making sure that there are no gaps uncovered.
7. Place the alaskas in the oven for 5–8 minutes, or until they are golden-brown.
8. Warm the reserved rumtopf liquor in a small saucepan and pour into a sauce-boat. Transfer the alaskas to individual plates and serve immediately, with the rumtopf sauce handed separately.

 *ASTI SPUMANTE*

PASTRIES, PIES AND TARTS

CANDIED CITRUS SAVARIN

SERVES 4

125g/4½oz plain flour
a pinch of salt
15g/½oz yeast
2 teaspoons sugar
5 tablespoons warm milk
2 eggs
45g/1½oz butter, softened
grated zest of 1 lemon

For the syrup
thinly pared zest of 1 orange
thinly pared zest of 1 lemon
thinly pared zest of 1 lime
170g/6oz granulated sugar
210ml/7½fl oz water
2 tablespoons Grand Marnier
2–3 teaspoons caster sugar

To serve
150ml/¼ pint Greek yoghurt

1. Sift the flour and salt together into a warmed bowl.
2. Cream the yeast and sugar together until frothy. Stir into the milk.
3. Make a well in the middle of the flour and add the yeast mixture and the eggs. Stir together to form a soft dough. Beat the dough in the bowl for 5 minutes. Transfer to a lightly oiled bowl, cover and leave to rise until doubled in bulk.
4. Cream the butter and lemon zest together until very soft.

5. Preheat the oven to 200°C/400°F/gas mark 6.
6. Stir the butter into the dough and work together with your hand until the ingredients are very well mixed.
7. Generously butter a 1.1litre/2 pint ring mould. Tip the dough into the mould, cover and leave to prove for 15–20 minutes.
8. Bake on the top shelf of the preheated oven for 25–30 minutes, or until well risen and golden-brown.
9. Make the syrup: cut the citrus zest into very thin needle shreds. Blanch in boiling water for 5 minutes. Drain and refresh in cold water.
10. Dissolve the sugar in the water in a saucepan over a very low heat. Bring to the boil, then add the citrus zest needle shreds and simmer for 20–25 minutes, or until transparent.
11. Lift the zest from the syrup with a slotted spoon. Add the Grand Marnier to the syrup and keep hot. Toss the needle shreds in the caster sugar and allow to dry for a few minutes.
12. When the savarin is cooked, do not turn out of the mould immediately. Prick it all over at intervals with a skewer. Pour over the hot syrup and allow to stand for 20–30 minutes in the ring mould.
13. Loosen the savarin carefully and turn on to a serving plate. Arrange the candied citrus zest on top. Spoon the yoghurt into the centre and serve.

 *SAUTERNES*

BLOOD ORANGE AND STEM GINGER MERINGUE PIE

SERVES 6–8

170g/6oz flour quantity pâte sucrée (see page 645)

For the filling
juice of 2 blood oranges
15g/½oz cornflour
grated zest of 3 blood oranges
juice of 1 lemon
2 pieces of stem ginger, chopped
85g/3oz butter, diced
225g/8oz granulated sugar
3 eggs, lightly beaten and strained
6 blood oranges, peeled and segmented

For the meringue
3 egg whites
85g/3oz soft light brown sugar
85g/3oz caster sugar

To serve
double cream or crème fraîche

1. Preheat the oven to 190°C/375°F/gas mark 5.
2. Roll out the pastry and use to line a 20cm/8in flan ring. Chill for 30 minutes. Bake the pastry blind (see page 640). Remove the lining paper and beans. Reduce the oven temperature to 170°C/325°F/gas mark 3.
3. Make the filling: mix the blood orange juice with the cornflour until there are no lumps. Put the mixture with all the remaining filling ingredients except the orange segments, into a heavy-based saucepan or double boiler and heat gently, stirring all the time, until the mixture is thick. Pour into a bowl and leave to cool.
4. Pour the mixture into the pastry case and arrange the blood orange segments on top.
5. Make the meringue: mix both sugars together. Whisk the egg whites until stiff. Add 1 tablespoon of the sugar and whisk again until very stiff and firm. Fold the remaining sugar

into the egg white mixture. Pile the meringue on to the pie. It is essential to cover the filling completely or the pie will weep. Dust with a little extra sugar.
6. Bake in the preheated oven for 10–15 minutes, or until the meringue is pale biscuit colour. Allow to cool for 5 minutes before serving.

 AUSTRALIAN BOTRYTISED RIESLING

DEEP TREACLE TART WITH WHISKY CREAM

SERVES 10–12

For the pastry
225g/8oz plain flour
a pinch of salt
30g/1oz caster sugar
140g/5oz butter
1 egg yolk
6 tablespoons very cold water

For the filling
675g/1½lb golden syrup
grated zest and juice of 1 large lemon
340g/12oz fresh white breadcrumbs

For the whisky cream
290ml/½ pint double cream, lightly whipped
2 tablespoons whisky

1. Preheat the oven to 200°C/400°F/gas mark 6. Place a baking sheet in the oven to heat.
2. Sift the flour with the salt and sugar into a large bowl. Rub in the butter with the fingertips until the mixture resembles coarse breadcrumbs.
3. Mix the egg yolk with the water and add to the mixture.
4. Mix to a firm dough with a knife, then with the fingers of one hand. It may be necessary to add more water, but the pastry should not be too damp. (Though crumbly pastry is more difficult to handle, it produces a shorter, lighter result.)

5. Roll out the pastry to the thickness of a £1 coin and use to line a 28cm/11in loose-based flan case 2.5cm/1in deep. Chill for 30 minutes to relax. (This prevents the pastry from shrinking during baking.)

6. Warm the syrup with the lemon zest and juice until liquid. Stir in the breadcrumbs and set aside to cool. Tip into the flan case and spread evenly.

7. Place the tart on the hot baking sheet and bake near the top of the oven for 20 minutes, then reduce the oven temperature to 180°C/ 350°F/gas mark 4 for 30 minutes, or until the pastry is golden-brown (if the pastry is browning too fast, move it to a lower shelf in the oven).

8. Make the whisky cream: carefully fold the whisky into the cream and pile into a jug.

9. Serve the tart warm with the whisky cream handed separately.

 *AUSTRALIAN LIQUEUR MUSCAT OR TOKAY ASZU*

WALNUT, HONEY AND CANDIED ORANGE TART

SERVES 6

170g/6oz flour quantity pâte sucrée (see page 645)
110g/4oz walnuts, roughly chopped

For the candied orange zest
thinly pared zest of 2 large oranges and a little juice
225g/8oz granulated sugar
6 tablespoons water
1 tablespoon clear honey

To serve
4 tablespoons crème fraîche

1. Preheat the oven to 190°C/375°F/gas mark 5.

2. Roll the pastry into a 30cm/12in circle and place on a baking sheet. Decorate the edges with a fork or the point of a sharp knife pressed

broad side into the pastry, or by pinching between fingers and thumb. Prick lightly all over with a fork. Gently press the walnuts on to the pastry. Chill for 15 minutes to relax (this prevents the pastry from shrinking during baking).

3. Bake in the preheated oven for about 15 minutes, or until the pastry is a pale biscuit colour and the walnuts lightly browned.

4. Loosen with a palette knife and allow to cool slightly and harden on the baking sheet. Slip on to a wire rack and leave to cool completely.

5. Meanwhile, prepare the candied orange zest: cut the orange zest into strips 5mm/¼in wide. Put into a small saucepan with enough water to cover and boil for 5 minutes to remove the bitter taste. Drain and refresh under cold running water.

6. Bring the sugar and water to the boil in the saucepan, stir in the orange zest and allow to boil for 5 minutes, then remove from the heat. Leave to stand for 1 hour. Lift the orange zest from the syrup and allow to drain on a wire rack. Reserve the syrup.

7. Mix together the orange zest, honey, 4 tablespoons of the syrup and 1–2 tablespoons orange juice.

8. Spoon on top of the walnuts. Cut into wedges to serve, with the crème fraîche handed separately.

 *AUSTRALIAN ORANGE MUSCAT*

LIME TART WITH ALMOND PASTRY

SERVES 6

225g/8oz flour quantity pâte frollée (see page 646)
juice of ½ lemon
grated zest and juice of 4 limes
85g/3oz butter
225g/8oz granulated sugar
4 eggs, beaten
3 tablespoons double cream

To serve
290ml/½ pint crème fraîche

1. Roll out the pastry and use to line a 22.5cm/9in flan case. Chill for about 45 minutes to relax (this prevents the pastry from shrinking during baking).
2. Preheat the oven to 190°C/375°F/gas mark 5.
3. Bake the pastry case blind in the preheated oven. Leave to cool.
4. Reduce the oven temperature to 150°C/300°F/gas mark 2.
5. Make the lime curd: put the lemon juice and lime zest and juice, the butter, sugar and eggs into a heavy-based saucepan. Cook over a low heat, stirring constantly with a wooden spoon, until the sugar has dissolved and the mixture has thickened sufficiently to coat the back of the spoon. On no account allow the mixture to boil, or it will curdle. Strain the curd through a sieve into a chilled bowl and stir in the cream. Allow to cool.
6. Pour the lime curd into the pastry case. Bake in the preheated oven for 25–35 minutes, or until the filling has set (when it should barely move if gently shaken).
7. Transfer the tart to a wire rack and leave to cool. Just before serving, spread the crème fraîche on top of the tart.

 *AUSTRALIAN LIQUEUR MUSCAT*

PEAR AND PECAN NUT TATIN

This recipe was kindly given to us by Alison Cavaliero, Co-Vice Principal of Leith's School.

SERVES 4

For the pastry
170g/6oz plain flour
55g/2oz fine polenta
140g/5oz butter
55g/2oz caster sugar
1 egg, beaten

For the topping
110g/4oz butter
110g/4oz caster sugar
6–8 ripe Comice pears, peeled and quartered
grated zest of 1 lemon
110g/4oz pecan nuts

To serve
290ml/½ pint Greek yoghurt

1. Preheat the oven to 190°C/375°F/gas mark 5.
2. Make the pastry: sift the flour and polenta together into a food processor, add the butter and pulse on and off until the mixture resembles fine breadcrumbs. Add the sugar and half the egg and continue to pulse on and off, adding the remaining egg if it looks a little dry.
3. Turn the mixture on to a work surface and draw it together. Put the pastry between 2 pieces of clingfilm and roll out to a 22.5cm/9in circle. Chill for 30 minutes to relax (this prevents the pastry from shrinking during baking).
4. Meanwhile, make the topping: melt the butter in an ovenproof 22.5cm/9in frying pan, add the sugar and stir over a low heat for 2–3 minutes.
5. Arrange the pears on top of the butter and sugar mixture and sprinkle with the lemon zest. Set over a medium heat and allow the butter and sugar to begin to caramelize around the pears, turning the frying pan from time to time to prevent the mixture from browning unevenly.
6. When the mixture has caramelized, remove the pan from the heat and put on to a baking sheet. Sprinkle the pecan nuts over the pears and put the pastry on top, trimming off any excess.
7. Bake on the top shelf of the preheated oven for 25–30 minutes, or until the pastry is golden-brown.
8. When the tatin is cooked, allow to stand for 1 minute before inverting on to a serving plate. Hand the yoghurt separately.

 *SAUTERNES*

CHOCOLATE SHORTBREAD TORTE WITH STICKY CRANBERRY GLAZE

SERVES 6

For the shortbread base
170g/6oz unsalted butter
85g/3oz caster sugar
30g/1oz cocoa powder
225g/8oz plain flour

For the filling
225g/8oz full-fat cream cheese
5 tablespoons double cream
140g/5oz plain chocolate
2 eggs
1 egg yolk
1 teaspoon coffee essence
2 tablespoons rum

For the topping
85g/3oz granulated sugar
5 tablespoons water
170g/6oz cranberries
5 tablespoons soured cream
icing sugar for dusting

1. Preheat the oven to 190°C/375°F/gas mark 5.
2. Make the shortbread base: melt the butter in a saucepan and stir in the sugar and cocoa powder. Remove from the heat and allow to cool for 2 minutes. Sift the flour and mix into the cooled butter mixture. Press the mixture on to the bottom of a 20cm/8in spring-form mould.
3. Bake in the preheated oven for 20–25 minutes, then remove from the oven and allow to cool for 5 minutes. Reduce the oven temperature to 150°C/300°F/gas mark 2.
4. Make the filling: beat the cream cheese until smooth.
5. Heat the cream and chocolate together in a small saucepan over a low heat until just melted. Stir into the cream cheese with the eggs,

egg yolk, coffee essence and rum. Beat well until smooth and pour on to the cooled crust.
6. Return to the middle of the oven and bake for about 30 minutes, or until the filling has set. Remove from the oven and allow to cool.
7. Meanwhile, make the topping: heat the sugar and water together in a saucepan until dissolved. Add the cranberries and bring to the boil, then lower the heat and simmer for 5–7 minutes, or until the liquid has reduced to a glaze. Remove from the heat and allow to cool.
8. Spread the soured cream over the top of the torte and arrange the cranberries on top. Dust with icing sugar and serve.

 *SAUTERNES*

DEEP FILLED RICH BRANDY MINCE PIES

MAKES 8

340g/12oz flour quantity sweet shortcrust
  pastry (see page 642)
1 egg white
caster sugar

For the filling
85g/3oz sultanas
85g/3oz raisins
85g/3oz currants
30g/1oz chopped mixed peel
85g/3oz shredded beef or vegetable suet
55g/2oz chopped almonds, toasted
grated zest and juice of 1 large orange
grated zest and juice of 1 lemon
1 teaspoon ground mixed spice
85g/3oz soft light brown sugar
4 tablespoons brandy

To serve
1 quantity brandy cream (see page 618)

1. Make the filling: mix all the ingredients together in a bowl, cover and leave to macerate overnight.
2. Roll out the pastry to a thickness of about

3–4mm/⅛in and cut out 10 large discs to line individual deep patty tins and smaller discs for the lids. Place the large discs in the patty tins.

3. Spoon the filling into the pastry cases. Brush the edges of the lids with a little water and press them into place on top of the filling, sealing the edges.

4. Make 2 small slits in the top of each pie. Chill the pies for 30 minutes.

5. Preheat the oven to 190°C/375°F/gas mark 5.

6. Brush the tops of the pies with a little egg white and sprinkle over a little sugar. Bake the pies at the top of the preheated oven for 20–30 minutes, or until golden-brown.

7. Allow to cool slightly on a wire rack before serving with the brandy cream.

 AUSTRALIAN LIQUEUR MUSCAT

CAKES AND PÂTISSERIE

OLD-FASHIONED ROAST CHESTNUT CAKE

SERVES 10–12

*340g/12oz chestnuts, peeled, or 200g/7oz peeled
   chestnuts*
240g/8½oz butter, softened
225g/8oz soft dark brown sugar
450g/1lb sultanas
170g/6oz glacé cherries, halved
55g/2oz ground almonds
grated zest of 1 orange
225g/8oz plain flour
½ teaspoon baking powder
3 eggs, beaten
2 tablespoons sherry or brandy
2 tablespoons milk

1. Preheat the oven to 180°C/350°F/gas mark 4.
Line a 20cm/8in deep cake tin with silicone
paper.
2. Place the chestnuts on a baking sheet with
15g/½oz of the butter and roast in the
preheated oven for 10–15 minutes, or until pale
golden-brown. Tip the chestnuts on to a plate
to cool, then cut them into quarters.
3. Cream the butter in a bowl until soft. Add
the sugar and beat until light and fluffy.
4. Put the roasted chestnuts into a large bowl
with the sultanas, cherries, ground almonds and
orange zest. Sift the flour and baking powder
together and stir them into the fruit, making sure
there are no clumps of dried fruit stuck together.
5. Add the creamed butter and sugar to the fruit
with the eggs, sherry or brandy and milk. Mix
everything together and add a little more milk if
necessary to achieve a dropping consistency.
Tip the mixture into the prepared cake tin and
bake in the middle of the preheated oven for
1½–2 hours, or until the cake is golden and a
skewer inserted into the centre comes out clean.
Allow to cool in the tin.
6. This cake is best kept in a sealed container
for a few days before eating.

UPSIDE-DOWN TOFFEE GINGERBREAD

SERVES 6

For the toffee topping
55g/2oz unsalted butter
85g/3oz soft light brown sugar
½ teaspoon ground ginger

6 dried figs, roughly chopped
8 dried pears, roughly chopped
70g/2½oz macadamia nuts

For the gingerbread
110g/4oz butter
110g/4oz soft light brown sugar
110g/4oz black treacle
225g/8oz plain flour
2 teaspoons ground ginger
2 eggs
100ml/3½fl oz milk
1 teaspoon bicarbonate of soda
2 tablespoons stem ginger, chopped

1. Grease a 20cm/8in moule-à-manqué tin or
round cake tin.
2. Preheat the oven to 180°C/350°F/gas mark 4.
3. Make the toffee topping: melt the butter in a
small saucepan and stir in the sugar and ginger.

Pour into the prepared tin.

4. Arrange the dried fruit and nuts on the toffee mixture.

5. Make the gingerbread: heat the butter, brown sugar and treacle gently together in a saucepan, until melted. Do not allow to boil. Remove from the heat and leave to cool.

6. Sift the flour and ground ginger together in a large bowl. Make a well in the centre and pour in the beaten eggs and treacle mixture. Gradually draw in the flour and mix to a batter.

7. Gently warm the milk, add the bicarbonate of soda and pour into the batter with the stem ginger. Mix well.

8. Pour the mixture carefully on to the fruit and nuts. Bake in the preheated oven for about 45 minutes, or until a skewer inserted into the middle of the cake comes out clean.

9. While still warm, turn the cake upside-down on a wire rack and leave to cool.

MAPLE, ORANGE AND PECAN CHELSEA BUNS

MAKES 12

15g/½oz fresh yeast
45g/1½oz caster sugar
450g/1lb strong plain flour
1 teaspoon salt
grated zest of 2 large oranges
55g/2oz butter
1 egg
225ml/8fl oz lukewarm milk
110g/4oz butter quantity sweet orange butter
    (see page 504)
110g/4oz pecan nuts, chopped
55g/2oz cranberries, roughly chopped and
    mixed with 55g/2oz caster sugar (optional)
oil for brushing
8 tablespoons good-quality maple syrup,
    warmed

1. Cream the yeast with 1 teaspoon of the sugar.

2. Sift the flour with the salt into a warmed mixing bowl and add the orange zest. Rub in the butter with the fingertips and stir in the sugar.

3. Beat the egg and add to the yeast mixture with the milk.

4. Make a well in the centre of the flour and pour in the liquid. Using first a knife and then the fingers of one hand, gradually draw the flour in from the sides of the bowl and knead until smooth.

5. Cover the bowl with lightly oiled clingfilm and leave to rise in a warm, draught-free place for about 1 hour, or until doubled in bulk.

6. Preheat the oven to 200°C/400°F/gas mark 6.

7. Knock down the dough and roll into a 30–35cm/12–14in square. Spread the sweet orange butter evenly over the dough and sprinkle with the pecan nuts and cranberries mixed with the sugar, if using.

8. Roll the dough up like a swiss roll and cut into 12 slices. Arrange the slices cut side up, 2.5cm/1in apart, in a 30 × 20cm/12 × 8in lightly greased roasting tin. Cover loosely with oiled clingfilm and leave in a warm, draught-free place to prove (rise again) for 15 minutes.

9. Bake the buns in the preheated oven for 20–25 minutes, or until golden-brown and firm to the touch.

10. Generously brush the buns with warmed maple syrup. Leave the buns to cool in the tin before serving warm or cold.

PETITS FOURS

The following selection make good Christmas presents and a stylish end to a formal dinner party.

GINGER AND CHOCOLATE TRUFFLES

MAKES ABOUT 24

285g/10oz chocolate couverture, roughly
    chopped
5 tablespoons double cream
2 pieces of stem ginger, finely chopped
1–2 teaspoons stem ginger syrup
30g/1oz unsalted butter

To finish
1 teaspoon ground ginger
2 teaspoons cocoa powder
2 teaspoons icing sugar
30g/1oz white chocolate, melted

1. Melt the chocolate in a heatproof bowl set over, not in, a saucepan of simmering water. Remove from the heat and leave to cool.
2. Put the cream into a saucepan, add the ginger and bring to scalding point. Remove from the heat and leave to cool.
3. Beat the butter until very soft. Mix it into the melted chocolate, add the cream and refrigerate until firm.
4. Put the mixture into a piping bag fitted with a 1cm/½in plain nozzle and pipe sticks about 5cm/2in long on to silicone paper.
5. Sift the ginger, cocoa and icing sugar together and dust over the chocolates. Drizzle with the melted chocolate and leave to set.

BOULES DE NEIGE
(Snowballs)

MAKES 24

30g/1oz ground almonds
30g/1oz ground hazelnuts
110g/4oz icing sugar
1 egg white, broken up with a fork

To glaze
1 egg white, whisked
3 tablespoons sifted icing sugar

1. Preheat the oven to 180°C/350°F/gas mark 4.
2. Sift the almonds, hazelnuts and icing sugar together into a bowl. Moisten with enough egg white to bind, but do not make the mixture too wet. Pound the ingredients together to form a paste.
3. Divide the mixture into 24 small balls the size of a walnut. Roll in the egg white, then the icing sugar. Place in paper petits fours cases.
4. Arrange on a sheet of silicone paper and bake in the preheated oven for 12–15 minutes.

Remove from the oven and leave to cool, then transfer to clean petits fours cases to serve.

NOTE: If the mixture is too wet, they tend to swell and burst during baking.

ORANGE AND LIME FORK BISCUITS

MAKES 12

110g/4oz unsalted butter
grated zest of 1 lime
grated zest of 1 orange
55g/2oz caster sugar
170g/6oz self-raising flour
a pinch of salt

To serve
icing sugar

1. Preheat the oven to 190°C/375°F/gas mark 5.
2. Cream the butter, lime and orange zest and sugar together in a bowl until light and fluffy.
3. Sift the flour with the salt into the mixture and stir together to form a dough.
4. Divide into 12 equal balls. Arrange a little apart on a baking sheet and flatten each with a wet fork. Chill for 15 minutes.
5. Bake the biscuits in the preheated oven for 10–12 minutes, or until light golden-brown. Remove from the oven and leave to cool on the baking sheet for 2 minutes, then transfer to a wire rack and leave to cool completely. Dust with icing sugar before serving.

PEANUT BUTTER BROWNIES

MAKES 24

225g/8oz unsalted butter
85g/3oz soft dark brown sugar
285g/10oz granulated sugar
3 large eggs

2 tablespoons brandy
170g/6oz plain flour
340g/12oz peanut butter
225g/8oz curd cheese
110g/4oz white chocolate, chopped
110g/4oz plain chocolate, chopped

1. Preheat the oven to 180°C/350°F/gas mark 4. Lightly grease a 30 × 20cm/12 × 8in roasting tin.
2. Cream the butter and sugars together until light and fluffy.
3. Mix the eggs together in a separate bowl, and gradually beat into the creamed mixture a little at a time, adding 1 tablespoon of the flour if the mixture begins to curdle.
4. Fold in the brandy and flour.
5. Mix together the peanut butter, curd cheese and chocolate and stir into the butter and flour mixture.
6. Bake the mixture in the prepared roasting tin for 45–50 minutes. The brownies should be very sticky (a skewer should not come out clean when inserted).
7. Cool on a wire rack and cut into squares for serving.

PETITS FOURS AUX AMANDES

MAKES 16

110g/4oz ground almonds
85g/3oz caster sugar
2 egg whites
almond or vanilla essence

To decorate
split almonds
glacé cherries

For the glaze
1 tablespoon caster sugar
2 tablespoons milk

1. Preheat the oven to 180°C/350°F/gas mark 4.
2. Sift the ground almonds and sugar together into a bowl.

3. Whisk the egg whites until stiff but not dry, then fold into the almonds and sugar with a few drops of almond or vanilla essence.
4. Put the mixture into a piping bag fitted with a 1cm/½in star nozzle. Pipe into a selection of shapes (rosettes, fingers, etc.) on a greased baking sheet.
5. Decorate the shapes with almonds or glacé cherries. Bake in the preheated oven for 12–15 minutes. Mix together the sugar and milk.
6. Remove the petits fours from the oven and immediately brush with the sugar and milk glaze.

PAINS DE SEIGLE

These resemble tiny rye bread loaves.

MAKES 24

110g/4oz ground almonds
110g/4oz caster sugar
30g/1oz plain flour
1½ egg whites
55g/2oz praline (see page 664)

1. Preheat the oven to 180°C/350°F/gas mark 4. Line a baking sheet with silicone paper.
2. Sift the ground almonds, sugar and flour together into a bowl. Moisten with enough egg white to bind but do not make the mixture too wet. Pound the ingredients together to form a paste.
3. Add the praline to the mixture and divide into 24 small balls the size of a walnut. Roll in the egg white, then in the icing sugar.
4. Arrange on the prepared baking sheet and bake in the preheated oven for 12–15 minutes. Transfer to a wire rack to cool.

NOTE: If the mixture is too wet, the petits fours tend to swell and burst during baking.

LES MAGALIS

MAKES 24

1-egg quantity pâte sucrée (see page 645)
1 quantity crème ganache (see following recipe)
450g/1lb chocolate fondant icing (see page 662)
browned ground almonds
browned shredded almonds or gold leaf

1. Preheat the oven to 190°C/375°F/gas mark 5.
2. Roll out the pastry thinly and use to line tiny tartlet tins. Chill for 15 minutes. Bake the pastry blind (see page 640) until just beginning to colour. Remove the tartlet cases from the tins and cool on a wire rack.
3. When cold, fill with the crème ganache and allow to harden.
4. Melt the fondant icing in a heatproof bowl set over, not in, a pan of simmering water, then remove the bowl from the pan and allow to cool. Ice the tops of each magali with a little of the fondant. Allow to set.
5. Sprinkle the edge of each magali with the browned ground almonds and place a thin shred of browned almond or gold leaf in the centre.

CRÈME GANACHE

MAKES 2 PETIT FOURS

70g/2½oz plain chocolate
20g/¾oz unsalted butter
4 tablespoons cream
2 teaspoons rum

1. Chop the chocolate into small pieces. Put into a heatproof bowl set over, not in, a pan of simmering water, and add the butter and cream. Cook until thick.
2. Flavour with the rum, remove the bowl from the pan and allow to cool. Use as required.

LES COLETTES

MAKES 24

1 full quantity crème ganache (see previous recipe)
24 petit-four size chocolate cases, using 55g/2oz chocolate (see page 606)

To decorate
gold leaf or finely chopped pistachio nuts

1. Put the crème ganache into a piping bag fitted with a fine pâtisserie nozzle. Pipe the chocolate cases full with the ganache.
2. Decorate with gold leaf or pistachio nuts.

TARTELETTES AMANDINES

MAKES 8

2-egg quantity pâte sucrée (see page 645)
2-egg quantity frangipane (see page 349)
30g/1oz flaked almonds
4 tablespoons warm apricot glaze
white praline (see page 605)

1. Roll out the pâte sucrée and use to line 8 tartlet tins or bateaux moulds. Fill with the frangipane and scatter the tops with the almonds. Chill.
2. Preheat the oven to 190°C/375°F/gas mark 5.
3. Bake the tartlets on the top shelf of the preheated oven for 12–15 minutes, or until the pastry is pale golden-brown and the frangipane is firm.
4. Remove from the tins and brush the tops with apricot glaze. Decorate the edge of each tartlet with the praline.

PETITS JAPONAIS

MAKES 8–10

85g/3oz ground almonds
170g/6oz caster sugar
3 egg whites
1 quantity fondant icing (see page 662)
1 quantity crème au beurre (see page 663)
2 tablespoons browned ground almonds or
    hazelnuts
2 tablespoons white praline (see following
    recipe)
whole toasted hazelnuts

1. Preheat the oven to 140°C/275°F/gas mark 1.
Line a baking sheet with silicone paper.
2. Sieve the ground almonds and sugar together
into a bowl.
3. Whisk the egg whites until stiff but not dry.
Fold in the almonds and sugar until just mixed,
do not overfold.
4. Spread or pipe the mixture into 5cm/2in discs
on the prepared baking sheet.
5. Bake in the preheated oven for 45–50
minutes, or until the discs lift easily from the
paper. Allow to cool on a wire rack.
6. To assemble: warm the fondant and ice half
the discs. Allow to cool and set. Spread the
remaining discs with the crème au beurre and
sandwich the discs together. Spread more cream
round the sides and press on ground almonds,
hazelnuts or praline. Finish with a rosette of
crème au beurre and a whole hazelnut.

WHITE PRALINE

MAKES 225G/8OZ

225g/8oz loaf sugar
120ml/4fl oz water
110g/4oz ground almonds

1. Dissolve the sugar in the water and turn up
the heat until the sugar syrup temperature
reaches 130°C/250°F. Remove from the heat
and allow the bubbles to subside.
2. Add the ground almonds and stir briefly until
the mixture resembles sand. Pass through a sieve
while still warm and store in an airtight container.

MARRONS GLACÉS

These chestnuts are time-consuming to prepare,
but nicer than the commercially prepared ones.

MAKES ABOUT 24

900g/2lb large chestnuts in their skins
570ml/1 pint milk
1 vanilla pod, split
570ml/1 pint water
450g/1lb granulated sugar
225ml/8fl oz liquid glucose

1. Put the chestnuts into a large saucepan and
cover with water. Bring to the boil, then simmer
gently for 5 minutes. Remove from the heat.
2. Remove the chestnuts one by one and peel,
taking care to remove the inner membrane of
the chestnut as well as the skin. It is easier to
peel the chestnuts while they are still hot.
3. Put the peeled chestnuts into a clean saucepan,
pour over the milk and add the vanilla pod. Bring
to the boil, then cook the chestnuts over a low
heat for 5 minutes, or until completely soft, but
not breaking up. Lift the chestnuts out of the milk
with a slotted spoon and leave to dry on kitchen
paper. Rinse and reserve the vanilla pod.
4. Meanwhile, make the syrup: put the water,
sugar and liquid glucose into a saucepan.
Dissolve the sugar over a low heat, then bring
to the boil. Simmer for 5 minutes. Add the
chestnuts to the pan with the vanilla pod and
bring back to the boil. Simmer for 1 further
minute. Pour the chestnuts and syrup into a
bowl and leave to cool overnight.
5. The following day, put the chestnuts back
into the saucepan, bring back to the boil and
simmer for 1 minute. Cool overnight. Repeat
this process once more the following day.
6. Lift the chestnuts out of the syrup with a
slotted spoon and leave to drain on a wire rack
overnight.
7. Place each chestnut in a petit four case and
store in a sealed container in a cool, dry place.

CHOCOLATE CHERRIES

These chocolates should be made a week in advance to allow the full flavour of the brandy to be infused into the cherries. You will need 24 small foil cups to make these sweets.

MAKES 24

24 black cherries, pitted
5 tablespoons brandy
225g/8oz chocolate couverture
170g/6oz fondant icing (see page 662)

1. Put the cherries into a bowl. Heat up the brandy and pour it over the cherries. Leave to stand for as long as possible.
2. Break up the chocolate into even pieces and place in a heatproof bowl set over, not in, a saucepan of simmering water. When the chocolate has melted, use a teaspoon to line the little foil cups with it. Pour out any excess chocolate. Leave to dry.
3. Melt the fondant with 2 teaspoons of the brandy from the cherries in a heatproof bowl set over, not in, a saucepan of simmering water.
4. Pour in enough fondant to come a third of the way up each foil cup.
5. Drain the cherries very well. Add one to each cup. Fill almost to the top with more fondant. Leave to harden for 5–10 minutes.
6. Spoon over enough chocolate, swirling it to seal the edges, to cover the fondant icing completely. Leave to cool and harden. Serve in the foil cups.

MISCELLANEOUS

Drinks
Preserves
Breads
Sauces and Garnishes

DRINKS

MULLED WINE

The important ingredient in mulled wine is, rather surprisingly, the water. Without it it can be far too rich and sickly. This recipe is just a guideline and can be altered according to individual tastes.

FOR 20 PEOPLE YOU WILL NEED ABOUT:

4 × 75cl bottles of full-bodied red wine
1.7 litres/3 pints water
20 cloves, wrapped in a J-cloth
3 oranges, sliced
3 lemons, sliced
225g/8oz granulated sugar (you may need to
   add extra sugar according to taste)
2 cinnamon sticks

1. Put all the ingredients into a large saucepan and dissolve the sugar over a low heat.
2. Bring up to simmering point and keep warm for at least 15 minutes. Do not boil or the alcohol will evaporate.

LEMON AND ORANGE CORDIAL

This recipe is taken from *The Penguin Freezer Cookbook* by Helge Rubinstein and Sheila Bush.

MAKES 3.5 LITRES/6 PINTS

5 oranges, washed
5 lemons, washed
30g/1oz citric acid
30g/1oz Epsom salts
55g/2oz tartaric acid
2.3kg/5lb granulated sugar
1.7 litres/3 pints boiling water

To serve
ice cubes
sprigs of fresh mint (optional)

1. Cut the oranges and lemons in half and squeeze out the juice, reserving the pips and pulp. Roughly chop the rind into 1cm/½ in pieces.
2. Put the juice and rind into a large non-metallic bowl with all the pips and pulp. Add the remaining ingredients and stir well until the sugar has dissolved.
3. Cover with a clean tea-towel and allow to cool.
4. When the mixture is quite cold, stir well and strain through a sterilized jelly bag or fine sieve, pressing as much juice as you can from the rinds.
5. To serve: dilute with water, adding ice cubes and a sprig of fresh mint to each glass if desired. Pour the cordial that is not for immediate use into plastic bottles and store in the freezer until required.

NOTE: The cordial will keep well in the refrigerator for up to 3 weeks, but as it is much easier to make in large quantities, we suggest freezing the extra until needed.

CRANBERRY AND ORANGE CRUSH

SERVES 2

6 large oranges, squeezed
225g/8oz frozen cranberries
a large dash of vodka (optional)
lemonade to sweeten (optional)

To serve
ice cubes
2 orange wedges
a few cranberries
2 sprigs of fresh mint

1. Whizz the orange juice, cranberries and
vodka, if using, in a blender until smooth.
Strain into a glass jug. Taste the juice and add a
little lemonade if you find it a little sour, or
need a mixer to serve more people.
2. To serve: thread the orange wedges with a
few cranberries and the sprigs of mint on to
2 × 15cm/6in wooden barbecue skewers.
3. Put some ice cubes into the bottom of 2
glasses and pour in the juice. Place a skewer in
each and serve immediately.

SHIRLEY HEIGHTS RUM PUNCH

SERVES 1

1 large measure dark rum (preferably Cavalier
    or Mountgay)
juice of 1 lime
a dash of grenadine syrup
ice cubes
1 glass of pineapple juice
freshly grated nutmeg

1. Put the rum, lime, grenadine and ice cubes in
a glass. Top up with pineapple juice.
2. Sprinkle with nutmeg and drink immediately.

NOTE: This is a speciality of Antigua in the
Caribbean.

PRESERVES

LEMON AND LIME MARMALADE

MAKES 1.6KG/3½LB

450g/1lb lemons, washed
450g/1lb limes, washed
2.8 litres/5 pints water
1.6kg/3½lb preserving sugar, warmed

1. Cut the lemons and limes in half and squeeze the juice into a large bowl. Remove the pips and tie them up in a piece of muslin or a clean J-cloth.
2. Slice the lemon and lime rinds thinly into 2.5cm/1in strips and add them to the juice with the bag of pips and the water. Cover and leave to soak for 24 hours.
3. Transfer to a preserving pan or large saucepan and simmer gently for about 2½ hours, or until the rind is soft and transparent-looking.
4. Pour the sugar into the saucepan and stir until it has dissolved. Bring slowly to the boil, then lower the heat and simmer until setting point is reached (106°C/222°F). (To test for setting point, put a teaspoon of the marmalade on to a chilled saucer and leave for a minute. Gently push the edge of the marmalade with a finger and if a skin has formed and it wrinkles, it is ready. If the marmalade is not ready, continue testing at 3-minute intervals.)
5. Allow the marmalade to cool for 10 minutes (this will prevent the fruit from rising to the top of the jars), then pour into warm, dry, sterilized jars (see page 277). Cover with jam covers and leave until cold. Label and store in a cool, dark, airy place.

NOTE: Soaking overnight helps to soften the fruit. It may be dispensed with, but longer simmering will then be necessary.

CHUNKY BLOOD ORANGE MARMALADE

MAKES 1.6KG/3½LB

900g/2lb blood oranges
2 lemons
2.8 litres/5 pints water
1.6kg/3½lb preserving sugar, warmed

1. Cut the oranges and lemons in half and roughly squeeze them into a large bowl. (It is not necessary to extract all the juice: squeezing is done simply to make removing the pips easier.)
2. Remove the pips and tie them up in a piece of muslin or a clean J-cloth.
3. Slice the orange and lemon rinds into chunks and add them to the juice with the bag of pips and the water. Leave to soak for 24 hours.
4. Transfer to a preserving pan or a large saucepan and simmer gently for about 2 hours, or until the orange rind is soft and transparent-looking.
5. Add the sugar and stir well while bringing the mixture slowly to the boil.
6. Once the sugar has dissolved, boil rapidly until the setting point is reached (106°C/222°F). This may take as long as 20 minutes, but usually less. Test after 5 minutes by putting a teaspoon of the marmalade on to a chilled saucer. Leave for a minute, then push the edge of the marmalade with your finger. If a skin has formed and it wrinkles, the marmalade is ready.

If the marmalade is not ready, continue testing at 3-minute intervals.

7. Allow the marmalade to cool for 10 minutes (this will prevent the fruit from rising to the top of the jars), then pour into warmed, dry, sterilized jars (see page 277). Cover with jam covers and leave for 24 hours.

8. Label and store in a cool, dark, airy place.

NOTE: Soaking overnight helps to soften the fruit. It may be dispensed with, but longer simmering will then be necessary.

SPICED DARK SEVILLE ORANGE MARMALADE

MAKES 3 × 450G/1LB

900g/2lb Seville oranges
grated zest and juice of 3 lemons
3 cinnamon sticks
85g/3oz fresh root ginger, peeled and chopped
5 star anise
12 cardamom pods
2 dried red chillies
1 teaspoon coriander seeds
2.3 litres/4 pints water
2kg/4½lb soft dark brown sugar

1. Wash the oranges. Cut in half and squeeze the juice. Collect the pips. Scrape as much pith as possible from the fruit and set aside. Put the prepared fruit into a large non-metallic bowl and pour over the orange juice, add the lemon zest and juice, cinnamon sticks and ginger.

2. Mix the reserved pips and pith together with the remaining spices and tie up securely in a piece of muslin or clean J-cloth.

3. Pour the water over the fruit and submerge the muslin bag in the liquid. Set aside to soak for 24 hours.

4. Put the entire contents of the bowl into a large heavy-based saucepan or preserving pan. Bring to the boil, then lower the heat and simmer gently for 1½–2 hours, or until the pith is very soft, making sure that the muslin bag is submerged at all times. Allow to cool, then

shred the fruit to the desired thickness (thin- or thick-cut).

5. Preheat the oven to 150°C/300°F/ gas mark 2.

6. Put the sugar into a roasting tin. Put into the oven to heat for 10 minutes.

7. Remove the muslin bag and cinnamon sticks from the saucepan. Squeeze as much liquid from the muslin as possible, then discard.

8. Add the warmed sugar to the shredded fruit and liquid in the saucepan. Bring to the boil, then lower the heat and simmer for 7–10 minutes, or until setting point is reached (106°C/220°F). To test for setting point, put a teaspoon of marmalade on to a chilled saucer and leave for a minute. Gently push the edge of the marmalade with a finger and if a skin has formed and it wrinkles, the marmalade is ready. If the marmalade is not ready, continue testing at 3-minutes intervals.

9. Allow the marmalade to stand for 30 minutes (this will prevent the fruit from rising to the top of the jars), then pour into the warm, dry, sterilized jars (see page 277). Seal and label. Allow to mature in a cool, dark and airy place for 1–2 weeks before use.

VODKA-MACERATED RAISINS

MAKES 3 × 225G/8OZ

450g/1lb large Valencia raisins
570ml/1 pint vodka
5 tablespoons soft light brown sugar

1. Pack the raisins into sterilized jam jars (see page 277).

2. Mix the vodka and sugar together and pour over the raisins. Cover, label and store for 3–4 weeks. Once opened, store in the refrigerator.

BREADS

FENNEL AND SUNFLOWER SEED BRIOCHE

MAKES 1 LARGE OR 12 INDIVIDUAL BRIOCHES

7g/¼ fresh yeast
2 teaspoons caster sugar
2 tablespoons warm water
225g/8oz plain white flour
½ teaspoon salt
2 eggs, beaten
55g/2oz butter, melted and cooled
30g/1oz sunflower seeds
2 tablespoons fennel seeds
½ teaspoon cayenne pepper

To glaze
1 egg, beaten with a pinch of salt

1. Grease a large brioche mould or 12 small brioche tins.
2. Mix the yeast with the sugar and water and leave until frothy.
3. Sift the flour with the salt into a mixing bowl. Make a well in the centre. Drop in the eggs, yeast mixture and melted butter and mix with the fingers of one hand to a soft but not sloppy paste. Knead on an unfloured board for 5 minutes, or until smooth. Put into a clean bowl, cover with a damp cloth or lightly oiled clingfilm and leave to rise in a warm, draught-free place for about 1 hour, until doubled in bulk.
4. Turn out and knead again on an unfloured board for 2 minutes. Mix together the sunflower and fennel seeds and the cayenne and knead into the dough until well distributed.

5. Shape the dough neatly and place in the brioche mould. If making individual brioches, divide the dough into 12 pieces. Take three-quarters of each piece, roll into small balls and place in the brioche tins. Make a dip on top of each brioche. Roll the remaining dough into 12 tiny balls and press them into the prepared holes. Push a pencil or thin spoon handle right through each small ball into the brioche base, to anchor the balls in place when baking.
6. Cover with lightly oiled clingfilm and leave in a warm place to prove (rise again) until risen to the top of the mould or tin (about 30 minutes for the large brioche, 15 minutes for individual ones).
7. Preheat the oven to 200°C/400°F/gas mark 6.
8. Brush the brioches with beaten egg. Bake the large one in the preheated oven for 20–25 minutes, the small ones for 10 minutes, or until well risen and golden-brown.

FOUNDATION BREAD DOUGH

450g/1lb plain flour
110g/4oz caster sugar
a large pinch of salt
150ml/¼ pint milk
30g/1oz fresh yeast
110g/4oz butter, softened
2 eggs, beaten

1. Sift the flour and half the sugar with the salt into a warmed mixing bowl.
2. Warm the milk to blood heat and add to the yeast and butter in a jug. Stir until dissolved, then mix in the remaining sugar and eggs.
3. Make a well in the centre of the flour, pour in

the liquid ingredients and mix until smooth, first with a wooden spoon, then with the fingers of one hand. When the dough comes away cleanly from the sides of the bowl, turn it on to a floured board and knead until it becomes elastic. Place the dough in a greased bowl (turn it in the bowl so that it is lightly greased all over), cover with a damp cloth and leave in a warm, draught-free place to rise for 45–50 minutes, or until doubled in bulk.

4. Knock down the dough, pull the sides to centre and turn it over, cover and let it rise again for 30 minutes before shaping and baking it as required. Add fruit when indicated in the recipe.

SWEDISH TEA WREATH

½ QUANTITY FOUNDATION DOUGH (see page 613)

For the filling
30g/1oz butter, softened
110g/4oz caster sugar
55g/2oz raisins
1 teaspoon ground cinnamon

For the icing
thin glacé icing (see page 662)
flaked almonds
glacé cherries, halved

1. Prepare the foundation dough (see previous recipe) and after the second rising turn it on to a floured board and roll out to a 23cm × 45cm/ 9 × 18in rectangle.

2. Spread with the butter, then sprinkle with the sugar, raisins and cinnamon.

3. Roll the dough up tightly from one long edge and seal by pinching the edges together. Place the roll on a greased baking sheet, forming it into a ring and joining the ends together. Cut two-thirds through the ring at 2.5cm/1in intervals with a sharp knife and turn each section on a diagonal. Cover with a damp cloth and prove (rise again) in a warm, draught-free place for 35–40 minutes.

4. Meanwhile, preheat the oven to 200°C/400°C gas mark 6.

5. Bake for 25–30 minutes, or until golden-brown. While still warm, brush with the icing and decorate with almonds and cherries.

HUNGARIAN COFFEE CAKE

This is called a coffee cake as it is traditionally served with coffee.

SERVES 6

450g/1lb plain flour
1 teaspoon salt
55g/2oz caster sugar
20g/¾oz fresh yeast
225ml/8fl oz lukewarm milk
55g/2oz butter, softened
1 egg, beaten

For the filling
170g/6oz caster sugar
1 teaspoon ground cinnamon
55g/2oz almonds, finely chopped
110g/4oz butter, melted
1 handful of seedless raisins

1. Preheat the oven to 190°C/375°F/gas mark 5.

2. Sift the flour with the salt into a mixing bowl.

3. Dissolve the sugar and yeast in the milk in a jug, add the butter and stir until melted, then add the egg.

4. Make a well in the centre of the flour, tip in the liquid ingredients and beat until smooth and elastic.

5. Place the dough in a greased bowl. Turn it over, cover with a damp cloth and leave to rise in a warm, draught-free place for 45–50 minutes until doubled in bulk.

6. Knock down the dough and leave to prove (rise again) for 30 minutes.

7. Turn the dough on to a floured board and divide it into pieces the size of walnuts. Cover and leave for a further 15 minutes.

8. Meanwhile, make the filling: mix together the sugar, cinnamon and almonds.

9. Grease a 23cm/9in tube tin well with some of the melted butter.

10. Shape each piece of dough into a neat ball and roll it first in the melted butter, then in the sugar and almond mixture.

11. Place a layer of the balls, barely touching, in the bottom of the prepared tin. Sprinkle with the raisins and press down lightly. Leave to prove (rise again) in a warm, draught-free place for 40 minutes.

12. Loosen the cake from the tin, invert on to a plate and leave until the butter mixture trickles down and the cake has cooled.

BAGELS

MAKES 8

450g/1lb strong plain flour
2 teaspoons salt
15g/½oz fresh yeast
225ml/8fl oz milk and water mixed, at room
  temperature
1 teaspoon caster sugar
2 tablespoons melted butter
1 egg, separated

To finish
sesame seeds or poppy seeds

1. Sift the flour with the salt into a large bowl.
2. Cream the yeast with the milk and water. Add the sugar.
3. Pour the yeast mixture into the flour and salt. Add the butter.
4. Break up the egg white with a fork and add to the flour mixture. Bring together with the fingers of one hand and knead for 10 minutes until smooth and elastic.
5. Place in a greased bowl, cover with greased clingfilm and leave in a warm, draught-free place for about 1½–2 hours, or until doubled in bulk.
6. Knock back the dough and divide into 12 equal balls. Flatten each ball into a neat round. Make a hole in the centre of each round and swing around your finger. The hole must be at least 2.5cm/1in diameter.
7. Place the bagels on a greased baking sheet and cover with greased clingfilm.

8. Leave to prove (rise again) in a warm, draught-free place for 20 minutes or until nearly doubled in size.
9. Preheat the oven to 200°C/400°F gas mark 6.
10. Grease a steamer tray and steam 3–4 bagels at a time for 1 minute, then return them to the baking sheet. Glaze with the beaten egg yolk and sprinkle with sesame or poppy seeds. Bake in the preheated oven for 20–25 minutes, or until the bagels sound hollow when tapped on the underside. Transfer to a wire rack and leave to cool.

ITALIAN BREAD WITH PARMESAN AND TRUFFLE OIL

SERVES 8

450g/1lb strong plain flour
2 teaspoons salt
55g/2oz Parmesan cheese, freshly grated
30g/1oz fresh yeast
225ml/8fl oz warm water
8 tablespoons truffle oil

1. Sift the flour with the salt into a large bowl. Stir in 45g/1½ oz of the Parmesan cheese.
2. Dissolve the yeast in the warm water and pour into the flour with 3 tablespoons of the truffle oil.
3. Gradually draw in the flour, and when all the ingredients are mixed to a soft dough, knead for 8 minutes until smooth and elastic. Put into a lightly oiled bowl, cover with clingfilm and leave in a warm place until 1½ times the original bulk.
4. Preheat the oven to 230°C/450°F/gas mark 8.
5. Punch the dough back into the bowl to knock out the air, then transfer to an oiled baking sheet and push the dough out to form a large oval. Cover with oiled clingfilm and leave to prove (rise again) in a warm, draught-free place for 10 minutes.
6. Press a floured finger irregularly into the top of the dough to form a pattern, then spoon over the remaining truffle oil.

7. Bake on the top shelf of the preheated oven for 10 minutes, then reduce the oven temperature to 180°C/350°F/gas mark 4 and bake for a further 10 minutes.

8. Sprinkle over the remaining Parmesan cheese and bake for a final 5–10 minutes, or until the loaf is golden-brown and sounds hollow when tapped on the underside. Remove to a wire rack and leave to cool.

SAUCES AND GARNISHES

SAUCE MALTAISE

SERVES 4

3 tablespoons wine vinegar
6 black peppercorns
1 bay leaf
2 strips of thinly pared orange zest
1 blade of mace
2 egg yolks
salt
110g/4oz unsalted butter, softened
grated zest and juice of 1 blood orange
2 tablespoons double cream, lightly whipped

1. Place the vinegar, peppercorns, bay leaf, orange zest and mace in a small heavy-based saucepan and reduce by simmering to 1 tablespoon.
2. Cream the egg yolks with a pinch of salt and a nut of the butter in a small heatproof bowl. Set the bowl over, not in, a saucepan of gently simmering water. Using a wooden spoon, beat the mixture until slightly thickened, taking care that the water immediately around the bowl does not boil. Mix well.
3. Strain on the reduced vinegar. Mix well. Stir over the heat until slightly thickened. Beat in the softened butter piece by piece, increasing the temperature as the sauce thickens but taking care that the water does not boil.
4. When the sauce has become light and thick, remove from the heat. Check the seasoning and add the orange zest, juice and cream. Keep warm by standing the bowl in hot water. Serve warm.

CRANBERRY, KUMQUAT AND PORT SAUCE

SERVES 8

225g/8oz fresh or frozen cranberries
8 kumquats, thinly sliced
55g/2oz granulated sugar
150ml/¼ pint port

1. Put all the ingredients into a small heavy-based saucepan. Stir over a low heat until the sugar has dissolved.
2. Cover the pan with a close-fitting lid and poach the cranberries and kumquats over a very low heat for 20 minutes, or until the kumquats are soft. Be careful not to boil the sauce or the cranberries will completely lose their shape, though this will not affect the final taste.
3. Check for sweetness and add a little more sugar if necessary. Serve warm or cold.

ICED VANILLA SAUCE

This can either be made overnight in a freezer or in an ice-cream machine ready to serve immediately.

SERVES 4

290ml/½ pint double cream
1 vanilla pod, split lengthways
4 large egg yolks
45g/1½oz caster sugar
3 tablespoons brandy

1. Put the cream and vanilla pod into a small

saucepan and bring to simmering point. Turn off the heat, cover the pan and leave to infuse for 30 minutes.

2. Scrape the vanilla seeds from the pod into the cream, using a blunt knife. Discard the pod.

3. Beat the egg yolks and sugar together in a bowl and stir in the vanilla cream.

4. Pour the cream mixture into a clean heavy-based saucepan and cook over a low heat, stirring continuously with a wooden spoon until the custard thickens. On no account allow the custard to boil. Immediately strain the custard into a clean bowl.

5. Add the brandy and taste the custard – it should be slightly too sweet and with a fairly prominent alcohol flavour. Add more sugar or brandy accordingly.

6. Transfer to a freezerproof container and allow to cool before freezing overnight.

7. To serve: tip the frozen custard on to a chopping board and cut into 2.5cm/1in cubes. Whizz in a food processor, using the pulse action, until the ice crystals have just broken down.

8. Transfer to a chilled serving jug and serve immediately.

NOTE: If using an ice-cream machine, the custard can be churned to the desired consistency at the end of stage 5.

VANILLA GREEK YOGHURT CREAM

SERVES 4

290ml/½ pint crème anglaise (see page 661)
150ml/¼ pint Greek yoghurt
1–2 teaspoons icing sugar (optional)

1. Allow the crème anglaise to cool, stir in the yoghurt and sweeten to taste with icing sugar if necessary. Pour into a sauce-boat and serve as required.

BRANDY CREAM

MAKES 290ML/½ PINT

290ml/½ pint extra thick double cream
55g/2oz icing sugar, sifted
4–5 tablespoons brandy

1. Mix the cream and icing sugar together in a bowl.

2. Gradually add the brandy. Check for sweetness, adding more brandy and/or sugar if desired.

3. Whip the cream until it holds its shape and chill for 30 minutes before serving.

MENU IDEAS

WINTER MENUS

Ensuring that a menu is well balanced is one of the most important
skills that a cook must learn.
Our suggested menus for winter entertaining are as follows:

Informal Supper

Dry-spiced pigeon breast with celeriac rösti
Crushed butternut squash
Lychee and star anise sorbet
White chocolate and macadamia nut biscuits

Formal Dinner Party

Game broth with wild mushrooms and pearl barley
Roast mallard with glazed limequats
Braised red cabbage with olives and garlic crisps
Pear and pecan tarte tatin with nutmeg and bay leaf ice cream
Petits fours:
Boules de neige
Les Magalis

New Year's Eve Dinner

Cappuccino of white truffle
Italian bread with parmesan and truffle oil
Warm pheasant mousse and port essence
Grilled wasabi salmon with lime mayonnaise
Pomegranate, spinach and bacon salad
Roast figs in port with iced vanilla sauce

Christmas Lunch

Marinated fresh tuna with soy and lime
Festive roast goose
Cranberry and kumquat sauce
Winter game chip baskets
Braised red cabbage with raspberry vinegar
Deep filled rich brandy mince pies with brandy cream
Vanilla, cinnamon and ginger sorbet

Buffet Party

Galantine of duck with foie gras
Pressed tongue with hot mustard chutney or raspberry and sultana chutney
Salsify, leek and blue cheese filo pie
Barley, apple, beetroot and smoked Cheddar salad
Christmas cracked wheat
Deep treacle tart with whisky cream
Roast figs in port with iced vanilla sauce

Winter supper

Roasted game soup with haricots blancs
Baked celeriac rarebit
Green salad
Hot citrus salad with shortbread

BASIC RECIPES

STOCKS

BROWN STOCK

900g/2lb chicken and veal bones
1 onion, peeled and chopped, skin reserved
1 carrot, roughly chopped
1 stick of celery, chopped
green part of 2 leeks, chopped (if available)
fresh parsley stalks
a few mushroom peelings (if available)
2 bay leaves
6 black peppercorns

1. Preheat the oven to 220°C/425°F/gas mark 7.
2. Put the bones into a roasting tin and brown in the oven (up to 1 hour).
3. Brown the onion, carrot, celery, and leeks, if using, in the oil in a large stockpot. It is essential that they do not burn.
4. When the bones are well browned add them to the vegetables with the onion skins, parsley stalks, mushroom peelings, if using, bay leaves and peppercorns. Cover with cold water and bring very slowly to the boil, skimming off any scum as it rises to the surface.
5. When clear of scum, simmer gently for 6–8 hours, or even longer, skimming off the fat as necessary and topping up with water if the level gets very low. The longer it simmers, and the more liquid reduces by evaporation, the stronger the stock will be.
6. Strain, cool and lift off any remaining fat.

NOTE: Lamb stock can be made in the same way with lamb bones but is only suitable for lamb dishes.

GLACE DE VIANDE

570ml/1 pint brown stock (see previous recipe),
absolutely free of fat

1. In a heavy-based saucepan reduce the brown stock by boiling over a steady heat until thick, clear and syrupy.
2. Pour into small pots. When cold cover with clingfilm or jam covers and secure with rubber bands.
3. Store in the refrigerator until ready for use.

NOTE: Glace de viande keeps for several weeks and is very useful for enriching sauces.

WHITE STOCK

onion, sliced
celery, sliced
carrot, sliced
chicken or veal bones
fresh parsley
fresh thyme
bay leaf
black peppercorns

1. Put all the ingredients into a saucepan. Cover generously with water and bring to the boil slowly. Skim off any fat and/or scum.
2. Simmer for 3–4 hours, skimming frequently and topping up the water level if necessary. The liquid should reduce to half the original quantity.
3. Strain, cool and lift off all the fat.

HAM STOCK

The best-flavoured ham stock is generally the well-skimmed liquor from boiling a ham or gammon, but this recipe works well with a cooked ham bone.

1 cooked ham bone
1 onion, chopped
1 carrot, chopped
1 bay leaf
fresh parsley stalks
black peppercorns

1. Place all the ingredients together in a large saucepan. Cover with cold water and bring gradually to the boil. Skim off any fat and/or scum. Simmer for 2–3 hours, skimming frequently and topping up the water level if necessary.
2. Strain and use as required.

NOTE: Ham stock is usually salty and should not be reduced.

GAME STOCK

1 onion, thickly sliced
1 leek, thickly sliced
1 carrot, thickly sliced
1 tablespoon oil
carcass leftovers from cooked game, such as
    pheasant, grouse or partridge
1 teaspoon black peppercorns
1 faggot of tied fresh herbs, such as parsley,
    thyme, sage, mushroom peelings
1 blade of mace

1. Brown the onion, leek and carrot in the oil in a large stockpot. It is essential that they do not burn. Add the cooked game carcass and remaining ingredients. Cover the contents with cold water.
2. Bring the water to the boil, then lower the heat and simmer gently for 4–5 hours, skimming off the fat as necessary and topping up with water if the level gets very low. The longer it cooks, and the more liquid reduces by evaporation, the stronger the stock will be.
3. Strain, cool and remove any traces of fat. Discard the carcass and vegetables.

COURT BOUILLON

1.1 litres/2 pints water
150ml/¼ pint wine vinegar
1 carrot, sliced
1 onion, sliced
1 stick of celery
12 black peppercorns
2 bay leaves
salt

1. Bring all the ingredients to the boil in a large saucepan and simmer for 20 minutes. Allow to cool, then strain.
2. Use as required.

WHITE FISH STOCK

onion, sliced
carrot, sliced
celery, sliced
fish bones, skins, fins, heads or tails of white
    fish
fresh parsley stalks
bay leaf
a pinch of chopped fresh thyme
6 black peppercorns

1. Put all the ingredients together into a saucepan, with water to cover, and bring to the boil. Turn down to simmer and skim off any scum.
2. Simmer for 20 minutes if the fish bones are small, 30 minutes if large. Strain.

NOTE: The flavour of fish stock is impaired if the bones are cooked for too long. Once strained, however, it may be strengthened by further boiling and reducing.

BROWN FISH STOCK

This is not a classic stock but can be used when a stronger flavour is required. It is a good alternative to chicken stock.

2 shallots
½ bulb of Florence fennel
½ carrot
1 stick of celery
2 tablespoons oil
2 teaspoons plain flour
1 litre/1¾ pints water
fish bones, skins, fins, etc. and crustacean and
*   mollusc shells*
1 bouquet garni
1 clove of garlic
½ teaspoon tomato purée

1. Cut the vegetables into large even dice.
2. Heat the oil in a large saucepan and add the vegetables. Cook over a very low heat until the vegetables are soft but not coloured.
3. Add the flour to the pan and continue to cook until the flour and the vegetables are a good russet-brown. Do not allow the vegetables to burn.
4. Remove the pan from the heat and add the water, fish bones, trimmings and shells, the bouquet garni, garlic and tomato purée.
5. Bring up to the boil, then reduce the heat and cook for 30 minutes. Skim regularly.
6. Strain and use as required.

SHELLFISH STOCK

1 onion, sliced
1 carrot, sliced
1 stick of celery, sliced
a selection of crustacean and mollusc shells,
*   such as prawn shells, mussel shells, lobster*
*   or crab cases*
1 bouquet garni
6 black peppercorns

1. Put all the ingredients into a saucepan. Cover with water and bring to the boil, then reduce the heat and simmer for 30 minutes. Skim regularly. Strain and reduce to two-thirds of the original quantity by boiling rapidly. Use as required.

FISH GLAZE

Fish glaze (glace de poisson) is simply very well-reduced, very well-strained fish stock, which is used to flavour and enhance fish sauces. It can be kept refrigerated for about 3 days or frozen in ice cube trays and used as required.

ROAST SHELLFISH STOCK

1 onion, sliced
1 carrot, sliced
1 stick of celery, sliced
a selection of crustacean and mollusc shells,
*   such as prawn shells, lobster or crab cases,*
*   roasted*
1 bouquet garni
6 black peppercorns

1. Put all the ingredients into a saucepan. Cover with water and bring to the boil, then reduce the heat and simmer for 30 minutes. Skim regularly. Strain and reduce to two-thirds of the original quantity by boiling rapidly and use as required.

VEGETABLE STOCK

MAKES 290–425ML/½–¾ PINT

4 tablespoons oil
1 onion, roughly chopped
1 leek, roughly chopped
1 large carrot, roughly chopped
2 sticks celery, roughly chopped
a few cabbage leaves, roughly shredded
a few mushroom stalks
2 cloves of garlic, crushed
a few fresh parsley stalks
6 black peppercorns

sea salt
1 large bay leaf
6 tablespoons dry white wine
570ml/1 pint water

1. Heat the oil in a large saucepan. Add the vegetables, cover and cook gently for 5 minutes or until softening.
2. Add the garlic, parsley stalks, peppercorns, salt, bay leaf, wine and water and bring to the boil. Reduce the heat and simmer for 30 minutes or until the liquid is reduced by half.
3. Strain the stock through a sieve, pressing hard to remove as much of the liquid as possible. Discard the vegetable pulp. Allow to cool and skim off any fat.
4. Use as required.

NOTE: The stock can be kept, covered, in the refrigerator for up to 1 week. It can also be frozen.

SAVOURY SAUCES, BUTTERS AND FLAVOURINGS

WHITE SAUCE

This is a quick and easy basic white sauce.

20g/¾oz butter
20g/¾oz plain flour
a pinch of dry English mustard
290ml/½ pint creamy milk
salt and freshly ground white pepper

1. Melt the butter in a heavy saucepan.
2. Add the flour and the mustard and stir over the heat for 1 minute. Remove the pan from the heat, pour in the milk and mix well.
3. Return the sauce to the heat and stir continuously until boiling.
4. Simmer for 2–3 minutes and season with salt and pepper.

BÉCHAMEL SAUCE

290ml/½ pint creamy milk
1 slice of onion
1 blade of mace
a few fresh parsley stalks
4 white peppercorns
1 bay leaf
30g/1oz butter
20g/¾oz plain flour
salt and freshly ground white pepper

1. Place the milk with the onion, mace, parsley, peppercorns and bay leaf in a saucepan and slowly bring to simmering point.
2. Remove from the heat and leave for the flavours to infuse for 8–10 minutes.

3. Melt 20g/¾oz of the butter in a heavy saucepan, stir in the flour and stir over the heat for 1 minute.
4. Remove from the heat. Strain in the infused milk and mix well.
5. Return the sauce to the heat and stir or whisk continuously until boiling. Add the remaining butter and beat very well (this will help to make the sauce shiny).
6. Simmer, stirring well, for 3 minutes.
7. Season to taste with salt and pepper.

NOTE: To make a professionally shiny béchamel sauce, pass through a tammy strainer before use or whizz in a blender.

MORNAY SAUCE (CHEESE SAUCE)

20g/¾oz butter
20g/¾oz flour
a pinch of dry English mustard
a pinch of cayenne pepper
290ml/½ pint milk
55g/2oz Gruyère or strong Cheddar cheese,
  grated
15g/½oz Parmesan cheese, freshly grated
salt and freshly ground black pepper

1. Melt the butter in a saucepan and stir in the flour, mustard and cayenne pepper. Cook, stirring, for 1 minute. Remove the pan from the heat. Pour in the milk and mix well.
2. Return the pan to the heat and stir until boiling. Simmer, stirring well, for 2 minutes.

3. Add all the cheese, and mix well, but do not reboil.

4. Season with salt and pepper as necessary.

VELOUTÉ SAUCE

20g/¾oz butter
20g/¾oz flour
290ml/½ pint white stock, strained and well
    skimmed (see page 625)
2 tablespoons double cream
salt and freshly ground white pepper
a few drops of lemon juice

1. Melt the butter in a heavy-based saucepan, add the flour and cook, stirring, over a low heat until straw coloured. Remove from the heat. Add the stock and mix well.

2. Return to the heat. Bring to the boil, stirring, and simmer until slightly syrupy and opaque. Stir in the cream. Season to taste with salt, pepper and lemon juice.

SAUCE ESPAGNOLE

4 tablespoons oil
1 small carrot, diced
1 small onion, diced
1 stick of celery, diced
2 teaspoons plain flour, browned
570ml/1 pint brown stock (see page 625)
½ teaspoon tomato purée
a few mushroom stalks
1 bouquet garni (2 fresh parsley stalks, bay
    leaves, blade of mace, tied together with
    string)

1. Heat the oil in a heavy-based saucepan, add the vegetables and fry until they begin to soften.

2. Stir in the flour and continue to cook slowly, stirring occasionally, scraping the bottom of the pan to loosen the sediment. Cook to a good russet-brown.

3. Remove from the heat, add three-quarters of the stock, the tomato purée, mushroom stalks and bouquet garni.

4. Return to the heat and bring to the boil, then simmer for 30 minutes.

5. Skim twice to remove scum: add a splash of cold stock to the boiling liquid to help bring the scum and fat to the surface. Tilting the pan slightly, skim the surface with a large metal spoon. Strain.

NOTE: The flour can be browned in the oven (200°C/400°F/gas mark 6). This gives the sauce a good colour.

DEMI-GLACE SAUCE

Demi-glace sauce is a refined sauce espagnole. Simmer together equal quantities of sauce espagnole and brown stock. Reduce by boiling to half the original quantity. Skim off impurities as they rise to the surface. Pass through a fine chinois (conical strainer), reboil and check seasoning.

MADEIRA SAUCE

3 tablespoons Madeira
1 teaspoon glace de viande (see page 625)
290ml/½ pint sauce espagnole (see above)
a nut of butter

1. Place the Madeira and glace de viande together in a small heavy-based saucepan. Boil until reduced by half.

2. Add the sauce espagnole and heat through.

3. Beat in the nut of butter.

WILD MUSHROOM SAUCE

30g/1oz butter
2 shallots, chopped
110g/4oz wild mushrooms, such as horn of
    plenty, chanterelles, etc.
55g/2oz flat mushrooms, sliced
425ml/¾ pint brown stock (see page 625)

100ml/3½fl oz dry white wine
170g/6oz unsalted butter, chilled and cut into
small pieces

1. Melt the butter in a sauté pan, add the shallots and cook until soft. Increase the heat and cook until golden-brown.
2. Add the mushrooms and cook for 1–2 minutes.
3. Add the stock and wine. Remove the mushrooms with a slotted spoon and reserve. Boil the stock and wine until reduced to about 150ml/¼ pint. Lower the heat under the pan.
4. Using a small wire whisk and plenty of vigorous continuous whisking, gradually add the butter, piece by piece. This process should take about 5 minutes and the sauce should become thick and creamy. Check the seasoning.
5. Return the mushrooms to the sauce and serve.

SORREL SAUCE

This is particularly good served with grilled salmon.

225g/8oz fresh sorrel leaves
15g/½oz butter
150ml/¼ pint fish stock (see page 626)
55ml/2fl oz double cream
30g/1oz unsalted butter
juice of 1 lemon
salt and freshly ground black pepper

1. Wash the sorrel leaves and drain well. Remove any thick stalks.
2. Melt the butter in large saucepan, add the sorrel leaves and cook gently until wilted and softened. Remove from the pan and drain well. Put the leaves into a bowl.
3. Reduce the liquid remaining in the saucepan until it becomes syrupy. Add to the sorrel leaves.
4. Purée the sorrel in a food processor or push through a sieve.
5. Heat the stock in a saucepan and whisk in the sorrel purée until it is evenly distributed. Add the cream and whisk in the butter and lemon juice. Season to taste with salt and pepper.

BREAD SAUCE

This is a very rich sauce. The quantity of butter may be reduced, and the cream is optional.

1 large onion, peeled
6 cloves
290ml/½ pint milk
1 bay leaf
10 white peppercorns, or a pinch of freshly
ground white pepper
a pinch of freshly grated nutmeg
salt
55g/2oz fresh white breadcrumbs
55g/2oz butter
2 tablespoons single cream (optional)

1. Cut the onion in half. Stick the cloves into the onion pieces and put with the milk and bay leaf into a saucepan.
2. Add the peppercorns, nutmeg, and a good pinch of salt. Bring to the boil very slowly, then remove from the heat and leave to infuse for 30 minutes. Strain.
3. Reheat the milk and add the breadcrumbs, butter and the cream, if using. Mix and return to the saucepan.
4. Reheat the sauce carefully without boiling. If it has become too thick, beat in more hot milk. It should be creamy. Check the seasoning.

ASPIC

1 litre/1¾ pints well-flavoured white stock (see
page 625)
15–30g/½–1oz powdered gelatine, as necessary
2 egg shells, crushed
2 egg whites

1. Lift or skim any fat from the stock.
2. Put the stock into a large saucepan and sprinkle on the gelatine, if using. If the stock is liquid when chilled, use 30g/1oz gelatine; if the stock is set when chilled, gelatine will not be necessary. Dissolve over a low heat, then allow to cool.
3. Put the shells and egg whites into the stock.

Place over the heat and whisk steadily with a balloon whisk until the mixture begins to boil. Stop whisking immediately and remove the pan from the heat. Allow the mixture to subside. Take care not to break the crust formed by the egg white.

4. Bring the aspic just to the boil again, and again allow to subside. Repeat this once more (the egg white will trap the sediment in the stock and clear the aspic). Allow to cool for 2 minutes.

5. Fix a double layer of fine muslin over a clean basin and carefully strain the aspic through it, taking care to hold the egg white crust back. When all the liquid is through (or almost all of it) allow the egg white to slip into the muslin. Then strain the aspic again – this time through both egg white crust and cloth. Do not try to hurry the process by squeezing the cloth, or murky aspic will result.

NOTE: When clearing, the saucepan, sieve and whisk should be scalded before use.

HORSERADISH CREAM

150ml/¼ pint double cream
1–2 tablespoons grated fresh horseradish
2 teaspoons white wine vinegar
½ teaspoon made English mustard
salt and freshly ground white pepper
sugar to taste

1. Put all the ingredients into a bowl and whisk to the required consistency.

AÏOLI

This is a speciality of Provence.

6 cloves of garlic, peeled and crushed
3 egg yolks
3 tablespoons fresh white breadcrumbs
salt and freshly ground white pepper
4 tablespoons white wine vinegar
290ml/½ pint good-quality olive oil
1 tablespoon boiling water

1. Put the garlic, egg yolks, breadcrumbs, salt, pepper and vinegar into a food processor. Whizz to a paste.

2. With the motor running, add the oil slowly to make a thick, emulsified sauce. Add the boiling water. Season to taste and use as required.

MAYONNAISE

2 egg yolks
salt and freshly ground white pepper
1 teaspoon dry English mustard
290ml/½ pint olive oil, or 150ml/¼ pint each
    olive and salad oil
a squeeze of lemon juice
1 tablespoon white wine vinegar

1. Put the yolks into a bowl with a pinch of salt and the mustard and beat well with a wooden spoon.

2. Add the oil, literally drop by drop, beating all the time. The mixture should be very thick by the time half the oil is added.

3. Beat in the lemon juice.

4. Resume pouring in the oil, going more quickly now, but alternating the dribbles of oil with small quantities of vinegar.

5. Season to taste with salt and pepper.

NOTE: If the mixture curdles, another egg yolk should be beaten in a separate bowl, and the curdled mixture beaten into it drop by drop.

TARTARE SAUCE

150ml/¼ pint mayonnaise (see above)
1 tablespoon chopped capers, rinsed
1 tablespoon chopped gherkins, rinsed
1 tablespoon chopped fresh parsley
1 shallot, finely chopped
a squeeze of lemon juice
salt and freshly ground black pepper

1. Mix all the ingredients together. Check the seasoning.

NOTE: Chopped hardboiled eggs make a delicious addition.

RÉMOULADE SAUCE

150ml/¼ pint mayonnaise (see page 632)
1 teaspoon Dijon mustard
½ tablespoon finely chopped capers
½ tablespoon finely chopped gherkins
½ tablespoon finely chopped fresh tarragon or
  chervil
1 anchovy fillet, finely chopped

1. Mix all the ingredients together.

NOTE: Rémoulade sauce is a mayonnaise with a predominantly mustard flavour. The other ingredients, though good, are not always present.

HOLLANDAISE SAUCE

3 tablespoons wine vinegar
6 black peppercorns
1 bay leaf
1 blade of mace
2 egg yolks
salt
110g/4oz unsalted butter, softened
lemon juice

1. Place the vinegar, peppercorns, bay leaf and mace in a small heavy saucepan and reduce by simmering to 1 tablespoon.
2. Cream the egg yolks with a pinch of salt and a nut of the butter in a small heatproof bowl. Set over, not in, a saucepan of gently simmering water. Using a wooden spoon, beat the mixture until slightly thickened, taking care that the water immediately around the bowl does not boil. Mix well.
3. Strain on the reduced vinegar. Mix well. Stir over the heat until slightly thickened. Beat in the softened butter bit by bit, increasing the temperature as the sauce thickens and you add more butter, but take care that the water does not boil.
4. When the sauce has become light and thick remove from the heat and beat or whisk for 1 minute. Check the seasoning and add lemon juice, and salt if necessary. Keep warm by standing the bowl in hot water. Serve warm.

NOTE: Hollandaise sauce will set too firmly if allowed to get cold and it will curdle if overheated. It can be made in larger quantities in either a blender or a food processor: simply put the eggs and salt into the blender and blend lightly. Add the hot reduction and allow to thicken slightly. Set aside. When ready to serve, pour in warm melted butter slowly, allowing the sauce to thicken as you pour.

BEURRE BLANC

225g/8oz unsalted butter, chilled
1 tablespoon chopped shallot
3 tablespoons white wine vinegar
3 tablespoons water
salt and freshly ground white pepper
a squeeze of lemon juice

1. Cut the butter in 3 lengthways, then across into thin slices. Keep cold.
2. Put the shallot, vinegar and water into a heavy sauté pan or a small shallow saucepan. Boil until reduced to about 2 tablespoons. Strain and return to the saucepan.
3. Lower the heat under the pan. Using a wire whisk and plenty of vigorous continuous whisking, gradually add the butter, piece by piece. The process should take about 5 minutes and the sauce should become thick, creamy and pale – rather like a thin hollandaise. Season to taste with salt, pepper and lemon juice.

TAPENADE

110g/4oz black olives, pitted
2 tablespoons capers, rinsed
1 medium clove of garlic, chopped
85ml/3fl oz olive oil
freshly ground black pepper

1. Put the olives, capers and garlic into a food processor and process until smooth. While the motor is still running, pour in the oil. Season with pepper.

3. With the motor running pour the oil on to the paste to form an emulsion, it should not be smooth.

4. Store in a covered bowl in the refrigerator and use within 4–5 days.

BASIC VINAIGRETTE

MAKES ABOUT 150ML/¼ PINT

45ml/1½fl oz white wine vinegar
juice of 1 lemon
1 tablespoon Dijon mustard
1 clove of garlic, crushed
1 teaspoon mixed dried herbs, rubbed
salt and freshly ground black pepper
a pinch of sugar
150ml/¼ pint olive oil

1. Whizz all the ingredients together in a blender. Leave to stand for 15 minutes, then check the seasoning. Refrigerate until needed.

NOTE: This dressing should be strong but balanced in flavour.

HARISSA PASTE

30g/1oz dried red chillies
2 fresh red chillies, de-seeded and chopped
2 large red peppers, grilled and skinned
4 cloves of garlic, crushed
juice of 1 lemon
1 teaspoon salt
2 teaspoons caraway seeds
2 teaspoons coriander seeds
2 teaspoons ground cumin
freshly ground black pepper
150ml/¼ pint extra virgin olive oil

1. Soak the dried chillies for 15 minutes in hot water. Drain, cut in half and remove the seeds.
2. Put into a food processor with the fresh chillies, peppers, garlic, lemon juice, salt and spices. Process together to form a smooth paste.

RED PESTO

2 cloves of garlic
1 small bunch of fresh basil
55g/2oz pinenuts
55g/2oz sun-dried tomatoes, chopped
150ml/¼ pint olive oil
55g/2oz Pecorino cheese, finely grated
salt and freshly ground black pepper

1. In a food processor or blender, whizz the garlic and basil together to a paste.
2. Add the nuts and sun-dried tomatoes and whizz in, then add the oil slowly with the motor still running. Add the cheese and whizz quickly.
3. Season to taste with salt and pepper. Keep in a covered jar in a cool place.

PESTO SAUCE

2 cloves of garlic
2 large cups of fresh basil leaves
55g/2oz pinenuts
55g/2oz Parmesan cheese, freshly grated
150ml/¼ pint olive oil
salt

1. In a blender or mortar, grind the garlic and basil together to a paste. Add the nuts, cheese, oil and plenty of salt. Keep in a covered jar in a cool place.

NOTE: Pesto is sometimes made with walnuts instead of pinenuts, and the nuts may be pounded with the other ingredients to give a smooth paste.

PARSLEY PESTO

2 cloves of garlic
a large handful of freshly picked parsley,
    roughly chopped
30g/1oz blanched almonds
150ml/¼ pint olive oil
55g/2oz Cheddar cheese, finely grated
salt and freshly ground black pepper

1. Process or liquidize the garlic and parsley together to a paste.
2. Whizz in the nuts, then add the olive oil slowly with the motor still running. Whizz in the cheese quickly. Season to taste with salt and pepper.
3. Keep in a covered jar in a cool place.

DILL PESTO

a large handful of fresh dill
55g/2oz blanched almonds
2 cloves of garlic
30g/1oz Parmesan cheese, freshly grated
150ml/¼ pint extra virgin olive oil
salt and freshly ground black pepper

1. Put the dill, almonds and garlic into a food processor and whizz to a paste. Add the cheese and continue to blend until well mixed.
2. With the motor running, gradually pour the oil into the herb mixture in a steady stream. It should be well emulsified. Season to taste with salt and pepper.
3. Keep in a covered jar in a cool place.

ROCKET PESTO

55g/2oz rocket
55g/2oz blanched almonds
85ml/3fl oz olive oil
55g/2oz Parmesan cheese, freshly grated
salt and freshly ground black pepper

1. Put all the ingredients into a blender and process until smooth. Season to taste with salt

and pepper. If the paste begins to look oily and too thick, add 1 tablespoon water.

ROUILLE

The traditional accompaniment to Bouillabaisse.

3 cloves of garlic, crushed
1 red chilli pepper, de-seeded and chopped
1 green pepper, halved, de-seeded and blanched
1 red pepper, halved, de-seeded, grilled and
    peeled
6 tablespoons olive oil
2 tablespoons fresh white breadcrumbs
salt and freshly ground pepper
Tabasco sauce

1. Blend the garlic, chilli and green and red peppers in a liquidizer until smooth. With the motor still running, very slowly pour the oil on to the purée. Add the breadcrumbs to bind the sauce.
2. Season to taste with salt, pepper and Tabasco.

TOMATO SAUCE

1 × 400g/14oz can of tomatoes
1 small onion, chopped
1 small carrot, chopped
1 stick of celery, chopped
½ clove of garlic, crushed
1 bay leaf
fresh parsley stalks
salt and freshly ground black pepper
juice of ½ lemon
a dash of Worcestershire sauce
1 teaspoon caster sugar
1 teaspoon chopped fresh basil on thyme

1. Put all the ingredients together in a heavy-based saucepan, cover and simmer over a medium heat for 30 minutes.
2. Liquidize and sieve the sauce and return it to the pan.

3. If it is too thin, reduce by boiling rapidly. Check the seasoning, adding more salt or sugar if necessary.

SALSA PIZZAIOLA

This recipe has been taken from *A Taste of Venice* by Jeanette Nance Nordio.

1 onion, chopped
2 tablespoons olive oil
3–4 cloves of garlic, chopped
1kg/2¼lb canned plum tomatoes
2 tablespoons tomato purée
2 teaspoons dried oregano
1 teaspoon dried basil
1 bay leaf
2 teaspoons sugar
salt and freshly ground black pepper

1. In a saucepan, sweat the onion in the oil until transparent.
2. Add the garlic and cook for 1 further minute, then stir in the tomatoes with their liquid, the tomato purée, oregano, basil, bay leaf, and sugar. Season to taste with salt and pepper. Bring to the boil, then cook very gently for about 1 hour.
3. Remove the bay leaf and check the seasoning. This sauce should be quite thick and rough but you may purée it if you wish.

PRAWN BUTTER

55g/2oz butter, softened
shells from 225g/8oz cooked prawns
½ teaspoon ground mace
1 teaspoon lemon juice
salt and freshly ground black pepper

1. Put all the ingredients into a food processor. Whizz, pulsing on and off, until the shells are well chopped but not completely puréed.

2. Push the ingredients through a sieve until as much as possible of the butter has come through. Discard the remaining shells.
3. Chill and use as required.

HERB BUTTERS

Flavoured butters have always been traditionally served with grilled food, to season and to replace moisture lost in cooking. Often the butter is made with a variety of herbs, which enhance the flavour without masking it. Salmon and sage are a good combination, and thyme, rosemary, oregano and basil, as well as parsley, chervil, chives and tarragon, also work well with fish.

GARLIC BUTTER

55g/2oz butter
1 large clove of garlic, crushed with salt
2 tablespoons lemon juice
salt and freshly ground black pepper

WATERCRESS BUTTER

2 sprigs of watercress
1 small bunch of fresh tarragon
1 sprig of parsley
55g/2oz butter
1 shallot, minced
salt and freshly ground black pepper

1. Blanch the watercress, tarragon and parsley for 30 seconds in boiling salted water. Refresh under cold running water. Drain well and pat dry. Chop very finely.
2. Cream the butter and beat in the shallot, watercress and herbs. Season with salt and pepper. Chill.

NOTE: Sorrel or spinach can be used instead of watercress.

CLARIFIED BUTTER

METHOD 1: Put 225g/8oz butter into a pan with 75ml/2½fl oz water and heat until melted and frothy. Allow to cool and set solid, then lift the butter, now clarified, off the top of the liquid.

METHOD 2: Heat the butter until foaming without allowing it to burn. Pour it through fine muslin or a double layer of J-cloth.

METHOD 3: Melt the butter in a heavy pan and skim off the froth with a perforated spoon.

NOTE: Clarified butter will act as a 'seal' on pâtés, and is useful for frying as it will withstand great heat before burning.

SEASONED FLOUR

Plain flour seasoned with salt and pepper is a useful way of coating fish and seasoning it at the same time. The flour coating stops the fish from sticking during frying and it also gives colour as the flour browns. Once used, seasoned flour must be discarded, so only make a small quantity for immediate use: 2 tablespoons plain flour to ½ teaspoon each of salt and pepper is enough to coat 4 small fillets of fish. Other seasonings may include cayenne pepper and paprika.

CURRY POWDER

There is no beating freshly made curry powder. Toasting and blending all the spices together makes a very good blend that can be used for all our recipes specifying curry powder. This mixture is quite hot; to increase or lessen the heat, adjust the quantity of chillies accordingly. The art of good curry powders is in the toasting; when the seeds are split by the heat, their full flavour comes through. Take care not to burn the seeds or the powder will taste bitter. To keep the curry powder fresh it is best stored in the freezer or a cool, dark place. Use within 3 months; any longer and the spices lose their flavour.

This quantity makes enough powder for several curries, halve the amount of seeds to make a smaller quantity. The spices can be bought from specialist grocers and some supermarkets.

6 tablespoons coriander seeds
4 tablespoons cumin seeds
6 dried red chillies
1 tablespoon black peppercorns
1 tablespoon mustard seeds, preferably black
3 tablespoons ground turmeric
3 teaspoons ground fenugreek

1. Heat a large frying pan. Add the coriander seeds and toss and toast over a medium heat until they begin to pop and colour. Transfer to a plate to cool.
2. Add the cumin seeds and chillies and toast in the same way until the cumin pops and the chillies turn dark reddish-brown in colour. Add them to the coriander and allow to cool.
3. Toast the peppercorns and mustard seeds individually in the same way and allow to cool.
4. When all the seeds are cold, put into a spice/coffee grinder or mortar. Pound together until a fine powder is formed. Stir the turmeric and fenugreek into the powder. Transfer to an airtight container and store until required.

GARAM MASALA

Garam masala (literally, 'mixed spice') does not store well, therefore it is best made fresh. This recipe makes about 3 tablespoons. Keep any excess in an airtight container in a cool, dark place, or freeze it.

20 cardamom pods
5cm/2in piece of cinnamon stick
1 teaspoon cumin seeds
1 teaspoon whole cloves
1 teaspoon whole black peppercorns
1 teaspoon fenugreek seeds
½ teaspoon freshly grated nutmeg
½ teaspoon chilli powder

1. Break open the cardamom pods and remove the seeds.

2. Put all the spices in a spice/coffee grinder and whizz to a fine powder. Store in an airtight container until required.

RED CURRY PASTE

3 red chillies, de-seeded and chopped
2 dried red chillies, de-seeded
1 canned cap pimiento, drained and sliced
1 tablespoon caraway seeds
1 tablespoon ground coriander
2 sticks of lemon grass, chopped
2.5cm/1in piece of galangal, peeled and chopped
2 shallots, chopped
2 teaspoons nam pla

1. Put all the ingredients into a blender and whizz to a smooth paste.

2. Store the paste in a sealed jar in the refrigerator. It will keep for 2–3 days.

NOTE: This paste is quite hot. For a milder version, decrease the amount of chilli used.

PICKLED GINGER

Gari, the pink preserved ginger that is traditionally served with many Japanese dishes, is quite difficult to find. This is an alternative.

225g/8oz frozen root ginger, peeled
150ml/¼ pint rice wine vinegar
1 drop of red food colouring
1 tablespoon chopped crystallized ginger

1. Using a peeler, shred the ginger into thin strips.

2. Put the vinegar and food colouring into a saucepan with the ginger. Bring to the boil, then remove from the heat and allow to cool.

3. Mix the crystallized ginger with the vinegar mixture. Store in a covered jam jar for 2–3 days before using.

PRESERVED LEMONS

These are delicious served with grilled meats and fish, as a garnish or as an integral part of the dish. They are traditionally served in this way in Morocco.

TO FILL A 570ML/1 PINT KILNER JAR

6 lemons
5 tablespoons coarse sea salt
1 teaspoon paprika
1 teaspoon cayenne pepper
12 cloves
1 cinnamon stick
570ml/1 pint olive oil

1. Sterilize the kilner jar by washing and heating in a warm oven for 15 minutes.

2. Cut each lemon into either 1cm/½in slices or wedges. Remove the membrane and any pips.

3. Put a layer of the lemons in the bottom of the jar, sprinkle with a generous amount of salt and a little paprika, cayenne and cloves, followed by more lemon slices. Continue to layer the lemons and seasonings until the jar is full.

4. Lay the cinnamon stick on top of the last layer to help wedge them in and pour the oil over the top, making sure that the lemons are completely submerged.

5. Seal the jar tightly and store in a cool, dark place for at least 3–4 weeks before using.

PASTRY, PASTA AND BATTERS

Pastry comes in many forms. All of them are made from a mixture of flour and liquid, and usually contain fat. Variations in quantities and the ingredients themselves give each type its distinctive texture and taste. The three commonest types of pastry are short, flaky and choux, all of which have variations. The degree of shortness (or crisp crumbliness) depends on the amount and type of fat (the shortening factor) incorporated into the flour, and the way in which the uncooked pastry, or paste, is handled.

THE INGREDIENTS

FATS Butter gives a crisp, rich shortcrust pastry with excellent flavour. Solid margarine gives a similar result that is slightly less rich and flavourful. Lard gives very short but rather tasteless pastry. It gives excellent results when used in combination with butter. Solid cooking fat and vegetable shortening give a crust similar to that produced by lard. Suet is used only in suet crust, which is a soft and rather heavy pastry. A raising agent is usually added to the flour to combat the pastry's doughiness, and to make it more cake-like in texture.

FLOUR in shortcrust pastry is usually plain, all-purpose flour. Weak or cake flour is also suitable for pastry-making. Wholemeal flour produces a delicious nutty-flavoured crust, but is more absorbent than white flour and will need more liquid, which makes it harder and heavier. For this reason, a mixture of wholemeal and white flour, usually half and half, is generally used to make 'wholemeal' pastry. Self-raising flour is occasionally used in pastry-making. It produces a soft, thicker, more cakey crust. It is also sometimes used to lighten cheese dough and other heavy pastes like suet

crust. Whatever the flour, it should be sifted, even if it has no lumps in it, to incorporate air and give the pastry lightness.

The less liquid used in pastry-making the better. Some very rich doughs, such as almond pastry, which contains a high proportion of butter and eggs, can be kneaded without any water or milk at all. Others need a little liquid to bind them. Water gives the pastry crispness and firmness. Too much makes pastry easy to handle but gives a hard crust that shrinks in the oven. The addition of egg or egg white instead of water will give a firm but not hard crust. Egg yolk on its own produces a rich, soft and crumbly crust.

MAKING PASTRY

RUBBING IN Shortcrust pastry is made by rubbing fat into sifted flour and other dry ingredients with the fingertips, then adding other ingredients such as egg yolks and any liquid. Everything should be kept as cool as possible. If the fat melts, the finished pastry may be tough. Cut the fat, which should be firm and cold but not hard, into tiny pieces using a small knife and floured fingers. The flour prevents the fat from sticking to the fingers and beginning to melt, and the smaller the pieces of fat, the better the chances of even distribution. Mix the pieces of fat into the flour, then rub in, handling the fat as quickly and lightly as possible so it does not stick to the fingertips. Pick up a few pieces of floury fat and plenty of flour with the fingertips and thumbs of both hands. Hold your hands about 25cm/10in above the bowl, thumbs up and little fingers down, and gently and quickly rub the little pieces of fat into the flour, squashing the fat lightly as you go. Do not try to mash each piece of fat; a breadcrumb texture, not doughy lumps, is what is required. Drop the floury flakes of fat from a height; this cools the fat and aerates it, making the finished pastry lighter. Shake the bowl regularly so that the unrubbed pieces of fat come to the surface. Stop when the mixture resembles very coarse – not fine – breadcrumbs.

ADDING LIQUID Rich shortcrust pastry, with a higher proportion of fat, needs little, if any, water added. Although over-moist pastry is easy to handle and roll out, the baked crust will be tough and may well shrink in the oven as the water evaporates in the heat. The drier and more difficult to handle the pastry is, the crisper the shortcrust will be. Add only as much water as is needed to get the pastry to hold together, and sprinkle it, 1 teaspoonful at a time, over as large a surface as possible.
Mixing should be kept to a minimum. Mix the pastry with a fork or knife so you handle it as little as possible. As soon as it holds together in lumps, stop mixing. Lightly flour your hands and quickly and gently gather into a ball, rolling it around the bowl to pick up crumbs.

RELAXING It is important to chill pastry for at least 30 minutes before rolling it out, or at least before baking. This allows cells to swell and absorb the liquid evenly. 'Relaxed' pastry will not shrink drastically or unevenly as just-made pastry will. Most pastries benefit from chilling, especially in hot weather, or if they are used to line tart tins, when shrinkage can spell disaster. Relaxing is less important, though still a good idea, for pastes used to cover pies. To prevent the surface of the pastry from drying out and cracking in the dry atmosphere of the refrigerator, cover it lightly with clingfilm or a damp cloth. Ideally pastry is relaxed before and after rolling.

ROLLING OUT Lightly dust the work surface with flour. Do not use much as this can alter the proportion of flour to the other ingredients. Once rolled, allow the pastry to relax in a cool place before baking, especially if it was not relaxed before rolling out.

BAKING BLIND Line the raw pastry case with a piece of kitchen foil or a double sheet of

greaseproof paper and fill it with dried lentils, beans, rice or even pebbles or coins. This is to prevent the pastry bubbling up during cooking. When the pastry is half cooked (about 15 minutes) the 'blind beans' can be removed and the empty pastry case further dried out in the oven. The beans can be re-used indefinitely.

TYPES OF PASTRY
SHORTCRUST: See recipe on page 642.
RICH SHORTCRUST: See recipe on page 642.

SUET CRUST PASTRY This is made like shortcrust pastry except that the fat (suet) is generally chopped or shredded before use. Because self-raising flour (or plain flour and baking powder) is used in order to produce a less heavy dough paste, it is important to cook the pastry soon after making it, while the raising agent is at its most active. During cooking the raising agent causes the dough to puff up and rise slightly and as it hardens, air will be trapped. This makes the suet crust lighter and more bread-like (see page 643).

PÂTE SUCRÉE, ALMOND PASTRY AND PÂTE À PÂTE These and other very rich pastries are extreme forms of rich shortcrust, with all the liquid replaced by fat or eggs. Traditionally they are made by working together the egg yolks and fat, and sometimes sugar, with the fingertips until soft and creamy. The flour is then gradually incorporated until a soft, very rich paste is achieved. To mix the paste, use only the fingertips of one hand. Using both hands, or the whole hand, leads to sticky pastry. The warmth of the fingertips is important for softening the fat, but once that is done, mixing and kneading should be as light and quick as possible. The pastry can be brought together very quickly by using a palette knife. Because of the high proportion of fat, no water is added.
Modern food processors enable the most unskilled cook to make these pastries in seconds. Simply put all the ingredients (the fat in smallish pieces) into the machine and process until the paste forms a ball. This may take a minute or so. The mixture first becomes crumbly, then as it warms up the butter softens

and largish lumps appear. When these are gathered into one or two cohesive lumps the paste is made. Do not over-process as the paste will become sticky and taste greasy. The speed of the processor makes for very good pastry which becomes crisp as it cools. When biscuit-coloured and cooked it will feel soft in the centre. When completely cool, slide off the baking sheet using a palette knife.

HOT WATERCRUST This is made by heating water and fat together and mixing them into the flour. Because of the high proportion of water, this pastry is inclined to be hard. Its strength and firmness allow it to encase heavy mixtures, such as an English pork pie, without collapsing. Also, as the fat used is generally lard, the pastry can lack flavour, so add plenty of salt. Many old recipes recommend throwing the pastry away uneaten once it has done its duty as container. Our recipe for Turkey, ham and stilton raised pie (see page 538) is a better-tasting modification of hot watercrust, containing butter and egg.

Do not allow the water to boil before the fat has melted. If the water reduces by boiling, the proportion of water to flour will not be correct. Quickly mix the water and melted fat into the flour in a warmed bowl, then keep it covered with a hot damp cloth. This prevents the fat from becoming set and the pastry from flaking and drying out.

CHOUX PASTRY Like Yorkshire pudding batter, this pastry contains water and eggs and depends on the rising of the steam within it to produce a puffy, hollow pastry case. It is easy to make if the recipe is followed closely. The following points are particularly important:

1. Measure ingredients exactly. Proportions are important with choux.

2. Do not allow the water to boil until the butter has melted, but when it has, bring it immediately to a full rolling boil. Boiling the water too soon will cause too much evaporation.

3. Having the sifted flour ready in a bowl so that the minute the rolling ball is achieved, you can tip in the flour, all in one go.

4. Beat fast and vigorously to get rid of lumps before they cook hard.

5. Do not over-beat. Stop once the mixture is leaving the sides of the pan.

6. Cool slightly before adding egg, otherwise it will scramble.

7. Do not beat in more egg than is necessary to achieve dropping consistency. If the mixture is too stiff, the pastry will be stodgy. If it is too thin, it will rise unevenly into shapeless lumps.

8. Bake until it is a good, even brown, otherwise the inside of the pastry will be uncooked.

9. If the pastry is to be served cold, split the buns/rings, or poke a hole in each of them with a skewer, to allow to steam inside to escape. If steam remains trapped inside, the pastry will be soggy and a little heavy. Opened-up pastry or small buns with holes in them can be returned to the oven, hole uppermost, to dry out further.

10. Serve the pastry on the day it is made (or store frozen), as it stales rapidly and does not keep well in a tin.

FLAKY PASTRY AND PUFF PASTRY These are begun in rather the same way as the first stage for preparing shortcrust pastry, though the consistency is initially softer and less short, as they contain a high proportion of water. Then more fat, either in a solid block or in small pieces, is incorporated into the paste, which is rolled, folded and re-rolled several times. This process creates layers of pastry which, in the heat of the oven, will rise into light thin leaves. For instance, puff pastry, which is folded in three and rolled out six times, will have 729 layers.

As the whole aim is to create the layers without allowing the incorporated fat to melt, start with everything cool, including the bowl, the ingredients, and the work surface if possible. Short, quick strokes (rather than long steady ones) allow the bubbles of air so carefully incorporated into the pastry to move about while the fat is gradually and evenly distributed in the paste. Work lightly and do not stretch the paste, or the layers you have built up will tear and allow the air and fat to escape. Chill the pastry between rollings or at any point if there is a danger of the fat breaking through the pastry, or if the pastry becomes sticky and warm. It sounds like a complicated business, but it is a lot easier done than said: follow the instructions on page 643 (puff pastry) and page 644 (rough puff pastry).

Pastry rises evenly to a crisp crust in a steamy atmosphere. For this reason flaky and puff pastries (which are expected to rise in the oven) are sometimes baked with a roasting pan full of water at the bottom of the oven, or on a damp baking sheet. The oven temperature is set high to cause rapid expansion of the trapped layers of air and quick cooking of the dough before the fat has time to melt and run out.

STRUDEL PASTRY This differs from most other pastries in that it actually benefits from heavy handling. It is beaten and stretched, thumped and kneaded. This treatment allows the gluten to expand and promotes elasticity in the dough. The paste is rolled and stretched on a cloth (the bigger the better) until it is so thin that you should be able to read fine print through it. Keep the paste covered and moist when not in use. When the pastry is pulled out, brush it with butter or oil to prevent it cracking and drying, or keep it covered with a damp cloth. Strudel pastry can be bought in ready-rolled leaves from most supermarkets. Called phyllo or filo pastry, it is used to make the Middle Eastern baklava. Detailed instructions for strudel pastry appear on page 647.

SHORTCRUST PASTRY (PÂTE BRISÉE)

170g/6oz plain flour
a pinch of salt
30g/1oz lard
55g/2oz butter
very cold water to mix

1. Sift the flour with the salt into a large bowl.
2. Rub in the fats until the mixture resembles coarse breadcrumbs.
3. Add 2 tablespoons water to the mixture. Mix to a firm dough, first with a knife, and finally with one hand. It may be necessary to add more water, but the pastry should not be too damp. (Though crumbly pastry is more difficult to handle, it produces a shorter, lighter result.)
4. Chill, wrapped, in the refrigerator for 30 minutes before using. Or allow to relax after rolling out but before baking.

RICH SHORTCRUST PASTRY

170g/6oz plain flour
a pinch of salt
100g/3½oz butter
1 egg yolk
very cold water to mix

1. Sift the flour with the salt into a large bowl.
2. Rub in the butter until the mixture resembles breadcrumbs.
3. Mix the egg yolk with 2 tablespoons water and add to the mixture.
4. Mix to a firm dough, first with a knife, and finally with one hand. It may be necessary to add more water, but the pastry should not be too damp. (Though crumbly pastry is more difficult to handle, it produces a shorter, lighter result.)
5. Chill, wrapped, in the refrigerator for 30 minutes before using. Or allow to relax after rolling out but before baking.

NOTE: To make sweet rich shortcrust pastry, mix in 1 tablespoon caster sugar once the fat has been rubbed into the flour.

SWEET PASTRY

170g/6oz plain flour
a large pinch of salt
½ teaspoon baking powder
100g/3½oz unsalted butter
55g/2oz caster sugar
1 egg yolk
55ml/2fl oz double cream

1. Sift the flour with the salt and baking powder into a large bowl.
2. Rub in the butter until the mixture resembles coarse breadcrumbs. Stir in the sugar.
3. Mix the egg yolk with the cream and add to the mixture.
4. Mix to a firm dough, first with a knife and finally with one hand. Chill, wrapped, in the refrigerator for 30 minutes before using, or allow to relax after rolling out but before baking.

SUET PASTRY

As suet pastry is most often used for steamed puddings, instructions for lining a pudding basin are included here. Use the pastry as soon as it is made.

butter for greasing
340g/12oz self-raising flour
salt
170g/6oz shredded beef suet
very cold water to mix

1. Grease a 1.1 litre/2 pint pudding basin.
2. Sift the flour with a good pinch of salt into a large bowl. Stir in the suet and add enough water to mix, first with a knife, and then with one hand, to a soft dough.
3. On a floured surface, roll out two-thirds of the pastry into a round about 1cm/½in thick. Sprinkle the pastry evenly with flour.
4. Fold the round in half and place the open curved sides towards you.
5. Shape the pastry by rolling the straight edge away from you and gently pushing the middle

and pulling the sides to form a bag that, when spread out, will fit the pudding basin.
6. With a dry pastry brush, remove all excess flour and place the bag in the well-greased basin.
7. Fill the pastry bag with the desired mixture.
8. Roll out the remaining piece of pastry and use it as a lid, damping the edges and pressing them firmly together.
9. Cover the basin with buttered greaseproof paper, pleated in the centre, and a layer of pleated kitchen foil. (Pleating the paper and foil allows the pastry to expand slightly without bursting the wrappings.) Tie down firmly to prevent water or steam getting in during cooking.

NOTE: Occasionally suet pastry is used for other purposes than steamed puddings, in which case it should be mixed as above and then handled like any other pastry, except that it does not need to relax before cooking.

PUFF PASTRY

225g/8oz plain flour
a pinch of salt
30g/1oz lard
120–150ml/4–5fl oz iced water
140–200g/5–7oz butter

1. If you have never made puff pastry before, use the smaller amount of butter: this will give a normal pastry. If you have some experience, more butter will produce a lighter, very rich pastry.
2. Sift the flour with the salt into a large bowl. Rub in the lard. Add enough water to mix with a knife to a doughy consistency. Turn on to a floured board and knead quickly until just smooth. Chill, wrapped, in the refrigerator for 30 minutes.
3. Lightly flour the board and roll the dough into a rectangle about 30 × 10cm/12 × 4in.
4. Tap the butter lightly with a floured rolling pin to shape it into a flattened block about 9 × 8cm/3½ × 3in. Put the butter on the rectangle of pastry and fold both ends over to

enclose it. Fold the third closest to you over first and then bring the top third down. Press the sides together to prevent the butter escaping. Give it a 90-degree anti-clockwise turn so that the folded, closed edge is on your left.

5. Now tap the pastry parcel with the rolling pin to flatten the butter a little; then roll out, quickly and lightly, until the pastry is 3 times as long as it is wide. Fold it very evenly in 3, first folding the third closest to you over, then bringing the top third down. Give it a 90-degree anti-clockwise turn so that the folded, closed edge is on your left. Again press the edges firmly with the rolling pin. Then roll out again to form a rectangle as before.

6. Now the pastry has had 2 rolls and folds, or 'turns' as they are called. It should be put to rest in a cool place for 30 minutes or so. The rolling and folding must be repeated twice more, the pastry again rested, and then again given 2 more turns. This makes a total of 6 turns. If the butter is still very streaky, roll and fold it once more.

ROUGH PUFF PASTRY

225g/8oz plain flour
a pinch of salt
140g/5oz butter
120–150ml/4–5fl oz very cold water to mix

1. Sift the flour with the salt into a chilled bowl. Cut the butter into pieces about the size of a sugar lump and add to the flour. Do not rub in but add enough water to just bind the paste together. Mix first with a knife, then with one hand. Knead very lightly.

2. Chill, wrapped, for 10 minutes.

3. On a floured board, roll the pastry into a strip about 30 × 10cm/12 × 4in long. This must be done carefully: with a heavy rolling pin, press firmly on the pastry and give short, sharp rolls until the pastry has reached the required size. Take care not to over-stretch and break the surface of the pastry.

4. Fold the strip into 3 and turn so that the folded edge is to your left, like a closed book.

5. Again roll out into a strip 1cm/½in thick.

Fold in 3 again and chill, wrapped, for 15 minutes.

6. Roll and fold the pastry as before, then chill again for 15 minutes.

7. Roll and fold again, by which time the pastry should be ready for use, with no signs of streakiness. If it is still streaky, roll and fold once more.

8. Roll into the required shape.

9. Chill again before baking.

VOL-AU-VENTS

MAKES 1 or 2

225g/8oz flour quantity puff pastry (see page 643)
a pinch of salt
beaten egg, to glaze

1. Preheat the oven to 220°C/425°F/gas mark 7.

2. Roll out the pastry to 1cm/½in thickness and cut into a round about the size of a dessert plate. Place on a damp baking sheet. Using a cutter half the size of the pastry round, cut into the centre of the pastry, but take care not to cut right through to the baking sheet.

3. Flour the blade of a knife and use this to knock up the sides of the pastry: try to slightly separate the leaves of the pastry horizontally; this enables the edge to flake readily when baking; it counteracts the squashing effect of the cutter used to cut out the round, which may have pressed the edges together, making it more difficult for the pastry to rise in even layers.

4. Mix the salt into the beaten egg. Brush the pastry carefully with this egg wash, avoiding the knocked-up sides (if they are covered with egg, the pastry will not rise).

5. With the back of the knife blade, make a star pattern on the borders of the vol-au-vent case and mark a lattice pattern on the inner circle. (The back rather than the sharp edge of the blade is used as this will not cut into the pastry; the idea is to make a pattern without cutting through the surface of the pastry.)

6. Bake in the preheated oven for 30 minutes, then carefully lift off the top of the inner circle.

Keep this for the lid of the case when filled. Pull out and discard any partially cooked pastry from the centre of the case.

7. Return the case to the oven for 2 minutes to dry out. The vol-au-vent is now ready for filling. Ideally the heated pastry case is filled with hot filling, and then served.

NOTE: Flaky or rough puff pastry is also suitable, but the method of cutting is different: cut the pastry into 2 rounds the size of a side plate. Stamp a circle right out of the centre of one of them. Brush the uncut round with egg and place the ring of pastry on top. Bake the middle small round of pastry too, and use it for the vol-au-vent lid.

POLENTA PASTRY

170g/6oz plain flour
a pinch of salt
85g/3oz polenta (coarse cornmeal)
140g/5oz butter
30g/1oz Parmesan or Gruyère cheese, grated
1 egg, beaten

1. Sift the flour, salt and polenta into a large bowl. Rub in the butter until the mixture resembles breadcrumbs.
2. Add the cheese and the egg and bind to a dough.
3. Roll into a circle 1cm/½ in thick to fit the top of a 25cm/10in frying pan. Chill in the refrigerator.

CHOUX PASTRY

85g/3oz butter
200ml/7fl oz water
105g/3¾ plain flour, well sifted
a pinch of salt
3 eggs

1. Put the butter and water into a heavy-based saucepan. Bring slowly to the boil so that by the time the water boils the butter is completely melted.

2. Immediately the mixture is boiling really fast, tip in all the flour with the salt and remove the pan from the heat.
3. Working as fast as you can, beat the mixture hard with the wooden spoon; it will soon become thick and smooth and leave the sides of the pan.
4. Stand the bottom of the saucepan in a bowl or sink of cold water to speed up the cooling process.
5. When the mixture is cool, beat in the eggs, a little at a time, until it is soft, shiny and smooth. If the eggs are large, it may not be necessary to add all of them. The mixture should be of a dropping consistency – not too runny.
('Dropping consistency' means that the mixture will fall off a spoon rather reluctantly and all in a blob; if it runs off, it is too wet, and if it will not fall even when the spoon is jerked slightly, it is too thick.)
6. Use as required.

PÂTE À PÂTE

225g/8oz plain flour
½ teaspoon salt
155g/5½oz butter, softened
2 small egg yolks
3–4 tablespoons water

1. Sift the flour with the salt on a work surface. Make a large well in the centre and put the butter and yolks in it. Work the yolks and butter together with the fingers of one hand and draw in the surrounding flour, adding the water to give a soft, malleable, but not sticky paste.
2. Chill, wrapped, in the refrigerator for 30 minutes. Use as required.

PÂTE SUCRÉE

170g/6oz plain flour
a pinch of salt
85g/3oz butter, softened
3 egg yolks
85g/3oz sugar
2 drops of vanilla essence

1. Sift the flour with the salt on to a board. Make a large well in the centre and put the butter in it. Place the egg yolks and sugar on the butter with the vanilla essence.

2. Using the fingertips of one hand, mix the butter, yolks and sugar together. When mixed to a soft paste, draw in the flour and knead just until the pastry is smooth.

3. If the pastry is very soft, wrap and chill, before rolling or pressing out to the required shape. In any event the pastry must be allowed to relax for 30 minutes either before or after rolling out, but before baking.

ALMOND PASTRY (PÂTE FROLLÉE)

Care must be taken when making this because if it is over-kneaded the oil will run from the almonds, resulting in an oily paste.

110g/4oz plain flour
a pinch of salt
45g/1½oz ground almonds
85g/3oz butter, softened
45g/1½oz caster sugar
1 egg yolk or beaten egg
2 drops of vanilla essence

1. Sift the flour with the salt on to a board or work surface. Scatter over the ground almonds. Make a large well in the centre and put in the butter, sugar, yolk or beaten egg and vanilla essence.

2. Using one hand only, mix with your fingertips. When creamy, gradually draw in the flour and almonds.

3. Knead gently to a paste. Chill, wrapped, in the refrigerator for 30 minutes before baking.

CINNAMON PUFF PASTRY

225g/8oz plain flour
2 tablespoons ground cinnamon
30g/1oz icing sugar
a pinch of salt
30g/1oz lard
150ml/¼ pint iced water
170g/6oz butter

1. Sift the flour, cinnamon, sugar and salt together. Rub in the lard. Add the iced water and mix with a knife to a dough. Turn on to a work surface and knead quickly until just smooth. Wrap in clingfilm and leave in the refrigerator for 30 minutes to relax.

2. Lightly flour the work surface and roll out the dough into a rectangle about 10 × 30cm/ 4 × 12in long. Roll out the pastry on either side of the centre third of the rectangle to form 2 flaps which will be used to enclose the butter.

3. Place the butter between 2 sheets of greaseproof paper and beat out with a rolling pin to form a flattened block about 6 × 7cm/ 2½ × 3in. Put the butter on the centre of the pastry rectangle and fold both flaps up over it. Fold up the bottom third of the pastry and then fold down the top third. The butter should now be completely enclosed. Give the pastry a 90-degree anti-clockwise turn so that the folded, closed edge is on the left. Press the edges firmly with the rolling pin to prevent any butter escaping.

4. Gently roll out the pastry, quickly and lightly, until the pastry is 3 times as long as it is wide. Fold up the pastry into 3 as before. Turn it 90 degrees anti-clockwise and repeat the rolling and folding once more. Wrap the pastry in clingfilm and chill for 30 minutes.

5. Repeat the rolling and folding 4 more times until the butter is no longer streaky. The pastry is now ready to use.

NOTE: If at any time butter breaks through the surface of the pastry, fold up the pastry, wrap it in clingfilm and chill for 30 minutes before further rolling and folding.

FILO OR STRUDEL PASTRY

285g/10oz plain flour
a pinch of salt
1 egg
150ml/¼ pint water
1 teaspoon oil

1. Sift the flour with the salt into a large bowl.
2. Beat the egg and add the water and oil. First with a knife and then with one hand, mix the water and egg into the flour, adding more water if necessary to make a soft dough.
3. The dough has now to be beaten: lift the whole mixture up in one hand and then, with a flick of the wrist, slap it on to a lightly floured board. Continue doing this until the dough no longer sticks to your fingers, and the whole mixture is smooth and very elastic. Put it into a clean floured bowl. Cover and leave in a warm place for 15 minutes.
4. The pastry is now ready for rolling and pulling. To do this, flour a tea-towel or large cloth on a work surface and roll out the pastry as thinly as possible. Now put your hand (well floured) under the pastry and, keeping your hand fairly flat, gently stretch and pull the pastry, gradually and carefully working your

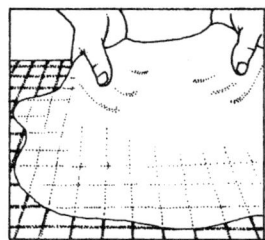 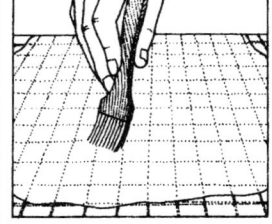

Stretch and pull until almost transparent; brush with butter

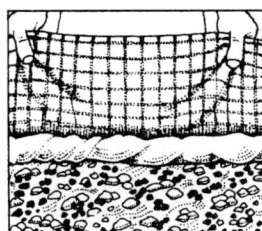

After filling, roll up (using the tea-towel)

way round until the paste is paper-thin. (You should be able to see through it easily.) Trim off the thick edges.
5. Use immediately, as strudel pastry dries out and cracks very quickly. Brushing with melted butter or oil helps to prevent this. Or the pastry sheets may be kept covered with a damp cloth.

NOTE: If the paste is not for immediate use wrap it well and keep refrigerated (for up to 3 days) or frozen. Flour the pastry surfaces before folding up. This will prevent sticking.

DANISH PASTRY

When rolling out Danish pastry, care should be taken to prevent the butter breaking through the paste and making the resulting pastry heavy. Use a heavy rolling pin, bring it fairly firmly down on to the paste and roll with short, quick, firm movements. Do not push it. Avoid using too much flour. If the paste is becoming warm and unmanageable, wrap it up and chill well in the refrigerator before proceeding.

For the pastry
15g/½oz fresh yeast
1 tablespoon caster sugar
100ml/3½fl oz warm milk
225g/8oz plain flour
a pinch of salt
1 egg, lightly beaten
110g/4oz unsalted butter, softened
1 egg, beaten, to glaze

1. Dissolve the yeast with 1 teaspoon of the sugar and the milk.
2. Sift the flour with a pinch of salt into a bowl. Add the remaining sugar. Make a well in the centre and drop the egg and the yeast mixture into it.
3. Using a round-bladed knife, mix the liquids, gradually drawing in the surrounding flour to make a soft dough. If extra liquid is required, add a little more water.
4. When the dough leaves the sides of the bowl, turn it on to a floured work surface and bring together gently until fairly smooth. Roll into a longish rectangle 5mm/¼in thick.
5. Divide the butter into hazelnut-sized pieces

and dot it over the top two-thirds of the dough, leavng a 1cm/½ in clear margin round the edge. Fold the pastry in 3, folding the unbuttered third up over the centre section first, and then the buttered top third down over it. You now have a thick 'parcel' of pastry. Give it a 90-degree turn so that the former top edge is on your right. Press the edges together.

6. Dust lightly with flour and roll again into a long rectangle. Fold in 3 as before. Chill in the refrigerator for 15 minutes.

7. Roll and fold the pastry once or twice again, turning it in the same direction as before, until the butter is worked in well and the paste does not look streaky. Chill for at least 30 minutes, or overnight, before proceeding.

WALNUT AND OAT PASTRY

55g/2oz rolled oats, ground in a food processor
225g/8oz plain flour, sifted
salt
85g/3oz walnuts, finely ground
140g/5oz butter, cubed
1 egg, beaten

1. Mix the oats with the flour, salt and walnuts in a large bowl.

2. Rub in the butter until the mixture resembles coarse breadcrumbs.

3. Add the egg to the flour mixture. Mix first with a knife and then with one hand to a firm dough. Chill, wrapped, in the refrigeritor for 10 minutes before using as required.

SHORTBREAD

MAKES 6–8

110g/4oz butter
55g/2oz caster sugar
110g/4oz plain flour
55g/2oz rice flour

1. Preheat the oven to 170°C/325°F/gas mark 3.

2. Beat the butter until soft, add the sugar and beat until pale and creamy.

3. Sift in the flours and work to a smooth paste. Chill for 15 minutes.

4. Place a 15cm/6in flan ring on a baking sheet

and press the shortbread paste into a neat circle. Remove the flan ring and flatten the paste slightly with a rolling pin. Crimp the edges. Prick lightly.

5. Mark the shortbread into 6–8 wedges, sprinkle lightly with a little extra caster sugar and bake for 40 minutes, until a pale biscuit colour. Leave to cool for 2 minutes, then transfer to a wire rack to cool completely.

FLAVOURED SHORTBREADS

Shortbread can be stamped into biscuits or made into petticoat tails and put into attractive tins. Many variations can be created by adding different ingredients to the basic recipe (see above).

ALMOND SHORTBREAD
Replace the flour with the equivalent weight of ground almonds.

HAZELNUT SHORTBREAD
Add 30g/1oz roughly chopped, browned and skinned hazelnuts with the flour to the creamed butter and sugar.

GINGER SHORTBREAD
Add 1 teaspoon ground ginger and 55g/2oz chopped crystallized stem ginger with the flour.

ORANGE SHORTBREAD
Add the finely grated zest of 2 oranges to the creamed butter and sugar before adding the flour.

OATMEAL AND POLENTA BISCUITS

MAKES 15

110g/4oz fine oatmeal, ground in a blender
110g/4oz polenta
1 teaspoon salt
85g/3oz butter, diced
1 egg
3–4 tablespoons water
plain flour

1. Mix the oatmeal, polenta and salt together in a large bowl. Rub in the butter until the mixture resembles course breadcrumbs.

2. Mix the egg with the water. Using a blunt

knife, stir in a little egg at a time until the mixture binds.

3. On a floured work surface, roll out the pastry into a thin layer and cut discs using a 8cm/3in pastry cutter. Place the biscuits on a greased baking sheet and chill for 30 minutes.

4. Meanwhile, preheat the oven to 180°C/350°F/gas mark 4.

5. Bake the biscuits in the preheated oven for 10–15 minutes, or until pale golden-brown.

6. Transfer to a wire rack and allow to cool before serving. Store in an airtight container.

BACON AND BANANA MUFFINS

MAKES 10–12

110g/4oz rindless smoked streaky bacon rashers
1 tablespoon sunflower oil
310g/11oz plain flour
3 teaspoons baking powder
a pinch of salt
225ml/8fl oz milk
2 large ripe bananas, mashed
2 eggs, lightly beaten
2 tablespoons caster sugar
55g/2oz butter, melted

1. Preheat the oven to 200°C/400°F/gas mark 6. Lightly oil a muffin tin.

2. Fry the bacon in the oil until golden-brown and crisp. Pour the bacon fat into a large bowl and tip the bacon bits on to a plate to cool slightly.

3. Sift the flour with the baking powder and salt and set aside.

4. Mix the milk, banana, bacon, eggs, sugar and butter into the bacon fat. Sift the dry ingredients for a second time on to the banana mixture and fold everything together until just mixed.

5. Fill the muffin tins three-quarters full and bake in the centre of the preheated oven for 15–20 minutes or until well-risen and golden-brown. Transfer the muffins to a wire rack to cool slightly before serving.

SAVOURY DAMSON BISCUITS

MAKES 24

These biscuits would be ideal to serve with a cheeseboard or with a dip before a meal.

225g/8oz damsons, semi-dried (see page 377)
170g/6oz plain flour
55g/2oz fine semolina
a pinch of salt
2 teaspoons caster sugar
85g/3oz butter, melted
½ egg, beaten
flour for rolling

1. Roughly chop the semi-dried damsons.

2. Sift the flour with the semolina and salt into a large bowl. Add the damsons, sugar, butter and egg and mix to a stiff dough.

3. Roll the dough out to the thickness of a £1 coin and cut out discs using a 5cm/2in pastry cutter. (The damsons will squash a little while the pastry is being rolled out, this is to be expected and is not a problem.)

4. Preheat the oven to 190°C/375°F/gas mark 5.

5. Arrange the biscuits on 2 greased baking sheets and chill for 20 minutes.

6. Bake the biscuits in the preheated oven for 10–12 minutes, or until pale golden. Transfer to a wire rack and allow to cool before serving.

QUICK CHIVE BLINIS

MAKES 24

110g/4oz self-raising flour
a pinch of salt
freshly ground black pepper
1 egg, beaten
100ml/3½fl oz milk
2 tablespoons finely chopped fresh chives
30g/1oz butter

1. Sift the flour with the salt and pepper into a large bowl.

2. Mix the egg and milk together. Make a well in the centre of the flour and pour in half the egg and milk mixture.

3. Stir the liquid and gradually draw in the flour from the sides of the bowl. Stir in the remaining egg and milk until the mixture is the consistency of thick cream and will just run from the spoon.

4. Stir in the chives, then cover and leave to stand for 10 minutes.

5. Meanwhile, heat a heavy-based frying pan and add a little of the butter. When the butter is really hot and has foamed, drop teaspoonfuls of the batter on to the surface, keeping them well separated.

6. Cook for 1 minute, or until bubbles have risen to the surface and the batter looks set on the top. Use a palette knife to turn the blinis over and cook for 1 further minute, or until both sides are lightly browned.

7. Continue to cook the remaining batter in the same way, wiping the pan out with kitchen paper between each batch to prevent the butter from burning.

CRANBERRY AND THYME DUMPLINGS

These dumplings are for adding to a casserole or soup to make it more substantial or simply more exciting. Dried cranberries are now widely available in large supermarkets over the Christmas season, but can be replaced with dried apricots if unavailable.

SERVES 4

170g/6oz self-raising flour
a pinch of salt
freshly ground black pepper
85g/3oz beef suet, shredded
55g/2oz dried cranberries, roughly chopped
1 tablespoon chopped fresh thyme
grated zest of 1 lemon
1 teaspoon caster sugar
120ml/4fl oz water

1. Sift the flour and salt into a bowl and season with pepper. Mix in the suet, cranberries, thyme, lemon zest and sugar.

2. Make a dip or well in the flour. Add three-quarters of the water to the well and, using a knife, mix in the surrounding flour. Draw the mixture together with your hands and knead gently to a soft dough, adding extra water if needed.

3. With floured hands, shape the mixture into dumplings about the size of a walnut.

4. To cook: put the hot soup or casserole into a deep ovenproof dish. Arrange the dumplings over the top and bake in the oven preheated to the specified temperature for 30 minutes, or until the dumplings have swollen up and are firm to the touch and golden-brown on top.

NOTES: Dumplings absorb a fair amount of liquid so it is important to make sure the casserole or soup into which they are going has enough liquid to accommodate them.

If you prefer the dumplings not to have a crunchy texture, cover the casserole with a lid when you put it into the oven.

FRESH HERB DUMPLINGS

MAKES 12

170g/6oz self-raising flour
salt and freshly ground black pepper
85g/3oz shredded beef suet
1 tablespoon chopped fresh thyme
2 tablespoons chopped fresh oregano
2 tablespoons chopped fresh parsley
2 tablespoons chopped fresh chives
about 4 tablespoons cold water

1. Sift the flour, salt and pepper into a bowl. Mix in the suet and herbs.

2. Make a well in the centre of the flour mixture. Add a little water to the well and, using a knife, mix in the surrounding flour. Draw the mixture together with your hands and knead gently to a soft dough.

3. With floured hands, shape the dough into dumplings about the size of a ping-pong ball.

4. To serve: add the dumplings to a hot soup or casserole (e.g. oxtail and damson stew, see page 446) and either poach over a direct heat or bake in a hot oven for 30 minutes, or until puffed up, light and cooked through.

REASONS FOR FAILURE IN PASTRY-MAKING

Shortcrust, rich shortcrust, etc.

Shrinkage	Over-handled, stretched too much during rolling, not chilled sufficiently, not cooked on top shelf.
Tough texture	Too much water, over-handled, heavy-handed rolling.
Greasy appearance	Overworked, hot hands, cooked at too low a temperature.
Grey appearance	Not baked blind for long enough, or not covered well in the refrigerator.

Rough puff, flaky, puff pastry

Tough pastry	Too much water, over-handling, fat not cold enough.
Fat escaping	Fat has not been incorporated correctly, pastry not chilled enough, fat not cold enough.
Poor rising	Incorrectly rolled and folded, final pastry rolled too thin.
Uneven rise	Uneven pressure when rolling.

Choux pastry

Flat, cracked appearance	Panada beaten too much when the flour was added.

Suet pastry

Grey, oily, unrisen	Water has not been boiling throughout cooking.
Tough, heavy texture	Over-handling, too much liquid.

Yeasted pastry

Tough pastry	Over-handling, too much liquid.
Greasy appearance	Butter has been melting while the pastry is made.
Poor rising	Too much sugar or salt, stale yeast, liquid too hot when added to the mixture.

ROCKET PASTA I

SERVES 4

225g/8oz strong 'OO' flour
2 large eggs
2 tablespoons olive oil
1 handful of rocket leaves, washed and dried
salt and freshly ground black pepper

1. Sift the flour into a large bowl, make a well in the centre and drop in the eggs and 1 tablespoon of the oil. Using the fingers of one hand, mix together the eggs and oil and gradually draw in the flour to form a soft dough.

2. Knead until smooth and elastic (about 15 minutes). Wrap in clingfilm and leave to relax in a cool place for 1 hour before using. (The pasta can be used at this stage for ravioli see page 154.)

3. Cut the dough in half and roll each half out until paper thin, using plenty of flour to prevent sticking. Lay the leaves of rocket out over one half and sandwich them together with the remaining half of pasta.

4. Roll out the 'sandwich' until 1mm/¹⁄₁₆in thick. Cut the pasta into 10cm/4in squares and lay out on a wire rack to form a crust (about 15–30 minutes).

5. To serve: bring a large saucepan of salted water to the boil, drop in the pasta squares and simmer for 3–5 minutes, or until the pasta is *al* *dente*. Drain well and toss with the remaining oil and season with salt and black pepper. Serve immediately.

NOTE: For all pasta recipes use strong 'OO' pasta flour if available.

ROCKET PASTA II

This recipe is used for making rocket ravioli with garlic and goat's cheese (see page 154).

SERVES 4

225g/8oz rocket, cooked (as for spinach)
340g/12oz strong 'OO' flour
a pinch of salt
2 eggs

1. Chop or liquidize the rocket and push through a sieve to make a fairly dry paste.
2. Sift the flour with the salt on to a board. Make a well in the centre and put in the eggs and rocket. Using the fingers of one hand, mix together the eggs and rocket, gradually drawing in the flour, to make a stiff dough.
3. Knead until smooth and elastic (about 15 minutes). Wrap in clingfilm and leave to relax in a cool palce for 30 minutes before using.

EGG PASTA

SERVES 4

450g/1lb strong 'OO' flour
salt
4 large eggs
1 tablespoon oil

1. Sift the flour and salt on to a wooden board. Make a well in the centre and put in the eggs and oil.
2. Using the fingers of one hand, mix together the eggs and oil and gradually draw in the flour, to make a very stiff dough.
3. Knead until smooth and elastic (about 15 minutes). Wrap in clingfilm and leave to relax in a cool place for 1 hour.
4. Roll out one small piece of dough at a time until paper-thin. Cut into the required shape.
5. Allow to dry (unless making ravioli); hanging over a chair back if long noodles, or lying on a wire rack or dry tea-towel if small ones, for at least 30 minutes before cooking. Ravioli is dried after stuffing.

NOTE: If more or less pasta is required the recipe can be altered on a pro-rata basis, for example, a 340g/12oz quantity of flour calls for a pinch of salt, 3 eggs and 1 scant tablespoon of oil.

COMMONEST NOODLE SHAPES

Spaghetti: originally made by pulling the dough into thin strands, now usually made by machine.
Macaroni: made commercially into short tube-like pieces.
Tagliatelle (fettuccine): thin ribbons of pasta, usually served with a sauce.
Ravioli: flat sheets used to form small stuffed envelopes, which are then boiled and served with or without sauce.
Tortellini: Small stuffed pasta shaped like curled half moons.
Cannelloni: rectangles about the size of a side plate. They are rolled and generally stuffed (like a pancake) after boiling, then reheated.

SHAPING TORTELLINI

1. Cut the rolled-out pasta dough into 7.5cm/3in rounds. Put a teaspoon of stuffing into the middle of each round. Moisten the edges with water.
2. Fold over to form stuffed semi-circles. Press the edges together.
3. Take each half-circle in both hands and curve it gently round the middle of the index finger. The ends should almost, but not quite, touch.
4. Roll the sealed curved edge of the tortellini over to make a groove around the edge.
5. Slip the tortellini off the finger and press the ends of the curled half-moon firmly together so that the tortellini cannot unroll.

GREEN PASTA

SERVES 4

225g/8oz spinach, cooked
340g/12oz strong 'OO' flour
a pinch of salt
2 eggs
1 tablespoon double cream

1. Chop or liquidize the spinach and push through a sieve to get a fairly dry paste.
2. Sift the flour with the salt on to a board. Make a well in the centre and put in the eggs, spinach and cream. Using the fingers of one hand, mix together the eggs, spinach and cream, gradually drawing in the flour, to make a stiff dough.
3. Knead until smooth and elastic (about 15 minutes). Wrap in clingfilm and leave to relax in a cool place for 30 minutes.
4. Roll out one small piece of dough at a time until paper-thin. Cut into the required shape. Allow to dry (unless making ravioli); hanging over a chair back if long noodles, or lying on a wire rack or clean tea-towel if small ones, for at least 30 minutes before cooking. Ravioli is dried after stuffing.

SPICE PASTA

This recipe works well using any ground spice such as nutmeg, ginger or cardamon.

SERVES 2

225g/8oz strong 'OO' flour
2 teaspoon ground cinnamon
2 eggs
1 egg yolk
1 tablespoon olive oil

1. Sift the flour and cinnamon into a food processor.
2. Add the eggs, yolk and oil and pulse on and off until the mixture resembles breadcrumbs. Turn on to a board and knead for 2-3 minutes or until smooth. Wrap in clingfilm and leave to stand at room temperature for 30 minutes. Use as required.

CINNAMON AND ALMOND PASTA

SERVES 2

225g/8oz strong 'OO' flour
2 eggs
3 egg yolks
2 teaspoons ground cinnamon
5 tablespoons ground almonds
2 teaspoons icing sugar
1 tablespoon sunflower oil

1. Put all the ingredients into a food processor and use the pulse action until the mixture forms a dry dough. (If a food processor is not available, sift the flour into a bowl, make a well in the centre and add the eggs, egg yolks, cinnamon, ground almonds, icing sugar and oil. Gradually mix the flour into the liquid, using your hand. Eventually draw it together into a ball of dough and knead until elastic.)
2. Roll out the pasta as thinly as possible. Dust with flour and roll up like a Swiss roll. Cut as thinly as possible into slices crossways. Unravel the pasta, dust with the flour and place on a tray to dry slightly. Use as required.
NOTE: Making the pasta is quicker and easier in a pasta machine.

ORANGE PASTA

SERVES 2

225g/8oz strong 'OO' flour
1 tablespoon icing sugar
2 eggs
3 egg yolks
grated zest of 2 large oranges
1 teaspoon vanilla essence
1 tablespoon hazelnut or sunflower oil

1. Sift the flour on to a wooden board. Make a well in the centre and put in the icing sugar, eggs, egg yolks, orange zest, vanilla essence and oil.
2. Using the fingertips of one hand, mix together the eggs and oil and gradually draw in the flour, to make a stiff dough.

3. Knead until smooth and elastic (about 15 minutes). Wrap in clingfilm and leave to relax in a cool place for 1 hour before using.

FLAVOURED PASTA

Follow the recipe for egg pasta (see page 652) and add the flavourings with the eggs.

Tomato Pasta Add about 2 teaspoons tomato purée.
Herb Pasta Add plenty of chopped very fresh herbs to taste, such as parsley, thyme, tarragon.
Beetroot Pasta Add 1 small cooked, puréed beetroot.
Saffron Pasta Add 1 packet of infused saffron strands.
Chocolate Pasta Add 55g/2oz melted plain chocolate.

SAFFRON NOODLES

SERVES 2

225g/8oz strong 'OO' flour
2 eggs
3 egg yolks
1 tablespoon olive oil
½ teaspoon saffron filaments, dry-fried
salt and freshly ground white pepper

1. Put all the ingredients into a food processor and process until the mixture forms a dough. (If a food processor is not available, sift the flour into a bowl, add the salt and pepper, make a well in the centre, add the eggs, oil and saffron liquid. Gradually mix the flour into the liquid, using your hand. Eventually draw it together into a ball of dough and knead until elastic.)
2. Roll the pasta as thinly as possible. Dust with flour and roll up like a swiss roll. Cut as thinly as possible. Unravel the pasta, dust with the flour and place on a tray to dry slightly. (This is much easier if you have a pasta machine.)

HALF-HOUR PASTA

With a food processor and a pasta machine you can be eating pasta half an hour after you thought about it. Use the same ingredients as for the traditional egg pasta recipe on page 652. While the dough is resting make your favourite quick pasta sauce and sit down to enjoy the best fast food there is.

SERVES 4

450g/1lb strong 'OO' flour
a pinch of salt
4 eggs
1 tablespoon oil

1. Put the flour, salt and the flavouring of your choice (see box) into a food processor and blend well. Beat the eggs and oil together, and with the motor running, gradually add them to the flour until the mixture resembles breadcrumbs. Remove from the processor. Bring a small amount of the mixture together with your fingertips. It should come together easily, but not be too wet. If it does feel wet, add a little extra flour.
2. Knead the dough briefly to bring it together, wrap it in clingfilm and leave it to relax for 10 minutes. Pass it through the widest setting of the pasta machine three or four times, then roll it through the different settings of the machine until you can get it through the narrowest gauge. Cut the pasta into the required shape and drop it straight into a large saucepan of boiling salted water.
3. Cook until *al dente*, then drain and serve with the sauce of your choice.

FRENCH PANCAKES (CRÊPES)

MAKES ABOUT 12

110g/4oz plain flour
a pinch of salt
1 egg
1 egg yolk

290ml/½ pint milk, or milk and water mixed
1 tablespoon oil
oil for cooking

1. Sift the flour with the salt into a bowl and make a well in the centre, exposing the bottom of the bowl.
2. Put the egg and egg yolk with a little of the milk into this well.
3. Using a wooden spoon or whisk, mix the egg and milk and then gradually draw in the flour from the sides as you mix.
4. When the mixture reaches the consistency of thick cream, beat well and stir in the oil.
5. Add the remaining milk; the consistency should now be that of thin cream. (Batter can also be made by placing all the ingredients together in a blender for a few seconds, but take care not to over-whizz or the mixture will be bubbly.)
6. Cover the bowl and refrigerate for about 30 minutes. This is done so that the starch cells will swell, giving a lighter result.
7. Prepare a pancake pan or frying pan by heating well and wiping with oil. Pancakes are not fried in fat – the purpose of the oil is simply to prevent sticking.
8. When the pan is ready pour in about 1 tablespoon batter and swirl about the pan until evenly spread across the bottom.
9. Place over heat and, after 1 minute, using a palette knife and your fingers, turn the pancake over and cook again until brown. (Pancakes should be extremely thin, so if the first one is too thick, add a little extra milk to the batter. The first pancake is unlikely to be perfect, and is often discarded.)
10. Make up all the pancakes, turning them out on to a tea-towel or plate.

NOTES: Pancakes can be kept warm in a folded tea-towel on a plate over a saucepan of simmering water, in the oven, or in a warmer. If allowed to cool, they may be reheated by being returned to the frying pan or by warming in the oven.

Pancakes freeze well, but should be separated by pieces of greaseproof paper. They may also be refrigerated for a day or two.

CRISP BEER BATTER

MAKES 290ML/½ PINT

85g/3oz plain flour
a pinch of salt
1 egg yolk
2 teaspoons oil
100ml/3½fl oz brown ale

Make the batter: sift the flour and salt into a bowl and make a well in the centre. Put the egg yolk, oil and beer into the well and mix to make a smooth batter. Cover and refrigerate for 30 minutes.

FRITTER BATTER

SERVES 4

125g/4½oz plain flour
a pinch of salt
2 eggs
290ml/½ pint milk
1 tablespoon oil

1. Sift the flour with the salt into a bowl.
2. Make a well in the centre, exposing the bottom of the bowl.
3. Put 1 whole egg and 1 yolk into the well and mix with a wooden spoon or whisk until smooth, gradually incorporating the surrounding flour and the milk; the consistency should be thick and creamy.
4. Add the oil. Allow to rest for 30 minutes.
5. When ready to use the batter, whisk the egg white until stiff but not dry. Fold it into the batter with a large metal spoon. Use the batter to coat the food and fry immediately.

WAFFLES

MAKES 8–10

2 eggs
170g/6oz plain flour

a pinch of salt
1 tablespoon baking powder
30g/1oz caster sugar
290ml/½ pint milk
55g/2oz butter, melted
vanilla essence
extra melted butter

To serve
butter
honey, maple syrup or jam

1. Separate the eggs.
2. Sift the flour, salt, baking powder and sugar together into a large bowl. Make a well in the centre and put in the egg yolks.
3. Stir the yolks, gradually drawing in the flour from the edges and adding the milk and melted butter until you have a thin batter. Add the vanilla essence.
4. Grease a waffle iron and heat it.
5. Whisk the egg whites until stiff but not dry and fold into the batter with a large metal spoon.
6. Add a little melted butter to the hot waffle iron, pour in about 4 tablespoons of the mixture, close and cook for 1 minute on each side.
7. Serve hot with butter and honey, maple syrup or jam.

NOTE: The first waffle always sticks to the iron and should be discarded.

TEMPURA BATTER

MAKES 425ML/¾ PINT

225g/8oz plain flour
2 small egg yolks
340ml/12fl oz water
a pinch of slat

1. When the oil is hot, mix the batter ingredients together – it should not be smooth.

BREADS

WHOLEMEAL BAPS

MAKES 12 BAPS

20g/¾oz fresh yeast
290ml/½ pint warm milk
1 teaspoon caster sugar
225g/8oz wholemeal flour
225g/8oz strong plain white flour
2 teaspoons salt
55g/2oz butter
1 egg, lightly beaten
sesame seeds

1. Dissolve the yeast with a little of the milk and the sugar in a teacup.
2. Sift the flours with the salt into a warmed mixing bowl. Rub in the butter as you would for pastry.
3. Pour in the yeast mixture, the remaining milk and nearly all the beaten egg and mix to a fairly slack dough.
4. When the dough will leave the sides of the bowl, press it into a ball and tip it out on to a floured board. Knead it until elastic, smooth and shiny (about 15 minutes).
5. Put the dough back into the bowl and cover it with a piece of lightly greased clingfilm. Put it into a warm, draught-free place (on a shelf above a radiator, in the airing cupboard or just in a draught-free corner of the kitchen). Leave it there until the dough has doubled in size (a least 1 hour).
6. Take the dough out of the bowl, knock down and knead again for 10 minutes.
7. Preheat the oven to 200°C/400°F/gas mark 6.
8. Divide the dough into 12 equal pieces and shape them into flattish ovals, using a rolling pin if you like. Place on a floured baking sheet

and prove (allow to rise again) for 15 minutes. Brush with the remaining beaten egg. Sprinkle with the sesame seeds.
9. Bake in the preheated oven for 20 minutes, or until firm. Leave to cool on a wire rack. Covering the baps with a tea-towel will ensure a very soft crust.

WHOLEMEAL BREAD

This wholemeal bread is simple to make as it has only one rising. As with all bread made from purely 100% wholemeal flour it will be heavier than bread made from a mixture of flours. The flour and water quantities are approximations as wholemeal flours vary enormously. The dough should be moist but not sticky. Use the smaller quantity called for and then add extra flour or water as necessary.

560g–620g/1lb 4oz–1lb 6oz stoneground 100%
*   wholemeal flour*
2 teaspoons salt
3 tablespoons buttermilk
290–340ml/10–12fl oz warm water
15g/½oz fresh yeast

1. Warm the flour with the salt in a large mixing bowl in the bottom of a low oven for about 5 minutes. Warm 2 × 675g/1½ lb non-stick loaf tins.
2. Mix the buttermilk with the warm water. Add a little of the liquid to the yeast with a pinch of flour.
3. Make a well in the centre of the flour, pour in the yeast mixture and nearly all the water and buttermilk. Mix to a dough. Add extra flour or liquid as required. Knead well.

4. Fill the warmed tins three-quarters full of dough. Smooth the tops and cover with a piece of lightly oiled clingfilm. Leave in a warm, draught-free place for 45 minutes, or until the dough has risen to the top of the tins.

5. Meanwhile, preheat the oven to 230°C/450°F/gas mark 8.

6. Bake the bread in the preheated oven for 15 minutes. Turn down the oven temperature to 190°C/375°F/gas mark 5 and bake for a further 25 minutes.

7. The bread should sound hollow when it is tapped on the underside. If it does not or feels squashy and heavy, then return to the oven, without the tin, for a further 5–10 minutes. Leave to cool on a wire rack.

ITALIAN BREAD

This is a basic olive oil bread which can be easily adapted by adding a variety of herbs such as rosemary or sage or grated cheese.

SERVES 4

30g/1oz fresh yeast
225ml/8fl oz warm water
450g/1lb strong plain flour
2 teaspoons salt
2 tablespoons olive oil

1. Dissolve the yeast in the warm water.

2. Sift the flour with the salt into a large bowl and make a well in the centre. Pour in the dissolved yeast and the oil. Gradually draw in the flour and when all the ingredients are well mixed, knead the dough for 8 minutes.

3. Put the dough into a lightly greased bowl. Cover with clingfilm and leave to rise in a warm, draught-free place (about 1 hour).

4. Shape as required. Cover again with clingfilm and leave to prove (rise again) until 1½ times its original size.

5. Preheat the oven to 230°C/450°F/gas mark 8.

6. Place the loaf on a baking sheet and bake in the preheated oven for 10 minutes. Turn the oven temperature down to 190°C/375°/gas mark 5 and bake for a further 45 minutes. Transfer to a wire rack and leave to get completely cold.

MELBA TOAST

SERVES 4

6 slices of white bread

1. Preheat the grill to its highest setting and preheat the oven to 150°C/300°F/gas mark 2.

2. Grill the bread on both sides until well browned.

3. While still hot, quickly cut off the crusts and split the bread in half horizontally.

4. Put the toast in the oven and leave until dry and brittle.

NOTE: Melba toast can be kept for 1–2 days in an airtight tin but it will lose its flavour if kept longer, and is undoubtedly best served straight from the oven.

RICE AND POTATOES

SWEET VINEGAR RICE

This is the recipe for the rice used in sushi. As with any cooked rice dish, keep refrigerated and eat within 24 hours of cooking.

MAKES ENOUGH FOR 15 PIECES OF SUSHI

225g/8oz Japanese sushi short-grain rice
425ml/¾ pint water
1 piece of kombu seaweed
75ml/2½fl oz rice wine vinegar
1 tablespoon caster sugar
2 teaspoons salt

1. Put the rice into a sieve and rinse under cold running water for 1 minute, to remove excess starch.
2. Put into a saucepan, cover with the water, add the kombu and allow to soak for 45 minutes.
3. After the soaking time, cover the saucepan with a well-fitting lid and bring to the boil. Reduce the heat and continue to cook the rice for 10–12 minutes or until cooked through.
4. Meanwhile, put the vinegar into a small saucepan, add the sugar and salt and heat slowly until dissolved. Remove from the heat and allow to cool.
5. When the rice is cooked, turn it on to a flat plate and remove and discard the kombu.
6. Pour the sweetened vinegar over the rice, toss with a fork and allow to cool. Use as required.

THAI STICKY RICE

In Thailand, sticky rice is traditionally served unseasoned; salt may be added if liked. The following recipe is a suitable accompaniment to many curries.

AROMATIC STICKY RICE

SERVES 4

225g/8oz Thai jasmine rice
425ml/¾ pint water
1 stick of lemon grass
1 red chilli
2.5cm/1in piece of fresh root ginger, peeled and bruised
1 clove of garlic

1. Put the rice, water, lemon grass, chilli, ginger and garlic into a large saucepan and allow to stand for 5 minutes.
2. Cover the pan and bring to the boil, then reduce the heat and cook over a low heat for 10 minutes, until the water is absorbed.
3. Remove the pan from the heat and allow to stand, covered, for 5 further minutes.
4. Remove the flavourings, if wished, and pile into a serving dish. Serve very hot.

POMMES ANNA

SERVES 4

675g/1½lb potatoes, peeled and thinly sliced
55g/2oz butter, clarified (see page 637)
salt and freshly ground black pepper
freshly grated nutmeg

1. Preheat the oven to 200°C/400°F/gas mark 6. Brush a heavy ovenproof pan with the clarified butter.
2. Arrange a neat layer of overlapping potato slices on the bottom of the pan. Brush the potatoes with butter and season well with salt, pepper and nutmeg.

659

3. Continue to layer the potatoes, butter and seasoning until all the potatoes have been used. Finish with butter and seasoning.

4. Set the pan over direct medium heat for 2 minutes to brown the bottom layer of potatoes.

5. Remove from the heat and cover with greased greaseproof paper and a lid or kitchen foil. Bake in the preheated oven for about 45 minutes or until the potatoes are tender.

6. Invert a serving plate over the pan and turn the potatoes out so that the neat first layer is on top.

SWEET SAUCES AND ICINGS

CRÈME PÂTISSIÈRE

290ml/½ pint milk
2 egg yolks
55g/2oz caster sugar
20g/¾oz plain flour
20g/¾oz cornflour
vanilla essence

1. Scald the milk by bringing it to just below boiling point in a saucepan.
2. Cream the egg yolks with the sugar and a little of the milk and when pale, mix in the flours. Pour on the milk and mix well.
3 Return the mixture to the pan and bring slowly to the boil, stirring continuously. (It will go alarmingly lumpy, but don't worry, keep stirring vigorously and it will become smooth.) Allow to cool slightly, then add the vanilla essence.

CRÈME ANGLAISE (ENGLISH EGG CUSTARD)

290ml/½ pint milk
1 vanilla pod or a few drops of vanilla essence
2 egg yolks
1 tablespoon caster sugar

1. Heat the milk and vanilla pod, if using, and bring slowly to the boil.
2. Beat the yolks in a bowl with the sugar. Remove the vanilla pod, and pour the milk on to the egg yolks, stirring steadily. Mix well and return to the pan.
3. Stir over a low heat until the mixture thickens sufficiently to coat the back of a spoon (about 5 minutes). Do not boil. Strain into a chilled bowl.
4. Add the vanilla essence, if using.

SUGAR SYRUP

285g/10oz granulated sugar
570ml/1 pint water
thinly pared zest of 1 lemon

1. Put the sugar, water and lemon zest into a saucepan and heat slowly until the sugar has completely dissolved.
2. Bring to the boil and cook to the required consistency (see page 662). Allow to cool.
3. Strain. Keep covered in cool place until needed.

NOTE: Sugar syrup will keep unrefrigerated for about 5 days, and for several weeks if kept chilled.

CARAMEL SAUCE

225g/8oz granulated sugar
290ml/½ pint water

1. Place the sugar in a heavy saucepan with half the water.
2. Dissolve the sugar slowly without stirring it or allowing the water to boil.
3. Once all the sugar has dissolved, turn up the heat and boil until it is a good caramel colour.
4. Immediately tip in the remaining water (it will fizz dangerously, so stand back).
5. Stir until any lumps have dissolved, then remove from the heat and allow to cool.

STAGES IN SUGAR SYRUP CONCENTRATION

TYPE OF SUGAR SYRUP	BOILING POINT	USES
Vaseline	107°C/220°–221°F	Syrup and sorbets
Short thread	108°C/225°–226°F	Syrup and mousse-based ice creams
Long thread	110°C/230°–235°F	Syrup
Soft ball	115°C/235°–240°F	Fondant, fudge
Firm ball	120°C/248°–250°F	Italian meringue
Hard ball	124°C/255°–265°F	Marshmallows
Soft crack	138°C/270°–290°F	Soft toffee
Hard crack	155°C/300°–310°F	Hard toffee and some nougat
	160°C/318°F	Nougat
Spun sugar	152°C/305°–308°F	Spun sugar

RASPBERRY COULIS

340g/12oz raspberries
juice of ½ lemon
75ml/2½fl oz sugar syrup (see page 661)

1. Whizz all the ingredients together in a food processor or blender, and push through a conical strainer.

NOTE: If it is too thin, the coulis can be thickened by boiling rapidly in a heavy saucepan. Stir well to prevent it catching.

GLACÉ ICING

225g/8oz icing sugar is enough to ice an 18cm/7in sponge.

225g/8oz icing sugar
boiling water to mix

1. Sift the icing sugar into a bowl.
2. Add enough boiling water to mix to a fairly stiff coating consistency. The icing should hold a trail when dropped from a spoon but gradually find its own level. It needs surprisingly little water.

NOTE: Hot water produces a shinier icing than cold. Also, the icing, on drying, is less likely to craze, crack or become watery if made with boiling water.

FONDANT ICING

225g/8oz loaf sugar
120ml/4fl oz water
½ teaspoon liquid glucose, or a pinch of cream
 of tartar plus 1 teaspoon water

1. Dissolve the sugar in the water over a low heat without boiling.
2. Mix in the glucose or the cream of tartar and the water. Cover and bring to the boil. Boil to the soft ball stage (115°C/235°–240°F on a sugar thermometer). At this point, a spoonful of the sugar syrup dropped into a bowl of cold water will form a soft ball when rolled between the fingers. Stop the sugar syrup from cooking any further by dipping the bottom of the pan into a bowl of cold water. Let it cool slightly.
3. Moisten a cold hard surface and pour the sugar syrup on to it in a steady stream. With a metal spatula, fold the outsides of the mixture into the centre.

4. Continue to turn with a spatula and work until the fondant becomes fairly stiff. Knead into balls. Place in a bowl and cover with a damp cloth for 1–2 hours.

5. If the fondant is to be stored, place in a screwtop jar. When ready to use, put it into a heatproof bowl and set it over a saucepan of simmering water to melt.

NOTES: A sugar thermometer is almost essential to get the syrup exactly the right consistency: not too liquid, nor too hard.

To make chocolate fondant icing, proceed as above but add 30g/1oz melted dark chocolate to the sugar syrup before pouring on to the work surface.

MARZIPAN OR ALMOND PASTE (UNCOOKED)

225g/8oz caster sugar
225g/8oz icing sugar
450g/1lb ground almonds
2 egg yolks
2 eggs
2 teaspoons lemon juice
6 drops of vanilla essence

1. Sift the sugars together into a bowl and mix with the ground almonds.

2. Mix together the egg yolks, whole eggs, lemon juice and vanilla essence. Add to the sugar mixture and beat briefly with a wooden spoon.

3. Lightly dust the work surface with icing sugar. Knead the paste until just smooth (overworking will draw the oil out of the almonds, giving a too greasy paste).

4. Wrap well and store in a cool place.

COOKED MARZIPAN

This recipe gives a softer, easier-to-handle paste than the more usual uncooked marzipan.

2 eggs
170g/6oz caster sugar
170g/6oz icing sugar
340g/12oz ground almonds
4 drops of vanilla essence
1 teaspoon lemon juice
icing sugar for kneading

1. Beat the eggs lightly in a heatproof bowl.

2. Sift the sugars together and mix with the eggs.

3. Place the bowl over a saucepan of boiling water and whisk until light and creamy or until the mixture just leaves a trail when the whisk is lifted. Remove from the heat and whisk until the bowl is cold.

4. Add the ground almonds, vanilla and lemon juice.

5. Lightly dust a very clean work surface with icing sugar. Carefully knead the paste until just smooth. (Overworking will draw out the oil from the almonds giving a too greasy paste.) Wrap well and store in a cool place.

CRÈME AU BEURRE

This is a rich, creamy cake filling.

110g/4oz granulated sugar
8 tablespoons water
4 egg yolks
grated zest of 1 lemon
110g/4oz unsalted butter
110g/4oz salted butter

1. Dissolve the sugar in the water and when completely dissolved boil rapidly to the short thread stage, about 108°C/225°F on a sugar thermometer. At this point a little sugar syrup, pulled between finger and thumb, will form a thread. Remove from the heat immediately.

2. Whisk the yolks and lemon zest and pour on

the syrup. Keep whisking until thick.

3. Soften the butter and whisk gradually into the mixture. Allow to cool.

NOTE: This makes quite a small quantity of icing. However, it is very rich.

CREAM CHEESE ICING

MAKES ENOUGH FOR A 20CM/8IN CAKE

170g/6oz medium-fat cream cheese
55g/2oz butter, softened
55-85g/2–3oz icing sugar, sifted
a few drops of vanilla essence

1. In a bowl, beat the cream cheese until soft. Stir in the butter, icing sugar and vanilla essence.
2. Taste and add more vanilla essence or icing sugar if required.

CHOCOLATE CARAQUE

30g/1oz plain, milk or white chocolate

1. Melt the chocolate on a heatproof plate over a saucepan of boiling water. Spread thinly on a marble slab or other hard cold surface and leave until just set.
2. Use a long knife to shave off curls of chocolate: hold the knife with one hand on the handle and one hand on the tip of the blade. Hold it horizontally and scrape the chocolate surface by pulling the knife towards you. Chill the curls to harden them.

PRALINE

a few drops of oil
55g/2oz unblanched almonds
55g/2oz caster sugar

1. Oil a baking sheet.
2. Put the almonds and sugar into a heavy saucepan, and set over a low heat. Stir with a metal spoon as the sugar begins to melt and brown. When thoroughly caramelized (browned), tip on to the oiled sheet.
3. Allow to cool completely, then pound to a coarse powder in a mortar or blender.
4. Store in an airtight jar.

NOTE: Whole praline almonds, as sold in the streets of Paris, are made in the same way, but are not crushed to a powder. They are sometimes used for cake decoration.

ICE CREAMS AND MERINGUES

RICH VANILLA ICE CREAM

This ice cream is made with a mousse base.

SERVES 6–8

70g/2½oz granulated sugar
8 tablespoons water
1 vanilla pod, split lengthways
3 egg yolks
425ml/¾ pint double cream

1. Put the sugar, water and vanilla pod into a heavy saucepan and dissolve the sugar over a low heat, stirring.
2. Beat the egg yolks well. Half whip the cream.
3. When the sugar has dissolved completely, boil rapidly to the short thread stage (when a little syrup is placed between a wet finger and thumb and the fingers opened, it should form a sticky thread 2.5.cm/1in long). Remove from the heat and allow to cool for 1 minute. Remove the vanilla pod.
4. Whisk the egg yolks and gradually pour in the sugar syrup. Whisk until the mixture is very thick and will leave a trail when the whisk is lifted.
5. Cool, whisking occasionally. Fold in the cream, pour into a freezer container and freeze.
6. When the ice cream is half frozen, whisk again and return to the freezer.

CHOCOLATE ICE CREAM

This ice cream is made with a custard base.

SERVES 4

340g/12oz plain chocolate, cut up into small
    pieces
570ml/1 pint milk
1 egg
1 egg yolk
55g/2oz caster sugar
570ml/1 pint double cream
1 teaspoon vanilla essence

1. Dissolve the chocolate in the milk in a heavy saucepan over a low heat.
2. Whisk the egg and egg yolk with the sugar in a heatproof bowl set over, not in, a saucepan of simmering water. Whisk until light and fluffy.
3. When the chocolate has melted and the milk nearly boiled, pour on to the egg mixture and whisk well. Strain and allow to cool.
4. Whip the cream lightly and fold it into the chocolate mixture with the vanilla essence. Pour into a bowl and freeze.
5. When half frozen, whisk again and return to the freezer.

MERINGUES (SWISS MERINGUES)

This quantity makes 50 miniature or 12 large meringues.

4 egg whites
a pinch of salt
225g/8oz caster sugar

For the filling
double cream, whipped

1. Preheat the oven to 110°C/225°F/gas mark ½.
2. Line 2 baking sheets wih silicone paper.
3. Whisk the egg whites with a pinch of salt until stiff but not dry.
4. Add 2 tablespoons of the sugar and whisk again until very stiff and shiny.
5. Fold in the remaining sugar.
6. Drop the meringue mixture on to the lined baking sheets in spoonfuls set fairly far apart. Use a teaspoon for tiny meringues, a dessertspoon for large ones.
7. Bake in the preheated oven for about 2 hours until the meringues are dry right through and will lift easily off the paper.
8. When cold, sandwich the meringues together in pairs with whipped cream.

PAVLOVA

SERVES 4–6

4 egg whites
a pinch of salt
225g/8oz caster sugar
1 teaspoon cornflour
1 teaspoon vanilla essence
1 teaspoon white wine vinegar or lemon juice
290ml/½ pint double cream, lightly whipped
450g/1lb soft fruits

1. Preheat the oven to 140°C/275°F/gas mark 1.
2. Line a baking sheet with silicone paper.
3. Whisk the egg whites with a pinch of salt until stiff. Gradually add the sugar, whisking until you can stand a spoon in the mixture.
4. Add the cornflour, vanilla and vinegar or lemon juice.
5. Pile the mixture on to the prepared baking sheet, shaping to a flat oval or circle 3cm/1½ in thick. Bake in the preheated oven for about 1 hour. The meringue is cooked when the outer shell is pale biscuit-coloured and hard to the touch. Remove from the oven, carefully peel off the lining paper and leave to cool completely on a wire rack.
6. When quite cold, spoon on the whipped cream and sprinkle on the fruit.

BREAKFAST DISHES

BREAKFAST MUESLI

SERVES 4

110g/4oz jumbo oats
290ml/½ pint plain yoghurt
150ml/¼ pint orange or apple juice
30g/1oz hazelnuts, skinned and toasted
30g/1oz mixed pumpkin and sunflower seeds,
   toasted
55g/2oz mixed dried fruit, chopped

1. Mix the oats in a large bowl with the
yoghurt, fruit juice, hazelnuts, sunflower and
pumpkin seeds and the dried fruit. The mixture
should look fairly wet at this stage. Chill for 15
minutes before serving.

NOTE: This is delicious served with a
colourful, crisp fresh fruit salad (see following
recipe).

BRIGHT BREAKFAST SALAD

SERVES 4

This simple salad is to go with breakfast muesli
(see previous recipe).

1 small pineapple
110g/4oz fresh strawberries, hulled
1 Granny Smith apple, cored and cut into
   chunks
1 ripe pear, cored and cut into chunks
55g/2oz seedless grapes
1 banana, thickly sliced
150ml/¼ pint freshly squeezed orange juice

1. Top and tail the pineapple and cut away the
skin. Cut the pineapple into quarters
lengthways and remove the core. Cut each
quarter into 2cm/¾in chunks.
2. Mix all the fruit together with the orange
juice and chill for 30 minutes before serving.

SELECT BIBLIOGRAPHY

SELECT BIBLIOGRAPHY

Fresh Produce Desk Book 1998 (published by the *Fresh Produce Journal*)

Baker, Harry, *R.H.S. Fruit* (Mitchell Beazley, 1980)

Matthew Bigg's Complete Book of Vegetables (Kyle Cathie Ltd., 1997)

Clarke, Ethne, *The Art of the Kitchen Garden* (Michael Joseph, 1998)

Jane Grigson's Vegetable Book (Penguin, 1978)

Larkcom, Joy, *The Salad Garden* (Frances Lincoln, 1984)

Leverett, Brian, *Country Wines, Beers and Beverages* (The Crowood Press, 1988)

The National Federation of Women's Institutes, *Home-Made Wines, Syrups and Cordials* (1966)

Rubinstein, Helge and Bush, Sheila, *The Penguin Freezer Cookbook* (Penguin Books, 1975)

Sainsbury's Book of Food (Frances Bissell, 1989)

Seddon, George and Radecka, Helena, *Your Kitchen Garden* (Mitchell Beazley, 1975)

Simmons, Alan F., *Growing Unusual Fruit* (David and Charles, 1972)

Information about apples from Common Ground.

INDEX

INDEX

INDEX